**Manufacturing Strategy**
**Text and Cases**

Second edition

Also by Terry Hill:

*Small Businesses: Production/Operations Management* (Macmillan, 1987)

*The Essence of Operations Management* (Prentice Hall International, 1994)

*The Strategy Quest* (AMD Publishing, 1998)

*Manufacturing Strategy: Text and Cases* (Irwin/McGraw-Hill, 3rd edn, 2000)

*Operations Management: Strategic Context and Managerial Analysis*
(Macmillan, 2000)

# Manufacturing Strategy

## TEXT AND CASES

### Second edition

**Terry Hill**

palgrave

First published 2000 by
PALGRAVE
Houndmills, Basingstoke, Hampshire RG21 6XS and
175 Fifth Avenue, New York, N.Y. 10010
Companies and representatives throughout the world

PALGRAVE is the new global academic imprint of St. Martin's
Press LLC Scholarly and Reference Division and Palgrave
Publishers Ltd (formerly Macmillan Press Ltd).

ISBN 0–333–76222–3 paperback

This book is printed on paper suitable for recycling and
made from fully managed and sustained forest sources.

A catalogue record for this book is available
from the British Library.

Editing and origination by
Aardvark Editorial, Mendham, Suffolk

10   9   8   7   6   5   4   3   2
09  08  07  06  05  04  03  02  01

Printed in Great Britain by
Antony Rowe Ltd, Chippenham, Wiltshire

# Contents

# Preface

Currently in many industrial companies, strategic developments are predominantly based on corporate marketing decisions at the front end of the debate with manufacturing being forced to react to these at the back end of the process. Since manufacturing managers come late into these discussions, it is difficult for them to successfully influence corporate decisions. All too often, the result is the formulation and later development of strategies which manufacturing is unable to successfully support. That is not to say that this happens for lack of trying; the work ethic is strong in the manufacturing culture. However, if the basic link between the manufacturing processes and infrastructure (that is, manufacturing strategy) and the market is not strategically sound, then – by definition – the business will suffer.

The many reasons why this happens are addressed in this book. Significant among them is that typically the attention of manufacturing managers primarily focuses upon the day-to-day part of their task. It concerns operations detail and is output-oriented, while in strategic terms their role is seen as being reactive.

The purpose of this book is twofold. First it is to help manufacturing executives to recognize and undertake the strategic dimension of their task. It is intended to help them think, analyse and discuss corporate issues and to formulate a functional strategy in line with the needs of a firm's markets.

Second, it is to provide the wherewithal for executives in other functions to relate to, understand and discuss manufacturing's strategic role and contribution to supporting a company's agreed markets. The way in which the book fulfils this purpose is to introduce and explain the concepts, ideas and language that underpin the emerging subject area of manufacturing strategy.

In this way it helps provide insights and evaluates manufacturing's corporate contribution through strategic perspectives, rather than just through operational performance. It not only helps manufacturing managers to develop and provide appropriate corporate level inputs, but also enables other executives to recognize and appreciate the strategic perspectives which emanate from manufacturing and which need to be given due consideration within the business debate.

The strategic perspective of manufacturing forms the basis on which the book is written, but the approach places these issues within the rightful context of the corporate whole. Thus, it recognizes that in today's world the majority of companies will be unable to sustain success over a long period of time if their strategy is based upon a single function's view of what is important. The book, therefore, emphasizes the essential requirement to link manufacturing's strategy to those of marketing and other functions in order to determine the best strategies for the business as a whole. In summary, the book is written as an attempt to:

1. Close the gap between manufacturing and marketing in terms of corporate strategy formulation.

2. Provide a set of principles and concepts which are pragmatic in nature and designed to be applied to each different part of a business.

3. Offer an analytical approach to the development of manufacturing strategy rather than advocate a set of prescriptive solutions. Each business and each part of each business is different. The resolution of strategy through prescription, therefore, is by definition inappropriate. Furthermore, the complexity in manufacturing is such that it encourages companies to take strategic short cuts. As a consequence, prescriptive approaches seem doubly attractive. The book argues strongly against such approaches. In suggesting a means of developing a manufacturing strategy and raising essential issues throughout, it provides a way of coping with this complexity. The principles and concepts outlined provide a basis for placing operational detail in an essential strategic framework.

Outlined in the book is a basic approach to developing a manufacturing strategy which has been used successfully in many companies throughout the world. It provides a logical, practical and effective way for manufacturing to interface with marketing in formulating corporate strategy. In so doing, it ensures that the 'front-end' debate concerns not just the outward-looking stance of marketing, but the outward-looking stance of the business as a whole. This thereby reduces the number of situations in which marketing-led strategies may be adopted which – in overall terms – will be harmful to the business. It does this by emphasizing the consequences for the total business of different decisions – a technique which is a prerequisite for developing sound strategic direction.

Many executives shy away from discussions of manufacturing because they see it as an area of technology and/or complex detail. This is because, traditionally, manufacturing is presented in this form. The approach in this book is to group together relevant operational detail into key strategic issues, and to provide an understanding of how these apply in companies. The development of a strategic language also gives the opportunity to move away from what often constitutes current practice – a discussion of operational problems. This is not only an inappropriate manufacturing contribution at the executive level, but also has the effect of dulling the interest of other functions in examining the corporate manufacturing issues involved. Strategic language, on the other hand, helps to orient and maintain the debate at the appropriate level. It stimulates executive interest and enables others to address the complexity by creating a manageable number of manufacturing variables.

The book comprises eleven chapters. Chapter 1 sets the scene by drawing some important international comparisons at national, industry and plant levels. The figures embody a growing awareness of the fact that those countries which clearly emphasize the importance of manufacturing's contribution to business success have consistently outperformed other developed countries with a sound industrial tradition.

The core of the book is in the nine central chapters. The headings highlight some key developments within manufacturing strategy. Together they form the substance of the language development as well as the methodologies to be used in its formulation. Chapters 2, 3 and 4 provide the context and content on the approach to be adopted when developing a manufacturing strategy and detail what needs to be undertaken at each step. They includes some illustrations to help with this explanation. Chapter 5 deals exclusively with the choice of manufacturing process, the basis for that choice, and the business implications that follow. Chapter 6 introduces the concept of product profiling which provides companies with a methodology for testing the current or anticipated future level of fit between the characteristics of their markets and those of their manufacturing processes and infrastructure. Chapters 7 and 8 deal with the concept of focus and the need to assign plants or parts of a plant to a defined set of tasks. The latter provides a detailed methodology statement on how to undertake this development. Chapter 9 examines the implications behind supply chain decisions. Companies need to address where they should position themselves on the process spectrum while realizing that both in-house and suppliers' processes fall within the remit of a firm's manufacturing strategy as both will impact how well a company can meet the needs of its markets.

Although at first sight these last three chapters appear to concern solely manufacturing process decisions, it is important to recognize that they are also a critical part of infrastructure formulation, since the size and shape of plants are significant factors in what constitutes an appropriate infrastructure, the subject of Chapter 10. This chapter introduces some important concepts as a way of providing a business with the insights necessary to formulate developments in the wide range of functions within manufacturing. This approach will enable these important, expensive and time-consuming tasks to be designed in order to support the requirements of a business. It will enable them to be given strategic shape and direction rather than emanating from specialized perspectives.

The final chapter concerns the area of accounting and finance, which is important because it provides some of the essential basic data used in the formulation of strategic decisions. As with Chapter 10, it is not intended to be a comprehensive statement of the area, but only to represent some production management views of serious shortcomings in this essential information provision. The professional accountant may find the approach provocative; it is intended, however, to be more constructive than that. The issues raised aim to challenge current practice and ideas as a way to stimulate improvement.

Finally, I trust that all who use the book will find it helpful. It is vital that manufacturing take its full part in strategic formulation if industrial companies are to prosper in the face of increasing world competition.

TERRY HILL

# 1

# International Comparisons

A new stark reality emerged in the 1980s – the impact of industrial competition. In most industrial nations, the struggle to survive had become, by then, an integral part of each manufacturing company's way of life. To downsize, once an anathema to business, had become an acceptable course of action, demanded by necessity or some comprehensive corporate strategic decision. The economic world of the 1980s was very different from that of the 1960s and 70s. The 1990s continued the trend. The new millennium has increased the pace.

For the most part, however, production decision making in manufacturing firms has not changed to meet these new challenges. In most Western companies, manufacturing management is still subordinate in strategy making to the marketing and finance functions. It continues to concern itself primarily with short-term issues. The underlying argument of this book is that a strategic approach to manufacturing management is essential if companies are to survive, let alone hold their own and grow by competing effectively in domestic and world markets.

This chapter provides some national and corporate comparisons. It shows how some nations with strong industrial traditions have been outperformed, illustrates the extent of the changes that have taken place and compares different approaches to the management of manufacturing. The final section focuses on manufacturing strategy, not only to link this chapter to the remainder of the book but also to highlight the increasing awareness of manufacturing as a strategic force at both national and corporate levels.

## Manufacturing Output

Trends in a nation's performance within its wealth-creating sectors reflect its overall prosperity. Since manufacturing is, for most countries, the most significant activity in this regard, reviewing it provides an insight into a country's general wellbeing.

Comparative figures on manufacturing output in the 1970s through to the late 1990s reveal the mixed fortunes of major industrial nations. Some countries of manufacturing repute have lost ground particularly in the 1970s, while others (for example, Japan, the US and Germany) have maintained sound growth throughout (see Exhibit 1.1).

1

**Exhibit 1.1**    Comparative manufacturing output, 1975–98 (1990 = 100)

| Country   | 1975 | 1980 | 1995 | 1998[2]  |
| --------- | ---- | ---- | ---- | -------- |
| Australia | 80   | 89   | 106  | 110[1]   |
| Canada    | 74   | 84   | 111  | 124      |
| France    | 77   | 91   | 98   | 106      |
| Germany   | 70   | 84   | 97   | 106      |
| Italy     | 70   | 90   | 107  | 107      |
| Japan     | 53   | 68   | 95   | 94       |
| UK        | 89   | 85   | 103  | 104      |
| US        | 61   | 77   | 118  | 137      |

*Notes*
1. The 1998 figure for Australia is based on 1997.
2. The 1998 figure for Canada and the UK is a Q1 and Q2 average, for all
   others it is a Q1, Q2 and Q3 average.

*Source:* OECD, Indicators of Industrial Activity, 1979, 1985, 1992 and 1998

**Exhibit 1.2**    Percentage share of world trade in manufactured goods for selected countries, 1980–96

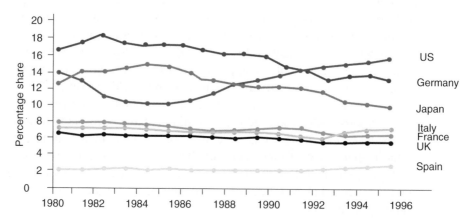

*Source:* OECD and UK Department of Trade and Industry for relevant years

However, of equal concern to these nations is how well they fared within the increasingly competitive markets they serve. Exhibit 1.2 shows the trends in percentage share of world trade in manufactured goods gained by selected countries from 1980 to 1996. The yearly performances of these different countries vary noticeably, particularly at the extremes. The US's strong export position after losing ground in the 1980s strengthened in the 1990s to reach a period high in 1996. Germany and Japan, while declining in the period, were still major performers in terms of world trade. The UK, the world's number one manufacturing nation at the start of the last century, revealed a gradual decline to around 5 per cent. And, in between, the steady improvement by several European countries sets an important benchmark as the major economic blocs of North America, the Asia Pacific and Europe took shape in the 1990s and strengthen into the 21st century.

To complete this initial review, export–import trade ratios are given in Exhibit 1.3 to provide an insight into the relative trading performances of main manufacturing nations, while Exhibit 1.4 provides similar data on all manufacturing for North America and the European Union. This review is further supplemented by Exhibit 1.5, which highlights one of the more recent and important sectors of manufacturing, that of electronics. It shows that several emerging nations are effectively competing in export markets with markedly improving trade balances in this key sector. Both the US and Europe as a whole show a worsening competitive picture in terms of their position in world markets.

The growing prosperity of emerging nations is built on developing their wealth-creating sectors such as manufacturing. Successive UK administrations have tended to act on the often painful premise that exposure to overseas competition is a necessary ingredient for the development of a strong, domestic manufacturing base.

**Exhibit 1.3**  Export–import ratio for selected sectors (1984 and 1995) and total manufacturing (1972, 1984 and 1995)

| Country | Aerospace | | Electronic industry | | Office machinery and computers | | Drugs | | Total manufacturing | | |
|---|---|---|---|---|---|---|---|---|---|---|---|
| | 1984 | 1995 | 1984 | 1995 | 1984 | 1995 | 1984 | 1995 | 1972 | 1984 | 1995 |
| Australia | 0.11 | 0.38 | 0.07 | 0.17 | 0.04 | 0.27 | 0.34 | 0.46 | – | 0.54 | 0.51 |
| Canada | 0.65 | 1.34 | 0.47 | 0.47 | 0.40 | 0.59 | 0.34 | 0.30 | – | 1.01 | 1.01 |
| France | 2.21 | 2.35 | 1.12 | 0.97 | 0.69 | 0.68 | 1.93 | 1.25 | 1.10 | 1.11 | 1.08 |
| Germany | 1.05 | 1.08 | 1.45 | 0.93 | 0.87 | 0.59 | 1.74 | 1.51 | 1.53 | 1.42 | 1.28 |
| Italy | 1.09 | 0.99 | 1.19 | 0.64 | 0.74 | 0.81 | 0.97 | 0.97 | 1.31 | 1.24 | 1.30 |
| Japan | 0.10 | 0.26 | 10.55 | 3.07 | 5.61 | 1.97 | 0.27 | 0.40 | 2.82 | 2.78 | 1.74 |
| UK | 1.43 | 1.53 | 0.73 | 0.87 | 0.73 | 0.97 | 2.14 | 1.74 | 1.09 | 0.81 | 0.90 |
| US | 2.98 | 3.20 | 0.52 | 0.65 | 1.83 | 0.59 | 1.70 | 1.12 | 0.84 | 0.63 | 0.73 |

*Note*
– = not available.

*Source:* OECD, Main Science and Technology Indicators, 1974, 1984 and 1998

**Exhibit 1.4**  Export–import ratio, total manufacturing by region

| Region | Total manufacturing | |
|---|---|---|
| | 1990 | 1995 |
| North America | 0.71 | 0.69 |
| European Union | 1.10 | 1.25 |

*Source:* OECD, Main Science and Technology Indicators, 1998

**Exhibit 1.5**   Trade balance for electronic equipment and components[1] for
selected countries by value ($bn)[2] for 1985, 1993 and 1998

| Country | 1985 | 1993 | 1998 |
|---|---|---|---|
| | $bn | | |
| Australia | (2.6) | (4.6) | (7.7) |
| Canada | (6.7) | (7.5) | (11.4) |
| France | (1.5) | (4.1) | (3.9) |
| Germany | (0.7) | (7.1) | (4.4) |
| Hong Kong | 1.3 | 2.1 | (0.5) |
| Italy | (2.1) | (4.3) | (9.4) |
| Japan | 37.1 | 75.2 | 58.9 |
| Malaysia | 0.7 | 9.0 | 16.9 |
| Singapore | 1.1 | 11.4 | 22.5 |
| South Korea | 2.0 | 11.3 | 17.1 |
| UK | (3.0) | (6.0) | (4.4) |
| US | (14.5) | (29.1) | (50.4) |
| Total Europe | (10.7) | (32.2) | (27.0) |

*Notes*
1. Electronic equipment includes electronic data processing, office equipment,
   controls and instruments, medical, industrial, military, communications, consumer
   and telecommunications. Components comprise active, passive and other.
2. These trade balances are calculated by subtracting the value of imports from the
   value of exports. Figures in brackets indicate an unfavourable balance.

*Source: Yearbook of World Electronic Data*, 1988 and 1993, Vols 1 and 2 (Elsevier
Advanced Technology, Oxford, UK) and 1999, Vols 1 and 2 (Reed Electronics
Research, Sutton, UK)

Of deep concern, however, is that manufacturing industry's response to that exposure has been woefully slow. Many firms have complained about 'unfair' external competition and focused on domestic rather than overseas competitors. They have adopted inadequate, reactive strategies because they have not appreciated the consequences for manufacturing. Typically, they have filled capacity by chasing sales, increasing variety and reducing order sizes, leaving overseas competitors with substantial advantages in the higher-volume segments of their markets. One outcome has been the loss of high-volume markets such as motorcycles, automobiles, trucks and shipbuilding: the nations that are prospering have often built their wealth base in these sectors. Exhibit 1.6 provides one illustration of the consequences of failing to respond quickly and adequately to the growing competitive forces of international competition in world markets.

Many businesses failed to recognize, until too late, that the sellers' markets of earlier years have long since passed. They became entangled in a long period of transition that often lasted into the 1990s. Businesses now need strategies that aim to gain and maintain specific and significant advantages against the most, not least, powerful competitors.

**Exhibit 1.6**  The challenge of world competition: the North American auto lesson in the 1990s

| Implants | | | Closures | | |
|---|---|---|---|---|---|
| Firm | Location | Capacity (000s cars) | Firm | Location | Capacity (000s cars) |
| Honda | Marysville | 360 | General Motors | Detroit | 212 |
| | East Liberty | 150 | | Norwood | 250 |
| | Alliston | 100 | | Leeds | 250 |
| | | | | Pontiac | 100 |
| Nummi | Fremont | 100 | Chrysler | Kenosha | 300 |
| Toyota | Georgetown | 240 | General Motors | Framington | 200 |
| | Cambridge | 50 | | Lakewood | 200 |
| Nissan | Smyrna | 480 | | Pontiac | 54 |
| Mazda | Flat Rock | 240 | Chrysler | Detroit | 21 |
| *Total implant capacity* | | *1720* | *Total closure capacity* | | *1817* |

*Note*
NUMMI = New United Motor Manufacturing Inc., a joint venture between General Motors and Toyota.

While nations such as the US, the UK and others with long manufacturing traditions were being buffeted by this growing surge in competition, some countries seemed to move from strength to strength. Of deeper concern are the facts underlying these trends, especially that of comparative productivity.

## Productivity: National Comparisons

A nation's prosperity depends on its comparative productivity. The past two decades of increasing competition have brought this sharply into focus. Although not a precise measure, it affords a way of assessing trends both for the performance of individual countries and their relative positions in appropriate world rankings.

Thus, there are two important dimensions of a productivity slow-down for any nation. The first is the rate of the slow-down itself; the second is the cumulative effect of the slow-down on the comparative level of productivity between a country and its competitors.

When a nation's growth rate lags substantially behind that of other industrialized countries for a protracted period, its standard of living will decline and companies will find themselves at a serious competitive disadvantage. If this condition goes unchecked, recovery will be increasingly difficult to achieve and breaking free from the downward spiral will be a major task. For the first time in its history, the US is facing the real prospect that its next generation will fail to enjoy a marked improvement in living standards compared with today and may even experience a decline.

Productivity measures the relationship between outputs (in the form of goods and services produced) and inputs (in the form of labour, capital, material and other resources). Although in practice productivity is not so simple to measure because of the global nature of the figures involved, it does provide an overall review of improvement that lends itself to trend analysis. Two types of productivity measurement are commonly used: labour productivity and total-factor or multifactor productivity. Labour productivity measures output in terms of hours worked or paid for. Total-factor or multifactor productivity not only includes the labour input but also all or some of the plant, equipment, energy and material input. However, when there is a change in a single-factor productivity ratio, it is important not to attribute the change solely to that one input. Owing to the interrelated nature of the total inputs involved, the change may well be influenced by any or all of the many variables that could contribute to the change. For example, production methods, capital investment, process technology, labour force, managerial performance, capacity utilization, material input/usage rates, capacity scale and product mix are all potential contributors to productivity improvements. Furthermore, the relative importance of these will vary from nation to nation, industrial sector to industrial sector, company to company, plant to plant and time period to time period.

Although it may be difficult to get a consensus on the quantitative dimensions of productivity measurement, the qualitative conclusions on the differing levels and trends within nations are clearly shown in Exhibits 1.7 and 1.8. They signal the steady, often significant, growth of some nations throughout the period, a fact reflected in the earlier data on performance. The comparative slow-down in the US signals its lead is shrinking with a resulting levelling off in living standards and a corresponding decline in its competitive position.

**Exhibit 1.7**    Trends in outputs per hours in manufacturing for selected countries, 1960–98 (1992 = 100)

| Country | 1960 | 1970 | 1980 | 1990 | 1995 | 1998 |
|---|---|---|---|---|---|---|
| Belgium | 18 | 33 | 65 | 97 | 109 | 122 |
| Canada | 41 | 59 | 75 | 95 | 108 | 112 |
| France | 23 | 46 | 71 | 99 | 114 | 128 |
| Germany | 29 | 52 | 77 | 99 | 111 | 127 |
| Italy | 20 | 37 | 44 | 93 | 114 | 114 |
| Japan | 14 | 38 | 64 | 95 | 109 | 121 |
| Netherlands | 20 | 39 | 70 | 99 | 120 | 133 |
| Sweden | 28 | 53 | 74 | 95 | 122 | 137 |
| UK | 30 | 43 | 54 | 89 | 107 | 105 |
| US | 53 | 62 | 94 | 98 | 115 | 127 |

*Source: Monthly Labor Review,* Bureau of Labor Statistics, US Department of Labor, August 1999

**Exhibit 1.8**  Annual percentage growth in output per hour and total-factor productivity for selected nations, 1950–96 and 1973–96

| Country | Growth in output per hour | | Growth in total factor productivity | |
|---|---|---|---|---|
| | 1950–1996 | 1973–1996 | 1950–1996 | 1973–1996 |
| | % per year | | % per year | |
| France | 4.73 | 3.60 | 3.33 | 2.52 |
| Germany | 4.77 | 2.93 | 2.88 | 1.86 |
| Japan | 6.33 | 4.47 | 2.91 | 2.23 |
| UK | 3.86 | 3.19 | 2.72 | 2.39 |
| US | 2.48 | 2.20 | 1.56 | 1.21 |

## Productivity: Plant-level Comparisons

In the 1990s, the level of competition in major regions such as North America, the Asia Pacific and Europe increased noticeably in most markets. Strong 'domestic' companies in each region were challenged by the big battalions from the powerful industrial nations around the world as market competition moved on apace. The new millennium is witnessing similar trends.

Setting aside arguments concerning trade practices, it is comparative productivity and relative performance on other relevant market factors that will determine which companies gain ground and market share.

The auto industry, a core sector in many industrial nations given the combined size of its assembly activity and supply-chain requirements, is one example of the fierce fighting that is taking place. The overall challenge from the Far East and its effect on the US auto industry was clearly shown earlier in Exhibit 1.6. With regional and global overcapacity at high levels, competition is and will remain fierce and productivity will continue to be a key factor in the comparative success of companies. To be successful in the future, car companies will need to increase efficiency to compete against new rivals and fresh benchmarks. Exhibit 1.9 illustrates the marked differences that exist and the task that lies ahead. The gap for some is enormous, while the challenge from Japan and South Korea is clearly demonstrated. Furthermore, these differences are company rather than location related as shown in Exhibit 1.10. This takes the data in the previous exhibit and presents this by location for both the parent company and manufacturing plant. The best and worst productivity figures again highlight the marked contrasts provided by Asia Pacific and the more established manufacturing nations of North America and Europe.

**Exhibit 1.9**    Productivity in some of the world's car plants, 1997 and 1998

| Automaker and location | | | Vehicles (000s) produced | Vehicles per employee | |
|---|---|---|---|---|---|
| | | | **1998** | **1997** | **1998** |
| **Canada** | GM | Oshawa[1] | 459.4 | 57 | 57 |
| | Toyota | Cambridge | 171.7 | – | 83 |
| **Czech Republic** | Skoda | Mlada Boleslav | 287.5 | 31 | 35 |
| **France** | Renault | Douai | 385.1 | 61 | 68 |
| | PSA | Aulnay | 262.0 | 52 | 58 |
| | PSA | Sochaux | 237.0 | 26 | 31 |
| **Germany** | GM | Eisenach | 174.8 | 77 | 76 |
| | Ford | Saarlouis | 290.4 | 59 | 59 |
| | VW | Emden | 329.7 | 28 | 37 |
| **Italy** | Fiat | Melfi | 383.0 | 70 | 73 |
| | Fiat | Mirafiori | 416.0 | 54 | 61 |
| **Japan** | Mitsubishi | Mizushuma | 521.0 | 147 | 163 |
| | Honda | Suzuka | 567.8 | 123 | 116 |
| | Toyota | Takaota | 450.0 | 122 | 103 |
| | Honda | Sayama | 484.8 | 112 | 114 |
| | Mitsubishi | Okazaki | 173.4 | 111 | 113 |
| | Nissan | Kyushu | 429.7 | 99 | 119 |
| **South Korea** | Daewoo | Changwon | 247.5 | 165 | 165 |
| | Hyundai | Ulsan #2 | 157.0 | 62 | 65 |
| **Spain** | VW | Navarra | 311.1 | 70 | 76 |
| | SEAT | Martorell | 498.5 | 69 | 69 |
| | Renault | Valladolid | 213.6 | 59 | 64 |
| **UK** | Nissan | Sunderland | 288.8 | 98 | 105 |
| | Honda | Swindon | 112.3 | 62 | 64 |
| | Ford | Dagenham | 250.4 | 62 | 61 |
| | Toyota | Burnaston | 172.3 | 58 | 72 |
| | Rover | Longbridge | 281.9 | 34 | 31 |
| **US** | Toyota/GM | NUMMI | 361.9 | 87 | 87 |
| | Honda | East Liberty | 238.7 | 85 | 87 |
| | Honda | Marysville | 456.0 | 82 | 88 |
| | Ford | Wayne | 226.5 | 79 | 72 |
| | Toyota | Georgetown | 475.3 | 78 | 83 |
| | Ford | Atlanta | 257.0 | 75 | 84 |
| | Nissan | Smyrna | 308.8 | 72 | 56 |
| | Ford | Chicago | 255.3 | 69 | 81 |
| | GM | Doraville | 257.2 | – | 51 |

*Notes*
1. GM's Oshawa figures are for two car plants.
2. – = not available.

*Source:* Motor Business Europe (Q4, 1999), Motor Business International (Q4, 1999) and Motor Business, Japan (Q4, 1999). The Economist Intelligence Unit (UK) 1999

**Exhibit 1.10** Best and worst productivity levels by automaker and regional location (1998)

| Regional location | | Vehicles per employee (1998) | |
| --- | --- | --- | --- |
| Parent company | Manufacturing plant | Best | Worst |
| European | Europe | 76 | 31 |
| Japanese | Europe | 105 | 64 |
| | Japan | 163 | 103 |
| | North America | 88 | 56 |
| North American | Europe | 76 | 59 |
| | North America | 84 | 51 |
| South Korean | South Korea | 165 | 65 |

# Why Has This Happened?

The reasons why this has happened are many and varied, and are discussed below. Some are unsubstantiated opinions, others are supported by fact. Some will be more relevant to some nations, sectors and companies and others less. However, learning from past failures is a step towards determining how to build a more successful competitive future.

## Failure to Recognize the Size of the Competitive Challenge

Consciously or otherwise, industry and society at large have failed to recognize the size of the competitive challenge, the impact it was having and would have on our very way of life and the need to change.

The significant loss of market share in smokestack industries by major industrial nations since 1950 is the most vivid example of those nations' misunderstanding of the size of the competitive challenge. And the challenge will continue. In the shadow of Japan, there are now many other competitors eager to take a larger share in world manufacturing output. Exhibit 1.11 provides one such example.

## Failure to Appreciate the Impact of Increasing Manufacturing Capacity

World manufacturing capacity up to the mid-1960s was, by and large, less than demand; in this period companies could sell all they could make. With the rebuilding of some industrial nations and the emergence of others, output in both traditional and new industrial nations began to outstrip total demand. At first, the more traditional sectors (such as shipbuilding and steel) were caught in the bind of overcapacity. Since then this has spread into other sectors such as automobiles and

**Exhibit 1.11**  Production of machine tools without parts and accessories for selected countries (millions of Ecu, index for 1997)

| Country | 1985 | 1990 | 1995 | 1997[2] | 1997 (1990 = 100) |
|---|---|---|---|---|---|
| Belgium | 130 | 224 | 189 | 213 | 95 |
| China | – | 645 | 1242 | 1380 | 214 |
| Denmark | 58 | 67 | 61 | 58 | 87 |
| France | 695 | 920 | 601 | 833 | 91 |
| Germany | 4401 | 6872[1] | 5579 | 5993 | 87 |
| India | – | 180 | 164 | 217 | 121 |
| Italy | 1535 | 2889 | 2537 | 3040 | 105 |
| Japan | 7399 | 8629 | 6992 | 8594 | 100 |
| South Korea | 248 | 669 | 695 | 776 | 116 |
| Netherlands | 50 | 106 | 95 | 125 | 118 |
| Spain | 350 | 800 | 506 | 719 | 90 |
| Taiwan | 381 | 737 | 1266 | 1550 | 210 |
| US | 3668 | 2660 | 3520 | 4054 | 152 |
| UK | 1010 | 1179 | 753 | 978 | 83 |

*Notes*
1. Up to 1990 the data for Germany includes the former DDR.
2. 1997 figures are all estimates.
3. – = not available.

*Source:* CECIMO Statistical Overview of the Machine Tool Industry 1985–97 (1998)

semiconductors. The most significant and consistent outcome has been the impact on competition. Overcapacity has contributed to the competitive nature of markets. The results have added to the dynamic nature of current markets both in terms of the form that competition takes and the timescales of change experienced.

## Willingness to Invest in Research and Development (R&D)

The pressure to market more and better products has heightened in recent years because of increasing competition and shorter product life cycles. One significant factor to help meet this growing need is to invest in R&D. Exhibit 1.12 reflects the clear commitment of major manufacturing nations in this regard. It shows the relative size of spend and trends over time for selected countries and regions. By 1989, Japan headed the list for the first time* and it continues to do so. Finally, the South Korean figures show a real growing commitment to technical development, a fact in keeping with several emerging and increasingly competitive economies.

---

\* The detail is not included in Exhibit 1.12 but was 2.98 per cent compared with the US at 2.88 per cent for 1989.

**Exhibit 1.12** Gross domestic expenditure on R&D as a percentage of gross domestic product (GDP)

| Country | 1981 | 1985 | 1992 | 1995 | 1997 |
|---|---|---|---|---|---|
| Australia | – | 1.27 | 1.59 | 1.62[1] | 1.68[2] |
| Canada | 1.23 | 1.44 | 1.55 | 1.62 | 1.64 |
| France | 2.01 | 2.25 | 2.42 | 2.34 | 2.26 |
| Germany | 2.45 | 2.72 | 2.48 | 2.30 | 2.39 |
| Italy | 1.01 | 1.13 | 1.20 | 1.01 | 1.05 |
| Japan | 2.32 | 2.77 | 2.95 | 2.98 | 2.83[2] |
| South Korea | – | – | 2.08 | 2.68 | 2.79[2] |
| UK | 2.42 | 2.31 | 2.13 | 2.02 | 1.94[2] |
| US | 2.45 | 2.93 | 2.74 | 2.61 | 2.64 |
| Total North America | – | – | 2.43 | 2.34 | 2.36 |
| Total EU | – | – | 1.92 | 1.84 | 1.84[2] |

*Notes*
1. 1995 figure for Australia is for 1994.
2. 1997 figures for Australia, Japan, South Korea, UK and Total EU are for 1996 respectively.
3. – = not available.

*Source:* OECD, Main Science and Technology Indicators for relevant years

**Exhibit 1.13** Technology balance of payments – coverage ratio

| Country | 1984 | 1990 | 1992 | 1994 | 1996 |
|---|---|---|---|---|---|
| Australia | 0.22 | – | 0.54 | 0.52 | 0.62 |
| Canada | 0.85 | – | 1.07 | 1.15[1] | 1.27[2] |
| France | 0.90 | 0.76 | 0.72 | 0.73 | 0.75 |
| Germany | 0.77 | 0.83 | 0.72 | 0.80 | 0.75 |
| Italy | 0.29 | 0.58 | 0.55 | 0.58 | 0.77[2] |
| Japan | 0.99 | 0.91 | 0.91 | 1.25 | 1.56 |
| Mexico | – | – | 0.18 | 0.16 | 0.34 |
| UK | 1.05 | 0.75 | 1.08 | 1.17 | 1.19[2] |
| US | 5.52 | 5.26 | 3.89 | 4.04 | 4.27[2] |

*Notes*
1. 1994 figure for Canada is for 1993.
2. 1996 figures for Canada, Italy, UK and the US are for 1995 respectively.
3. Figures >1 show receipts greater than payments.
4. – = not available.

*Source:* OECD Main Science and Technology Indicators for relevant years

The final perspective on issues of R&D expenditure is provided by Exhibit 1.13. Many countries with the committed R&D levels of spending shown in Exhibit 1.12 further supplement this by importing technology at a rate higher than that at which they sell. The US is the notable exception.

## Top Management's Lack of Manufacturing Experience

Top management's lack of experience in manufacturing has further ramifications for a business. Since manufacturing accounts for some 60–70 per cent of assets, expenditure and people, senior executives must fully appreciate the arguments and counter-arguments in manufacturing, ensuring that they consider the accompanying wide range of perspectives when making important manufacturing decisions. Once a company has made large investments, rarely does it invest a second time to correct any mistakes. There is no such lack of experience in Japan and Germany, where a full and perceptive insight into manufacturing is a prerequisite for top management.

However, the consequences of this knowledge gap do not stop here. As Wickham Skinner observes:

> to many executives, manufacturing and the production function is a necessary nuisance – it soaks up capital in facilities and inventories, it resists changes in products and schedules, its quality is never as good as it should be, and its people are unsophisticated, tedious, detail-oriented and unexciting. This makes for an unreceptive climate for major innovations in factory technology and contributes to the blind spot syndrome.[1]

And this brings with it many important consequences. One is that senior executives do not perceive the strategic potential of manufacturing. Typically it is seen in its traditional productivity-efficiency mode with the added need to respond to the strategic overtures of marketing and finance. The result is that manufacturing concentrates its effort and attention on the short term while adopting its classic, reactive posture towards the long-term strategic issues of the business.

## The Production Manager's Obsession with Short-term Performance Issues

The emphasis within the production manager's role has, in turn, been directed towards short-term issues and tasks. The overriding pressures to meet day-to-day targets and the highly quantifiable nature of the role and the output measures have reinforced the tendency of manufacturing executives to concern themselves with this feature to the exclusion of the important long term. The skills of production managers are high on short-term tasks such as scheduling, maintaining efficiency levels, controls and resolving labour problems.

Skinner rightly observed this twenty years ago when he commented that:

> most factories were not managed very differently in the 1970s than in the 1940s and 1950s. Manufacturing management was dominated by engineering and a technical point of view. This may have been adequate when *production* management issues centered largely on efficiency and productivity and the answers came from industrial engineering and process engineering. But the problems of operations managers in the 1970s had moved far beyond mere physical efficiency.[2]

This trend has continued in line with the fast-changing nature of markets. By the turn of the century, the production job had changed from one that concerned maintaining steady-state manufacturing by sound day-to-day husbandry to one that is now multidimensional. It is increasingly concerned with managing greater complexity in product range, product mix, volume changes, process flexibility, inventory, cost and financial controls and employee awareness because of the more intensive level of domestic and international competition.

This is the nature of the new task in the new millennium. No longer are the key issues solely confined to operational control and fine-tuning the system. The need is for broad, business-oriented manufacturing managers. But, companies have produced too few of them. The use of specialists as the way to control our businesses has increasingly led to a reduction in the breadth of a line manager's responsibilities, that has narrowed the experience base. Furthermore, many manufacturing managers, outgunned by specialist argument, have found themselves unable to cope with the variety of demands placed on them. The response by many has been to revert increasingly to their strengths. This has, therefore, reinforced their short-term role and their inherently reactive stance to corporate strategic resolution.

Manufacturing executives do not, on the whole, explain the important, conceptual aspects of manufacturing to others in the organization. Seldom do they evaluate and expose the implications for manufacturing of corporate decisions so that alternatives can be considered and more soundly based decisions can be reached. This is partly because of a lack of developed language to help explain the corporate production issues involved. Lacking, therefore, in strategic dimension, manufacturing has often been forced into piecemeal change, achieving what it can as and when it has been able. The result has been a series of intermittent responses lacking corporate coordination.

## Manufacturing Strategy

In the past decade and a half, countries such as Japan, Germany and Italy, as well as emerging industrial nations such as South Korea and Taiwan, have gained competitive advantage through manufacturing. The Japanese, in particular, have gone for existing markets and provided better goods with few, if any, inherent benefits derived from material and energy resources. The earlier examples serve to illustrate this.

One of the keys to this achievement through manufacturing has been the integration of these functional perspectives into corporate strategy debate, and it is appropriate now to explain what this embodies and how it differs from the conventional approaches to the management of production. In broad terms, there are two important roles that manufacturing can offer as part of the strategic strengths of a company.

The first is to provide manufacturing processes that give the business a distinct advantage in the marketplace. In this way, manufacturing will provide a market edge through unique technological developments in its process and manufacturing operations that competitors are unable to match. This is quite rare and examples are hard to find. One such is Pilkington's float-glass process.[3]

The second is to provide coordinated manufacturing support for the essential ways in which products win orders in the marketplace that is better than such support provided by the manufacturing functions of its competitors. Manufacturing must choose its process and design its infrastructure (for example, controls, procedures, systems and structures) that are consistent with the existing way(s) that products win orders, while being able to reflect future developments in line with changing business needs. Most companies share access to the same processes, and thus technology is not inherently different. Similarly, the systems, structures and other elements of infrastructure are equally universal. What is different is the degree to which manufacturing matches process and infrastructure to those criteria that win orders. In this way, manufacturing constitutes a coordinated response to the business needs that embraces all those aspects of a company for which manufacturing is responsible.

To do this effectively, manufacturing needs to be involved throughout the whole of the corporate strategy debate to explain, in business terms, the implications of corporate marketing proposals and, as a result, be able to influence strategy decisions for the good of the business as a whole. Too often in the past, manufacturing has been too late in this procedure. Corporate executives have tended to assume that competitive strategies are more to do with, and often in fact are one and the same as, marketing initiatives. Implicit, if not explicit, in this view are two important assumptions. The first is that manufacturing's role is to respond to these changes rather than to make inputs into them. The second is that manufacturing has the capability to respond flexibly and positively to these changing demands. The result has been manufacturing's inability to influence decisions, which has led to a posture that appears to be forever complaining about the unrealistic demands placed upon production.

The need for a manufacturing strategy to be developed and shared by the business is not only to do with the critical nature of manufacturing within corporate strategy but also a realization that many of the decisions are structural in nature. This means that they are hard to change. If the business does not fully appreciate the issues and consequences, it can be locked into a number of manufacturing decisions that will take years to change. These can range from process investments on the one hand to human resource management practices and controls on the other. Decisions not in line with the needs of the business can contribute significantly to a lack of corporate success. To change them is costly and time consuming. But even more significant, they will come too late. The development of a corporate policy consisting of a coordinated set of main function inputs will mean that a business would be able to go in one consistent, coherent direction based on a well-argued, well-understood and well-formed strategy. This is achieved, in part, by moving away from argument, disagreement, misunderstanding and short-term, parochial moves based on inter-functional perspectives to the resolution of these differences at the corporate level. Currently, marketing-led strategies leave the aftermath to be resolved by manufacturing, which without adequate, appropriate guidance or discussion and agreement at the corporate level, resolves the issues as best it can largely from its unilateral view of what is best for the business as a whole.

In the majority of cases, manufacturing is simply not geared to a business's corporate objectives. The result is a manufacturing system, good in itself, but not designed to meet company needs. Manufacturing left in the wake of corporate decisions is often at best a neutral force, and even sometimes inadvertently pulls in the opposite direction. Seen as being concerned solely with efficiency, the question of production's strategic contribution is seldom part of the corporate consciousness.

What does all this mean for production managers? One clear consequence is the need to change from a reactive to a proactive stance. The long-term inflexible nature of manufacturing means that the key issues, and there are many of them, involved in process choice and infrastructure development need to be reflected in business decisions, with the business being made aware of the implications for manufacturing of proposed corporate changes. When this is achieved, the strategy decisions that are then taken reflect what is best for the business as a whole. So manufacturing management's attention must increasingly be towards strategy. This does not mean that day-to-day operations are unimportant, but the balance and direction of management activity needs to reflect the relative impact on business performance of both strategy and operations while recognising that both need to be done well. Top management have, by and large, perceived corporate improvements as coming mainly through broad decisions concerning new markets, takeovers and the like. However, the building blocks of corporate success are to be found in creating effective, successful businesses where manufacturing supports the market requirements within a well-chosen, well-argued and well-understood corporate strategy.

# Conclusion

There is a growing and consistent awareness that the emphasis in successfully managed manufacturing functions is increasingly towards issues of strategy. Early evidence was provided in the Advisory Council for Applied Research and Development's 1983 booklet entitled *New Opportunities in Manufacturing: The Managements of Technology*. This specifically recommended that 'companies in manufacturing should review the balance of their senior management (team) and ensure that the role of a suitably qualified board member includes responsibility for manufacturing strategy'.[4] In the 21st century, this board level contribution is even more crucial to the continued success and growth of companies.

Top management needs to pay a great deal more than lip service to the task of ensuring that manufacturing's input into the strategic debate is comprehensive and that the agreed corporate decisions fully reflect the complex issues involved. Much determination will need to be exercised to ensure that the more superficial approaches to incorporating the wide-ranging aspects of manufacturing into corporate decisions are avoided. The rewards for this are substantial.

Manufacturing executives must begin to think and act in a more strategic manner. In an environment traditionally geared to meeting output targets, the pressure on manufacturing has been to manage reactively and to be operationally efficient rather than strategically effective. It has been more concerned with doing things right (efficiency) than doing the right things (effectiveness). Over the years, this has been seen as the appropriate manufacturing task and contribution. Furthermore, it has given rise to the related assumption that any other posture would imply negative attitudes, with manufacturing appearing to be putting obstacles in the way of achieving key corporate objectives. At times, this puts manufacturing in the vicious circle of corporate demands on manufacturing, manufacturing's best response, a recriminating corporate appraisal of that response, new corporate demands for improved manufacturing performance and so on. The purpose of this book is to help to avoid the all-too-common corporate approach to manufacturing by providing a set of concepts and approaches that together create a platform from which manufacturing can make a positive contribution to developing powerful competitive strategies. But, manufacturing executives must first accept that they need to manage their own activities strategically and this is almost as much a change in management attitude as it is an analytical process.

The purpose of thinking and managing strategically is not just to improve operational performance or to defend market share. It is to gain competitive advantage and it implies an attempt to mobilize manufacturing capability to help to gain this competitive edge. Kenichi Ohmae, a leading Japanese consultant with McKinsey,[5] suggests that when managers are striving to achieve or maintain a position of relative superiority over competitors, their minds work very differently from when the objective is to make operational improvements against, often arbitrarily set, internal objectives.

This chapter has highlighted manufacturing's tendency to emphasize operational efficiency more than competitive advantage. The danger for the business is that manufacturing gets so used to absorbing and responding to demands that reacting becomes the norm. Each crisis is viewed as a temporary situation, that often militates against recognizing the need to review strategies fundamentally. By the time this need becomes obvious, the business is often at a serious competitive disadvantage.

The aims of this book are to help manufacturing reverse its reactive tendencies and change its short-term perspective; that is, to explain manufacturing from a strategic perspective by identifying the managerial and corporate issues that need to be addressed to establish competitive advantage.

There is much evidence that in many traditional manufacturing nations the capability exists to turn domestic manufacturing around and to challenge and beat overseas competition in both home and world markets. There are already examples of that turnaround in competitive performance, but the key ingredients include tough, professional management, combining strategic analysis of key issues with the intuitive, creative flair that for so long has been directed primarily towards solving operational problems.

It is imperative that manufacturing managers take the initiative. For some organizations or functions with a business, the *status quo* even suits them. In those same organizations, manufacturing is played off against a forever-changing set of objectives and targets, and it hurts. If manufacturing waits for other corporate initiatives they will not come soon enough. The lack of empathy and understanding by top management towards manufacturing often means that, when difficulties arise, the preferred course of action is to get rid of the problem by selling off the business or buying in from outside. The causes of the problem are seldom addressed. Companies should realize that there are no long-term profits to be made in easy manufacturing tasks – anyone can provide these. It is in the difficult areas where profits are to be made. Furthermore, selling off inherent infrastructure can lead to an inability to compete effectively in future markets. The critical task facing manufacturing managers is to explain the essential nature of manufacturing in business terms, and this must embrace both process technology and infrastructure development.

# Notes

1. W. Skinner, 'Operations Technology: Blind Spot in Strategic Management', Harvard Business School working paper 83–5 (1983), p. 11.
2. W. Skinner, 'Operations Technology', p, 6. These views are also confirmed by the author in his book entitled *Operations Management, Strategic Context and Managerial Analysis,* Basingstoke, UK: Macmillan Business, 2000.
3. The development of the float-glass process in the 1950s by Pilkington, a UK glass manufacturer, was a remarkable step forward in the technology of float-glass making. The costly grinding and polishing operations in the conventional manufacture of glass were eliminated and the result was plate glass production at a fraction of the cost.
4. Advisory Council for Applied Research and Development, *New Opportunities in Manufacturing: The Management of Technology*, London: HMSO Cabinet Office, October 1983, p. 48.
5. K. Ohmae, *The Mind of the Strategist*, New York: McGraw-Hill, 1982, pp. 36–7.

# 2 Developing a Manufacturing Strategy – Principles and Concepts

Companies invest in a wide range of functions and capabilities in order to make and sell products at a profit. Consequently the degree to which a company's functions are aligned to the needs of its markets will significantly affect its overall revenue growth and profit. The appropriate investment in processes and infrastructure in manufacturing is fundamental to this success. The reality is that a lack of fit between these key investments and a company's markets will lead to a business being well wide of the mark. If a firm could change its manufacturing investments without incurring such penalties as long delays and large reinvestments, then the strategic decisions within manufacturing would be of little concern or consequence. However, nothing could be further from the truth. Many executives are still unaware

> that what appear to be routine manufacturing decisions frequently come to limit the corporation's strategic options, binding it with facilities, equipment, personnel, basic controls and policies to a non-competitive posture, which may take years to turn round.[1]

The compelling reasons to ensure fit are tied to the very nature of manufacturing process and infrastructure investments, which are invariably large and fixed. They are large in terms of the size of the investment (£s) and fixed in that it takes a long time to agree, sanction and implement these decisions in the first instance and even longer to agree to change them. Companies having invested inappropriately cannot afford to put things right. The financial implications, systems development, training requirements and the time to make the changes would leave the company, at best, seriously disadvantaged. To avoid this, companies need to be aware of how well manufacturing can support the marketplace and be conscious of the investments and time dimensions involved in changing current positions into future proposals.

## Functional Strategies within the Context of a Firm

Four levels of strategy are present within the overall context of a firm and its environment. The degree to which each will impact a company's competitiveness will vary depending, for instance, on the industrial sector(s) involved and the arena of competition such as domestic, regional or world markets.[2]

- *Industrial level strategy* – of concern here are issues that appertain to an industrial sector or reflect the level and nature of government intervention. They include dimensions such as trade barriers, investment incentives, national security, cost of capital, government and banking relationships with industry and government policies on inflation, employment and intervention.

- *Corporate level strategy* – this concerns the market sectors in which a company, as a whole, decides to compete, the degree of importance it attaches to each sector and the priority given to each sector in terms of investment and other allocations of resources.

- *Business level strategy* – companies typically comprise many businesses. In many companies there is an increasing level of independence between the parts that make up the corporate whole. Car companies (and others with similar levels of commonality in terms of products and markets) are the exception rather than the rule. Most companies are marked with diversity. Business level strategies invariably, therefore, concern identifying the markets in which each of the several (often many) businesses compete and the dimensions of competition involved.

- *Functional level strategy* – at this level, different functions have the principal or shared responsibility for supporting those factors in a company's markets on which it competes. Invariably, a company will compete in several markets and hence each function will need to develop a strategy appropriate to each of these markets. Functional strategies concern investing in and developing the necessary capabilities to bring this about.

This book concerns the strategy of the manufacturing function. It is about how to develop manufacturing strategies to support (with the other relevant functions in a business) agreed markets. However, this requires coordination both on the horizontal dimension (across functions) and also on the vertical dimension (linking functional strategies with the business and corporate levels).

## Functional Executives: Strategy versus Other Roles

Executives have several sets of responsibilities. These tasks embrace:

- *management and control* – the requirement to manage and control the various aspects of their function
- *efficiency* – the need to undertake the various tasks and responsibilities at lowest cost
- *strategy* – the requirement to develop functional strategies that support the relevant needs of a company's markets.

Whereas the first two tasks are invariably recognized as being an integral part of an executive's role, the third is not. In part this is due to a failure to separate the sets of tasks involved. Thus, while the first two form part of the corporate and executive's own expectations, the third does not.

In corporate terms, the first two concern efficiency. Both are essential but they are predominantly operational tasks. Functional strategies, on the other hand, concern the prioritizing of developments and investments within a function in terms of supporting a company's agreed markets. Thus a function's strategic role is to develop the processes, procedures, systems, people and other capabilities for which it has responsibility in line with the needs of agreed markets. In some instances, a function will have sole responsibility for supporting a given market need, and in others this will be shared by two or more functions.

## Functional Strategies

In most companies, corporate strategy statements are a compilation of functional strategies and nothing more. They are derived independently both of one another and the corporate whole (see Exhibit 2.1).

**Exhibit 2.1**    Functional strategies are developed independently of one another and the corporate whole

---

\* Manufacturing here includes supplier relations, purchasing, distribution and other operations activities – also, see Chapter 9.

**Exhibit 2.2**    Integrating functional strategies and forging the corporate strategic outcome

Charged with developing strategies for their own parts of a business, functions such as research and development, marketing, manufacturing* and engineering prepare such statements independently. The result is a comprehensive list of functional statements that are then put together as the strategy for the corporate whole. However, company-wide debate rarely concerns how these fit together or assesses their support of agreed markets. Congruence is assumed and is given credence by the use of broad descriptions of strategy that, instead of providing clarity and the means of testing fit, wash over the debate in generalities.

Through debate and challenge, functional strategies must be developed that support agreed markets with consistency between the various parts of a business. Only in this way can coherent strategies be forged that align all functions to support the business. Thus, corporate strategy is the outcome of functional strategies and can only be achieved by integration across the functional boundaries; corporate strategy, then, is both the binding mechanism for and the end result of this process (see Exhibit 2.2). Thus, all the functions within a business need to be party to agreeing the blueprint of corporate strategy. They are then party to the debate and its resolution that facilitates the identification of the individual strategies necessary to support agreed direction and for which each function takes responsibility.

---

* See footnote on p. 20

## Strategies versus Philosophies

Strategies concern supporting markets. Therefore those functions that have the principal or shared responsibility for providing the needs of markets have to develop a strategy to undertake those tasks. Many companies, however, have failed to recognize this link. Consequently, all functions (irrespective of whether or not they have responsibility for directly supporting a company's markets) have been asked to provide strategic statements as an input into the overall strategy of the firm. Companies have failed to distinguish between strategies (actions to directly support markets) and philosophies (preferred ways of accomplishing tasks or approaches to elements of management).

This has added to the confusion. Philosophies have been mixed in with strategies. For example, R&D's strategic inputs may concern issues such as product design and material substitution; marketing's issues may include branding, pricing and customer relations; manufacturing's may include delivery reliability, price and quality conformance; and engineering's may include process development and technical support. However, other functions do not have a strategic role *per se*.

For example, human resources, accounting and finance provide essential inputs to a business but, invariably, they have neither the principal nor shared responsibility for any factors in a company's markets. Therefore they would not have a strategic role. However, that is not to say that their role is insignificant. On the contrary, their inputs are essential and far reaching. They are, though, in the form of philosophical statements about approaches that enhance the overall ability of a company to undertake and fulfil its operational and strategic tasks.

Why argue for this distinction? The reason is to increase a company's awareness of what strategy is, which functions are responsible for providing the relevant dimensions and the key role of other functions to help in this task. Until companies sharpen their awareness of the necessity to understand markets, identify the functions with prime responsibility for providing relevant market needs and harness the support of the whole organization in that provision then they will continue to be disadvantaged in a world where the level of competition continues to increase. Without this, strategy will continue to be expressed and explained in a broad, generic manner, fail to provide direction and give functions no option other than do what they think best. Motherhood and apple pie have good attributes in themselves but are not necessarily strategic in their origins or orientation.

## Functional Dominance within Corporate Strategy

In broad terms, the changing world demand/capacity balance has brought with it a change in the fortunes of different functions. Up to the mid-1960s, many industries had enjoyed a capacity/demand relationship that favoured manufacturing's position in the sphere of strategic influence. This, together with postwar growth, helped create the dominance of the manufacturing function in many corporations. As the demand/capacity balance began to even out and selling into existing and new markets became more difficult, the power base of corporate influence began to swing away from manufacturing, heralding the rise of marketing. Then by the mid-1970s, the impact of recessions and energy crises had, in turn, opened the door to the influence of accounting and finance. These varying fortunes, however, rarely seemed to be based on what was best for the total good of the business, but more on which functional perspective appeared to provide the key to corporate success or salvation. As a result, those functions out in the cold themselves were left without due corporate influence.

These events reinforced the functional bias within corporate strategy debate explained in the last section. The independent formulation of functional strategies and the failure to cross-relate them continues to be the order of the day. This failure to debate strategy has led to essential perspectives and contributions of key functions being left out of strategic outcomes.

However, the existence of increasing world competition, overcapacity in many sectors of manufacturing industry, increasing scarcity of key resources and decreasing product life cycles make it all the more logical for businesses to incorporate the key functional perspectives when determining policy decisions. Why then, does this not happen? In many organizations, manufacturing adopts or is required to take a reactive stance in corporate strategy discussions. Yet how can the perspectives of the function that controls such a large slice of the assets, expenditure and people, thus underpinning the very welfare of a company, be omitted?

## Reasons for Manufacturing's Reactive Role in Corporate Strategy Formulation

The importance of manufacturing's contribution to the success of a business is readily acknowledged. The prosperous nations of today owe their success to their wealth-creating sectors, of which manufacturing is a key part. Why then do manufacturing executives typically adopt a reactive role within strategic debate? Why does this situation not improve?

## How Operations Executives See Their Role

A prime reason why manufacturing's strategic contribution is reactive is that this is how operations managers view their strategic role. They define their role as requiring them to react as well as possible to all that is asked of the operations system. They feel they must:

- exercise skill and experience in effectively coping with the exacting and varying demands placed on manufacturing
- reconcile the trade-offs inherent in these demands as best they can.

Rarely do they see as an integral part of their role the need to contribute appropriately to corporate decisions that will impact the demands on manufacturing and its ability to provide the necessary market support.

They do not explain the different sets of manufacturing implications created by alternative policy decisions and changes in direction. By not contributing at the corporate level, they fail to help the company arrive at decisions that embrace all the important business perspectives.

## How Companies See Manufacturing's Strategic Contribution

Companies themselves often reinforce operations executives' emphasis on the short-term operational aspects of manufacturing. They too see manufacturing's role as involving day-to-day operations and signal this orientation through discussion and required contributions.

Companies also reinforce such an orientation by the way in which they develop managers within manufacturing. Many companies typically promote operators to supervisors, supervisors to managers, and managers to executives, with scant regard for the change in emphasis that needs to take place. They provide little help to make this transition a success. One major company, recognizing the important corporate contribution to be made by its manufacturing executives, instituted a series of tailor-made programmes in manufacturing strategy. During the first of these, 16 plant managers reflected that as a group their aggregate company service exceeded 300 years, yet the collective training they had received to help them prepare for their manufacturing executive roles was less than 30 days.

The outcome is that the short-term, 'minding the store' role is reinforced by corporate expectations. Thus, the accepted and required contribution of manufacturing executives tends to be confined to the day to day, and the reactive role in strategy decision making continues to be the reality.[3]

## Too Late in the Corporate Debate to Effectively Influence Strategic Outcomes

Manufacturing executives typically are not involved, or do not involve themselves, in corporate strategy decisions until these decisions have started to take shape. Before long, this point of entry into the strategy debate becomes the norm. The result is that manufacturing has less opportunity to contribute and less chance to influence outcomes. As a consequence, operations managers always appear to be complaining about the unrealistic demands made of them and the problems that invariably ensue.

## Failure to Say 'No' when Strategically Appropriate

The 'can't say no' syndrome is still the hallmark of the operations culture. But this helps no one. Manufacturing executives tend to respond to corporate needs and difficulties without evaluating the consequences or alternatives and then explaining these to others. Any senior executive, including those in manufacturing, must be able to say 'no' from a total business perspective and with sound corporate-related arguments. In typical situations, operations managers accept the current and future demands placed on the systems and capacities they control, then work to resolve them. In this way, they decide between corporate alternatives, but only from a narrow functional perspective of what they believe to be best for the business. It is essential that this changes. Resolving corporate-related issues in a unilateral way is not the most effective method to resolve the complex alternatives at hand. This resolution needs corporate debate to ensure that the relevant factors and options are taken into account so an appropriate corporate decision can be concluded.

Strategic decisions need to encompass the important trade-offs embodied in alternatives that have their roots in the process and infrastructure investments associated with manufacturing and are reflected in the high proportion of assets and expenditures under its control.

## Lack of Language to Explain, and Concepts to Underpin, Manufacturing Strategy

On the whole, operations managers do not have a history of explaining their functions clearly and effectively to others in the organization. This is particularly so for manufacturing strategy issues and the consequences that will arise from the corporate decisions under discussion. On the other hand, marketing and financial executives are able to explain their function in a more straightforward and intelligible manner.[4] By talking about how strategic alternatives will affect the business, they can capture the attention of others regarding the issues at hand and their strategic outcomes.

However, the reasons for this difference in perspective and presentation are not solely attributable to manufacturing executives themselves. The knowledge base, concepts and language essential to highlighting corporate relevance and arresting attention have not been developed to the same level within manufacturing as within other key functions. Consequently, shared perspectives within manufacturing, let alone between functions, are not held, which contributes to the lack of interfunctional understanding.

For evidence of this last point, compare the number of books and articles written and postgraduate and postexperience courses provided in the area of manufacturing strategy to those for the other major functions of marketing and accounting/finance. Relatively few contributors address this fundamental area. The result is that manufacturing executives are less able to explain their essential perspectives. Hence, executives from other functions are less attuned to the ideas and perspectives that form the basis for understanding manufacturing's strategic contribution.

## Functional Goals versus Manufacturing's Needs

In many organizations, the managers of different functions are measured by their departmental efficiency (an operational perspective) and not overall effectiveness (a business perspective). Furthermore, their career prospects are governed by their performance within the functional value system. As a consequence, managers make trade-offs that are suboptimal for the business as a whole. Typically, the performance of these specialist departments is measured by their own functionally derived goals and perspectives rather than those of line management and hence the requirements of the business itself. Getting adequate and timely resources committed to manufacturing's needs normally proves difficult.

Competing in different value systems, being measured against different performance criteria and gaining prominence and promotion through different departmental opinions of what constitutes important contributions has gradually fragmented the functions making up a business. It has created a situation where shared perspectives and overlapping views are left to individual accomplishment and endeavour rather than in response to clear corporate direction.

**Exhibit 2.3**   The dichotomy of business views illustrated by the different figures included on typical customer-order paperwork

Source: T. Hill, *Manufacturing Strategy: The Strategic Management of the Manufacturing Function*, New York: Macmillan, 1993, p. 30 (with permission)

Exhibit 2.3 illustrates this dichotomy. An accountant or salesperson, when receiving a customer order, will typically look at one figure as being the most significant measure of business relevance – the total value (£s) of the order placed.

Given the same document, manufacturing managers will look at the order make-up. For them, the business relevance of an order is not its value, but the product mix, volumes and delivery requirements it embodies. This aspect determines the ease with which an order can be made in terms of the process configurations already laid down and the process lead times involved. It will reflect manufacturing's ability to meet the cost base and delivery schedule of the product(s) ordered, and hence the profit margin and delivery performance that will result.

Where marketing is measured by the level of sales revenue achieved, each £ of sales in their value system will carry the same weight as any other £ of sales. Hence all sales are deemed equal. In reality, all orders are not of the same value to a business. The higher the level of fit between product mix and anticipated volumes and actual sales, the more that target level will normally be met. Product costs based on one level of volumes or process configurations based on a given product mix are rarely, if ever, realigned with incremental volume and mix changes. Even the costing base that underpins initial forecasts is rarely, if ever, adjusted each time the market picture alters. A great business divide, therefore, separates the two realities of marketing and manufacturing. The simplistic measure of total sales value disguises those market characteristics so essential to manufacturing's ability to sustain cost and profit-margin structures in a business and other order-winners that create long-term growth.

## Length of Tenure

Since the mid-1960s, there has been a growing practice to reduce the length of tenure for job incumbents. Introduced under the umbrella of executive development, it has been seen as a way of broadening perspectives and signalling the company's level of regard for an executive's future within the corporation. However, the significant drawbacks of this trend have largely gone unnoticed. Managerially and strategically it goes against the overall corporate good. It militates against executives developing the areas of responsibility within their control and contributing to the essential long-term strategic requirements of a business. For without the necessary level of continuity to see through developments and without sufficient understanding of the essential functional perspectives within the strategic debate, executives are discouraged from taking the longer-term corporate perspective. In fact, to start developments in key areas without the timeframe to see their completion is arguably irresponsible.

The result is an inclination to maintain the *status quo* and to meet functional goals above all else. In times of change, neither of these promotes the corporate good. Instead, managers will make decisions that are based on how they will politically affect themselves in the future rather than how they will affect the business's competitive position.

## Top Management's View of Strategy

The authors of business plans and corporate marketing reviews look outwards from the business. Top executives associate themselves with these activities, seeing them as essential components in developing corporate strategy. The result is that they give adequate and appropriate attention to the external environment in which the business operates.

Manufacturing plans typically address stated business needs and are based on the internal dimensions of the processes involved, and top executives are not likely to take part in developing these plans. The result is that executives request and receive a manufacturing strategy statement without becoming involved in its structure, development or verification. They see manufacturing as not having an external dimension and assume, therefore, that the corporate strategy debate need not embrace these perspectives. Rather, they focus on manufacturing outcomes of strategic alternatives such as capacity and costs.

But manufacturing plays a vital role in supporting a company's chosen markets. Assessing the investment and time required for such support and which markets to grow is fundamental to strategic debate and agreed outcomes. In many companies, however, top management has abdicated the key task in corporate strategy of linking markets and manufacturing or is not even aware that such a linkage should be made.

## The Content of Corporate Strategy

The failure of companies to incorporate functional perspectives into their corporate strategy debate stems in part from the approaches to strategy development as advocated by leading researchers and writers in the field. The training of both executives charged with strategy development and specialists who provide relevant support reinforces such failure. This problem is apparent in the content of corporate strategy statements and manifests itself in a number of ways.

## Strategy Statements are General in Nature

Since strategy is general in nature, using all-encompassing statements to express it is deemed appropriate. The result is that expressions of strategy typically use words with more than one meaning. This broadbrush manner assumes that these general perspectives are universal in both nature and relevance. But what typifies markets today is difference not similarity. Thus general statements are inaccurate and misleading. By ignoring the differences that exist within markets, functional strategies in turn become general in nature and are driven by their own rather than a business perspective.

General statements may underpin theory and provide broad overviews of potential scenarios. But companies compete in their own markets and in which specific order-winners and qualifiers will prevail. Thus strategy, like management, is an applied field where specific and not generalized reviews are required. The key to understanding a business then is to determine the ways in which it competes in its different segments. And of this you can be sure, segments will require functional strategies to reflect these differences.

## Strategy Debate and Formulation Stops at the Interface

Functional strategies are typically not linked to one another. Most companies require each function to provide a strategic statement but fail to integrate them. The result is that corporate strategies stop at the interface between functions.

This approach is also re-enacted in many large corporations at the next level. Often, multinationals seem unable or unwilling to incorporate individual company statements into a strategy for the whole group. This failure to link, either by default or intent, is a consistent and comprehensive weakness in strategy formulation. The result is that in increasingly dynamic and competitive markets, companies systematically fail to realize their strategic potential and consequently are outperformed.

Furthermore, this apparent lack of need to integrate strategies is paralleled in the literature. A review of books on strategic marketing and corporate strategy will confirm that the link between the marketing-related dimensions of strategy and those of manufacturing is not made. The implication is, therefore, that it is unnecessary. Or if necessary, its impact is of insufficient consequence to be an integral part of the review process.

Articles and books on marketing strategy were recently reviewed. Of the 1,250 pages covered by the nine articles and three books, less than one per cent concerned manufacturing. A similar review of ten books in the field of corporate strategy revealed that of the 4,000 pages written, only two per cent concerned manufacturing. Thus strategy formulation as advocated and undertaken by leading researchers in the fields of corporate and marketing strategy also stops at the interface. Methodologies are put forward that lead companies into making major decisions and committing a business for many years ahead without requiring the essential interface between the company or business unit and corporate levels and between the functions that make up the firm (see Exhibits 2.1 and 2.2).

The consequences are enormous. First, the risks associated with such approaches in today's markets are substantial. The high level of risk is not a result of the uncertainty of future markets and the unknown moves of competitors but of the process of internal strategy formulation. Second, such approaches consistently result in the failure to create the type of strategic advantage that comes directly from embracing key functional perspectives and arriving at commonly agreed and understood corporate directions.

## Whole versus Parts

The underlying rationale for these advocated and adopted methodologies appears to be based on the assumption that corporate improvement can be accomplished by working solely on the corporate whole. Although reshaping the whole is an important facet of strategic resolution, the necessary links to constituent parts and the role of those parts in bringing about agreed directions and change is fundamental. Unless companies forge these links when choosing what is best for the business and agreeing on directions to pursue, they are unlikely to arrive at appropriate decisions essential for their growth and prosperity over time.

## Typical Outcomes

The results of this lack of integration are documents and statements that have the trappings, but not the essence, of corporate debate. With functional strategies independently derived, the nearest they get to integration is that they sit side by side in the same binder. The title 'corporate strategy' for most companies is a misnomer. In reality, the strategy is no more than a compilation of functional strategies separated, as in the binder, one from another.

Furthermore, even a department's presentation of its strategy it is not intended to and does not, in fact, spark corporate-based discussion. Those companies that justify this procedure on the grounds that it requires executives to engage in rigorous, functionally oriented debate are not only guilty of false rationalization but also are missing the point. In today's markets, companies that fail to harness the resources of all facets of their business will be seriously disadvantaged. Not only will they miss out, they may well be in danger of missing out altogether.

## Developing a Manufacturing Strategy

Companies require a strategy not based solely on marketing, manufacturing or any other function, but one that embraces the interface between markets and functions. Thus, what should and must be the link between functional strategies is the markets a business serves or intends to serve. One illustration is the link between marketing and manufacturing. Both functions must have a common understanding and agreement about company markets. Only then can the degree of fit between the proposed marketing strategy and manufacturing's ability to support it be known at the business level and objectively resolved within corporate perspectives and constraints.

For this to take place, relevant internal information explaining the company's manufacturing capabilities needs to be available within a business, as well as the traditional marketing information that is primarily concerned with the customer and the market opportunities associated with a company's products. It is not sufficient that such information should be available – and often it is not. To be effective, the owner-

**Exhibit 2.4**   The steps to help link manufacturing to marketing with corporate strategy development

| Steps |
| --- |
| **1** Define corporate objectives |
| **2** Determine marketing strategies to meet these objectives |
| **3** Assess how different products qualify in their respective markets and win orders against competitors |
| **4** Establish the appropriate process to manufacture these products (process choice) |
| **5** Provide the manufacturing infrastructure to support production |

ship of its use must be vested in top management. As with other functions, manufacturing strategy is not owned by manufacturing. It requires corporate ownership.

Senior executives need to understand all the strategic inputs in the corporate debate for without this understanding the resolution between conflicting or non-matching functional perspectives cannot be fully investigated and resolved. Without this individual functions must themselves handle the trade-offs involved as best they can.

Typically, top executives inappropriately delegate this task. But leaving it to others borders on being irresponsible. Developing and agreeing strategy is top management's key task. In fact, it is the one task that cannot be delegated. If it is, top executives will find themselves only able to exercise control over decisions taken in a global, after-the-event way.

## Strategic Integration – Linking Manufacturing to Marketing

There is no short cut to moving forward. There are, however, five basic steps that provide an analytical and objective structure in which the corporate debate and consequent actions can be taken, as shown in Exhibit 2.4.

These are, in one sense, classic steps in corporate planning. The problem is that most corporate planners treat the first two as interactive with 'feedback loops' and the last two as linear and deterministic. While each step has substance in its own right, each impacts the others – hence the involved nature of strategy formulation. This is further exacerbated by the inherent complexity of manufacturing and the general failure to take account of the essential interaction between marketing and manufacturing strategies. What is required, therefore, is an approach that recognizes these features and yet provides an ordered and analytical way forward.

The suggested approach to linking manufacturing with corporate marketing decisions is schematically outlined in Exhibit 2.5. It is presented in the form of a framework to help outline the stages involved. A glance at the exhibit will reveal a gap between columns 2 and 3. This is to indicate the corporate objectives/marketing strategy interface that typically takes place as part of a firm's corporate planning procedure and often as a separate corporate exercise. Column 3 highlights the need for companies to understand their markets (the criteria listed here are typical of

**Exhibit 2.5**   Framework for reflecting manufacturing strategy issues in corporate decisions (steps involved)[1]

| Corporate objectives | Marketing strategy | How do products qualify and win orders in the marketplace? | Manufacturing strategy | |
| --- | --- | --- | --- | --- |
| | | | process choice | infrastructure |
| Growth<br><br>Survival<br><br>Profit<br><br>Return on investment<br><br>Other financial measures | Product markets and segments<br><br>Range<br><br>Mix<br><br>Volumes<br><br>Standardization versus customization<br><br>Level of innovation<br><br>Leader versus follower alternatives | Price<br><br>Quality conformance<br><br>Delivery<br>  speed<br>  reliability<br><br>Demand increases<br><br>Colour range<br><br>Product range<br><br>Design<br><br>Brand image<br><br>Technical support<br><br>After-sales support | Choice of alternative processes<br><br>Trade-offs embodied in the process choice<br><br>Role of inventory in the process configuration<br><br>Make or buy<br><br>Capacity<br>  size<br>  timing<br>  location | Function support<br><br>Manufacturing planning and control systems<br><br>Quality assurance and control<br><br>Manufacturing systems engineering<br><br>Clerical procedures<br><br>Compensation agreements<br><br>Work structuring<br><br>Organizational structure |

*Note*

1. Although the steps to be followed are given as finite points in a stated procedure, in reality the process will involve statement and restatement for several of these aspects will impinge on each other.

some that may relate to a firm's various markets) as this forms the basis of manufacturing's task to support the needs of agreed markets. And just as there are typically different markets, there will be different tasks that call for different strategies.

The approach provides the key to stimulating corporate debate about the business in such a way as to enable manufacturing to assess how it needs to and the degree to which it can support products in the marketplace and to identify the developments and investments it needs to undertake as part of its strategic role. It has been researched and tested successfully in many industries and businesses of different sizes.

## How it Works

How to use the methodology outlined in Exhibit 2.5 will be covered in two sections of the book. The following sections will overview the basic steps. Chapter 3 will cover the methodology to be followed when undertaking these types of analyses. Specifically, it will:

■ provide background for analysing the cases included in this text by explaining what data are reviewed and why
■ give an approach for students to follow if their course requires an in-plant review
■ help executives undertake reviews of this kind within their own businesses.

The objective of using this framework is to produce a manufacturing strategy for a business (steps 4 and 5). In all instances this will include a review of existing products plus a review of proposed product introductions. Furthermore, the review will be based on current and future market expectations. This is because manufacturing needs to support a product (that is, with after-sales service and supply) over the whole and not just a part of its life cycle and hence the business needs to address this total decision. As product requirements change, so will manufacturing's task. The range of support requirements, therefore, will invariably affect the choice of process (step 4) and infrastructure (step 5) considered appropriate for the business over the whole life cycle of each product or product family. Levels of investment will also need to reflect this total support, and the varying degrees of mismatch over the life cycle between the product requirements and manufacturing process and infrastructure capability will need to be understood and agreed. In this way, the business will make conscious decisions at the corporate level. It will exercise its due responsibility for resolving trade-offs between the investment required to reduce the degree of mismatch and the ramifications for the business by allowing the mismatch to go unaltered.

However, to get to steps 4 and 5 the three earlier steps need to be taken. With some understanding of what is to be achieved in a manufacturing strategy statement, it is now opportune to go through each step in turn and then to explain how the necessary interrelations between these parts come together as a whole to form a corporate strategy for a business.

**Step 1**    **Corporate Objectives**
Inputs into corporate strategy need to be linked to the objectives of the business. The essential nature of this link is twofold. First, it provides the basis for establishing clear, strategic direction for a business and demonstrates both the strategic awareness and strategic willingness essential to corporate success. Second, it will define the boundaries and mark the parameters against which the various inputs can be measured and consistency established, thus providing the hallmarks of a coherent corporate plan.

For each company, the objectives will be different in essence and emphasis. They will reflect the nature of the economy, markets, opportunities and preferences of those involved. The important issues here, however, are that they need to be well thought through, hold logically together and provide the necessary direction for the business. Typical measures concern profit in relation to sales and investment, together with targets for both absolute growth and market-share growth. Businesses may also wish to include employee policies and environmental issues as part of their overall sets of objectives.

**Step 2**    **Marketing Strategy**
Linked closely to the provision of the agreed corporate objectives, a marketing strategy needs to be developed and will often include the following stages:

1. Market planning and control units need to be established. Their task is to bring together a number of products that have closely related market targets and that often share a common marketing programme. This will help to identify a number of manageable units with similar marketing characteristics.

2. The second stage involves an analysis of product markets that includes:

   ■ determining current and future volumes
   ■ defining end-user characteristics
   ■ assessing patterns of buying behaviour
   ■ examining industry practices and trends
   ■ identifying key competitors and reviewing the business's relative position.

3. The final stage concerns identifying target markets and agreeing objectives for each. This will include both a broad review of how to achieve these and the short-term action plans necessary to secure the more global objectives involved.

In addition, a company should agree on the level of service support necessary in each market and assess the investments and resources needed to provide these throughout the business.

The outcome of this will be a declaration to the business of the product markets and segments that the strategy proposes and the identification of the range, mix and volumes involved. Other issues pertinent to a business will include the degree of standardization/customerization involved within each product range, the level of innovation and product development proposed, whether the business should be a leader or follower in each of its markets and the extent and timing of these strategic initiatives.

**Step 3**     **How Do Products Qualify and Win Orders in the Marketplace?**

Manufacturing's strategic task is to meet the qualifiers* for which it is responsible and to provide, better than the manufacturing functions of competitors, those criteria that enable the products to win orders in the marketplace. As stressed in the footnote to Exhibit 2.5, the debate initiated by this methodology is iterative in nature. This is both appropriate for and fundamental to strategic resolution. Thus the company as a whole needs to agree on the markets and segments within these markets in which it decides to compete.

In no way can these critical decisions be the responsibility or prerogative of a single function. Typically, however, most companies develop strategy through a marketing perspective (see steps 1 and 2). Although the marketing debate is pre-eminent in corporate strategy procedures, the problem is that this is where the debate ends. As a function, marketing will have an important and essential view. But it is not the only view and in no way should it be allowed to dominate corporate strategy resolution. Functional dominance, no matter of what origin, is detrimental

---

* Suffice here to say that qualifiers get and keep companies in markets but do not win orders.

**Exhibit 2.6**    How order-winners link corporate marketing decisions
with manufacturing strategy

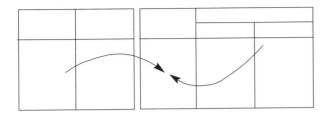

to today's business needs and must be avoided. One essential perspective of a firm's markets has to come from manufacturing. This perspective is established by determining those order-winners and qualifiers* that manufacturing needs to provide. The procedure is, in reality, to ask the marketing function questions that require manufacturing answers. This step, therefore, is the essential link between corporate marketing proposals and commitments and the manufacturing processes and infrastructure necessary to support them (see Exhibit 2.6).

However, not only are the relevant order-winners and qualifiers of differing levels of importance in different markets but the degree of importance will also change over time. The procedure to be followed and the important issues to be addressed are covered in some detail later in this chapter.

**Step 4**    **Process Choice**
Manufacturing can choose from a number of alternative processes to make particular products. The key to this choice is volume and associated order-winners. Each choice, therefore, needs to reflect the current and future trade-offs involved for the various products. The issues embodied in these trade-offs are both extensive and important. Chapter 5 has been devoted to process choice and will examine in detail the implications of this fundamental decision.

**Step 5**    **Infrastructure**
Manufacturing infrastructure consists of the non-process features within production. It encompasses the procedures, systems, controls, compensation systems, work-structuring alternatives, organizational issues and so on within manufacturing. Chapter 10 discusses and illustrates some of the major areas involved.

Although the five steps discussed above comprise the elements of manufacturing strategy development, it is not intended here to treat the first two steps in other than a somewhat superficial way – they are dealt with rigorously in other textbooks.[5] The purpose of including them is both to demonstrate the integral nature of strategy formulation and to reinforce the interactive nature of the procedures involved. The

---

* See footnote on p. 34.

remaining three steps mentioned above are all dealt with extensively in later chapters. Step 3, which concerns the order-winners and qualifiers of different products, is now discussed in general terms. A more detailed review is provided in Chapter 3.

## Order-winners and Qualifiers

Some order-winning criteria do not fall within the jurisdiction of manufacturing. For example, after-sales service, being the existing supplier, technical liaison capability, brand name and design leadership are features provided by functions other than manufacturing. It is a corporate decision, therefore, whether or not to allocate resources to provide one or more of these particular features. However, within the mix of order-winners over a product's life cycle, manufacturing-related criteria will normally be the most important.

The rationale for establishing the order-winners for different products is to improve a company's understanding of its markets. Before outlining the procedure for doing this, the following section will describe some important characteristics and issues involved to give essential background and context.

## Define the Meaning

To understand a business requires that relevant discussion is both comprehensive and clear. As mentioned earlier, many companies perceive strategy to be broadly based and are content with arriving at all-embracing but essentially unclear statements. Given that difference rather than similarity characterizes today's markets, a company must understand its markets to achieve adequate and clear outcomes from strategic discussion. A prerequisite is that the dimensions that characterize a company's markets are clearly defined and agreed. Using words that convey more than one meaning will only lead to misunderstanding and an inadequate base on which to establish agreed direction.

Therefore companies that use descriptions of the success factors in their markets such as *customer service* are ill-served. Customer service can mean any number of things. The key is to agree which dimension of customer service is the important criterion. The reason is simple. Without this level of clarity, executives will walk away from the strategy debate with their own idea of which dimension of a particular factor is the most critical to the business. Furthermore, reviewing the importance of the same factor in the different markets served by a company can also embody similar misunderstandings. Most, if not all, companies today are selling products in markets characterized by difference and not similarity and these essential insights need to be clearly identified as a prerequisite for sound strategy development.

Two words illustrate these points: *quality* and *delivery*. It is essential, for instance, to separate the dimension of *design* from that of *quality conformance*. Both are related, but whereas the former concerns creating a product specification, the latter describes the task of meeting the given specification. Although one is the task of the design function, the other is a distinct manufacturing task. While the perspectives are interrelated, the point being highlighted is that the tasks form part of different functional offerings.

Similarly, take the aspect of *delivery*. Separating the issue of 'on time' from that of 'speed' (that is, short lead times) is an essential part of understanding the key dimensions of a market. Describing both under the one word *delivery* will hide essential insights.

## Strategy is Time and Market Specific

It is not appropriate to discuss strategy as a set of stereotypes. To do so may simplify the process but will confuse the outputs. Two dimensions of markets that highlight this are a recognition that order-winners and qualifiers are both time and market specific. That is the order-winners and qualifiers in a given market will change over time and the order-winner and qualifier outcomes of the debate on one market are specific to that market and cannot be deemed revelant (and hence transferred) to another market. Recognizing this will prevent stereotypes from being applied and help create and sustain the essential dimension of clarity emphasized earlier.

## Definitions of Order-winners and Qualifiers

The last two sections have emphasized the need to distinguish differences as part of the strategy formulation. To this end, an essential part of manufacturing's task is to recognize and apply the concept of order-winners and qualifiers.

- **Qualifiers** are those criteria that a company must meet for a customer to even consider it as a possible supplier. For example, customers increasingly require suppliers to be registered under the ISO 9000 series. Suppliers, therefore, who are so registered have only achieved the right to bid or be considered. Furthermore, they will need to retain the qualification in order to stay on the shortlist or be considered as a competitor in a given market. However, providing or attaining these criteria do not win orders.

- **Order-winners** are those criteria that win the order.

## Order-winners versus Qualifiers

The need to identify difference is further underscored by recognizing the essential difference between these two dimensions in a market. To provide qualifiers, companies need only to be as good as competitors; to provide order-winners, they need to be better than competitors. However, qualifiers are not less important than order-winners – they are different. Both are essential if companies are to maintain existing share and grow.

The need to distinguish between those criteria that win orders in the marketplace and those that qualify a product to be there is highlighted in the following example. When Japanese companies entered the colour television market, they changed the way in which products won orders from predominantly price to quality conformance and the reliability of products in service. The relatively low product quality conformance and reliability in service of existing television sets meant that in the changed competitive forces of this market, existing producers were losing orders through the dimension of quality to Japanese companies; that is, existing manufacturers were not providing the criteria that qualified them to be in the marketplace. By the early 1980s, manufacturers that lost orders raised product quality conformance so that they were again qualified to be in the market. As a result, product quality conformance and reliability in service became qualifiers again and the most important order-winner in this market reverted back to price.

Manufacturing, therefore, must provide the qualifiers to get into or stay in the marketplace. But these alone will not win orders. They merely prevent a company from losing orders to its competitors. Once the qualifiers have been achieved, manufacturing then has to turn its attention to the ways in which orders are won with the aim of providing these better than anyone else.

Also, if price is not the predominant order-winner, it does not mean that a company can charge what it wishes. Although it needs to recognize that it does not compete on price and, therefore, should exploit this opportunity, it has to keep its exploitation within sensible bounds. Failure to do so will result in a company losing orders increasingly to those who are more competitively priced. Hence, in this situation a company will have turned a qualifying criterion (that is, a product highly priced within some limits) into an order-losing criterion where the price has become too high.

## Differentiating between Order-winners and Qualifiers

Having identified and separated order-winners from qualifiers, it is now necessary to distinguish between the importance of one criterion and another. This is done differently for each category.

- **Order-winners** – once order-winners are agreed, appropriate weightings (points out of a hundred) are allocated to each (see Exhibits 2.7, 2.8 and 2.9).

- **Qualifiers** – less definition of importance is required for qualifiers. If a company needs to qualify in one market segment on both quality conformance and delivery reliability, then it needs to attain the necessary levels in each. However, some qualifiers will be more critical in terms of a customer's/market's requirements and these are distinguished by labelling them as order-losing sensitive qualifiers (see Exhibits 2.7, 2.8 and 2.9).

**Exhibit 2.7** US graphics company: order-winners and qualifiers for selected customers

| Criteria | Customer A | | | Customer B | | |
|---|---|---|---|---|---|---|
| | 1999 | 2000 | 2001 | 1999 | 2000 | 2001 |
| Design (product specification) | 40 | 40 | 40 | 30 | 40 | 50 |
| Price | Q | Q | Q | 40 | 20 | Q |
| Delivery – reliability | QQ | QQ | QQ | QQ | QQ | QQ |
| – speed | 30 | 20 | Q | 30 | 20 | Q |
| Quality conformance | QQ | QQ | QQ | QQ | QQ | QQ |
| R&D support services | 30 | 40 | 60 | – | 20 | 50 |

*Notes*
Q denotes qualifier.
QQ denotes an order-losing sensitive qualifier.

**Exhibit 2.8** European battery company: order-winners and qualifiers for selected products sold in Europe

| Criteria | 1998 | 2000 | 2002 |
|---|---|---|---|
| *Product type 10A* | | | |
| Design | 40 | 30 | 20 |
| Quality conformance | Q | Q | Q |
| Delivery – reliability | QQ | QQ | QQ |
| – speed | 25 | 20 | 20 |
| Price | 35 | 50 | 60 |
| *Product type C80* | | | |
| Quality conformance | 20 | 20 | 15 |
| Delivery – reliability | QQ | QQ | QQ |
| – speed | 20 | 20 | 10 |
| Design | 60 | 50 | 40 |
| Price | Q | 10 | 35 |

*Notes*
Q denotes a qualifier.
QQ denotes an order-losing sensitive qualifier.

## Direct Customer versus End-user Reviews

Some companies manufacturing end products may need to recognize the criteria relating to their own (direct) customers and also those relating to the eventual end user. They will both have a bearing on what a company needs to recognize and, in turn, on the functional strategies which need to be developed to support their markets.

**Exhibit 2.9**   European engineered sealing systems company: order-winners and qualifiers
for selected customers

| Criteria | Customer A (France) | |
|---|---|---|
| | **1999** | **2002** |
| Price | 20 | 30 |
| Delivery – reliability | QQ | QQ |
|     – speed | 35 | 40 |
| Quality conformance | QQ | QQ |
| Design | Q | Q |
| Technical support | 20 | 20 |
| Brand name | 25 | 10 |

| | Customer B (France) | |
|---|---|---|
| | **1999** | **2002** |
| Price | 50 | 60 |
| Delivery – reliability | QQ | QQ |
|     – speed | 20 | 20 |
| Quality conformance | QQ | QQ |
| Design | Q | Q |
| Technical support | 20 | 20 |
| Brand name | 10 | Q |

| | Customer C (Switzerland) | |
|---|---|---|
| | **1999** | **2002** |
| Price | Q | 10 |
| Delivery – reliability | Q | QQ |
|     – speed | 10 | 20 |
| Quality conformance | QQ | QQ |
| Design | 35 | 30 |
| Technical support | 25 | 15 |
| Brand name | 30 | 25 |

*Notes*
Q denotes a qualifier.
QQ denotes an order-losing qualifier.

## Monitoring Actual/Anticipated Change over Time

Since markets are dynamic, order-winners and qualifiers and/or their associated
weightings will change over time. Thus to monitor this change, relevant criteria and
their weightings are agreed over time. The next section deals with how this is
accomplished.

## The Procedure for Establishing Order-winners and Qualifiers

To create the essential interface between marketing and manufacturing, a business must understand its markets from the viewpoints of both these functions. Classically, companies fail to distinguish clearly between the market (business) and marketing (functional) perspectives. This lack of clarity shows itself in several ways. For instance, in many companies the strategy debate typically ends when steps 1 and 2 of the framework (see Exhibit 2.5) have been accomplished. The assumption is that marketing's view of the market is how the market is. The key nature of step 3 lies in facilitating the important distinction between the function and the business by asking market-oriented questions requiring manufacturing answers. These questions ask how different products qualify and win orders in their respective markets.

In developing a manufacturing strategy, the identification of relevant order-winners for different products or customers is a key step. This helps companies move from what is often a vague understanding of its many markets to a new and essential level of awareness. Too often, companies describe their business as composed of relatively large segments and, in so doing, make the assumption that all products within a segment have similar qualifiers and order-winners because they have similar names, are sold to similar customers or belong to the same segment from the viewpoint of marketing. But products win orders in different ways from one another; they will typically have more than one order-winner and the order-winners will change over time. Unless the company recognizes these differences, it will not achieve the level of clarity essential to increasing business understanding and on which to base major investment decisions.

The procedure used to gain these insights is now discussed:

- Marketing is requested to separate the business into different segments as it perceives them. The procedure, as with other aspects of strategy debate, is iterative in nature. Thus marketing's separation of the business provides relevant insights and market distinctions for the debate that follows, but they are reconsidered and very often revised as the strategy formulation progresses.

- To focus discussion, marketing chooses sample products and/or customers to represent these market segments. This step serves three purposes. First, it helps to test whether the segments chosen are sufficient to distinguish the market differences that exist. Second, it enables the debate to be oriented towards the particular rather than the general. Third, it allows specific data to be collected and analyses to be completed on the representative sample of products or customers chosen for each segment. In turn, this provides essential insights into the real nature of the different market segments. As Exhibit 2.10 illustrates, there is invariably a marked difference between the contractual requirements of customers and the actual requirements of customers. Handled by different people who typically do not interface within their own organizations, the reality of what

**Exhibit 2.10** Contractual versus actual customer requirements

customers actually need is invariably different from what was agreed in a contract. In part this often stems from the aggregation of requirements by a customer to enhance its negotiating stance *vis-à-vis* the diversity of the actual requirements of the parts that make up the whole. Only by checking details can the essential perspectives of reality be identified. In this way, market reality replaces market perception and customer behaviour replaces customer voice.

- Marketing is also required to establish two future time periods for each segment. Note that the selected periods may not be the same as they are chosen to reflect the characteristics of each segment.

- The next step is to provide actual and forecast sales volumes for chosen representative products or customers, based on current and future time periods.

- When this information has been gathered, marketing identifies the qualifiers and order-winners relevant to each of the sample products customers choose. Three illustrations are provided in Exhibits 2.7, 2.8 and 2.9. Weighted percentages for relevant order-winners have to be assessed for both current and relevant future time periods.

- This information now provides the initial input into this part of the strategic debate. In turn, marketing's opinion will be contested both by other functions and by the information relating to the issues highlighted by the selection and importance attached to the relevant qualifiers and order-winners. This enables the company to have a clearer and more informed view of what manufacturing must provide to compete effectively in chosen markets. Only when this is clearly understood can manufacturing strategy be formulated and appropriate decisions made about process and infrastructure investments and developments.

Chapter 4 provides a more detailed review of the methodology to be used in developing a manufacturing strategy and will include a further explanation of the procedure outlined above.

## Understanding the Criteria Chosen and Their Relative Weightings

As explained above, marketing is asked to determine the weightings for each relevant order-winner. This involves allocating percentage points to each criterion for both current and future time periods. In this part of the procedure, the discussion concerns not only the individual weights but also the reasons why any changes in emphasis are anticipated in the future.

Where changes do occur, the business must support the full range of criteria together with the changes in emphasis involved. As explained earlier, whereas some of these will be non-production features, the major thrust will in fact be from manufacturing. Certainly the provision of any significant changes in emphasis anticipated in the future will typically be manufacturing based, and the need to reconcile the process and infrastructure investments appropriate to meet the changing requirements will have to be fully discussed, understood and eventually agreed on by all concerned.

A final word concerns the order-winners put forward by marketing and the percentage weightings proposed. When this procedure is first adopted, there is a distinct tendency for marketing to include a host of criteria and, partly as a result of not distinguishing between their relative importance, will often spread the percentage points, thus failing to identify the critical order-winning feature(s). Understanding the criteria and weightings selected is necessary to ensure that this situation does not arise. Marketing's clear identification of how orders are won is an essential first step in developing an appropriate corporate manufacturing strategy. As explained earlier, this debate is then fuelled by the views of other functions and the collection of relevant data. The company will achieve the necessary level of understanding and essential insights only if such rigorous debate is maintained throughout the strategy-making process.

Invariably, the challenge to marketing's views made by other functional perspectives and the data collected for representative products and customers will change the initial view of the market. The need to verify and understand the criteria and respective weightings continues to be a task at the very core of the strategy process. This rigorous approach provides essential insights and the involvement in these debates and outcomes results in functions gaining an essential understanding of the company's markets and their strategic role in supporting them.

## Identifying Qualifiers with the Potential to Become Order-winners

Part of step 3 is to identify any qualifiers associated with the different sets of products or customers with the potential to become order-winners (for instance, the earlier example of the changed role of quality conformance in the colour television market). Once a company identifies such criteria, it must decide whether to invest in manufacturing to initiate this change. The impact it would have on market share, the time it would take for competitors to catch up and the investments involved in bringing about this change would be some of the issues to be addressed in this corporate strategy decision.

## Identifying Qualifiers That Are Order-losing Sensitive

The final phase of step 3 is to identify any qualifiers that are order-losing sensitive. Manufacturing must be fully aware of any qualifier that if it failed to provide might quickly result in lost orders. Where these are identified, the discussion that follows is aimed at determining the degree of order-losing sensitivity and the degree of risk the business is prepared to take. The company can make appropriate decisions once it understands the trade-offs between associated costs, investments and sales.

## The Outputs of Manufacturing Strategy

Two outputs accrue from the use of this framework.

### The First Output

This concerns a review of the implications for manufacturing processes and infra-structure support of selling products in current and future markets, as depicted in Exhibit 2.11. It involves assessing the degree of match between what exists in manufacturing and those processes and infrastructure features needed to provide the order-winners and qualifiers of a company's markets.

This check should also be done for all future product proposals or new customer agreements. So should the essential regular review be used to pick up any volume or order-winner/qualifier changes, that may be significant as measured against the relevant base year. In this way, by checking on and assessing competitors' moves and actions and reviewing customer behaviour changes and trends, the relative levels of match and mismatch are monitored, thus detecting incremental marketing changes that have occurred over time and often otherwise go unnoticed. Only by reviewing current and future requirements against the original decisions can the full change be assessed.

**Exhibit 2.11**  Assessing the implications for manufacturing processes and infrastructure of order-winners

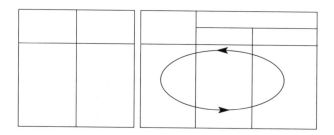

**Exhibit 2.12**  Manufacturing's input into the corporate strategy debate

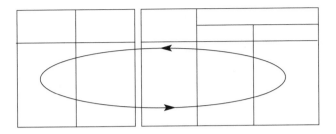

**The Second Output**

Once determined, the manufacturing strategy and the necessary investments and time period for change form part of the corporate strategy debate, as illustrated in Exhibit 2.12.

As a consequence, the company as a whole is now required to review the business in both marketing and manufacturing terms. It changes the style and substance of corporate decisions from functionally based arguments and perspectives to ones that address functional differences by resolving at the business level the trade-offs involved. This corporate resolution therefore leads to an agreed understanding of what are the:

- business objectives,
- marketing strategy, and
- manufacturing strategy.

In reality, it will lead to one of five positions based on the degree of fit between the marketing and manufacturing strategic interface.

1. Where the interface is sufficiently close and requires little, if any, adjustment.

2. Where the interface is not sufficiently close, but the corporate decision is not to invest the required time and money to bring it closer to 1 above.

3. Where the interface is not sufficiently close, and the decision is to change the marketing strategy to reduce the mismatch and move towards 1 above.

4. Where the interface is not sufficiently close and the decision is to allocate the time and investment to enable manufacturing to bring its processes and infrastructure to that required to support the marketing strategy and so move towards 1 above.

5. A combination of alternatives 3 and 4 to move towards position 1.

In situations 3 and 4, the company decides to reposition marketing and manufacturing, respectively, to bring about the position described in 1. In the case of 2, it is essential that the reality of the mismatch is translated into manufacturing targets and budgets to present a manageable, achievable and hence controllable task. In this way, the inadequacies of manufacturing's performance against budget are separated from the consequences of the corporate strategy decision to accept the mismatch involved. The business is, therefore, able to learn the extent of the consequences resulting from the manufacturing/marketing interface mismatch and use this vital information in its future strategic decisions.

Chapter 4 discusses the outputs described here and provides examples of different strategy applications.

## Manufacturing Typically Develops more than One Strategy

As markets are different, the order-winners and qualifiers relating to these markets will also be different. Consequently manufacturing (as well as other functions) will need to develop different strategies to support these different sets of market needs.

Typically. in the past this has neither been recognized nor provided. The failure of corporate strategy approaches to identify difference has led, in turn, to general strategic approaches being adopted by manufacturing. If markets are deemed to be the same, generic support for these makes sense. Rarely is this so.

Corporate debate needs to direct its attention to highlighting the differences inherent in markets. Clarity of meaning and distinguishing between order-winners and qualifiers are all part of achieving this. As markets are the key to the continued success and growth of companies then no effort should be spared in rooting out these essential differences. Manufacturing's task is, then, to develop different strategic responses required to support a company's different markets.

## Conclusion

To be effective, strategies must display the following characteristics that are central to the procedure and the outcomes:

- *Congruence of purpose and function* – The markets in which a company competes should link functional strategies. Otherwise functions will base strategies on their own perspectives and understanding, which would disrupt the essential gains of coherent direction of the parts and the whole. Congruence of purpose and function, therefore, is an essential ingredient of strategy formulation and implementation.

- *A focus on key priorities* – The coherent direction in which functional strategies need to be formed will lead to an agreement on which developments and investments are the most important for supporting given markets. Priorities for timescales and costs are agreed on and functions base subsequent actions and activities on these outcomes. This prioritizing mechanism is a key characteristic of effective strategies. It gives essential context, orients actions, keeps the list of tasks small and manageable, focuses attention on what is critical and promotes coordination and cooperation between the different functions in the core task of being competitive within agreed markets.

■ *Commitment through understanding* – Knowing where the company is going and why is essential if strategies are to be effective. In addition, knowing where and why builds commitment among participants. An understanding of the rationale underpinning the strategies to be taken and the priorities to be pursued gives essential and appropriate direction in the short term while providing the basis for strategic rethinking that the future will undoubtedly demand.

■ *Routine performance measurement* – Strategy leads to appropriate direction, the pursuit of priorities and the essential commitment to see them through. As part of the continuous reappraisal of strategy decisions, performance needs to be monitored on a regular basis. Routine checks are vital in themselves. Adherence to and progress towards agreed strategies is essential for all developments and close and continuous monitoring of performance is integral to a successful strategy. Furthermore, strategy is not a once-and-for-all development that remains unaddressed between one review time and the next. Continuous reassessment needs to be undertaken and the routine measurement of performance is an integral part of this procedure.

## Market- or Marketing-led?[6]

Many companies do not keep in sharp focus the critical differences between being market-led and being marketing-led. To substitute the business (market) perspective with a functional (marketing) perspective will invariably lead to distorted strategies and eventually to corporate disadvantage. Checking the characteristic of a strategy based on the perspectives of a single function against those listed above clearly underscores these essential differences. Furthermore, in many businesses, this way of handling market reviews and strategy formulation is made worse by the fact that marketing is becoming increasingly characterized by the perceived role of creating ideas. Generating ideas often becomes an end in itself, with the rigour of testing business fit left to others. Many businesses, however, fail to appreciate that the most significant orders are the ones to which a company says no. For this marks the boundaries of the markets in which it competes and this defines the context in which manufacturing's strategic response needs to be made. To be able to say no means that a company has agreed and understands the markets in which it competes. And this can only be resolved through rigorous corporate debate about markets.

## Manufacturing Strategy

In the past, companies have seen manufacturing's role as being the provider of corporate requests. Corporate-strategy debate has stopped short of discussing the implications of decisions for manufacturing. This behaviour has been based on two incorrect assumptions.

1. Within a given technology, manufacturing is able to do everything.
2. Manufacturing's contribution concerns solely the achievement of efficiency rather than also including the effective support of market needs.

The result for many companies is that not only have the profit margins they once enjoyed been eroded, but also the base on which to build a sound and prosperous business in the future is no longer available. A company is exposed and vulnerable without the frequent manufacturing strategy checks necessary to evaluate the fit between the business and manufacturing's ability to provide the necessary order-winners and qualifiers of its various products and customers. In times of increased world competition, being left behind can be sudden and fatal. In many cases, averting the end is the only option left. Turning the business around, however, will only be achieved by switching from an operational to a strategic mode, which will require a corporate review of the marketing and manufacturing perspectives and of the financial implications of the proposals.

Manufacturing strategy comprises a series of decisions concerning process and infrastructure investment, which, over time, provide the necessary support for the relevant order-winners and qualifiers of the different market segments of a company. It is built on keeping the strategic developments relevant to the business, that is, it must reflect the aspects of manufacturing critical to those segments of the firm under review. Identifying the pertinent aspects, and setting aside those that are not, provides for a strategy that is oriented to the market and the simplicity and clarity of direction this affords.

On the other hand, manufacturing strategy is not:

- A list of all aspects typically comprising a manufacturing function and an attempt to develop a strategic statement about each. Differentiating the important from the less important aspects in terms of market needs is a key feature of sound strategy development

- An exhortation that the strategic perspectives of the manufacturing function should be paramount.

Manufacturing's strategic task is to transform, over time, support for a company's market into an appropriate collection of facilities, structures, controls, procedures, and people. This chapter has provided essential insights into the principles and concepts that underpin this task. The next looks in some depth at order-winners and qualifiers and the chapter after that at the procedures to follow.

## Notes

1. W. Skinner, 'Manufacturing – Missing Link in Corporate Strategy,' *Harvard Business Review*, May–June 1969, p. 13.
2. These perspectives are well covered in S. Kotha and D. Orne, 'Generic Manufacturing Strategies: a Conceptual Analysis', *Strategic Management Journal*, 1989, **10**: 211–231.
3. Also refer to W. Skinner, *Manufacturing – The Formidable Competitive Weapon*, New York: John Wiley & Sons, 1985. The section entitled 'Wanted: A New Breed of Manufacturing Manager' provides insights into developments in production management in the period 1980 to 1984 and the changing task to meet, among other things, the strategic role in manufacturing.
4. This argument was put forward in T. J. Hill, 'Manufacturing Implications in Determining Corporate Policy', *International Journal of Operations and Production Management*, 1(1): 4.
5. These include D. A. Aaker, *Developing Business Strategies*, New York: John Wiley, 1988; H. I. Ansoff, *Corporate Strategies*, New York: Penguin, 1987; P. J. Below *et al.*, *The Executive Guide to Strategic Planning*, San Francisco: Jossey-Bass, 1987; A. C. Hax and N. S. Mailuf, *Strategic Management: An International Perspective*, Englewood Cliffs, NJ: Prentice Hall International, 1984; B. Houlden, *Understanding Company Strategy*, 2nd edn, Basil Blackwell, Oxford, 1996; G. Johnson and K. Scholes, *Exploring Corporate Strategy*, 4th edn, Englewood Cliffs, NJ: Prentice Hall International, 1997; M. E. Porter, *Competitive Strategy*, New York: The Free Press, 1980, and J. Quinn *et al.*, *The Strategy Process*, 2nd edn, 1993.
6. See Terry Hill, *The Essence of Operations Management*, Englewood Cliffs, NJ: Prentice Hall International, 1993, p. 25.

## Further Reading

Buffa, E. S. *Meeting the Competitive Challenge: Manufacturing Strategy for US Companies*. Homewood, IL: Richard D. Irwin, 1984.

Gunn, T. G. *Manufacturing for Competitive Advantage*. Cambridge, MA: Ballinger, 1987.

Mather, H. *Competitive Manufacturing*. Englewood Cliffs, NJ: Prentice Hall International, 1988.

Samson, D. *Manufacturing and Operations Strategy*. Sydney: Prentice Hall, 1991.

Skinner, W. *Manufacturing in Corporate Strategy*. New York: John Wiley, 1978.

Slack, N. *The Manufacturing Advantage*. London: Mercury Books, 1991.

Voss, C. A. (ed.) *Manufacturing Strategy*. London: Chapman & Hall, 1992.

# 3 Order-winners and Qualifiers

The last chapter introduced the concept of order-winners and qualifiers, discussed the rationale behind these perspectives and outlined their distinguishing characteristics. This chapter examines these dimensions more fully, explaining specific criteria in some detail.

The essence of strategy stems from the need for companies to gain a detailed understanding of their current and future markets. Functions are then required to develop strategies based on supporting the characteristics of agreed markets. However, functions should not be reactive within this procedure. On the contrary, they must be proactive in strategic debate, explaining their perspectives so that the rest of the business understands them. This ensures that these perspectives form part of the discussion and the decision. Manufacturing strategy, therefore, consists of the strategic tasks manufacturing must accomplish to support the company's order-winners and qualifiers for which it is solely or jointly responsible.

## Strategic Scenarios and Approaches

As highlighted in Chapter 2, strategic formulation tends to be expressed in general terms. Key reasons include:

- Since strategy implies a broad review, companies also perceive the underlying characteristic of strategic outputs to be broad.

- Companies appear to seek strategies that are uniform in nature. This offers apparent clarity in the form of consistent strategic statements that are easy to express, explain and address. A level of uniformity has inherent attractions no matter what the company's size.

It is not surprising then that typical expressions of corporate strategy include such general terms such as 'service', 'responsiveness' and 'meeting the customer's needs'. In addition researchers, writers and advisors have proffered generic statements concerning corporate strategy formulation with expressions such as 'low cost', 'differentiation' and 'critical success factors'. The use of general terms similar to these brings two major drawbacks. First, difference is not brought into focus but is blurred. Second, decisions concerning the nature of the market segments in which a company wishes to compete are not resolved at the strategic level. A company may not recognize that orders for products, often within the same market segment, are won in different ways. This lack of clarity brings conflicting demands on manufacturing, which reinforce that function's tendency to be reactive in strategic formulation and disperses the essential coherence necessary to provide strategic thrust, guidance and advantage.

Furthermore, this lack of clarity is considered adequate in markets that are increasingly characterized by difference and not similarity. However, ask chief executive officers whether the markets served by the group of companies under their control are similar in nature – the answer would be 'no'. Ask if the markets served by a typical company are the same – the answer would again be 'no'. How is it then that companies continue to expect or believe that manufacturing's support (in terms of process and infrastructure investments) for these would be common? If that is not so, then why do companies apply the same manufacturing approaches to support their different markets not only in one plant but in all their different plants?

The strategic process, therefore, needs to be based on an exact understanding of markets and differences within a market. As highlighted earlier, all too often companies debate strategy in general terms and undertake strategy using general courses of action. This invariably and increasingly leads to a lack of fit between functional strategies and corporate markets. Where this happens, companies will find themselves at a serious disadvantage.

Before moving on to how companies need to understand markets, let us review what typically happens to firms in the absence of clear, well-defined strategic debate.

## Strategic Vacuum

The absence of a manufacturing strategy within a business typically leads to a strategic vacuum and into that void a raft of solutions – panaceas or flavour-of the-month initiatives – continues to be drawn.

This type of response is underpinned by a basic logic. Executives recognize that manufacturing, as a significant part of the company, should be making and needs to be making a significant contribution to the overall success of the business. There is, therefore, due pressure on manufacturing to respond to these corporate demands and expectations. Without strategic context, manufacturing has traditionally responded by undertaking currently popular solutions. In this way, companies seek to achieve parity in manufacturing by modelling operations on best practice. However, although a solution may be good in itself, its application to a specific problem is often inappropriate. Given manufacturing's reactive nature and the existence of corporate initiatives, it is easy to see why most companies have invested regularly and significantly over the years in responses that, by and large, are eventually discarded. The cause of their abandonment is principally their lack of relevance to the solution in the first place.

## Understanding Markets

To formulate functional strategies, a company must first clearly understand and agree on the markets in which it wishes to be today and tomorrow. This critical, initial step provides the two essential dimensions for the formulation of sound and effective strategies.

1. The in-depth debate about the markets in which a company decides to compete is a prerequisite to strategy formulation. The clear identification is based on a well-articulated understanding of market needs and the implications of these for all functions. It is through this mechanism that functional differences are reconciled with each other, and markets and corresponding segments are delineated. Furthermore, since markets are dynamic, strategic debate must be ongoing.

2. With this agreement, functions need to be geared towards meeting the requirements of a firm's current and future markets. Thus each function's strategic contribution is expressed in terms of priorities, developments and investments.

The first step, therefore, is to understand markets. To do this adequately, companies need to set aside generic, broad-based statements and seek to identify the level of difference that exists and the relevant dimensions of each segment in which they wish to compete.

## Characteristics of Today's Markets – Difference and Speed of Change

As emphasized in Chapter 2, whereas past markets were characterized by similarity and stability, current markets are characterized by difference and change.

The characteristics of today's markets place a greater need on understanding than in the past, and one theme in this book is the need to attain this necessary level of understanding. The last two chapters have outlined a framework for gaining more detailed market insights. A wide range of methodologies has been put forward by academics, consultants and other advisers specifying approaches that would lead to strategic insights and appropriate answers. Driven by a need for generic solutions the approaches advocated have too often set aside the overriding difference that exists in companies in order to offer a universal way of developing a corporate strategy. Failing to recognize and cope with difference and avoiding the essential interface between corporate, business unit and functional strategies and also between functions themselves has resulted in approaches that appear complete but which, when applied, are unable to cope with the complex nature of today's business and their markets. The solution is not that easy.

All that is common for companies is that current and future markets are the essence of strategy and provide the agenda on which to base functional strategic responses. Companies will be unable to arrive at successful and workable strategic decisions unless they understand their markets better. Only in this way will they be able to identify the strategic alternatives to meet the needs of their different markets and thus move away from prescriptive approaches and solutions. The viable solutions developed by academics and consultants are most attractive in what they offer. The all-embracing and solution-oriented characteristics of these approaches neither provide executives with the insights necessary to cope with their complex businesses nor warn them that the approach has limitations and that the resolution will be difficult, time consuming and necessitate many months of exacting work. The approaches also invariably fail to start with sufficient emphasis on understanding markets. As a result, executives typically remain impeded by their failure to complete this fundamental task. Also, as with most aspects of management, the essential ingredient in doing a task well is hard work. Understanding today's varied and fast-changing markets is no exception.

Identifying relevant order-winners and qualifiers, and the relative weightings to be attached to them, helps companies to achieve these critical insights. The following sections describe what these criteria are and how they work.

## Order-winners and Qualifiers – Basic Characteristics

This section outlines important background for the discussion of the specific criteria in the next section. A company should keep in mind the following characteristics and issues:

- General statements about markets embody imprecise meanings. As a result, executives take away from corporate strategy discussions their own understandings that are typically and understandably based on their own functional perspectives. Thus, a prerequisite for sound corporate strategy development (that is, agreement by all on what markets the company is and should be in and the characteristics of those markets) is missing.

- Order-winners and qualifiers are both market and time specific. Thus, the criteria relating to a market will need different levels of emphasis and will change over time. It follows, therefore, that there can be few general rules.

- When developing order-winners and qualifiers, companies must distinguish the level of importance for individual criteria for each market. To do this, they weight order-winners by allocating a total of 100 points; for qualifiers, a distinction is made between a qualifier and an order-losing sensitive qualifier, or one that will cause a business to lose customers' orders quickly. Examples of these dimensions were given earlier in Exhibits 2.7, 2.8 and 2.9 together with supporting text.

- Order-winners and qualifiers and their relative weightings will change over time. To assess these potential changes, a company must weight each criterion for the current period and two future periods. The latter will need to reflect the nature of the market, for example, for a printing company the future time periods may be next year and the year after, but for an aerospace company they would need to be three and seven years, respectively. Again Exhibits 2.7, 2.8 and 2.9 illustrate these points.

■ In most instances, differences exist between the criteria needed to retain existing customers and those needed to increase market share or gain prospective customers. These differences will need to be reflected in the relevant order-winners and qualifiers and their respective weightings.

■ Similarly, the criteria that relate to winning orders for a primary supplier will differ from those for a secondary or other supplier categories. Although customers tend to infer that the criteria are the same, common sense challenges that logic. The large percentage share of demand that typically goes to a primary supplier creates very different contractual demands and opportunities than those for other suppliers. Thus the way in which secondary or other suppliers win their part of the contract needs to reflect this.

■ Not all order-winners and qualifiers are related to manufacturing. However, over time manufacturing-related criteria will often come to the fore – for example, price and on-time delivery.

## Order-winners and Qualifiers – Specific Dimensions

As mentioned earlier, there is a range of order-winners and qualifiers, and not all of them form part of manufacturing's strategic function. This section, therefore, separates the different categories and reviews typical criteria within each category. As stressed earlier, strategy is market and time specific and, therefore, not all order-winners and qualifiers will relate to or be of the same importance to all companies.

## Manufacturing-related and Manufacturing-specific Criteria

This category concerns those order-winners and qualifiers that are specific to manufacturing and will, where relevant, form part of manufacturing's strategic role.

*Price*

In many markets, and particularly in the growth, maturity and saturation phases of a product life cycle (see Exhibit 3.1), price becomes an increasingly important order-winning criterion. When this is so, manufacturing's task is to provide the low costs necessary to support the price sensitivity of the marketplace, thus creating the level of profit margin necessary to support the business investment involved and create opportunity for the future. As in many of the pertinent analyses in manufacturing,

**Exhibit 3.1**   Generalized product life cycle

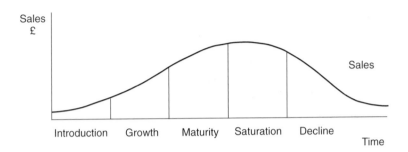

highlighting the pockets of significant cost will give direction to the areas where resource allocation should be made and management attention given.

In most manufacturing companies in North America, Europe and other developed industrial nations direct labour is only a small part of the total cost. Materials followed by overheads are usually the two main areas of cost that should be reflected in the provision of information, allocation of resources and frequency of review. The likelihood, however, is that they are not.

Since price has been an omnipresent factor in most markets, companies are reticent to consider that it may not be a relevant order-winner. This misunderstanding often stems from the fact that price comparisons with alternatives will typically form part of a customer's evaluation of a product. However, for price to be an order-winner, margins must be low. Only in such situations will low-cost manufacturing be a priority. Where margins are high, price is not an order-winner. In these types of market, customers will compare one price to another, not to seek the lowest price but to check that the quoted price is within an acceptable range. Therefore, companies need to recognize the key difference between being price competitive (a qualifier) and competing on price (an order-winner).

The evaluation described here is not unique to the criterion of price. Customers will typically cross-check all relevant criteria. In the case of qualifiers, this is to ensure a ballpark fit, whereas for order-winners, customers will typically be looking for a 'better than' performance.

As explained earlier, qualifiers get a company into and maintain it within a market. As such, they do not win orders but are essential prerequisites for a company to be considered as a potential supplier. Where price is a qualifier, a company cannot simply charge whatever it wishes. The company must price the product according to what the market will bear, keeping exploitation within sensible bounds. Failure to do so will result in an increase of orders lost to those competitors that are more price competitive. Hence in this situation a company will have turned a qualifying criterion (that is, a product highly priced within acceptable limits) into an order-losing criterion (the price has become too high).

Where price is an order-winner, low (or anticipated low) margins give manufacturing the clear task of reducing costs in order to maintain or improve available margins. Also, when a company decides to reduce price significantly, thus altering its role or its importance as an order-winner, it must similarly change related elements of manufacturing strategy. Companies that elect to alter the role of price would need, therefore, to assess the lead times involved, investment implications that result and the cost-reduction potential. Making a strategic decision to reduce price without assessing these factors will invariably lead companies into inappropriate strategies, for the decision to reduce price, although difficult to evaluate, is easy to make. Cost reduction, on the other hand, is easy to evaluate but difficult to achieve.

## Cost Reduction

Many companies do not concentrate their efforts in the area of greatest cost. In many instances, companies direct the most effort towards reducing direct labour cost. Although an organization must improve productivity at all levels, focusing on the area of greatest cost will tend to yield the best results. Since overheads and materials together typically account for some 85–90 per cent of total costs, giving these the *pro rata* attention they deserve makes sense but often is not done. The traditional emphasis on the control and reduction of direct labour cost still attracts most of the resources allocated to the overall cost-reduction task. Tradition and experience of what to do still seem to reinforce these practices. (The effect of process lead-time reduction on elements of overhead costs is highlighted in a later section.)

Furthermore, concentrating on one aspect of cost rather than total costs can lead to lost opportunities. For instance, Heinz had undertaken a labour cost-reduction plan at its Starkist tuna factories in Puerto Rico and American Samoa. With increasing competition from low labour-cost areas, this policy seemed to make sense. But a study revealed that the workers were so overworked that each day they were leaving tons of meat still on the bone. Adding workers, slowing down production lines, increasing supervision and retraining increased costs by $5m but cut waste by $15m, thus saving $10m each year.[1] A similar example is provided by a Dutch-based food-preparation company. The growing importance of high-volume demand from large supermarket chains in Europe had brought an increased emphasis on price as an order-winner. The company's response was to seek direct labour productivity improvements. But this diverted attention from controlling costs elsewhere. Further reviews revealed high levels of waste in preparation. For example, lettuce loss was four times higher than the standards set. Additional training and close monitoring of actual performance compared to standards soon got waste down to acceptable levels and with it, associated costs.

Many organizations have undertaken continuous improvement efforts to increase productivity.[2] The key areas for re-evaluation, however, are broadly based, reflecting the more significant areas of expense and cost-reduction opportunity. Typical lists include eliminating waste (sources of waste include doing necessary tasks wrong the first time – a source related to quality conformance – and doing unnecessary tasks; estimates for the costs associated with these range from 20 to 30 per cent and 10 to 20 per cent respectively), product design, quality at source, process redesign, just-in-time (JIT) production control systems, set-up reduction, overhead reduction and the involvement of people.[3] The outcomes create significant improvements and typically separate out the high performers. Examples of this are increasingly common. One such study investigated the relative importance of 18 automotive component plants, nine of which were located in Japan and nine in the UK. Exhibit 3.2 shows the difference between those plants categorized by the report[4] as being 'world class' (note that all 'world-class' plants were Japanese but not all Japanese were 'world class') and the remainder of the sample.

**Exhibit 3.2**   Relative average performance of 'world-class' and other plants against selected dimensions

| Dimension | Relative plant performance | |
| --- | --- | --- |
| | World class | Other |
| Units per (100 = best) | | |
| ■ hour | 95 | 54 |
| ■ square metre of floor space | 89 | 64 |
| Level of rework (% direct labour time) | 1.5 | 4.1 |
| Hours of inventory | 11 | 75 |

## Experience Curves

Evidence clearly shows that as experience accumulates, performance improves, and the experience curve is the quantification of this improvement. The basic phenomenon of the experience curve is that the cost of manufacturing a given item falls in a regular and predictable way as the total quantity produced increases. The purpose of this section is to draw attention to this relationship and its role in the formulation of manufacturing strategy. It is helpful to note that while the cost/volume relationship is the pertinent corporate issue, some of the examples will in fact relate price to volume because the information, not being company derived, uses average industry price as a convenient substitute.

The price of a new product almost always declines after its initial introduction and as it becomes more widely accepted and available. However, it is not so commonly recognized that over a wide range of products, costs follow a remarkably consistent decline. The characteristic pattern is that the cost declines (in constant £s) by a consistent percentage each time cumulative unit production is doubled. The effects of learning curves on labour costs have been recognized and reported over the past 40 years beginning with studies on airframe production in the United States prior to the Second World War. However, experience curves are distinctly different from this. The real source of the experience effect is derived from organizational improvement. Although learning by individuals is important, it is only one of many improvements that accrue from experience. Investment in manufacturing processes, changes in production methods, product redesign and improvements in all functions in a business account for some part of the significant experience-related improvements.

The experience curve is normally drawn by taking each doubling of cumulative unit production and expressing the unit cost or price as a percentage of the cost or price before doubling. So an 80 per cent experience curve would mean that the cost or price of the one-hundredth unit of a product is 80 per cent of that of the fiftieth; of the two-hundredth, 80 per cent of that of the one-hundredth and so on. Exhibits 3.3 and 3.4 show the experience curve for colour film and colour paper produced by Japanese companies in the period 1965 to 1990.[5] Exhibit 3.4 also illustrates the basic features of these curves, explained as follows:[6]

1. The horizontal axis measures the cumulative quantity produced on a logarithmic scale. Exhibit 3.5a and b shows the same information plotted on a linear and logarithmic scale, respectively. The information on Exhibit 3.5a reveals a smooth curve and the implied regularity of the relationship between unit cost and total volume. However, Exhibit 3.5b shows the same information plotted on double logarithmic scales. This presentation shows percentage changes as a constant distance, along either axis. The straight line on the log–log scale in Exhibit 3.5b means that a given percentage change in one

**Exhibit 3.3**    Experience curves for colour film produced by Japanese companies, 1965–90, 1969–90 and 1976–90

*Source: Photo Electric News* and the *Japanese Economic Journal* for relevant years

**Exhibit 3.4**    Experience curve for colour paper produced by Japanese companies 1965–1990

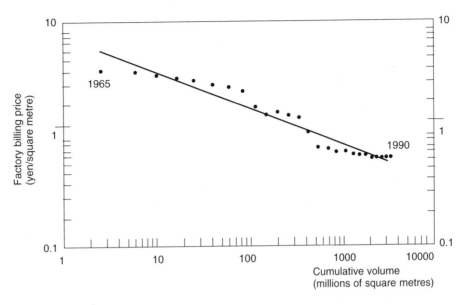

*Source: Photo Electric News* and the *Japanese Economic Journal* for relevant years

factor has resulted in a corresponding percentage change in the other. The nature of that relationship determines the slope of the line that can be read off a log–log grid.

2. Returning to Exhibits 3.3 and 3.4 the logarithmic scale shows that many doublings of production can be achieved early on, but later vastly larger quantities are needed to double the cumulative unit volumes then involved. This implies, as one would expect, that movement down the experience curve slows with time. Initially, additional growth in annual volumes can offset this, but the levelling in demand associated with the mature stage in a product life cycle and the eventual saturation and later decline through technical obsolescence will slow the rate of progress down the curve.

3. The vertical axis of an experience curve is usually cost or price per unit and is also expressed logarithmically. However the cost or price per unit must be adjusted for inflation to allow comparisons to be drawn over time; Exhibits 3.3 and 3.4 show that improvements further down the curve become, in absolute terms, quite small. Thus as progress is made down the curve each incremental movement will both take longer and yield less.

The characteristic decline in cost or price per unit was established by the Boston Consulting Group's (BCG) work in the 1960s and early 1970s as between 20 and 30 per cent for each doubling of cumulative production. Although the BCG claims that

**Exhibit 3.5**  Cost/volume or price/volume relationship expressed on a linear and a log–log scale

**(a) Linear scale**

**(b) Log–log scale**

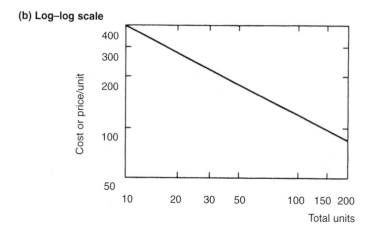

this can go on (in constant £s) without limit and despite the rate of experience growth, in reality this tends not to happen for the reasons given earlier.

Furthermore, it is important to stress that the experience curve characteristics are phenomenological in nature. They portray a relationship between cost or price and volume that can, but does not necessarily, exist. Consequently, the BCG concludes that:

> these observed or inferred reductions in costs as volume increases are not necessarily automatic. They depend crucially on a competent management that seeks ways to force down costs as volume expands. Production costs are most likely to decline under this internal pressure. Yet in the long run the average combined cost of all elements should

decline under the pressure for the company to remain as profitable as possible. To this extent the relationship is of normal potential rather than one of certainty.[7]

Many people today advocate different approaches to reducing cost. While some companies strive for dramatic breakthroughs, many are now returning to approaches based on '*Kaizen*', a Japanese term meaning 'continuous improvement'. Used by many Japanese and now Western companies, the approach has resulted in significant ongoing improvements. For example, let us look at Toyota.

- The sub-compact Terce 1 is the smallest Toyota sold in the United States. The car contributes modestly at best to profits. Even so, Toyota made the 1992 model faster, roomier and quieter than its predecessors – it weighs less, achieves equally good mileage (32 mpg on the highway) and, remarkably, is similarly priced under $8,000 for a basic four-door sedan. It is $100 cheaper than General Motors' new Saturn and as much as $1,600 less than other competing models.[8]

- In 1997, Toyota launched three products as part of its range in the US car market. All three failed to meet the needs of the segment in which each competed. By 1998, Toyota had learnt from its product mistakes, recalibrated and launched again, as shown in Exhibit 3.6.

**Exhibit 3.6**  Continuous improvement: learning to make it better with examples from Toyota

| Model/year | Details |
|---|---|
| Previa LE 1997 | Highly engineered, it was powered by a small engine under the floor. Buyers found it sluggish and expensive at $30,000 |
| Sienna XLE 1998 | Run-of-the-mill engineering, this van is made in the US with a larger engine using conventional technology. Price $22,000 |
| Lexus GS300 1997 | A sport sedan with moderate performance (a V-6 engine with acceleration of 0 to 60 mph in 8.3 seconds), a tiny trunk and a high price ($44,800) |
| Lexus GS400 1998 | The upgraded GS400 with a V-8 engine and 0 to 60 mph in 6.0 seconds. A sizeable trunk but little increase in price on the GS300 |
| T100 1997 | This version of the T100 was uncompetitive on size, power and price. Built in Japan, some models cost $25,000 |
| T100 1998 | The new design has a bigger cab and engine but lower price. Built in the US, there is no 25 per cent import duty |

*Delivery Reliability*

On-time delivery (OTD) means supplying the products ordered on the agreed due date. It, therefore, is a major concern both of the manufacturing and distribution functions. In many businesses this criterion now constitutes a qualifier. Very often, it is an order-losing sensitive qualifier, meaning that if companies continue to miss due dates, customers will increasingly stop considering them as potential suppliers. Thus unless these firms improve their on-time delivery, they will not get the chance to compete. There is a growing recognition of the importance of delivery reliability as a criterion in most markets. Its change towards being a qualifier is part of that competitive perspective. Increasingly, then, OTD performance is a competitive factor,[9] and its measurement by customer, sector and overall is key in most businesses. The need to identify different OTD expectations is a critical step here as with other order-winners and qualifiers.

For the manufacturing function, this involves consideration of capacity, scheduling and inventory, principally for work-in-progress and finished goods. This must be supplemented by regular reviews of those dimensions affecting a company's record on delivery reliability, such as completed line item reviews (product mix made as measured against the production plan) and checks on lead-time performance throughout the total process.

The exactness of the due date can vary from an appointed hour on a given day to delivery of the agreed quantity starting, and finishing, in an agreed week. The level of data collection and the timing and proactive nature of the feedback to customers will need to form part of this decision. As a rule, the more exact the delivery is, the more proactive a supplier should be in the data collection and the more regular the performance summaries and feedback to customers should be.

These data are the source of information about the size of 'call-offs' (what a customer actually wants rather than the total quantities expressed in any contract or agreement) and the lead times associated with the delivery. The former concerns the issue of costs and price agreements, the latter leads into the criterion of delivery speed.

*Delivery Speed*

A company may win orders through its ability to deliver more quickly than competitors or to meet the delivery date required when only some or even none of the competition can do so. Products that compete in this way need a manufacturing process that can respond to this requirement. There are two perspectives to the issue of delivery speed. One is where the process lead time, while being shorter than the delivery time required by the customers, is difficult to achieve because the current forward order load (or order backlog) on manufacturing capacity plus the process lead time to complete the order is greater than the delivery time required (see Situation 1, Exhibit 3.7). This is resolved through either a short-term increase

**Exhibit 3.7**    Situations where delivery speed is an order-winning criterion to be provided by
manufacturing

**Situation 1**
Order point

Customer's delivery requirement

Existing order backlog
or forward load

Process lead time
in manufacturing

**Situation 2**
Order point

Customer's delivery requirement

Process lead time in manufacturing

**Exhibit 3.8**    Where delivery speed is not an order-winning criterion

Order point

Customer's delivery requirement

Existing order backlog
or forward load

Process lead time
in manufacturing

in capacity (for example, overtime working), a rescheduling of existing jobs or a combination of both.

The other is where the process lead time is greater than the customer delivery requirement (see Situation 2, Exhibit 3.7). In these situations, manufacturing (for a given process technology) can only meet the customer's requirements by either increasing short-term capacity or holding inventory and thus reducing the process lead time by completing part of manufacturing before the order point and hence in anticipation of winning these types of orders. Schedule changes may facilitate the accomplishment of the task but will not in themselves resolve this type of situation.

Where process lead time and existing order backlog do not exceed the customer's delivery requirement, delivery speed is not an issue (see Exhibit 3.8).

With regard to delivery, it is important to distinguish between delivery promise (that is, committing the company to deliver in line with a customers' requirements) and delivery speed. The former can be a commitment in any of the situations described by Exhibits 3.7 and 3.8, whereas the latter only appertains to situations similar to those given in Exhibit 3.7.

**Exhibit 3.9**   Superfast producers

| Company | Product | Time from order to finished goods (weeks) | | Percentage reduction |
| --- | --- | --- | --- | --- |
| | | Old | New | |
| GE | Circuit breaker boxes | 3.0 | 0.6 | 80 |
| Motorola | Pagers | 3.0 | 0.1 | 97 |
| Hewlett-Packard | Electronic test equipment | 4.0 | 1.0 | 75 |
| Brunswick | Fishing reels | 3.0 | 1.0 | 67 |

*Source:* Based on B. Dumaine, 'How Managers Can Succeed Through Speed', *Fortune*, 13 February 1989, pp. 5–29.

**Exhibit 3.10**   Typical improvements in production flow times

| Example | | Before | After | Percentage reduction |
| --- | --- | --- | --- | --- |
| Japan | | | | |
|    Washing machines (Matsushita) | Hours | 360 | 2 | 99 |
| United States | | | | |
|    Motorcycles (Harley-Davidson) | | 360 | 3 | 99 |
|    Motor controllers | Days | 56 | 7 | 88 |
|    Electric components | | 24 | 1 | 96 |
|    Radar detectors | | 22 | 3 | 86 |

*Source:* Based on G. S. Stalk Jnr and T. M. Hout, *Competing against Time: How Time-based Competition is Reshaping Global Markets,* New York: Free Press,1990, p. 67

Increasingly, companies are reducing lead times. Some are endeavouring to shorten them reactively, if not proactively, in line with their perception of their markets or to get a competitive edge. The levels of improvement that can be achieved are substantial, as testified by Exhibits 3.9 and 3.10.

An organization's response to reducing lead times needs to be corporate wide, and often the lead times associated with before and after manufacturing can be a substantial part of the time it takes from order entry to customer delivery. For example the time needed for Toyota to schedule a dealer's order is one day, compared to Detroit's five; Milliken, the large US textile manufacturer, has been collaborating with General Motors on car interiors, with Sears on upholstery fabrics and with Wal-Mart on clothing. Working now as partners rather than separate parts of the operation, Milliken and its customers have been able to reduce, among other things, the lead time required to fill an order by 50 per cent.[10]

One principal contributor in this important dimension of reducing lead time, however, is manufacturing. (Note that lead-time reduction in product development is addressed under the section on design covered later in the chapter.) From the moment an order reaches the factory, all elements of lead time need to be reviewed with the aim of reducing each component involved in the total process. To succeed, companies must transform themselves and simply break the paradigms that hold current procedures and norms in place.[11]

Companies can knowingly offer short lead times to customers by holding excess capacity, maintaining low- or zero-order backlogs or holding inventory at any or all stages in the process. However, in these situations, such decisions are not manufacturing's, as they should emanate from corporate-based agreement. Furthermore, such circumstances will not constitute a delivery-speed requirement as defined above. Manufacturing's role, however, would be to maintain the various elements on which such decisions are based. A supplier's promise to deliver by an agreed date then leads to the aspect of delivery reliability, which was described in the last section.

With customers typically reducing their own lead times, many companies are finding that the element of delivery speed is becoming an increasing factor in their markets. Consequently, customer lead times are shorter than the combined lead times of material purchase and manufacture (see Exhibit 3.7). A firm's response to delivery speed, as with all criteria, can be either reactive or proactive. By being reactive, a company will cope with the necessary lead-time reduction as and when it occurs, by some combination of changing priorities, expediting, increasing short-term capacity or living with some level of failure to deliver on time. By being proactive, a company will reduce its own lead times, thereby obviating delivery speed from being an internal factor while exploiting short lead times in the marketplace. Possible scenarios in which companies may be involved are outlined in Exhibit 3.11. This sets out a series of time-related alternatives and firms need to determine their current and preferred position by market as the first step to establishing a strategic response. Companies' potential opportunity to reduce lead times will depend on the nature of their markets (for example, whether they sell standard or special products and offer a design-and-manufacturing, or manufacturing-only, capability) and their decisions to hold different levels of raw materials/components, work-in-progress and finished goods inventory. As a company moves (or is able to move) from point 1 to 5 in Exhibit 3.11, overall lead times will reduce. However, as explained above, any repositioning is a corporate decision directly affecting the element of delivery speed. Adjusting its position on this continuum so as to eliminate or reduce the impact of delivery speed would then need to be supported by shortening each element of lead time within the overall process. This would involve a whole range of decisions including capacity, inventory holdings and set-up reduction.

Finally, time-based management has a further, significant advantage. Compared with the more traditional, bureaucratic or entrepreneurial approaches it leads to reductions in overhead costs as shown in Exhibit 3.12.

## Quality Conformance

Quality as a competitive criterion has been thrust centre stage since the late 1970s. Although its importance has been recognized throughout this period, many compa-

**Exhibit 3.11** Alternative responses to markets and their lead-time implications

| Initial positions | Length of lead times |
|---|---|
| 1. *Design to order* – new product response where companies design and manufacture a product to meet the specific needs of a customer. | Long |
| 2. *Engineer to order* – changes to standard products are offered to customers and only made to order. Lead times include the relevant elements of engineering design and all manufacturing. | |
| 3. *Make to order*[1] – concerns manufacturing a standard product (any customization is nominal and does not increase total lead times) only on receipt of a customer order or against an agreed schedule or call-off. | |
| 4. *Assemble to order* – components and subassemblies have been made to stock. On receipt of an order (or against an agreed schedule or call-off), the required parts are drawn from work-in-progress/component inventory and assembled to order. | |
| 5. *Make to stock* – finished goods are made ahead of demand in line with sales forecasts. Customers' orders are met from inventory. | Short |

*Note*

1. Some customers require companies to make to print (that is, make a product in line with a given drawing). In such markets, lead times only include raw materials purchase/supply and manufacturing. They do not include design, but some customer-induced redesign during the process will often be involved.

**Exhibit 3.12** Overhead costs incurred in time-based management approaches compared with those involved in classic structures: industrial component suppliers

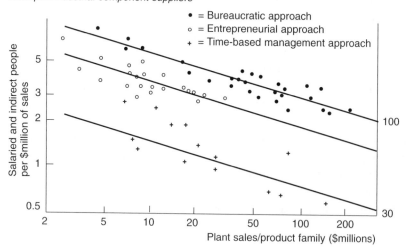

*Example: Industrial component suppliers*

• = Bureaucratic approach
o = Entrepreneurial approach
+ = Time-based management approach

*Source:* Based on G. S. Stalk, Jnr and T. M. Hout, *Competing against Time: How Time-based Competition is Reshaping Global Markets*, New York: Free Press, 1990, p. 54

nies have failed to compete on this dimension. In part this is because the definition of the word 'quality' has been broadened to encompass many dimensions. The result has been a lack of understanding and subsequent lack of direction, the hallmark of generic statements that characterize strategy formulation. Exhibit 3.13 lists eight dimensions of quality and identifies the function(s) that would typically assume prime responsibility for their provision.[12] However, in many instances and as recognized here, by separating criteria into 'manufacturing-related and manufacturing-specific', 'manufacturing-related but not manufacturing specific', and 'non-manufacturing-related', there is overlap. Single and joint provision is, therefore, the outcome.

One reason companies do not compete successfully in the quality domain is their failure to clarify which dimension(s) of quality will provide the best results in given markets. Identifying the different dimensions involved is the first step. The next is to agree which, and to what extent each, needs addressing.

In the context of this section, the aspect of quality that concerns manufacturing provision is conformance – making a product to specification. Linked closely to design (which determines the specification itself – see Exhibit 3.13), quality within this definition is a key manufacturing task. Its role in most markets has now been changed from an order-winner to a qualifier.[13] In part this has been brought about by Japanese companies that, as a facet of their competitive thrust in several industrial markets, made products to a high level of quality conformance. The result has been similar to the colour television example given in Chapter 2. Companies, in order to stay in relevant markets, needed to improve the quality conformance dimension of

**Exhibit 3.13** The dimensions of quality and the functions typically responsible for their provision

| | Dimensions of quality | Function(s) responsible |
|---|---|---|
| Performance | A product's primary operating characteristics | Design |
| Features | Secondary characteristics, the 'bells and whistles' | |
| Reliability | The probability of a product malfunctioning within a given period | |
| Aesthetics | How the final product looks | |
| Durability | A measure of a product's life in terms of both its technical and economic dimensions | |
| Conformance | The degree to which a product is manufactured to the agreed specification | Manufacturing |
| Serviceability | The ease of servicing (planned or breakdown) to include the speed and provision of after-sales service | Design and after-sales |
| Perceived quality | How a customer views the product | Marketing and design |

*Source:* Based on D. A. Garvin, 'Competing on the Eight Dimensions of Quality', *Harvard Business Review*, November–December 1987, pp. 101–19

their products. Having done so, the role of quality conformance then changed from an order-winner to a qualifier. Today, customers expect products to be of a high quality, thus recognizing (at least intuitively) that quality conformance is a given.

One example of this importance of conformance quality within a market is provided by automobiles. The growth in Japanese companies' share within the volume and luxury sectors of this market has been outstanding.[14] This is partly due to the continued high levels of quality conformance achieved compared to principal competitors. Link this to their superior productivity performance shown in Exhibits 1.9 and 1.10) and the reasons for their success begin to emerge.

The recent attention attracted by quality-based approaches in management has further highlighted the emphasis on the advantages of completing tasks correctly the first time. This, in part, has been an extension of the improvements in the quality conformance of products and the significant benefits that have been secured. Much has been written on the approaches that have underpinned success.[15]

### Demand Increases

In some markets, a company's ability to respond to increases in demand is an important factor in winning orders. These sales may reflect the high seasonality of customers' requirements or be of a spasmodic or one-off nature. This factor concerns the level of predictability surrounding demand itself as well as others such as product shelf life and the frequency of product modifications in line with market requirements. All will affect manufacturing's response.

Knowing seasonal demand makes it possible to reach agreement between supplier, manufacturer, distributor and customer about inventory holdings throughout the process, process capacity and planned increases in labour (for example, overtime working or additional shifts). With one-off or spot business (for example, during an influenza epidemic when demand is for the same product that may have a short shelf life, thus limiting viable inventory levels, or where a product is customer specified at some point in the process and, therefore, cannot be made ahead of demand, or a significant order for a product over and above agreed call-off quantities or simply an unexpected, sizable order for a given product), holding materials or forms of capacity, arranging short-term increases in labour capacity (for example, through overtime), rearranging priorities or some combination of these will typically be a supplier's response.

The phenomena described here provide another example of the way that a lack of essential clarity can lead to serious levels of corporate misunderstanding. The generalized discussion surrounding these key aspects of a business typically involves words such as 'flexibility'.[16] However, the extent to which a company intends to respond to these significant increases in demand is a strategic decision of some magnitude. To allow each function to respond according to its own interpretation invariably leads to major mismatches.

*Product Range*

As highlighted earlier, markets are increasingly characterized by difference, not similarity. However, the balance between levels of customization and the volume base for repetitive manufacturing has to be addressed by the business as a whole. That markets are increasingly segmenting is a given. Manufacturing's role is to continue to develop processes that can cope with product-range differences and provide low-cost results. It needs to be able to bridge these essential differences in order to retain the volume base so essential to efficient manufacturing.

Thus, where product ranges are widening, process developments need to reflect the broadening nature of the product base and the lower-volume implications that tend to go hand in hand with these trends. The former needs to be recognized at the time when process investments are made. The latter is reflected in reduced set-up times, whether manual or automated (for example, a numerically controlled facility), so enabling companies to cope with the lower-volume nature of these changes while retaining the necessary levels of cost.

Examples of these trends are seen in the automobile industry. The pressure on car makers at the lower end of the volume scale is to continue to differentiate their products as a way of competing not only with their traditional competitors but with makers at the higher end of the volume scale as well. BMW's 7 Series offers a marked uplift in customization, more akin to the very low-volume luxury car makers such as Rolls-Royce and Aston Martin. Handcrafted leather interiors and its 'any colour' option are examples of this. Competition based on increasing the product and option range is also coming from traditional, high-volume car companies. Several Japanese car makers (for example, Toyota) have been and are continuing to develop a production system capable of responding to individual customer requirements. As a result, to support increases in product range options successfully, manufacturing needs to develop its processes to provide these in a cost- and time-efficient way.

## Manufacturing-related but not Manufacturing-specific Criteria

Although businesses separate clusters of activities into different functions, in reality they are, and need to form, part of the same whole. Thus, many functions within a company will directly support manufacturing or will undertake tasks that link or directly affect that function's strategic and operational roles.

*Design*

The links between design, manufacturing and markets are the very essence of a business. The way that these interrelate, therefore, is fundamental to sound strategy development and implementation. Both design and manufacturing's aim is to provide products according to their technical and business specifications. In addition, these two functions combine to provide the product development phase that comes before the ongoing selling/manufacturing activity that forms the commercial substance of companies. Three of the more important dimensions involved are addressed in this section and have been chosen because they are fundamental to this basic corporate activity.[17]

## Low Cost

Design is becoming increasingly important in providing essential support for several criteria relevant to today's markets. Products have to be designed both with process characteristics and cost reduction in mind. Thus design not only concerns functionality, it has a critical impact on product costs. With direct materials typically accounting for some 40–60 per cent of the total, the opportunities to reduce costs at source are substantial. In addition, this essential link reinforces the need to meet the design for manufacturing requirements in terms of labour-cost reduction through increased automation and other labour-saving opportunities. For many years, corporate appeals by Western firms to design for manufacture have been more exhortation than accomplishment, a view confirmed by a committee of the National Research Council in the early 1990s.[18] It found the overall quality of engineering design – the process of turning a concept into a finished product or determining how to make a new toaster, dress or computer as efficiently as possible – to be poor. Long before a product reaches the store, 70 per cent or more of its cost is determined by its design.

Any third-rate engineer can design complexity. In many companies, the emphasis to make it simple is neither part of the designer's make-up nor part of the corporate demands placed on this function. In the new millennium, pressure on price will continue to be an important competitive factor in many segments. Thus, design's role in the total corporate response is fundamental in more ways than one.

## Product Range

The increasing level of product diversification has already been recognized as an important factor in today's increasingly competitive markets and central to this provision is the design function. The pressure on design will vary from market to market and the interpretation and execution of these is central to a company's ability to remain competitive. The tendency for Western designers to be more interested in functionality than the commercial facets of design is in marked contrast to competitors, particularly the Japanese. As Hiroyuki Yoshida, head of Toyota's design centre, reflected, 'Whatever the merits of a design, it has to be robust enough to go through our engineering and manufacturing system. The commercial point of design has not been lost. We are in the business to make low-cost high-quality cars for a mass market. We are making cars, not art.'[19]

Within this context, as highlighted elsewhere, markets are increasingly segmenting. Design needs to be able to meet these changes and to recognize, certainly in terms of attitude and speed of response, that change is a fundamental charateristic of today's markets. For example, Honda had to move from developing its Accord range as a world car (the same model selling into all markets) in the early 1980s to designing two distinct ranges for its home and US markets.

It is now the age of diversification and those companies unable to keep pace with this growth of diversity will decline. Many companies, therefore, are directing much more attention to incorporating the perspectives and preferences of customers into future designs. A classic example of this is provided by Toyota and Mazda. Both have built complexes in Tokyo that incorporate vehicle-design studios in which the visitors are invited to 'design' their own cars. Thus ideas on what constitutes a potential customer's ideal vehicle are included as inputs into future designs.

However, the demand for styling and product features has to be reconciled with other pressures. Environmentally friendly products are not only a growing concern of customers but also high on the agenda of legislative bodies. For example, clean-air legislation in the US and the European Union is at the forefront of changing pressures on vehicle design. Their requirements for minimum percentage sales of low-emission vehicles (LEVs) and ultra-low-emission vehicles (ULEVs) has been an added stimulus for improvements on all car emission standards. The targets for the next five years will mean that unless there is a major breakthrough in existing engine technology, companies will have to develop a viable electric car in the first five years of this century.

Most major car makers have recognized the need to harness design capabilities to meet these environmentally stimulated developments. General Motors, Ford and Chrysler concluded an agreement with the US government under which a total of $1bn is to be spent in the period to the year 2003 on developing advanced battery technology.

## Lead Times

The reduction of lead times within the manufacturing process has already been highlighted as an increasingly important order-winner. Similarly, speed to market with new product designs and developments has become a significant competitive factor. The increasing priority of speed is based on a recognition that it can simply negate the competition. The results of such improvements, as shown in Exhibit 3.14, speak for themselves. In addition, companies receive a number of distinct advantages from reducing product design and development lead times, including the following:

1. **Benefits of double gain.** Being first in the market brings advantages of both higher volumes and higher margins – the opportunity for double gain – as explained below.

    a. *Product life cycles are extended* – If a product is introduced sooner, rarely will it become obsolete sooner. This advantage accrues even more so where customers incur high switching costs. The usual outcome of early product introduction is to gain more customers who, in turn, stay longer (see Exhibit 3.15).

**Exhibit 3.14**  Examples of reduction in product development lead time

| Company | Product | Development time (months) | |
|---|---|---|---|
| | | Old | New |
| AT&T | Telephones | 24 | 12 |
| Hewlett-Packard | Computer printers | 54 | 21 |
| Honeywell | Thermostats | 48 | 12 |
| Ingersoll Rand | Air-powered grinders | 42 | 14 |
| Warner Electric | Clutches and brakes | 36 | 9 |

**Exhibit 3.15**  The increased sales revenue element of the benefits of double gain

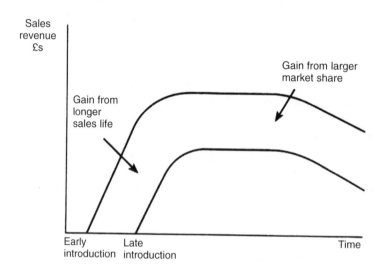

b. *Increased market share* – The first producer will, in the beginning, command 100 per cent market share. Thus, the earlier a product appears, the more likely the prospect of obtaining a large market share. Link this to the previous factor and the impact on total life cycle volumes is marked.

c. *Higher profit margins* – A company will naturally enjoy a higher level of pricing freedom in the early stages of a product's life cycle. This will, therefore, provide higher margins in the early stages with the opportunity for manufacturing to provide lower costs in light of the volume advantages highlighted above (see Exhibit 3.16 and also the earlier section on experience curves).

d. *Double gain* – The first three factors combine to give a situation of double gain – companies gain higher sales and also achieve a higher margin on each sale.

**Exhibit 3.16**  The higher profit margin element of the benefits of double gain

2. **Technology, consumer preference and corporate image**. Reductions in product-development lead times also provide opportunities for companies to sustain technology leadership and corporate image:

   a. *Exploiting technology opportunities* – If an organization can develop products quickly, it is more able to synchronize its product developments with the latest technologies and thus exploit these opportunities fully.

   b. *Matching consumer change* – Short product-development lead times help a business to match market changes, thereby tracking more closely changes in consumer preferences and demands.

   c. *Corporate image* – Developing products more quickly will help a firm to maintain its corporate image of being a progressive front-runner in developments and technology excellence.

3. **Reduction in design costs**. Compressing development lead times also results in a reduction in design costs. This is achieved in part by increased levels of cooperation, which reduces misunderstandings and ensures the incorporation of functional perspectives throughout. In addition, the changed role and contribution of design within the process also leads to less time being spent within the design stages with associated reductions in cost.

Exhibit 3.14 provided examples of what can be achieved, while Exhibit 3.17 shows how this is accomplished. A glance at the latter shows a two-pronged approach to reducing lead times:

■ shorten the total time to complete the steps in the process
■ starts the steps earlier, running some in parallel.

**Exhibit 3.17**  Digital Equipment Company's (DEC) reduced completion time for
a new product development

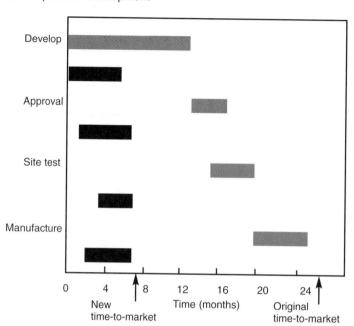

*Source:* R. Reeve, 'Profiting from Teamwork' *Manufacturing Breakthrough*, January–February 1992, p. 22 (with
permission)

Although some steps in the revised approach are much shorter, the gain is more
cumulative in nature and a combination of the two elements above, as clearly
shown in Exhibit 3.18. This compares approaches to product development by
Japanese, North American and European car makers. A close look at the details
provided illustrates the two-pronged approach mentioned above, and reflects
different approaches and values of those involved, as explained below:

- Western designers typically expect to develop products that require little or no
  modification. As perfection is rarely, if ever, achieved, any necessary changes
  must be identified in later phases. However, also part of the typical design function's attitude is a resistance to change since, given the perfection syndrome, a
  need for change implies failure. The result is long first-phase lead times, that are
  subsequently further increased because of the inherent resistance to change.

- The Japanese alternative is based on a different set of expectations. Knowing
  that perfection is impossible, designers conclude their proposals much more
  quickly than their Western counterparts and, ready to accept change, respond to
  the demands of the modification stages with appropriate expectations and corresponding speed. The result is a significant overall reduction in development
  lead times.

**Exhibit 3.18** Average project lead times and stage length in Japanese, US and European car makers[1]

| Development phase | Japanese | | | United States | | | European | | |
|---|---|---|---|---|---|---|---|---|---|
| | Begin | End | Stage length | Begin | End | Stage length | Begin | End | Stage length |
| Concept study | 42 | 34 | 8 | 62 | 44 | 18 | 62 | 47 | 15 |
| Product planning | 38 | 29 | 9 | 57 | 39 | 18 | 57 | 40 | 17 |
| Advanced engineering | 42 | 27 | 15 | 56 | 29 | 26 | 52 | 39 | 13 |
| Product engineering | 30 | 6 | 24 | 40 | 12 | 28 | 39 | 16 | 23 |
| Process engineering | 28 | 6 | 22 | 31 | 6 | 26 | 38 | 8 | 30 |
| Pilot run | 7 | 3 | 4 | 9 | 3 | 6 | 9 | 3 | 6 |
| Total | – | – | 82 | – | – | 122 | – | – | 104 |

*Note*
1. Data in months before start of production; figures have been rounded. Sample sizes are Japan, 12; United States, 6; and Europe, 10.

*Source:* B. Clark and T. Fujimoto, 'Overlapping Problem-solving in Product Development', in K. Ferdows (ed.) *Managing International Manufacturing*, Amsterdam: Elsevier Science, 1989

A look back at the examples of product-development lead-time reduction clearly illustrates the shared responsibility for two or more functions to provide this criterion. This joint provision is highlighted as Exhibit 3.19.

Competing on time is a key aspect in many markets and has several dimensions. Delivery speed and product-development lead times have been highlighted so far. Another aspect, however, is also emerging: plant start-ups. In the late 1980s, the National Bicycle Industrial Company took only seven months from the day the company president raised a query about the possibility of increasing the levels of

**Exhibit 3.19** Shared functional provision of relevant order-winners and qualifiers

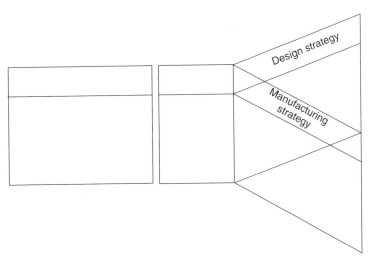

**Exhibit 3.20** Comparative change-over times to produce a new model, American and Japanese car makers

| Plant | Car model | End and start dates of the car model | | Elapsed times (days) |
|---|---|---|---|---|
| | | Old | New | |
| *North American* | | | | |
| Oshawa, Ontario | Chevy Lumina | 19 Nov 93 | 14 Feb 94 | 87 |
| Kansas City | Ford Contour/ Mercury Mystique | 20 May 94 | 19 Jul 94 | 60 |
| *Japanese* | | | | |
| Georgetown, Kentucky | Toyota Camry | 16 Aug 91 | 03 Sep 91 | 18 |
| Marysville, Ohio | Honda Accord | 27 Aug 93 | 30 Aug 93 | 3 |

customization of its range of high-volume bicycles to the actual plant start-up in July 1987. Similarly a *Business Week* article[20] highlighted the gap between Japanese and North American car makers in terms of the length of time needed to change over a factory to produce a new model. Exhibit 3.20 shows the significant differences, part of which comes from the insistence by Japanese car makers that their engineers adapt designs to a plant's existing capabilities.

### Distribution

Distribution's role in quick and reliable delivery has been mentioned earlier. As part of the total process, distribution plays an essential role in delivery.

In addition, the costs of this facet of overall provision (including those of storage, warehouse administration and movement) typically have been rising both in themselves and as a percentage of the total. Highlighting the potential source of cost reduction inherent in distribution-related activities has not, however, received the attention that other supply-chain activities have.

## Non-manufacturing-related Criteria

It is not unusual for companies to be in markets whose relevant order-winners are not directly related to manufacturing. In these types of markets, manufacturing typically will be required to support one or more qualifiers. Some of the more important criteria that frequently characterize markets are now briefly discussed. In all instances each function responsible for the criterion reviewed would have the task of providing and maintaining the required level of support.

## Design Leadership

The role of design and its relationship to competitive issues such as product-development lead times and product costs have already been discussed. However one of the design function's principal roles concerns the development of products in terms of features, aesthetics, perceived levels of design in specification and reliability (including costs) while in service (see Exhibit 3.13). Furthermore, where frequent design introductions offer a competitive edge, this requirement will be at the forefront of the function's performance priorities. Linked to the need for shorter product-development lead times, this criterion is increasingly emerging as a major competitive factor in today's markets. For example, responding to the challenge from Yamaha, Honda almost doubled its range of motorcycle models in less than two years, eliminating Yamaha's short-lived advantage. Liz Claiborne (a designer/manufacturer of separates and sportswear) introduced two additional clothing seasons to reflect more clearly consumer buying patterns. Seiko has increased its dominant role in the watch market with a highly automated factory capable of producing new models each day. In semiconductors, the competitive factor is largely the speed with which new product technologies can be applied to chips. Other companies (for example, Ford Europe), introduced major retraining programmes in the mid-1990s to 'spark creativity'.[21]

The importance of product design has always been recognized. Markets can be dominated by this dimension and unique design, particularly in the past, has been considered the principal order-winning provision of this function. However, companies are increasingly recognizing the other contributions that the design function can make in winning orders, the key elements of which have been discussed in earlier sections.

## Being an Existing Supplier

Where a company is an existing supplier, it may continue to win orders in part, or solely, because of this factor. The criterion tends to be relevant to both low-volume and spares markets. In the former, manufacturing needs to continue to support the relevant order-winners and qualifiers. In the latter, it needs to recognize the impact that its performance on relevant criteria will have on orders for any new or existing products in the future.

## Marketing and Sales

The marketing and sales functions' principal orientation is towards the marketplace. Its important links to customers and its insights into the characteristics of relevant market segments – including issues of pricing, competitive threats, growth and/or decline of existing segments, and identification of new opportunities – is an essential part of a company's strategic provision.

*Brand Name*

Through a variety of activities, including design, advertising and increasing or maintaining market share, companies seek to establish brand names for their products. Where this has been achieved and maintained, companies will win orders partly due to the image its products have in the markets in which they compete.

*Technical Liaison and Support*

In certain markets, customers will seek technical liaison from suppliers during the precontract phase and technical support thereafter. The quality and extent of a supplier's in-house technical capability to support product development, particularly towards its introduction in the early stages of its manufacture, will be an important criterion in these markets.

*After-sales Support*

Furthermore, companies may look for ways of differentiating their total product by offering, for instance, a high level of customer support (see Exhibit 3.13). One example is BMW. The company has a fleet of 30 cars funded jointly with its dealers and strategically placed throughout the UK. The purpose is to go to the support of any BMW that has broken down by the roadside. The company will continue to increase this standby fleet until it can sufficiently deal with the 80 per cent of breakdowns occuring in all the BMWs in the UK that can actually be solved at the roadside.

A further example of after-sales is the motor repairs sector. Compact discs enable a mechanic to call up information on any component or car by typing in the relevant part or the vehicle's chassis number. In repair procedure terms, the mechanic can find out which faults cause which problems and what procedures should be followed. Service sales staff are similarly able to investigate customer details and vehicle records to help in their service-support provision. Companies already using these customer support systems include Volkswagen, BMW, Opel, PSA (Peugeot and Citroen), General Motors and Toyota.

# Benchmarking[22]

The failure of a company to assess and monitor its competitors is at best a mark of corporate complacency and at worst a sign of strategic naivety. For a company, such a monitoring process has two important dimensions:

- A continuous updating of the level and dimensions of competition within its markets.
- Proactivity, seeking to improve its own business performance by learning from other companies about what can be done and how to do things better.

Benchmarking is an approach that was identified and highlighted in the mid-1980s and that many companies believe is essential to help to continue enhancing their competitive position in the new millennium. It does this by redirecting the corporate spotlight from assessing internal performance (typically using internal measures) to checking externally how current (albeit improved) performance compares with best practice. In this way it reinforces the clear need to identify market requirements, to differentiate importance and to establish the level of performance that needs to be achieved within each competitive dimension.

As shown in the earlier section on experience curves, all companies tend to learn and improve through time, but the key question is whether the rate of improvement is adequate to become and/or remain competitive. Benchmarking forces companies to look outwards and recognize this external perspective as the appropriate way to identify the levels of performance that need to become their new targets. Furthermore, checking against performance in other businesses (and particularly in unrelated sectors) leads to some distinct advantages:

- It describes the 'what' rather than the 'how'. Thus, companies are presented with targets not solutions, which in turn increases the aspect of ownership. The panacea syndrome mentioned earlier also identifies the inappropriateness of solution-oriented approaches.

- Having targets to aim for helps to create a uniform response from all parts of a business. When goals are common, improvement becomes a shared task.

- It reinforces the executive role, rather than that of support staff as the key element for bringing about sustained performance improvements.

- External, and particularly ex-sector, comparisons are often perceived as being more objectively derived and therefore more readily accepted.

- It opens up new improvement horizons that frequently represent a stepped change in performance. In so doing, it provides the opportunity to leapfrog competitors in selected and relevant dimensions of performance.

Benchmarking is concerned with the search for best practices, whatever their source, in order to achieve superior performance. It therefore involves continuously measuring a company's products, services and practices both against competitors and the leaders in any business sector. It is, however, not an end in itself but a means to help to achieve levels of competitiveness. In this way, it offers an important dimension within the domain of order-winners by ensuring that corporate performance against relevant criteria is measured against externally derived, best-practice norms. Benchmarking, therefore, moves a company from having an inward bias to incorporating external perspectives, which invariably introduces a stepped change in terms of performance. These external antennae help a company to assess what is going on and also to manage itself within its own environment.

Implementing benchmarking starts with determining the key functions within a business that need to be reviewed. When the relevant performance variables to measure these functions have been agreed, then identifying best-in-class performances sets the target. What follows is the task of assessing the action programmes to bring corporate performance into line with and then to surpass that achieved by the best-in-class companies.

For benchmarking to be successfully implemented, some key elements need to be in place. These include:

- *Rigour.* It is essential that companies ensure that the targets to be achieved are set high enough. Targets need to be derived from knowledge and not intuition.

- *Overcoming disbelief.* In the initial phases of this process, companies often need to convince themselves that they can not only do better but can meet the often daunting tasks that benchmarking reviews typically identify.

- *Accountability.* Benchmarking represents an ongoing procedure for measuring performance and ensuring improvement. A prerequisite for this is to instil in everyone the responsibility and authority for identifying, checking and implementing the changes necessary to achieve this improvement.

- *Culture change.* Managers typically spend most of their time on internal issues. Reorienting companies to be externally rather than internally focused is an essential facet of the successful introduction and ongoing development of this approach and associated improvements.

## Best-in-class Exemplars

The need for companies to assess themselves against externally derived standards has been stressed throughout this book. Thus, examples need to be identified from a number of different company classifications, including:

- Other parts of the same company – internal benchmarking[23]
- Direct competitors
- Companies in the same industrial sector but not direct competitors
- Latent competitors
- Companies outside the industry.

Recognizing the different categories enables a firm to identify a broader range of potential best-in-class sources, thereby improving the quality and representative nature within this critical phase. An example that illustrates the advantages of using best-in-class exemplars is afforded by Exhibit 3.21 showing how IBM's use of outside-the-industry perspectives helped it to identify its future targets.

In the same way, Jack Welch (Chairman and CEO of General Electric Company) set a corporate goal in 1995 to become a six-sigma quality company by the new millennium:

> which means a company that produces virtually defect-free products, services and transactions. Six sigma quality is a level of quality that to date has been approached by only a handful of companies, among them several in Japan, with Motorola being the acknowledged leader in this country... We want to make our quality so special, [he explained] so valuable to our customers, so important to their success that our products become their only real 'value choice'.[24]

## Ways to Close the Gap then Surpass Exemplars

Improving performance is the result of a number of coordinated actions in line with the key functions already identified. The particular improvements will need to reflect the tasks on hand. However, companies must recognize the different levels of achievement that exist:

**Exhibit 3.21**  Benchmarking quality helped IBM identify its best-in-class, six sigma target[1]

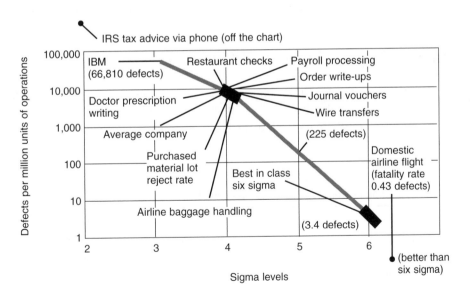

Note

1. At the beginning of 1990, IBM admitted its overall defect rate was around 3 sigma, or 66,810 defects per million operations.

*Source*: B. C. P. Rayner 'Market-driven Quality: IBM Six-sigma Crusade', *Electronic Business*, 15 October, 1990, p. 28 (with permission)

- *Try harder* – This is a classic approach that, if adopted, implies a failure to recognize the principles underpinning benchmarking.
- *Emulate* – This involves setting achievement targets on a par with competitors and/or best-in-class examplars.
- *Leapfrog* – This means setting targets higher than existing exemplar norms.
- *Change the rules of the game* – This entails setting the pace in driving the order-winners and qualifiers in relevant markets.

These dimensions constitute target levels of change. The difficulty many companies face at the beginning is in identifying the different levels of achievement. Many find that looking outside helps to identify more clearly levels of higher achievement as shown in Exhibit 3.22.

## Competitors are Moving Targets

Earlier, the need to recognize that order-winners and qualifiers change over time was stressed. This is because markets are dynamic and competitors are moving targets. Companies that set their sights without taking into account these dimensions may find themselves further behind. By failing to identify the rate of improvement of competitors, companies may set themselves targets only to find that the goalposts have moved. The result is that at best they have closed the gap. More typically a company that fails to incorporate the future rate of improvement of its competitors will find itself even further behind and less able to catch up.

## **Determining Order-winners and Qualifiers**

For companies to gain an understanding of their markets takes time. In fact, strategy debate has a calendar time base that cannot be circumvented. The characteristics of markets and the perspectives of functions must be allowed adequate time, both in

**Exhibit 3.22**  Source and levels of targeted achievement

|  | Level of achievement | |
| --- | --- | --- |
| **Exemplar** | **Emulate** | **Change the rules of the game** |
| Internal benchmarking | 80 | 20 |
| Direct competitors | | |
| Industry sector but not competitor | | |
| Latent competitor | | |
| Outside the industry | 20 | 80 |

their explanation and reception. Going away for a corporate strategy weekend or arranging one-off discussions will lead to generalized statements and little insight.

The strategy facet of order-winners and qualifiers is similarly bound by these characteristics. Seeking to clarify and understand these key insights will take time and requires soundings from the following different sources.

- *Functional perspectives* – The internal perspectives of those functions that are engaged in the provision of products or that interface with the marketplace hold important insights into customer requirements. Often, however, companies limit this internal review to that of the marketing function. In part, this is based on the historical perception that marketing's view of the market represents the market. Within this context, other functions have failed to assess customers and markets in terms of what they represent from their alternative perspectives. The consequence has been that companies have given undue weight to marketing's view, which has emphasized the need to respond to customers' actual or perceived wishes and demands. Checking the impact on a business has not usually been part of a firm's overall assessment of a market, segment or customer.

- *Customers' views* – Checking with customers on what they believe they require can invariably lead to a distorted view of reality. Setting aside the aspect of self-interest, customers place orders on suppliers in one system and make demands on supplier's plants in another. Furthermore, customers are unlikely to acknowledge that the business they offer to a supplier is anything other than favourable. Equally, customers often fail to make distinctions concerning different criteria – it is safer to ask for everything at the highest level or provision.

  Most times, those involved in agreeing contracts do not know the critical dimensions of the contracts being discussed. Few have attempted to find out. All present their business in its best light. Thus, to seek the views of customers can only be one part of an assessment of a company's market.

- *Actual orders* – The real demands on a supplier are embodied in the characteristics of the individual orders, call-offs, and/or scheduled deliveries placed by customers. Tracing the volumes, lead times, margins and other relevant aspects of these will bring an essential perspective when evaluating opinion. Many companies, however, fail to analyse the key data that are an inherent by-product of their system and that contain the characteristics of the commercial transactions representing the very nature of their markets.

- *Customer reviews* – Working with customers is essential to maintain and grow sales. Discussion with customers, therefore, is a key component of this process. However, seeking customers' views is typically restricted to the sales and marketing function and is characterized by the criticisms listed in the section 'Customers' views' above. This traditional approach needs to be replaced. Reviews of customers should be undertaken by executives from sales/marketing, operations and other relevant functions, be based on data that analyse the real demands of customers (see the section 'Actual orders' above) and be ongoing in nature and frequent in occurrence.

The purpose of such reviews is to highlight the nature of the actual demands made by customers, to discuss ways to improve customer support (including possible changes in a customer's own activities and procedures), to proactively develop customer relationships that are business rather than functionally based and to agree the improvement priorities for functions that would now form part of a coordinated corporate approach.

# Conclusion

In today's markets, it is increasingly less likely that companies will have a sustainable competitive advantage. To compete effectively and continue to be successful, firms need to understand their markets.

However, strategy debate has been and continues to be general in nature. Typical outcomes are general descriptions that foster independent responses from functions. But companies that fail to provide coherent strategies will continue to lose out. Unless individual functions are able, and are required, to develop strategies that directly support their markets, these firms will lose substantial and essential advantage.

Distinguishing and weighing order-winners and qualifiers forms a key element of this strategic provision. Without such insights, agreement on what constitutes markets is replaced by individual views grounded in the biases and preferences of different functions. This leads to unsophisticated responses and allows, even encourages, unrelated functional initiatives to be developed.

For manufacturing, investments in both processes and infrastructure are expensive and fixed. Once commitments have been made it is difficult – sometimes impossible – to make changes, certainly within the allowable timeframes of current commercial environments. The overall effect on corporate performance is significant. In the short term it can lead to substantial disparity in performance, in the long term it can be at the root of overall corporate success or failure.

# The Capsizing Effect

The need for companies to be proactively alert stems from the nature of today's markets. Whereas companies in the past could recover from being outperformed and strategically outmanoeuvered, this is increasingly less likely. An ever-increasing phenomenon of the current competitive environment is the capsizing effect. Companies find that one day they are confident, secure and well directed and the next capsized, bottom up and sinking. The capsizing effect is often due to a lack of corporate awareness of competitive performance. Not being alert to the dimensions and extent of competitive performance leaves a company vulnerable to significant reversals of fortune and hence irretrievably disadvantaged.

To avoid being competitively outmanoeuvered (or sinking altogether), a company must understand its markets with sufficient insight and undertake this task on an ongoing basis. This not only provides understanding of sufficient adequacy on which to base corporate strategic directions but gives the essential inputs from which coordinated functional strategic outputs are formed.

## Hitting Singles versus Home Runs

One essential feature of management that is singularly omitted from its many descriptions is hard work. Clearly identifying markets, establishing functional strategies to support these and implementing the outcomes is a demanding role. One characteristic essential for completing these necessary parts is persistence. Winning teams build on hitting singles and do not rely on home runs.

## Little is New, Even Less is Complex

Earlier is was pointed out that any third-rate engineer can design complexity. The same holds true for strategy. Moving from what is complex and uncertain to what is understood and clear is the result of hard work – the same as required of a designer to get from the complex to the simple.

Sound foundations for strategy are built on understanding; to respond to changing markets, a company must know where it is. In the past, companies have tolerated an inadequate understanding of their markets, with the result that they have been unable to respond and lost market share or even lost out all together. Complexity is an inherent feature of most aspects of business and none more so than markets. But it need not be so.

Similarly, nothing is new. The issues and criteria (even the aspect of time) discussed in this chapter are not revolutionary. For example, nearly 70 years ago Henry Ford highlighted the 'meaning of time' as an essential and integral competitive factor in all stages of his business from raw materials to distribution.[25] With ore-extraction to sold-product lead times at a little over four days and average shipping times between factory and branches of just over six days, the meaning of time was well understood and exercised as long ago as the 1920s. What is new is the need to identify markets in terms of what wins orders and then to develop functional strategies to support these. Every long journey begins with a first step – in strategy this first step is understanding your markets.

## Notes

1. R. Henkoff, 'Cost Cutting: How to Do it Right', *Fortune,* 9 April 1990, pp. 40–9.
2. For example, the Peugeot car company in Coventry (UK) has adopted a lean manufacturing and just-in-time (JIT) philosophy with significant results – see C. Gooding, 'On the Road to a Slicker Operation', *Financial Times,* 22 July 1993, p. 16.

3. For example, refer to Henkoff (1990) or Terry Hill *Operations Management: Strategic Context and Managerial Analysis,* Basingstoke, UK: Macmillan, 2000, Chapters 3, 5, 9, 10, 12 and 13.

4. 'The Lean Enterprise Benchmarking Project', Andersen Consulting, Cardiff (UK), Business School and University of Cambridge (UK).

5. Other examples of experience curves include those for the crushed-bone and limestone industry, 1925 to 1971, in the *Boston Consulting Group Perspective* 149, 'The Experience Curve Reviewed v. Price Stability'; 'The Model T Ford, 1909 to 1923', in W. J. Abernathy and K. Wayne; 'Limits of the Learning Curve', *Harvard Business Review,* September–October 1974, pp. 109–19; and random access memory (RAM) components, 1976 to 1984, in P. Ghemawat, 'Building Strategy on the Experience Curve', *Harvard Business Review,* March–April 1985, pp. 143–9.

6. The computation of an experience curve is clearly detailed in 'Experience and Cost: Some Implications for Manufacturing Policy', Harvard Business School paper, 9–675–228 (revised July 1975).

7. *Perspectives in Experience,* Boston Consulting Group, 1972, p. 12.

8. A. Taylor III, 'Why Toyota Keeps Getting Better and Better and Better', *Fortune,* 19 November 1990, pp. 66–79. Also refer to D. Imai, *Kaizen,* New York: Random House, 1986.

9. Several authors have stressed the importance of delivery reliability. For example, J. E. Ashton and E. X. Cook, Jnr, 'Time to Reform Job Shop Manufacturing – Organize Your Factor for Quality and On-Time Delivery', *Harvard Business Review,* March–April 1989, pp. 106–11, and A. Kumar and G. Sharman, 'We Love Your Product but Where Is It?', *The McKinsey Quarterly,* 1992, **1**: 24–44.

10. Referred to in J. L. Bower and T. M. Hout, 'Fast-cycle Capability for Competitive Power', *Harvard Business Review,* November–December 1988, pp. 110–18.

11. Further details and approaches are to be found in G. S. Stalk, Jnr and T. M. Hout, *Competing Against Time: How Time-based Competition is Reshaping Global Markets,* New York: Free Press, 1990; R. W. Schmenner, 'The Merit of Making Things Fast', *Sloan Management Review,* Fall 1988, pp. 1–17; and J. D. Blackburn, *Time-based Competition; The Next Battleground in American Manufacturing,* Homewood, IL: Business One Irwin, 1991. Other references include P. Goldsburgh and P. Deane, 'Time is Money', *Management Today,* September 1985, pp. 132–9; and B. Dumaine, 'How Managers Can Succeed through Speed', *Fortune,* 13 February 1989, pp. 54–9.

12. These eight dimensions of quality were first listed by D. A. Garvin in 'Competing on the Eight Dimensions of Quality', *Harvard Business Review,* November–December 1987, pp. 101–19.

13. C. A. Voss, 'Quality in a Manufacturing Strategy', *Total Quality Management,* June 1990, pp. 149–52, elaborates on the role of quality conformance as a qualifier.

14. Survey, 'Executive Cars', *Financial Times,* 30 April 1993, p. II.

15. Books or articles that specifically address approaches to quality conformance include R. Caplan, *A Practical Approach to Quality Control,* London: Business Books, 1971; J. M. Juran, *Quality Control Handbook,* Maidenhead: McGraw-Hill, 1974; P. B. Crosby, *Quality is Free,* Maidenhead: McGraw-Hill, 1979; J. M. Juran and F. M. Gryna, *Quality Planning and Analysis,* New York: McGraw-Hill, 1980; W. E. Deming, *Quality, Productivity and Competitive Position,* Cambridge, MA: MIT Press, 1982; A. V. Feigenbaum, *Total Quality Control: Engineering and Management,* 3rd edn, Maidenhead: McGraw-Hill, 1983; G. Taguchi, *Designing Quality into Products and Processes,* Asian Productivity Organization, 1986; F. Price, *Right First Time: Using Quality Control for Profit,* Aldershot: Wildwood House, 1986; and B. G. Dale (ed.) *Managing Quality,* 2nd edn, Hemel Hempstead: Prentice Hall, 1994.

16. The basic misunderstandings surrounding the word 'flexibility' are highlighted in T. J. Hill and S. H. Chambers 'Flexibility: A Manufacturing Conundrum', *International Journal of Operations and Production Management,* 1991, **11**(2): 5–13.

17. The dimensions of quality listed in Exhibit 3.13 that relate to design function are addressed in a later section.
18. C. W. Hoover, Jnr, co-chaired the committee that studied engineering design in the United States. The critical findings were embodied in his article, 'US Products Designed to Fail', *Chicago Tribune*, 6 July 1991, p. 15.
19. Quoted in C. Leadbetter, 'Toyota's Conundrum: Creating a Global Car for a Niche Market', *Financial Times*, 17 July 1991, p. 16.
20. J. B. Treece, 'Motown's Struggle to Shift on the Fly', *Business Week*, 11 July 1994, p. 103.
21. J. McNamara, 'Ford's Engineers Become Lateral Thinkers', *Financial Times*, 10 May 1993, p. 12.
22. Readings on benchmarking include R. Osterhoff *et al.* 'Competitive Benchmarking at Xerox' in M. J. Stahland and G. M. Bounds (eds) *Competing Globally Through Customer Value*, New York: Quorum Books, 1991, pp. 788–98; A. S. Wellbeck *et al.,* 'World-class Manufacturing: Benchmarking World-class Performance', *The McKinsey Quarterly*, 1 November 1991, pp. 3–24; K. A. J. Leibfried and C. J. McNair, *Benchmarking; A Tool for Continuous Improvement*, HarperCollins, 1992; R. Cross and P. Leonard 'Benchmarking: a Strategic and Tactical Perspective' in B. G. Dale (ed.) *Managing Quality*, 2nd edn, Hemel Hempstead: Prentice Hall, 1994 and M. Zaire, *Benchmarking for Best Practice: Continuous Learning Through Sustainable Innovation*, Oxford: Butterworth-Heinemann, 1998.
23. Internal benchmarking is an idea based on identifying the best-in-class within one's own total company in terms of concepts, usefulness and speed of introduction.
24. Extract from John J. Welch Jnr's presentation at General Electric Company's 1996 Annual Meeting at Charlottesville, Virginia, 24 April 1996.
25. H. Ford, *Today and Tomorrow*, Cambridge, MA: Productivity Press, 1998, particularly Chapter 10, 'The Meaning of Time'.

## Further Reading

Spendolini, M. J. *The Benchmarking Book*, New York: American Management Association, 1992.
Stahl, M. J. and G. M. Bounds (eds) *Competing Globally Through Customer Value*, New York: Quorum, 1991.

# 4 Developing a Manufacturing Strategy – Methodology

The last two chapters introduced the concepts and principles underpinning the development of a manufacturing strategy. They also discussed the key strategic task of developing a clear understanding of how a company competes. This chapter addresses the question of how you develop a manufacturing strategy.

Functions manage, control and develop the resources for which they are responsible at both the operational and strategic levels. These roles are the two sides of the same coin. The operational tasks concern managing and controlling the day-to-day, short-term aspects of a business. The strategic task concerns investing in and developing those capabilities to provide the qualifiers and order-winners that relate to agreed current and future markets and Exhibit 4.1 provides an overview of what is involved.

Knowing how a firm competes in relevant markets is a prerequisite for sound strategy development. Without it, functions may pursue good practice but not necessarily sound strategy. They will, in terms of strategic direction, be simply working in the dark. That today's markets are different rather than similar has been

**Exhibit 4.1** From markets to manufacturing strategy

| Markets | How do you qualify and win orders? | Manufacturing's | | |
|---|---|---|---|---|
| | | strategic task | current performance | strategy |
| Agree the current and future markets in which a company competes | Determine the order-winners and qualifiers for each market segment both today and in the future | Translate the relevant order-winners and qualifiers into the equivalent manufacturing tasks | Assess how well manufacturing currently provides the order-winners and qualifiers for which it is solely or jointly responsible | Prioritize the investments and developments to better support the needs (order-winning and qualifying criteria) of current and future markets for which manufacturing is solely or jointly responsible |

stressed through these early chapters. A basic task is to determine what these differences are so that appropriate context and direction can be established and on which functional strategies can be based.

That companies must support their markets is clearly acknowledged. What comprises markets, however, is inadequately established by most companies. As clearly understanding markets is a prerequisite for functional strategy development, a detailed and comprehensive review of a company's current and future markets is the first step in sound strategy formulation.

Why then do companies typically not provide this essential clarification? One common cause is that most companies undertake and work with general reviews of markets that typically provide descriptions (for example, the standard industrial code of a company is a commonly used method of segmenting customers) but do not address the question 'how do you qualify and win orders in that segment or customer group?' The result is that companies do not know any other way and are unable to undertake reviews that identify the competitive factors within different segments.

## Generic Strategies: Today's Version of the Alchemist's Stone

Academics, consultants and other third-party advisers seek generic strategies in much the same way as those who sought to change base metal into gold. Perhaps this quest will only be set aside when firms realize that, despite best intentions, the reality they need to manage embodies a diversity and dynamism that makes categorization impossible and hence irrelevant.

That markets are inherently and increasingly different leads to a simple conclusion: by definition there cannot be some way of overlaying this diversity and its dynamic nature with a process that seeks the selection and application of one or more generic options.

What, then, is the alternative? If markets are dissimilar then strategies need to match this diversity. Consequently functions have to develop different strategies to match the needs of their different markets. Arguing for generic strategies is not only inappropriate by being simplistic in nature and origin but also results in the failure to align strategies to a firm's various markets.

Niche, low cost, core competence-type arguments are seductive in their apparent offerings. The promise of uniformity is appealing to those with the task of developing strategies for businesses which are typified by difference not similarity. In fact, such approaches purport to identify a corporate similarity which, though desirable, is inherently not available. The alternative is to recognise difference and develop multi-strategies to address these separate needs... For, strategy is not a process leading to generalisations... It's a distillation process with the task of identifying the very essence of what comprises a business.[1]

## The Nature of Strategy: Directional and Iterative

To assume or believe that companies can forge strategic understanding to the point that it will not require development and/or adoption is unrealistic. Strategy is directional. It points the way and, assuming that the debate is rigorous, involves the relevant functional perspectives and has opinion challenged and verified by data analysis, then it gives sound direction. However, the dynamic and changing nature of today's markets and the need to adjust and readjust introduces an iterative and emerging dimension to the way in which strategy unfolds over time. However, the emergent element concerns the nature of strategy. It does not imply that firms should follow an approach that is largely without direction at the start and gradually evolve a strategy as one emerges. The essence of strategy is to provide direction. This does not imply that the chosen direction is correct. It may be wrong (in whole or part) in itself or need adjustment as markets change and/or opportunities/threats emerge. However, direction is as essential to sound strategy as is the ability to recognize the need to change as markets are better understood and in response to the changes inherent in the nature of today's business environment. The task, then, is to discuss, check and agree markets on a continuous basis. And, by definition, this strategic thrust is (and often needs to be) a combination of being market-driving as well as being market-driven. Monitoring and responding to the needs of markets and customers invariably has to combine a reactive (market-driven) and a proactive (market-driving) dimension.

With these thoughts in mind, let us now return to the approaches to follow when undertaking the development of a manufacturing strategy.

## Checking Markets

To gain the essential understanding of markets requires a detailed review. Only analysis of this depth will yield the insights essential to fulfilling this task. Given that corporate strategy and the functional strategies of which it is comprised are the end result, a company should not have to justify giving adequate time, attention, and resources to undertake the task. Strategy is hard work, often painstaking in its execution and needs top management's full attention. Furthermore, it is an ongoing task. Simply, without this commitment, firms take risks, especially in difficult environments. The need is obvious. Who would thank an airline crew who did not plan their route with care? Corporate recognition of this need is not well established and its execution is, therefore, often lacking.

## Substituting Customers' Behaviour for Customer's Voice

The purpose of collecting data and verifying the nature of a customer's orders is best summed up as moving from a recognition that the nature of markets is not what a customer says it is but to how a customer actually behaves. I have yet to have a customer declare that the agreed price for a product is too low or that the nature of the business on offer is troublesome and difficult to support. The reality is only known once the demands placed on a supplier by a customer's orders unfold. Unless these are checked then the nature of the business on hand (and what functional strategies have to support) will not be clear. While the needs of customers are met at the level of execution and order fulfillment (customer behaviour), what these comprise are not known without relevant supporting analyses that in turn are essential data to form part of the strategic debate.

## The Most Important Orders are the Ones to Which You Say 'No'

Once markets and their characteristics are agreed, a company starts to gain control of its strategy. Then it is able to judge whether a piece of business fits its strategic direction. Thus, from there on in, the most important orders are the ones to which a company says 'no'. These mark the boundaries by declaring the segments of a market in which a company decides it does not wish to compete. Without this level of clarity, all orders are deemed to be equally attractive. By definition that cannot be. But without a mechanism for knowing how to judge, appropriate decisions cannot be made.

## Form and Nature

An introduction to the form and nature of market reviews was provided in Chapter 2, together with the examples given in Exhibits 2.7, 2.8 and 2.9. It will help now to discuss these three different applications to illustrate the form and nature of these outputs.

### US Graphics Company

The example given in Exhibit 2.7 shows the order-winners and qualifiers for two customers in one of this company's markets. At the time of the analysis the sales revenue derived from Customer A was four times that of Customer B. As you will guess, the company supplies to a whole range of customers that, in turn, are in different markets themselves. The market review, therefore, would need to establish the order-winners and qualifiers for all customers in all markets. Very often, customers will have similar order-winners and qualifiers, a fact that must be clearly established as part of the analysis. The grouping together of customers with similar order-winners and qualifiers is then completed at the next stage. Assumptions on the similarity of segments must be avoided. Analysis will establish the level of similarity or difference that exists in a company's markets, and approaches to strategy formulation based on analysis and verification need to replace the broad-brush overviews that characterize current practice.

What then does Exhibit 2.7 reveal? Without adequate discussion and analysis, companies tend to work on the assumption that the needs of customers are the same. However, Exhibit 2.7 shows that there are marked differences. For Customer A, the predominant order-winners concern the technical offering of the company and the proposed strategy is to increase this emphasis in the future such that in two years after this analysis was completed, the product specification and R&D support would consistute the only order-winners. Throughout, price has remained a quali-fier (that is, the company enjoys high margin business with Customer A) and support for Customer A's short lead-time requirements is clearly recognized. In addition, part of its manufacturing strategy is to create a capability where this becomes a prerequisite for doing business with this customer.

Customer B on the other hand is distinctly more price sensitive than Customer A, a factor signalled by the 40 point weighting given at the time of the analysis. Equally, the importance of the technical dimension of design and R&D support is much lower than with Customer A. However, a glance forward shows how the company intends to change Customer B's view of this business to bring it more into line with Customer A. In this way, the company is moving from being market-driven to being market-driving, and thereby capitalizing on the strengths of its R&D and technical support functions. Manufacturing's strategic role will increas-ingly be to support the key qualifiers of price, delivery reliability, delivery speed and quality conformance.

## European Battery Company

Exhibit 2.8 shows the order-winners and qualifiers for two products. Companies may assume that products of the same type (in this instance, batteries) will win orders in a similar way to one another. The analysis completed here shows how very different they are for these two selected products. The current and anticipated price sensitivity of Product Type 10A is in marked contrast to that of Product Type C80. The role of design reflects the non-price-sensitive nature of sales at the time the analysis was completed and the high margins they attract. However, as competitors match the C80 design, price is expected to become an increasingly important order-winner. Delivery speed remains an order-winner while on-time delivery is an order-losing sensitive qualifier in both instances with both forming part of manufacturing's strategic task. Finally, the aspects of quality conformance for C80 reflects manufacturing's capability to make this product to specification and is recognized as forming part (with design) of the technical dimension being offered. For Product Type 10A, making to specification (that is, quality conform-ance) is a qualifier and constitutes a process capability that is not in any way unique to the company.

## *European Engineered Sealing Systems Company*

This company supplies engineered sealing systems to a range of customers throughout the world, three of which are given in Exhibit 2.9. The examples again illustrate how segments can differ from one another. In fact, in this instance, the company wins orders from these customers in very different and sometimes opposing ways. In 1999, price ranged from a qualifier for Customer C to being the dominant order-winner for Customer B. Similarly, the role of design was markedly different for Customer C compared to Customers A and B, as was the importance of delivery speed in winning orders from Customer A compared to the other two customers. Meanwhile the criteria of delivery reliability, quality conformance, technical support and brand name are more similar to all three customers in terms of role and weighting.

These three examples bring out a number of important points to bear in mind while reading the following sections that describe the methodology to use when undertaking this work.

1. Markets are characterized by increasing difference. The key to understanding markets lies in being able to identify and highlight these differences so as to be able to develop functional responses to support them.

2. Marketing segments markets from the point of view of identifying differences in customer buying behaviour. The examples given as Exhibits 2.7 to 2.9 illustrate how different order-winners and qualifiers may be present within a given marketing segment. Reversing the segmentation process by identifying manufacturing-related differences is, therefore, an essential first step in developing a manufacturing strategy.

3. Order-winners and qualifiers invariably change over time. Hence, strategy is both time- and market-specific and this necessitates identifying differences both today and tomorrow.

4. The process of identifying the order-winners and qualifiers relevant to a company's markets involves all functions as well as appropriate analysis with which to test initial opinions and assumptions. Only by sound, in-depth discussions will the essential characteristics of a company's markets be revealed. In this way, functions are required to explain their perspective and, once agreed, the essential support from manufacturing and other functions (for example design and marketing) is clearly identified. This, in turn, forms the basis on which functional strategies need to be developed, leading to greater coherence within a business and the essential support for agreed markets and customers.

The key to all these points is the in-depth discussion that needs to take place, a style very different from the form and nature of today's strategic debate in many firms. Only by statement, explanation, analysis and re-explanation will more accurate and better understood strategic insights be shared by all concerned. Without this, companies will invariably revert to functionally based strategic alternatives that will typically pull a business in different directions.

## Reviewing Relevant Order-winners and Qualifiers

Let us now turn to how discussions are structured and the types of analysis needed to test views and to help distinguish essential differences within a company's chosen markets. To facilitate the strategy debate, it is necessary to start with some stated view of the market as a focal point for discussion.

The best place to start is to seek the views of marketing. To do this, marketing should be asked to:

■ Segment the market from a marketing point of view and choose products or customers that represent each chosen segment.

■ Establish for each segment appropriate future planning horizons that reflect the relevant timescales involved. Normally, this is given as two future time periods similar to the examples in Exhibits 2.7 to 2.9.

■ Select and weight the order-winners and qualifiers for each segment for both the current and future time periods, using the products and customers that represent each segment as part of this step.

Marketing's inputs then form the basis for discussion and are challenged by:

■ The opinions of other functions
■ The data collected to test the initial views on how a company wins orders in its markets.

Using the initial views of marketing as the inputs to and focus of debate, other functions express opinions, ask questions, and seek clarification of why segments work the way marketing suggests. The outcomes include an improved understanding between functions and a revised understanding of the markets in which a company competes. This may alter the weightings attributed to particular order-winners and qualifiers or change them altogether.

The more significant inputs into this important debate come from collecting the data and completing the analysis relevant to the markets under review. The purpose of this step is to enable companies to replace opinions with facts. This helps the strategic debate reach sound conclusions based on the needs of the overall business rather than being unduly swayed by the forceful arguments of individual functions. The discussion also seeks to identify the further analysis necessary to verify the opinions and views expressed as part of a continuous evaluating process.

Throughout it is important to use functional opinions within the strategy debate, not as sets of arguments and counter-arguments but as a means of directing analysis. When functional views are raised the question to follow should be 'what data need to be provided to check whether this view holds?' Only in this way can companies move to a level of debate that provides the essential quality and yields the necessary insights on which to make sound strategic decisions.

A review of some of the necessary analyses follows. The principal purpose is to explain the approach and its underlying rationale so as to enable this way of working to be transferred to other areas of analysis and to other companies.

## *General Issues*

As explained earlier, when a company undertakes the initial review of its markets it asks marketing to identify products or customers that represent each chosen segment. Subsequent analysis is based on these, as analysing representative products or customers equates to analysing the relevant segment. The assumption underlying the concept of segmentation is that everything that falls within the selected groupings is similar. The purpose of the analysis is to test this perception, not only as a checking mechanism but also to:

■ improve a company's understanding of its markets
■ allow it to review its markets or parts of them
■ change its decisions on the relative importance of these parts
■ form the basis of functional strategies by prioritizing investments and developments.

The outcomes affect all parts of the business as would be expected and as emphasized earlier.

## Analyses to be Completed

What follows is a list of analyses that will provide key insights. However, in using them there are two points to bear in mind.

1. The analyses will not be of equal value in all situations. Some may be difficult to undertake due to data availability, while others will not identify differences that would yield further insights.

2. The checks listed below will sometimes overlap. Thus undertaking a customer-related review may duplicate (in part) the analysis involved in one of the manufacturing-related checks.

Although these points are not significant in themselves, being aware of these issues is useful background. Often analysis leads nowhere but still needs to be completed as knowing this outcome is important in its own right.

## Manufacturing-related Analysis

The key role of analysing markets in strategic debate has been stressed throughout. As mentioned earlier, however, many companies confine their review of markets to the perspectives held by marketing and consequently limit their analysis to customer surveys, statements on the size and share of current and future markets, competitor analyses, SWOT reviews[2] and other classic marketing-oriented approaches.

The purpose of these manufacturing-related analyses is to review markets from a manufacturing perspective in terms of the stated order-winners and qualifiers. Thus the market review moves from an external customer perspective to an internal one that considers what actually happens in a business. This internal review supplements the more subjective judgements of customers and externally oriented marketers by adding perspectives based on the reality of the orders placed by customers and the demands these make on the organization in meeting their business specifications. This then allows companies to verify functional views and modify them on the basis of analysis rather than opinion.

Finally, when undertaking this investigation, it is essential that the customer orders and/or contracts reviewed are chosen and verified by the executives involved. Seeking their knowledge of what is representative is essential in order to ensure that the findings are relevant and usable. Once this step is agreed, the following analyses need to be completed. This section covers all the criteria that relate to manufacturing. Which ones to undertake in a particular company will reflect the criteria that are relevant to that firm's markets. Similar analyses would need to be undertaken to test other non-manufacturing-related criteria, the provision of which is the responsibility of functions other than manufacturing.

## Price

Where price is a criterion, companies need to review the actual costs and margins associated with the orders involved. In many instances, companies use their own form of standard costs as the basis for reviewing margins and making comparisons between one customer or order and another. However, these cost calculations are invariably inaccurate, distorting the decisions based on them. It is essential, therefore, that companies analyse the actual costs incurred in completing the orders under review. Also, in many instances they should increase the order sample being checked to provide a wider basis for comparisons.

The inaccuracies that result from assumptions are thus exposed. For example, Exhibit 4.2 compares the actual contribution for a representative group of products

**Exhibit 4.2**    A comparison of actual contribution for a group of representative products to the order-winner weighting given to price

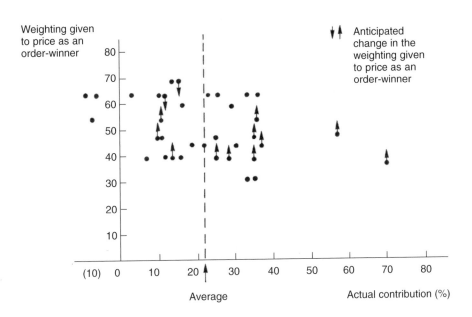

to the weighing given to price as an order-winner and shows the noticeable inconsistency between these two related factors.

Similarly Exhibit 4.3 compares the estimated contribution for a number of representative products to the actual contribution recorded when orders for these products were made on relevant processes.

More accurate cost information provides fresh insights and essential details on the relative value of different customers or orders. The data given in Exhibits 4.2 and 4.3 result from summaries of such analyses and give an overview of the differences that typically exist between actual and estimated contributions and between reality and opinions. A company would use the individual data entries and, where necessary, would complete further analyses to verify different perspectives and trends before reaching a decision.

To improve the quality of cost data, a company must identify direct costs other than labour and materials wherever possible; for example, delivery charges where a direct delivery service is provided. In addition, it is important to supplement the analysis to give further critical insights where possible. For example, where different orders are processed on the same equipment, and where this is a scarce resource, an additional calculation should be made to identify the contribution earned per machine hour. Contribution as a percentage of the selling price does not give the best insight into the relative value of orders as it assumes that all other non-direct factors involved are of the same relative importance.

**Exhibit 4.3**    Actual versus estimated contribution for a number of representative products

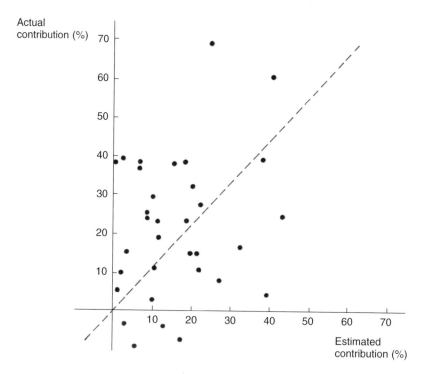

Contribution per machine hour, or other scarce resource, relates the contribution earned to the use made by each order of a given process, where, in effect, a company is selling available machine capacity. As illustrated by Exhibit 4.4, the two analyses give very different insights into the worth of these orders. Whereas contribution as a percentage of price gives one rank-order listing, contribution per machine hour gives another.

As highlighted previously, the segmentation of markets from a marketing perspective implies that the customers/orders within each segment are similar. From a marketing perspective this is so; it is the very premise on which the principle of marketing segmentation is built. But companies, lacking other insights, extend this similarity concept to other pertinent dimensions of the business, more through a lack of rigour than an overt statement. The key step in manufacturing strategy is to add those missing dimensions that are relevant to manufacturing. By so doing it checks how orders are won and the uniform nature of relevant criteria within each segment. Without this, functional strategies will be pursued that typically are not consistent with how orders are won for different subsegments or customers.

Part of this clarifying process tests perceptions of markets, as shown in Exhibits 4.2 and 4.3 and Exhibit 4.5 goes one step further. In addition to testing initial perspectives, it also checks on the level of consistency within a segment. As the data show, customers within a segment yield markedly different levels of contribution from one another.[3]

**Exhibit 4.4**  Contribution percentage and contribution per machine hour. Comparisons for representative orders[1]

| Order reference | Price (£) | Direct costs (£) | Contribution (£) | Contribution (%) | Machine hours | Contribution per machine hour (£) |
|---|---|---|---|---|---|---|
| 631 | 220 | 44 | 176 | 80 | 1.5 | 117 |
| 205 | 568 | 114 | 454 | 80 | 3.9 | 116 |
| 216 | 1 246 | 269 | 977 | 78 | 11.2 | 87 |
| 470 | 244 | 56 | 188 | 77 | 4.0 | 47 |
| 298 | 1 960 | 462 | 1 496 | 77 | 9.3 | 161 |
| 607 | 3 612 | 830 | 2 782 | 77 | 13.3 | 209 |
| 512 | 134 | 32 | 102 | 76 | 1.5 | 66 |
| 483 | 4 010 | 1 004 | 3 006 | 75 | 21.5 | 140 |
| 658 | 166 | 42 | 124 | 75 | 0.7 | 107 |
| 313 | 1 134 | 306 | 828 | 73 | 5.7 | 145 |
| 284 | 864 | 246 | 618 | 72 | 2.1 | 294 |
| 182 | 724 | 65 | 159 | 71 | 4.7 | 14 |
| 573 | 1 066 | 320 | 746 | 70 | 3.1 | 240 |
| 417 | 3 345 | 1 140 | 2 205 | 66 | 7.9 | 279 |

*Note*
1. All data are actuals.

**Exhibit 4.5**  Contribution percentage of sales and contribution per machine hour for representative orders for two segments

| Customer | Actual contribution[1] | |
|---|---|---|
| | % sales | per machine hour |
| *Segment 1* | | |
| Hulton | 41.8 | 918 |
| Avis Robins | 24.6 | 431 |
| MKC | 8.6 | 288 |
| Clairelle | 12.4 | 152 |
| Artiste | 30.7 | 714 |
| *Segment 2* | | |
| Prelpac | 14.0 | 243 |
| JRR | 8.6 | 186 |
| Sheuks | 16.1 | 115 |
| Dells | (1.0) | (64) |
| Avenols | 22.3 | 408 |

*Note*
1. Customer data is the average for a representative sample of orders.

From a marketing point of view, the segments chosen remain valid as they reflect essential marketing differences that are clustered together. From a manufacturing view, however, the segments do not constitute the same level of similarity. These fresh insights challenge the initial views on segment groupings and the level of company awareness of what constitutes above- and below-average business from a contribution-earning point of view. Again, the contribution percentage of sales and contribution per machine analyses provide essential and often different insights into this strategic review. Thus, decisions on which market segments, customers or orders should receive priority in terms of growth, development investment and support can now be made at a more informed level and on a corporate rather than distinctly functional basis.

The need to collect actual data has been stressed throughout. Shopfloor records are often kept outside the formal system. These records need to be sought and, where they do not exist, a once-off arrangement needs to be made to capture the actual labour, materials and other direct costs incurred in completing an order or making a given quantity of relevant products. With price known, the calculations are straightforward and the outcomes then form part of the debate on a particular segment or the business as a whole.

## Quality Conformance

Many analyses within companies are completed in a general format. Typical of these is the measurement of quality conformance. However, while its overall effect on costs is relevant, the external dimension of quality is not general but is particular to a customer. Thus the key dimension here is not average quality conformance level but the actual customer level provided.

Reviewing quality conformance by product, order or customer yields essential insights. Such analyses will also build into the direct material dimension of costs addressed in the last section.

## Delivery On Time

As with quality conformance, on-time delivery (OTD) tends to be measured in aggregate, if at all. Not only does this fail to distinguish the importance of individual customers, it also fails to identify the differing delivery needs of customers.

What constitutes on time cannot be covered by a simple definition. Customers' needs can range from given hourly slots on a stated day to any day within a given week or even longer period. Others may not want delivery before a given time but will accept delivery any time thereafter, within stated limits. Furthermore, delivering the perfect order also includes providing all line items on the order at the correct quantities. Moreover, the dimensions of on-time, order-fill accuracy and being error free are interlinked in terms of the level of overall delivery reliability.

Being 95 per cent on time with an order-fill rate of 90 per cent and an error-free rate of 98 per cent results in an overall delivery performance of less than 84 per cent.

The task of checking delivery reliability, therefore, must be preceded by defining what constitutes OTD and the other dimensions that need to be measured. Measurement of delivery reliability should reflect performance by customer and segment and relate to its perceived role in winning orders. In most companies, delivery reliability will be a qualifier rather than an order-winner; in many, it will be an order-losing sensitive qualifier. Knowing what to measure and its relative importance are as critical as the performance record itself. Where OTD is a relevant criterion, companies should define and measure it as discussed above. Tracking actual orders provides the dimension of reality in the discussion on markets.

*Delivery Speed*

The definition of delivery speed was given earlier (see Exhibits 3.7 and 3.8). Assessing its presence in markets involves comparing the total lead time normally required by all relevant stages of the process – order processing, material/component purchasing, material/component delivery, manufacturing, assembly, packing and shipping – against the lead time given by the customer (that is, the time between order placement and required delivery).

In some instances customers will pull forward the required delivery date part way through the process. Companies must identify how such an action affects delivery speed in only part of the process by comparing the remaining elements of lead time to the revised customer lead time.

Many companies have consistently responded to the growing importance of delivery speed in their markets by shortening lead times through actions such as set-up reductions, eliminating delay and investing in inventory ahead of time. When checking the extent of delivery speed within its markets, a company should note the level of ongoing investment within the business that is a direct result of its response to meeting the demands of this criterion. Such continuing costs should then be set against relevant customers and form part of a company's overall evaluation of these sales.

Once again, only by checking specific orders and customer requirements can the reality of markets be exposed. This increased understanding provides a more informed view of a business and the reality of how it competes.

In terms of performance, checks on the overall lead time from receipt of customer order to the point of payment (the cash-to-cash cycle) give key insights. Checks within these then need to be made. Comparing actual processing time and overall lead time at each step identifies the extent and size of delays and highlights the areas where actual processing needs reviewing and delays need to be eliminated. (These reviews should adopt a business re-engineering approach in order to ensure that the whole as well as the parts are reviewed. This, in turn will lead to the best opportunity to reduce the time and costs involved.[4])

## Other Criteria

As discussed in the last chapter, there are many different order-winning and qualifying criteria besides those addressed above. Checks on the extent of their provision
and the level of ongoing performance achieved will take, in principle, a form
similar to the approaches outlined in more detail for the four criteria addressed here.
This is not to imply that some criteria are more important than others. The ones
chosen are typically present more often in markets, are related specifically to manufacturing and provide suitable illustrations of general approaches to follow.
Knowing the dimensions to look for and using orders as the basis of analysis will
yield the essential insights that companies need to have to succeed in today's
competitive environment.

## Customer and Product-related Analysis

As explained in the previous section, very often the purpose of the analyses is to
give insights concerning products, ranges of products and customers. As the earlier
examples in the chapter illustrate, products within a range and customers within a
segment are based on a marketing perspective and, from an operations' viewpoint,
are not necessarily the same as one another. Also, orders from the same customer
are often significantly different from one another. Sometimes this is linked to the
fact that orders are received from different parts of a customers' total business,
although in other instances difference still exists even though the orders come from
the same customer source, as in Exhibit 4.6.

**Exhibit 4.6**   The insights gained into the nature of the mix of business received from customers
regarding gross margin percentage, quality conformance levels and associated
inventory levels

|  | Products | |
|---|---|---|
| **Aspect** | **All** | **Top 17 by annual sales value** |
| Parts supplied | 94 | 10 |
| Total annual quantity for all products supplied (mm units) | 1.3 | 0.6 |
| Average gross margin (%) | 10 | 30 |
| Level of quality conformance – customer demerits awarded | | |
| number of parts given one or more demerits | 23 | 2 |
| total demerits awarded[1] | 102 | 21 |
| % total inventory holding for Customer A's products | 100 | 31 |

*Note*
1. The higher the number of demerits, the worse the performance on meeting the agreed product specification.

**Exhibit 4.7**     Customer reviews: lead times allowed by three companies in terms of the date an order or schedule was received compared to the required delivery

| Company | Lead times (days) – # stock-keeping units[1,2,3,4] | | | | | | | | | | | Total |
| | Current day minus[5] | | | | Current day | Current day plus | | | | | | |
| | 11+ | 7–10 | 4–6 | 1–3 | | 1–3 | 4–6 | 7–10 | 11–20 | 21–30 | 31+ | |
|---|---|---|---|---|---|---|---|---|---|---|---|---|
| A | – | 1 | 1 | – | 2 | 2 | 1 | 9 | – | 2 | 52 | 70 |
| B | – | – | – | 25 | – | – | 18 | – | 51 | 40 | 112 | 246 |
| C | – | 4 | – | 6 | 5 | – | 12 | – | – | – | 24 | 51 |

*Notes*
1. The review was taken at a specific point in time and includes all orders waiting to go into production and already in work-in-progress. Calculations for the latter were based on the original receipt date of the order or schedule.
2. A stock-keeping unit (SKU) is a distinct product with its own unique reference number.
3. The figures also include where a customer reschedules delivery dates. Here the original lead time was taken out of the sample (the order date no longer being relevant) and the new requirement was added to the review.
4. The lead-time calculations are based on the date the order or schedule was received (for telephoned orders, the date used was that of the telephone call and not that of the confirmation order) compared to the date of the required delivery.
5. Current day minus figures mean that the date the order or schedule was received was one or more days after the required delivery date specified on the paperwork.

As you can see from Exhibits 4.6 and 4.7 and also the illustration given earlier in the chapter, the insights provided play a key role in formulating views of a given company's markets and face-to-face discussions with customers in terms of prices and elements of customer support. Reviewing the whole range of products supplied will typically provide a different picture to the one based on the sample of products/issues that customers invariably select for discussion. This in part goes back to an earlier section. Firms need to check a 'customer's behaviour' rather than only listening to a 'customer's voice'.

## Outcomes of the Market Debate

Checking and debating markets leads to a number of both general and specific outcomes.

### General Outcomes

First, it improves the level of understanding between functions. Functions typically develop strategies independently of one another. While data such as forecast sales and their capacity implications traditionally form part of the forward-looking debate, the nature of markets and the key insights into their differences do not. Thus shared approaches are not systematically reviewed and agreed.

Second, debate helps bridge the interface between functions at the strategic level. Functional views, supplemented by data, enable the different dimensions to form the basis for discussion. In this way, essential differences and perspectives are exposed and explored. Set within the context of a company's markets, the debate is moved from views typically expressed from the singular dimension of functions to the corporate-wide perspectives essential to arriving at strategic decisions.

## *Specific Outcomes*

The first specific outcome of market debate is that it modifies initial views of markets. Bringing other perspectives and relevant data to the discussion raises a company's insights into its markets to the desired level of detail that enables key distinctions to be made. This then helps a firm to modify its initial views of its markets and the relevant order-winners and qualifiers within each segment. In this way, a company's view of its markets is improved and is also based on shared agreement between functions.

Second, debate forms the basis for developing a manufacturing strategy. The order-winners and qualifiers within a company's markets are the dimensions of a business that manufacturing, as well as all other functions, needs to support. The remainder of the book will address manufacturing-related dimensions and responses. These concern the process and infrastructure-related issues outlined in Exhibit 2.5 as well as issues concerning coping with difference (Chapters 7 and 8) and the links with the perspectives of accounting and finance (Chapter 11).

## Relating Manufacturing to Agreed Markets

The last section explained the way to verify the importance of relevant criteria within chosen markets. The next steps are to test manufacturing's support of these (see Exhibit 2.11) and also to link manufacturing's strategic response to those of other functions, particularly marketing (see Exhibit 2.12), through the common denominator of supporting agreed markets.

The data and ongoing discussion result in a clearer and more accurate understanding of a company's markets. Bear in mind that strategy development needs to be an ongoing debate involving continuously tracking the changing nature of markets. With this essential step completed, the company can establish the strategic role of manufacturing and other functions. Operationalizing strategy is an integral part of the task. With the direction set, manufacturing's task is to prioritize the developments and investments it will undertake and the measures it will use to check performance. And the priorities will be different because the needs of the market segments will be different.

The section that follows highlights further analyses that may reveal important trends or identify relevant issues that then need to be addressed. It also gives a flavour of the tasks that manufacturing would typically undertake to support relevant order-winners and qualifiers. However, the nuts and bolts of how to secure these improvements is the province of the production/operations management area, dealt with elsewhere in relevant literature.[5] What a manufacturing strategy provides, therefore, is the priority list that links markets to developments, investments and tasks and forms the key performance dimensions on which manufacturing should be measured. Strategy statements on their own are of little value. Unless they translate into actions and result in continuous improvement, they are without purpose.

# Price

What follows is a flavour of the analyses that may be undertaken to check ongoing trends or identify current positions on a number of cost-related dimensions. As explained earlier, these are provided to illustrate the types of analysis designed to give further insights into current or potential problems and to highlight areas for improvement.

## Annual Plant Volumes

At the plant level, distinguishing annual volumes (or annual quantities where items are similar in work content) per product or stock-keeping unit (SKU) enables a check to be made on plant volume orientations. Exhibit 4.8 shows the spread of volumes in four North American plants producing pharmaceutical products. It was part of an analysis to show the broad orientation of the plants at the time of the review. The subsequent realignment of products would require the same analysis for individual SKUs.

**Exhibit 4.8**  Annual quantities per SKU for four plants manufacturing similar products

| Dimensions | Plant 1 | Plant 2 | Plant 3 | Plant 4 |
|---|---|---|---|---|
| Annual units (in millions) | 55.4 | 128.1 | 47.6 | 91.3 |
| Number of SKUs | 316 | 1 642 | 852 | 260 |
| Annual units per SKU (in thousands) | 175 | 78 | 56 | 351 |
| Number of active compounds | 25 | 72 | 45 | 28 |

## Annual Quantities – Volumes per Product

Many companies fail to assess the degree of incremental change that has taken place in their business over time. Typically, they compare the current year with the one before and in so doing overlook the level of change that may have taken place over a longer relevant period. One example of such a review is given in Exhibit 4.9.

**Exhibit 4.9**   SKUs/annual quantity (units in thousands)

| Year | Number of SKUs | | | |
|---|---|---|---|---|
| | ≤250 | 250–750 | 750–1 000 | 1 000+ |
| Current | 41 | 6 | 6 | 5 |
| Current minus 3 | 18 | 5 | 3 | 4 |
| Current minus 6 | 8 | 2 | 2 | 4 |

## *Length of Production Runs*

Identifying the length of production runs over time as an average for different processes, departments or plants shows relative volumes during the chosen period. An analysis of the processes needed to manufacture one of the high demand ($ revenue) products of a US consumer plant revealed that in the previous six years the average production run size (in hours) had fallen to 38 per cent of the first full year of production. Checking manufacturing's responding change-over or set-up reductions and inventory holdings then forms a further part of the strategic review.

## *Contribution per Machine Hour*

Relating actual contribution per machine or process hour to other dimensions such as production run lengths (in hours) and units per hour also checks how these factors influence the level of actual contribution earned on a process and within the whole plant. Exhibit 4.10 shows customer-order data identify the contribution per machine hour for four customers representing different segments. In this instance, the analysis provided an unexpected perspective on these segments.

**Exhibit 4.10**   Actual contribution per machine for different segments

| Segment/key order-winner | $ per machine hour |
|---|---|
| Very high volume/price | 625 |
| High volume/price | 415 |
| Delivery speed | 593 |
| Low volume/non-price[1] | 380 |

*Note*
1. Orders won predominantly on non-manufacturing criteria.

# Pricing

As illustrated in the last section there will often be significant differences in contribution between one product or customer and another. The source of these differences is not, however, restricted to the nature of the associated manufacturing costs; often the source can be the pricing structure used by a company. Established sometime in the past and typically in markets that have since changed in terms of the pattern of demand and customer order mix, the pricing mechanism is typically extended without revision. The outcome often leads to inappropriate pricing which results in below-average business increasingly being undertaken. The details given in Exhibit 4.6 illustrate this point. The product tail for Company A comprised low price products (some 56 per cent, on average, of the top 17 products) as well as the associated inventory and quality conformance problems. Subsequent discussions brought agreement with the customer to increase the price on 46 of the 77 'tail-end' range.

# Quality Conformance

Checks on quality conformance levels need to be made that reflect products, orders, customers and segments. Again, assessing how well the specific needs of different parts of the market are being met is the underlying basis for the review. General reviews provide important perspectives, but specific reviews normally yield essential insights.

One analysis that is also important to the price-related dimension concerns the correlation between production run lengths/sizes and net output per hour. Exhibit 4.11 plots these relations for one process, showing higher unit outputs per hour as run sizes increase. However, this also directs attention to why this general, although not unexpected, trend exists and also why there are some distinct exceptions to this relationship. Exhibit 4.11 shows some low run-size orders achieving high net

**Exhibit 4.11** Correlation between the size (units) of a production run and the net output (units) per hour

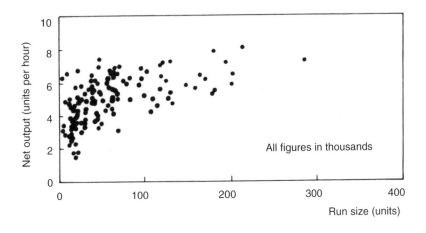

outputs per hour and vice versa. Investigation as to why will undoubtedly reveal key insights that, in this instance, may relate to quality conformance factors.

## Delivery Reliability

Overall checks on the relative levels of delivery reliability must be avoided. They need, on the one hand, to identify the dimensions of on time, error levels and order-fill rates referred to earlier, while on the other they need to be customer- or order-related.

Collecting data on levels of performance must then seek to identify any patterns that exist between levels of delivery reliability and, for instance, order size, customer lead times (including schedule changes), process lead times and material deliveries. Establishing these relationships will often provide insights in terms of why above- or below-average performance is being achieved and, in so doing, highlight the actions to take to improve this key dimension of customer support.

## Delivery Speed

Relationships between customer and total lead times are the essence of delivery-speed reviews and also relate to the last section. Other relevant checks to this dimension include:[6]

- Creating a throughput efficiency index that compares the standard hours to make a product with the actual lead times involved from start to finish.
- Measuring changeover/set-up times as a percentage of the total time taken (process time plus set-up time).

## Conclusion

The purpose of these checks is to verify various functions' opinions and to move the debate on the essential insights into markets from one based primarily on subjective views to one based primarily on information. The outcomes are twofold, as explained below:

1. The fresh perspectives and essential insights challenge or verify the views held of segments, products and/or customers for each relevant manufacturing-related dimension (such as price, quality conformance , delivery reliability and delivery speed). This will identify the demands of customers and confirm the importance of each dimension's contribution to the business as a whole. Typically companies will then replace some 10 per cent of existing sales revenue with 'better' margin business. The impact on the total is invariably dramatic.

2. Manufacturing's performance is consistently measured against clearly stated requirements of those customers a company has agreed to supply and support. This leads to a priority list of activities relevant to each dimension (for example, reducing cost, improving quality conformance, reducing total lead times, reducing set-up or changeover times and supporting product range. In this way, manufacturing's strategic response is set both within the context of the business and within its own priorities.

## Process Versus Content

Many strategists place too much emphasis on process and too little on content. Discussion, while an essential part of corporate strategy development, will lead to poor outcomes unless the content of the discussion is of the highest quality. Without a rigorous review using data to verify and replace opinion then market definitions and strategic outcomes will be of little value. Generic strategies, while promising much, deliver little.

## Corporate Context

Finally, it is essential that the analyses completed for customers/products are set within an overall corporate context. Identifying the relative importance of a customer/product in terms of current and future total corporate profit/contribution levels is essential in arriving at decisions in the best interests of the overall business. Supporting below-average customers today in the belief that they will become above-average customers tomorrow makes good corporate sense. However, checking that this type of transition takes place is a key dimension of implementing strategy.

The following chapters will point the ways forward, offering essential insights into how a company may respond to meet the ever-changing demands of today's dynamic and highly competitive markets. These responses, however, need to be within the context of agreed markets that are clearly understood as to their relevant order-winners and qualifiers.

## **Notes**

1. Taken from T. Hill *The Strategy Quest*, AMD Publishing 1998, Bristol, pp. vi and vii. This book, written in the form of a novel, addresses the issues in this chapter as well as those in Chapters 7 and 8 on focus.
2. A SWOT analysis determines the strengths, weaknesses, opportunities and threats relating to a company in its chosen markets. The limitations of SWOT analysis are brought into question by T. J. Hill and R. K. Westwood's (1997) article 'SWOT Analysis: It's Time for a Product Recall', *Long Range Planning*, **30**(1): 46–52.

3. Further analyses can also be completed that test the level of consistency within a customer's portfolio of orders.

4. Several books and articles are available on the topic of business re-engineering. They include T. H. Davenport and J. E. Short, 'The New Industrial Engineering: Information Technology and Business Process Redesign', *Sloan Management Review*, 1990, **31**(4): 11–26; T. H. Davenport, *Process Innovation: Reengineering Work Through Information Technology*, Cambridge, MA: Harvard Business School Press, 1993; M. Hammer and J. Champy *Reengineering the Corporation: A Manifesto for Business Revolution*, New York: Harper Business, 1993; H. J. Johansson, P. McHugh, J. Pendlebury and W. A. Wheeler III, *Business Process Reengineering*, New York: John Wiley, 1993; D. C. Morris and J. S. Brandon, *Reengineering your Business*, New York: McGraw-Hill, 1993; E. Obeng and S. Crainer, *Making Re-engineering Happen*, London, Pitman Publishing, 1994 and J. Champy, *Reengineering Management – the Mandate for New Leadership*, New York: HarperCollins, 1995.

5. For example, L. J. Krajewski and L. P. Ritzman, *Operations Managements: Strategy and Analysis*, 5th edn, Reading, MA: Addison-Wesley, 1998; R. G. Schroeder, *Operations Management: Decision-making in the Operations Function*, 4th edn, New York: McGraw-Hill, 1993; and T. Hill, *Operations Management: Strategic Context and Managerial Analysis*, Basingstoke, UK: Macmillan, 2000.

6. See also the earlier section on delivery speed.

# 5 Process Choice

The way a business decides to make its products is a choice many executives believe to be based on the single dimension of technology. As a consequence, they leave this decision to engineering/process specialists on the assumption that they – the custodians of technological understanding – are best able to draw the fine distinctions that need to be made. The designation of these specialists as the appropriate people to make such decisions creates a situation in which the important manufacturing and business perspectives are at best given inadequate weight and, in many instances, omitted all together.

Manufacturing is not an engineering- or technology-related function. It is a business-related function. Whereas products need to be made according to their technical specifications, they also have to be supplied in ways that win orders in the marketplace. This business dimension is the concern of manufacturing. When making process investment decisions, therefore, companies need to satisfy both the technical and business perspectives. The former is the concern of engineering; the latter is the concern of manufacturing.

This chapter describes the manufacturing and business implications of process choice and highlights the importance of these issues when making investment decisions. In this way, it helps to broaden the view of manufacturing currently held by senior executives[1] and provides a way of reviewing the manufacturing implications of marketing decisions, hence facilitating the manufacturing input into corporate strategy. This ensures that the necessary marketing/manufacturing interface is made and that the strategies adopted are business rather than functionally led.

## Process Choice

When choosing the appropriate way in which to manufacture its products, a business will take the following steps:

1. Decide on how much to buy from outside the company, which in turn determines the make-in task.

2. Identify the appropriate engineering-technology alternatives to complete the tasks embodied in each product. This will concern bringing together the make-in

components with the bought-out items to produce the final product specification at agreed levels of quality conformance.

3. Choose between alternative manufacturing approaches to completing the tasks embodied in providing the products involved. This will need to reflect the market in which a product competes and the volumes associated with those sales. The present processes in many existing factories are often not ideal. This issue is dealt with later in the chapter, when the important insights into process choice have been covered.

The choice of process concerns step 3 in this procedure. It will need to embody the decisions made in the other two steps and recognize any constraints imposed by them. However, while these constraints alter the dimensions within the decision (for example, what is involved) they do not alter its nature. The essence of the choice is linked to the appropriate way to manufacture, given the market and associated volumes involved.

Having stressed the optimal nature of process choice, there are certain constraints that have an overriding impact on this decision. What these are and how they limit business options will be explained in the next section.

## The Manufacturing Function

The principal function of the manufacturing process is to take inputs (materials, labour and energy) and convert them into outputs (products). To complete this, a business usually must choose between different modes of manufacturing. They choose one or, as is often the case, several ways. The fundamental rationale for this decision must be that the chosen process is the one best able to support a company competitively in the marketplace. There are several important perspectives to be taken into account. Each choice of process will bring with it certain implications for a business in terms of response to its markets, manufacturing capabilities and characteristics, level of investment required, unit costs involved and the type of control and style of management that are appropriate. To help understand these, it is necessary to review the process choices available.

There are five generic types of manufacturing process: *project*, *jobbing*, *batch*, *line* and *continuous processing*. However, in many situations, hybrids have been developed that blur the edges between one process and the next. What these hybrids are, how they relate to the classic types and what they mean for a business will also be discussed.

Before going on to describe the process choices involved, it is worth noting here that two of them (project and continuous processing) are associated with a particular product type (civil engineering and foods/liquids, respectively), a point addressed later in the chapter. A firm may find that in reality it has little option but to choose the one appropriate process (for instance, oil refining and continuous processing are to all intents and purposes inextricably linked). However, a company must be clearly aware of the precise nature of the business implications involved in the choice it is 'forced' to go along with and that the trade-offs associated with these dimensions are fixed.

An important factor to note at this time is that companies do not invest then reinvest progressively as demand increases, as, for example, to reflect product life cycles. It is simply too expensive. Neither will they wish to reinvest as demand decreases later in the cycle. Companies, therefore, invest to reflect anticipated demand levels, a factor which relates to both Chapters 6 and 7, on 'Product Profiling' and 'Focus' respectively.[2]

## The Generic Types of Process Choice

*Project*

Companies that produce large-scale, one-off (that is, unique), complex products will normally provide these on a project basis. Examples include products involved in civil engineering contracts and aerospace programmes. A project process concerns the provision of a unique product requiring the coordination of large-scale inputs to achieve a customer's requirement. The resource inputs will normally be taken to where the product is to be built, since it is not feasible to move it once completed. All activities, including the necessary support functions, will usually be controlled by a total system for the duration of the project. Resources allocated to the project will be reallocated once their part of the task is complete or at the end of the project.

The selection of project as the appropriate process is based on two features. First, the product is a one-off, customer-specified requirement; second, it is often too large to be moved or simply cannot be moved once completed. The second criterion is such an overwhelming facet of this decision that products of this nature will always be made using the project choice of process. However, businesses will also be concerned with determining how much of the product to make away from site and how best to provide the parts or sections that go into the structures made on site. These will, in turn, often be produced using a different choice of process than project. These decisions need to be based on other criteria, which will become clear in the descriptions of these other choices that follow.

Some confusion arises in the use of the word *project*. It commonly refers to a one-off complex task and/or the managerial style used to control such an event. This needs to be distinguished from its use here, which identifies a distinct process of making a product, the very characteristics of which (for example, moving resources to and from a site) are detailed above.

*Jobbing*[3]

A jobbing process is used to meet the one-off order requirements of customers; for example, purpose-built tooling. The product involved will be of an individual nature. This requires the supplier to interpret the customer's design and specification and apply relatively high-level skills in the conversion process. A large degree of this interpretation will normally be made by skilled employees, whose experience in this type of work is an essential facet of the process. Once the design has been specified, one skilled person – or possibly a small number of them, if the task is time consuming – is assigned the task and is responsible for deciding how best to complete and carry it out. This may also include a level of responsibility for scheduling, liaison with other functions and some involvement with arrangements for the subcontracted phases, where necessary.

This one-off provision means that the product will not again be required in its exact form, or if it is, the demand will tend to be irregular, with long time periods between orders. For this reason, investment in the manufacturing process (for example in jigs, fixtures and specialist plant) will not normally be warranted.

### Jobbing versus Job Shop

It is worth noting here that confusion often arises around the terms *jobbing* and *job shop*. While the former refers to a choice of process as explained above, the latter is a commercial description of a type of business. For example, a small printing business may often be referred to as a job shop or even a jobbing printer. This is intended to convey the nature of the business involved or market served, that is, it describes that the printer undertakes work, typically low volume in nature, that meets the specific needs of a whole range of customers. However, printing is in fact a classic example of a batch process, which is explained in the next section. Thus, from a commercial standpoint, such a firm takes on low-volume orders (hence the term *job*) from its customers but, from a manufacturing perspective, uses a batch process to meet these requirements.

### Special versus Customized versus Standard Products

Finally, it is also important to distinguish between special, customized and standard products. The word *special* is used to describe the one-off provision referred to earlier in this section – that is, the product will not again be required in its exact form or, if it is, the demand will be irregular, with long time periods between orders. The phrase *standard product* means the opposite – the demand for the product is repeated (or the single customer order is of such a large volume nature) and thus warrants investment.

The word *customized* refers to a product made to a customer's specification. However, the demand for a customized product can be either special (that is, not repeated) or standard (that is, repeated). An example of the latter is a container of a particular shape and size, as determined by a customer. Although customized, the demand for such a container (for example, Coca-Cola or other soft drink products) will be high and of a repeat nature. The appropriate choice of process will, therefore, be determined by volume and not the customized nature of the product.

Furthermore, some businesses are by their very nature the producers of customized products. The earlier example of the printing firm is such a case. Here products normally will be customized in that the printed material may include the logo, name, product and other details of the customer in question. However, a printer will find a significant level of similarity between the demands placed on manufacturing by the different customer orders. In fact the differences will be in the plate containing the specific images and writing and the ink colours and paper size in question. To manufacturing, therefore, the customized jobs are not specials (as defined earlier) but standards. Thus, it will select a process other than jobbing to meet the requirements of the markets it serves. In the printing example this would be batch and the rationale for this and what is involved become clear in the next section.

## Batch

A company decides to manufacture using batch processes because it is providing similar items on a repeat basis, usually in larger volumes – quantity × work content – than associated with jobbing.[4] This type of process, however, is chosen to cover a

**Exhibit 5.1**  Process choice related to volumes[1]

*Note*
1. Volume on the horizontal axis refers to order-quantity size.

*Source:* Terry Hill *Operations Management: Strategic Context and Managerial Analysis*, Basingstoke, UK: Macmillan, 2000, Chapter 4

wide range of volumes, as represented in Exhibit 5.1 by the elongated shape of batch, compared to other processes. At the low-volume end, the repeat orders will be small and infrequent. In fact, some companies producing very large, one-off items will adopt a batch rather than a jobbing process for their manufacturing. When this happens, the work content involved will be high in jobbing terms, while the order quantity is for a small number of the same but unique items. At the high-volume end, the order quantities may involve many hours, shifts, or even weeks of work for the same product at one or more stages in its designated manufacturing route.

The batch procedure divides the manufacturing task into a series of appropriate operations, which together will make the products involved. The reason is simply to determine the most effective manufacturing route, so that the low-cost requirements of repeat, higher-volume markets can be best achieved. At this stage, suitable jigs, fixtures and equipment will typically be identified to help reduce the processing times involved, the investment in which is justified by the total product output over time.

Each order quantity is manufactured by setting up that step of the process necessary to complete the first operation for a particular product. The whole order quantity is completed at this stage. Then, the next operation in the process is made ready, the total order quantity is completed and so on, until all stages required to make a product are completed. Meanwhile the process used to complete the first operation for the product is then reset to complete an operation for another product and so on. Thus capacity at each stage in the process is used and reused to meet the different requirements of different orders.

Examples (in addition to printing mentioned earlier) include moulding processes. Here the mould to produce an item is put into a machine. The order for that component or product is then produced, the mould is taken off, the raw materials may have to be changed, a mould for another product is put into the machine and so on. Similarly in metal machining processes a machine is set to complete the necessary metal cutting operation for a product and the whole order quantity is processed. When finished, the machine in question is reset to do the required metal cutting work on another item, while the order quantity of the first product goes on to its next stage, which is completed in another part of the process. At times an order quantity may have more than one stage completed on the same machine. Here the same principle applies, with the process reset to perform the next operation through which the whole order quantity will be passed.

## Line

With further increases in volumes (quantity × work content), investment is made to provide a process dedicated to the needs of a single product or a given range of products. The width of the product range will be determined at the time of the investment. In a line process (see Exhibit 5.1) products are passed through the same sequence of operations. The standard nature of the products allows for this. Hence, changes outside the prescribed range of options (which can be very wide, for example, with motor vehicles) cannot be accommodated on the line itself. The cumulative volume of the product range underpins the investment.

As explained in a later section, it is important clearly to recognize the fundamental differences in what constitutes volume. In a car assembly plant, for instance, customer order quantities are normally small. The eventual owner of a car orders in units of one, which the dealership passes on to the assembly plant as an order for a single car or cumulates with one or more other orders for single units. In manufacturing terms, however, all orders for single cars are for products that the production process interprets as being the same product. Hence the order quantity of a car assembly plant comprises the cumulative volume of all orders over a given period. This constitutes the high-volume nature of this business, making line the appropriate process.

Normally the wider the product range, the higher the investment required in the process to provide the degree of flexibility necessary to make these products. Where the options provided are very wide and the products involved are costly or bulky, the company is more likely to make them on an order basis only. For example, there will normally be a longer delay when purchasing an automobile (especially if several options are specified)[5] than say a domestic appliance. The underlying reason is the different degree of product standardization involved. The automobile will be made against a specific customer order and the domestic appliance to stock.

In summary, in a line process all products (irrespective of the options involved) are perceived to be standard. Thus the process does not have to be stopped to meet the requirements of the products made on the line. However, in order to accommodate another product in batch (which, for example, may only involve a different colour moulding), the process has to be stopped and reset.

## Continuous Processing

With continuous processing, a basic material is passed through successive stages or operations and refined or processed into one or more products. Petrochemicals is an example. This choice of process is based on two features. The first is very high volume demand; the second is that the materials involved can be moved easily from one part of the process to another, for example, fluids, gases and foods.

The high-volume nature of the demand justifies the very high investment involved. The processes are designed to run all day and every day with minimum shutdowns, due to the high costs of starting up and closing down. Normally the product range is quite narrow and often the products offered are purposely restricted in order to enhance volumes of all the products in the range. For example, oil companies have systematically restricted the range of octanes offered and hence increased the volumes of all those grades provided. Another feature in continuous processing is the nature of the materials being processed. Whereas in line there are manual inputs into the manufacture of the products as they pass along, in continuous processing the materials will be transferred automatically from one part of the process to the next, with the process monitoring and often self-adjusting flow and quality conformance levels. The labour tasks in these situations predominantly involve checking and some adjusting of the system but typically do not involve manual inputs into the process as they would on a line.

## *Choice of Processes within a Business*

The five generic processes have been described separately because they are discrete choices. However, most businesses will select two or more processes as being appropriate for the products they manufacture, a fact that reflects the different volume requirements of components, subassemblies and products. One illustration of this is the use of batch processes to make components and line processes to assemble those components into final products. This occurs because although the quantity required in both operations may be the same (and frequently it is larger in the first, as two or more of the same component may be required for each assembly), the work involved in making a component is much smaller than that in building the final product. The result is that the volume requirements (quantity × work content) for components is insufficient to justify the level of investment for a more dedicated process such as line.

A second example is the construction of standard housing (where price is typically an order-winner) which would be completed using a combination of project and batch processes. Project processes would be used in that resources need to be brought to the site and reallocated to other sites once their part in the task is complete or at the end of the building programme, while batch processes would be used as several houses would typically be built in parallel. This is feasible as the houses are standard (basic structures with a list of options) and their construction known ahead of time. This is desirable as it shortens building lead times and reduces labour costs. For batch processes to be used, the construction of a house is broken down into a number of steps. Each step is then completed on several houses before the next step in the programme is commenced. Hence the foundations and footings would be completed on several houses and then the next step would start and so on. Completing the same stage of a number of houses at the same time or within the same period increases the utilization both of the skilled workers involved and any specific equipment necessary at a particular stage. In the same way, the level of prefabrication (for example, roof timbers, walls and partitions, doors, doorframes and windows) would be maximised to reduce material costs as well as the labour cost in construction.

# Markets and Product Volumes

As emphasized throughout the preceding sections, the underlying factor in choosing which of the five processes is most appropriate to manufacturing a product is volume (that is, quantity × work content). The link between the demand for a product and the investment in processes to complete this task is fundamental to this decision. It is important, therefore, clearly to distinguish what is meant by volume.

Although companies express forecast sales in terms of a period (typically a year), manufacturing does not make annual volumes – it makes order quantities. Thus contracts, based on agreed total sales in a given period, but not the size of actual orders (or call-offs), can be very misleading. On the other hand, manufacturing often cumulates orders from different customers (using order-backlog/forward-load principles) or decides to make products for finished goods inventory to be sold in the future, in order to enhance volume. The choice is restricted by the degree of customization of the product and factors such as current forward load, seasonality of sales and lead times in supplying customers' requirements. Hence, the horizontal axis in Exhibit 5.1 concerns order quantities placed on manufacturing. In project and jobbing, products are only made to customer order. In batch, decisions to cumulate demand, or make to stock, relate to appropriate volumes for the process investments in place and the actual sales-order volumes required.

The term *flexibility* is used to describe several different requirements. Two of these relate to volume. One concerns demand increases and the other alludes to the ability of a process to manufacture low quantities (as well as higher volumes) at required levels of cost. In turn, the latter concerns the relationship between set-up and process time. Thus where a company experiences reducing order volumes but has already invested in a high-volume process designed to manufacture products at fast output speeds, it will need appropriate investment to ensure that it can keep set-up times sufficiently short to maintain the order quantity (hours) and set-up time ratio at an acceptable level. Current research work in many manufacturing companies provides numerous illustrations of where annual sales for a product may be similar to those in the past but actual order quantities (or call-offs) have reduced significantly. The link between this section and the previous one is fundamental in terms of process investment.

## Technical Specification versus Business Specification

As volumes increase, the justification for investing in processes dedicated to make that product increases. High utilization of plant underpins the investment. Similarly, if processes will not be highly utilized by one product, they need to be chosen so that they can meet the manufacturing and business needs of other products. Therefore, firms, when choosing processes, need to distinguish between the technology required to make a product and the way the product is manufactured. On the one hand, the process technology choice concerns the engineering dimension of providing a process that will form, shape, cut and so forth a product to the size and tolerances required (the technical specification). On the other hand, the manufacturing dimension concerns determining the best way to make a product. This decision needs to be based on volumes and relevant order-winners and qualifiers (the

**Exhibit 5.2** The constituents of customer orders when choosing processes and the function responsible for their clarification

| Specification | Responsible function |
|---|---|
| *Technical specification*<br>The fundamental requirements of a product including its physical dimensions | Research and development or engineering |
| *Business specification*<br>The order quantities and relevant order-winners and qualifiers of the markets in which it will compete | Manufacturing |

business specification) – see Exhibit 5.2. As volumes rise, the appropriate choice will change, as illustrated in Exhibit 5.1.

When companies invest in processes, they typically specify the technical requirements. This is recognized as fundamental, and appropriately so. But they typically fail to specify the business requirement the process investment has to meet, a requirement crucial to the success of a firm. However, in the past, manufacturing has failed to develop these critical, strategic arguments and insights. The consequences for many companies have been serious, leading to premature reinvestment of a considerable size or even the closing down of parts of its business. Leaving the choice of these investments to be made against the single dimension of the technical specification has led to inappropriate decisions, based on the narrow base of technology. Manufacturing's failure to realize that it is the custodian of these decisions has indirectly supported this approach.

The choice of process needs to be understood, not in engineering terms (the technical specification), but in terms of manufacturing constraints and other dimensions of the business specification. Understanding how well a process can support the order-winning criteria of a product, the implications of the process for a company's infrastructure and other relevant investments is fundamental to this strategic decision. These issues are dealt with in the following section.

## Business Implications of Process Choice

It has already been explained that market characteristics (order-winners and qualifiers) and product volumes are the underlying factors in choosing the appropriate process. In addition, the nature of the product is also a factor in this decision in terms of the two extremes in Exhibits 5.1 and 5.3, namely project and continuous processing.

Hence the procedure used is first to assess the market-volume dimension. This then forms the basis for choosing which process is appropriate to best meet these critical business needs. The engineering dimension provides the initial set of alter-

**Exhibit 5.3**   The engineering, manufacturing and business dimension phases involved
in process choice

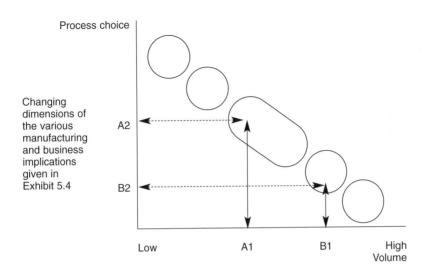

Phase 1 links the market/volume to the process choice.

Phase 2 picks up the corresponding manufacturing and business implications of the many
dimensions given in Exhibit 5.4, and that go on the vertical axis. The above diagram shows volumes
A1 and B1, the appropriate process choice and their corresponding points on the manufacturing and
business implications dimensions, A2 and B2.

natives concerning the ways to meet the technical requirements of the product.
However, at this juncture the engineering dimension finishes and the manufacturing
and business dimensions start. Phase 1 links the market volumes to the process
choice (the manufacturing dimension, which also takes into account the engineering dimension described earlier) – A1 and B1 in Exhibit 5.3. Phase 2 automatically picks up the corresponding point on each of the various manufacturing and
business implications given in Exhibit 5.4, A2 and B2 respectively in Exhibit 5.3.
However, many companies recognize the technical dimension but not the manufacturing and business dimensions. The engineering proposal currently underpins the
major part of process investment decisions, which in turn are based on the forecast
market volumes that form part of the corporate marketing strategy. The manufacturing and business implications embodied in a proposal are typically given scant
recognition. But it is these issues that bind manufacturing and regulate its ability to
respond to the business needs. Once the investment is made, not only are the
processes fixed but also the whole of the manufacturing infrastructure is fixed. The
result is that this decision dictates the extent to which manufacturing can support
the needs of the marketplace, the essence of business success.

When Phase 1 in Exhibit 5.3 is completed, the choice of process is designated.
However, at the same time it stipulates the position on the vertical dimensions that

**Exhibit 5.4**  Selected business implications of process choice

| Aspects | Project | Jobbing | Batch | Line | Continuous processing |
|---|---|---|---|---|---|
| | | | **Typical characteristics of process choice** | | |
| **Products and markets** | | | | | |
| Type of product | Special/small range of standards | Special | → | Standard products | Standard products |
| Product range | Wide | Wide | → | Narrow | Very narrow |
| Customer order size | Small | Small | → | Large | Very large |
| Level of product change required | High | High | → | Low and within agreed options | None |
| Rate of new product introductions | High | High | → | Low | Very low |
| What does a company sell? | Capability | Capability | → | Standard products/commodities | Standard products/commodities |
| How are orders won? | | | | | |
| Order-winners | Delivery speed/unique design capability | Delivery speed/unique design capability/repeat business | → | Price | Price |
| Qualifiers | Price/on-time delivery/quality conformance | Price/on-time delivery/quality conformance | On-time delivery/quality conformance | Design/on-time delivery/quality conformance | Design/on-time delivery/quality conformance |
| **Manufacturing** | | | | | |
| Nature of the process technology | Oriented towards general purpose | Universal | → | Dedicated | Highly dedicated |
| Process flexibility | High | High | → | Low | Inflexible |
| Production volumes | Low | Low | → | High | Very High |
| Dominant utilization | Mixed | Labour | → | Plant | Plant |
| Changes in capacity | Incremental | Incremental | → | Stepped change | New facility |
| Key manufacturing task | To meet specification/delivery schedules | Responsive to specification/delivery date requirements and changes | → | Low-cost production | Low-cost production |

**Investment and Cost**

| | | | | | |
|---|---|---|---|---|---|
| Level of capital investment | Low/high | Low | → | High | Very high |
| Level of inventory | | | | | |
| Components/raw material | As required | As required/low | Often medium | Planned with buffer stocks/low | Planned with buffer stocks |
| Work-in-progress | High¹ | High¹ | Very high | Low | Low |
| Finished goods | Low | Low | → | High² | High³ |
| Percentage of total costs | | | | | |
| Direct labour | Low | High | → | Low | Very low |
| Direct materials | High | Low | → | High | Very high |
| Site/plant overheads | Low | Low | → | High | High |

**Infrastructure**

| | | | | | |
|---|---|---|---|---|---|
| Appropriate organizational | | | | | |
| Control | Decentralized/centralized | Decentralized | → | Centralized | Centralized |
| Style | Entrepreneurial | Entrepreneurial | → | Bureaucratic | Bureaucratic |
| Most important operations management perspective | Technology | Technology | → | Business/people | Technology |
| Level of specialist support to manufacturing | High | Low | → | High | Very high |

*Notes*

1. This would depend on stage payment arrangements.
2. However, many businesses here only make against customer schedules or on receipt of a customer order.
3. The finished-goods inventory in, for instance, oil refining is stored in the postprocessing stages of distribution and at the point of sale.

will accrue as a result. Hence Phase 2 is inextricably tied to Phase 1. Therefore the decisions in Phase 1 cannot be taken in isolation. The choice has to embrace both Phase 1 and Phase 2. Only in this way will an organization avoid falling into the Cyclopean trap from which it may take years to extricate itself. Only in this way will a business take into account the short- and long-term implications that emanate from the decision to manufacture using one choice of process as opposed to another.

To help explain the business implications of process choice, the perspectives involved have been placed into four categories – products and markets, manufacturing, investment and cost and infrastructure. Furthermore, the issues for illustration and discussion have been chosen on the basis of their overall business importance. However there are many other issues equally important to understand, and these have distinct operational rather than strategic overtones.[6]

The critical issue embodied in Exhibit 5.4 is how each perspective reviewed changes between one choice of process and another. Thus when a company decides to invest in a process it will at the same time have determined the corresponding point on each dimension within these four categories. It is necessary for companies to understand this and be aware of the trade-offs embodied in that choice.

Exhibit 5.4 contains many generalized statements that are intended to relate the usual requirements of one type of process to the other four. In almost all cases there is an arrow drawn between jobbing and line. This is intended to indicate that as a process moves from jobbing to low-volume batch to high-volume batch through to line, the particular characteristic will change from one form to the other. The reason for this approach is to help explain the implications of these choices and examine the consequences that normally will follow.

Companies selling products typically made using the project process will need to make decisions on how much is made away from the site and transported in. Today, for instance, many parts of a civil engineering structure are made off-site by jobbing, batch or line processes, then brought in as required. Similarly, products with the fluid, semifluid or gaseous characteristics necessary to avail themselves of continuous processing may also be made on a batch process basis. Thus the changing business characteristics displayed in Exhibit 5.4 illustrate the sets of alternatives embodied in these choices as well.

Finally, Exhibit 5.4 has been arranged to illustrate the linked relationship between jobbing, batch and line choices as opposed to the more distinct process–product relationship existing in project and continuous processing, described earlier. The section that follows adopts this division.

## Selected Business Implications

This section further explains the implications of the dimensions provided in Exhibit 5.4. The four categories of products and markets, manufacturing, investment and cost and infrastructure are explained under each of the process choice headings, helping to link them. To emphasize the separate natures of project and continuous processing and the linked natures of jobbing, batch and line, the following sections discuss project first, followed by jobbing, batch and line in one general section, and then continuous processing at the end. Despite their link, jobbing, batch and line nevertheless differ from each other. Hence each is discussed in a separate subsection. But since batch often links the change in dimensions between jobbing and line, the latter two processes are dealt with first to help to describe batch within this overall perspective.

# Project

## Products and Markets

Companies choosing project processes sell capability. They sell their experience, know-how and skills to provide for a customer's individual needs. Hence they are in a market that will require a high level of product change and new product introductions. Its product range will be wide, with low unit-sales volume. It will win orders on aspects such as unique design capability or delivery speed, with price normally acting as a qualifier rather than an order-winner. Through the competitive nature of today's markets, criteria such as quality conformance and on-time delivery have typically changed from being order-winners to qualifiers, as signalled by their presence in all types of market.

## Manufacturing

Oriented towards general purpose equipment, with specialist plant to meet particular product, design or structural features, project processes are highly flexible in coping with the low product volumes of the market and design changes that will occur during production. Changes in capacity mix, or in total, can be made incrementally, with the key tasks being on-time completion and meeting the specification as laid down by the customer.

## Investment and Cost

The capital investment in plant and other processes will tend to be low. But there will be some high-cost items that may be purchased or hired, depending on their potential usage, availability, costs and similar factors. Due to the opportunity to schedule materials, the inventory at this stage will be on an as-required basis. Work-in-progress levels will be high but normally much of this will be passed on to customers through stage payment agreements. In a make-to-order situation, finished goods are small, with immediate delivery on completion. The key cost will normally be materials, and sound purchasing arrangements, material usage and work-in-progress control are essential.

*Infrastructure*

> Due to the uncertainties in the process and the need to respond quickly to any customer-derived changes, the organizational control should be decentralized and supported by an entrepreneurial, rather than a bureaucratic, style. In addition, once the business grows, the company must centrally control the key items of plant, internal specialist/engineering skills and other outsourced commodities or skills to ensure they are effectively scheduled by project and between projects. The operations manager must understand the relevant technology to appreciate and respond to unforeseen difficulties and problems, both technical and non-technical, and to use the local and centrally based specialist support effectively.

# Jobbing

*Products and Markets*

> In essence a jobbing business sells its capability to manufacture a customer's requirements. It is restricted only by the range of skills of its workforce or by its process capabilities. Thus it handles a wide product range, competing on aspects other than price. This does not mean that a business can charge any price it decides. But if the price is within what is reasonable for the market – and that includes provisions for additional delivery speed or poststart modifications – then price is a qualifier rather than an order-winner.

*Manufacturing*

> As a consequence of the products it provides and markets it serves, the manufacturing process must be flexible. Its major concern is the utilization of its labour skills, with process being purchased to facilitate the skilled operator to complete the task. Changes in capacity can be achieved incrementally. The order-backlog position that exists in make-to-order markets will allow manufacturing to undertake any foreseen adjustments in capacity ahead of time. The key manufacturing task is to complete the item to specification and on time, since normally this one-off item forms an integral part of some greater business whole, as far as the customer is concerned.

*Investment and Cost*

> Although some of the equipment used in jobbing can be very expensive, generally this investment is low compared to batch and line. In addition, material will tend to be purchased only when an order has been received, with material delivery forming part of the total lead time. Work-in-progress inventory will be high with all jobs, on

average, being half-finished, while the make-to-order nature of its business means that products are dispatched once completed. There will tend to be few specialist and other support functions, which leads to a relatively lower plant/site overhead cost. These specialist tasks will be largely part of the skilled worker's role, which, together with the high labour content, normally makes this the highest portion of total costs. Material costs will tend to be low; any expensive materials involved will invariably be on a customer-supplied basis.

### Infrastructure

Organizational control and style need to be decentralized and entrepreneurial in nature, so as to respond quickly and effectively to meet the inherent flexibility requirements of this market. For this reason, the production executive has to understand the technology involved, as this forms an important part of his contribution to business decisions (for example, in accepting an order, agreeing estimated costs and resulting prices, confirming a delivery quotation or providing part of the specialist inputs into a business).

## Line

### Productions and Markets

A line process reflects the other end of the spectrum to jobbing. The business sells standard products that, to be successful, are typically sold on price and are associated with large customer orders. The level of product change is usually prescribed within a list of options; outside this, the product is not normally available. Product design and quality are determined at the outset to meet the perceived needs of the customer, with on-time delivery a qualifier in today's markets.

### Manufacturing

To provide low manufacturing costs, the process is dedicated to a predetermined range of products. It is not geared to be flexible outside this range, due to the high costs of change. This provides the opportunity to maintain the necessary quality conformance levels throughout the process. Production volumes need to be high to achieve the level of plant utilization necessary to justify the investment and to underpin the cost structures involved. As explained earlier, it is the cumulative volume of products made within the period that constitutes the volume dimension justifying investments. Output changes are more difficult to arrange, due to the stepped-change nature of capacity alterations.

*Investment and Cost*

The key to low manufacturing costs is high process investment, which goes hand in hand with line. The volumes involved allow schedules of raw materials and components to be planned with associated buffer stocks to cover the uncertainty of supply. Work-in-progress inventory will be low. Although finished goods will tend to be high, many businesses, as part of a decision to keep inventory investment as low as possible, will only make standard products against customer schedules or on receipt of an order. Also, products offering many optional extras (such as motor vehicles) will tend to have a policy of only making to a specific order. Hence, even in times of relatively low sales, if the new car selected includes an unusual set of options and consequently is unlikely to have been built in anticipation of an early sale, delivery will be delayed. Finally, the high areas of cost tend to be in materials, bought-out components and site/plant overheads, with direct labour a relatively small part of the total.

*Infrastructure*

Since the choice of a line process represents a high-volume business, then a more centralized organization, controlled by systems, is more appropriate. On the manufacturing side, the key production executive task concerns the business/people aspects of the job, with specialist support providing the technical know-how for products and processes.

# Batch

*Products and Markets*

Between jobbing and line, comes batch. This is chosen to cover a very wide range of volumes as illustrated by the elongated shape depicted in Exhibits 5.1 and 5.3. Batch links the low/high volume, special/standard products and make-to-order/make-to-stock businesses. In most cases, the choice of batch, rather than jobbing, as the appropriate way to manufacture products signals that production volumes (that is, quantity × work content) have increased and are of a repeat nature but insufficient to dedicate processes solely to them, as would be the case in line. Some unique high-volume orders may also be done on a batch basis.

At the low-volume end of batch, the processes are able to cope with a high degree of product change and a high level of new product introductions. Here, the business is oriented towards selling capability, with price starting to become a more important order-winner, due to the volume and repeat nature of the products. At the high-volume end of batch, products have become increasingly standard, order sizes larger and product change lower, all of which illustrate the shift in product-market characteristics toward line. As mentioned earlier, market pressures typically have changed quality conformance and on-time delivery from order-winners to qualifiers.

## Manufacturing

It can be deduced from the product-market features that batch processes usually have to cope with a wide range of products and production volumes. To handle this task these processes must be of a general nature, offering a high degree of flexibility. With some items of equipment the utilization will be low; with others plant will have been purchased to meet the needs of a product or to offer distinct process advantages (for example, numerical control (NC) machines, machining centres and flexible manufacturing systems, each of which will be described in a later section). In these cases, high investment will be justified normally on a usage basis and the aim will be to utilize the capacity to the fullest.

To help underpin the total process investment many companies adopt a deliberate policy of increasing the utilization of a plant in three ways:

1. putting a wide range of products through the same set of processes.

2. manufacturing many of the same products in a single order quantity or batch quantity (hence the name). In this way, the number of set-ups is reduced, which decreases the setting costs and increases effective capacity.

3. making products wait for processes to become available. This policy, together with the order-quantity decisions above, leads to a work-in-progress inventory investment that, in relation to the size of the business, tends to be very high compared to jobbing and, particularly, line.

## Investment and Cost

To be competitive in markets moving towards the high-volume end, a business will increasingly invest in its batch processes to achieve the low manufacturing cost requirement of these markets. As explained earlier, many companies exploit this still further by putting more products through the same processes and, hence, increasing overall utilization. However, the major trade-off associated with this policy is the very high investment in work-in-progress inventory. The raw materials, components, and finished goods inventory levels will in turn be associated with the make-to-order or make-to-stock nature of the business. As with all companies in this mid-volume markets, the nearer it is to a make-to-order situation the more the characteristics of that market will prevail and vice versa. The make-up of total costs is no exception.

*Infrastructure*

As the business moves away from the low-volume end of the continuum, central-ized controls and a bureaucratic style become more appropriate. The increasing complexity of this growth will change the nature of the specialist functions, with design and production engineering becoming an ever-important support to manu-facturing. The production manager's role will be bound up with appreciating and recognizing the critical business issues involved, providing coordination through-out and spearheading the development of manufacturing systems.

At the low-volume end of batch, the characteristics, although not the same, will in many situations be more akin to those in jobbing. Therefore it is important to recog-nize the extent and trends in these changes and make the necessary adjustments.

## Continuous Processing

*Markets and Products*

At the other end of the volume spectrum, companies that choose continuous processing will sell a narrow range of standard products in markets where product change and the rate of product introductions are low. The company will sell standard products rather than capability and large customer orders will be won principally on price.

*Manufacturing*

In a price-sensitive market, the key manufacturing task will be low-cost production. To help keep costs low, the process will be highly dedicated, with the cost of struc-ture based on high production volumes, leading to a need to achieve high plant utilization. The fixed nature of capacity also creates restrictions when increases or decreases in output are required, with the decision based on whether or not to build a new facility on the one hand or how often to run the plant (known as campaigning) on the other.

*Investment and Cost*

The high plant investment and high volume output associated with continuous processing offers the opportunity to keep raw material inventory on a planned usage basis, with built-in buffer stocks to cover uncertainties. Work-in-progress will be relatively low, with inventory in finished goods high. This is because of the need to maintain output levels at all times against fluctuating sales patterns. In many cases, however, finished goods are held in the extensive distribution system of a business and sometimes at its own retail outlets (for example, petrol stations).

Owing to the high process investment, direct labour costs are small, with the highest cost usually in materials. Site/plant overheads in this process will be high owing to the need to support the process and handle the high output levels involved.

### Infrastructure

The high-volume nature of these businesses lends itself to a centralized, bureaucratic organization control and style. Manufacturing performance is measured against budgets, variance analysis is the order of the day and investment proposals are centrally monitored. An understanding of the process and product technology is important when running a production unit, together with the ability to coordinate the high level of specialist support provided for manufacturing.

## An Overview of Process Choice

To help clarify the issues involved in process choice, an overview of how these alternatives link to one another is now described. The first important fact to stress is that each of the choices embodies a totally different approach to manufacturing a product. Although described in some detail in the chapter, a short explanation of these differences will serve to reinforce this important point.

- **Project** – this is used for one-off products that have to be built on site because it is difficult or impossible to move them once they have been made. Consequently, the resources involved need to be brought to the site and released for reuse elsewhere when they are no longer needed.

- **Jobbing** – this is used for one-off products that can be moved once completed. The responsibility for making the product is normally given to a skilled person, who decides how best to make it and then completes all or most of the operations involved, including checking quality conformance at each stage.

- **Batch** – with an increase in volumes and the repeat nature of products, companies select batch as the effective way to meet the requirements involved. Because the products are repeated, companies can consider investment at each of the manufacturing steps to make them. This includes engineering time to decide how best to make a product, jigs and fixtures to facilitate the completion of certain operations and equipment purchased with an eye to making these and other products with similar characteristics. However, the volumes involved do not warrant the purchase of dedicated equipment. The operations necessary to complete a product are, therefore, not linked and are said to be decoupled.

- **Line** – when demand is sufficient to justify dedicating equipment solely to making a specified range of products, a line process is normally chosen. The operations necessary to complete a specified range of products are linked together so that each product goes from one operation directly to the next and so on. The operations necessary to complete a product in this instance are said to be coupled. The operators involved will physically take part in assembling the products.

■ **Continuous processing** – when the demand for a product is such that the volume required necessitates a process being used all day and every day, further investment is justified. The equipment in this instance is designed to automatically transfer the product from one stage to the next, check the quality conformance within the process and make adjustments where necessary. The investment associated with this is warranted by the volumes involved.

To emphasize these distinctions Exhibit 5.5 shows the gap between the five choices. It also makes the point that whereas there will sometimes be a transition from jobbing to low-volume batch, from low-volume to high-volume batch, from high-volume batch to line or from high-volume batch to continuous processing, the same will not apply between project and jobbing or from line to continuous processing. Similarly, when volumes reduce towards the end of a product's life cycle, the reverse movement may take place, but again it would only go as illustrated in Exhibit 5.5.

**Exhibit 5.5**    Potential transitions between the different choices of process

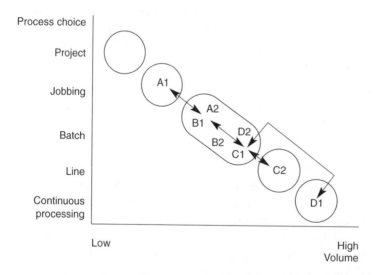

This shows four potential volume transitions that typically may face a business. The first example shows a move from one off[1], low-volume (A1) to repeat order, low-volume demand (A2) for a product or vice versa and the change in manufacturing process that should ideally accompany this movement. Examples B1 to B2, C1 to C2 and D1 to D2 show similar demand changes at different points on the volume scale and requiring similar decisions concerning the realignment of the process choice.

*Note*
**1.** One-off is a description of uniqueness, not order quantity.

Transition in these instances refers to the possibility that, as volumes increase or decrease, a business may change its choice of manufacturing accordingly. However, project and continuous processing are prescribed by the nature of the product itself and the volumes involved. In this way, businesses with these characteristics are precluded from considering any other process in a transitional movement, as described here and shown in Exhibit 5.5. Those products that lend themselves to being produced using continuous processing (for example, fluids, gases and foods) are often produced on a batch basis, where the production volumes involved are not adequate to justify the high investment associated with continuous processing.

When product volumes increase or decrease, companies should ideally realign their choice of process as appropriate to the new levels of volumes. However, many companies find themselves unable, or unwilling, to commit the fresh investment necessary to complete this realignment, especially where the volume movement is downward.[7]

# Hybrid Processes

As mentioned earlier, many companies have developed hybrid processes to better enable them to support the characteristics of their markets. Some comprise a mix of two of the five generic processes; others are developments within an existing process type, often based on the use of numerical control (NC) machines. Some of the more important hybrid developments are now explained, and to help position these in relation to the generic processes, they are included together in Exhibit 5.6. However, the list includes some (for example, machining centres) that have been generally applied and are provided as standard items[8] from a supplier's catalogue.

Finally, as with all hybrids. there is a root stock. Thus although each hybrid format will comprise a mix of two process types, it will still be classified as belonging to one or the other. This phenomenon is highlighted by the headings of 'batch-related' and 'line-related' in the sections that follow. These hybrids have batch and line roots, respectively. What happens is that they alter some of the trade-offs described in Exhibit 5.4. Some will improve and some will worsen. What a company seeks is an overall set of trade-offs that are better for the business as a whole than those provided by the current process(es) provision.

## Batch-related Hybrids

### *Numerical Control (NC) Machines*

An NC system[9] is a process that automatically performs the required operations according to a detailed set of coded instructions. Since mathematical information is

**Exhibit 5.6**   The position of some hybrid processes in relation to the five generic choices
of process

the base used, the system is called numerical control. The first applications were to
metal cutting processes such as milling, boring, turning, grinding and sawing, but in
recent years the range of NC applications includes tube bending, shearing and
different forms of cutting. The operation of machine tools is from numerical data
stored on paper or magnetic tapes, tabulating cards, computer storage or direct
information. Compared with conventional equipment, NC machines offer increased
accuracy, consistency and flexibility to meet specification changes, even with the
need to meet very complex manufacturing requirements. Thus design changes and
modifications require only a change in instruction, nothing more.

In reality, an NC machine is a development of a batch process; it is also low
volume in nature. It is batch because the machine stops at the end of one process
and is reset for a new job or stopped while a new programme is being loaded. It is
low volume because the set-up times are short, hence providing an acceptable ratio
between set-up times and the length of the run before the next set-up. The position
of NC machines on Exhibit 5.6 illustrates this.

However the trade-off against conventional plant operations is the increased
investment associated with NC processes. In addition, the introduction of the new
technology and associated changes can create problems for the operators, setter,
and supervisor in terms of their roles, the level of specialist support and changing
skill requirements.

## Machining Centres

Machining centres first appeared in the late 1950s. They combine NC operations previously provided by different machines into one machine centre. With tool changing automatically controlled by instructions on the tape and carousels holding up to 150 tools and more, the underlying rationale for this development is to maximize the combination of operations completed at a single location.

A machining centre typically embraces several metal cutting facilities (for example, milling, boring and drilling) that are applied to a given piece of work in a predetermined sequence reflected in the NC programme. The relevant range of tools is stored in a magazine. The appropriate tool is then selected and the particular operation completed. The hybrid nature of this process is that several operations are completed before the item of work is removed. Thus a machining centre completes many operations in sequence, without removing the item from the process. This reflects aspects of line within what is, in reality, still a batch process. (That is, the process stops and resets itself not only between operations but between one item and the next.)

In this way, a machining centre changes the pattern of work-in-progress inventory associated with the generic process that could be adopted as an alternative, namely batch. Just as in line, a part now goes through a number of operations in sequence and thus changes the process design from functional to product layout. However, in most companies, the pre- and postmachining operations are performed on another process choice (for example batch). This use of a combination of processes would change the relevant point on the dimensions shown in Exhibit 5.4. Machining centres, like all NC-based processes, increase volume flexibility (for example, reduced set-ups and the resulting ability to meet, for example, the low-volume requirements of products) in relation to an alternative non-NC process, due to the nature and level of the capital investment involved. This is reflected in Exhibit 5.6.

Thus, machining centres are a hybrid between batch and line; as a consequence, the position on some trade-offs (see Exhibit 5.4) changes. For instance, work-in-progress inventory within the machining centre will decrease compared to completing the same operations at individual and unconnected work stations. Similarly, the relative level of investment will increase. As you will note, both these changes are more towards a line process. However, as explained earlier regarding hybrids, the root process is still batch.

## Flexible Manufacturing Systems

Whereas a machining centre is best suited to low volumes, a flexible manufacturing system (FMS) is appropriate to mid-volume requirements – see Exhibit 5.6. This too is designed to complete a given number of operations on an item before it leaves the system. However, rather than the item being contained in a single centre, in an

FMS the workpiece is automatically transferred from one process to the next. Besides volume differences, the physical dimensions of the items to be machined are typically much larger than those completed by machining centres.

Flexible manufacturing systems are a combination of standard and special numerical control (NC) machines, automated materials handling, and computer control in the form of direct numerical control (DNC)[10] for the purposes of extending the benefits of NC to mid-volume manufacturing situations.[11] Whereas NC equipment and particularly machining centres accommodate relatively low-volume demand, much less attention has been given to improving manufacturing's approach to mid-volume, mid-variety products, although this accounts for a large part of the products that would fall into the batch range of volumes.

FMSs are designed around families of parts. The increased volumes associated with bringing together the individual requirements of a range of products and treating these as one volume justify the investment. This, combined with the inherent flexibility of the NC equipment creates the rationale for using FMSs in the mid-volume segment of demand. Classic families of products are:

1. **By assembly** – grouping parts together that would be required to make a single assembly (for an example an engine). The system would be designed to allow the user to order against an assembly requirement, rather than scheduling order quantities for each part through an appropriate series of functionally laid-out processes.

2. **By type** – categorizing parts by type for a range of similar products. This would relieve higher-volume production processes of the low-to mid-volume part numbers and thus reduce the number of change-overs involved. This aggregate family demand justifies the capital investment, with the inherent flexibility within the FMS allowing a relatively wide range of products to be considered and facilitating the balancing and rebalancing of the workload as product mix and volumes change.

3. **By size and similar operations** – the specification of the FMS in this situation reflects the physical size of the parts and the particular operations that need to be completed. Again, the flexibility within the system extends the range of work with which it can cope and allows high utilization owing to its ability to handle product mix and volume changes.

A typical series of events in processing a part in FMS (see Exhibit 5.7) is as follows:

■ A DNC system directs a cart carrying an empty fixture to a load station and also advises the loader which part is to be loaded.
■ On completion, the loader signals that it is ready; the computer directs the part to the first operation, selecting, if available, the lowest backlog potential.
■ The part is automatically unloaded, the appropriate NC programme selected, and the work completed.

**Exhibit 5.7**    An example of a 15-station random FMS provided as a three-stage installation

*Source:* Kearney & Trecker Corporation, Milwaukee, WI, *KT's World of Advanced Manufacturing Technologies*, 2nd edn, Milwaukee, WI

■ This procedure will be followed until the part is finished, whence it goes to the unloading area and out of the system.

The hybrid nature of FMS is based on logic similar to that described for machining centres, that is, maximizing the combination of operations completed at a single location. The additional capital investment will bring with it both lower cost and lower work-in-progress inventory advantages, trade-offs more akin to line. However, the root process is still batch.

## Group Technology

The first three hybrid processes concerned the use of NC equipment as the basis for the process change. However, alternative hybrid processes can be adopted that use conventional or non-NC equipment. Three are described here. The first is a batch-line hybrid known as group technology.

The underlying difference between the choice of batch and line processes is one of associated volumes. Group technology gains for batch processes some of the advantages inherent in high-volume line situations. It does this by changing the process or functional layout associated with batch manufacturing into the product layout associated with line (see Exhibit 5.8).

The approach involves separating out those processes that do not lend themselves to the application of group technology because of such factors as the level of investment and health considerations (for example noise or process waste/fumes). The next step is to group together families of like products. The criteria for this selection are similar to those outlined for FMS. However, note that the process flexibility inherent in group technology application is not of the same order as in FMS.

The third step is to determine the process configuration necessary to manufacture each product family involved and to lay out the cell or line to reflect the required manufacturing routings. The final stage is to complete a tooling analysis within each family, with a twofold aim. The first is to group together those parts within the family that can use the same tooling. This forms the basis for scheduling to reduce setting time. The second is to include this feature as part of the design prerequisites for future products.[12]

As shown in Exhibit 5.6, group technology moves a business's volumes toward the high end. In so doing, group technology changes the process on many of the Exhibit 5.4 dimensions from batch to line. Most important, it creates an inherently less flexible process in that to reuse any spare capacity brought about by a decrease in product family volumes will not be easy, or even possible, without moving the location of the plant; a form of process investment. The key advantages to be gained from group technology include reduced lead times and lower work-in-progress inventory. There is also a series of advantages associated with any form of small-scale manufacturing unit. A detailed review of these issues is provided elsewhere.[13]

**Exhibit 5.8**    Group layout and the transition from a functional (batch) to product (line) layout

Functional layout

Lathe shop — Milling section — Drilling section — Grinding section

All products take their own operation sequence through the different sets of capacities

Group layout

Group 1 — Group 2 — Group 3 — Group 4

All operations to make each product within the family are completed within a group of processes

Product layout

Series of work stations in operational sequence to complete a given range of products

## Linked Batch

As with most of the developments discussed in this section, linked batch is a hybrid of batch and line. However linked batch does not need to encompass a large number of processes, which is more typical in the examples given earlier. In some instances, only two or three sequential processes may be linked; in others, for example, food packing, the whole of the process may be linked. Whereas in the other illustrations the investment decisions are typically made as part of a complete process review, linked batch is undertaken on a more piecemeal or evolutionary basis. That is, where only two or three processes are linked, decisions are typically piecemeal in nature; linking the whole set of processes is quite often the result of changing volumes over time and adaptive use of existing capacity to meet the process requirements of other products. The sequential processes, although physically laid out in line (that is, one operation follows another), are run as a batch process (that is, when product change is required, all the linked operations have to be stopped and reset to accommodate this change). Irrespective of the length of the set-up changes, the fact that the process has to be stopped makes it a batch process.

## *Dedicated Use of General Purpose Equipment*

Where the volume of a specific part is sufficient, manufacturing can justify the allocation of a process to its sole use. This dedication is not in the plant itself but in the use of a general purpose process. Thus, the potential flexibility and other characteristics illustrated in Exhibit 5.4 of a general purpose process are retained and they will be reclaimed when volumes reduce. Characteristically, then, the process is not altered. Hence the process is still batch and therefore general purpose in nature. What becomes dedicated is the use of the process, which reflects the volume requirements for the product in question.

Thus the hybrid stems from a change in use (as explained earlier) to reflect the high-volume demand for a product and not a physical change to the process itself. It remains a batch process, even though during the period in which its use is dedicated to the manufacture of a given product it may (for example, for colour changes) or may not be reset.

# Line-related Hybrids

Just as the last section discussed developments and hybrids rooted in batch processes, this section reviews hybrids related to line.

## *Mix Mode Assembly Lines*

A line process that can cope with a broad range of products without stopping is known as a mix mode assembly line. In reality, companies determine the product range for all line processes when they make the process investment. However, the term *mix mode* has been used to reflect processes in which companies have made systematic and purposeful investments to increase the product range involved. Typically this entails programming the line to make small quantities of different products in a predetermined sequence.

The origins of a mix mode assembly line are twofold. On the one hand, a reduction in demand for existing products releases capacity, which a company may wish to reuse. This, in turn, can lead to the adaptation of an existing line process to accommodate other products. On the other, a mix mode assembly line may be developed to handle the operations necessary to complete a number of products currently completed in other ways (for example using linked-batch processes). What makes the root here a line process is that it does not have to be stopped and reset to accommodate the next product.

Mix mode assembly lines are designed to cope with a range of products in any scheduled combination. This is achieved by the use of computer-controlled flow lines that schedule work according to the overall production requirements and the short-term workloads at the various stations. The increased range of products that can be accommodated justifies the investment necessary to achieve a high level of this aspect of flexibility. In this way, a mix mode assembly line is an alternative process to batch that could be used to meet the required level of volume of the products in question.

As can be deduced from this explanation, a mix mode assembly line is not technically a hybrid, in that the characteristics of another process have not been combined with those of line. Instead, it is a line process that can accommodate the requirements of a wider range of products than typically can be made on a classic line process. It has been included here to illustrate how process investment can change certain relevant trade-offs in a business.

*Transfer Lines*

The last hybrid process to be discussed is transfer lines. Where the volume demand for products is very high, further investment is justified. Transfer line is a hybrid between line and continuous processing. However, its root process is still line because it can be stopped without major cost. The position of transfer lines on Exhibit 5.6 illustrates the features of this process. The high demand justifies investment designed to reduce the manual inputs associated with a line process and to move more towards a process that automatically transfers a part from one station to the next, positions it, completes the task and checks for quality conformance. Furthermore, deviations from the specified tolerances will be registered and automatic tooling adjustments and replacements will often be part of the procedure. To achieve this, the process is numerically controlled in part or in full, which provides the systems control afforded, in part at least, by the operator in the line process.

# Review of the Use of Numerical Control (NC) in Hybrid Processes

Whereas linked batch, group technology, and the dedicated use of as general purpose process are derived from alternative uses of conventional, non-NC processes, the other four hybrid processes are based on the concept of numerical control in one form or another.[14]

The last section explained, and Exhibit 5.6 illustrated, that the basis for the choice between one NC hybrid process and another is volume. As with choices between the five generic processes outlined in Exhibit 5.4, the implications for these choices have to be understood and taken into account at the time of their selection (see Exhibit 5.9). The NC base of these processes brings with it a level of flexibility that is far greater than that inherent with non-NC alternatives. This means that the process is more able to cope with a wider range of products and to handle product mix changes over time. However dedication in these alternatives starts to be introduced when processes are brought together to meet the needs of a given range/family of products. In order to reuse these thereafter, further and often substantial investment will have to be made to relocate, adapt or change existing processes and their configuration to meet the needs of other products. This change

**Exhibit 5.9**    Hybrid NC process choice related to volume

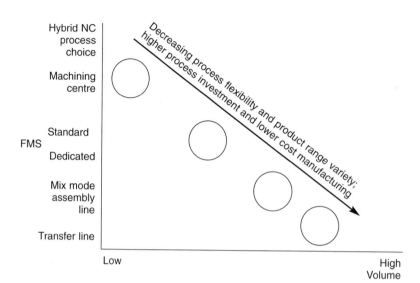

is illustrated by the gap between machining centres and FMS. As the choice moves to the other end of the spectrum, the implications of dedication will begin to take hold.

Exhibit 5.9 illustrates the rationalized use of NC-based processes as they relate to volume. As with the generic processes described earlier, while volume is the basis for choice, two other equally important dimensions must form part of this decision. The first is the change in volume expected over time. The second is the host of implications to the business that must be understood and taken into account when arriving at this decision. Some of these are shown in Exhibit 5.9, but Exhibit 5.4 provides a more complete list.[15]

## Corporate Manufacturing Responses to Similar Markets

Different approaches are used in the same industry. Companies making similar products may choose similar processes yet manage the total manufacturing task in significantly different ways. Thus process choice, as shown in Exhibit 2.5, is only part of manufacturing's strategic response. For example, providing support for the criterion of delivery speed necessitates reducing lead times throughout the supply chain and not just in the manufacturing elements of lead time (see Exhibit 5.10). Manufacturing's contribution to achieve competitive advantage must reflect the mix of all parts of the total process.

**Exhibit 5.10** Elements of operations lead time and typical actions to reduce the length of time involved

| Steps in the supply chain | Typical activities to reduce lead times |
|---|---|
| Customer order processing | Shorten administrative procedures |
| Material lead times | Purchasing-based negotiations to reduce lead times including consignment inventory arrangements |
| Order backlog/forward load | Adjusting short-term capacity to reduce the length of the order backlog or forward load |
| Process | Decreasing lead time through a combination of:<br>■ reducing set-ups<br>■ shortening process lead times<br>■ holding inventory to move increasingly towards an assemble-to-order and make-to-stock position |
| Postprocess tasks | Reducing the overall time it takes to complete:<br>■ testing<br>■ packaging<br>■ despatch arrangements/documentation<br>■ delivery |

As explained earlier, Japanese car makers schedule their plants in accordance with sales forecasts and work on make-to-stock rather than on order-backlog, make-to-order principles. Furthermore, given little order backlog, these companies are now offering to make and deliver a car to a customer's specification in a much shorter time.

As stressed throughout, coherence between the many elements involved results in an integrated strategy. By raising the car specification a company keeps options low and thereby reduces customer choice. This in turn leads to fewer schedule adjustments. In many instances, the automobile specified may be already planned or even in stock. Similarly, reducing lead times in all parts of the process is a significant factor (see Exhibit 5.10) in helping to achieve this difference.[16] Thus recognizing the order-winners and qualifiers in relevant markets becomes the focus of activity and facilitates coherent functional support for key criteria.

# Technology Strategy

Advances in computer control have brought fresh opportunities for the United States and other Western manufacturers. The potential for innovation in manufacturing is greater now than it has ever been. Advanced manufacturing technologies (AMT) have provided a viable option to sourcing manufactured components and products from other parts of the world. There is no doubt about the potential, and applications such as robotics and complete computer-aided design are growing at up to 30 per cent per year with the result that annual sales for the entire AMT industry are about $40bn.

The approach to the use of technology and ensuring the suitability of its application creates the most concern. Tripping over engineering white elephants in the past should make companies understandably wary, not of technology improvements themselves, but of approaches that lead to sizeable investments in inappropriate technologies. However, the preoccupation with the search for panaceas may well lead companies to duplicate yesterday's mistakes. Indeed, the case for a technology strategy in itself should sound warning bells. Articles advocating technology–strategy links abound. These articles concern, for the most part, descriptions of the technologies and illustrations of specific applications and resulting improvements. But they fail to explain how to select technological investments that best support a business. Without this conceptual base, companies are unable to make assessments to draw distinctions. As a result, they have to fall back on hunches, or support the judgment of specialists, who are devotees of technological innovation and advantage, rather than business-oriented executives trying to ensure fit with the market and viewing process investment in a supportive role.

To some extent, the emerging call for companies to develop technology strategies has its roots in recent process innovations and computer applications in manufacturing. Historically, the clear link between manufacturing and the marketplace, which developed in the growth years following the Second World War, led to a well-understood manufacturing strategy that was appropriately reflected in the activities and developments within the process, production and industrial engineering functions. Not only was the status of engineering clearly reinforced but it also evolved that engineers were perceived to be the custodians of determining appropriate process and relevant elements of infrastructure investments.

This postwar role also led to, or reinforced, the low status of manufacturing management, with the attendant difficulties discussed in Chapter 2. These role characteristics in manufacturing were established in relations with other specialist functions, with similar consequences, some of which are discussed in later chapters on process positioning, infrastructure and accounting.

## Flexibility – A Strategic Cop-out?

For many businesses, past investments in dedicated processes have proved inappropriate for current markets. New investment requirements have been brought about, in part, by pressures of competition. But the response has often been to purchase new equipment with sufficient flexibility for a wide range of products and to cope with low order-quantity requirements. However, decisions that are not based on assessments of the marketplace and evaluations of alternatives are tantamount to strategic cop-outs! 'If in doubt, resolve the doubt' has become 'if in doubt, buy flexibility'.

One company, after witnessing an overall decline in volumes throughout the parent group, committed itself to the purchase of flexible processes to cope with an environment of change. An analysis of processes, product life cycles, and order-winners clearly showed that the purchase, in part, of dedicated plant would best meet these requirements. This eliminated a $0.25m investment on unnecessary flexibility. As another illustration, three companies, each manufacturing in different segments of engineering, were using expensive NC machines primarily on high-volume products. Discussions revealed failures in the companies to separate comparisons of process capability of holding tight tolerances (current versus early 1980s technology) and the business needs of the process (low cost based on high volumes).

## Technology Push versus Pull Strategies

Process investments can be used on either technology push or pull strategies. In a push strategy, the rationale for process investments comes from technology-based arguments; pull strategies reflect technology investments based on defined market needs. It is critical that companies with push strategies see arguments concerning the corporate potential to sell the spin-offs from the proposed technology invest-ments as being only *part* of the evaluation. They must also be sure to evaluate such investments on their own merits.

## Manufacturing Strategy and Technological Opportunities

Current process innovations present an important opportunity for companies to compete effectively in worldwide business.

However, committing scarce resources to investments based primarily on the perspectives of specialists or in search of a panacea to update and realign manufac-turing presents enormous and unnecessary risks. It is essential that technology alter-natives form part of manufacturing strategy developments, as discussed in this and the previous chapter. A business must link investments with a well-argued under-standing of its markets if it is to avoid inappropriate major capital expenditure.

# Conclusion

Assessing the level of mismatch between its current processes and current busi-ness, determining the adjustment it must or is able to achieve and making the appropriate choice of process for future products are difficult and critical produc-tion management tasks – difficult, in that the decision is complex; critical, in that the process investment will be substantial and changes will be expensive and time-consuming to implement.[17]

## The Nature of Markets and Manufacturing

One of the core problems facing companies is that markets are inherently dynamic and manufacturing is inherently fixed. Markets are continually changing in response to internal initiatives and external pressures, while manufacturing remains fixed in terms of the trade-offs embodied in its investments. Thus, whereas market change is an inherent outcome of time, manufacturing will not change unless a conscious decision is made and additional investment is committed. A company that fails to make these commitments will have a manufacturing function less able to support its chosen markets.

## Manufacturing's Strategic Response

Typically, companies have responded to the need to choose manufacturing processes by leaning solely on the engineering/technology dimension. But an engineering solution is not what is required. The engineering input concerns providing alternative technology options that will enable the product to be manufactured. However, the choice of process concerns how manufacturing is then completed. Such choice will involve the product/market, manufacturing investment/cost and infrastructure dimensions that have been examined in this chapter.

Engineering proscriptions, technology solutions seeking problems or the belief that panaceas are on hand have been instrumental, in part, for the uncompetitive position in which many manufacturing companies currently find themselves. Couple this with a marketing-led strategy in some business that has overreached itself or the more universal impact of incremental marketing changes that, over time, have altered business without companies recognizing the strategic consequences involved, and the result has been the erosion of large, traditional markets by overseas competitors. Other companies, persuaded by the apparent desirability of new markets or the short-term solution to get out of tough manufacturing industries, have also left the way clear in these high-volume, established markets. However, there is no long-term future in easy manufacturing tasks. The short run may appear attractive but learning and relearning how to be competitive is essential to the long-term wellbeing of companies and nations.

Successful manufacturing nations have been systematically picking off many of the existing markets of long-established industrial nations by a combined marketing/manufacturing strategy thus creating, at the expense of its competitors, a sound industrial base essential to a nation's long-term prosperity and growth. The Japanese have, in fact, built their manufacturing base on traditional smokestack industries. And, more recently emerging nations are now doing the same.

# Notes

1. One of the reasons for manufacturing's reactive role in corporate strategy was discussed earlier in Chapter 2

2. This issue is specifically addressed by T. J. Hill, R. Menda and D. M. Dilts, 'Using Product Profiling to Illustrate Manufacturing/Marketing Misalignment', *Interfaces*, 1998, **28**(4): 42–63.

3. Also sometimes called unit or one-off.

4. Companies do manufacture order quantities of one on a batch basis. In this instance, what underlies their process decision is the repeat nature of a product, not the size of an order quantity.

5. Whereas this is typically the case in Western motor vehicle plants, Japanese car makers schedule their manufacturing plants on the bases of sales forecasts and make-to-stock rather than order-backlog, make-to-order principles.

6. Many of these additional issues are illustrated and discussed in Terry Hill, *Operations Management: Strategic Context and Managerial Analysis,* Basingstoke, UK: Macmillan, 2000, Chapter 4.

7. A point examined in detail in T. J. Hill, R. Menda and D. M. Dilt's *Interfaces* article referenced in note 2 above.

8. In reality, some customization may be offered but the substance of this equipment is standard.

9. More advanced NC systems were introduced in the late l960s in the form of computer numerical control (CNC), which replaced the hard-wired control unit of the NC system with a stored programme using a dedicated minicomputer. Hence, the memory storage rather than paper-tape input makes the process more reliable and more flexible in programme changes. Direct numerical control (DNC) systems consist of a number of NC and/or CNC machines connected to a centralized computer. The centralized source of information provided by DNC helps in the control of manufacturing. Flexible manufacturing systems (FMS) combine the DNC principle together with the other features described in a later section.

10. See note 9.

11. P. R. Haas, 'Flexible Manufacturing Systems – A Solution for the Mid-Volume, Mid-Variety Parts Manufacture', 2SME Technical Conference, Detroit, April 1973, and J. J. Hughes *et al.*, 'Flexible Manufacturing Systems for Improved Mid-Volume Productivity', *Proceedings of the Third Annual AIEE Systems Engineering Conference*, November 1975.

12. A fuller explanation is given in Terry Hill, *Operations Management: Strategic Context And Managerial Analysis*, Basingstoke, UK: Macmillan, 2000, Chapters 4 and 5. Also refer to G. A. B. Edwards, *Readings in Group Technology*, Machinery Publishing Company, 1971, and J. L. Burbidge, *The Introduction of Group Technology*, Portsmouth, NH: Heinemann Educational Books, 1975.

13. Ibid.

14. NC refers to the operation of machine tools from numerical data stored on paper or magnetic tape, punched cards, computer storage or direct information. The development of machining centres results from the concepts of NC. In a machining centre, a range of operations is provided using a carousel with up to 200 tools or more (that is, embodied in the centre) from which the programme will select as required, with some taking place simultaneously as necessary. Consequently, a machining centre is not only able to cope with a wide range of product requirements, it can also be scheduled to complete one-offs in any sequence desired. More advanced NC systems include computer numerical control (CNC) systems using a dedicated minicomputer to perform NC functions and direct numerical control (DNC), which refers to a system having a computer controlling more than one machine tool. A DNC system includes both the hardware and software required to drive more than one NC machine simultaneously. To do this, DNC uses a computer, which may be a minicomputer,

several minicomputers linked together, a minicomputer linked to a large computer, or a large computer on its own.

15. See note 6.

16. The lead time taken by typical US car makers from receipt of a dealer's order to the start of the manufacturing process is three times longer than the time taken by Toyota.

17. This issue is further highlighted in the pharmaceutical industry where the gamble on plant investment not only concerns the potential level of demand but also whether a drug will be accepted by relevant drug authorities and which formulae will eventually be best received in the market. See V. Griffiths, 'No Cure for Risk', *Financial Times*, 7 April 1994, p. 13.

## Further Reading

Blois, K. J. 'Market Concentration – Challenge to Corporate Planning', *Long Range Planning,* 1980, **13**: 56–62.

Bolwijn, P. T., Boorsma, J., van Breukelen, Q. H., Brinkman, S. and Kumpe, T. *Flexible Manufacturing; Integrating Technical and Social Innovations,* Amsterdam: Elsevier Science Publishers BV, 1986.

Burbridge, J. L. 'The Simplification of Material Flow Systems', *International Journal of Production Research*, 1980, **20**: 339–47.

Dale, R. G., Burbridge, J. L. and and Cottam, M. J. 'Planning the Introduction of Group Technology', *International Journal of Operations and Production Management*, **4**: 34–7.

Zelenovie, D. M.'Flexibility – A Condition for Effective Production Systems', *International Journal of Production Research*, 1980, **20**(3): 319–37.

# 6 Product Profiling

A company needs to have a comprehensive understanding of how well manufacturing can support its business as alternative processes are chosen. The size of and timescales involved in these process investments create issues that must be addressed in the corporate strategy debate. Chapter 5 discussed the implications of process choice, provided insights and, consequently, outlined some of the blocks on which to build manufacturing's strategic dimensions. Assessing how well existing processes fit an organization's current market requirements and making appropriate choices of process to meet future needs are critical manufacturing responsibilities, owing to the high investment associated with the outcomes of these decisions.

When companies buy processes, however, they often fail to appreciate the business trade-offs embodied in those investments (see Exhibit 5.2). Product profiling enables a company to test the current or anticipated level of fit between the characteristics of its market(s) and the characteristics of its existing or proposed processes and infrastructure investments – the components of manufacturing strategy – see Exhibit 2.5. The purpose of this assessment is twofold. First, it provides a way to evaluate and, where necessary, improve the fit between the way in which a company wins orders in its markets and manufacturing's ability to support these criteria (that is, manufacturing's strategic response). Second, it helps a company move away from classic strategy building characterized by functional perspectives separately agreed, without adequate attempts to test the fit or reconcile different opinions of what is best for the business as a whole (as illustrated in Exhibits 2.1 and 2.2).

In many instances though, companies will be unable or unwilling to take the necessary steps to provide the degree of fit desired because of the level of investment, executive energy and timescales involved. However, sound strategy is not a case of having every facet correctly in place. It concerns improving the level of consciousness a company brings to bear on its corporate decisions. Living with existing mismatches or allowing the level of fit to deteriorate can be strategically sound if a company is aware of its position and makes these choices knowingly. Reality can constrain strategic decisions. In such circumstances, product profiling will help increase corporate awareness and allow a conscious choice between alternatives. In the past, many companies have not aspired to this level of strategic alertness.

## The Need to Expand Manufacturing Strategy's Language Base

Manufacturing has had difficulty expressing important perspectives in a manner that provides for corporate insight and discussion. Unless it can do this, other business functions will find difficulty in embracing the issues on hand and, in turn, being party to their resolution. Intuition, experience and gut-feeling must give way to business-related concepts and explanations. This is not to imply that the former are of little value. On the contrary, they form an integral part of sound management practice. However, at the strategic level they need to be explained in a way that other executives can understand, so allowing them to become part of the ongoing corporate debate and strategic outcomes. In fact one of the key tests for the usefulness of management theory is whether or not it crystalizes the intuitive insights of experienced executives. In this way it contributes to the essential intellectual nature of the management debate – intellectual not in the sense of theory but reflecting the complex and applied nature of the management task.

Each business will require its own approach and resolution. The examples described in the following sections met the specific needs of those businesses to which they relate. They should not be considered universally applicable. The conceptual base on which these analyses rest, however, can be transferred to other corporate scenarios and used to prepare similar analyses that will yield their own profiles.

## Product Profiling

Inconsistency between the market and the capability of the manufacturing process to support the business specification of its products can be induced by changes in the market or process investment decisions or a combination of both. In all instances, the mismatch results from the fact that while manufacturing investments are inherently large and fixed (once a company has purchased them, it will have to live with them for better or for worse for many years) markets are inherently dynamic. In addition, corporate marketing decisions can often be relatively transient should a business so decide. The inherently changing nature of markets and a company's ability to alter marketing perspectives to allow for change and repositioning are in opposition to manufacturing decisions that bind a business for years ahead. A company must reconcile this, which requires strategic awareness, recognition and action.

Product profiling is a way to ascertain the level of fit between the choices of process and infrastructure investment that have been or are proposed to be made and the order-winners and qualifiers of the product(s) or customers under review. The sections that follow describe situations and, to some extent, different dimensions of the same problem.

## Levels of Application

Product profiling can be undertaken at either the level of the company or level of a process. Company-based applications provide an overview of the degree of fit between all or significant parts of a business and existing manufacturing facilities or its proposed manufacturing investments and developments. Process-based applications provide a check of the fit between the products that the equipment under review is to provide.

## Procedure

The procedure used in product profiling is outlined below. This details the basic steps to follow but the essential direction of the analysis needs to reflect the match/mismatch issues within the whole or parts of a business. Remember, the purpose of profiling is to draw a picture to help identify the current or potential problem, hence allowing discussion of and agreement on what steps should be taken to improve a company's strategic position.

1. Select relevant aspects of products/markets, manufacturing, investment/cost and infrastructure as outlined in Exhibit 5.4. This choice must meet two over-riding requirements:

   ■ The criteria selected must relate to the issues on hand and reflect the strategic dimensions of relevant markets. Thus dimensions other than those given in Exhibit 5.4 will often be selected, as the examples that follow illustrate.

   ■ The number of criteria selected must be kept small enough to allow the picture illustrating the issues to show through. Choosing too large a list will blur the essential clarity required and detract from the facilitating role that this approach plays within strategic discussion and formulation.

2. Display the trade-offs of process choice that would be typical for each criterion chosen in 1 above. This provides the backdrop against which the product(s) or customer(s) can be profiled.

3. The purpose of profiling is to provide comparison. The next step then is to profile the products, product groups, customers or companies involved. This is done by positioning the selected product(s), group(s) of products or companies on each criterion selected. Remember, this is a comparative technique; therefore you are looking to show the relationship of one product or customer to another, to compare a company today with what it was (or would be) in a selected earlier (or later) period or to review one business with another. The purpose is to test the correlation between market requirements and manufacturing's current or proposed response to their provision. Thus the profiling (the position on each

chosen dimension where what is being reviewed is placed) is to display a comparative picture and not become an issue or concern of exactness.

4. The resulting profile illustrates the degree of consistency between the characteristics of the market(s) and the relative position of the processes and infrastructure within manufacturing. The more consistency that exits, the straighter the profile will be. Inconsistencies between the market and manufacturing's inherent ability to meet these needs will result in a dogleg-shaped profile.

Remember throughout that the purpose of a profile is to display the issues relevant to a business and enable a company to review the degree of alignment that exists. This pictorial representation of those dimensions relevant to a business allows the executives responsible for strategic decisions to recognize the issues, their origins and the corrective action to take.

The examples that follow illustrate the points above and afford the opportunity to discuss particular applications.

## Company-based Profiles

### Inducing Mismatch with Process Investments

As emphasized in the last chapter, all process choices include fixed business trade-offs that can be changed only by further investment or development. Thus, a company's investment in a process embodying trade-offs inconsistent with part or all of its markets induces mismatches between process and market unless the company changes its markets. The degree of mismatch would correspond to the relative size and importance of the process(es) involved and the associated level of reinvestment.

A company producing a range of cartons, for example, decided to invest $6m in part of its processes. These processes were core to a range of its products that accounted for about 30 per cent of total sales revenue. Based on the current level of activity, the investment would have been payed back in 5.5 years. However, to meet the parent group's return-on-investment, four-year norms, the company needed to increase the output of these products by about 50 per cent.

For some time, the company's marketing strategy had been to position itself in the higher-quality end of all its markets. However, to gain the larger volumes necessary to justify this process investment, the company had to go for business won on price. Soon the company had almost 15 per cent of its total business with distinct low-cost needs, while having to meet the schedule-change needs of a further 30 per cent of sales. The consequences were significant and the ramifications substantial. Within a short space of time, the process investment had introduced manufacturing conflict in a large part of its total business.

**Exhibit 6.1**   A product profile illustrating mismatch between the market and manufacturing induced by process investment

| Some relevant aspects | | Typical characteristics of process choice | | |
|---|---|---|---|---|
| | | jobbing | batch | line |
| Products and markets | Product range | wide | | narrow |
| | Customer order size | small | | large |
| | Level of schedule changes required | high | | low |
| | Order-winners | delivery speed/ unique capability | | price |
| Manufacturing | Process — technology | general-purpose | | dedicated |
| | Process — flexibility | high | | low |
| | Production volumes | low | | high |
| | Key manufacturing task | response to specification and lead-time change | | low-cost manufacturing |

● ◑  Position of existing products on each of the chosen dimensions and resulting profile ─────────

○ ◑  Position of new products on each of the chosen dimensions and resulting profile ‐ ‐ ‐ ‐ ‐ ‐ ‐ ‐

Product profiling can draw attention to the sort of mismatches involved here, by graphically representing key marketing and manufacturing differences that the single set of processes had to accommodate (see Exhibit 6.1).

In the example given above, the $6m process investment was, in terms of its point on the jobbing-batch-line continuum in Exhibit 6.1, consistent with its existing processes and chosen to support its existing business. However, the additional price-sensitive business required different process and infrastructure support. The straight line and dogleg relationships in the figure reflect this.

## Applying the Same Manufacturing Strategy to Two Different Markets

The last example concerned the impact of a process investment on the fit between a company's market and its manufacturing capability. Without a well-developed manufacturing strategy, the company was unconsciously driven by other functional (in this instance, financial) norms and arguments into an inappropriate major investment. Failure to recognize that investment decisions need to be based on strategy, and not functional perspectives and prerequisites, is a common contributor to poor corporate performance.

However an equally important source of inappropriate investment decisions is the assumption that to meet different corporate requirements a similar manufacturing strategy approach can be applied. Typically, this happens where specialists' views form the basis of initiatives, rather than a manufacturing strategy formulated to the requirements of individual markets. Again, product profiling can provide a graphic description of the resulting mismatch and help explain these differences.

Faced with a decline in markets and profits, a company undertook a major internal review of its two manufacturing plants. To provide orientation for its business, it decided to manufacture different products at each of its two sites; each plant then manufactured distinct products and associated volumes. Four or five years later, the number of product types handled by Plant B was eight times as many as Plant A, and, as one would expect, product volume changes were reflected in this

**Exhibit 6.2**    A product profile illustrating the level of match and mismatch between two plants and their respective markets induced by applying the same manufacturing strategy to both plants

| Some relevant aspects for this company | | | Typical characteristics of process choice | | |
|---|---|---|---|---|---|
| | | | jobbing | batch | line |
| Products and markets | Product | type | special | | standard |
| | | range | wide | | narrow |
| | Customer order size | | small | | large |
| | Level of product change required | | high | | low |
| | Rate of new product introductions | | high | | low |
| | Order-winner | | delivery speed/ unique capability | | price |
| Manufacturing | Process | technology | general-purpose | | dedicated |
| | | flexibility | high | | low |
| | Production volumes | | low | | high |
| | Key manufacturing task | | response to specification and lead-time changes | | low-cost manufacturing |
| Investment | Level of capital investment | | low | | high |

○ ◖ Position of Plant A on each of the chosen dimensions and the resulting profile ———

● ◖ Position of Plant B on each of the chosen dimensions and the resulting profile - - - - - -

This figure reflects the consistency of products and process for Plant A, and the inconsistencies for Plant B reflected by a straight line and dogleg shape, respectively.

decision. While in Plant A, average volumes for individual products rose by 60 per cent, in Plant B they decreased by 40 per cent. In addition, to redress the decline in profits, the company also embarked on major manufacturing investments at each plant, involving identical process investments and infrastructure changes. Exhibit 6.2 illustrates how these changes fitted Plant A's markets, while they led to a significant mismatch for Plant B.

The procedure followed is similar to the one outlined in the previous section. Again, the first step is to describe, in conceptual terms, the characteristics of product/markets, manufacturing, investment/cost and infrastructure features pertinent to the business. The dimensions selected for these two plants are detailed in Exhibit 6.2. First, the characteristics that reflect the change between jobbing, batch and line need to be described. Thus, the product range associated with jobbing is wide and becomes increasingly narrow as it moves through to line, whereas customer order size is small in jobbing and becomes increasingly larger as it moves through to line and so on. These dimensions represent the classic characteristics of the trade-offs embodied in process choice. Plant A's profile shows a straight-line relationship between the products and markets and the manufacturing and infrastructure provision. However, Plant B's profile shows a dogleg shape due to the difference in markets compared to the similar process and infrastructure investments made in each of the two plants.

Based on Exhibit 6.2, Exhibit 6.3 provides a further illustration and additional insights into the extent of the mismatch brought about by applying the same manufacturing strategy to Plants A and B described here. Whereas Plant A had appropriate

**Exhibit 6.3** The level of inconsistency on all points of the dimensions on the vertical axis

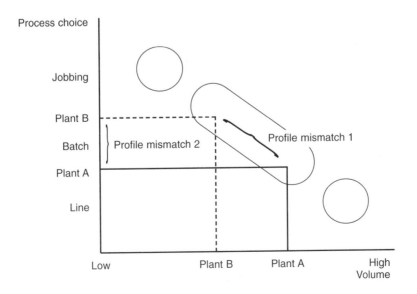

process investments in line with its product volumes, Plant B did not (referred to as 'Profile mismatch 1' on Exhibit 6.3). As a consequence, whereas Plant A was appropriately positioned on each dimension on the vertical axis (see Exhibits 6.2 and 6.3), again Plant B was not (referred to as 'Profile mismatch 2' on Exhibit 6.3).

## *Incremental Marketing Decisions Resulting in a Mismatch*

For many companies, changes in market requirements happen over time, and these incremental changes are more typically the source of mismatches in a business. Product profiling provides an important way of describing these changes and their overall impact on a company.

As highlighted earlier, while markets are inherently dynamic, manufacturing is inherently fixed. This is not, however, a result of attitudes or preferences – markets will simply change over time whether or not a company so desires, whereas the manufacturing investments will stay as they are unless deliberately changed by development or further investment.

Product profiling is a way of mapping the fit between the requirements of current markets and the characteristics of existing processes. The key to identifying these differences lies in the recognition that while the needs of the market may have changed, the characteristics of the manufacturing process and infrastrucure investments will not. These, as emphasized in Chapter 5, will remain fixed, unless there is further, appropriate investment.

To illustrate, let us consider a European-based business finding itself under pressure from its US parent company to grow sales and profits. Its response was to adopt a marketing strategy to broaden its product range. Process investments had already been updated and there was excess capacity over and above current sales levels. Supporting the required sales growth would consequently not incur significant investments. As the strategy developed, the product range widened, while the customer order size decreased and the number of production schedule changes increased. Now, several years into their marketing strategy, the company is experiencing problems in terms of manufacturing's ability to support current markets and provide profit at required levels. To explain the causes of this problem it is necessary to compare the current year with the year in which the manufacturing process and infrastructure investments were made. This is because when a company invests in processes or infrastructure, it does so to reflect the characteristics of its markets as perceived at that time. As shown in Exhibit 6.4, at the time prior to the marketing strategy change, there is a match between the characteristics of the company's products and markets, manufacturing and infrastructure. The incremental marketing changes in the ensuing period had the cumulative effect of moving the company's position to the left on several, relevant product/market dimensions. The implications for manufacturing of the incremental marketing changes in these years are revealed when drawing the equivalent profile for the current year. Again, the profile mismatch illustrates that manufacturing had become increasingly less able to support the changing marketing trends, which the dogleg profile illustrates (see Figure 6.4).

**Exhibit 6.4** A product profile of a company's mainstream products to illustrate the impact of incremental marketing decisions

| Some relevant aspects for this company | | | Typical characteristics of process choice | | |
|---|---|---|---|---|---|
| | | | jobbing | batch | line |
| Products and markets | Product range | | wide | | narrow |
| | Order size | | small | | large |
| | Frequency of changes | product | high | | low |
| | | schedule | high | | low |
| | Order-winners | | delivery speed/ unique capability | | price |
| Manufacturing | Process technology | | general-purpose | | dedicated |
| | Production volumes | | low | | high |
| | Ability to cope with change | product | easy | | difficult |
| | | schedule | easy | | difficult |
| | Set-ups | number | many | | few |
| | | expense | inexpensive | | expensive |
| Infrastructure | Engineering orientation | | product introductions | | process improvements |

○ ◑ Company's original position on each of the chosen aspects and the resulting profile ————————

● ◑ Company's current position on each of the chosen aspects and the resulting profile ------------

The current year profile illustrates the dogleg shape, which reflects the inconsistencies between the high-volume batch processes and infrastructure purchased in the past, and the current market position.

## Reallocation of Products Due to Downsizing

Companies faced with a reduction in overall demand often decide to downsize total manufacturing capacity as a way of meeting future profit expectations. This decision involves the reallocation of products from one plant to another, thereby enabling one plant to downsize or close while improving current machine utilization in the other. Debates of this kind are based on two checks:

- A technical specification fit between the products to be made and the processes available.
- The financial implications of the different decisions.

Often, however, companies fail to check whether the business specifications of the products to be transferred match the processes. There were many illustrations of this source of mismatch in the 1990s. The resulting profile is similar to that in Exhibit 6.4 but is due to stepped rather than incremental changes. It results from the failure to recognize that different units of capacity, although meeting similar technical specifications, do not have the same business specifications (see Exhibit 5.2).

## Internal Sourcing Decisions Based on Unit Costs

Often within a group of companies the same product will be manufactured in two or more locations. Executives with profit responsibility for a region will understandably look to sourcing costs as a major factor in profit performance. Where two or more plants make the same product, differences in unit price will attract some sister companies within the group to place their business with the least-cost company. In the mid-1990s, a North American multinational was under pressure to maintain its record of profit performance; the various parts of the business were required to match or even improve their own performance. The result was that executives switched their internal source of products on the basis of lowest cost as an important way of maintaining or improving their own individual profit performance. Within a short time, however, the least-cost plant found that it could no longer maintain its previous cost levels. Attracting volumes of differing (often low) levels and required to meet different market needs led to this 'best' plant grossly underperforming. A product profile showed why, with reasons similar to those described in the last two examples, although with different origins.

## Process-based Profiles

Company-based profiles help reflect changes at the corporate level and identify the varying degrees of match or mismatch that exist or will exist if market needs and characteristics are not reflected in manufacturing. Process-based profiles provide similar insights but concern the review of a single process (or group of similar processes) in relation to the products produced on it (them). There can be more than one processed-based profile completed within a single plant.

A prime reason why mismatches develop is that as demand for a product(s) changes, capacity is released. The typical result is that companies will allocate other products to that process on the basis of a technical specification check but not a business specification check. These may be either derivations of products already made in that process or new products. In both instances the product range widens, overall individual order quantities decrease and the process stops and starts more often.

The outcome is that the process will increasingly be required to support the business specification of two or more products that have order-winners or other market characteristics different from one another. Profiles based on a format similar to those given earlier will help explain this to a business so that decisions are changed or expectations realigned.

A US-based pharmaceutical company located the manufacture of a major new product in its Kansas City plant. The initial sales of this product justified forecasts, and following this initial success the company introduced product variants to maximize total sales revenue. These variants took the form of dosage, package size and labels/leaflets in several languages. Sales continued to grow, and the company purchased further packaging equipment, similar to the existing processes, to meet increased capacity requirements. Variants continued and so did total sales. Although not competing on price (brand name and product patents were important factors for these products in winning orders), margins deteriorated. Furthermore, as competing products entered the market and price levels were revised, overall profit levels fell short of expectations.

The profile in Exhibit 6.5 helps explain why. A mismatch between marketing and manufacturing resulted from engineering and manufacturing's orientation shifting away from exploiting the potential cost advantages associated with volumes towards that of product introductions necessitated by the variations strategy. The process investment and manufacturing orientation were misaligned with the needs of the market and the profit potential associated with reducing costs. Consequently profit margins were short of the level necessary to support the high R&D expenditure essential to secure future growth and market penetration in pharmaceutical markets.

## Using Product Profiling

The examples given in the previous sections illustrate the role product profiling may play in helping a company to check its existing product and process choice relationship and allow, where relevant, comparisons to be made between similar applications or to measure trends over time. However the reviews given were based on hindsight, not on the forward-looking characteristics of strategy. When a company is able to illustrate current positions and future alternatives, it can discuss alternatives and determine which strategic direction best meets the needs of the business. In this role, product profiling helps companies determine the business perspectives of manufacturing.

However, companies that are, for whatever reason, experiencing a mismatch between their current market needs and existing manufacturing processes and infrastructure face a number of choices. These are:

1. Live with the mismatch.
2. Redress the profile mismatch by altering the marketing strategy.

**Exhibit 6.5**　　A profile of the product variants packed on a number of similar packaging lines

| Some relevant aspects | | | Typical characteristics of process choice | | |
|---|---|---|---|---|---|
| | | | jobbing | batch | line |
| Products and markets | Product range | | wide | | narrow |
| | Frequency of changes | product | high | | low |
| | | schedule | high | | low |
| | Order-winners | | delivery speed/unique capability | | price |
| Manufacturing | Process technology | | general-purpose | | dedicated |
| | Production volumes | | low | | high |
| | Ability to cope with change | product | high | | low |
| | | schedule | high | | low |
| | Set-ups | number | high | | low |
| | | expense | low | | high |
| Infrastructure | Engineering-orientation | | product introductions | | process improvements |
| | Manufacturing management's key task | | product interpretation and meeting deadlines | | low cost, increased efficiency |

○ ◖　Initial position on each of the chosen aspects and resulting profile ————————

● ◖　Current position on each of the chosen aspects and resulting profile -------------

3. Redress the profile mismatch by investing in and changing manufacturing and its infrastructure.
4. A combination of 2 and 3.

Alternative 1 affords companies the opportunity consciously to make a decision on the trade-offs involved. This may be the correct strategic choice. It does bring a company's expectations more in line with reality, makes it aware of the real costs of being in different markets, changes the measures of performance by distinguishing between those based on business-related decisions and those based on functional achievement and raises the level of corporate consciousness about the overall consequences of maintaining product profile *status quo* or the decision to improve or widen any *mismatch* that may exist. Furthermore, future decisions concerning new products are now more able to incorporate these essential perspectives; such decisions reconcile the diverse functional perspectives under the mantle of what is best for the business overall.

Alternatives 2 and 3 concern ways of straightening existing mismatches or consciously avoiding the widening of existing or creating of new ones. These decisions may be taken independently or in unison. Alternative 2 involves influencing corporate policy through changes or modifications to existing or proposed marketing strategies. In this way, the implications of marketing decisions for manufacturing are addressed and included as an integral part of the corporate strategy debate. Thus, manufacturing is able to move from the reactive stance it currently takes to a proactive mode, so essential to sound policy decisions.

Alternative 3 involves a company's decision to invest in the processes and infrastructure of its business, either to enable manufacturing to become more effective in its provision of the order-winners/qualifiers and support in the marketplace for existing products or to establish the required level of support for future products. Like Alternative 2, it enables manufacturing to switch from a reactive to a proactive response to corporate marketing decisions. Thus, by receiving pertinent inputs at the strategic level, the business becomes more aware of the implications involved and is able to arrive at strategic options based on the relevant and comprehensive inputs necessary to make sound judgments at the strategic level.

# Conclusion

The reasons companies fail to incorporate the manufacturing perspectives into the strategy debate are many. For one, manufacturing is traditionally presented as a technical- or engineering-related function. This not only creates barriers to discussion, it also misrepresents the key perspectives a company needs to address. A major thrust within manufacturing strategy is to reorient its contribution from a technical/engineering to a business perspective. This not only opens the debate by providing meaningful insights, it also introduces those manufacturing perspectives that can contribute to the success of a business. In this way, it helps create the link with other functions by using the common denominator of the market to create interest in and highlight the relevance to other functions. The results are business-based discussions leading to essential strategic outcomes.

Product profiling is one such development. By translating process investments into business issues, companies are able to assess the fit between these major resources and the markets they are required to support. In addition, being able to explain trends, mismatches and options in picture form enhances the power of the message and increases its role in corporate understanding and debate. It leads to sound strategy developments by enabling functions to explain themselves in corporate terms and provides a language to enhance essential discussion and agreement.

# 7 Focused Manufacturing – Principles and Concepts

Manufacturing is inherently a complex task and managing this complexity is a key corporate role. The complexity involved, however, does not emanate from the nature of the individual tasks that the job comprises. In all but highly technical, special product market segments, it is not difficult to cope with the technology of the product or process. In most situations, the process technology and wherewithal to make the product involved have been purchased from outside, with appropriate engineering and technical know-how provided inside to support the manufacturing requirement and underpin any necessary development. In a similar way, product design and the associated technology falls under the auspices of the customer and/or design function. Hence, neither process nor product technologies are generally difficult to understand or manage from the viewpoint of the manufacturing function.

The complexity in manufacturing stems from the number of aspects and issues involved in the task, the interrelated nature of these and the level of fit between the manufacturing strategy task and the internal process capability and infrastructure.

In all instances, the level of complexity is derived largely from, or can be controlled by, the corporate strategy decisions made within the business itself. However, whereas past research has identified the number and interrelated nature of the tasks and issues involved as being a fundamental characteristic of complexity (the small-is-beautiful syndrome[1]), the fit between the manufacturing strategy task, the internal process capability and infrastructure has only recently received close attention. These latter issues come under the heading of 'focused manufacturing'.

## Focused Manufacturing

Focused manufacturing concerns linking an organization's manufacturing facilities to the appropriate competitive factors of its business(es), with the aim of enabling that company to gain greater control of its competitive position. One of the most difficult tasks in managing manufacturing is responding to the different market demands made on the production facilities. This is due to the wide and often diverse nature of these demands and the level of complexity generated in the corresponding parts of the manufacturing function, including suppliers. Many companies are now finding that focusing the demands to which individual facilities must respond can markedly reduce the level of complexity involved in managing those operations and results in an improved overall performance.

When explaining focus, the words *narrow* or *narrowing* are often used. For example, Skinner, who was the first to expound the benefits of focused plants, argues that 'a factory that focuses on a narrow product mix for a particular market niche will outperform the conventional plant, which attempts a broader mission'.[2] However, taken at face value, this argument can be misleading. Many companies do not have the 'narrow product mix' alternative referred to here. The issue of focus, therefore, is more accurately explained in Skinner's fuller definitions, which formed part of his fourfold view for effecting basic changes in the management of manufacturing. Two of these were:

> Learning to focus each plant on a limited, concise, manageable set of products, technologies, volumes, and markets.

> Learning to structure basic manufacturing policies and supporting services so that they focus on one explicit manufacturing task, instead of on many inconsistent, conflicting, implicit tasks.[3]

The emphasis here is on a limited and consistent set of tasks, which will often be far from the layman's definition of narrow. So, to avoid confusion and the implication of a simplistic resolution of the infinitely complex reality of business, the dimension of narrow should be omitted. It is the homogeneity of tasks and the repetition and experience involved in completing these that form the basis of focused manufacturing. Thus, focusing the demands placed on manufacturing will enable resources, efforts and attention to be concentrated on a defined and homogeneous set of activities, allowing management to prioritize the key tasks necessary to achieve a better performance. In most plants, however, a meaningful level of plant focus is rarely understood, let alone achieved. There are several factors that have contributed to this position over the past 15 to 20 years.

## Principle of Economies of Scale in Markets Characterized by Difference

For many years it has been (and still is) argued that the principle of economies of scale is a sound and appropriate way of organizing and managing businesses. As an underlying approach, it is highly attractive. However, for most organizations today this approach no longer works well. The advantages that can accrue from applying economies of scale are no longer being realized because the markets and the necessary corporate response to and support for them have changed. While markets in the past were characterized by similarity, today's markets are characterized by difference.

Economies of scale are most appropriate for and best applied to high-volume, steady-state markets (that is, where similarity is the hallmark). However, for most companies these conditions no longer reflect the nature of their businesses. For many, these prerequisites are far from their own realities. In fact, if anything, the opposite applies. Their markets are low volume and dynamic in nature (that is, where difference is the hallmark). The key reasons why the conditions have changed are now discussed.

## Marketing

Marketing-led strategies are invariably based on principles of growth through extending the product range. Invariably, new products (even those requiring new technologies) are manufactured, partly at least, on existing processes, and almost always within the same infrastructure. The logic for this is based on the principle of the economies derived from using existing plant capacity where possible and being supported by the existing overhead structure. Over time, the incremental nature of these marketing changes will invariably alter the manufacturing task. The result is complexity, confusion and worst of all a production organization that, because it is spun out in all directions by a kind of centrifugal force, lacks focus and a doable manufacturing task.[4]

When asked to provide the different order-winners for a range of products, a factory must make a series of compromises.

## Increases in Plant Size

Faced with a shortage of capacity, companies find the attractions of on-site expansion irresistible. The tangible arguments of cost and overhead advantages, plus the provision of a better hedge against future uncertainty, provide the basis against which companies measure the alternatives. They rarely take into account the costs of the associated uplift in complexity and the bureaucracy that develops as factories try to cope. These changes are further hidden or disguised by their piecemeal or incremental nature. Schmenner concludes that:

> Big plants usually have formidable bureaucratic structures. Relationships inevitably become formal, and the worker is separated from the top executives by many layers of management. All too often, managers are shuffling the paperwork that formal systems have spawned... Although there has to be some formality in plant operations, too much can wipe out the many informal procedures that keep plants nimble and able to adapt to change.[5]

## Manufacturing

To aggravate the situation of compromise described in the last section, manufacturing in these circumstances will rarely have a definition of its task. It will be required to perform on every yardstick, with these often changing from one day to the next, depending on the pressures from within and outside the business. The result is that manufacturing, without an agreed strategy, will respond as best it can, independently deciding on the best corporate compromises or trade-offs involved. Invariably the result is reduced plant performance.

## Plant Utilization

Embodied in these scale principles is the argument concerning improving the utilization of plant and equipment. As capacity is released due to a fall off in demand for a product(s), companies typically reutilize the spare capacity by introducing new products. In most companies, the justification for purchasing new processes or equipment will usually be based partly on total volumes. Companies, by planning to use existing process capacity to complete some or all of the operations for new products, will more easily meet this investment hurdle. However, when evaluating the suitability of processes for a product, companies invariably only check that technical specifications are met. They rarely check the consistency of the business requirement (that is, manufacturing task) for each of the new products involved. Furthermore, this check is necessary not just for current requirements; it must be made over time as products go through their life cycles and relevant order-winners change correspondingly.

## Specialists as the Basis for Controlling a Business

Management perceives the use of specialists as the appropriate way to control a business. 'These professionals, quite naturally, seek to maximize their contributions and justify their positions. They have conventional views of success in each of their particular fields. Of course, these objectives are generally in conflict.'[6] Furthermore, the essential link between the activities of specialists and the major functions of a business requires close cooperation and understanding. Too often, that is not present. The failure of companies clearly to define the focus of their business exacerbates this problem. Without this direction, there is insufficient shared understanding of what is required. Thus, support systems, controls, information provision and other features of infrastructure are not developed in line with the appropriate and agreed corporate needs. Trade-offs are not made, therefore, against the shared understanding of the business. They are assessed on the fragmented and uncoordinated views and advice of specialists and based on what seems best at the time, rather than on an agreed strategic appreciation of competitive performance.

## Looking for Panaceas

Emanating somewhat from the last point is the approach by many businesses to seek resolution to problems through panaceas. The search for which of the many

**Exhibit 7.1**　　In pursuit of a panacea – which three-letter acronym next?

*Source*: Operations Institute, Johnson & Johnson with permission.

three-letter acronyms is the key to success has become the strategic pastime of many firms (see Exhibit 7.1). Most companies can recall their own redundant solutions. The latest example of a long line in manufacturing is exhorting businesses to adopt the best of the Japanese system as a matter of course rather than one effective way of meeting a defined need. Although in themselves such developments can contribute substantially to business success, they need to be derived from strategic discussion and in line with appropriate and agreed direction.

There are two prerequisites to achieving this potential, both of which successful Japanese companies have met. First, developments in manufacturing, as well as other functions, need to fit the market needs of a business. Japanese companies undertook developments in response to requirements placed on their manufacturing functions to improve given activities recognized as critical to the overall success of the business. The result was just-in-time (JIT), total quality management (TQM) and other concepts and approaches.

The second prerequisite concerns time. To undertake, develop and fit major initiatives into existing structures requires adequate time. After all, it took those Japanese companies some 30 years to perfect their ideas and to adapt these approaches carefully to the needs of their business. Characteristically, Western companies expect and even demand their implementation and successful adoption to be achieved overnight. The rushed nature of this approach results in inappropriate applications and unrealistic expectations.

The panacea approach will at best only distract management from the essential resolution of its strategic direction; at worst it will imply that there is no longer any need to be concerned – all is in hand.

# Trade-offs in Focused Manufacturing

The choice of focused manufacturing implies trade-offs. In arriving at this decision, companies must distinguish between the gains associated with size reduction and manageable units and those that accrue from the approach adopted towards achieving focused manufacturing. A reduction in size may well go hand in hand with the decision to focus; however companies must differentiate the advantages resulting from any decision to reduce size and those unique to each choice.

## Downsizing versus Focused Plants

It is important to separate the concepts of downsizing (that is, reducing the size of plants) and focusing. Focusing manufacturing businesses will lead invariably to reduction in plant sizes. There are, however, advantages and disadvantages to these reductions. Smaller plants will bring such advantages as the potential for improved communication, greater orientation towards a well-understood and agreed set of business objectives, simpler and more appropriate forms of control and managerial style, higher levels of employee participation and motivation, shorter process lead times, lower work-in-progress inventory, reduced complexity of the production-control and scheduling task and a more accurate assessment of financial performance. On the other hand, smaller plants run contrary to the concept of economies of scale and may well lead to the need to increase or duplicate certain processes or parts of the infrastructure such as procedures and specialist capabilities.

Since these advantages and disadvantages result directly from the change in size itself, companies must base their choice of approach on the characteristics of each alternative. There are three approaches to focusing facilities. The characteristics of each are listed in Exhibit 7.2 and summarized below.

# Alternative Approaches to Focused Manufacturing

There are three alternative approaches to focused manufacturing:

### Based on Products/Markets

This orients relevant parts of the manufacturing facilities towards a particular customer or generic group of products, a basis for focus that reflects the breakdown of actual or forecast sales typically used by companies. Typifying a market perspective, such a focus often mirrors this function's view of the business.

### Based on Processes

This groups together products that are made with similar processes. The principal rationale is to gain advantages such as concentrated expertise and improved utilization of manufacturing processes. It accomplishes this by identifying like products on the basis of their process requirements.

Companies that make repeat or standard products with insufficient volume to go to line (a common situation) will choose batch as the appropriate process. This enables spare capacity to be utilized and reutilized by any product requiring an operation(s) to be completed by the process in question. The approach to focus described here is based on a similar rationale. Products needing the same process will go into the same manufacturing unit, thereby avoiding the potential duplication of investment. However, when plants are broken down into two or more focused units, no matter what the basis for achieving this, the process capacities allocated to the smaller units will never be utilized as fully as they are when using a batch process. The latter arranges processes on a functional basis (that is, all equipment providing similar technical capabilities to be put into the same geographical area and managed as a whole unit). This arrangement facilitated the utilization and reutilization of process capability.

Breaking plants down on the basis of processes enables a company to minimize plant duplication, as shown in Exhibit 7.2. This principle is known as group technology, which was identified as a hybrid process in Chapter 5.

### Based on Manufacturing's Strategic Task

This approach allocates products to a particular unit on the basis of different order-winners and qualifiers that manufacturing needs to provide – the strategic task of manufacturing. By focusing parts of a manufacturing unit, this approach creates conditions where the task (that is, what manufacturing has to do well to support particular order-winners and qualifiers) is consistent. Often this orientation is paral-

**Exhibit 7.2**   Characteristics of alternative approaches to focusing facilities

| Characteristics | | Alternative approaches | | |
|---|---|---|---|---|
| | | **Products/markets** | **Processes** | **Manufacturing task** |
| Orientation | basis | Product/market name | Processes | Manufacturing's strategic task |
| | rationale | Marketing's view of the markets | Plant utilization | Order-winners and qualifiers to be provided by manufacturing |
| Principal functional stimulus | | Marketing | Engineering | Manufacturing |
| Minimizes duplication of processes and equipment involved | | No | Yes | No |
| Need to support a wide range of | volumes | Yes | Yes | No |
| | order-winners | Yes | Yes | No |
| Products stay in the same unit for all or most of their life cycle | | Yes | Yes | No |
| Greatest potential for orienting and evaluating appropriate levels of infrastructure within the units | | – | – | Yes |

leled by differences in volume levels, but this is not always the case. As shown in Exhibit 7.2, breaking down plants into two or more units provides the best conditions for creating a consistent and coherent set of manufacturing requirements, tasks and priorities.

In reality many businesses are best served by adopting a combination of approaches when focusing plants, as explained more fully in the next chapter. Of primary concern to a company is how to achieve focus. To give this its due weight, the next chapter has been devoted to explaining the steps involved in detail. It gives examples of different applications to help illustrate how the outcomes reflect the realities of different plants. Meanwhile, the sections that follow continue to examine the principles on which focus is based.

## Plant-within-a-plant Configuration

As stressed throughout, one important trade-off (implicit if not explicit) in focused manufacturing is that of plant size versus the economies of organizational scale. Although the ideal would be plants individually focused to the needs of markets and arranged on the basis of the alternatives given in Exhibit 7.2, this is often not practical on two counts. First, many companies own existing sites, with sizable investments in the bricks and mortar, utilities, plant, offices and other facilities. Second, as businesses change, there is a real danger that the manufacturing complexity associated with a lack of focus could gradually permeate some of the plants. Where rearrangement is constrained by the size of initial plants, their geographical location and the distribution difficulties involved, process and infrastructure support considerations and so on, the flexibility of overall size (the larger the factory, the greater the permutations available) can often be to a company's advantage. However, although this second aspect may not be a major issue for many companies, the first is.

The way to provide focus in these situations (as implied in the earlier example of the supplier to the vehicles markets) is to adopt a plant-within-a-plant (PWP) configuration. This involves physically dividing sites (even to the point of using partitions and different entrances and other facilities), thus providing a 'separate' plant within which manufacturing is focused to the needs of different parts of its total business. This reduces units to a more manageable task, attracting the advantages both of focus and smaller size.

Although the trade-off for these distinct and often critical gains is the apparent loss of economies of organization size, PWP provides an opportunity to review overheads in line with each focused manufacturing plant. These judgments are much easier to make, owing to the improved clarity between business needs, direction and overhead requirements. The amorphous mass takes on shape, which in turn allows each part of the business to reflect its needs in terms of overhead provision. The total business can then assess the relative contribution of each part to its overall success.

Over a number of years, a telecommunications switchgear company had developed its products to match the evolving technologies within telecommunications as it changed from mechanical to electromechanical and then to electronic. Irrespective of the underlying technology, all its products performed the same task for the customer – more sophisticated, but the same task. As is often the case, there was a considerable overlap between the life of one product and that of another. As a result, it was necessary to manufacture more than one product at a time, plus spares for each range. The spares service was part of the company's commitment to the past, as well as demonstrating to its current customers that they would be provided for in the future. In order, therefore, to establish the total manufacturing task, the company had to review the whole of the market requirements, as only this would provide a true picture of the issues involved – see Exhibit 7.3.

Product A, based on a mechanical technology, no longer sold as part of a new contract. Sales were restricted to spares or replacement equipment for existing installations. The processes required to make this product were specific to this range, as the other three products were based on electronic product technology and required different processes.

**Exhibit 7.3**  Changes over time in production volumes and manufacturing's strategic task

| Aspect | | Product | | | |
|---|---|---|---|---|---|
| | | **A** | **B** | **C** | **D** |
| Production volumes | current | low – spares volumes | low | high | low/medium |
| | in 2–3 years | low – little change | decreasing | decreasing | increasing |
| Manufacturing's strategic task based on agreed order-winners and qualifiers | current | delivery speed | delivery speed | cost reduction | quality conformance and delivery on time |
| | in 1 or 2 years | delivery speed | delivery speed | cost reduction | cost reduction |

Product B was also no longer sold as part of a new contract and had been superseded by Products C and D. These two products had been introduced within a relatively short time after Product B, a fact that reflected the rapid advances that had been made in product technologies within telecommunications applications.

The company, while maintaining the process capability unique to meeting the spare parts and replacement equipment sales of Product A, currently produced Products B, C and D on the same processes. As sales for Product D increased, manufacturing experienced greater difficulty.

The origin of these problems can be explained through the principle of process and product focus.[7] This concept helps a company look at its present and future product decisions for manufacturing by considering what type of focus would best suit the corporate market needs.

Being *process focused* means that the manufacturing facility is designed on a general-purpose basis and is thus able to meet the needs of a relatively wide range of volumes. These requirements typically would include product development, low volumes, intermittent, uncertain demand patterns and delivery speed.

When a plant is *product focused*, it is designed to meet the needs of what is often (compared with a process-focused plant) a relatively narrow range of products, normally with high volumes and/or similar process requirements. Such a plant is, therefore, specialized in order to meet the low-cost requirements of what typically would be a price-sensitive market.

The manufacturing strategy adopted by this company for its electronic products had been based on the provision of a general-purpose production process. In that way it was able to meet the requirements of Products B, C and D using the same facilities. This decision had to be taken to meet three main objectives:

■ To handle known product development within an existing facility and so avoid the need to plan for new facilities at each stage.

■ To minimize total product costs for all items, accepting that this may not be possible for individual products.

■ To be better able to handle volume fluctuations due to variable demand patterns from major customers.

However, by the very nature of general-purpose processes, each product will be assumed to have similar order-winners and hence a similar manufacturing task will be appropriate. In this situation, these processes would be suboptimal in meeting the cost-reduction requirements of Product C and later those of Product D.

A facility to provide the existing and future market requirements would need to encompass the characteristics of both a process- and product-focused plant as described earlier. To provide these in one process will always lead to compromise. However where this trade-off is between the key order-winners of different products, the company must make alternative provisions for focused manufacturing.

Focused manufacturing creates a structure in which each plant or PWP has is own facilities where it can concentrate on every element of the manufacturing task. Each part of the facility comprises its own processes and infrastructure, which are developed in line with each task. This not only provides significant gains in sustaining, qualifying and meeting the order-winning criteria, it also decreases the likelihood of the agreed focus being undermined, which is known as *focus regression.*

## Focus and the Product Life Cycle

An earlier section examined the three principal approaches to focusing manufacturing, summarized in Exhibit 7.2. However, where possible, companies should seek to focus plants on the basis of providing manufacturing with a consistent task (that is supporting similar order-winners). Splitting on the basis of products/markets or process typically results in the creation of a smaller version of the larger whole. Since downsizing will always result in the advantages of being smaller, the key is to gain, as much as possible, the many other advantages available, some of which were given in Exhibit 7.2.

As mentioned earlier, separating plants on the basis of order-winners and qualifiers will often be paralleled by differences in volume levels. The link between volume and order-winning criteria as presented in Exhibit 5.4 was clearly established and explained. An illustration of this concerns the nature of the product life cycle and the changes in volume and order-winning criteria that take place over time.

The distinction between product and process focus referred to earlier is shown in Exhibit 7.4 below. Establishing where a production facility stands on this spectrum and in which direction it is evolving will allow a firm to review where it is and where it should be in terms of manufacturing's support of its markets. In this way, it provides one of the essential inputs into the corporate strategy debate by highlighting the degree of match between the marketing and manufacturing strategies. It brings the company's attention to any current levels of difficulty and the possible ways to provide what is best for the business as a whole.

In developing its manufacturing strategy, the company in the boxed example became aware of the type of focused manufacturing appropriate to its products as they went through their life cycles (illustrated in Exhibit 7.5.)

**Exhibit 7.4**    Orientation of a particular manufacturing facility

Process focus
(general purpose
facility)

Product focus
(facilities dedicated
to products)

**Exhibit 7.5**   A typical product life cycle and its relationship to focus

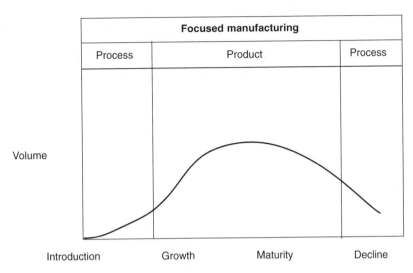

In the early stages of growth, manufacturing will be faced with less predictable sales volumes, product and process modifications, customer orientation and varying levels of delivery speed. The provision of these will usually best be met by the capability and flexibility characteristics inherent in process focus. In the period of maturity, with high-volume sales and when the product technology has been fixed, attention is totally directed toward processes, with low-cost manufacturing becoming predominant (that is, product focus). Finally, in the period of product decline, the manufacturing requirement will revert back to being a process-focused facility due to the change in volumes and order-winning criteria.

A look back at Exhibit 5.4 and relevant discussion will not only further illustrate these differences but also help to underpin the underlying rationale for focus. Companies will continue to find themselves needing to support different markets and their position will be one of continuous change. Manufacturing's effective support of these differences will be a key factor in overall corporate success.

## Progression or Regression in Focused Manufacturing[8]

By definition, a single manufacturing process cannot provide the aspects of process and product focus at the same time. The recognition of the critical trade-offs to support the corporate marketing requirements is an essential component of a sound manufacturing strategy. In practice every facility faces some variety in the market requirements for its products. A company must be aware of these fluctuations in variety and evaluate the consequences of these changes. The increase in product variety within the company described earlier and the associated differences required by these products over time led to an increased diffusion between products and processes. This, in turn, led to movement away from its preferred focus, known as *focus regression*. On the other hand, to become increasingly competitive a facility needs to take appropriate steps to achieve greater movement towards its preferred focus, known as *focus progression*. This would require the company described earlier to align Products B, C and D to their appropriate focus. Only in this way could the key task be addressed by manufacturing for the different products at the respective stages in their life cycles.

# Conclusion

Achieving and maintaining focused manufacturing needs to be an overt corporate activity. Focus does not occur naturally – in fact, there are normally forces at work that militate against it. These forces, as detailed below, need to be recognized so action may be consciously taken to ensure that improved focus is not inhibited through corporate neglect or traditional views of what is best for a business.

■ *Marketing* often stimulates the desire to create and maintain a broad product line. This is, and has been for some time, an integral part of marketing's strategy. Thus, it has become a felt need, with overtones of image, and frequently constitutes an important measure of the function's own performance.

■ *Sales* holds the understandable view that it is easier to sell a broader line. This is reinforced by commission schemes for salespeople, normally based on total sales value (£s). It implies that sales of all products are of equal value to the business and fails to recognize the need to differentiate one product sale from the next. This function will also argue that a review of total competition reveals a wide variety of features on offer, affording wider selection for the customer. It follows that as customers' preferences vary, a wide range better meets the total diverse needs. This may well be true some of the time but it does not usually hold true all the time. Often customers' preferences are based on unsubstantiated or non-technical rationales. In these circumstances, it is much harder to sell a product that meets customers' actual as opposed to perceived needs. Finally, in businesses experiencing seasonal or cyclical demand, there is often a strong argument to increase variety to help smooth out such patterns.

■ *Manufacturing* also inhibits focus for reasons such as being bound by past union agreements on work practices, high investment costs associated with the purchase/movement of processes and the risk of uncertain benefits.

■ *Accounting and finance* similarly stimulate forces that work against focus. These include capital restrictions and rationing, the overriding emphasis on short-term earnings and the prevalence of cost information that distorts reality by failing to provide data that allow sensitive insights to be gained.

■ *Corporate* forces also limit the steps taken, because of a general resistance to including the manufacturing perspective in the corporate strategy development and a reluctance to increase the interaction between marketing and manufacturing. The trend stems largely from divisions between specialists and executives within management and the predominance, at different times, of a single function in formulating strategy. The background and perspectives brought to strategy discussions by key managers, therefore, have been too narrowly based. This leads to corporate imbalance, in the first instance, and in the second, insufficient breadth on which to base appropriate revisions. The changed economic circumstances during the 1980s through into the 1990s have forced companies to arrive at strategy decisions based on what is best for the business as a whole. This change has been brought about by the increased level of corporate consciousness within the business. Strategies developed out of a single functional perspective, which were then superficially overlaid by particular perspectives as and when they arose, are rapidly being replaced by genuine corporate debate. However, until that happens, corporate forces will often drive out focus and other manufacturing strategy arguments, placing these functional perspectives in their customary reactive position.

## Supporting Markets Characterized by Difference

Failure to challenge how well existing concepts apply to the current and future needs of a business is at the root of today's problems for many companies. By continuing to use concepts and approaches developed for markets, the characteristics of which are very different from the needs of today and tomorrow, companies are finding increasing difficulty in competing effectively. With manufacturing measured on every yardstick and corporations failing to address the size and relevance of its enormous overhead expense, the process of determining appropriate strategic direction (and its effective pursuit) is inadequately managed.

Substituting one approach for another is not the answer. Making better use of large key resources is the aim. With markets characterized by difference rather than similarity, it is essential that firms learn to compete effectively in market segments that are different from one another. Markets based on different order-winners will present conflicting requirements for manufacturing to support only if facilities (processes and infrastructure) are not organized to meet these differences. Focus is an appropriate response to the increasing levels of difference that characterize today's markets. Thus focused approaches make more sense and lead to substantial improvements on every significant corporate dimension. Being able to fashion manufacturing facilities and supporting activities to the particular needs of various markets enables companies to compete effectively. An approach based on reducing or eliminating diversity within corporate portfolios as a strategy in itself is unsound. Advocates of these policies are not only turning their backs on today's reality but also on opportunities. Competing in diverse markets is not in itself strategically unsound. What makes such a business mix unsound is the failure to recognize and reflect the very differences that exist. Being competitive and successful in different types of markets is a prerequisite for a company today and the concept of focus offers principles by which to achieve this.

# Ways Forward – Halting the Drift into Unfocused Manufacturing

The development of a manufacturing strategy, as outlined in Chapter 2, provides one overriding advantage: it offers a meaningful and realistic way for manufacturing to communicate with the rest of the business. By doing this, it provides the base on which to build, creating a positive move to halt the drift into unfocused manufacturing.

The first step is to concentrate management attention and effort onto the core business areas. As a company adjusts to marketplace changes, then product lines, customer characteristics, customer preferences and order-winners all change. There must be a reference point from which, or around which, to build the corporate strategy. This reference point is the existing core of the business, in which a company has a clear competitive advantage. Concentration by production and marketing on the core business is essential. However there are several aspects, general and specific, that need to be addressed.

Overall, it is important to use the opportunity created by the strategic development procedure to redress some of the general inhibitors detailed earlier. The development of an appropriate manufacturing strategy will, in itself, induce a corporate strategy that embodies the marketing and manufacturing perspective. In so doing, it will get both these functions to pull in the same corporate direction, by matching production and marketing with the corporate need and measuring the achievement of both against the same corporate yardsticks. Similarly, capital budgeting needs to be couched within the long-term corporate plan and expenditure measured in terms of the agreed focus. Revisions also need to be made in the accounting system, in order to provide data more relevant to these decisions and the necessary information on which to base them and monitor future performance.

Now it is time to consider the tasks essential to achieving focused manufacturing. The fundamental purpose behind focus is to establish a plant mission, based on the development of an appropriate manufacturing strategy. In many instances, it will result in a split of processes and infrastructure of existing facilities and the establishment of plant-within-a-plant configurations. When these steps are taken principally to refocus existing plants, manufacturing must agree on and establish an optimum plant size. This will restrict the task to what is meaningful and manageable and limit the future potential for focus regression. But this is not enough. Manufacturing's task is to ensure that focus progression becomes an integral part of their strategic task. This is facilitated in two ways. The managerial consciousness of the importance and strategic strength derived through focus, and an annual programme to give direction to ensure its achievement.

## Notes

1. Brought to prominence in E. F. Schumacher's book, *Small Is Beautiful: Economics as if People Mattered*, New York: Harper & Row, 1975.
2. W. Skinner, 'The Focused Factory', *Harvard Business Review*, May–June 1974, pp. 113–21.
3. Ibid., p. 114.
4. Ibid., p. 118.
5. W. Schmenner, 'Every Factory Has a Life Cycle', *Harvard Business Review*, March–April 1983, p. 123.
6. Skinner, 'The Focused Factory', p. 115.
7. These different types are broad descriptions of approaches to focus. Although they do not always provide an appropriate strategic fit between the market and manufacturing, they are sound, generalizable explanations. They provide a useful insight into the key differences that exist for many products throughout their life cycles.
8. This concept was first introduced in an article by T .J. Hill and R. M. G. Duke-Woolley, 'Progression or Regression in Facilities Focus', *Strategic Management Journal*, 1983, **4**(2): 109–21.

# 8 Focus: Methodology

The principles and concepts underpinning focus were outlined in the last chapter. We now turn our attention to the steps to take when developing focused plants.[1]

As stressed throughout, today's markets are characterized by difference not similarity. The task facing manufacturing, therefore, is how to cope with the marked levels of difference that typically exist in a firm's markets. Increasingly, manufacturing is turning toward the design and development of focused plants or plant-within-a-plant configurations. However, before discussing the steps to achieve focus, we should consider the origins of existing plant structures, how they are currently arranged and the reasons for these decisions.

## Origins of Existing Plants

Driven by the concepts of economies of scale and control through specialists, resulting manufacturing plants are typically large, with process layouts based on functional similarity and centralized infrastructures. The outcomes are similar to that in Exhibit 8.1.

Processes are arranged so that products can share the available capacity as a way of facilitating higher levels of equipment utilization. Similarly, a firm's organization structure is based on line/executive functions (such as sales and manufacturing) with appropriate specialists undertaking advisory and support roles. The underlying rationale for these is economies of scale – higher process utilization is self-explanatory; similarly, one centralized function of specialists is the most cost-effective way of providing the set of capabilities and technical support for the whole business, as discussed earlier. The concept of focus challenges the relevance of the manufacturing application of these principles in support of today's markets.

## Moving to Focused Plants

The last chapter explained the concept of focus and the alternative approaches to achieve it. The idea is to arrange manufacturing in such a way as to create a consistent task within each focused unit. The steps to take in focusing existing manufacturing facilities are detailed below. However, before discussing the methodology, it is important to bear in mind the following:

178

**Exhibit 8.1**    Typical layout of existing plants based on economies-of-scale principles
(not to scale)

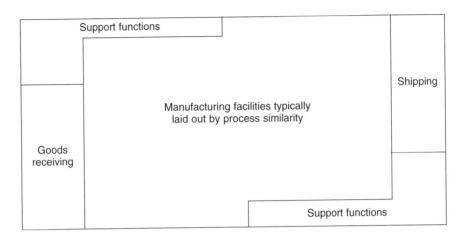

- Focus should not be seen as the preferred dogma on which to base manufacturing arrangements. Replacing one dogma with another will lead to inappropriate investments or future situations of misalignment through neglect or lack of knowing what to do and how to do it.

- In reality, companies will typically use two or more approaches when focusing plants. Some developments will combine economies-of-scale principles with those of focus. Others will use a combination of the approaches to focus explained in the last chapter, namely products/markets, processes and manufacturing's strategic task. Since combinations often yield the best overall results, companies must be pragmatic rather than dogmatic.

- Very often, companies will not be able to arrive at appropriate focused approaches for all parts of a business. When applying chosen approaches, companies may find that they are left with parts of the whole with which they can do little. Although requiring improvement, it can be difficult if not impossible to develop these remnants within the concept of focus because of insufficient similarity within the markets and manufacturing task.

- The principle of applying focus is to improve on what currently exists. Focusing parts of a business not only leads to gains within these parts but also simplifies that which remains unchanged, thus facilitating developments throughout.

- The final point is one of approach. It is often best to rearrange a business one part at a time and enlarge the scope of change one phase at a time. Choosing areas where the rationale is clearest helps to improve the rate of success, reduce the size of the task, maintain acceptable timescales and allow everyone to learn.

The underlying theme when focusing a business must be pragmatism. Thus if one approach to focus does not bring improvement in a particular situation, that facet should not be applied. In most businesses, combinations of approaches will secure the best level of overall improvement. Companies need to determine the desired extent of change in order to achieve what is best overall and be wary of the inertia and resistance to change that exist in most organizations. Furthermore, the process of change needs to be ongoing. As markets will continually change, manufacturing's response will need to reflect these fresh demands. In the past, many companies have failed to question existing approaches, in part because of the fundamental logic of the current approach but also because there has not been a viable, well-argued and well-articulated alternative. Focus provides one such challenge to existing organization arrangements, based on improving support for a company's markets.

## Steps Towards Focused Plants

This section outlines the steps to be followed when applying the concept of focus. As with most responses, it is iterative in nature and needs adequate time to work through the issues involved and the alternative outcomes under review.

## Process Review

The first task is to review the existing manufacturing processes to identify any that are too expensive to duplicate.[2] Examples of these will differ from one business or industry to the next. It may be a particular process such as heat treatment or clean, hygienic conditions to meet health and safety regulations, or coating and finishing facilities; or it could be a specific technical process requirement to make particular products. This technical sweep thereby identifies the realistic constraints in moving from economies of scale to focus as a basis for plant configurations. Those processes that are not to be duplicated will retain their batch-process, economies-of-scale organizational features.

In some companies products may well be tied to given processes. Any rearrangement, therefore, of the different manufacturing tasks involved would lead directly to process duplication, with potentially high additional investment. Upstream processes will often fall into this category. Downstream processes (for example, packing) are normally less likely to be affected by this constraint because of the lower levels of investment typically involved.

## Identifying Manufacturing Order-winners and Qualifiers

The next step is to identify the manufacturing-related order-winners and qualifiers. These will form the basis for determining any rearrangement of manufacturing, given the constraints identified in the process review.

These criteria need to be carefully evaluated, then matched to the relevant plant focus. Failure to do this will often lead to an inappropriate choice and to a lack of understanding of the rationale on which to base future decisions in line with ever-changing market needs. Throughout, the principle is to create (within the constraints of reality and what is best for the business) a coherent set of tasks for manufacturing within each plant configuration. The manufacturing task needs to be based on a set of similar order-winners and qualifiers wherever possible. Once the focus split is agreed, considerations of hardware (processes) and software (infrastructure) can proceed again.

## Process Rearrangement

Process rearrangement is then completed. Processes are allocated and physically moved to the agreed units in line with product requirements regarding capability and capacity. Those not to be duplicated will, as explained earlier, retain their batch-process features, still based on economies of scale. In this way, companies need to arrive at pragmatic decisions that best suit the business overall. Some processes are too expensive to duplicate, given the level of utilization that would result. These would still need to be managed, organized and controlled on a batch-process basis to serve the varying needs of the overall business.

## Infrastructure Rearrangement

The final stage concerns reviewing the infrastructure requirements of the different manufacturing units. The selection, while reflecting the market needs of each manufacturing unit, must be tempered by sensible constraints and principles. These are addressed in Chapter 10, which is concerned with the development of manufacturing infrastructure.

In this stage, companies reshape existing overheads by allocating relevant support/specialist functions (in terms both of capability and capacity) to each focused unit. This enables support to orient its activities to the particular needs of each different part of a business.

The two key principles that underpin this step are:

- **Activities versus functions** – as functions comprise groups of activities, the underlying principle involved in this step is to identify those activities (as opposed to functions) that are better allocated to a focused unit and those where keeping them centrally based makes more sense. Exhibit 8.2 provides some illustrations.

- **Location** – the overhead resources must actually be physically allocated (that is, relevant staff must be located at the site) and not merely nominally designated. In this way responsibility for how much specialist support is needed and the management and direction of the staff involved clearly belongs to the focused unit. Similarly, reporting structures for the specialists and their prime interests and drivers are centred on the focused unit and its operational and strategic tasks.

At the same time as reshaping existing overheads, companies also need to work up from the bottom of the organization. This means determining what elements of work would best constitute the shopfloor task. By working from both ends, companies can challenge existing paradigms and approaches, which will result in fresh insights into how best to reshape the 'soft side' of manufacturing's strategic response.

The issues of infrastructure and the job of work are dealt with in more detail in Chapter 10. Suffice to say that the first step in this stage (as explained earlier) is to identify those aspects of a support function's tasks that are truly specialist in nature and those that are candidates for being completed elsewhere. This then enables a

**Exhibit 8.2**  Examples of the activities split between specialist functions and focused units

| Function | Activities typically best allocated to a | |
| --- | --- | --- |
| | specialist function | focused unit |
| Quality | Quality assurance – agreeing sampling routines, laboratory testing and establishing checking procedures | Quality control – undertaking quality conformance checking procedures such as inspection |
| Operations planning, control and scheduling | Long-term tasks such as capacity planning | Day-to-day scheduling and control of manufacturing |
| Purchasing | Vendor selection and negotiating supply contracts | Arranging for call-offs of bought-out materials, components and other items in line with the manufacturing schedule |

company to consider who would best complete the latter, what would be their appropriate reporting structures (see Exhibit 8.2) and where they should be geographically situated.

The importance of this part of an organization's review is twofold:

- Overheads are typically a very large part of an organization's total resource provision. Thus orienting this to support the needs of its various markets will be a significant factor in the level of corporate success.

- Whereas process reallocations are constrained by issues such as investment, the opportunity to reshape and reposition overheads is usually not as restricted by such factors. Therefore this aspect of strategic review will often provide more opportunities to make the sizeable gains brought about through focus.

In reality companies often decide that a combination of these approaches best suits their needs because the duplication of investments alters the trade-offs under review. Thus certain advantages need to be foregone for the sake of the business overall. Similarly, companies could argue for greenfield provision as the ideal response to the market differences at the root of these proposals. However, companies' existing sites are usually an overpowering factor in the eventual decision. Approaches to meet these different realities include plant-within-plant configurations, a concept introduced in the last chapter.

## Focus Regression versus Focus Progression

As markets are dynamic, the relevant order-winners and qualifiers will invariably change over time both in themselves and as products go through their life cycles. Consequently focusing plants is not a one-off task. To avoid focus regression, companies need to continue to develop and reshape the fit between market needs and manufacturing as an ongoing task.

Very often this is best accomplished by moving products from one focused unit to another. In this way the lack of fit between the change in order-winners and the basis of the focused unit in which a product is currently manufactured can be erased. Thus alignment between market and manufacturing and the preservation of consistency in manufacturing task (the heart of focus) can be retained over time.

As markets are inherently dynamic (they will change whether you want them to or not) and manufacturing is inherently fixed (it will not change unless you deliberately change it) then focus regression is an inherent characteristic in today's business environment. Recognizing this is essential. Restoring these links and thereby maintaining the consistency of manufacturing's task is a fundamental part of manufacturing strategy.

A major supplier of components and products to the private, commercial and off-highway home and export vehicle markets was reviewing one of its principal manufacturing facilities. The company's attempts to cope with product range increases, volume changes and the growing original equipment (OE)/spares mix resulted in accumulated complexity. Its factory was difficult to manage, had high work-in-progress inventory and was increasingly unable to meet customers' delivery needs or earn a satisfactory level of return on its investment.

To reduce the manufacturing task to a manageable size, it decided to create several units based on a product/market split. These units, the company argued, would best reflect customers' needs while reducing work-in-progress inventory requirements. To test the validity of the approach, the company initially took the smallest manufacturing unit within the product/market split and, as it was convenient, relocated its processes and infrastructure within an unused part of the existing site. The first review highlighted a series of gains that, as a subsequent analysis showed, resulted from the manageability of the small size. A more testing analysis, however, showed that the order-winners for different parts of this and the other product/market units were not being addressed any more specifically than before the reorganization. The company had merely created smaller versions of the larger whole that, in fact, mirrored the problems of the bigger manufacturing units except those associated with overall size. The high and low volumes linked to OE and spares demand, respectively, called for different order-winning criteria. The appropriate split here would have been to separate units by order-winners and qualifiers that would have created the necessary link between the manufacturing task and the market. The gains owing to small size would automatically follow.

## Implementing Focus: Examples and Illustrations

This section provides examples of focus. They are intended not only to show approaches to meet different needs, but also to illustrate some of the issues raised so far.

A large European electronics manufacturer was facing the decision on where to site its thick-film facility. It had two manufacturing units in geographically separate sites but it needed to double its overall capacity in the near future to meet the anticipated growth in thick-film application. The alternatives were either to spread the increase over both sites or to re-examine its process needs and reflect these in the plant selection. On reviewing this problem, the company recognized two issues as fundamental to the choice. The first concerned the increasing quality conformance demands of its products; the second, the extent to which each location could attract an adequate level of engineering and development infrastructure support. Through discussions on the effects of these implications, the company saw that in this instance the exacting product specifications, low volumes, development activities and necessary high calibre of engineering and specialist support came together to form a coherent set of process and infrastructure requirements. The demands on the process and support staff for products with a lower specification but higher volumes required a different set of processes and infrastructure. With this now clearly established and the availability and likelihood of attracting sufficient engineering and specialist staff at each location identified, the choices fell into place. In addition, by keeping separate the process capabilities for the two groups of products, the problems of establishing, identifying and maintaining the quality requirements for items with very different levels of product specification were considerably reduced. Therefore, choosing the plant focus on the basis of process split enabled the company to recognize, appreciate and take account of the key practical constraints involved. These were reflected in the focused manufacturing decision, thus aligning the plant to the different market segments.

A large food company had grown from its beginnings at the same manufacturing site. Over the years, it had developed an organizational structure designed to realize the benefits of having selected a site that was sufficiently large to contain expansion and well placed to access the local labour pool and relevant distribution channels.

Like many companies, although enjoying good profits and steady growth in real sales, it continually questioned its cost base and the appropriateness of its organizational set-up. One outcome was that it decided to move away from its traditional and well-established style of centralized

*cont'd*

support functions and apply the concept of focus. In process terms, it found that the technical requirements of groups of products meant that these could only be made on certain processes. Therefore, this prevented any opportunity to cross-link different products by markets or order-winners. Furthermore, it could not justify duplicating plant because of the equipment, buildings and space costs involved. However, the company reviewed its products' order-winners and adjusted current arrangements to create a consistent manufacturing task within its market segments. In this way, therefore, the marketing/manufacturing interface (see Exhibit 8.3) led to improved business fit primarily through realigning markets rather than changes in manufacturing.

However, the real gains came when the company reviewed its infrastructure. It recognized that the centralized specialist and other overhead functions were not aware of the distinct differences within its markets nor, consequently, of the different manufacturing tasks required. A review of information provision and supporting activities and priorities revealed a marked inconsistency between what was needed and what was provided. By reallocating specialist and other staff, where appropriate, to the separate manufacturing units, the company tailored support to the particular needs of each part of the business. This led to significant reductions in overheads caused by unnecessary duplication of procedures and systems and unwanted provision of support staff. Such gains could not have been achieved with the inadequate direction provided by the company's traditional centralized approach.

## Focused Plants – Outcomes

To help reinforce the points raised in the earlier sections, illustrations of typical outcomes from focusing manufacturing are now provided.

### Focused Plants

A US-based pharmaceutical company decided to review its European manufacturing facilities. These supported all sales in Europe as well as the Middle East and Africa (EMEA). At the time, the company had five manufacturing units in Europe each of which supported the whole range of demand for the products made in their respective plants. Two of these facilities (Plants 1 and 2) were much larger than the other three and, although these two larger plants manufactured many high-volume products, they also supported the demands for products for all the countries and distribution outlets in the EMEA region and at all stages in each product's life

**Exhibit 8.3**    Allocation of products to Plants 1, 2 and 5

| Products | | Plants | | Plant |
|---|---|---|---|---|
| | | 1 | 2 | 5 |
| High volume | high volume | ✓ | ✓ | |
| | low volume | | | ✓ |
| Low volume | | | | ✓ |

cycle. As you can imagine, this included the low-volume demand from smaller countries in the region and for products in the latter stages of their life cycles. Two of the other smaller plants (Plants 3 and 4) also had similar mixed volumes while Plant 5 made products the demand for which was at the low end of the volume spectrum. Looking as well to reduce costs, the company decided to close Plants 3 and 4 and focus the remaining three facilities as follows. Plants 1 and 2 would handle the high-volume end of product demand while investment would be made in Plant 5 to handle all low-volume products and also the low demand requirements (particularly in parts of the Middle East and Africa) of products made in Plants 1 and 2 – see Exhibit 8.3. In this way, the company focused its plants by manufacturing task and this allowed them to better support relevant markets. In an environment where price was not an order-winner the manufacturing task was to make products available to customers where unavailability would result in lost sales and potential switches in brand loyalty.

Plants 1 and 2 could orient their priorities around process throughput speeds meeting growing customer demand and always delivering on time, while Plant 5 prioritized reducing set-up times in line with the low-volume dimension of its markets and a fast response capability to meet the delivery speed characteristics of demand.

### Plant-within-a-plant

As highlighted earlier, the investment implications of existing plants and infrastructure means that companies cannot justify relocating and setting up greenfield sites. The only viable alternative for them is to adopt a plant-within-a-plant (PWP) approach to focus.

A multinational packaging company has several manufacturing plants in Europe and North America. These covered a wide range of packing from labels through to injection and blow moulding. One of its Canadian moulding companies concluded that the most appropriate manufacturing support for its diverse markets was to move to a PWP arrangement with each unit supporting a different set of market needs.[3] Before the change, the processes and infrastructure were organized in a way similar to that in Exhibit 8.1. The revised approach is shown in Exhibit 8.4. Within each PWP, the necessary processes in terms of capability and capacity were allocated together with these support activities originally completed by

**Exhibit 8.4**    Plant-within-a-plant arrangement of the facilities outlined in Exhibit 8.1

| Support functions | | Shipping |
|---|---|---|
| Goods receiving | PWP1 – processes and infrastructure | Shipping |
| Goods receiving | PWP2 – processes and infrastructure | Shipping |
| Goods receiving | PWP3 – processes and infrastructure | Support functions |

centralized specialists that were considered to be better provided within each PWP unit. A glance at Exhibit 8.4 shows that some activities are still provided by centralized, support functions, where this expertise is more sensibly arranged as a single provision. In addition, when the process allocations were made additional processes were purchased in order to provide adequate capacity within this new arrangement.[4]

# Conclusion

Focused plants, whether individual units or plant-within-a-plant configurations, offer to many companies real improvements sufficient to justify the investments involved. The increasing levels of difference within today's markets are exposing the inappropriateness of yesterday's approaches in the form of reduced competitiveness and loss of market share. Firms are increasingly questioning the approaches taken in the past while searching for sensible developments that will bring more appropriate manufacturing responses and improved support for the differing sets of market needs.

Introducing focus is one alternative, with the best outcomes often resulting from a mixed approach based on fit and pragmatism. But companies must understand the revelance of focus as a way forward before introducing it. Moreover, the rate of its introduction needs to be tempered by what can be achieved and the challenges these ideas bring.

Many companies need to review their manufacturing provision with some urgency. Splitting out those parts of a business that more readily lend themselves to focus is the place to start. However, avoiding the dogmatic use of these approaches is essential in order to gain the substantial and lasting benefits that can accrue. But the dynamics of markets will necessitate continuous review and revision in order to avoid the drift into focus regression that is inherent in all organizations.

## Notes

1. In his book *The Strategy Quest*, AMD Publishing, Bristol, 1998, Terry Hill depicts the procedures and concerns that characterize the development of a plant-within-a-plant business. Written as a novel it is intended to help overcome the marked and understandable misgivings and questions raised when this issue is considered by any organization. While the style of the book is unusual, the issues addressed and debates pursued are commonplace.
2. In some instances, there may be other factors, for example space constraints, but often these also constitute cost-related reasons for not duplicating existing capabilities.
3. This is described in detail in *The Strategy Quest*, 1998.
4. A factor discussed in Chapter 7.

# 9 Make or Buy and Managing the Supply Chain

Companies rarely, if ever, own the resources and activities necessary to make a product from start to finish including delivery to customers. The decision on what to make and what to buy and the task of managing the supply chain that results are, therefore, key strategic issues within manufacturing. They concern the width of a firm's internal span of process (how much of a product it makes in-house), the degree and direction of vertical integration alternatives and its links and relationships at either end of the process spectrum with suppliers, distributors and customers.

Both the make-or-buy decision and the supply chain management task have major ramifications for the business itself. They are essential for growth and success and crucial for survival. However the current position and corporate response on both these key issues are typically not the result of strategic debate but the outcome of earlier decisions and attitudes that lack adequate strategic context and involve insufficient recognition of the integrated nature of supply chains. What a company decides to make or buy will impact its potential to be successful in its current markets while restricting or facilitating its ability to change direction in the future. Having made the decision, a company in managing its supply chain often fails to appreciate that the various elements involved directly impact many of the order-winners and qualifiers in its markets. Traditional corporate approaches thus singularly fail to recognize the integrated nature of the whole and the need to manage proactively all elements in line with the needs of its markets. Developing cooperation and improving coordination are not just good things to do but are essential if a company is to compete successfully now and in the future.

## Reasons for Choosing Whether to Make or Buy

Although in theory every item can be made or bought, in reality the choice is far more restricted. In many instances companies may have no alternative other than to subcontract the making of a material, component, subassembly or even final product due to barrier-to-entry reasons, such as not having the in-house technical capability or the unjustifiably high levels of process investment that would be involved. However, few businesses when they consider their past decisions find that the current make-or-buy position has been reached according to a well-considered and consistent set of criteria developed and readdressed over time.

This section discusses the factors to be considered when deciding whether to make or buy. It also highlights some of the actual reasons that underpin such decisions which companies should be aware of and should avoid.

## Retaining Core Technology Elements of the Business

Most companies choose to keep in-house those processes that represent the core technology elements of their business. For instance, a company that manufactures its own finished items will invariably retain the assembly-onward end of the production process. The reasons include the wish to retain immediate control of product identity, design security, final product quality and the ultimate link with its customers.

In the same way, companies will seek to protect aspects of their products that reflect advantage. Design security has already been highlighted and, in the same way, retaining control over process technology developments will typically lead to a decision to retain that stage in-house.

## Strategy Considerations

Make-or-buy decisions need to be made within the strategic context of a business. The order-winners and qualifiers (for example, price, delivery reliability, delivery speed and quality conformance) that relate to a company's markets and that make-or-buy decisions affect need to be reflected in such actions and their outcomes. For example, Dell Computer Corporation developed the capability to assemble personal computers quickly in response to customers' orders but found that ability constrained by component suppliers' long lead times.[1] However, other companies alert to key market-related issues incorporate these into their make-or-buy and sourcing decisions. For example, Lego, the privately owned Danish manufacturer of building kits and other toys, has for years concentrated its production in Europe and the US, arguing that this best satisfies its design and quality conformance requirements. And Lego is not alone in basing decisions on strategic rather than cost-alone factors. Motorola's decision to set up cellular phone production in Germany and Benetton's decision not to source garments in the Asia Pacific but to retain local (Italian) suppliers, who would meet the fast response needs of its supply chain support for its fashion-based marketplace, are further examples of strategy-based make-or-buy decisions.

A key factor, then, is how current and future positions on the make-or-buy continuum impact manufacturing's ability to support those market criteria for which it is solely or jointly responsible. Similarly, issues concerning relevant process and product technologies need to be considered as stressed in the last section. Whether or not a company makes in-house, supply-chain performance regarding relevant order-winners and qualifiers will directly impact a company's ability to retain customers, grow share and make money. The issues involved will be addressed in detail in the later section on managing the supply chain, where the fundamental nature of this decision is clearly highlighted, fully discussed and appropriately illustrated.

## Span of Process and Product/Process Technology

The earlier sections highlighted situations where companies retained relevant product and process technologies. In cases where there is a significant stepped change in product technology, the very opposite can happen. Where a company applies new technology developments to its existing products or on the introduction of new, if similar, products into its current range, it may find itself without the in-house process capability to meet all of the new and more complex product technology requirements. The result is that it buys the technology in the form of components. Normally, this narrowing takes place in the earlier upstream stages of a process where the new technology developments are the most radical; the later downstream processes are kept in-house because the technology associated with them is more in line with existing manufacturing expertise and is also closer to the final product itself.

The IT sector provides a classic example of this. With the rapid rate of component development, IT companies often have no alternative than to buy in the technology from outside in the form of chips and other parts in order to keep pace with competition and changing technical developments. As Exhibit 9.1 illustrates, although such companies may have had a wider internal span of process for earlier products, with technology developments this is correspondingly reduced.

**Exhibit 9.1**    The reduction in span of process with increases in the technology of the product (not to scale)

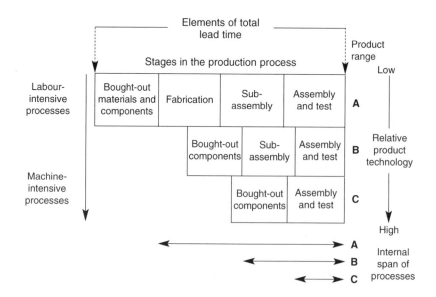

In this illustration, a company when producing only product range A had developed in-house much of the process technology to make the products involved. The advent of product range B and, later, product range C heralded a distinct technology change. Not having the manufacturing process capabilities to provide these new requirements, the company brought them in from outside in the form of components. The narrowing of the internal span of process that resulted is shown in Exhibit 9.1.

In such situations, when and by how much to widen the span of process, after the initial narrowing, is a significant strategic decision which in practice is often treated as an operational issue. A classic example of this was provided in the 1970s in the hand-held calculator market. Bowmar, one-time market leader, failed to successfully integrate backwards into integrated circuit production and eventually withdrew from the business, while Texas Instruments (TI) successfully integrated forwards into calculators and took over the market leadership. One major reason for TI eventually displacing Bowmar was that its comparative process position gave it more opportunity to reduce costs and exploit potential experience curve gains, and that is what it did. Bowmar, restricted to assembly cost gains, was constrained by its suppliers' price reductions for a large part of its costs. TI, on the other hand, had no such limitations.

In the 1990s and through to the early part of the 21st century, the dominance of the Intel Corporation in PC design and the supply of chips such as microprocessors has redressed, if not revised, the supplier/customer relations within the IT sector. Intel's increasingly powerful position as a supplier of chips has strengthened its opening position *vis-à-vis* customers and greatly changed the nature and results of subsequent negotiations within the board sector of the IT industry.[2]

## Product Volumes

Companies faced with the different tasks involved with manufacturing high and low volumes can adopt a plant-within-a-plant alternative, as reviewed in Chapter 7. A company may also consider buying out those products with a low-volume demand, for instance, and that would, in turn, normally lead to a narrowing of the internal span of process. An example of this decision involved a manufacturer of engine parts for agricultural and diesel trucks. When the low-volume spares demand was reached in a product's life cycle, the company increasingly subcontracted component manufacturing where the machining processes involved were only used on operations for components for that product or for products with similar low volumes. In that way, it reduced its span of processes and kept the manufacturing task within agreed bounds.

## The Globalization of World Trade

Trade barriers across much of the world have declined sharply. It is estimated, for example, that the average tariff by 1990 stood at 7 per cent or less than one-fifth of the level in 1960. Simultaneously a range of new markets, notably in Asia and eastern Europe, has opened up to foreign investment. This has made global manufacturing much more possible. One outcome is the reduced need for many overseas plants. Markets that previously demanded local production facilities because of high tariff levels can now be supplied by imports. A good example of this is the Australian automotive sector. In the 10 years to 1997, tariffs on imported cars dropped from 57.5 per cent to 22.5 per cent, while imported cars rose from 15 to about 50 per cent of the market.[3] Domestic car plants (for example, Nissan) have already started to close.

## The Reality of Make-or-buy Decisions

The previous sections identified some of the principal reasons that may form the basis of make-or-buy decisions. In reality, many companies approach this critical task and base the strategic decision involved on reasons that are less rational and seldom sound. The more common of these are now discussed.

### History: Continuing Yesterday's Decisions

Make-or-buy decisions taken at one moment in time are often not reconsidered at a later date. Inertia, a reluctance to add additional executive tasks and avoiding possible short-term problems militate against taking appropriate reviews. Once made, make-or-buy decisions often remain unchallenged.

Over the last 30 years, a reduction in product life cycles, rapid changes in product and process technologies and growing world competition have increased the size of the management task. One result has been that executives, while responding to changes that demand immediate attention, have deferred addressing other key, longer-term issues. In some areas this has resulted in companies taking their eye off the ball and failing to undertake periodic reviews regularly and within reasonable timescales. In key areas such as the make-or-buy decision, the corporate impact, especially in times of accelerating change, can be irreparable.

### The Dominance of Cost and Technology Arguments

The format used to address the question whether to make or buy typically centres around issues of technology and cost. The initial consideration is whether or not a company has the process technology to make a component or product. Where the technical capability is not already in-house, the automatic response is to buy from outside.

Where process technology is not a barrier, the next consideration is the cost of provision. While a most important dimension in itself, taken without addressing the requirements of markets and relevant order-winners and qualifiers (such as delivery speed, quality conformance, ability to ramp up and deliver on time) it will lead to inappropriate decisions and have a potentially damaging impact on a firm's short-term let alone long-term strategic position.

### Shedding Difficult Manufacturing Tasks

Over recent years companies have tended to shed difficult manufacturing tasks by subcontracting or divestment. Many firms approach this decision with an eye more on the difficulties embodied in the task rather than on the strategic consequences of the make-or-buy decision they are about to take. Short-term gains, taken on their own, look most attractive. However, the accompanying loss of skill, essential manufacturing know-how and infrastructure may limit a company's ability to respond in the future. A maxim to bear in mind is, 'if the manufacturing task is easy, then any company can do it.' The key to manufacturing success is to resolve the difficult manufacturing issues, for this is where high margins are to be made.

Some companies have, in the ongoing evaluation of these decisions, omitted related costs and investments, thus distorting the picture. One large company established an offshore manufacturing capability to avail itself of the low costs inherent in that decision. In its subsequent assessment of that investment, however, the company failed to recognize that the established costing and financial procedures did not allocate appropriate costs and inventory holdings to the offshore site. Consequently, all rework costs and in-transit inventory were charged against the home-based plant. The distorted figures reinforced the buy decision that had been taken, encouraging similar decisions in the future. However, when the accounting rules were changed, future options became less attractive.

These types of decision often given inadequate weight to important strategic issues. Aspects such as surrendering the ownership of costs and quality conformance and the need for an appropriate infrastructure base from which to launch changes in direction are ignored and thus lost as future options. Proponents of such strategies typically have the superficial understanding of business development that is associated with an analysis of figures, rather than a grasp of reality.

## Issues Involved in Changing Make-or-buy Decisions

For many years, changes in make-or-buy decisions were associated principally with the widening of a company's initial span of process. More recently many businesses have considered reducing process spans. Faced with a decline in demand and associated capacity requirements, companies have, possibly for the first time in their recent histories, been confronted with the necessity to decrease their span of process and often on many major business fronts. Coupled with well-received arguments about identifying core competencies and shedding other investments and process capabilities, this has accelerated the move by companies towards span reduction.

When repositioning, whether for growth or contraction, a business must fully assess the issues involved. In particular, it needs to determine whether or not the estimated costs and investments in process and infrastructure are realistic. Additional sizeable investments are often incurred after the event. Although not included in the original decision they form an integral part of securing the benefits of the original undertaking. Assessments based on previous experience need to form part of current estimates. Similarly, the benefits assumed to accrue from divestment may not be achieved when anticipated and sometimes not at all. An illustration that typifies this problem concerns the support functions within a firm's overhead structure. The extent of the overhead support necessary to effectively sustain the new process investment and/or growth into new products is often understated, while the anticipated reduction in overheads, associated with a narrowing of a firm's internal span of process, is generally overestimated.

It is also necessary to separate the issues involved in these decisions between those that essentially support strategy and those that do not. To ensure that span-of-process decisions are consistent with key corporate objectives (or if not, are recognized as not being consistent) is an essential step in the procedure. Decisions can all too often be taken without this appropriate level of clarity. Differentiating issues provides an opportunity to review these manufacturing decisions in the light of relevant corporate strategy considerations. It allows comparisons between options to be made on the basis of appropriate information. Separating strategic arguments into their functional derivatives will add further clarity to the corporate understanding that should form the context in which these important manufacturing decisions need to be addressed.

Particular issues will differ from one case to another and the level of importance of issues will also vary. Some of the more important advantages and disadvantages are listed here. How effectively a business is able to achieve the mix of benefits and risks involved, yet offset costs wherever possible, depends on a functionally capable and alert management team and the level of understanding and agreement they have reached on the strategic issues involved.

## Costs and Investments

One of the fundamental sets of trade-offs involved in span-of-process decisions concerns costs and investments.[4] The level of investment will determine the width of process internal to a business and in so doing will have a direct bearing on the levels of cost involved. The principal areas of cost associated with span-of-process decisions are:

■ Transaction costs concerned with the buying, selling and physical handling of materials throughout relevant processes.

■ The costs associated with improving the coordination between the supply, production and distribution activities.

■ The costs associated with combining similar overhead activities. Companies can do this when they widen their span of process. However, centralizing activities makes it difficult to achieve the apparent overhead gains when the internal span of process is narrowed. In these situations, companies must assess whether or not the *vertical slicing* into those overheads attributable to a proposed reduction in span is in fact achievable (see Exhibit 9.2).

■ The investment in hardware, controls, procedures and other relevant infrastructure requirements. Although the tangible costs of plant and equipment are readily identified and agreed to in principle, the costs resulting from changes in the less tangible areas are not as apparent nor as easily quantified. In turn, decisions on them are subject to judgement and require close examination. Invariably, these areas of projected costs are made on the assumption, or based on the argument, that the existing infrastructure can or will have to cope.

In situations of process widening many companies neither clearly identify all the investment and associated requirements involved nor hold a shared view of the strategic relevance of the proposed span-of-process changes. Invariably in these circumstances, sufficient allowances will not have been provided or the necessary allocations will have been squeezed out of the proposals as a result of the apparent conscientiousness of those involved. The outcome will be an underestimation of the investment needs in the short term that will normally result in a number of further investments in the future. The final tally will sometimes be well in excess of that on which the initial strategic decision was based.

**Exhibit 9.2**   Corresponding overhead support to the process under review (which will form part of the corporate decision on process narrowing – known as *vertical slicing*)

Two further important ramifications of widening the internal span of process concern a company's ability to adopt different options. First, the capital used up in these moves prevents its use elsewhere. Second, the implied commitment to a market and the product and process technologies and life cycles involved can be highly risky. The inherent inflexibility accumulated in these strategies may result in a sluggish response to change, high levels of unplanned capital expenditure and often sizeable write-offs.

## Strategic Considerations

Although decisions on process repositioning usually embody their own set of specific strategic issues, there are some important general considerations that help form the basis for strategic action.

■ *High entry barriers* – in industries where a wide span of process brings a set of distinct entry barrier advantages, increasing the internal span will raise the financial and managerial resources required for a company to enter and compete effectively with existing businesses. Established firms may, therefore, raise the stakes, thus discouraging new entrants.

■ *Supply assurance* – the supply of critical materials may well be of such importance to a company that this gain alone would be sufficient justification for the investment involved. As with all forms of backward integration, the issue of whether or not a company decides to keep process capacity solely in balance with its internal needs raises its own set of advantages and disadvantages.

■ *Secured outlets* – in the same way as supply can be assured by integrating backwards, securing outlets can result from integrating forwards. Additional advantages also accrue with this move – improved feedback leads to a position of being more aware of demand changes and provides an opportunity to increase the accuracy of forecasts.

## The Managerial Task

Changes in span of process will invariably lead to a change in the total management task within a business. The dimensions of change involved come under three broad headings:

■ *The level of complexity* – one important consequence that invariably comes from a widening of process span is the increase in complexity and the hidden costs associated with these incremental uplifts. The associations of synergy are probably more apparent in the level of complexity than elsewhere. Here, one and one really are greater than two.

■ *The question of balance* – when companies increase their span of process they face the questions of the trade-offs involved between whether or not to keep the supply or outlet in balance with the rest of the business. A large group of manufacturing companies, deciding on a policy of expansion, asked the individual companies involved to put forward proposals relevant to their own business. One such company, a cable maker, proposed integrating backwards into wire drawing. To limit the investment involved, it purchased a local site and installed capacity roughly in line with its own needs. With the high price of copper, neither part of the business wanted high material inventory. As a consequence, the production runs on which the drawn-wire cost structure had been based, and which sustained the investment rationale, could not be maintained. This was because of the programme changes necessary to meet cable sales and the low inventory planned for in the overall investment. Since one part of the business was not adequately decoupled from the next, even shorter runs and overtime working in the wire-drawing plant could not prevent cable delivery dates being missed. Eventually, the company had to re-examine issues of capacity balance and decoupling inventory levels.

■ *The manufacturing task* – span-of-process changes bring corresponding changes in the manufacturing management task. The cable-making/wire-drawing example had one further important rider. The management team assumed that their knowledge of cable making together with existing internal organizational and control systems would be sufficient to anticipate likely difficulties and to cope with any that were unforeseen in the processes involved in drawing wire. They underestimated the change in the manufacturing management task, which partly contributed to the wire-drawing unit's failure to break even in the first 20 months let alone meet the projected return on investment.

The traditional argument for ownership has been based, at least in part, on the economies of large scale. In the past two or three decades, this argument has been a major thrust within existing accounting perspectives. Based on inadequate analysis of what the new reality would bring, the economies-of-large-scale rationale has often been the principal distorting factor in these critical decisions. In many companies, the impact has been further disguised by the build-up of complexity associated with incremental process widening. In most situations, it is not the technology considerations but the control and other infrastructure features of the manufacturing task that are affected.

# Levels of Vertical Integration

The previous sections introduced some of the important perspectives, issues and context concerning make-or-buy decisions. The following sections address alternative strategies. This first section concerns dimensions of vertical integration, what is entailed and the benefits and disadvantages involved. The next main section flags up a growing problem for many industrialized nations: the hollowing of the manufacturing sector. The final section discusses a company's alternatives to widening the span of process. These sections offer a mix of the advantages associated with the approaches discussed in the two previous sections.

## Dimensions Involved

The principal dimensions of vertical integration are the breadth and level of activity and the form it takes. *Breadth* addresses decisions on which of the principal activities a firm decides to perform in-house. This involves functions such as design, manufacturing and distribution. Closely linked to this is the decision on the amount, or *level*, of each activity to be undertaken in-house and how much will, therefore, be subcontracted. Finally, the *form* concerns the level and type of ownership, trading partnership arrangements and other issues that are addressed in the following sections.

## Benefits of Vertical Integration

All make-or-buy decisions bring a mix of internal and external benefits and costs. In particular, decisions on vertical integration offer firms a number of inherent competitive advantages that are linked to increased knowledge of markets and technology, improved control over its environment and increased opportunity to support the characteristics of its markets. These include:

■ *Improved market and technological intelligence* – this increases the ability to forecast more accurately trends concerning key aspects of a business from demand patterns to technology and cost changes. Furthermore, it provides guarantees for supplies and markets which, in turn, strengthen a firm against known and opportunistic competitors.

■ *More readily available technological innovations and options* – this leads to greater coherence and transfer within the total organization, that is, sharing technology initiatives and opportunities by collaboration. In addition, it enables companies to transfer experience, thereby increasing the level of knowledge of events and so reducing some areas of uncertainty.

■ *Increased control over relevant aspects of a firm's environment* – these opportunities can take the form of backward integration to reduce dependency of supplies and forward integration to help to gain market penetration or acceptance. Instances of the latter range from overcoming strong entry (even monopoly) barriers, to gaining acceptance of new products. With regard to the former, St Gobain, a French glass-maker, purchased the UK-based glass processor and merchant, Solaglass, as a way of entering the UK glass market, which at the time was dominated by Pilkington Glass. The advent of both aluminium and rayon provide examples of the way vertical integration facilitated the acceptance of the use of these new materials as substitutes in existing markets.

■ *The provision of low-cost opportunities* – this is accomplished by generating internal demand and thereby contributing to the high-volume requirement for low-cost manufacturing. One example of this is the semiconductor market. Japanese companies such as Fujitsu, Hitachi, Mitsubishi, NEC and Toshiba have progressively outcompeted their US rivals partly through the high level of integration that characterizes their businesses. Semiconductors were invented in the 1950s, and since then four decades of accelerating growth produced by the year 2000 a worldwide industry of over $100bn, more than treble what it was in the mid-1980s. However, the highly integrated Japanese semiconductor manufacturers are able to make their products at increasingly lower costs than their competitors throughout the rest of the world. A substantial part of this is the result of the high-volume base created by internal, corporate demand. Japanese giant *zaibatsus* make semiconductors along with everything else from robots to cars and satellites. The result is that Japan currently has 50 per cent of the world semiconductor market, with the US at 37 per cent and Western Europe at 11 per cent.

■ *The differentiation of products* – this can occur in all aspects of production from product customization to the availability and use of alternative new materials as a way of meeting a product's technical, cost and other requirements.

## Benefits of Outsourcing

On the flip side of this key decision are the benefits to be gained from outsourcing. These primarily concern cash, costs and technology and include the following:

■ *Freed resources* – buy decisions reduce or more often eliminate the associated resources necessary to make the component, subassembly or final assembly involved. One result is that resources are freed, making funds available to be used elsewhere in a business.

■ *Reduced operating costs* – with less being made internally the process technology requirements and associated support are reduced together with the operations management and control tasks that typically accompany manufacturing.

■ *Easier to control costs* – with buy decisions, the dimension of cost control is simplified to one of a supplier's unit price. Although contract negotiations demand their own set of skills, the task of cost control for the materials, components, subassemblies or assemblies involved is, in itself, simplified.

■ *Access to world-class capabilities* – purchasing from selected vendors creates the opportunity to source from potentially world-class capabilities. It gives access to the technologies and expertise that make up a provider's primary business.

■ *Increased focus on own core tasks* – the reverse side of the last point, it allows a company to increase its attention, in terms of development time and investment, on its own primary business and associated core tasks.

## Disadvantages of Outsourcing

To some extent the disadvantages of outsourcing are the inverse of the benefits discussed above and supplement the 'benefits of vertical integration' section. They include:

■ *May lose control of important capabilities* – outsourcing brings with it the possibility of losing control of key capabilities. For example, dimensions such as quality conformance, delivery speed and delivery reliability are now, in part, within the processes and systems of suppliers. Managing the whole supply chain, as discussed later, becomes an increasingly important priority.

■ *Reversability* – the decision to subcontract is invariably irreversible. This is due, in part, to a reluctance to reconsider and then change direction on previous outsourcing decisions coupled with the stepped nature of such a change in terms of buying in technical capability and expertise from a zero base.

■ *New management skills* – managing a supply chain requires different, and often more demanding, skills than those to handle in-house manufacturing. Often, and particularly in the past, purchasing and related functions within a business have been allocated 'Cinderella' status with corresponding levels of resource and management talent. Integrating the essential links within a supply network requires skills of a high order to secure the essential contribution to meeting the needs of a firm's markets.

## Assessing the Appropriate Level of Vertical Integration

The degree of success of vertical integration depends on how well it has been thought through and fits the needs of the enlarged business. In instances in which it has not been thought through, rationalization tends to replace strategic rationale. In addition, vertical integration is based on the assumption that the potential benefits are tangible and achievable rather than illusory. In some instances, companies may integrate because the opportunity to do so was available and timely. Those that fail to separate the action itself from the rationale underpinning that action may unknowingly incur significant disadvantages.

To determine the appropriate level of integration needs sound data. Without knowing what is involved at each level, deciding where is best is not possible. Not only is a realistic assessment of costs and benefits required but also the timescales involved both in terms of current decisions and future changes.

## Level of Integration[5]

The final dimension concerns the level of integration a firm chooses to undertake. At the extreme, firms may decide on a *fully integrated strategy*, where all their requirements for a given material, product or service are bought internally. In these instances, the supplying units are usually fully owned subsidiaries. This alternative works best where:

- the level of price competition does not require companies to pursue the lowest cost alternatives to compete effectively in a market
- the advantages derived from accessibility to scarce resources outweigh other factors
- capacity increases are not stepped in nature, which can create investment obstacles in terms of changing demand and associated volumes.

## Taper-integrated Strategy

The more usual level of integration is referred to as a *taper-integrated strategy*.[6] With this, firms rely on outsiders to provide a portion of their requirements, which enables the integrated facilities to secure a high level of capacity utilization by alternating the make-or-buy decision to advantage. However, such strategies, especially when exercised to the full, incur a number of disadvantages, including:

- alternating the make-or-buy decision to advantage militates against developing good customer/supplier relations. In the long run it may alienate suppliers, as such strategies often do not provide them with adequate lead times to enable resources to be switched, capacity to be reduced or alternative sales to be secured.

- by definition a taper-integrated strategy implies splitting volumes and dilutes those conditions that maximize low-cost opportunities.

- alert suppliers may charge a price premium where volumes are low and subject to fluctuations.

The forms of integration discussed in this section entail at least some degree of internal provision. However there are alternatives to integrated strategies, as explained in a later section.

# The Hollow Corporation

There is an increasing recognition of and growing concern about a phenomenon referred to as the *hollow corporation*.[7] Where companies have considered the question of how manufacturing should best be organized to meet the dynamics of their markets, many have shied away from addressing and incorporating the manufacturing dimension within the debate concerning the appropriate short- and long-term strategy for a business. The attraction of low-cost manufacturing opportunities in the Far East, Eastern Europe and Mexico has lured many European and North American manufacturers to subcontract substantial parts of their existing processes without regard for, adequate understanding of, or sufficient in-depth debate about the long-term implications of these critical and often irreversible decisions. Exhibit 9.3 illustrates this continuing trend. The simplistic rationale of problem avoidance has such siren-like qualities as to make the decision difficult to argue against.

**Exhibit 9.3**   Trends in component sourcing for US manufacturers

| Levels of outsourcing | Percentage of US manufacturers | | | |
| --- | --- | --- | --- | --- |
| | 1988 | | 2000 | |
| | Actual | Cumulative | Estimated | Cumulative |
| Percentage components outsourced | | | | |
| 81–100 | 8 | 8 | 9 | 9 |
| 61–80 | 8 | 16 | 14 | 23 |
| 41–60 | 14 | 30 | 20 | 43 |
| 21–40 | 23 | 53 | 25 | 68 |
| 1–20 | 36 | 89 | 25 | 93 |
| None | 11 | 100 | 7 | 100 |
| Percentage components made outside the US | | | | |
| 81–100 | 1 | 1 | 4 | 4 |
| 61–80 | 2 | 3 | 5 | 9 |
| 41–60 | 7 | 10 | 15 | 24 |
| 21–40 | 14 | 24 | 25 | 49 |
| 1–20 | 42 | 66 | 34 | 83 |
| None | 34 | 100 | 17 | 100 |

*Source:* Department of Trade and Industry Report, 'Manufacturing into the Late 1900s', PA Consulting Group, HMSO, 1989, p. 46

However, as mentioned in the previous section, the long-term consequences of these decisions to companies and to nations seems neither to have been fully recognized nor adequately assessed. Such decisions bring the instant rewards of solution and profit. For many organizations, moving offshore becomes a last resort to offset sizeable structural disadvantages. The alternative is to become competitive in the relevant dimensions such as design, price, quality conformance and delivery performance, but usually the impact of this short-term thinking has not been fully assessed. To the nation as a whole there is an increasing dependency on imports, compounded by a loss of technological know-how and ownership, which will invariably lead to being driven out of some businesses altogether.

Companies pursuing this rationale rarely do so as a way of buying time to enable them to strategically regroup. For most it is a comprehensive solution in its own right, with an apparent disregard for the long-term implications and inherent constraints imposed on future strategic options.

Furthermore, the ripple effect means that for every $1bn of imports there is a further substantial loss to a nation's economy as a whole.[8] In addition, as time goes on these offshore plants will draw the service jobs that surround manufacturing and at a company level, the effects are similar. Once skills have been transferred out, that know-how will eventually be lost to that company.

The trend towards outsourcing on a larger scale has gathered momentum partly on the back of increased corporate moves towards downsizing that took a strong hold on business strategy direction from the mid-1980s through most of the 1990s. Bolstered by doctrines such as core competence that were in favour at the time, the benefits and rewards offered by solution-based approaches have a unique appeal to unquestioning recipients. The attraction of such offerings as fixed-asset freedom, cash infusion, capital fund availability and lower overhead cost structures was much heeded at the economic altar of financial markets.

The decision on whether or not to outsource is a sound one to address. What is of concern are the bandwagon consequences of panacea solutions, the failure to review the decisions within the context of the overall business and to assess the strategic impact over appropriate timescales. Exhibit 9.4 humourously depicts one ultimate outcome with the commentary, as always, aimed at exposing and questioning, in this instance, the potential folly of the underlying trend.[9]

At the extreme, the postindustrial company could be vertically disaggregated, relying on other companies for manufacturing and many essential business functions.[10] They become industrial, corporate shells. And there are strong forces pushing companies this way. In the short term, these decisions offer fixed-asset freedom and dynamic networking, both arguably suited to meeting the characteristics of today's markets. Such arrangements allow companies to respond quickly to exploit new markets and new technologies. The organizations become more agile, flexible and responsive. Typically, firms need less capital, carry lower overhead costs and can better tap into outside technology. In essence, they are more entrepreneurial.

One outcome of this is that manufacturing companies of a new kind are evolving – those that do little manufacturing. They import components and assemble them or import the products themselves and sell them. The result is a hollowing of once-powerful manufacturing companies. Following a strategy of this kind, companies become trapped in a position where their ability to compete is increasingly undermined by their own and their competitors' actions. Unchecked, this will invariably lead to the abandonment of their status as strong industrial

**Exhibit 9.4**    A hint of satire in this comment on the trend towards outsourcing by highlighting the
potentially simplistic approach to these key strategic decisions. In this instance, the UK
utility giant, British Gas, and the outsourcing of its IT provision including the human
dimension of this decision was the stimulus. © Roger Beale (with permission)

companies and the retardation of their capacity for innovation and productivity
improvement. The erosion of a nation's wealth-creating activity is the aggregate
effect of these policies, which in the end reduces the standard of living enjoyed by
its people.

On a more serious note, outsourcing no matter what form it takes presents a new
risk to companies. Sensitive information needs to be shared on the one hand and
providing the opportunity for new entrants to gain expertise presents risk on the
other. It is important for firms to look long and hard before turning to suppliers for
engineering help. If the technical dimension in all its forms is part of a company's
competitive advantage then giving it away means having less of an edge in the
marketplace. In today's competitive environment this could be a significant, long-
term disadvantage. Examples from the past illustrate the consequences while more
recent ones point to the potential involved.

- In the 1960s, the then-dominant US television industry gave the technology to build picture tubes to low-cost Asian suppliers. Some time later, Asian companies began making entire TV sets and the US industry nearly went out of business.

- Similar concerns are surfacing in the aerospace industry. Since the 1980s Boeing (the giant US aircraft company) has let Japanese suppliers get close to fuselage design practices on wide-body jets. Boeing has long advocated partnerships as a way of controlling the Japanese but there is growing concern that such practices will help stimulate an Asian aircraft industry. And, given Japanese engineering prowess in other sectors, aerospace is for them a ready-made extension of their current expertise.

The full impact of the disaggregation philosophy on the welfare of corporations and nations is only now being realized. Many firms are finding themselves hamstrung. They are increasingly exposed to competition from suppliers yet have less security of supply and control of production; they lose design and manufacturing expertise, which forms the essential springboard from which to launch their strategic response. Furthermore, having once taken this strategic option, it is difficult to alter course. Strategic options become increasingly restricted and future positions reinforce original rationale, subsequent logic and chosen outcomes. To rebuild alternatives has infrastructure and time dimensions that are unappreciated and consequently unaddressed.

In a recent interview, Hisashi Sakamaki, who oversees all Canon's (the Japanese photo and printer giant) manufacturing, recalled the important lessons learned from US companies' mistakes as described by the MIT Commission on Industrial Productivity.[11] 'The key for us,' he says, 'has been to figure out how to benefit from production overseas without losing our capacity to develop production at home. Most American firms rushed abroad and lost that knowledge.'[12]

## Alternatives to Widening Internal Span of Process

The discussion so far has implied that the choices companies must make also involve an ownership or non-ownership option. Either a company invests in the process through ownership or it buys out its requirements from suppliers. Many companies perceive that in certain situations they have only two viable options or even just Hobson's choice.[13] To them being reliant on suppliers is not a feasible alternative.

However, where greater control is necessary, companies need to consider alternatives to widening the internal span of process. In assessing whether or not the decision should be by investment, companies must separate strategic from tactical issues and trace the strategic arguments to their functional source. Only in this way will a business be able to establish clearly whether or not a decision has to be through investment ownership.

The alternatives are based on an appropriately high degree of liaison between those involved. Some involve legal agreements or arrangements of some kind. Others attempt to exploit opportunities with links that are beneficial to all concerned.

## Joint Ventures

Companies often have to exploit opportunities, particularly in areas such as applied technology and research. Where companies have similar needs and both can benefit from combining, a joint venture is a sensible alternative.

Joint ventures are separate entities sponsored by two or more actively involved firms. Because joint ventures draw on the strengths of their owners, they have the potential to tap the synergy inherent in such a relationship and the improved competitive abilities that should accrue. Since the late 1970s joint ventures have increased substantially in Europe and the US, particularly in industries such as communications systems, IT and services.

This trend is continuing and domestic joint ventures have become an important way of improving the strengths and reducing the weaknesses of cooperating businesses. Companies willing to undertake the high degree of commitment and cooperation that is necessary in joint ventures can exploit opportunities from which they previously would have been debarred, due to investment or lead-time barriers.

However joint ventures should not be seen as a convenient means of hiding weaknesses. If used prudently, such ventures can create internal strengths. They can be resource-aggregating and resource-sharing mechanisms, allowing sponsoring firms to concentrate resources where they possess the greatest strengths. Exhibit 9.5 provides a comprehensive list of reasons for forming joint ventures and is classified into operational and strategic uses.

Joint ventures, therefore, not only share investment but, often more importantly, provide direction and make fresh opportunities possible.

Identifying the areas in which to focus attention, with the knowledge that the developments will have a commercial outlet, can give substance to this decision. Reducing risk in this way while also limiting the investments required to bring the activity to fruition is an ideal solution. By providing this mix, a joint venture is a sensible alternative to the owner/non-owner options.

**Exhibit 9.5**   Reasons for forming joint ventures[14]

| | Advantages |
|---|---|
| **Operational** | ■ Reduces uncertainty<br>■ Shares investment and risk<br>■ Process capacity sharing<br> – increases utilization<br> – avoids process duplication<br> – wider product ranges<br>■ Shares facilities in other parts of the supply chain; for example, distribution channels<br>■ Increases technological know-how by<br> – facilitating information exchange<br> – potentially creating critical mass in areas such as research and development<br> – broadening expertise in, for instance, engineering and IT systems<br>■ Strengthens market intelligence<br>■ Helps retain key staff<br> – increased job scope<br> – better career opportunities |
| **Strategic** | ■ Strengthens current strategic position by<br> – pioneering developments into new segments<br> – rationalizing existing segments<br> – reducing competitive volatility<br>■ Pre-empts competitors<br> – facilitates access to new markets and customers<br> – supports growth in market share<br> – strengthens negotiating position<br> – gains access to global markets<br>■ Augments strategic position<br> – creates and develops synergies<br> – technology and skill transfers<br> – diversify: divest existing and/or leverage investments and capabilities |

# Non-equity-based Collaboration

Companies unwilling or unable to cope with joint-venture arrangements can resort to an appropriate form of non-equity-based collaboration to meet their needs. These mechanisms provide the means of establishing cooperative working arrangements that need a long-term base if the collaboration is to yield meaningful and useful results. Such arrangements include:

■ Research and development consortia to enhance innovation and the exploitation of results.

- Cross-marketing agreements to provide opportunities, such as utilizing by-products, widening product lines and sharing distribution channels.
- Cross-production agreements to avoid facilities duplication, provide vertical integration opportunities and transfer technology know-how.
- Joint-purchasing activities to enhance buying power in terms of price gains and increased supplier allegiance.

## Managing the Supply Chain

The make-or-buy decision is not only critical in itself but it also governs the size and nature of the supply chain and the resulting management tasks. However, whether a company makes or buys, the need to effectively manage the whole supply chain has increasingly been recognized as a key executive role and one that directly impacts a company's ability to compete in its chosen markets. The task of managing the in-house or internal phase of the chain is addressed throughout this book. This section deals with the key issues and approaches that relate to managing the external parts of a supply chain.

The concept of a totally integrated supply chain – from material producer through to end customer – is bringing great changes to the way businesses operate. Increasingly companies no longer compete just with each other but rather they compete through their supply chains (see Exhibit 9.6). To bring this about companies need a supply chain that is managed as an integrated whole to secure maximum support for the competitive factors in their markets and that is underpinned by responsive and adaptive systems and procedures. This, in turn, requires meaningful collaboration and fuller relationships to provide the essential basis for cooperation and joint developments.

## Supply-chain Management Issues

In the 1980s companies turned their attention to fixing their manufacturing problems but few addressed total supply-chain costs. By the early 1990s firms started to

**Exhibit 9.6**    The changing basis of competition

|  | Basis of competition |
|---|---|
| Yesterday | Manufacturing company versus Manufacturing company |
| Today | Manufacturing company's supply chain versus Manufacturing company's supply chain |

realise the need to shift emphasis. With shortening product life cycles, more customer choice and reducing lead times set within the context of growing world competition, it became essential to review the whole supply chain, identify opportunities and manage these improvements. As most companies expect outsourcing to increase in future years,[15] the need to manage the supply chain effectively has to be high on the corporate agenda. Whether you make or buy the responsibility for managing the whole chain can no longer be ignored as it was in the past. Some of the key management issues involved are now discussed.

## Globalization

With trade barriers easing and markets opening up, the globalization of business activity has accelerated. Two key issues result from this – a widening choice of offshore suppliers and the need to manage the global supply chain that emerges.

The growing manufacturing base of regions and countries such as the Far East, Eastern Europe, Mexico and South America has received high exposure in part, if not exclusively, due to the low-cost manufacturing provision they offer. While for some companies low cost is consistent with their market needs it is essential that market requirement and not unit cost drives choice. The notion of low cost is typically a small part of the business picture and companies are clearly beginning to recognize this. For example, in the mid-1990s developed countries took almost two-thirds of foreign direct investment inflows, while developing countries accounted for the remainder.[16]

There is an increasing emphasis on global capability. In order to take full advantage of this opportunity companies need to manage the processes and interfaces involved. It is essential to avoid the scenario of gaining advantage in one phase of a supply chain and losing the benefits in the next. Key to this is globalizing total customer relations from design through logistics to the end user.

## Incorporating Uncertainty

Today's markets are characterized by shortening product life cycles and stiffening requirements for all aspects of customer service. Against this background large manufacturing companies are characterized by complexity as clearly illustrated by a review of the material flows for typical products. Multiple suppliers provide materials, parts and subassemblies to manufacturing sites with varying regularity. These are then processed through a number of stages that, in turn, are characterized by uncertainty. Finished products then go to a range of customers often with varying sets of demands. These patterns are further confused by the range of transportation options to meet the spread of customers around the world.

The real management problem within this complex network is, however, the uncertainty that characterizes it. But many companies still treat this task as if it were predictable. The planning and scheduling systems inadequately take account of

**Exhibit 9.7**   Rising level of mark downs in the retail sector

| Year | US department store mark downs as a percentage of dollar sales |
|------|:---:|
| 1970 | 8 |
| 1989 | 17 |
| 1997 | 20 |

*Source:* Financial and Operating Results of Department and Speciality Stores, National Retail Federation (US)

demand uncertainty. They are designed as if certainty rather than uncertainty was the reality with which they had to cope. And, as the situation today is increasingly less predictable than in the past, this leads to circumstances of unnecessary inventory and high obsolescence. To illustrate, data on the percentage of mark downs with US department and speciality stores is given in Exhibit 9.7. The levels since 1970 have risen dramatically.

Furthermore, all this is in the context, on the one hand, of IT developments such as electronic point-of-sale scanners that provide up-to-the-minute data on customer buying patterns and, on the other hand, manufacturing improvements concerning the production of smaller order sizes. But at the same time, the drive to meet customer requirements has typically widened product ranges dramatically even in industries that traditionally have not been considered fashion driven. The number of new-product introductions in the US food industry, for example, exploded ninefold from 1980 to the early 1990s.

But new-product introductions have two adverse side effects:

- average life cycles are reduced. This, in turn, shortens the relative duration of the more stable phase of demand in relation to the less-certain initial and end phases.
- total demand is spread over more stock-keeping units (SKUs).[17] The more items, the more difficult the task of forecasting sales.

Overall the result is a growing unpredictability that increases the need to manage each phase of the supply chain and the interface between them. As highlighted earlier, Dell Computer Corporation, having shortened its own assembly lead times in response to the delivery speed requirements of its customers, found itself constrained from meeting these needs by the long lead time of its component suppliers.

## Customer/Supplier Dependence

The relationship between customers and suppliers is influenced by the level of dependency of the one on the other – see Exhibit 9.8. Where customers and suppliers are positioned will impact potential relationship options as explained in the next section.

**Exhibit 9.8**   Customer/supplier dependence

## Types of Supplier Relations

Part of the make-or-buy decision is how best to structure relationships with suppliers. Customers can position themselves in a number of ways within the constraints of dimensions such as the 'dependence factor' introduced in the last section. Characteristics of these different types of supplier relationships are now reviewed.[18] Which one a company should choose needs to reflect the characteristics of the materials or components involved and of the marketplace in which a company operates.

■ *Trawling the market* – here suppliers are held at arm's length with a growing amount of business completed using computerized interaction. For example, General Electric (GE) in the US increasingly purchases components over the Internet where it posts details of parts electronically and prequalified vendors then quote for the contract. Here, there is little face-to-face interaction and the key order-winner is price. Delivery on time and quality conformance are qualifiers and form part of the listing prerequisites. Gains also include reduced processing costs – for example, GE quotes a 90 per cent reduction compared to traditional paperwork procedures. Finally, this phase may entail placing a significant amount of business with competitors.

■ *Ongoing relationships* – these involve establishing medium-term contracts with suppliers, developing relations in terms of information sharing and require sound management by customers.

- *Partnerships* – involve long-term contracts characterized by the extensive sharing of information and increased trust. For example, since 1988 the US car maker Chrysler's average contract length with suppliers has more than doubled.

- *Strategic alliances* – the trend in sourcing is towards strategic alliances that are characterized by the increased depth and breadth of the whole customer/supplier relationship. A prerequisite of more cooperative relationships is a dramatic reduction in the supplier base and a recognition by customers of the fact that their costs, quality conformance levels and lead times are partly within the processes of their supplier. For example, Xerox has reduced its suppliers from over 5,000 to about 400, while Chrysler in the mid-1990s saved more than $0.5bn from supplier-generated ideas.

  Strategic alliances are marked by long timescales, extensive sharing of information, increased trust, joint development of products and processes and the intent to work together over an extended period. Boeing has strategic alliances with GE, Rolls-Royce and Pratt & Witney, partly to reduce the financial risk of new aeroplane programmes and partly to cope with the complex technical interfaces between engines and airframes that have to be designed in conjunction with each other.

- *Backward integration* – the final step is to change from relationship to ownership. This leads to the full sharing of information and the transfer of goals and culture.

## Offshore Manufacturing Plants

Often foreign manufacturing plants are established for the classic benefits of tariff and trade concessions, lower labour costs, subsidies and reduced logistic costs. As a consequence they are assigned a limited range of tasks and responsibilities that typically reflect the prime reason for which they were built. Companies are now reviewing this classic perspective and broadening their expectations of offshore plants and the way they manage and measure them (see Exhibit 9.9).

It is important for companies to exploit these opportunities and Exhibit 9.10 lists some potential roles for foreign factories.

**Exhibit 9.9**   Examples of companies seeking and gaining additional roles from offshore plants

| Company | Location | Tasks |
|---|---|---|
| Hewlett-Packard | Guadalajara (Mexico) | ■ Assembles computers<br>■ Designs memory boards |
| 3M | Bangalore (India) | ■ Manufactures software<br>■ Writes software |
| Motorola | Singapore | ■ Manufactures pagers<br>■ Designs pagers |

**Exhibit 9.10** Progressive roles of offshore manufacturing plants[19]

| Development phase | Characteristics |
|---|---|
| Offshore factory | ■ Established to manufacture specific items at low cost |
| | ■ Technical and managerial investments kept to a minimum |
| | ■ Level of local autonomy is typically not extensive |
| Server factory | ■ Supplies specific national or regional markets |
| | ■ Typically located to overcome tariff barriers, reduce taxes, minimize logistic costs or cushion the business from exposure to foreign-exchange fluctuations |
| | ■ Provides a base from which to launch products into a market (for example, the European Union) |
| Contributor factory | ■ Serves a specific national or regional market |
| | ■ Responsibilities extend to product development and process engineering as well as the choice and development of suppliers |
| | ■ Potential site as a testing ground for new products, process technologies and computer systems |
| Lead factory | ■ Creates new products, processes and technologies for the company as a whole |
| | ■ Responsible for tapping into and collecting local knowledge and technological resources in general and for use in developing new products and processes |
| | ■ Key role with suppliers including choice and development |
| | ■ Whole range of external relationships including customers, process technology suppliers and research centres |
| | ■ Frequently initiates innovations |

## Logistics Costs

US companies spend almost 11 per cent of the gross domestic product (almost $700bn) to wrap, bundle, load, unload, sort, reload and move goods around. By 2002, the estimated logistics bill in Europe will be approaching $160m. With figures like these, the cost of making products is often not the area in which to seek savings. A typical box of cereals in the US is estimated to spend 140 days getting from factory to supermarket shelf. It goes through a procession of stages each of which has a warehouse. The resulting inefficiencies and logistic costs are staggering.

Companies, therefore, need to take into account their supply chains when making location choices and also seek potential savings where the berries will often be thickest and lowest. The lack of attention paid to supply chains in the past and the growing size of this element in terms of cost, quality conformance and lead times makes the potential benefits here attractive and high on most companies' priority list.

# Developing the Supply Chain

The goal of supply-chain management is to link the market, distribution channel, manufacturing process and supplier base such that customers' needs are better met at lower costs. As highlighted earlier, while many companies began fixing their manufacturing problems from the early to mid-1980s, few addressed the total cost of ownership. By the early 1990s, progressive companies had begun to realize the need to refocus from 'fixing' manufacturing to addressing how to better manage their supply chains, a fact confirmed by a 1996 European-based survey. This identified that 88 per cent of the companies reviewed had been carrying out significant overhauls of supply chains and saw supply-chain management as the focus for improvement in their overall performance.[20]

But, we should have learned from history that little ever changes. In 1929 Ralph Borsodi observed that in the '50 years between 1870 and 1920 the cost of distributing necessities and luxuries had nearly trebled, while production costs had come down by one fifth... what we are saving in production we are losing in distribution'.[21] The same scenario exists today.

## Origins and Evolution of Supply Chains

As emphasized earlier when discussing the concept of focus (Chapters 7 and 8), the origin of organizations in the 21st century is rooted in functional management and control with the subsequent result of split responsibilities. The outcome is a fragmented supply chain with an emphasis on vertical rather than horizontal processes as illustrated in Exhibit 9.11.

For most companies, developing a supply change is a multiphased task. It starts with integrating the steps within the internal supply chain as illustrated in Exhibit

**Exhibit 9.11**  Phase 1 – Typical initial position of functionally fragmented supply chains with built-in delays/inventory, vertical reporting structures and systems and the separation of suppliers, manufacturing and customers

**Exhibit 9.12** Phase 2 – Integration of the supply chain activities within a business

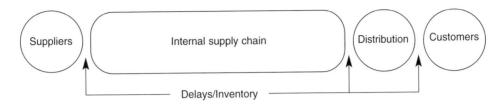

9.12. This internal coordination emphasizes the horizontal nature of the processes inherent in the basic tasks of procurement through to finished-goods provision and forges cooperation between the steps to create an integrated whole and the opportunity to reduce costs and delays on the one hand and improve responsiveness to customer needs on the other.

The next step concerns coordinating activities between businesses. As shown in Exhibit 9.13 this stage involves recognizing additional facets within the supply chain (for example, tier 1 and tier 2 suppliers and stages in the distribution channel) in order to ensure that these form part of the collaborative development between supply-chain partners.

The final phase is to synchronize the planning and execution of activities across the supply chain (see Exhibit 9.14). This requires partnership and strategic alliance arrangements that will include the transfer and access of data between businesses from design through to order fulfilment, call-offs and delivery schedules. Traditional roles and responsibilities will change dramatically with suppliers on the one hand at times taking responsibility for design through to the internal supply chain and deciding how much and when to ship goods to customers on the other.

The principles underlying these changes have their origins in a recognition that the whole, and not solely the internal phase, of a supply chain is the basis for today's competition. Given the extent and nature of the support for markets that is provided by operations, aligning the supply-chain provision with the requirements

**Exhibit 9.13** Phase 3 – Collaboration across the supply chain by coordinating activities between businesses

**Exhibit 9.14**  Phase 4 – Synchronized and real-time planning and execution of activities across the supply chain

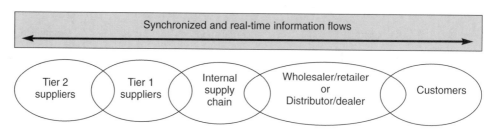

of agreed markets needs to be a central feature of strategy implementation. Key issues that result include:

- *Overcoming the barriers to integration* – functions within organizations and organizations themselves create barriers to integration. Viewing the supply chain as a whole is a prerequisite for rethinking how best to provide market support through the entire supply chain and overcoming these inherent obstacles.

- *Responding to short lead time* – delivery speed is an order-winner or qualifier in many of today's markets. Customers are seeking to reduce lead times and the strategic response of suppliers needs to match these quick response demands. To do this reliably requires developing lean logistics and managing the supply chain as an integrated whole.

- *Eliminating costs* – an integrated approach lowers costs by reducing inventory, simplifying procedures, eliminating duplication and other non-value-added activities together with associated overheads. Viewing the supply chain as a whole enables processes and procedures to be structured with the associated gains of reduced time and cost.

- *Moving information, not inventory and delays* – non-integrated approaches have built-in delays comprising time and inventory. By moving information, delays are reduced and subsequent parts of the chain can match real-time needs rather than using inventory to provide against uncertainty and the unknown.

One parallel to lean supply-chain management is provided by the revolutionary changes brought to high-peak climbing by Reinhold Messner. As Exhibit 9.15 explains, the 'direct alpine approach' he introduced changed the 'conventional mountaineering strategy' (one based on 'massive amounts of support including extra oxygen') to one using 'little equipment and no oxygen support to reach the top'. Messner argued that under the conventional approach, the slowest man set the pace, whereas his goal was 'speed of execution' – the final assault was made 'by himself, or with one other person, in a single day'.

**Exhibit 9.15** Lean supply chain works elsewhere and brings similar benefits[22]

'Reinhold Messner, the Italian climber, is one of the great sports heroes of Europe. His claim to fame is not so much that he climbed all 14 of the world's highest peaks. Messner's primary achievement is that he introduced a totally new way of climbing – the direct alpine approach – which uses little equipment and no oxygen support to reach the top.

Conventional mountaineering strategy is based on massive amounts of support, including extra oxygen, thought essential for climbs over 25,000 feet. Men such as Sir Edmund Hillary and Chris Bonington relied on hundreds of guides who carried food, oxygen and other supplies; an American expedition to climb Everest in 1963 included 900 porters trudging up the mountain with 300 tons of equipment.

Messner argues that under this strategy, the slowest man sets the pace. His goal is speed of execution. Although assisted by guides up the base of a mountain, Messner usually makes the final assault by himself, or with one other person, in a single day. He scaled the north face of Everest solo, without oxygen – one of the most severe mountaineering challenges ever attempted.'

## Aspects of Change

Underpinning the developments set out in the last section are a number of changes that need to be secured if the desired supply-chain management improvements are to be realized. The most important of these changes are now discussed.

### Effective consumer response

There is more to supply-chain management than hard-nosed procurement and tight controls over inventory levels. While effectively managing the supply chain concerns eliminating delays and reducing resources along the way, the orientation of such improvements needs to be towards more effective consumer response where market requirements and not traditional dimensions such as cost reduction underpin priorities and direction.

More effective consumer response combines a company's own internal improvements with seeking changes in all the external elements of the supply chain. These range from suppliers shouldering some or all of the associated development costs to smaller, more frequent deliveries necessitating suppliers to hold inventory or produce more often in smaller lot sizes. For most companies there is little choice but to seek more from suppliers because their own customers are exacting the same pressure on short lead times and sharing risk.

The result fosters closer relations with fewer suppliers. The greatest challenge is working both the internal and external dimensions of the chain in line with the needs of agreed markets. The key to making this happen is attitude and information, the topics of the next two sections.

### Changes in attitude

Relationships with suppliers have a history where cooperation was not the way in which customers behaved. Absolute control over aspects such as design and scheduling, pitting suppliers against each other and ruling by threat and fear are being abandoned in favour of long-term relationships often with single suppliers. Companies are also bringing suppliers on board much earlier in the design process, seeking technical help and contributions and even inviting suppliers to help in identifying future products.

To underpin these changes customers are reviewing the way they handle suppliers and the level of cooperation involved. The trend towards greater cooperation goes hand in hand with a more proactive style as illustrated in Exhibit 9.16.

**Exhibit 9.16**   Phases in changing customer attitudes to suppliers

| Changing customer attitudes to suppliers | |
|---|---|
| Threat and fear | Traditional stance. Perceptions based upon:<br><br>■ customer dominates the relationship with suppliers<br>■ suppliers respond to demands<br>■ customers pitted against each other<br>■ underpinned by the threat of the purchase orders and contracts being given to other suppliers on the one hand and a supplier's fear of losing the business on the other |
| Reward | First step towards cooperation and moving from a reactive to a proactive stance. Characterized by elements such as:<br><br>■ fewer suppliers<br>■ award of long-term contracts<br>■ customer is proactive in building a relationship with suppliers |
| Collaboration | Progressive move towards fuller and more cooperative relationships, the pace of which is set predominantly by the customer. Evolution through a series of steps such as a customer:<br><br>■ identifies improvements that a supplier can make<br>■ provides support and resources (for example, technical capability) to undertake improvements<br>■ gives actual help to improve suppliers including training a supplier's staff<br>■ starts to take into account the processes of its suppliers when designing products so as to help them improve their level of support<br>■ focuses attention on tier 2 suppliers as a source of improving tier 1 suppliers' support (see Exhibit 9.13). |
| Integration and synchronization | The final step is to integrate activities achieving benefits typically associated with ownership – the concept of virtual ownership. Based upon mutual respect and trust these include suppliers access to real-time information with customers harmonizing their suppliers' work and synchronizing their support. These changes include:<br><br>■ access to design-related information and responsibility for product design<br>■ suppliers responsibility for deciding when and how much to ship |

### Increasing use of IT

Since the early 1960s four major stepped changes in information technology developments have transformed the way that companies have conducted business and each wave of technology has radically altered the supply chain that links suppliers through to end users.

The initial phase of information technology application was based on main-frame computers. It began in the early 1960s and continued to be the dominant technology until the early 1970s. Business applications included material requirements planning and manufacturing resource planning (MRP and MRPII respectively). These enabled companies to standardize and systemize the day-to-day tasks in operations and parts of the supply chain. As a result, companies developed functional expertise supported by systems designed on the tasks of relevant functions.

The second phase was based on personal computers (PCs) that began in the 1970s and continued well into the 1980s. PC applications like word processors, spreadsheets and presentation software facilitated communication across functional boundaries. PCs also resulted in the power of computing being in the hands of employees, and businesses built on this opportunity by focusing on the development of cross-functional processes that brought benefits that were both functional and overall business in origin.

The third phase of computer-based IT applications was based on network computing. Starting in the mid-1980s it continues to have a dominant influence on how companies are managed and business is conducted. Network computing, customer/supplier applications, electronic data interchange (EDI), point-of-sale response and other forms of electronic mail are reducing the costs of handling information and transactions while speeding up information exchange that allows real-time systems and responses to be developed while leveraging the efficiencies of functional expertise (phase 1) and cross-functional business processes (phase 2).

The fourth phase is based on the Internet and World Wide Web. Providing a universal infrastructure, the Internet facilitates the interchange of information between businesses by not only reinforcing existing trends of cooperation but also helping companies to consider their supply chains as a whole, where their role is to manage and orchestrate process priorities and performance. By fostering better communication and interchange of information between companies, this phase enables fully integrated processes between businesses, not only customers to suppliers but also between suppliers.

One of the lasting effects of these technology applications is that they have facilitated the breakdown of barriers from cross-individuals to cross-corporations (see Exhibit 9.17).

### Focusing on non-value-added activities

Increasingly companies have focused attention on minimizing non-value-added activities while providing information and communication tools that allow employees to focus on the value-added and strategic activities within the business. As firms reduce non-value-added activity they redirect those newly released resources to

**Exhibit 9.17**  The evolving role of IT in managing a supply chain

| Phase | Aspects of change |
|---|---|
| 1. Cross-individuals | Broke down barriers between functional experts themselves and between these and the executives responsible for managing core parts of a business, particularly operations |
| 2. Cross-functional | Facilitated links between functions by requiring and helping the interchange between different parts of the same business |
| 3. Cross-businesses | Impacted the way companies conducted business by removing barriers within an organization and between parts of the immediate supply chain |
| 4. Cross-corporate | Continued the cross-corporate changes by facilitating cooperation of businesses within a supply chain including tier 2 suppliers |

the value-added and strategic dimensions of their business. For example, companies are increasingly using electronic intranet catalogues that enable office staff (the consumers) to order non-production goods (for example, office supplies and computer software) directly from agreed suppliers. Not only does this break down barriers but it also eliminates non-value-added activities such as data re-entry and checking, thus allowing more time for purchasing staff to focus on their value-added activities such as developing supplier relations and contract negotiations.

**Strategic partnering**

The need to be more competitive has led to a major drive to partner other companies in the supply chain. As stressed in the earlier section on 'changes in attitudes', customer/supplier relations continue to undergo major changes where the goal is to synchronize activities to the point where virtual integration is achieved (see Exhibit 9.16).

The extent to which this can be secured is not only constrained by the parties involved but also by the stage in a sector's evolution. For example, in the early days of the computing industry the major players had no option but to build the infrastructure to produce all the components and parts a computer needed. They had little choice. As the industry grew, more specialized companies developed to produce specific components. This allowed new entrants a choice. As Michael Dell (founder of Dell Computers) explained, 'as a new start-up, Dell couldn't afford to create every piece of the value chain. But more to the point, why should we want to? We concluded we'd be better off leveraging the investments others have made and focusing on delivering solutions and systems to customers... It's a pretty simple strategy.' Michael Dell continued, 'but at the time it went against the dominant "engineering-centric" view of the industry. The IBMs, Compaqs and HPs subscribed to a "we-have-to-develop-everything" view of the world. If you weren't doing component assembly you weren't a real computer company.'[23]

Strategic partnering is based on a conscious decision that sees its ultimate goal as virtual integration. This seeks to incorporate other parts of the supply chain as if they are part of one's own business – a long way from the not uncommon stance of outsourcing parts of a business that were, in fact, problem areas that a company could not fix.

On the delivery end of the chain, companies work with their customers to better understand their needs. In some partnerships, retail stores are sharing point-of-sale data to help suppliers better meet market trends and changes. On the sourcing end of the chain, suppliers are delivering more frequently, keeping consignment stock in a customer's warehouse (and only invoicing on use) and managing the replenishment cycle to reflect usage while helping to optimize their own schedules. While the customer frees up resources, the supplier has longer-term customer commitment, a barrier from competition that reduces sales and marketing effort and firm data on which to plan and schedule manufacturing and its own suppliers.

**Exhibit 9.18**  Examples of customer/supplier relationship developments in a range of industrial sectors

| End customer | Customer/supplier developments |
|---|---|
| Hitachi (VCR equipment) | ■ Six-monthly supplier meetings where Hitachi's CEO provides details of aggregate plans and policies to suppliers' top executives<br>■ Suppliers arranged into groups by categories of parts – cosmetic, electronic, mechanical and assembly. Each group has bi-monthly two-day meetings to resolve quality conformance, technical and delivery issues |
| Volvo (cars) | ■ 75 per cent of every car is made outside Sweden<br>■ Volvo collects parts from suppliers and ships them to Gothenburg<br>■ Suppliers required to maintain two to four weeks of stock<br>■ Pallets of parts not opened until moved to the assembly area, necessitating a guarantee on quality conformance and quantity<br>■ Volvo provides a 12-month forecast: first six weeks are firm, next 12 weeks can vary but Volvo accepts responsibility for materials and work-in-progress inventory |
| Boeing (passenger aircraft) | ■ Design-build teams used on the 777 passenger airliner<br>■ First plane off the assembly line – parts were so accurate that the nose-to-tail measurement was less than 23/1000 of an inch (0.6 mm) from design specification<br>■ Success built on computer-based design and the design-build teams used that included suppliers. Core to this success was the mutual respect and trust built up within the teams[24] |
| UK-based motor manufacturers | ■ Forum established comprising experts from General Motors, Honda, Nissan, Toyota and Volkswagen<br>■ Purpose is for these major competitors to cooperate in educating and improving tier 2 supplier base to the auto industry[25] |
| Canon (photocopiers and printers) | ■ Sent own engineers to Daisho Denshi (a $0.25bn maker of circuit boards and other parts) at a time when it was on the verge of bankruptcy<br>■ Improvements in efficiency, quality conformance and on-time delivery resulted<br>■ Led to Daisho Denshi cutting prices to Canon by 10 per cent[26] |

To illustrate the nature and extent of partnering arrangements and developments, Exhibit 9.18 provides examples of relationship developments in a range of industrial sectors.

## Summary Benefits

While some customer/supplier developments attract specific sets of gains, there are several benefit clusters that are invariably present, in full or part, in all such developments. This section summarizes these sets of general gains as a way of reflecting on the issues discussed in the last section and highlighting the potential benefits involved.

## Reducing Costs

Companies are becoming increasingly aware of an obvious truth, at least in hindsight – the maker of a part should be more able to design it at a lower cost than its customer. The expertise base and continuing transfer of ideas from one solution to another should always lead to lower-cost applications.

> 'In the Detroit research centre of Johnson Controls Inc., (a major supplier of automotive seats), a computer-operated shaking machine subjects the seats to the bumps and bangs encountered on a test track. In a nearby room, one Johnson team is devising seats for Chrysler's next generation of midsize cars, while teams in other rooms are doing the same job for Ford Motor Co., GM, Toyota Motor Corp., and the Mercedes-Benz unit of Daimler-Benz AG... Because a supplier can sell parts to an entire industry, the system becomes a vehicle for transforming new techniques from one manufacturer to another (with the result that) the maker of a part should be able to conceive a new one more cheaply than the final assembler that is responsible for the whole product.'[27]

A. T. Kearney Inc., a Chicago consulting firm, estimates that where manufacturers properly incorporate suppliers into their product development process they can cut their purchased parts and services costs by as much as 30 per cent.[28]

Working with suppliers can lead to cost reductions other than from the more traditional sources. Encouraging suppliers to come up with cost-cutting ideas and design innovations can lead to potentially large savings. As mentioned earlier, in 1996 Chrysler Corporation (the US car maker) took $1bn savings from the systems that it shared with its supplier.

## Shortening Lead Times

The importance of recognizing the value-creating potential of the supply chain is central to successful strategies into today's competitive environment. For many companies this, in turn, translates into the opportunities available in each phase – suppliers, internal supply chain, logistics and customers – and their roles in bringing about these gains. One key competitive dimension is lead-time reduction.

IKEA, the Swedish home furnishings retailer, has more than 100 stores and 1,800 suppliers in over 50 countries. The company's insistence on low cost from its suppliers has two key implications. First, the sourcing is widely dispersed and parts of finished items may be purchased from different locations. Second, items must be bought in large volumes. Both factors require an efficient system for ordering parts, integrating them into products and delivering them to stores, while keeping inventory levels low and meeting demand quickly. This is achieved by building on long-term supplier relations and a sophisticated logistics system, the centrepiece of which is IKEA's network of warehouses. Point-of-sale information at each retail outlet provides online sales data to the nearest warehouse and the operational head office in Almhult where information systems analyse sales patterns worldwide. In turn, the warehouses act as logistic control points and consolidate requirements. As transit hubs they work with retail stores to anticipate demand and eliminate shortages while keeping inventory (and corresponding floor space) low. Underpinning all this is the need for short lead-time provision. Working with suppliers as well as in-house supply-chain developments have enabled IKEA to meet the delivery speed needs of the fashion market it serves.

Reducing lead times has also been at the centre of the supply strategy of A. W. Chesterton Co. (a family-owned seal, pump and packings manufacturer in Massachusetts). Key to the substantial but essential improvements has been the company's management of its supply chain. This is well illustrated by the reduction in suppliers in the 1990s from 1300 to 125 and giving delivery reliability, short lead times and quality conformance twice as much importance as price when evaluating which suppliers to partner. For Chesterton, the demands of its own markets require putting pressures on its own suppliers. In the mid-1990s the delivery time for mechanical seal parts was 12 to 16 weeks. Today, it is down to days or even hours. To facilitate this the company has installed computer systems that allow customers to transmit drawings and engineering specifications directly to the plant floor where new process investments speed manufacturing.

But the lead times of other aspects of a business are equally critical to overall success. The emphasis is on getting suppliers to become more than just parts providers. One key area is to participate in and contribute to new designs particularly with regard to cutting costs and development lead-time reductions. Dana Corporation, a major supplier of truck axles, has an entire 60-engineer laboratory near Toledo dedicated to U-joints. Using a computer-aided design system Dana can design new products cheaply and quickly – in fact, prototypes for customers can be built in a few hours.

The Taiwanese Acer Corporation, with other PC makers, has had to reduce lead times in line with the short product life cycles of its market. The company works on a ten-month product life cycle, with three months allowed for product development and modifications, six months for sales of the product and one month to sell old inventory before the next cycle begins.

## Lower Inventories

The classic, uncoordinated approach to managing a supply chain typically results in each stage having enough raw material (or its equivalent) inventory not to run out and sufficient finished goods (or its equivalent) to ensure that customers would not be caught short. One result of each stage adopting these positions is excess inventory. And the longer the lead time the greater the likelihood of these ineffi- ciencies occurring in the process. Managing the supply chain as a whole means stitching together an entire business with external providers being treated as part- ners as if they were inside the company. Lower inventories result as the following examples illustrate.

Eastman Chemical's processes call for 1,500 different raw materials provided by 850 suppliers. To make sure that as little inventory as possible sat idle, Eastman devised what it calls 'stream inventory management'. This requires treating the whole supply chain as a pipeline. 'When an order comes in from the customer, we take one pound of product out of the tail end. We've then got the raw material func- tion working with the supplier to put another pound in on the other end. We want to achieve continuous flow' is how Eastman describes its approach.[29] And stream inventory management has paid off. Eastman can now monitor inventory while at its suppliers which, combined with more accurate production forecasts, means there is no longer the need to hold excess inventory that sits idle, just in case. Examples of the dramatic inventory reductions that have been achieved include:

■ wood pulp stock down from three months' supply to nine days with the next target set at four days

■ 20 years ago the company kept 18 million pounds of paraxylene, a material for polyethylene terephthalate (PET) plastic soda bottles, to support 520 million pounds a year of PET production in the US. Today, Eastman holds only 14 million pounds of paraxylene to support three times the volume of PET production

■ company-wide, the company's inventories as a percentage of sales had almost halved in the decade from the late 1980s. In 1998, total inventory had fallen to less than 11 per cent, with raw materials and supplies at less than 3 per cent of sales.

Michael Dell (founder of the Dell Computer Corporation) began in 1984 with a simple business insight: to sell direct to customers and make to order. Thus, in one swoop he eliminated the reseller's mark-up and the costs and risks associated with finished goods inventory. The 'direct business model', as it is known, gave Dell Computer a substantial cost advantage and directly contributed to growing a $12bn company in just 13 years.

To achieve this Dell uses technologies and information to blur the traditional boundaries in the supply chain from suppliers through to customers. In so doing, Dell is moving towards virtual integration (as Michael Dell describes it) that combines individual strategies such as customer focus, supplier partnerships and just-in-time manufacturing into a coordinated whole. Virtual integration harnesses the economies-of-scale benefits of two traditional business models. On the one hand, it taps into the benefits of a coordinated supply chain traditionally only available through vertical integration while, on the other hand, it taps into the benefits of specialization where companies (in Dell's case, its suppliers) focus on what they are good at with the associated gains from volumes and technology investment.

There are many challenges facing Dell Computer to realize this potential and establish these collaborations. One key driver to do this is monitoring low inventories. In the fast-changing technology business, inventory carries more risk than in other sectors. The dimensions of risk in computing concern response time to launching product developments and protection from falling material prices. As Michael Dell explained:[30]

■ if I've got 11 days of inventory and my competitor has 80, and Intel comes out with a new 450 megahertz chip, that means I'm going to get to market 69 days sooner.

■ if the cost of materials goes down 50 per cent a year and you have two or three months of inventory versus 11 days, you've got a big cost disadvantage. And, you're vulnerable to product transitions, when you can get stuck with obsolete inventory.

For these reasons, Dell works closely with its suppliers to keep reducing inventory and increasing speed, as its arrangements with Sony exemplify. With Sony (considered a reliable supplier with defect rates on monitors of less than two per million) Dell now collects monitors daily in the quantities needed to meet its own customer orders and ships direct. The result is reduced lead times and no finished monitor inventory. Similarly, Dell has agreed with Airborne Express and United Parcel Services (UPS) to collect (say) 12,500 computers a day and the same quantity of monitors from Sony's plant in Mexico. Then they match the one with the other and deliver them directly to Dell's customers. To do this, Dell has developed real-time information on its own demand profile and links this into its suppliers, sometimes every few hours. With this insight and certainty, suppliers can meet Dell's five or six days of lead time. 'The greatest challenge in working with suppliers is getting them in sync with the fast pace we have to maintain. The key to making it work is information', explained Kevin Rollins, Vice-Chairman of Dell Computer Corporation.[31]

The outcome of all of this was that in 1998, inventory at Dell was only $233m to support $12.3bn of sales, with the number of days' supply in inventory falling from 31 in 1996 to just 7 days two years later.[31]

Efficient customer response (ECR) is a relation of just-in-time and partnership sourcing. Its central doctrine is that many practices that make good business sense to individual parts of the supply chain add cost and complexity from the perspective of the chain as a whole.

One central theme of ECR is co-managed inventory. Instead of sending out orders to suppliers as stock gets low, customers hand over to suppliers the task of generating orders. Both parties agree forecasts and suppliers take over the responsibility for replenishment using up-to-date sales information from the customer.

Somerfield (a UK supermarket chain) introduced these concepts in the late 1990s. Initial results showed a reduction in inventory of over 20 per cent while the times when shelves were empty decreased by almost 3 per cent.

VOAC, the Swedish-based division of the US manufacturer Parker Hannifin, makes mobile hydraulic equipment. In the 1990s VOAC reorganized its logistics. Originally the company had its head office and factories in Sweden and eight sales offices across Europe. All had their own warehouses and distribution set-ups. Inventories were high, the level of customer delivery performance variable, lead times were long and logistics costs were substantial. Its partner in changing the logistics organization was UPS Worldwide Logistics. It now has one European distribution centre in the Netherlands, online connections for all offices and direct order input. Electronically processed orders are then tracked from beginning to end with UPS providing vendor managed inventory (VMI) facilities that take into account future demand forecasts, manufacturing lead times and existing inventory levels. Improved supply-chain management has extended the customer order cut-off point during a working day from 3 pm to 6 pm and resulted in shorter delivery lead times and inventory reductions of 60 per cent.

# Conclusion

Whether to make or buy needs careful assessment and the factors that substantiate changes to span-of-process decisions need to be clearly understood. In the past, and carried on the winds of growth, many companies repositioned their point on the process span as a matter of course. Believing that they could manufacture anything, many companies decided to widen their process spans without an adequate understanding of strategic fit and the tactical consequences involved. Similarly, early entrants into new technology markets such as IT had little option at the time than to make the components involved. In recent times, subcontracting is in vogue. What often characterizes these trends is flavour-of-the-month rather than issues of strategic fit. It is essential when deciding whether or not to reduce process spans that companies undertake strategic and tactical analyses while being careful to avoid the lure of short-term gains without considering long-term, strategic outcomes.

When making process-positioning decisions companies need to establish the true extent of the costs and benefits involved. Understatement of costs and overstatement of benefits are all too often the basis on which companies make decisions and evaluate outcomes. But, such make-or-buy decisions are not only substantial but often final, at least within commercial timescales – when a company closes a plant it will never reopen it. Deciding whether to make or buy invariably commits a company for years ahead and consequentially is critical to the strategic positioning of a company.

Make or buy is the first part of a two-phased task. The second is that once the make-or-buy decision is made, companies have to recognize the need to manage both the internal and external dimensions of the supply chain. And this typically requires a company to make a fundamental shift in approach and thinking as summarized in Exhibit 9.19.

The format of the joint cooperation that is a core feature of strategic alliance developments is moving at a pace as the following boxed illustrations highlight.

**Exhibit 9.19**  Changing approach to managing supply chains

| Dimensions | | Approach | |
|---|---|---|---|
| | | **from** | **to** |
| Customers and suppliers | | Contractual relationships | Harness the power of partnerships |
| Organisation | structure | Functionally based activities | Process and cross-functional activities |
| | relationships | Functional orientation | Cooperation |
| Basis for competition | | Manufacturer | Supply chain |

Components account for some 60 per cent of the cost of a new car. Yet the component makers have traditionally shared relatively few of the risks of a new launch. The car makers, on the other hand, have to meet large fixed investments such as factories and capital equipment in what are increasingly uncertain markets. Part of the move to strategic alliances is now based on shared costs and shared uncertainty. At Volkswagen (VW)'s new bus and truck plant in Resende (some 150 km from Rio de Janeiro, Brazil) about 35 per cent of the fixed costs have been met by component suppliers. Resende is also co-managed by VW and its suppliers under a profit-sharing consortium.

> The Hambach plant in eastern France that builds the two-seater Mercedes-Benz sports car provides another example of the changing relationships within strategic alliance developments. Ten suppliers preassemble important sections. For example, steel bodies come from Magna International, the Canadian group. VDO, the German automotive electronics maker, builds fully assembled cockpits, including the instruments, while Ymos (the German component specialist) makes complete door assemblies, including trim, window winders and glass. But that is not all. The ten suppliers have invested almost $300m in the project.

> The assembly plant for Skoda's Octavia saloon is designed with six zones adjacent to the production line. The zones are also positioned on an outside wall so that the suppliers involved have direct truck access. The component suppliers are responsible for supporting the production schedule that includes the preassembly of parts just before they are required to go on to the car.

Other examples serve to illustrate the developments in supplier/customer relations that are changing the mind sets of those involved. From an almost wholly manual system in the 1980s, TNT (Europe's biggest freight and logistics company) launched an Internet service in early 1999 that enables its customers to track orders from beginning to end.[32] Quickshipper, as the Internet service is called, enables its customers to arrange the collection of consignments directly through the TNT web site. After planning their order, customers can then use the site to follow its progress to delivery. Quicker order processing also means faster deliveries.

Merloni, the Italian white goods company, now links its domestic appliances in people's homes with remote diagnostic centres around Europe via the telecommunications network. For an annual fee of about $50, a service centre will use computers to monitor appliances around the clock. Special software can detect such defects as electric motor malfunction or power failures and alert owners by telephone.[33]

As response time becomes a more important factor than low labour costs in keeping major customers, offshore manufacturers of everything from PCs to garments need to embrace e-commerce developments. Take Lite-on Technology Corporation, the Taiwanese manufacturer of computer hardware. In the mid- to late 1990s it typically had a month to execute orders from IBM, Compaq Computer and

**Exhibit 9.20** The short lead-time requirements of customers

| Item | Lead time to fill a US order |
| --- | --- |
| Colour monitors | 2 days |
| Notebook computers | 1 day |
| CD-ROM drives | 4 hours |

other overseas customers. Since then the required lead times have shrunk dramatically (see Exhibit 9.20).

How does Lite-on cope? By integrating its customers, factories, warehouses, accounting functions and parts suppliers into a single digital supply chain. This cuts lead times in all phases of the procedure from order taking, manufacturing scheduling, suppliers' deliveries and shipping. As Exhibit 9.21 shows, this is now a general development led by major companies as part of the way to better manage their supply chains.

With today's markets becoming more global and competitive in nature, companies need to rethink their response. As support for many order-winners and qualifiers is the responsibility of the manufacturing function, how it manages these responses is a key strategic task. But to do this effectively, it needs not only to manage the internal phase of the supply chain well but also the external elements including a proactive relationship with customers. In this way, a coordinated response that harnesses the potential of the whole supply chain will be looked for, identified and delivered. Without it, strategic advantage will be surrendered and the growth and prosperity of a company will be undermined.

**Exhibit 9.21** Customer-led developments to better manage their supply chains involving overseas suppliers

| Hooking up Asia | | |
| --- | --- | --- |
| **The problem** | **The solution** | **The application** |
| Asian manufacturers are under increasing pressure from US customers to turn around orders in record times. Hard-pressed Asian companies also need new customers to offset revenue shortfalls. | It is electronic. Digital links between customers, factories, parts suppliers and shippers can drastically shorten order time, while web sites can attract new business and help find new partners. | Companies like General Electric and IBM are wiring up Asian companies from India to Japan for electronic data interchanges, while Asian-based operators are offering web sites for e-commerce. |

*Source:* J. Moore and M. Kripalani, 'Racing to Get Globally Wired', *Business Week*, 20 April 1998, p. 26

# Notes

1. M. L. Fisher *et al.*, 'Making Supply Meet Demand in an Uncertain World', *Harvard Business Review*, May–June 1994, p. 84.
2. J. Moore and A. Reinhardt, 'Living With Intel', *Business Week*, 20 January 1997, pp. 24 and 25.
3. N. Tait, 'Handling the Sourcing Decisions: Lowest Cost is not Always the Answer', *Financial Times*, 15 October 1997, p. 13.
4. For example, refer to C. Batchelor's review of the gains secured through subcontracting and reported in his article, 'Lower Overheads and Increased Productivity', *Financial Times*, 23 April 1991, p. 14.
5. K. R. Harrigan, *Strategies for Vertical Integration*, Lexington, MA: Lexington Books, 1983, also addresses these issues.
6. Ibid., Ch. 2 discusses these alternatives and offers frameworks to help in their selection.
7. See, for example, a special report entitled 'The Hollow Corporation', *Business Week*, 3 March 1986, pp. 56–76.
8. The ripple effect concerns the real cost of imports to an economy. For each $1bn of foreign-made consumables it was estimated that the total costs to the US economy was $1.43bn on top of the $1bn imports themselves, as reported in the following table.

| Area of cost of the economy | $ Millions |
|---|---|
| Imported automobiles | 1,000 |
| Other vehicles engaged in hauling raw materials and finished products | 200 |
| Steel and fabricated metal parts | 184 |
| Machine tools | 98 |
| Rubber and plastics | 67 |
| Non-ferrous metals | 46 |
| Chemicals | 40 |
| Other manufacturing | 343 |
| Wholesale and retail margins, transportation, warehousing and utilities | 348 |
| Mining | 47 |
| Finances and insurance | 39 |
| Plant construction | 16 |
| Total | $2,428 |

*Source:* Data Resources Inc., *Business Week*, March 1988, p. 61

9. *Business Week*, March 1986, pp. 63–6 introduces the notion of postindustrial corporations that could subcontract everything from manufacturing to invoicing customers.
10. The article 'The Hollow Corporation' as early as the mid-1980s introduced the notion of postindustrial corporations that could subcontract everything from manufacturing to invoicing customers – the concept of virtual corporations.
11. E. W. Desmond, 'Can Canon Keep Kicking', *Fortune*, 2 February 1998, pp. 58–64.
12. Ibid.
13. Thomas Hobson, a Cambridge carrier, had a policy of letting out his horses in rotation, without allowing his customers to choose among them. Hence they had to take or leave the one on offer.
14. K. R. Harrigan, "Managing Joint Ventures – Part II', *Management Review*, February 1987, p. 29.

15. I. M. D. and A. T. Kearney's 1996 survey revealed that of the major European companies asked, 52 per cent anticipated increasing the level of outsourcing in the future.

16. N. Tait (1997), p. 13.

17. Products that are different to any other product in any way (including, for example, the number of units in an outer packing case) will have a unique company code number and are referred to as stock-keeping units (SKUs).

18. N. Tait (1997), p. 13.

19. Adapted from K. Ferdov's 'Making the Most of Foreign Factories', *Harvard Business Review*, March–April 1997, pp. 73–88.

20. Economist Intelligence Unit and KPMG Management Consultants report entitled 'Supply Chain Management: Europe's New Competitive Battleground', 1996.

21. R. Brosodi, 'The Distribution Age', D. Appleton & Co, 1929.

22. J. A. Blecke, 'Peak Strategies', *McKinsey Quarterly*, Spring 1989.

23. J. Margretta, 'The Power of Virtual Integration: An Interview with Dell Computer's Michael Dell', *Harvard Business Review*, March–April 1998, p. 74.

24. N. Templin and J. Cole, 'Manufacturers Use Suppliers to Help Them Develop New Products', *Wall Street Journal*, 22 December 1994, pp. 1 and 6.

25. A. Lorenz, 'Unique Alliances Drives Suppliers', *The Sunday Times*, 23 November 1997, p. 13.

26. E. W. Desmond (1998), pp. 58–64.

27. N. Templin and J. Cole (1994), p. 6.

28. Ibid., p. 6.

29. E. Brown, 'The Push to Streamline Supply Chains', *Fortune*, 3 March 1997.

30. J. Margaretta (1998), p. 76.

31. Ibid., p. 81.

32. C. Price, 'TNT Steps Up Web Delivery', *Financial Times*, 3 March 1999, p. 13.

33. P. Marsh, 'On-line Machines that Take the Worry out of Wash Day', *Financial Times*, 6 October 1998, p. 18.

## Further Reading

Armour, T. J. and Teece, D. H., 'Vertical Integration and Technological Innovation', *Review of Economics and Statistics*, August 1982, **62**: 470–4.

Arrow, K. J., 'Vertical Integration and Communications', *Bell Journal of Economics*, Spring 1975, **6**: 173–82.

Bailey, P. and Farmer, D., *Purchasing – Principles and Management*, 5th edn, London: Pitman, 1986.

Blois, K. J., 'Vertical Quasi-integration', *Journal of Industrial Economics*, July 1972, pp. 253–72.

Buzznell, R. D., 'Is Vertical Integration Profitable?', *Harvard Business Review*, January–February 1983, pp. 92–102. (Offers an analysis based on the profit impact of market strategies (PIMS) data to assess a number of relationships including vertical integration and profitability, vertical integration, investment intensity and return on investments, and vertical integration, relative market share and profitability.)

Cavinato, J. L., *Purchasing and Materials Management*, St Paul, MN: West, 1984.

Cherry, J. V., 'Vendor's Viewpoint: Quality, Response, Delivery', *Quality Progress*, 1988, **17**(11): 40–2.

Dempsey, W. A., 'Vendor Selection and the Buying Process', *Industrial Marketing Management*, 1978, **17**: 257–67.

DTI and Society of Motor Manufacturers and Traders, 'A Review of the Relationships Between Vehicle Manufacturers and Suppliers', February 1994.

Ford, H., *Today and Tomorrow*, Productivity Press, 1988.

Gale, B. T., 'Can More Capital Buy Higher Productivity?', *Harvard Business Review*, July–August 1980, pp. 78–90.

Harrigan, K. R., *Managing for Joint Venture Success*, Lexington, MA: Lexington Books, 1986.

Kraljic, P., 'Purchasing Must Become Supply Management', *Harvard Business Review*, September–October 1983, pp. 109–17.

Petit, P. E., 'Vendor Evaluation Made Simple', *Quality Progress*, 1984, **17**(3): 19–22.

Porter, M. E., *Competitive Analysis*, New York: Free Press, 1980. (Chapter 14 provides an extensive discussion of the potential benefits and limitations of vertical integration.)

Schonberger, R. J., *Building a Chain of Customers*, London: Hutchinson Business Books, 1990.

Schmalensee, R., 'A Note on the Theory of Vertical Integration', *Journal of Political Economy*, March–April 1973, pp. 442–59.

Williamson, O. E., 'The Vertical Integration of Production: Market Failure Considerations', *American Economic Review*, 1971, **61**: 112–23.

# 10 Manufacturing Infrastructure Development

The need for a business to resolve the issues of process choice in line with the manufacturing strategy requirement has been paramount in this book so far. To reiterate, companies must clearly understand which manufacturing processes can best meet the needs of the marketplace, or how well existing processes provide the order-winners and qualifiers for products and/or customers in different segments. However the task facing manufacturing is not simply to choose the process and necessary hardware. Once this has been analysed and the trade-offs reconciled, the emphasis shifts. The company must now ensure that the structure and composition of the component parts, or functions, that provide its necessary internal systems and communications are also developed in line with the manufacturing strategy requirement. Process choice concerns the features of hardware, the tangible ways in which products are manufactured. But the task is more than this. The supporting structures, controls, procedures and other systems within manufacturing are equally necessary for successful, competitive manufacturing performance.

These structures, controls, procedures and other systems are collectively known as the *manufacturing infrastructure*. This comprises the inner structure of manufacturing and necessarily includes the attitudes, experience and skills of the people involved. Together they form the basis of the manufacturing organization, charged with the task of providing the necessary support to the areas of responsibility involved.

As illustrated in Exhibit 2.5, manufacturing strategy comprises both processes and infrastructure. Getting one and not the other in line with market needs will lead to inconsistencies similar to the levels of mismatch illustrated in Chapter 6. Aligning process characteristics with market needs is insufficient in itself. The impact of infrastructure investments on sound manufacturing strategy provision is as critical as process choice and, in some companies, more so.

Infrastructure developments are also characterized by their high level of investment and their fixed nature. These decisions are as binding as their hardware counterparts and must be made with the same clear link to the needs of a company's markets. If not, problems will arise that are identical to those already highlighted for process decisions. Furthermore, companies need to parallel continuing market changes with appropriate developments in manufacturing. The inherently fixed nature of manufacturing infrastructure is often coupled with an inertia for change

stemming in part from the nature of corporate reviewing procedures that are typically built on functional goals and perspectives. Often those responsible for the
realignment of the essential components of manufacturing infrastructure are
unaware of, or unable to respond to, the growing need to make the necessary and
appropriate changes. One underlying message in Peters and Waterman's *In Search
of Excellence* is that success depends on awareness.[1] Building and developing infrastructure on a manufacturing strategy base does just that. It gives appropriate direction and allows a choice to be made between alternative sets of trade-offs. The
company then has a shared awareness of what is required in manufacturing if it is to
best support the current and future needs of the business, and the necessity of
linking manufacturing to the marketplace through its process hardware and organizational software is established. Thus the components of manufacturing strategy
must be inexorably linked to give them coherence and synergistic purpose, as illustrated in Exhibit 10.1.

Infrastructure represents part of the complexity inherent in manufacturing. To
develop an appropriate infrastructure to support manufacturing effectively, a
company must recognize two important dimensions. The first concerns the way the
company is structured internally and why it has evolved that way. The second
involves recognizing the key perspectives to be taken into account when developing
the important areas of infrastructure.

By themselves, most elements of infrastructure do not require the same level of
investment nor do they have the same impact on manufacturing's strategic role as
does process choice but taken collectively they do. Together, their importance in
providing the strategic support for the business cannot be overstressed. Similarly,
the difficulties experienced through the interaction of inappropriate systems and the
costs involved in effecting major changes can be of the same magnitude as those
decisions involving manufacturing hardware. The transformation over time of the
support for the marketplace into an appropriate collection of facilities, structures,

**Exhibit 10.1** The inexorable link of components of manufacturing strategy with each other and with the
market needs of a business

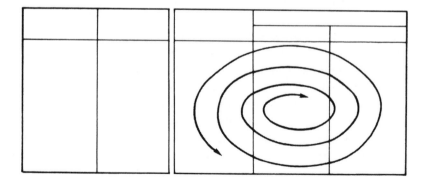

controls, procedures and people comprises the manufacturing strategy task. As Hayes and Wheelwright conclude:

> it is this pattern of structural [*process*] and infrastructural decisions that constitutes the 'manufacturing strategy' of a business unit. More formally, a manufacturing strategy consists of a sequence of decisions that, over time, enables a business unit to achieve a desired [*market-related*] manufacturing structure [*process choice*], infrastructure, and set of specific capabilities.[2]

In relation to corporate strategy, they recognize that 'the primary function of a manufacturing strategy is to guide the business in putting together the set of manufacturing capabilities that will enable it to pursue its chosen competitive strategy over the long term.'[3]

## Manufacturing Infrastructure Issues

Manufacturing infrastructure comprises a complex set of interacting factors. Western companies traditionally have coped with this by breaking their infrastructures into appropriate sets of responsibilities or functions and deploying people to provide the necessary support. To work effectively this requires a high degree of coordination linked to manufacturing's strategic tasks. However, reality does not bear out the theory. Typically, these parts or functions are managed separately and come together primarily at the tactical or operational interface. Developments within the various elements of the manufacturing infrastructure of a company are given the level of detailed attention they require at the points of application. It is at these levels where meaningful, in-depth discussion takes place, no doubt stimulated by the real need to make the particular area of infrastructure development work effectively. However, the merits of the individual parts and how they fit together are rarely encompassed by any strategic overview. For this reason, piecemeal developments, propounded in the main by specialists, lead to an uncoordinated approach to infrastructure design.

It is essential that the basic parts of the organizational framework reinforce and support the manufacturing task. This enables a company to get away from functionally based perspectives of what is appropriate and important. The only way to achieve this is to orient discussion on the requirements of the business, that is, to replace functional argument by a corporate resolution between alternatives and to replace unilaterally stimulated argument of what is best for the business by corporate-based argument of the same. This then provides a base on which to develop a comprehensive, coordinated and directed infrastructure to meet a firm's current and future needs. It not only enables a company to get its orientation right, but it also enables it to avoid being saddled with functions that are no longer required or are inappropriately weighted when related to the business needs. Changing the *status quo* is difficult, unless the firm knows why and how it wants or has to change. Only then is it able to move from subjectively based to objectively based analyses and decisions. This requires a very clear statement of what constitutes the manufacturing task – the manufacturing strategy appropriate to the company. Once functional managers understand and appreciate this, a company can reshuffle the *status quo*. It is then in a position to avoid situations where vested interests argue for the retention or growth in capabilities and capacities for their own sake rather than for their relative contribution to the current and future success of the business.

Questions stemming from these views concern why functions hold on to their current level of size and why they argue for their own retention and growth. In many instances they do so because it is the best perspective they have. Only when a business orients functions towards the outside (that is, to what the market requires) can it provide the opportunity for alternatives to be measured against corporate-related criteria. The provision of a common, relevant base enables functional arguments to be put into perspective. It shifts the evaluation of proposals from the use of subjective to objective criteria. It gives appropriate direction to which all infrastructure development must aspire, while also providing detailed checklists against which developments can be evaluated. In this way, these costly developments will meet manufacturing strategy requirements rather than functional or specialist perspectives. Furthermore, by looking outwards and forwards, developments will be made with a knowing eye on future competition and thus be more likely to incorporate the manufacturing needs of tomorrow.

If the functions charged with making effective infrastructure provision are not given strategic direction, there is the real possibility that specialist support functions will pursue their own points of view, a problem many businesses experience today. Firms need the functional and specialist capabilities to make sense of the complexity. Without these inputs, they cannot reach the level of effectiveness necessary to meet today's competitive pressures. The difference between an infrastructure based on a number of specialist views and one coordinated to meet the needs of a business by an appropriate strategy is significant for most firms and critical for many.

The review and incremental development of infrastructure within the strategic context of manufacturing is equally important – it concerns altering the balance or changing the focus of development so that it is in line with the manufacturing task and hence forms an integral part of manufacturing strategy. A firm's ability to backtrack on its decisions is also important at times. This activity, however, is often thwarted by the difficulties presented by specialists who are typically highly analytical people capable of arguing their case with great clarity and strength and protecting their own views and areas of responsibility in a vacuum. The existence of a manufacturing strategy provides the parameters for analysis and debate either to reconcile arguments or views or to redirect development activity.

# Infrastructure Development

Strategy comprises the development and declaration of a shared view of business direction. But unless a business regularly updates its strategy in response to market change deviations from supporting market needs will go unnoticed and individual interpretations of strategy, rather than the strategy statement itself, will become fact. In both instances, fragmentation will occur and the necessary coherence will diminish.

The successful development of infrastructure requires care. Many companies have adopted a piecemeal approach by resolving one facet at a time, as often stimulated by the apparent need of the moment as by a carefully selected priority. Picking off one area makes sense as a way of coping with the complexity involved. However, many organizations even in these situations do not undertake sufficient analyses before determining the area for development. This preliminary analysis need not become a complex debate; Exhibit 10.2 points to the essential issues – the need to determine the make-or-buy decision and define the size of the manufacturing units. Thus, rather than investing money, time and effort in resolving the current complexity, a company should define the level of complexity it wishes to handle. Only then is it able to decide how best to manage the chosen level and only then is it able to develop the infrastructure appropriate to its needs. For once a company understands its strategic manufacturing task and the organizational make-up involved (its *organizational profile*), the direction and content of any infrastructure development will become clear and comprehensible.

**Exhibit 10.2** Companies need to determine the level of manufacturing complexity before developing appropriate infrastructures

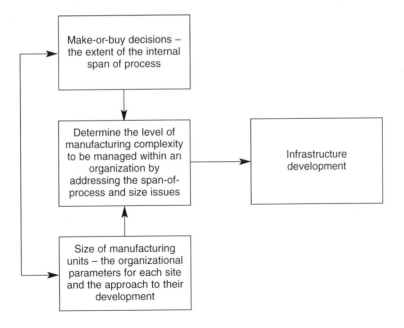

Many companies in the past have pursued the economies of large scale without fully evaluating the net gains involved (see Chapter 7 on focus). A classic approach to achieving these apparent gains sometimes has been to centralize at corporate and plant levels. This has led to centralized functions being created throughout an organization. Primary counter-arguments concern the increased complexity involved in large organizations and the difficulties of reshaping them in times of change. In many instances, the anticipated gains of centralized functions have proved to be an organizational El Dorado.

The chapter so far has emphasized the importance of appropriately developing manufacturing infrastructure and its significant contribution to providing the necessary manufacturing support to the marketplace. Before discussing some of the key areas of infrastructure design, it will be worthwhile to highlight practical, but general, considerations.

- It is most important to determine and agree on the important areas of infrastructure within manufacturing. A discretionary approach to change is essential to ensure that scarce development resources are used in those areas that will yield the best returns. The approach to change must reflect those areas that will have the most strategic impact, a point emanating from the concept of the 80/20 rule.[4]

- As with process choice, it is necessary to establish and then choose between sets of trade-offs that go hand in hand with each decision. The criteria, however, against which to measure the trade-offs must be concerned with manufacturing's strategic role.

- The essence of sound infrastructure design is that it must respond to the dynamics of reality. Although some areas will require major change, much of the necessary change can be achieved incrementally. After drawing this distinction, the company must regularly review areas of manufacturing infrastructure to effect the necessary developments, including the simplification and even withdrawal of controls, systems and procedures. It is most important, on the other hand, to avoid major change wherever possible. In many instances, the need for major change reflects the degree of mismatch between requirement and provision that has developed incrementally over time without corresponding appropriate adjustments. Often, sizeable and lengthy disruptions are required to put things right.

- Linked to the issue of avoiding situations of stepped change is the decision of determining what constitutes the job of work and what is the role of specialists within an organization. Although addressed later in the chapter, it is important to emphasize here that continuous development is easier to bring about where the responsibility for identifying and implementing improvements is locally based. Employee involvement creates conditions where changes are brought about by incremental developments. On the other hand, control through specialists can result in the need for changes being undetected or unattended. In such circumstances, the requirements for change will often be set aside and, when eventually addressed, the developments and tasks involved tend to be large.

## Important Infrastructure Issues

A company that fails to develop its infrastructure, as part of its response to meeting the needs of its marketplace, is likely to experience two linked consequences:

1. the business position may worsen because, among other things, the systems and controls will fail to give executives accurate and timely indicators to help them manage the business and initiate the necessary developments.

2. the key components of infrastructure necessary to help reshape or rebuild the business may not be in place when they are most necessary and most urgently required.

The approach to developing the separate parts of a manufacturing company's infrastructure involves two integrated steps. The first is determining the marketplace or competitive requirements, that is, each aspect of infrastructure must be built around the way products win orders. The controls, systems, procedures, attitudes and skills involved will then be oriented towards those manufacturing tasks pertinent to the order-winners and qualifiers of different products or customers. The second is ensuring that the necessary level of coherence and coordination exists in the various but related parts of manufacturing infrastructure. In this way all the software pulls in the same, appropriate direction and the company releases the synergy inherent in these substantial investments. In addition, those involved feel the consequential facilitating and motivating benefits of coherent direction.

The rest of the chapter concerns a number of organizational issues and some of the key areas of operational control. It was not easy to select which infrastructure issues to discuss here from the many that could warrant attention. Although the relevance and importance were factors in this decision, more than a small slice of subjective opinion was involved. Relevance, however, may not be so important because it will change between businesses; thus the discussion that follows is primarily meant to explain the principles of infrastructure design and development rather than to make a comprehensive statement on manufacturing infrastructure. The other important aspects of infrastructure, not covered here, will need to be similarly developed, using the same elements and procedures described in the following sections.

## Organizational Issues

The development investment and running costs required to maintain the support functions within a manufacturing business are high. The rationale for this high-cost provision is based, in part, on providing adequate and appropriate support to make manufacturing more effective and efficient. It is essential to ensure that this is achieved. Most organizations have treated the approach to developing relevant support for manufacturing as an operational and not as a strategic issue. Consequently the approach of many businesses to critical aspects of organizational design has not been based on the necessity to support manufacturing's strategic role. Some of the consequences of this are now discussed.

## Role of Specialists

Most manufacturing firms in developed economies make extensive use of specialists in running a business. The approach adopted by companies in the past has been to create functions comprising specialist staff to supply expert advice, guidance and activity in various relevant areas. The intention has been to provide the major line functions with necessary help. In the past three or four decades, this trend towards the employment of specialists has been growing in manufacturing and other sectors of the economy.

In the light of increasing world competition, companies must reassess the extent of the use made of specialists. Before discussing alternatives to the typical pattern of specialist provision currently used in most firms, it would be helpful to review some of the ways in which this concept of control has tended to evolve as one way of examining the current position, while providing some possible insights into the ways forward. The emphasis throughout will be towards the manufacturing function, although the points raised and suggestions made may well prove pertinent in other parts of a business.

## Specialists and Economies of Scale

The rationale underpinning the concept of control by specialists is to bring together staff to provide the capability, support and development deemed necessary to help line functions meet the needs of a business. This involves the principle of economies of scale, addressed in Chapter 7 on focus. Furthermore, the placement of these groups has traditionally been on a functional basis and, eventually, although not always initially, they have been positioned in a reporting structure that has been outside the main line functions.

Consequently many companies adopting this concept of control experience several major difficulties. Some of the reasons such control is not highly effective include:

- *The question of ownership* – the lack of a detailed understanding shared by line and staff functions of the important perspectives of each other is legendary. To redress this in the past few years, words such as *user-oriented*, *user-sensitive*, and *user-friendly* have become part of the standard approach in an attempt to overcome the inherent difficulties created by this organizational arrangement. However, attitudes and detailed insights are taking time to change.

■ *Role clarity* – the roles and relationships shared by line and staff functions within the common decision procedures in which they are involved has resulted, in certain instances, in a large measure of misunderstanding and criticism, leading even to acrimony and derision. This is due, in part, to the people themselves, the different salaries, reporting and working structures involved, the implied criticism of the specialist's activity, the high level of failures, apparent lack of interest or time allocation by specialists in the post-implementation period and the relative inexperience of specialists both in organizational and personal terms, which leads to a failure to appreciate that the only hard task in management is managing. However, the perceived roles of the line and support functions within the whole of these areas of development or day-to-day support procedures are too often not clarified either at the organizational or operational levels.

Line managers invariably see the specialist function as a means of improving an area of operational weakness. As busy executives, and not owning, in organizational terms, the time or control of the specialists involved, line managers often take a reactive role in the key periods of a development programme. But it is these managers who must make the final decision for the development to be effective. Hence, such decisions are often delayed until later when the problems invariably arise. The results are far from effective.

■ *Organizational relevance* – the principle of control through specialists and economies of scale is appropriate in high-volume and stable markets. The 1980s saw markets increasingly moving away from those characteristics, a trend that continued into the 1990s and still does so today. Companies, therefore, need to reconsider this basic tenet. It does not, however, mean that they should swing to the opposite end of the continuum. They need to avoid the 0–100 management[5] response that has characterized many changes in the past. There are other points on any continuum apart from 0 and 100 (that is, where a company is now and the point that represents the very opposite set of characteristics). It does mean, though, that companies should reconsider appropriate organizational responses to meet the changing and different needs of current and future markets. In most, simply distinguishing those tasks that are clearly specialist in nature from those that are operational will start the process of reconsidering what tasks should go where.

## Functional Silos

In many organizations the specialists' role and area of responsibility has grown. However, this growth has been determined more on the basis of perceived organizational neatness than on making best use of the specialists' contribution to meet the needs of the business. Typically, as illustrated in Exhibit 10.3, activities once within the province of the line functions have been drawn into the authority sphere of specialists (Phase 1). Classically, an independent reporting structure then evolves

**Exhibit 10.3**  Typical phases in the evolution of specialist functions in an organization

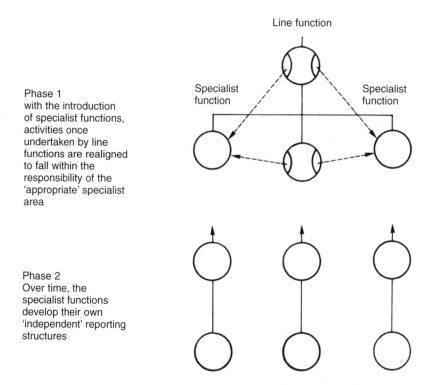

Phase 1
with the introduction
of specialist functions,
activities once
undertaken by line
functions are realigned
to fall within the
responsibility of the
'appropriate' specialist
area

Phase 2
Over time, the
specialist functions
develop their own
'independent' reporting
structures

(Phase 2). The result is that key sets of responsibilities that need to be integrated into the line activities are separated. The inherent difficulties associated with this structure when trying to redress the lack of necessary integration are now apparent in many companies. Functional silos have evolved in which individual functional goals and objectives tend to have higher priority for resource allocation than does the support of line activities.

## Control From a Distance

An invariable consequence of this approach is that companies evolve into organizations with too many people and too much control over manufacturing by financial analyses and reporting systems developed without adequately reflecting the business itself. This has been brought about, in part, by the belief that effective management can be maintained at a distance, using controls, systems and feedback developed by specialists. Often the hands-off controls being used have not reflected key trends, while those responsible for exercising and monitoring control have lacked the necessary knowledge of the business under review to enable them to detect changes and to ask penetrating questions at the opportune time. At best, this has contributed to the decline in performance; at worst it could accelerate this decline by emphasizing, for instance, short-term performance improvements at the expense of medium- and long-term strategic requirements. While this way of reviewing performance gathered momentum in the 1970s through into the 1990s, companies have been reassessing this practice in recent years. The practice was stimulated and given credence by the predominant role of specialists but companies are reconsidering the value of leaning too heavily, sometimes solely, on the views and contributions of these functions.

## Reward Systems

Companies need to reflect the relative importance and contribution of executives to a business by the level of remuneration and opportunity for advancement provided. Attracting able people into key jobs needs to be linked to an organization's reward system. Many companies, unfortunately, have failed to correlate executives' salaries with the direct effect those individuals have on the success of the business. What has unduly influenced salary structures and the opportunity for promotion are factors such as apparent scarcity, assumed contribution and market rates for salaries. Consequently all too often companies have offered higher salaries to those whose influence falls in the 20 per cent of the 80/20 rule. Thus the more able people have been attracted away from those line functions that affect the 80 per cent of what creates business success.

## Too Many Layers

One outcome of the extensive use of specialists is organizations with too many layers. At the head office, corporate staff can turn into an expensive bureaucracy. At plant level, divisional staffs, built up by middle management as they get promoted, are retained by their successors. Steward of McKinsey & Co. warned some 20 years ago that 'ever since the 1960s, when we started to believe that a professional manager can manage everything, we've been on the wrong track'. The random rotation of managers, based upon this belief, led to 'the new managers, unfamiliar with the businesses they were expected to run, [hiring] staff to advise them. When they moved on, a new manager repeated the cycle... The problem was compounded when companies started going international.'[6] Economies of large scale have also contributed to this problem. 'Along with bigness comes complexity... And, most big companies respond to complexity in kind, by designing complex systems and structures. They then hire more staff to keep track of all this complexity.'[7]

The results are reviewed in Exhibit 10.4, which illustrates the changes in layers of management that have taken place from the 1900s through to those anticipated by the year 2000.

**Exhibit 10.4** The number of levels within a typical organization at different times

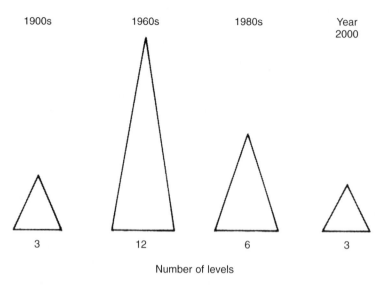

The way forward has been to reduce the layers and cut out the fat. The response at DuPont's Maitland plant (Ontario, Canada) is typical. During the 1980s, it reduced the number of layers in organizational hierarchy from 11 to 6 and shed 700 employees, many of them highly paid middle managers. As in most organizations, it was not that these employees were not doing a good job; but their roles slowed down procedures and constituted tasks that did not add value. Before the cut, a production manager at the Maitland plant supervised 90 workers through 6 foremen; today he has a staff of 40 and no foreman. Similarly, if workers needed a new tool the decision to purchase came from higher up. Today, they order it directly from the supplier. In addition, customers now telephone the plant directly about orders, speeding up the procedure that previously would have gone through DuPont's Toronto head office and four layers of bureaucracy. The result is that everyone benefits from this kind of organizational change.

The way forward for many companies is increasingly clear. The question to be answered is, 'which is the best approach to take?' For many companies, the classic response has been to implement across-the-board reductions. Having cut the workforce and dispensed with the frills, companies would request managers to reduce all round by an appropriate percentage. But these haphazard cuts left most corporate or central staff intact, the divisional ratios between managers and workforce rising and organizations more sluggish and less profitable.

This approach smacks of the specialists' view of an organization: to make the bottom line come right, just change the figures. This assumes that the existing structure will be appropriate in a reduced form. However, many businesses are realizing that the one thing they must not do is to take an axe to the job. Reshaping an organization requires careful surgery with reductions in line with business requirements. It needs to start with the business and build up from the bottom as well as down from the top. Many organizations in the past have only built top-down, without an assessment of the contribution of each part to the business as a whole. This has merely added to the layers. Reshaping an organization has to take into account the role of functions, establish the responsibility for decisions and boundaries of authority, and agree the appropriate level and reporting structure between the line and support functions involved. It helps to clarify that the line functions will in many instances routinely make the important decisions due to the authority/responsibility link that must exist. Also, support functions will in many instances provide a clerical/administrative backup filtering service or front position. For example, in recruitment the human resource function's role is advisory and usually, quite rightly, consists of drawing up a short list. In industrial relations negotiations, the specialist provides a first negotiating line to allow those with prime responsibility to take any necessary fall-back position.

The business-related approach, therefore, enables a company to develop its organization in line with its needs and it also provides the opportunity to change the perception of roles at all levels in the organization from top to bottom. Finally, not only is this procedure based on the business but it also blocks off any functional or personal escape routes that tend to be prevalent in many companies.

## Operational Effects of Structural Decisions

A significant consequence of the decision to use specialists extensively within a business is the effect it has at the operational level. One important issue concerns role definitions on the shopfloor and other similar jobs throughout an organization.

### The Operator's Job

The concept of an operator's job as perceived in most Western manufacturing companies is that of a 'making' or 'producing' task (for example, operating a machine or assembling a product). For this reason, when there are no appropriate making tasks to be completed, the dilemma facing the shopfloor supervisor is between recording a labour excess and completing work not required in the current period (that is, creating inventory). This problem is made even worse by process investment. Management reduces the job skills and the work involved when they invest in plant and equipment. In order to redress the reducing job interest and to capitalize on the opportunity to use the time released in an effective way, it is first necessary to change the concept of work.

The premise on which this change should be built revolves around the fact that work, in effect, consists of not only the doing task, but also the tasks of planning

**Exhibit 10.5**  The separation of the three facets of work and the gap between them created by the organizational structure

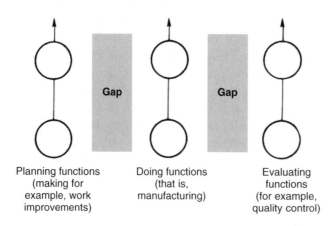

Planning functions
(making for
example, work
improvements)

Doing functions
(that is,
manufacturing)

Evaluating
functions
(for example,
quality control)

and evaluating.[8] In many companies work has been separated into these three components, with each part completed by a different function. The rationale for this is a by-product of the use of specialists and the development of support functions within an organization. Exhibit 10.5, therefore, is an extension of Phase 2 in Exhibit 10.3. It illustrates a typical structure, the separation of important activities at the operator level, and the inherent gap created by the structure between these three intrinsic parts of work. This has resulted from the development of organizational structures using specialists and functional reporting procedures. It has led to a situation where the inherent contribution of operators to work-improvement activities has been lost and the essential link between the responsibility for manufacturing and quality conformance has been severed.

## Strategy-based Alternatives

For many companies, the organizational structure consisting of line and support functions is proving less than effective. Structures designed for stable, high-volume markets increasingly fail to meet the needs of today's markets, which are characterized by low volumes and instability set in an environment of increasing competition, worldwide overcapacity and dynamic markets.

Any evaluation of structures and detailed roles, however, needs to ask, 'will it meet the requirements of the business?' The suggested areas of change that follow are intended to reflect more accurately existing responsibility structures or are designed to facilitate an appropriate and relevant contribution by people throughout the organization. If firms are to compete effectively in world markets, their structures need to be both dynamic and designed to tap the relative potential of all their employees.

## Functional Teamwork

Companies need to reconsider the currently held view of line and support functions. The alternative is to build specialist functions back into the line with them reporting within that authority/responsibility structure. The principal consequences of this would be:

■ changing the reporting structures removes the problem of the line management/specialist interface not working.
■ it clarifies the current role of specialists into those areas that:

(a) are primarily within the scope of the specialism – for example, quality assurance, the development of robotics within productivity improvement, and production planning

(b) should be under the auspices of the line management function – for example, quality control, internal efficiency activities and production control.[9]

This would enable an organization to build its structure around sets of coherent, interrelated activities rather than, as at present, around activities with similar names. It would not *per se* lead to reductions in people – although it invariably does – and in fact, would sometimes lead to increases of staff in certain functions. Although transferring decision-making activity from the centre to the plant and from specialists into the line may not change staffing levels, it would dramatically change the relevance of activities undertaken and assignment priorities established. The benefit, for instance, for manufacturing managers to have the opportunity to generate cost analyses in line with their own perspectives and requirements and in line with their contribution to corporate decisions has to be seen to be believed.

The process is one of reshaping overheads. To be successful, it will need to challenge fundamentally current structures, attitudes and expectations. Organizations that are functionally driven and controlled through specialisms are top heavy and unresponsive. They fail to capitalize fully on the abilities of their people and the time availability created by investment. This reconsideration is based on the rationale of continuous improvement. The result is that not only do organizations become more cost efficient, they also become more effective. The following sections address related issues.

## Structure of Work

As implied by the comments on what constitutes work, organizations need to build back into the doing task aspects of planning, evaluating and other elements of work currently undertaken by specialist, overhead functions. Enhanced by the *functional teamwork* concept described above, and as part of the rationalization of work and relative contributions by different employees, Exhibit 10.6 suggests how parts of

**Exhibit 10.6**  Incorporating appropriate planning and evaluating steps into the doing tasks

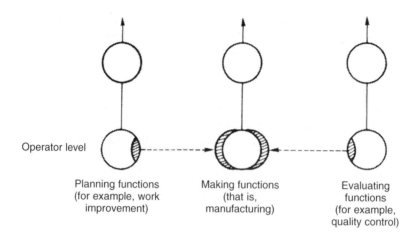

Operator level

| Planning functions (for example, work improvement) | Making functions (that is, manufacturing) | Evaluating functions (for example, quality control) |

such planning and evaluating activities, presently completed by support functions, should be reassigned to those currently responsible for the making tasks. In this way, not only does such an action lend support to the arguments put forward in the last section, but it also provides a tangible commonsense illustration of the effect this can have. These actions lead to greater productivity and, at the same time, create greater job interest for all concerned. Other areas where similar redefinitions of responsibility are taking place include work improvement (the subject of a later section) and maintenance. In the case of the latter, first level tasks such as oiling and greasing equipment and undertaking daily and weekly unskilled but essential maintenance are increasingly being completed by operators.[10]

It releases specialists from non-specialist work, often eliminates the need to coordinate activities with the attendant delays and waiting and gives operators work that involves the three important dimensions that make up meaningful tasks by broadening their responsibilities and allowing them both to plan and to evaluate the work they carry out.[11] Although these changes bring small returns in themselves, the cumulative effect can be enormous and a significant contribution made to providing manufacturing's strategic contribution.

Examples from DuPont's Maitland plant illustrate this. Under the previous system, a customer's quality conformance complaint was handled by head office. Now the operator who made the product goes to see the customer and decides how to correct the problem. Problems are cleared up more quickly and customers are happier. At the other end of the spectrum, 'staring at a bank of computers is not a stimulating way to spend a 12-hour shift. To make [an operator's] job more interesting and more useful to the company, [operators] are trained – in their off hours and at overtime rates – in computer technology. [They then become] responsible for maintaining computers in the plant's control room and for helping to develop expert systems.'[12]

A different perspective that reinforces this issue concerns payment systems used for operators. Typical systems pay the job not the person and are based on analyses and evaluations. Such approaches reinforce inflexibility and create barriers to change. An alternative to these is a skills-based system. This is built on the concept that individuals should be paid for their skills, a perspective that allows for and encourages change similar to that depicted in Exhibit 10.6.

## Cascading Overheads and Flattening Organizations

Linked both to the structure of work and the changing role of specialist functions within a business is the drive to cascade overheads and to flatten organizations. Companies should seek to push work as far down the organization as possible. Coupled to an investment by the firm in the training of the people involved, the systematic cascading of overheads will help increase the level of staff flexibility required, allow any spare time created as a by-product of process investments to be usefully absorbed and provide those involved with a more meaningful task.

This involves changing the levels at which decisions are made and allowing people to decide on how best to complete tasks once they have been given the relevant parameters and information. Bureaucracy is reduced, overhead costs decrease and decision-making lead times are shortened.

## Quality Circles or Productivity Improvement Groups

As part of the organizational changes advocated here, the introduction of quality circles or productivity improvement groups needs careful consideration. The necessary care in evaluation of the role and contribution of these developments, however, has not always been exercised by those Western companies that have adopted them. In many instances, they have been perceived as panaceas and as such have been evaluated and implemented at an operational level and not as part of a strategic organizational change to draw out the continuous improvement potential of the shopfloor.

The concept of quality circles emanates from Japanese business practice. The name derives from the fact that, after the Second World War, quality conformance was Japan's initial major manufacturing problem. Hence, some organizations have changed the name to productivity improvement groups to more accurately reflect the activities currently undertaken. Quality circles illustrate the impact of participation on the productivity increases that can be achieved in all aspects of performance. They systematically involve workers in the improvement of quality conformance, productivity and similar operations activities. This form of worker involvement in Japan continues to grow.

A review of the overall performance of many Japanese companies highlighted employee involvement as an important aspect of operations management style and consequently many other countries began adopting this approach. It was recognized as a way of providing the systematic involvement of the workforce and the returns on the investment of training given and time spent were numerous and impressive. However, the distinction in many firms has not been drawn between the use of these improvement initiatives as a major organizational change adopted as an operational response and one adopted as part of a strategy-led response to improving the effectiveness of manufacturing. This has led some reviewers to conclude that in many organizations quality circles are already in the adoption–disappointment–discontinuation cycle that has been characteristic of many other managerial fads.

The failure of European and US manufacturing companies to recognize the value of the shopfloor contribution is widespread. The use of quality circles or productivity improvement groups is an aid to redressing this imbalance and tapping what is probably a company's most underdeveloped asset – the ideas and contributions of its workers. For this to be effective, the company needs to be genuinely committed to the principle of continuous improvement and to accept that this can only be achieved by participative management. The structures then need to be developed to make the *principle* work in *practice* and then to support its development throughout while not interfering with the nature of that development. In this way, companies are able to start tapping into their collective wisdom. The change is a strategic one. It accepts that there are significant benefits to be derived from detailed operational improvements, that implementing improvements quickly and effectively must be on a participative basis and that people, as a group, have the ability to evaluate each others' ideas and develop them.

Participative management is not a soft style. It is both demanding and results oriented. The difference is embodied in the changed views of work and relative contribution of those involved. Functions, and groups of people who are high potential contributors, need to be clearly identified. Similarly, other functions and groups need to be placed in their relative positions on the continuum depicting business needs. Fulfilling potential or eliminating low contributors will bring noticeable improvements.

The improved results are marked. Exhibit 10.7 compares some key outcomes in terms of shopfloor problem-solving structures regarding automotive component plants classed as 'world class' and the rest.[13]

**Exhibit 10.7**  Shopfloor problem-solving structures and outcomes

| Aspect | Plant classification | |
| --- | --- | --- |
|  | World class | Other |
| Percentage participation | 80 | 54 |
| Meetings per month | 3.5 | 2.5 |
| Suggestions per employees | 16.7 | 12.3 |
| Percentage suggestions accepted | 79 | 13 |

# Operational Control

Infrastructure development is a wide-ranging area and, as explained earlier, the aspects addressed in this chapter are not meant to provide either a comprehensive or even a representative coverage. They have been chosen because they constitute some of the important aspects of manufacturing infrastructure. Also, their treatment is intended to offer guidelines on how to develop other areas within the manufacturing strategy of the company. In this section, therefore, only three facets of operational control are covered. The first, quality conformance, is selected because of its important role as either a qualifying or order-winning criterion. The second, inventory control, is chosen because it is typically a substantial asset in a manufacturing company's balance sheet. The final aspect, control of manufacturing, has been addressed because of its role in delivery performance, which concerns other important qualifying or order-winning criteria. In addition, the conclusion of the chapter discusses a payment system development chosen because of its inherent role in the motivation of people to achieve the relevant performance criteria to be provided by manufacturing and as an example of how all facets within infrastructure need to develop within a strategic overview the context of a functional strategy.

# Control of Quality[14]

In many instances quality conformance is a qualifier in manufacturing strategy terms and its impact on market share is more dramatic than probably any other single factor.

In many sectors, Japanese companies have systematically increased the level of quality conformance to such an extent that they have fundamentally changed customers' expectations not only in these markets but as a general rule. Initially challenging existing norms where quality conformance was a qualifier, they made and sold products with a markedly lower level of defects. The results were dramatic. Unable to meet the distinctive higher-quality levels, companies suddenly found that they were no longer qualifying to compete in their traditional markets. Loss of market share followed. To regain a place on customers' short lists, companies were required to reconsider their basic approach to quality conformance provision and to take on board the markedly higher expectations of their customers. Today, quality conformance has reverted to being a qualifier in many markets. Thus failure to meet existing quality conformance expectations or to track future improvements will lead to an order-losing scenario and attendant consequences.

Often in the past, companies did not recognize the potential strategic consequences of separating the responsibility for quality conformance from the person responsible for completing the task. In project and jobbing processes this division has rarely, if ever, been introduced. In continuous processing, quality checks have been built into the process, thus retaining the link between the doing and evaluating task within the process itself. However, in batch and line, the responsibility for

**Exhibit 10.8** Responsibility for quality control (that is, checking conformance to specification) and the type of process

| Process | Task | Responsibility for quality conformance |
|---|---|---|
| Project and jobbing | The making and quality conformance tasks are normally integrated in the skills of the person | Usually vested largely in the performance of the task or provision of the service; that is, the person responsible for this part of the process plus supervisory support |
| Batch and line | Work has been deskilled to reduce, among other things, labour costs; inspection and later quality control functions introduced | Theoretically vested in the person providing the task, with supervisory, quality control and inspection support; in reality, the quality control and inspection functions are primarily responsible for quality conformance levels |
| Continuous processing | Quality specification is determined by the process and, therefore, reintegrates quality conformance into the task | Usually an integral part of the process design; the facilities to monitor quality conformance are usually controlled by the person responsible for other aspects of the total task |

*Source:* Terry Hill, *Operations Management, Strategic Context and Managerial Analysis*, Basingstoke: Macmillan, 2000

completing the task and achieving the required levels of quality, while argued to be one and the same, are really two separate sets of responsibilities (see Exhibit 10.8).

The most appropriate time to check conformance to specification is when an item is made. However, under the systems still often used in batch and line processes, work is checked after its production. Either the length of time between production and quality conformance checks or when quality checks are taken will have a direct bearing on a company's ability to minimize the repercussions of below-quality work.

This raises two important issues concerning quality conformance that need to be agreed at the corporate level and then form part of manufacturing's response to this essential market requirement:

1. *A reactive or proactive approach to quality* – The first issue is to determine whether to adopt a reactive or proactive approach to quality. In the former, the emphasis is towards detection, with the objective of preventing faulty work being passed on to subsequent processes. This will minimize the costs involved in rectification, scrap, returned products and non-repeat business.

   A proactive approach emphasizes prevention rather than detection. It requires allocating resources to make products right the first time, more of the time.

This is achieved by reviewing the quality of design and conformance to identify the factors affecting these two features. Quality control is then designed around this analysis.

2. *The responsibility for quality conformance* – The responsibility for quality conformance concerns two separate issues. The first concerns defining the departmental responsibilities throughout the process; the second, the responsibility for measurement.

In recent years, the distinction between quality assurance and quality control (that is, checking conformance) has become more marked. Quality assurance is the function charged with the task of developing the quality structure, and the responsibilities and activities within that structure, together with establishing procedures to ensure the organization meets the agreed quality levels for its products. Quality control is that aspect of quality that concerns the practical means of securing product quality, as set out in the specification (that is, quality conformance). The separation of roles between the people completing the work and those given specific responsibility for checking the quality achieved, albeit as a backup activity, has been in force for a number of decades. This separation has been further emphasized by the reporting systems that have developed in many organizations (see Exhibits 10.3 and 10.5).

To facilitate manufacturing's task, an infrastructure change has to be implemented. Quality control needs to revert to the set of activities for which manufacturing is responsible, while the quality checks on conformance need to form part of the operator's role.

The importance of this essential change is gaining widespread recognition, as illustrated by the points allocated to this dimension under the categories 'Information and Analysis' and 'Human Resource Focus' and within the Baldrige Award[15] (see Exhibit 10.9). However, the extent to which Western companies have incorporated these fundamental changes in their pursuit of quality improvements is not as extensive as generally assumed. Although commitment to quality improvement from top management is high, Baldrige examiners report that applicants 'have been surprised to find they come up short at the other end of the organizational chart.

**Exhibit 10.9** Baldrige Award (points allocation by category)

| Category | Points |
| --- | --- |
| Information and analysis | 85 |
| Strategic planning | 85 |
| Leadership | 125 |
| Human resource focus | 85 |
| Information and analysis | 85 |
| Process management | 85 |
| Business results | 450 |
| Total | 1000 |

Many companies with high-profile reputations for quality have been told to do more to empower their employees as well as their upper ranks.'[16]

However, the importance of achieving high product quality is being clearly recognized. Respondents in Europe and the United States placed product quality as their number one competitive priority over the following five years, clearly signalling an overall recognition of this issue.[17] At the corporate level, companies clearly illustrate the importance they attach to achieving major improvements in quality. IBM, for instance, admitted at the beginning of 1990 that its overall defect rate was around three sigma, or 66,810 defects per million operations. IBM's aim is to reach six sigma, or 3.4 defects per million operations.[18]

The gains are considerable, not only in costs but also in customer relations and job interest. However, it will not happen overnight. Traditions die hard, and the investment in training needs to be clearly recognized. However, with the responsibility for good quality work now back where it belongs, companies can also move from the reactive approach that they invariably adopt, which are almost dictated by the existing departmental and online responsibilities for quality, to the proactive approach necessary to ensure that manufacturing will be able to provide the quality requirements demanded by current and future markets.[19]

## Control of Inventory

In most manufacturing companies, inventory is usually substantial, whereas the methods used to control it are typically inadequate. They lack the level of sophistication and insight appropriate for an item that stands at up to 30–40 per cent of many companies' total assets. While decisions to use funds for plant and equipment, for instance, are normally carefully monitored, the relative effort and attention given to the control of inventory is generally too little and too late. Increases in inventory happen and concern to exercise due control over this sizeable asset comes after the event. This is because inventory control is based on a number of operational activities without the strategic overview of control warranted by an investment of this size.

There are two general characteristics about inventory that illustrate, above all, the level of business disinterest in its control and the underlying perspectives on which existing controls are built. First, many companies take complete physical counts of stock on as few occasions as possible, often as little as twice a year to coincide with the financial accounting periods. Furthermore, as the date for stocktaking approaches, companies commonly create an unrepresentative picture of inventory inside the business by holding off purchases at the front end and moving existing inventory inside the business itself. The rationale for this is to reduce the inventory holding *per se* and so record a more favourable position in relevant financial statements. Such actions also reduce the size of the clerical task involved. On the whole manufacturing companies look on these tasks as a chore rather than an opportunity to collect valuable data essential to the control of what is one of the biggest single assets on their balance sheets.

Second, inventory breakdowns are normally expressed in terms of the stage the material has reached in the process: namely, raw materials/components, work-in-progress, and finished goods. This choice is made solely to facilitate the valuation of inventory as an input into the profit and loss account and balance sheet. Thus, the outcome of this data-collection exercise is viewed primarily as a provision of information to the accounts function and not as an important opportunity to create the basis for controlling this large asset.

The purpose of having inventory is to provide a set of advantages that reflect a business's needs. Depending on what constitutes the needs in the marketplace and the agreed manufacturing requirements within the business, the size and spread of inventory will differ. Effective control is based on an understanding of why inventory is held, where it is and what functions it provides. Currently, however, many companies attempt to control inventory by global, across-the-board mandates over short time periods. This approach neither reflects real control nor time dimensions.

## Causal Analysis as a Basis for Inventory Control

There are two broad categories of inventory: corporate and operations. Corporate is the type of inventory that does not provide a manufacturing function (often accounting for some 20 to 25 per cent of the total holding).[20]

The types of corporate inventory are numerous and reflect the nature of the manufacturing company involved. Typical of these are:

- Sales inventory to support customer agreements
- Sales inventory owing to actual sales being lower than forecast
- Marketing inventory to meet a product launch
- Purchasing inventory incurred to achieve quantity discounts
- Corporate safety stocks caused by uncertainty of supply (for example, possible national or international strikes)
- Slow-moving inventory under various related subheadings.

The control of corporate inventory requires information on the stock held by cause. Once the inventory category is determined and is separated into its appropriate type, the company can set targets in line with the business needs (and this may not always be a reduction), charge the appropriate function with responsibility for inventory control and monitor it. A company is then able to understand the return it receives for its investment, decide on the value for money associated with that holding and use this information as part of its overall review of functions, customers, policies and so on.

The function of operations inventory is to facilitate the manufacturing process at all stages. However, in order to exercise meaningful and effective control, the company must understand the types of inventory within this category and classify the relevant holding accordingly.

Several important principles and approaches are involved in the effective control of inventory, including:

1. **The dependent/independent demand principle** – When the rate of use for an item does not directly relate to the use of any other item, it should be treated as an independent pattern of demand. Examples include finished goods and factored items. Conversely, items with demand linked to the use of other items are said to have a dependent demand pattern. For example, components and subassemblies. This distinction enables companies to recognize that, whereas the demand for independent items will have to be arrived at through forecasting or similar techniques, the demand for dependent items can be calculated.

2. **The functions provided by operations inventory** – Holding operations inventory provides a number of distinct functions within manufacturing. These causes need to be distinguished and inventory data collected by category. The functions are:

   ■ *Decoupling inventory*. Separating one process from the next allows both to work independently of one another and decouples otherwise dependent parts of the total operations process. Decoupling inventory concerns materials waiting for processes so that each process can be most efficiently used. It is not found in jobbing, line or continuous processing because the person and process, respectively, move the inventory from one operation to the next on a continuous basis. It is, however, at the very essence of batch manufacturing.

   ■ *Cycle inventory*. This relates to the decision to manufacture a quantity of products (sometimes referred to as a lot or batch size) that reflects criteria such as set-up to production-run length, customer-order size and call-off patterns. The rationale for cycle inventory is to reduce set-up costs and to help maximize the use of process capacity by increasing production-run lengths.

   ■ *Pipeline inventory*. This is the inventory needed to be held when companies decide to subcontract one or more processes to an outside supplier at some time during the total process lead time. All the inventory associated with this decision is classed as pipeline.

   ■ *Capacity-related inventory*. One way to cope with anticipated sales is to plan production in line with sales forecasts. This, however, often leads to a situation of peak-capacity requirements being met by overtime, recruitment of additional labour and the holding of spare process capacity. Another way is to plan some sort of level production programme, stockpiling inventories in the low-sales periods for selling in the high-sales periods. This is known as capacity-related inventory and concerns transferring work from one time period to the next in the form of inventory. It provides one way of stabilizing production capacity in an environment of fluctuating sales levels.

   ■ *Buffer inventory*. This concerns the problem that average demand, by definition, varies around the average. In order to cope with this, companies hold higher levels of inventory to reflect this variation. Buffer inventory's function, therefore, is to help to protect the process core against the unpredictable variations in demand levels or supply availability. The higher the service level or the lower the level of stockout risk set up by a business, the greater the quantities of buffer inventory required. A decision to hold inventory in excess of this requirement, however, should be classed as safety stock and fall within a corporate inventory provision.

3. **Causal mapping of inventory** – When undertaking this control task, an agreed area of the business is selected for analysis – it is not necessary to review the whole business. The purpose of the analysis concerns identifying where large blocks of inventory occur and not with assessing the whole of the inventory holding and the level of exactness called for in an annual stocktake, the results of which go into published accounts. Inventory is then identified by position in the process and by its function.

- Position in the process is recorded as between the last process the material left to the one that will complete the next step.

- If a parcel of inventory provides more than one function (for example, those of cycle and decoupling), then an arbitrary split is made and the dual function recorded. As before, the data outcomes concern magnitude not exactness. Any large amounts of inventory are then further analysed and systematically reduced.

4. **Reducing inventory** – The key to inventory reduction concerns removing inventory that is not adding value. It eliminates the unnecessary and arrives at a level sufficient to support current systems, existing manufacturing processes and procedures and corporate commitments and decisions. To do this, companies need to identify the reasons why excess inventory has been generated, change the rules and procedures to stop this recurring and use up existing inventory while preventing inflows of inventory except those that are necessary.

Many companies, however, compare current inventory levels with those proposed using alternative manufacturing planning and control systems. By doing this they compare current inadequate control with best-practice control of proposed alternatives. But companies should first reduce inventory levels to necessary norms and then decide whether or not the reduction benefits accruing from alternative proposals are sufficient to justify the investments and changes involved. In this way, decisions are made on a like-for-like basis, thus enabling companies to identify the real sources of improvement.

5. **The 80/20 rule** – A review of inventory based on a Pareto analysis[21] will almost certainly reveal that some 20 per cent of the items will account for about 80 per cent of the value. Using this as the basis for an ABC classification allows a company to exercise tight control over the relatively few items that are high in value and classed as 'A' items in such a review. However, on the low-value

items, excess buffer inventory holdings allow the controls to be simple and the records to be minimal.

Based on these perspectives of inventory, the control exercised can now reflect the important, the large and the relevant. Once a business knows why and how much inventory is being held it can divert attention, effort and the level of control accordingly. Two examples to illustrate this approach will help to amplify the issues involved.

---

A US company making products for use in the construction, mining and steel industries adopted an across-the-board policy of providing a two-day delivery for all products. As a result, it held finished-goods inventory together with some work-in-progress to support a make-to-stock or assemble-to-order provision for its products. The rationale for this was based on a corporate marketing perspective that short lead times were an essential competitive factor in the company's markets.

A manufacturing strategy review identified the high level of inventory necessary to support the short lead times on offer. As part of this review, the delivery speed criterion was questioned especially in the context of static market share for key products. This included in-depth discussions with customers by manufacturing executives concerning how to support their needs and analyses of lead-time requirements stated on actual customer orders. The outcome was that less than 15 per cent of sales required a lead-time support of two days. For these, consignment stock (managed by the company on behalf of customers) was held. All other sales were then met on a make-to-order basis where delivery on time and shortening process lead times became the principal manufacturing strategy tasks. The overall result was a reduction in inventory of 46 per cent.

---

A plant that was part of a large group of companies received an across-the-board corporate directive to reduce inventory by 15 to 20 per cent in a given period. The plant involved manufactured optional features for vehicles. However, to make a sale, the customer required short delivery response to minimize the off-the-road time for any vehicle. To provide this distinct order-winning criterion, the products had been designed to have a high proportion of standard parts and subassemblies to gain some economies of scale and to maximize coverage of the wide range of products involved, while minimizing inventory holdings. To meet this short lead time, manufacturing needed to hold all parts in stock so as to reduce the overall process lead time and allow itself the time to respond to the market. Only when inventory's role within manufacturing strategy was explained was the corporate directive rescinded.

Finally, when reviewing inventory holdings it is important to look at Exhibit 5.4. It illustrates how the implications for inventory holdings of raw materials/components, work-in-progress and finished goods would differ with each choice of process. As a starting point the trade-offs involved between inventory investment, plant utilization, efficiency and other operational factors need also to be taken into account when reviewing the fundamental decisions addressed in Chapter 5. However, this in no way precludes a company from changing the mix in trade-offs that surround inventory investment. When doing so it needs to take into account the following:

■ *return* – inventory is an asset. Its evaluation, as with other assets, needs to concern the added value it brings to a business compared to the level of investment involved. Inventory is not an investment that, by definition, should always be reduced. The only inventory to be automatically eliminated is that which brings no return.

■ *evaluation* – when evaluating inventory, the value-added side of the equation needs to include both operational (the plant utilization and efficiency-type gains mentioned earlier) and strategic (support for order-winners and qualifiers, such as delivery speed) factors.

■ *alternatives* – inventory is not the only way in which a company can provide dimensions within a business. For example, set-up reduction enables companies to maintain the ratio between the length (hours) of set-ups (that is, lost capacity) and length (hours) of production runs (that is, productive capacity) and reduce inventory. Just-in-time production systems (described later) provide an alternative approach to managing processes. In so doing they pick up a fresh set of trade-offs for manufacturing and the business, which, on the plus side, include a sharp reduction in inventory levels. It is essential, therefore, that the manufacturing strategy debate concerning process choice and the role of inventory in this configuration (see Exhibit 5.4) explains and amplifies the implications for the business and the critical nature of the trade-offs involved.

# Control of Manufacturing[22]

Many firms see manufacturing investment and agreements on markets to be independent sets of decisions. Few appreciate the need to link the two. The result, which has been a theme throughout the book, is that firms have made and continue to make large investments in process and manufacturing infrastructure without setting them within a strategic context. However, the high cost and fixed nature of manufacturing investments, their key role in helping to secure the short- and long-term prosperity of a business and the dynamic nature of today's markets make this increasingly risky.

## *No Strategy, Poor Systems*

One such area that illustrates the general problem outlined above is that of manufacturing planning and control (MPC) systems. As a large infrastructure investment and as a critical function in the management of manufacturing this provides a classic example of the panacea-driven approach that has characterized past decisions in the manufacturing function. Material requirements planning (MRP), just-in-time (JIT) and optimized production technology (OPT) are recent illustrations. Bought more for their apparent benefits than business fit, it is not surprising that many companies still continue to experiece that these investments, large in nature and time-consuming to change and install, fail to realize their full benefits.[23]

---

A medium-sized US furniture company made high-volume standard products using simple process technologies, with few operations and little work-in-progress inventory. To support short customer lead times there were high levels of finished-goods inventory. The company controlled manufacturing using central scheduling and manual shopfloor controls supported by visual checking and verbal communications between departments. To improve equipment utilization, productivity and order tracking on the shopfloor, the company installed a computer-based shopfloor control system with automated order-tracking, queue-control and capacity-planned features costing about $0.75m. In business terms, the principal area for improvement was an increased level of sales support by fulfilling customer orders more quickly while keeping the finished-goods inventory under control. The key to achieving this would have been to improve the master production-scheduling function to better reflect actual sales in plant schedules, so avoiding imbalances in finished-goods inventory characterized by shortages and excess stockholdings. The investment in the shopfloor control system was not only unnecessary but resulted in added paperwork, with a corresponding increase in overheads. It also diverted key supervisory effort from other areas.

---

Responding to the technology developments in the telecommunications field, a European company moved from electromechanical to electronic-based products. While components for the old products were made in-house, using a range of batch processes and final assembly lines, the company purchased the new product technology in the form of components.

Beset with several dimensions of manufacturing change, the company retained its previous MRP system as a tested and proven device. However, in

*(Continued)*

doing so it overlooked the critical shift in manufacturing. Whereas the old products required the emphasis to be placed on the control of a broad range of complex, internal processes and the inherent work-in-progress inventory, the key control issues for the new products were vendor scheduling and component-inventory management. Retaining the previous MRP system led to a failure to switch resources to vendor scheduling and to highlight component as opposed to work-in-progress holding as the key area of inventory control. As a result, pressure was placed in the wrong areas, shortages increased and the control system was unable to cope with the new demands.

A UK aerospace company manufacturing a wide range of products at all stages in their life cycles invested in a comprehensive, standard computer-based MRP system to meet all its requirements. The complexity of the data, training needs and the system's running and support requirements were reflected in the costs involved – $8m over a two-and-a-half year period plus high running costs. A postinstallation review highlighted that although the system met the needs of original equipment manufacture (OEM) products, it did not meet the needs of the spares business. It was estimated that 60 per cent of the original database investment was not necessary. Instead, the planning and control needs of the spares business could have been better provided, at significantly less cost, by simplified master scheduling, materials planning and shopfloor controls; there was no need for the order-tracking, queue-control and priority-despatching features essential to the OEM part of the business.

## From Panaceas to Policy

The examples given in the last section show how firms may invest in planning and control systems that, although sound in themselves, do not fit the needs of the business. The outcome not only results in unnecessary expenditure but also leads firms to assume that this aspect of manufacturing has been resolved.

The way for companies to improve the fit of these investments to the needs of the business is to link markets to processes and to MPC systems. This not only requires clear understanding of markets and the subsequent link to manufacturing but also of the way that MPC systems differ in themselves and the key characteristics they embody.

The market debate has been a consistent theme and the steps involved have been highlighted earlier. With this complete, companies next have to link markets

**Exhibit 10.10** Linking manufacturing strategy to the design of the master production schedule

| Strategic variables | | | Master scheduling approach | | |
|---|---|---|---|---|---|
| | | | MTO[1] | ATO[1] | MTS[1] |
| Markets | Product | Type | Special | ⟶ | Standard |
| | | Range | Wide | ⟶ | Predetermined and narrow |
| | Individual product volume per period | | Low | ⟶ | High |
| | Delivery | Speed | Difficult | ⟶ | Easy |
| | | Reliability | Difficult | ⟶ | Easy |
| Manufacturing | Process choice | | Jobbing/low-volume batch | ⟶ | High-volume batch/line |
| | Managing changes in sales and mix | | Through order backlog | Through WIP[1] or FG[1] inventory | Through FG[1] inventory |
| | Meeting delivery speed requirement | | Through rescheduling requirements | Reduces process lead time | Eliminates process lead time |

*Note*
1. MTO = make-to-order; ATO = assemble-to-order; MTS = make-to-stock; FG = finished goods; WIP = work-in-progress

**Exhibit 10.11** Linking manufacturing strategy to the design of the materials planning approach

| Strategic variables | | | Materials planning approach | |
|---|---|---|---|---|
| | | | Time-phased | Rate-based |
| Markets | Product | Type | Special | Standard |
| | | Range | Wide | Narrow |
| | Individual product volume per period | | Low | High |
| | Ability to cope with changes in product mix within a period | | High potential | Limited |
| | Delivery | Schedule changes | Difficult | Easy |
| | | Speed | Through scheduling excess capacity | Through inventory |
| Manufacturing | Process choice[1] | | Batch | Line |
| | Source of cost reduction | Overhead | No | Yes |
| | | Inventory | No | Yes |

*Note*
1. In jobbing, shopfloor control is handled by the skilled operator

through manufacturing strategy to the design of the master production schedule (MPS). The conceptual base for explaining differences and appropriate responses is given in Exhibit 10.10. This shows how companies need to select the base type of MPS to reflect the characteristics of their markets while similarly matching other aspects of manufacturing on relevant dimensions. In this way, companies develop coordinated responses in line with market needs to improve the level of support within manufacturing.

In the same way, firms must review the other facets of planning and control systems to identify and develop relevant parts of the MPC system. Exhibit 10.11 identifies the market and the manufacturing implications in terms of the design of the materials planning approach. It helps to explain why time-phased or rate-based approaches are appropriate given the different market characteristics that manufacturing needs to support. In addition, it shows appropriate processes while identifying the orientation of selected key tasks in manufacturing. Finally, Exhibit 10.12 links these to the design of the shopfloor control system and illustrates the rationale

**Exhibit 10.12** Linking manufacturing strategy to the design of the shopfloor control system

| Strategic variables | | | Shopfloor control approach | |
|---|---|---|---|---|
| | | | **Push-type** | **Pull-type** |
| Markets | Product | Type | Special | Standard |
| | | Range | Wide | Narrow |
| | Individual product volume per period | | Low | High |
| | Accommodating demand versatility | Total volume | Easy/Incremental | Difficult/stepped |
| | | Product mix | High | Low |
| | Delivery | Speed | Achieved by schedule change | Achieved through finished goods inventory |
| | | Scheule changes | More difficult | Less difficult |
| Manufacturing | Process choice[1] | | Jobbing/low-volume batch | High-volume batch/line |
| | Source of cost reduction | Overheads | Low | High |
| | | Inventory | Low | High |
| | Changeover cost | | High | Low |
| | Control of manufacturing | Key feature | Order status | Flow of materials |
| | | Basis | Person/system[1] | System |
| | | Ease of task | Complex | Easy |

*Note*
1. In jobbing, shopfloor control is handled by the skilled operator.

**Exhibit 10.13**    The relevant manufacturing tasks and MPC system investments of two companies serving different markets

| Company | Market characteristics | Order-winners and qualifiers | Manufacturing strategy | | | | |
| --- | --- | --- | --- | --- | --- | --- |
| | | | **Manufacturing** | | **Manufacturing planning and control system** | | |
| | | | Task | Features | Master production scheduling | Material planning | Shopfloor control |
| Company A | ■ Customized products<br>■ Wide product range<br>■ Low volume per product<br>■ Make-to-order<br>■ Initial versus repeat orders<br>■ Future order call-offs | ■ Design capability<br>■ Delivery speed<br>■ Delivery reliability (QQ)[1]<br>■ Quality conformance (Q)[1]<br>■ Price (Q)[1] | ■ To reduce process lead time<br>■ Manufacture to engineering specifications and quality standards<br>■ To achieve delivery reliability | ■ Batch manufacturing<br>■ Long process routings<br>■ High precision work<br>■ Accommodate delivery and design changes<br>■ Labour cost equals 60 per cent<br>■ Control of actual costs<br>■ Process and product uncertainties | ■ Make-to-order/assemble-to-order<br>  – Customer orders<br>  – Anticipated orders<br>  – Forecast orders<br>■ Used for rough cut capacity planning due to long lead time impact on delivery<br>■ Customer order promising | ■ Time-phased material planning<br>■ Material is particular to customer orders<br>■ High obsolescence risk<br>■ Extra materials needed for scrapped items<br>■ Trade-off: shorter lead time versus raw material inventory | ■ Push system<br>■ Priority of scheduling of shop orders<br>■ System supported by dispatching and production control personnel<br>■ Capacity requirements planning by work centre<br>■ Order tracking and status information |
| Company B | ■ Narrow product range<br>■ Standard products<br>■ High volume per product<br>■ Seasonal demand<br>■ Sales from finished goods inventory at distributors<br>■ Introduction of new products<br>■ Changing product mix | ■ Price<br>■ Delivery speed (through finished-goods inventory in distribution divisions)<br>■ Quality conformance (Q)[1]<br>■ Delivery reliability (Q)[1]<br>■ Base design and peripheral design changes (Q)[1] | ■ To provide a low-cost manufacturing support capability<br>■ To support the marketing activity with high delivery speed through finished-goods inventory | ■ High-volume batch and line production process<br>■ Short set-up times; small batch sizes<br>■ Low-cost manufacturing<br>■ Low labour cost<br>■ High material cost<br>■ Inventory reduction (raw material, components, and WIP[2])<br>■ Overhead reduction (low MPC[2] costs) | ■ Make-to-stock<br>■ Manufacture to forecast<br>■ Level production<br>■ Three-month frozen planning horizon<br>■ Manufacture to replenish distribution inventories | ■ Rate-based material planning | ■ Pull system<br>■ Kanbam containers<br>■ JIT[2] flow of material<br>■ Low raw material, component, and WIP[2] inventory |

*Notes*

1. Q denotes a qualifier, a capability required in order for the company to enter and remain in its market; QQ denotes an order-losing sensitive qualifier, a capability that if not supported leads to a rapid loss of business.

2. MPC = manufacturing planning and control; JIT = just-in-time; WIP = work-in-progress.

for alternative control approaches. Once again, it shows how alternative shopfloor control approaches line up with different market features and also provide a link to key manufacturing responses and tasks.

Thus, Exhibits 10.10 to 10.12 provide an overview of MPC systems and illustrate the way in which market differences require different MPC system responses. They help to show how the elements of alternative systems are consistent within themselves and how the development of appropriate responses needs to be accomplished within all facets of this major aspect of manufacturing infrastructure provision. Companies that fail to make these essential links will invest in systems that are inappropriate for the markets in which they compete and hinder manufacturing's ability to meet customer needs.

## Why Don't Panaceas Work?

Solutions presuppose that market requirements and corporate characteristics are the same. But today nothing is further from the truth. Markets are not characterized by similarity but by difference. Therefore linking elements of manufacturing strategy to the actual needs of markets is fundamental to the task. Solutions obviate this requirement and this basic step. A sound manufacturing strategy, on the other hand, is one where decisions and investments in processes and infrastructure are consistent with the needs of a company's markets. Exhibit 10.13 provides an illustration of two companies competing in different markets. It shows the link between their markets and relevant order-winners and qualifiers, the corresponding manufacturing tasks and the supporting processes and manufacturing planning and control systems.

It starts by showing the key differences in the markets served by the two companies. Tracing across from these market characteristics to the manufacturing responses shows clear differences in the latter while illustrating how each set of responses is consistent with the market needs of each company.

This is how the task of manufacturing – in all facets of its support for the varied needs of markets – needs to be fulfilled. Without the critical step of linking clear market definition to an understanding of the conceptual phase of manufacturing process and infrastructure options, the relevant and consistent choices will not be made and the panacea-driven approaches will be perpetuated.

## Conclusion

The JIT production system within Toyota has all the classic hallmarks of strategic infrastructure development. It works well because Toyota has demonstrated that it understands the need to reconcile the three major phases in its business – the before phase (its suppliers), the owned phase (its own processes) and the forward phase (the sale of cars through its networks). It works because Toyota has managed its forward phase in such a way that it freezes schedules, thus demanding or requiring little change in its own or its suppliers' processes. In this way, it has cushioned its manufacturing core from the instability of the marketplace, thus preventing it from being exposed. The stability so created means that Toyota is able to demand exact deliveries, so much a feature of the JIT production system. It has earned this favoured position and can and does, therefore, demand these benefits from suppliers, thus forcing the inventory forward and out of the system, rather than the other way round.

Many Western car companies do not appreciate these essential links. They show due sensitivity in the forward phase because they must generate goodwill and motivate their distributors to sell more cars. In the before phase, the converse happens. Here they believe that threatening suppliers will bring best results and this is a very telling difference.

Providing a clear manufacturing strategy for the business enables those responsible for infrastructure development to work from a common base, in a common direction, to meet a common requirement. Historical, personal and, in some instances, almost esoteric views fall by the wayside to be replaced by a strategic underpinning of infrastructure. This provides relevance by meeting the needs of the business and continuity by ensuring that the long-term requirements are an integral part of current thinking and decisions. Without a strategy-based approach these wide multifunctional areas are open to personal judgements, prone to fixed ideas and swayed by arguments based on what specialists can readily provide rather than the inputs necessary to meet the actual dimensions of manufacturing. The interactive nature of the dynamics within manufacturing, not being the responsibility of any one specialist or support function, is not at the forefront of the argument or application. The responsibility for this is clearly and wholly manufacturing's. Thus underpinning these with a clear and well-argued manufacturing strategy will provide the direction and mechanism for common evaluation.

On an entirely practical basis, the development and introduction of a payment system illustrates how any facet of infrastructure can and needs to be designed to support a company's competitive strategy and not to be in keeping with the efficiency-oriented perception of manufacturing's strategic role. The example below illustrates this.

---

A medium-sized manufacturing company wished to replace its existing payment scheme for hourly-paid employees, which had fallen into disrepute. The initial proposals centred on a classic productivity-based scheme, involving individual bonus-related earnings. When it recognized the need to develop this in the context of a manufacturing strategy, the company postponed work on the scheme until the necessary, earlier work was completed.

*(Continued)*

> Three manufacturing-related order-winners and qualifiers were highlighted – delivery speed, delivery reliability and price. With these now forming the basis of the manufacturing task, the scheme that was eventually developed reflected these criteria. Delivery performance (speed and reliability) now accounts for half the potential performance earnings, while the other half is for improvements in productivity. Furthermore, to encourage a broader view of work, the payments were made twice a year on factory-wide achievement related to attendance time.
>
> The shape and emphasis now more accurately reflected the needs of the business and are consistent with manufacturing's strategic contribution in supporting the company's current and future markets by the way the scheme was designed.

On the need to challenge the way in which US companies organize themselves and to consider the definitions of role, responsibility, authority, specialists and all the other facets of infrastructure, the last word belongs to Mr Konsuke Matsushita.

The difference in views expressed in the following quotation is stark, and the challenge to rethink existing approaches is clearly stated. Although many changes and improvements have been introduced in the work patterns of business over the past decade, the gap in many organizations is still marked. One thing is certain, to be successful in the future, companies will need to be adaptive and effectively use all the resources within the business.

**The Last Word: 'Why the West will Lose'**

We are going to win and the industrial West is going to lose: there is nothing much you can do about it, because the reasons for your failure are within yourselves.

Your firms are built on the Taylor model; even worse, so are your heads. With your bosses doing the thinking, while the workers wield the screwdrivers, you are convinced deep down that this is the right way to run a business.

For you, the essence of management is getting the ideas out of the heads of the bosses into the hands of labor.

We are beyond the Taylor model: business, we know, is now so complex and difficult, the survival of firms so hazardous in an environment increasingly unpredictable, competitive, and fraught with danger that their continued existence depends on the day-to-day mobilization of every ounce of intelligence.

For us, the core of management is precisely this art of mobilizing and pulling together the intellectual resources of all employees in the service of the firm. Because we have measured better than you the scope of the new technological and economic challenges, we know that the intelligence of a handful of technocrats, however brilliant and smart they may be, is no longer enough for a real chance of success.

Only by drawing on the combined brain power of all its employees can a firm face up to the turbulence and constraints of today's environment.

This is why our large companies give their employees three to four times more training than yours; this is why they foster within the firm such intensive exchange and communication; this is why they seek constantly everybody's suggestions and why they demand from the educational system increasing numbers of graduates as well as bright and well-educated generalists, because these people are the lifeblood of industry.

Your 'socially-minded bosses', often full of good intentions, believe their duty is to protect the people in their firms. We, on the other hand, are realists and consider it our duty to get our own people to defend their firms, which will pay them back a hundred-fold for their dedication. By doing this, we end up by being more 'social' than you.[24]

# Notes

1. T. J. Peters and R. H. Waterman, Jnr, *In Search of Excellence: Lessons from America's Best-Run Companies*, New York: Harper & Row, 1982.
2. R. H. Hayes and S. C. Wheelwright, *Restoring Our Competitive Edge: Competing through Manufacturing*, John Wiley & Sons, 1984, p. 32.
3. Ibid., p. 33.
4. The 80/20 rule reflects the implied relationship between two sets of data or consequences. In this instance, it illustrates that 80 per cent of the total strategic benefits to be gained from infrastructure development will arise from 20 per cent of the areas of application. The use of the figures 80 and 20, however, is illustrative of the relationship implied in the selected phenomenon and not intended to be definitive.
5. This expression, 0–100 management, was developed to highlight the pendulum-like response to problems or disadvantages that typifies organizational action. Instead, companies need to reposition themselves on a gradual and continuous basis while clearly recognizing that the diverse nature of markets will require diverse responses.
6. 'A New Target: Reducing Staff and Levels', *Business Week*, 21 December 1981, pp. 38–41.
7. Peters and Waterman, *In Search of Excellence*, p. 306.
8. This and some of the other concepts discussed here are taken from a set of well-developed work-structuring principles that have been presented in various unpublished papers by P. C. Schumacher, Schumacher Projects, Godstone, Surrey, UK.
9. Refer to Exhibit 10.5.
10. See S. Senju (ed.) *TQC and TQM*, Tokyo: Asian Productivity Organization, 1992 and Y. Takahashi and T. Osada *TPM; Total Production Maintenance*, Tokyo: Asian Productivity Organization, 1990.
11. A key feature of quality circles is that those involved not only implement their ideas but also evaluate the gains they yield.
12. Stoffman, 'Less Is More', pp. 97–98.
13. 'The Lean Enterprise Benchmark Project', Anderson Consulting, Cardiff Business School (UK) and University of Cambridge (UK), 1993.
14. The dimension of quality referred to here is conformance.

15. The Malcolm Baldrige National Quality Award is a US government industry venture but supported solely by the industry-funded Baldrige Award Foundation. Started in 1988, the programme entails assessment against the criteria given in Exhibit 10.11.

16. P. Burrows, 'Five Lessons You Learn from (Baldrige) Award Entrants', *Electronic Business*, 15 October 1990, pp. 22–4.

17. Interestingly, Japanese respondents in the same Manufacturing Features survey placed product quality as their number four competitive priority. They are apparently now looking to other priorities to give them a competitive edge.

18. B. C. P. Rayner, 'Market-driven Quality: IBM's Six Sigma Crusade', *Electronics Business*, 15 October 1990, pp. 26–30.

19. There are many references to the advantages to be gained and examples of the results of such decisions. These include J. M. Juran, 'Product Quality – A Prescription for the West', *Management Review*, June 1981, pp. 9–20; Schonberger, *Japanese Manufacturing Techniques*, pp. 47–82 and 181–98; D. A. Garvin, 'Quality on the Line', *Harvard Business Review*, September–October 1983, pp. 65–75; C. Lorenz, 'A Shocking Indictment of American Mediocrity', *Financial Times*, 17 October, 1983; T. Kona, *Strategy and Structure of Japanese Enterprises*, New York: Macmillan, 1984, pp. 194–6; M. Imai, *Kaizen: The Key to Japanese Competitive Success*, New York: Random House, 1986, Ch. 3; T. G. Gunn, *Manufacturing for Competitive Advantage: Being a World Class Manufacturer*, Cambridge, MA: Ballinger, 1987; J. P. Alston, *The American Sumurai*, Berlin: Walter de Gruyter, 1989; B. G. Dale and J. J. Plunkett, *Managing Quality*, Hemel Hempstead: Philip Alan, 1990; N. Slack, *The Manufacturing Advantage*, London: Mercury, 1991; and M. J. Stahl and G. M. Bounds (eds), *Competing Globally through Customer Value*, New York: Quorum Books, 1991.

20. See Hill, *Operations Management*, Chapter 10 for a more detailed discussion on the types of corporate inventory and their control.

21. A Pareto analysis orders the data from highest down to lowest. The list provided then helps to show the 80/20 relationship that exists between the data being reviewed.

22. This section is based on W. L. Berry and T. J. Hill, 'Linking Systems to Strategy', *International Journal of Operations and Production Management*, 1992, **12**(10): 3–15.

23. Earlier research in the early 1980s alerted companies to the extent of this phenomenon. R. G. Schroeder, 'Materials Requirements Planning: A Study of Implementation and Practice', Falls Church, VA: American Production and Inventory Control Society, reported that 63 per cent of MRP applications studied cost as much as $5m, yet failed to realize their full benefits.

24. K. Matsushita, 'Why the West Will Lose: Extracts from Remarks Made by Mr Konosu Matsushita of the Matsushita Electric Industrial Company (Japan) to a Group of Western Managers,' Industrial Participation. Spring 1985, p. 8.

# 11 Accounting, Finance and Manufacturing Strategy

Two common denominators are used in manufacturing businesses as the basis for control and performance measurement. The first is the time base on which manufacturing principally works. Product mix and volumes, capacity, efficiency, utilization and productivity are all normally measured by time. The second common denominator is that of money. At the corporate level, forecast activity levels, performance measures, levels of investment and similar activities use the money base. The importance of getting the correct links between the time-based and money-based measures is self-evident – correct not only in terms of being accurate, but also in reflecting the key perspectives associated with the business itself.

The money-based denominator issues addressed in this chapter are controlled by what, in many companies, is frequently one of the least developed functions: accounting and finance. Based on approaches established when business activities were very different, this area has not really faced up to resolving many of the important changes in business with appropriate developments. This chapter highlights a number of areas that need to be addressed from the point of view of both manufacturing and overall strategy. It will link the areas of manufacturing and corporate strategy with accounting and finance and illustrate some of the key issues that need to be developed and the essential direction these improvements need to take. In addition, it will show the ways in which manufacturing strategy will influence and, in some cases, facilitate some of these changes, while also drawing attention to the essential nature of manufacturing's needs and the accounting and financial information provision.

The purpose of this chapter is to make a number of critical observations about the impact on manufacturing of finance and accounting practices. The observations are made from a manufacturing executive's perspective, hence they may well be provocative when examined by the professional accountant. If this causes debate between manufacturing and finance executives, the purpose of this chapter has been achieved. Solutions to the issues addressed must be worked out in the context of a company's own corporate and manufacturing strategies. Since the financial systems in a business can, and do, have a major impact on manufacturing's ability to develop and maintain effective competitive strategies, one essential objective of the finance function must be to give manufacturing the ability to measure and assess its performance accurately in relation to major competitors, the relative contribution of products, customers and manufacturing activity to overall profits and the competitive value of investment proposals. The chapter deals with two broad areas of interaction between finance and manufacturing: first, the effect on manufacturing strategy of investment appraisal methods; second, how management accounting systems critically affect the control and performance measurement of manufacturing operations.

# Investment Decisions

The approach to developing a manufacturing strategy was explained in some detail in earlier chapters. One important consideration highlighted in those explanations was the level of alternative investments associated with different decisions (see Exhibit 11.1). Many organizations, bounded by cash limitations, need to commit their scarce resources wisely. However, the criteria for assessing the level or nature of this critical corporate decision have rarely been arrived at with the care and in-depth analysis that is warranted. In many companies, investment decisions initially chosen or stimulated by corporate competitive requirements are finally evaluated solely by accounting measures and methods of appraisal. The effect of these financial measures on both strategy and the consequent investment decisions is illustrated by the framework introduced in Chapter 2. Accounting methods of investment appraisal are generally based on one important premise – the relative return on capital associated with each investment proposal under review. With capital investment in limited supply and capital rationing a widespread consequence, the argument to invest predominantly on the basis of return is not only built into the appraisal system itself, but invariably is reinforced by the discussion and argument that will take place. In this way, the figures will unwittingly support investment return as the predominant or even exclusive measure on which to assess these key corporate strategy decisions.

The consequences of this undue weighting have been felt by many companies, and the ramifications within manufacturing industry have been widespread. The necessity to question this view of investment decisions has stimulated a series of well-argued articles and papers that illustrate the simplistic nature of the accounting

**Exhibit 11.1**  Restrictions imposed at both ends of the manufacturing strategy process

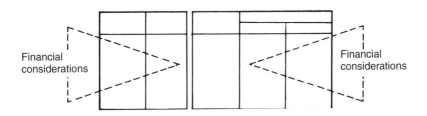

perspective and challenge its unevaluated application. As early as 1974, Dean declared that 'because of our obsessive concentration on short-term gains and profits, US technology is stalemated'.[1] Hayes and Abernathy's 1980 article said it all in the title, 'Managing Our Way to Economic Decline',[2] and again with Garvin, Hayes captured the essence of the issues in the article 'Managing as if Tomorrow Mattered'[3] in which they make, among other things, a concerted challenge on current accounting approaches to investment appraisal. They provide a detailed argument to support their view that companies have increasingly turned to sophisticated, analytical techniques to evaluate investment proposals. The long-term result has been that many of the managers involved have 'unintentionally jeopardized their companies' future'. As Hayes and Garvin conclude, 'investment decisions that discount the future may result in high present values, but bleak tomorrows'.

Since then, the basic criticisms have been taken on by others, particularly from the accounting profession. Of these, Kaplan well illustrates these growing concerns, as clearly shown in the title of his book with Johnson, *Relevance Lost: The Rise and Fall of Management Accounting*[4] and again with Cooper in the two articles, 'How Cost Accounting Distorts Product Costs'[5] and 'Measure Costs Right: Make the Right Decision'.[6]

## The Need for a Strategic View of Investments

When evaluating investments, companies need to make a strategy-based review. What constitutes a sound investment needs to be measured by its contribution to the agreed corporate strategy and not by how well it meets the criteria laid down by a set of accounting rules and evaluations. In one of several critiques of current management accounting, Simmonds observes that:

> the emphasis... accounting and finance have placed on return on investment over the years has subtly transmuted into a widely- and deeply-held belief that return comes from the investments themselves... The truth is much different. Sustained profit comes from the competitive market position. New production investment to expand sales must imply a change in competitive position, and it is this change that should be the focus of the investment review. Without it, the calculations must be a nonsense.[7]

This sleight of hand has been detected by all too few companies. Consequently, the key factor by which investment proposals have been assessed has increasingly swung away from strategy considerations towards levels of investment return *per se*. But return must be defined in terms of improved long-term competitiveness rather than just short-term measures.

Changing the basis of investment appraisal is complex and fraught with difficulties. It is one of those issues in which manufacturing executives have traditionally felt relatively weak, while those who control the cash are professionally very strong. The debate has, therefore, been one sided, with manufacturing the casualty by default. The arguments that investments must provide a quick payback are financially, and emotionally, attractive. They tend, however, to oversimplify the investment issues at stake and fail to drive executives towards determining and analysing those fundamental criteria that constitute the components of competitive strategy. Falling back on investment appraisal by financial numbers becomes the easy option. It simplifies the task, avoids the need to agree the strategic issues involved and dilutes the link between the decision making and subsequent evaluation. As the overriding reason for going ahead is based on perspectives provided by a function that does not carry the executive responsibility for making it happen, then this essential link is weakened.

A short section on investment can only begin to open up the debate from the manufacturing perspective by providing some guidelines that manufacturing can use to raise key questions. The hope is that finance executives will also use them to develop their own appreciation of the strategic issues involved in manufacturing investment decisions. Ten key contentions are made, each of which is expanded to give substance, but none can be claimed to be comprehensively examined. They are:

■ Investment decisions must be based on order-winners
■ Financial control systems need to be developed to meet the needs of the investment evaluation process
■ Investments are not separate decisions but need to be considered as part of a corporate whole
■ There can be only one given reason to substantiate an investment proposal
■ Excessive use of return on investment (ROI) distorts strategy building
■ Government grants are not necessarily golden handshakes
■ Linking investment to product life cycles reduces risks
■ Manufacturing must test the process implications of product life cycle forecasts
■ Investment decisions must quantify working capital and infrastructure requirements
■ Past audits capture learning and improve future decisions.

## Investment Decisions Must be Based on Order-winning Criteria

The impact of investment policies and appraisal methods on manufacturing strategy's contribution to the competitiveness of a business is clearly significant. If high hurdle rates are imposed, capital investment will invariably decrease. In times of capital rationing, the argument put forward in support of high return-on-investment thresholds is that they motivate a company to cream off the more attractive investment proposals and hence use available funds for the best opportunities. But this line of argument fails to assess the relevance of investment proposals in the context of an agreed corporate strategy. The result, at best, is hit-and-miss alignment of essential investments with manufacturing's strategic contribution; at worst, the investments essential for manufacturing to provide its contribution to market objectives are not even made.

For instance, delays in appropriate investment would lead to costs not declining as expected. Hence, achieved experience curve gains would fall off and if the delay itself and extent of the investment requirement were large, loss of market share would eventually follow.

Manufacturing strategy arguments for process investment to meet order-winners and qualifiers, other than price and the associated low-cost manufacturing task, come up against the difficulties of accounting and finance-based rationale. Proposals, for instance, to invest in processes that increase production flexibility when customer response and delivery speed are the key order-winners will be difficult to prepare in an appraisal system where return on investment is paramount. Similar forces will also work against facilities focus, irrespective of the importance of its role within manufacturing's support of the business needs. As explained in Chapter 7, focus will invariably lead to process duplication. However, investment appraisal systems often fail to incorporate as part of the evaluation procedure the need to orient facilities to better meet the order-winners and qualifiers of different markets. This, by implication, gives undue weight to return on investment or capacity utilization and will militate against focus in manufacturing.

Other accounting and financial perspectives will also work against the pursuit of focus in manufacturing. The accounting function's desire and argument to manage earnings and cash flows by smoothing cyclical business swings carries substantial corporate weight. However, focused manufacturing requires greater interaction between manufacturing and sales/marketing which leads to a higher level of shared dependence between these two prime parts of a business. This argues against smoothing, with the dynamics of sustaining and improving market share growing in significance and carrying more weight than the smoothing argument put forward by accounting and finance.

Investments such as computer-aided design (CAD) provide an example of the limitations in the accounting approach to investment appraisal. CAD is usually evaluated on the cost savings attributed to its introduction. However, a significant gain associated with this investment is the speed of response to customer changes, particularly in a make-to-order business. Often companies do not give due weight to the dimension of delivery speed as part of its competitive position within its chosen markets. So, the contribution that CAD can make in corporate strategy support will neither be evaluated as part of the investment appraisal nor systematically developed and exploited at all stages in the business.

In a reflective mood, Drucker pinpoints a belief in their own accounting figures as one of the common mistakes made by companies, which always leads to trouble.

> The conventions are very inadequate, inappropriate… It gives [companies] the wrong information. They don't know what the real savings are… Cost accounting gives you information on the cost of doing, but not on the cost of not doing – which is increasingly the bigger cost. Quality [conformance] and downtime are neither of them in the model.[8]

In developing a sound understanding of their need to compete effectively in different market segments, companies will recognize the importance of relevant order-winners and qualifiers. With these established and reflected in the evaluation of manufacturing performance, companies can assess their importance and take them into account when judging appropriate investments. Until then companies will continue to use apparently 'hard' data as the predominant, or even sole, arbitrator. Thus, in developing manufacturing strategy, companies must recognize the role of order-winners and qualifiers in the evaluation procedure and ensure that they reflect the business and not accounting conventions.

An assessment of current and future markets in terms of order-winners and qualifiers is essential in a company's investment proposal procedure, especially when investments are based on a forecast increase in sales. This will include a review of the way that both the existing and proposed capacity support relevant order-winners. In particular, it should identify levels of match or mismatch with an eye towards changing the way the company will win current and future orders.

## Financial Control Systems Must Meet the Needs of the Investment Evaluation Process

Financial control systems tend to be designed to meet the needs of accountants; consequently they are usually structured around a network of expense codes or account numbers, clinically constructed to facilitate electronic processing and the consolidation of final accounts and budget reports. From the accountant's viewpoint, this is a reasonable way of handling what are often complex analyses. The result, however, is that business transactions are then analysed on the basis of the account codes available and squeezed through a straitjacket of top-down apportionment to provide accountants with a view of expenditure and its relationship to business activity.

Taking such an approach, many financial control systems seek to trace actual expenditure to points of authorization and compare it to planned expenditure. The authorization provides the link on which to establish explanation and the formulation of corrective action. As highlighted in the last section, these evaluation procedures create major problems for a manufacturing company seeking to update its technology in response to relevant order-winners and qualifiers. These criteria may be one of two types:

- Product oriented; for example, quality conformance or lowest cost supply.
- Process oriented; for example, short lead times, widening product range or reducing customer order size.

Existing financial control systems tend not to provide management with a realistic basis for analysis against these criteria. In fact, in some instances, existing systems are misleading.

**Exhibit 11.2**   Typical financial control system provision versus investment evaluation requirement

| Dimension | Financial control system provision | Investment evaluation process requirement |
|-----------|-----------------------------------|-------------------------------------------|
| Direction | *Backward* – examine expected historical trading performance | *Forward* – project future performance |
| Orientation | *Internal* – examine and report on current business performance | *External* – evaluate current and future markets and competitors |
| Timescale | *Short-term* – review performance monthly | *Long-term* – examine expected performance over a given period |
| Expenditure base | *Revenue expenditure* – trace performance on the evaluation of revenue | *Capital expenditure* – evaluate investment in facilities to incorporate risk |
| Control base | *Return on investment* – assess return in respect of the net capital employed | *Cash-flow control* – relate expected cash flows to initial cash outlays |

Exhibit 11.2 provides a summary of some of the key differences between traditional financial analysis (geared to a steady state, low-variety, high-volume and slowly changing business environment) and the approaches to analysis required by the highly competitive nature of today's business environment.

## Investments Decisions – Not Separate but Part of a Corporate Whole

Companies with more than one site, particularly multinationals, need to review investments within the context of total corporate markets and total manufacturing provision. In the past, investments have tended to be taken as a series of separate decisions. At best companies have identified process overlaps but usually they have not reviewed corporate marketing and manufacturing strategies for the whole business. The result is that the link between current and proposed investments has not been forged. The outcomes of this include excess capacity, uncoordinated strategic responses, conflict and a failure to capitalize on corporate size and worldwide presence. One executive reflected on his company's failure to include separate decisions as part of a corporate whole: 'the outcome is that whereas the group has companies everywhere [global reach] it does not compete on a global basis'. Part of the problem – and one of the outcomes – for this company was that investments, being reviewed as separate decisions, did not require the corporate whole to be part of the essential context for these decisions. Overcapacity was rampant.

Given the increasingly competitive nature of global markets, companies need to move towards total reviews of their many businesses in order to assess within and between geographical regions. Only in this way can manufacturing's response be continuously reshaped. This will not only improve the fit between existing capacity, capabilities and chosen markets, it will also provide an overall view of existing manufacturing capabilities for current and future markets, the necessary investments and the appropriate location of these within the total business.

A cable maker decided to integrate backwards into wire-drawing. The opportunity to purchase an existing factory some distance away from the main cable-making facility had financial and practical advantages over expanding on the main site. The justification for the investment was reduced costs. Calculations based on well-established and publicly available drawn wire prices pointed to an acceptable return on investment.

In reality, while the calculations were based on drawn wire purchase prices, the supplier's costs were based on the high volume nature of its total business. Supplying solely to meet its parent company's cable-making demand, the wire-drawing schedule resulted in short runs over the wide range of drawn wire sizes required. The resulting high costs due to increased set-ups, lower throughput rates, lower effective capacity and resulting overtime working, higher waste and more frequent deliveries led to 18 months of losses before the new facility broke even.

## There Can Be Only One Reason to Substantiate an Investment Proposal

Investment appraisals submitted for review will typically include an extensive list of arguments and reasons for supporting a particular proposal. In many companies, the appraisal procedure has developed into an art form. Not only are the numbers massaged but also the rationale underpinning the investment typically encompasses a long list of arguments in the belief that the cumulative weight of these will win the day. Consequently, the essential clarity that should pervade these critical proposals is neither recognized as being essential nor required in the evaluating decision procedure.

This results in two major disadvantages:

■ **Stated reasons do not always reflect reality**. In many instances, proposals reflect the corporate norms and expectations recognized as being prerequisities for consideration let alone success. As Exhibit 11.3 shows,[9] key decisions are often taken for undisclosed reasons and the essential control of investments and agreement on their underlying support for a business is thus obviated.

■ **The essential argument needed to distill investment issues and insights is not considered necessary**. If investment proposals do not require a distinction to be drawn between prime and other reasons, the essential argument needed to distill the key issues is not an inherent part of these procedures. Hence, the rigour necessary for sound strategic argument is typically not undertaken. Furthermore, with the passage of time the real reasons for investments are lost and postinvestment evaluations, if undertaken at all, are set against incorrect strategic dimen-

**Exhibit 11.3** Documented and perceived reasons for all investments over a two-and-a-half year period – UK manufacturing company

| Purchase reasons | Documented | Perceived |
|---|---|---|
| Cost reduction | 50[1] | 19[2] |
| Update/introduce new technology | 37 | 55 |
| Increase throughput/productivity | 37 | 17 |
| Increase capacity | 37 | 27 |
| Part of a reorganization | 28 | 34 |
| Improve quality | 25 | 16 |
| Process dedication requirement | 25 | 21 |
| Reduce changeover times | 21 | – |
| Improve product flexibility | 20 | – |
| New process/existing technology | 18 | 1 |
| Reduce supervisory costs | 16 | 12 |
| Purchase of available machine | 15 | 17 |
| Improve material control | 10 | – |
| Reduce lead times | 6 | – |
| Process modernization | 5 | 22 |
| Automate process | 4 | – |

*Notes*

**1**. To be read: In 50 per cent of the cases cost reduction was documented as a reason for investment.

**2**. To be read: In 19 per cent of the cases, cost reduction was perceived to be a reason for investment. Perceived reasons were attained sometimes after investment had been made.

sions. The outcome is that 'before' and 'after' evaluations are typically not recognized as key steps in investment proposal procedures.

Companies, therefore, should adopt the maxim that there can be only one given reason to substantiate an investment proposal. The logic may appear at first to be simplistic but the rationale is sound. If one reason alone cannot support an investment, the substance and focus of the arguments need to be questioned. While such a procedure does not disallow listing secondary reasons, it will force strategic debate and clarify the essential rationale underpinning these key decisions.

## Excessive Use of ROI Distorts Strategy Building

Companies in developed economies such as Europe and North America, highly sensitive to the shareholders' view of short-term declines in profits, have become all the more prone to adopting a short payback posture. Furthermore, in times of low-profit performance, the pressure invariably increases to effect short-term recovery programmes as a way of demonstrating improvement and management action. In turn, the argument to set high thresholds can win the day when inadequate strategic direction and agreement have been reached or when the real need for investment has not been identified. Like drowning men clutching at straws, companies are attracted by the promise of higher returns. But investments in manufacturing processes and infrastructure taken out of their strategic context can commit a company for years ahead in an inappropriate direction. Although procedures require potential benefits to be clearly explained before investments are made, few companies rigorously assess the actual level of benefits achieved to determine the extent to which reality measured up to the proposals and to identify why any significant disparities arise. A UK survey in the early 1990s verified this practice. It found that while 96 per cent of respondents reported a requirement to demonstrate quantifiable future benefits from capital investment, only 58 per cent validated these after the fact.[10] While hindsight is not a substitute for foresight, such assessments provide a review of the effectiveness of these critical decisions. These analyses not only identify the actual level of return but also enable a company to measure the extent to which past investments have supported its corporate strategic requirements.

The approach to investment appraisal in Japan and Germany has a different basis. When they invest they are often prepared to sacrifice the short-term for longer-term profits that accrue from market share and increased volumes. In this way, they demonstrate two important differences in approach. First, they avoid the delusion that in an imprecise environment numbers are precise and thereby reliable, that is, they understand that the use of numbers does not reduce risk. Second, they accept that to run a successful business, risks must be taken.

Ohmae summarizes the clear difference in approach between Western and Japanese businessmen. Discussing the investments made by two Japanese companies, he concludes that 'in neither case... is any attention given to return on investment (ROI) or payback period, let alone to discounted cash flow. In both, the dominant investment criterion is whether the new business is good for the corporation as a whole.'[11] Ohmae illustrates these differences by posing the following questions:

> How many contemporary US corporations relying on ROI yardsticks would have embarked on the development of a business that required a twenty-year incubation period, as did Nippon Electric Company with its computer and semiconductor businesses?... Would Honda have so obstinately persisted in using its motorbike profits to bring its clean-engine vehicle to market if it were a corporation that measured the ROI of each product line and made its decisions accordingly? In fact, would any manufacturers be entering the four-wheel vehicle market in today's environment if ROI were the investment criterion?[12]

Similar questions and observations hold true today.

In many companies, a by-product of the emphasis on ROI in the corporate evaluation of investments has been an increasing tendency to view these proposals as a series of one-off, unrelated events and not, as they invariably are, characterized by strategic sequence. Only when companies review investment decisions in the light of their corporate strategies, and in turn their marketing and manufacturing strategies, will the essential cohesion be established. Until this happens, companies will be in danger of investing in ways that will not give them the necessary synergistic gains of strategic coherence. An example of what happens is provided by a company involved in the manufacture of office equipment and supplies. Over the years, the company had added on capacity in a piecemeal way. It eventually had seven manufacturing units in the same road, only two of which were interconnected. On paper, buying new sites as they were required made a better ROI than resiting the business. However, the costs of handling and transportation between units added complexity and overhead duplication. The position was only assessed when a new chief executive called a halt to the proposal to add another part to the 'rabbit warren'.

Perhaps the ultimate illustration of the excessive use of ROI and the distortion it brings is provided by Stephen Roach, Morgan Stanley's influential chief economist and the guru of downsizing (the cult of corporate shrinking that wiped out millions of jobs around the world in the name of efficiency and ROI). After a decade of arguing for and influencing businesses to pursue downsizing as a prerequisite to corporate, long-term success, he decided that he had got it wrong. He then declared that 'relentless cost cutting was bad for business. If you compete by building, you have a future, if you compete by cost cutting, you don't.' Carlin's article[13] commented on Roach's own reflections on his complete turnaround following a decade of advocating downsizing as the only path to follow. Roach observed that it had been 'a powerful learning experience for him and the debate had been a healthy one', to which Carlin's response was that even by the standard of a modern guru such a change was 'breathtaking'. 'So there we are' Carlin continued, 'this is the Age of Exoneration by Amazing Unforeseen Circumstances. No-one could have foreseen the effects of deforestation, artificially stimulated over-production or leaking water pipes.'

## Government Grants Are Not Necessarily Golden Handshakes

With disproportionately high unemployment rates in parts of many Western countries and the impact of declining primary and secondary sectors of the economy, most governments have, understandably, pursued policies to attract manufacturing and other activities to these areas to redress the regional imbalance. In a similar way, they have persuaded organizations to take on ailing companies or parts of companies to avert significant instances of primary and secondary redundancy. In addition, at plant level, governments have attempted to stimulate or support investment in manufacturing companies to help increase their competitiveness in world markets. In each instance, the carrot has been a generous system of grants and other awards. Many companies, attracted by the size of the handouts and the cash and return-on-investment gains they represent, have decided to take up the offer and relocate or establish all or parts of their business in one of a number of distressed areas, take on a relatively large piece of manufacturing capacity at one go or invest in state-of-the-art equipment to improve their manufacturing process capability. Companies that have not established clear strategic parameters and have evaluated proposals largely in terms of return or cash injection have all too often rued the decision. They are often bound by a minimum period of residence, by the relative size of the investments involved or by the desire to save face, at least in the short term or while the custodians of the decision still have responsibility for the business concerned. Examples are numerous.

---

A carpet company integrated vertically into yarn production instead of continuing its policy of buying from a number of yarn suppliers. The mill selected was in a remote area and some 100 miles away from the parent company's carpet plants. The deal included sizeable government grants and incentives as part of its regional policy and job creation and retention schemes. These investment benefits made the resulting ROI calculations highly attractive.

Besides the difficulties associated with recruitment at all levels in the mill and the distances involved in what was a linked process, the decision incurred one additional and fundamental problem. The rationale to split yarn and carpet manufacturing was made on the basis that it was a natural break in the processes involved. However, the company had established its niche in the quality end of the market. Separating the business at the natural break between the sets of processes involved had satisfied the investment-oriented arguments but, at the same time, the essential quality-control link had been broken between yarn spinning and carpet manufacture, both of which were now a corporate responsibility. Thus, a manufacturing split based on processes had ignored the essential qualifying criterion of producing high-design specification carpets. The quick feedback and opportunity for close liaison were not easy to exploit. In the early months, top management was preoccupied with justifying the investment from both parts of the total business. Reality, however, proved more difficult to handle than the statements in the integration proposals.

---

A medium-sized company decided to establish a subcontract machining facility. The company abandoned its first choice of industrial site for one some 25 miles away. The carrot offered was that the latter had a development classification attracting a high level of grant and expenditure exemptions. This alternative proved significantly more attractive to the

*(Continued)*

executives, banks and other financial institutions, who all developed a fixa-tion on the impact it made on ROI, profit and cash flows. However, when the order-winning criterion of delivery speed was introduced into the debate, these accrued financial advantages paled into insignificance. Without the sales, the calculations had no foundation.

A large manufacturing company that had great difficulty in achieving adequate profit margins was persuaded to absorb part of another group of companies. The cash injection offered as part of the government proposal to avert job losses swung the balance. The difficulties of absorbing such a large addition to manufacturing capacity, matching systems, controls and other parts of the infrastructure, besides the production processes involved, added to the company's already difficult task. The rationalization that ensued cast serious questions on the fit between the decision and the strategic needs and direction of the existing business. The outcome was added problems, less time and attention given to managing the base concern of unacceptable profit levels and an overall deterioration in its financial performance during the next two years.

## Linking Investment to Product Life Cycles Reduces Risk

Many companies entering markets for existing replacement or new products make decisions on process investment. These must reflect the forecast demands for those items at the various stages in their life cycles. As explained in Chapter 5, most prod-ucts do not move from jobbing to batch to line levels of volume over the life cycle. In fact, this rarely happens. Companies assess the market or base their forecast volume requirements with customers. They then have to plan their investments in accordance with the relevant volume parameters established by these procedures. It does not make sense for them to invest at one level of volume, then reinvest in response to subsequent market growth. The difficulty inherent in these decisions is the judgemental nature of predicting the future. Where a high level of certainty exists, there is less difficulty in matching the process investment to eventual product volumes. However, in areas of uncertainty, and given the characteristic ways of appraising investments and evaluating the various alternatives, companies invariably place themselves in a yes/no situation. Long delivery times for equip-ment further aggravate this position. Commitments have to be made months, some-

**Exhibit 11.4** Alternative approaches to investment decisions

times years, in advance of the scheduled launch. An alternative to this can be considered in many situations.

Exhibit 11.4 shows a projected life cycle for a product. At 1, process investment decisions would have to be made and purchase orders raised, in order for the plant to be installed and commissioned to meet the intended product launch at A. The alternative approach is to delay the process investment decision until 2, allowing sales forecasts to be amended in line with the actual sales to date. The trade-off embodied by adopting this second approach is that the process choice would be more in line with requirement. In this example, the new forecasts could be higher, lower or somewhere near the original forecast. Hence the eventual investments would be more in keeping with the actual sales levels. To do this, yet minimize investment, would require that existing processes could cope with the manufacturing task to point B. The company would, therefore, not be able to meet the level of manufacturing costs necessary to yield adequate margins. In this way, the trade-offs between loss of profits in the period between A and B and the risk of inappropriate investments being made would have to be assessed.

## Manufacturing Must Test the Process Implications of Product Life Cycle Forecasts

In many instances, investment proposals rarely cover each main phase of a product's life cycle. Yet manufacturing's task is to produce the product over each phase of this cycle and respond to the consequent variations in volumes, qualifiers and order-winners. Returning to Chapter 7 on focus, the importance of distinguishing between product and process focus (see Exhibit 7.4) brings with it the need to provide alternative sets of processes. However, not only does the production engineering function classically ignore the change in the manufacturing task towards the end of a product's life cycle but also the potential process investment requirements associated with this change are ignored. Hence many companies must retain a high-volume plant to meet low-volume requirements. Faced with this mismatch, manufacturing does the best it can. Unfortunately, many businesses do not recognize the need to look at the alternative approaches. What happens is that manufacturing unilaterally chooses the solution that makes most sense in the light of the production difficulties, constraints and performance measures within a company. However, the fit of the solution can then be changed in circumstances where the trade-offs involved have come under corporate scrutiny (for example, the inventory holding associated with making order quantities in excess of customer call-offs or requirements). Given that the order-winners associated with the volumes involved at these stages in a product's life cycle are invariably different (see Exhibit 11.5), the process choice appropriate to these stages should be realigned if manufacturing is to be able to provide the essential criteria at each stage of a product's life cycle. Thus, the investment proposal needs to include the processes necessary to manufacture effectively (in line with the varying needs of the market) throughout each stage.

The viability of a proposed product introduction should be over the whole of its life cycle and so include the investments necessary to cope with the same time period. This does not happen. Companies often assume that the process installed for the high-volume phase is the only requirement. Where existing processes can cope effectively with the change in volumes, the costs involved with this transfer (often quite high) also need to be recognized in the initial stages and included as part of the corporate assessment.

## Investment Decisions Must Quantify Working Capital and Infrastructure Requirements

Many investment decisions are distorted in two ways. On the one hand, they ignore intangible, difficult-to-evaluate reductions or benefits that accrue from the

**Exhibit 11.5**  Product life cycles, order-winning criteria and process investment interact

High-volume phase:

typical order-winning criterion of price requiring low-cost manufacturing processes

Low-volume phase:

typical order-winning criteria of delivery speed and reliability requiring flexible manufacturing processes

Volume

Process investment considerations

investment itself.[14] On the other, they underestimate the working capital needs associated with each proposal and often ignore altogether the infrastructure costs involved. The tangible nature of the investments associated with the equipment, plant and support services involved in a process have led to a clear identification of the costs involved. However many areas of investment directly associated with the capital expenditure being proposed have been overlooked or ignored in the past and, in many instances, are understated or assumed to be unnecessary at present. Only in the past 10 years have companies required a statement of the additional inventory necessitated by the process proposals under consideration. The drive by most companies to reduce inventory over the past 10 to 15 years has been an important stimulus for this change. Even so, many proposals understate inventory. This is because those involved in the preparation of a capital expenditure proposal are invariably not responsible for inventory levels within manufacturing. This leads to a significant underestimation of the levels actually needed to sustain manufacturing.

The effect on the infrastructure requirements that will emanate from particular manufacturing process investments is often either underestimated or not evaluated when expenditure proposals are prepared. As those who prepare the proposals are often not the people responsible for either the control of manufacturing or achieving the required levels of performance, an oversimplified review of infrastructure requirements is typically made. Consequently, companies do not recognize any increase in complexity and they assume that existing systems, controls and structures are not only adequate but also appropriate. The incremental nature of such assumptions leads to a deterioration in a company's ability to control and assess its manufacturing function and the eventual overhaul of one or more parts of its infrastructure. The costs associated with such developments can be high. For example, one company estimated that to install a revised manufacturing control system in a typical plant cost upwards of $500,000.

When a company is starting with a greenfield site on which to make a single product, its investment decisions will usually take full account of the need for services, systems and controls for the major aspects of infrastructure. However most companies are more complex and are generally investing in existing plants or introducing products to be made in already up-and-running processes. Investment considerations when introducing a product are usually more akin to the following examples:

■ The decision to enter a market will require an investment in all the processes necessary to manufacture the product in question. While similar to the greenfield site example referred to above, the product in this instance will be assumed to use existing site services, support systems and overheads. Such an assumption belies reality. It ignores the increase in complexity and corresponding demand placed on the non-process aspects of manufacturing that go hand in hand with the decision and the resulting deterioration of the effectiveness of existing systems and structures.

- Most product introductions generally use parts of the existing manufacturing processes. This compounds the current situation. It will increase inventory and make manufacturing more complex to manage by the shared use of existing processes and infrastructure and the interplay between them.

## Post-audits Capture Learning and Improve Future Decisions

Investment proposals contain details outlining the tasks involved and the benefits to be gained. By definition the proposal comprises estimates and projections, most of which will change when events unfold. As many of these are core to the proposal, its evaluation and its outcomes, post-implementation checks not only provide an audit but, more importantly, are a source of refining future estimates by testing them against what actually happens. In this way, reality checks capture the learning, increase the accuracy of projections and thereby directly improve future decisions.

Many companies do not undertake these audits as an integral part of their investment appraisal procedures. As a consequence, the detail demanded in the appraisal phase is in marked contrast to that undertaken after the event. Given the learning that could be transferred to future decisions in this key aspect of strategy, what actually happens is that jumping over financial hurdles becomes the area of attention and improvement, with the real issue of making sound and better investment decisions being relegated to a secondary activity.

## Operating Controls and Information

To assess its current performance, a company needs control information that reflects the key areas of its manufacturing task. Although there is a lot of information collected and recorded, many companies fail to separate clearly the difference between records and controls.[15] Furthermore, 'the development of the marketing orientation [in many companies] has led to an increase in the amount of market-based information available to management. In contrast, the paucity and limited availability of relevant internal information is striking.'[16] One key problem area is that of management accounting. Although money is used as the common denominator to assess current and future corporate performance, this function is often lacking in relevance and sensitivity towards changing circumstances.

## The Simplistic Nature of Accounting Information

The accounting information provided in most companies can be characterized in a number of ways (also refer to Exhibit 11.2). First, it is historically based. Although this is an inherent part of cost information, accountants, and thus the business, do not consider it to be of paramount importance in producing information that is relevant and close to reality. Second, invariably the information provided is primarily focused on management accounting relating to the business as a whole rather than the management control of manufacturing. This leads to the inadequate provision of critical information by which management can assess performances and make future decisions.

In broad terms, accountants work primarily on the basis of norms. They choose averages to simplify the measurement task. The procedure is then to compare each part of the business to a norm. However, the global nature of these comparisons hides the key to control. Failing to go back to the information from which the average has been drawn obscures the level of performance achieved. An average is a compilation of many parts but it is important to be able to assess the level of performance within each. The argument put forward in defence of the averaging approach is that to collect and update data for all parts would be very time-consuming and expensive. Therefore it is necessary to simplify the procedures and tasks involved to make some sense of reality and to be able to report within an acceptable timescale.

Reality, however, is complex. The controls need to reflect and measure reality. The accountants' approach is to simplify reality by simplifying the controls used. In this way, they are able to account for all the parts yet cope administratively with the task, that is, they meet the obligation of 'accounting for everything in a systematic way'. However, the basis for control in companies needs to reflect the complex business issues and not the tasks required by company law. Hence, the controls need to reflect the size and importance of the area concerned – detailed controls for the significant areas and simple, broadbrush controls for the insignificant areas.

Several general examples will serve to illustrate these points:

■  Most companies use total sales revenue as an indicator of successful performance. Invariably this leads to a situation where the contribution of individual products is not rigorously examined. In profit and loss account terms, the top line becomes the measure of sales performance and the bottom line, the measure of manufacturing performance. What fails to be clearly distinguished is that the two performances are inextricably linked. This consequently reinforces the argument by marketing of the need to retain all products. The simple measure of the marketing performance fails to distinguish the relative contribution of each product. Hence the conclusion that all sales are equally good business.

■  It is usual for manufacturing's task to be based on a proposed or forecast level of volumes. Invariably the volumes experienced differ from period to period and over time. However, rarely are costings provided for the different volume levels. It is essential to establish costings for the varying levels of throughput. In this way, the costings appropriate to the volume levels experienced will be used. This will then allow a company to assess a period's performance in a more exact way and to establish the reasons for the level of achievement or lack of achievement recorded.

**Exhibit 11.6**  Some accounting approaches, depending on the type of process

| Aspect | | Type of Process | |
| --- | --- | --- | --- |
| | | **General purpose** | **Dedicated** |
| Overhead | Recovery | Process or product oriented | Blanket rate per standard hour |
| | Control | Complex control: needs to assess the impact of product mix and volume changes, alternative routings and other similar factors | Simple variance control, derived from comparing actual to standard unit volumes |
| Costs | Set-ups | Direct to product | Overhead rate based on machine utilization |
| | Process scrap | Specific to the process or product | Blanket allowance |
| | Quality | Direct to product | Overhead rate established |
| | Tooling | Direct to product | Overhead rate established |
| | Maintenance | Direct to process | Overhead rate established |
| Basis for pricing | | Product cost basis | Contribution basis |
| Development of accounting procedures and controls | | Bottom up | Top down |

■ Accounting systems should reflect the type of processes being used. As shown in Exhibit 11.6, the treatment of costs, pricing and the development of accounting procedures and controls will vary. The costing structure and performance reporting system needs to take account of these differences in order to distinguish between the provision of sensitive cost information and the measurement of performance.

■ Plant decisions constitute a large business risk because of the size of the investment, the forecast sales basis for that decision and the flexibility/process cost trade-offs involved and their relationship to the market. However, the accounting policy on depreciation reinforces this risk when it is classified in relation to the type of plant rather than the life of the product for which the plant is to be purchased. Typically, the plant is depreciated by rule-of-thumb accounting classifications. For instance, one large manufacturing company used the rules in Exhibit 11.7 which were based on historical usage and precedents.

The gains accrued from having common accounting procedures belied the simplistic nature of this policy. Consequently, this sizeable asset becomes detached from its essential business orientation in order to accommodate the administrative requirements of the accounting function and policies involved.

**Exhibit 11.7** Rule-of-thumb accounting practices

| Item of plant | Typical length of depreciation in all parts of the company (in years) |
|---|---|
| Tool room equipment | 25 |
| Presses | 20 |
| Automatic lathes | 15 |
| Numerically controlled machines | 10 |
| Machining centres | 5 |
| Test | |
|     Dedicated | 5 |
|     General purpose | 10 |

# The Need for Accounting System Development

Demands for accounting system development are not new. Criticisms levelled at existing approaches have become both increasingly vocal and more broadly based. So far these overtures have resulted in little progress other than some tinkering at the edges. Some argue that the concerted pressure for these improvements has increased because of growing competition and loss of market share.[17] In part this is so. But the real reason is not one of blame.[18] To be able to assess options and alternative strategies, companies need insights and, in today's competitive climate, the pressure to make significant and speedy strategic responses has never been greater. However, accounting systems, even in their recording mode, do not provide information that helps the decision process. It is neither relevant nor timely. A far more fundamental question concerns accountants' perception of the role of accounting systems. Past history clearly marks them, at best, as being reactive. Hence their bean-counter/record-keeper image. What is needed is an executive response, proactively developing systems that fulfill the needs of the decision-making processes necessary to meet the demands of today's markets and competitive threats.

Revisions are being made. A UK survey in the early 1990s reported that in the previous five years 'significant revisions to cost-management systems were cited by 68 per cent of respondents'. However, the survey also reported that many of these revisions 'were "traditional" rather than "new" accounting techniques and practices'.[19] The implication drawn by the authors of the report was that 'introducing advanced cost-techniques and practices may not be the best costing improvement for many businesses'. The concern is that developing basic systems will not give a company the insights it requires. If traditional practices provided what was needed, then the essential criticism levelled against these systems would not be widespread and growing.

In their attempts to improve the competitive nature of their performance, many Western companies are paying greater attention to a whole range of improvements in quality conformance processes, inventory holdings and workforce policies. All are essential measures to effect this change. Not only is the level and urgency of response high but the approaches have challenged and are challenging the very basis of previous practice. The same cannot be said of accounting.

For example, in markets characterized by difference not similarity and by a rapid rate of change, 'most companies still use the same cost accounting and management control systems that were developed decades ago for a competitive environment drastically different from that of today'.[20] When trying to assess the level of contribution provided by each product as a prerequisite for judging what steps to take, many companies find that the accounting information provided fails to differentiate between them. While everyone knows that higher volumes decrease costs and product proliferation increases them, rarely are these essential trade-offs differentiated within accounting procedures. Classically, the core activities generate the substantial parts of a business. However, companies need appropriate information to assess sensibly the trade-offs associated with product breadth and focus. Non-core products are characteristically marginal in their contribution to a firm.

> Far worse than this, they may create added cost, which will be hidden by an average allocation to all products and customers. As a consequence, the essential core business may be deemphasized or overpriced, while the marginal extensions of the product line and customers served may be underpriced or overemphasized in their importance. This may be true even though a real competitive advantage exists in the core business while there is no comparable advantage in the extension coverage.[21]

The impact on business competitiveness can be significant.

## Working on the Left Side of the Decimal Point

> Information used in companies is not accurate. Plus or minus 10 per cent is the rule of thumb used by many. Accounting information is no exception. That these 'analyses are rarely, if ever, exact [and] all they can do is give a 'feel' for the financial dimensions of various activities and opportunities' is a realistic view.[22]

The typical presentation of accounting information is a giveaway. Figures to one or two decimal points give a spurious level of data accuracy. All that the system has provided is the refining of inaccurate data and accounting functions rarely remind those using the data that it is not as accurate as it may appear.

Working only on the left side of the decimal point brings significant advantages even using existing systems. The information is easier to use, its role in the decision-making process is reinforced, and the need to understand the issues and to ensure that all relevant perspectives are considered is highlighted.

## Assessing Current Performance

Companies control their businesses using different procedures in different time periods. At different periods, a company will have a strategic plan (usually agreed the previous year), budgets based on the strategic plan and revised budgets reflecting current events and levels of activity.

However, many companies then compare actual performance with the budget as the principal way of reviewing overall corporate performance.[23] But this comparison will not provide insights into performance. The company's revised plans are what need to be set against actual performance. This will, therefore, enable actual performance to be set against the actual plan. Budget changes that result from adjustments to strategic plans need to be reviewed separately in order to assess the planning procedure, the reasons for change and the impact or revisions on corporate expectations.

## Allocate, Not Absorb Overheads

Overheads are a large proportion of total costs. In most manufacturing companies they are between 25 and 50 per cent of total costs[24] and are usually increasing both in themselves and in terms of their relative size. Yet all too often the bulk of these are absorbed. A review of one manufacturing company revealed that some 80 per cent of total overheads were absorbed. As these costs accounted for over 40 per cent of the total, the implications were alarming. Overhead costs are predominantly absorbed because it involves less administrative work and system maintenance than alternatives. Many accountants abuse this principle still further, by using one overhead absorption rate for several parts of the business involved, and often absorbing on a single basis rather than the several necessary to reflect the business diversity and thus improve the relevance of the information provided. One company within a group of manufacturing companies had seven sites, with uses ranging from holding and distributing raw materials through spares, low-volume manufacturing and high-volume manufacturing to distribution of finished goods. Overheads for all seven sites were pooled and were then absorbed at one common rate for each site based on the single factor of direct labour hours. Faced with declining profits, the group executive turned to the basic performance evaluation of each site. The answers told them very little.[25] To decide how to redress the decline required financial information that was site specific and also reflected the products and their cost structure within each site.

To provide information that gives greater accuracy and insights, one key step is for accounting functions to adopt the policy of allocating overheads wherever possible.[26] As a general rule, a minimum target of allocating 80 per cent of total overheads should be the initial aim. The consequences would be that only a relatively small portion of total costs would then need to be spread on an absorption basis.

Information that provides more accurate insights is a prerequisite for making sound management decisions. This is particularly so regarding:

■ **Products** – decisions concerning pricing and the impact on margins, sales and growth potential are at the very core of commercial activity and will significantly influence the financial performance of a company.

■ **Opportunities for cost reduction** – when the sources and extent of costs are more clearly identified, the opportunity to reduce costs is improved. This opportunity is particularly enhanced by developments in activity-based costing addressed in the next section.

## Activity-based Costing

Activity-based costing (ABC) identifies costs on an activity rather than functional base. Many companies currently use the latter approach, which directly leads to the need to disperse these groups of cost using some allocation/absorption procedure. Identifying costs on the basis of activity eliminates the need for a two-stage procedure.

Thus in ABC, activities/transactions are the focus of the costing system, as it is they, not products, that cause costs to be incurred. While products consume direct materials and direct labour, activities consume overhead resources with products currently consuming activities. Thus, ABC is particularly concerned with understanding the cost of activities and their relationship to products and services. The approach taken is as follows:

■ Identify the major activities.
■ Determine the underlying factors that cause the activity to occur – known as *cost drivers*.
■ Create cost pools to collect activity costs that have the same cost driver. The major activities (see above) must therefore constitute a homogeneous set of tasks and costs such that cost variations in any pool can be explained by a single cause.
■ Attribute the costs of the activities gathered with each cost pool to the products/sources based on cost drivers (that is, how much of the activity has been used by the product/service in question).

In this way, ABC is a more sophisticated absorption/allocation system resulting in a more accurate identification of costs. There are two important but distinct uses of the information provided by ABC – product decisions and identifying opportunities to reduce costs.

*Product-Related Decisions*

Analysis of the cost structure of overhead activities enables a full review of products/services, customers, markets and profitability. It is used to support key decisions about

■ product pricing, and
■ growth, decline, renegotiation or exiting market segments, customers and/or products.

*Reducing or Reshaping Non-value Activities*

Once a company's key activities have been agreed, ABC identifies non-value-added activities. It determines whether types of activity are necessary in part or at all and whether each is efficiently provided. It thus ensures that the cost of non-value-added activities is visible and so enables management to review the size and shape of overhead costs as part of its operational decision-making process.

However, whereas companies investing in ABC always use the new information in product-related decisions, many do not use it to review non-value-added activity.[27] In fact, any organization that has not systematically reduced overhead costs as a direct result of ABC has failed to use this approach in the true sense of the word. Unfortunately, many businesses still fall into this category and thereby miss many of the real opportunities for overall improvement. The survey referred to earlier confirmed this. While 32 per cent of respondents had ABC in place, only 11 per cent were using cost drivers as performance measures.[28]

# Focused Manufacturing Helps to Identify Overhead Costs

The concern that the accounting functions have failed to develop systems that would improve key insights into product costs and non-value-added activities has been expressed earlier. The last two sections have addressed key perspectives and reviewed recent developments to meet these criticisms.

A significant reason why the accounting functions have been unable to provide adequate costing-system developments has been that the problem has become too complex to be handled by a single solution. However, unless companies find ways of driving out costs and arriving at sound product decisions, they will have problems in competing effectively in today's tough market conditions.

Adopting the manufacturing strategy principles of focus and plant-within-plant configurations (see Chapter 7) will also facilitate the provision of more accurate cost information. These approaches enable a company to identify more easily the overheads associated with each part of manufacturing and to assess the contribution provided by each part to the whole business. This change brings with it a shift from the principle of accounting for overheads on a functional basis to that of direct overhead allocation. Thus, instead of summarizing the costs involved in providing a support function as a total for that function, it accounts for those overheads that are dedicated to or are directly associated with a part of manufacturing. Not only does this now enable a company to assess more clearly the contribution of its different parts, but in times of change it will enable a company to take out or increase the vertical slice of overheads associated with that part of the process under review. It thereby allows change to take place in a more orderly and sensible way. It aligns accounting decisions with manufacturing strategy needs and avoids accentuating the already wide gap between the support needs of manufacturing activities and the perceived role of support functions. When overhead costs are clearly identified with a particular sector of manufacturing, the level and nature of support can be agreed to meet the current needs of that sector and to accommodate changes in the future.

A further refinement to these changes involves making any functional overhead into a business unit. This moves a business away from the position where an accountant or accounting procedure arbitrarily spreads the unallocated overhead to make the books balance to a position where each part of the business declares a budget for the amount it intends to purchase from each overhead function. The gains are obvious. Beware, however, of two possible developments:

■ The counter-argument put forward by accountants that these changes are difficult to accomplish and lack a high degree of accuracy. These changes will, in fact, enhance the relevance and accuracy of this information in the light of business needs.

■ Attaining accuracy as an end in itself. The corporate gain is providing information to help prioritize product decisions and cost-reduction activities.

## Create Business-related Financial Information

The key role of business-related financial information has been highlighted in the sections concerning cost-system developments. As an essential input into developing both a marketing and manufacturing strategy, accounting information is rarely designed specifically to provide analyses that would form an integral part of the formulation of either functions' strategic statement. Examples of key marketing information in addition to those specifically mentioned earlier include:

■ *customer sales and profitability* – an assessment both of the sales and total costs associated with selling to, and support for, major customers enables a company to establish the true worth of these relationships, and

■ *market share and profitability* – identifying the value of sales in each market, its relative size, associated costs to promote and support relevant activities and the level of profitability for each market segment are essential inputs into formulating a marketing plan.

For the manufacturing side of the business, information that is rarely provided by existing accounting systems but that would offer invaluable insights in the strategy formulation includes:

■ cost estimates of manufacturing at varying levels of throughput

■ capacity analyses identifying any bottleneck or limiting factor in the manufacture of each product (known as *analysis of contribution by limiting factor*). This enables companies to assess proposals to increase capacity and to decide how best to allocate existing capacity in the meantime (see Chapter 4), and

■ cost estimates for supplying items outside the normal product range.

Finally, the need to separate out those costs incurred by manufacturing but not induced by manufacturing decisions is seldom reflected in the control statements provided by the accounting system. Excess manufacturing costs incurred as a result of a change in schedule to meet a sales or customer request, for instance, are usually not shown under their own separate headings (for example, manufacturing excess cost due to customer schedule change).

## Provide Performance-related Financial Information

The final area of development concerns the provision of accurate performance-related information. As the measurement of actual performance needs to be set against targets that reflect reality, so levels of performance within a business will differ from one part to another. Not all products can be expected to achieve the same performance standards during each and every year of their lives. Therefore, why should products in different stages of their life cycles be forced to meet the same minimum standard each year? For this to be appropriate would require an unbalanced portfolio made up solely of products all in the same stage of their life cycles.

Once performance expectations have been resolved, the next issue concerns the level of expected activity. Budgets, by definition, are out of date by the time they are completed. It is necessary, therefore, to review the budget figure by using the latest information. In this way, the basis for establishing and assessing levels of performance is changed from a budget to a latest-estimate basis. One clear example of this is the use of flexible budgeting, which changes the cost base in line with actual volumes and alters the basis for related cost information (for example, overhead absorption either by traditional or ABC systems).

The last illustration concerns the distortions businesses experience as a result of the way in which they calculate inventory values. In many situations, inventory desensitizes cost information by becoming a cost buffer. Most accounting systems assume that costs are held in the value of work-in-progress inventory as calculated in the system. Often, accumulated cost excesses are discovered when the inventory is physically counted at the end-of-period stocktaking and then recorded as an inventory or stocktaking loss. Since many firms physically count inventory only twice a year, control or responsibility is not easy to establish.

# Conclusion

The growing criticism of existing accounting systems and investment appraisal procedures is more than justified. The accounting profession in the United States and many other Western countries has come to be responsible for providing financial information. Unfortunately, accounts have generally been reactive in responding to the changing needs of business and have spent too much of their time keeping records rather than providing information for, and partaking in, the control and development of the business. The description of bean-counter sits well.

Two general misconceptions have contributed to this:

- management concerns developing not just maintaining existing procedures, and

- like other functions, accountancy has failed to recognize that its role is subservient to that of the business. Its prime task is to respond to and meet the needs of a business. The *raison d'être* of a function exists through the business. Functions do not exist in their own right. Evaluating a function's contribution, therefore, needs to be set within this frame.

The potential contribution of accounting and finance functions is significant. The key insights and overall executive role it can bring to a business are considerable. However, to realize this level of effectiveness, companies must recognize changes in need and respond to them in an appropriate manner. This chapter has posed several issues that companies must address. Of these, three dimensions need to be at the forefront of accounting provision.

## Markets are Changing

The traditional perspective of productivity and evaluation of investment decisions needs to be modified in line with the needs of the business, reflecting how these needs are secured. The principle that should drive today's businesses is based on keeping existing customers and winning new ones, not lowering labour costs. Cutting lead times, boosting quality conformance levels, improving delivery reliability, reducing inventories and supporting product range are factors that top the list in these endeavours. Accounting systems and financial reviews need to reflect this.

# Businesses are Characterized by Difference, not Similarity

Difference not similarity characterizes today's businesses. Rules and procedures need to reflect and embrace this. Levels of control, therefore, should be established to ensure that the more difficult and complex a proposal, the less formal and bureaucratic the approach. Investment proposals for relatively small sums are well served by laid-out procedures and predetermined hurdles. Major investments on the other hand, are ill served by such approaches. Yet usually one set of rules applies, as characterized by the bureaucratic belief that the essence of control has its root in well-defined procedures.

Major investments need approaches that are the very opposite of current developments and executive behaviour. The maxim should be that the larger the investment, the more informal the approach and the lack of definition within the procedures used. Thus, major investments should be led by strategy and subject to open debate, ideally involving non-executive contributions to enhance neutrality. Putting forward functional proposals in line with agreed and structured procedures discourages strategic debate, stifles discussion and encourages rationalization – the very opposite of what is required to handle these complex and fundamental strategic decisions.

# Linking Process Investment Decisions and the Evaluation of Control Systems

In many companies, the link between process investment decisions and the need to provide supporting control systems is not appreciated. Decisions about processes are not only tangible, but they are also taken at a different phase in the decision sequence (see Exhibit 11.8). On the other hand, the sizeable investments associated with manufacturing process decisions of working capital and infrastructure are often obscured for exactly the opposite reasons – they are less tangible and occur in the operating phase of the installation.

Furthermore, when a process investment is installed on the shopfloor, a distinct accounting change takes place. At the preoperational stage highlighted in Exhibit 11.8, a process is singularly evaluated in great detail as part of the investment appraisal system and is cash-flow oriented. However once installed, this same process will no longer be treated as an individual item in accounting control terms. Instead it will be controlled by a number of broadbrush accounting systems based on profit. It will become just part of a functionally based set of assets and costs comprising a range of investments that differ in usage, degree of dedication to the manufacture of specific products and age and support-system requirements. The change in accounting treatment highlights the contrasts involved and the necessary high level of control in the preoperational phase compared with the lack of sensitivity in the global controls once the asset is being used.

**Exhibit 11.8** The three phases in an investment programme

| Phase | Timescale | Features of the investment | Tangible nature | Features of evaluation and control |
|---|---|---|---|---|
| 1. | Preoperation | Fixed assets in the form of plant, equipment and associated installation costs | High | Constitutes taking one investment in isolation. Traditional investment appraisal techniques used, which are *cash-flow* oriented. |
| 2. | Operating | Supporting working capital in the form of inventory | | The investment now becomes an integral part of the business summary. It reverts to revenue accounts that measure *profit* to investment as the basis of control or assessment. |
| 3. | Operating | The service and support overheads necessary to provide an appropriate level of infrastructure | Low | Control of individual investments now relatively loose – rarely have post-audits. |

## Ways Forward

What then are the ways forward? They involve changes at two levels in the organization. At the top, many executives have perceived their role in accounting and finance in a different form. Often they become involved in, or even spearhead, activities designed to generate earnings by financial transactions. This has the major drawback of diverting management effort and interest away from the business core. They become more distant from the prime profit-generating activities of a manufacturing business. They start to control from a distance. Without the understanding of each firm's strategies, they feel unable to contribute to the essential developments that must be made in the tough competitive climate that characterizes the manufacturing sector. They feel exposed and become less able to evaluate the necessary long-term alternatives. As a consequence, they increasingly exert pressure by short-term measures and assessments. Lower down the organization, plant executives being measured by the short-term success of the business often respond by adopting similar opportunistic patterns of behaviour such as reducing expenditure or withholding investments to increase profits and improve cash flow in the short term. Similarly, groups of companies often monitor investments centrally and against a common set of criteria. However, they leave the postinstallation assessment to be taken at the plant level. Seen as part of their role, the group executives' action reinforces the predominant role of financial measures when assessing investments and weakens the key responsibility link between the investment decision and its future evaluation. The need to decentralize these responsibilities could not be more strongly argued.

The way forward is through the emergence of strategy-based decisions and controls. Accounting and manufacturing need to determine together the investment criteria and day-to-day accounting control provision that should be adopted. Not only will this orient manufacturing towards its key tasks, it will also provide information that is both relevant and current. This growing awareness of the need for strategic management accounting must be accelerated if companies are to make sound manufacturing and other strategy decisions.[29] It is most necessary, therefore, that firms stem the apparent drift away from their manufacturing focus.

Perhaps a final lesson for Western European companies is that 'in Japan, perpetuation of the enterprise, not profit, is the driving force'. As Toshiba's Okano puts it: 'the company is forever'.[30] Although in no way implying that this should be adopted as the corporate value system. it highlights one essential difference. Strategy is the driving force; survival and success will only be achieved through a strategic orientation and this must become the pattern by which companies both give direction and assess current and future performance.

## Notes

1. R. C. Dean, Jnr, 'The Temporal Mismatch – Innovation's Pace versus Management's Time Horizon', *Research Management*, May 1974, pp. 12–15.
2. R. H. Hayes and J. Abernathy, 'Managing Our Way to Economic Decline', *Harvard Business Review*, July–August 1980, pp. 66–77.
3. R. H. Hayes and D. A. Garvin, 'Managing as if Tomorrow Mattered', *Harvard Business Review*, May–June 1982, pp. 71–9.
4. H. T. Johnson and R. S. Kaplan, *Relevance Lost: The Rise and Fall of Management Accounting*, Boston: Harvard Business School Press, 1987, includes important insights into accounting systems, for example, Chapter 8, 'The 1980s: The Obsolescence of Management Account Systems'.
5. R. Cooper and R. S. Kaplan, 'How Cost Accounting Distorts Product Costs', *Management Accounting*, April 1985, pp. 20–7.
6. R. Cooper and R. S. Kaplan 'Measure Costs Right: Make the Right Decisions', *Harvard Business Review*, September–October 1988, pp. 96–103.
7. K. Simmonds, 'Strategic Management Accounting', in R. Crowe (ed.), *Handbook of Management Accounting*, 2nd edn, Aldershot: Gower, 1988, pp. 25–48.
8. G. Foster, 'Drucker on the Record', *Management Today*, September 1987, pp. 58–9 and 110.
9. S. Parkinson, T. J. Hill and G. Walker, 'Diagnosing Customer and Competitor Influences on Manufacturing Strategy', in F. Bradley (ed.), *Marketing Thought around the World*, Proceedings of the 20th Annual Conference of the European Marketing Academy, Dublin, May 1991, pp. 741–55.
10. R. Davies, C. Downes and R. Sweeting, *UK Survey of Cost Management Techniques and Practices, 1990/91*, Price Waterhouse, London, 1991, p. 11.
11. K. Ohmae, 'Japan: From Stereotypes to Specifics', *The McKinsey Quarterly*, Spring 1982, pp. 2–33.
12. Ibid., p. 3.
13. J. Carlin, 'Guru of Downsizing Admits He Got It Wrong', *Independent on Sunday*, 12 May 1996, p. 1.

14. Davies *et al.*, *UK Survey*, p. 11, confirmed this point. Although 96 per cent of respondents were required to demonstrate quantifiable future benefits, only 55 per cent regarded intangible benefits as playing an important role in the justification process.

15. T. J. Hill and D. J. Woodcock, 'Dimensions of Control', *Production Management and Control*, 1982, **10**(2): 16–20.

16. K. J. Blois, 'The Manufacturing/Marketing Orientation and Its Information Needs', *European Journal of Marketing*, **14**(19): 354–64.

17. For example, refer to W. L. Ferrara, 'More Questions than Answers: Is the Management Accounting System as Hopeless as the Critics Say?', *Management Accounting*, October 1990, pp. 48–52.

18. Ibid., p. 48.

19. Davies *et al.*, *UK Survey*, p. 16.

20. R. S. Kaplan, 'Yesterday's Accounting Undermines Production', *Harvard Business Review*, July–August 1984, pp. 95–102.

21. Boston Consulting Group Perspective no. 219, *Specialization or the Full Product Line*, Boston, MA, 1979.

22. Ferrara, 'More Questions than Answers', 1990, p. 52.

23. Davies *et al.*, *UK Survey*, p. 11, reported that budget versus actual was employed by 98 per cent of respondents as a performance measure. However, only 35 per cent utilized flexible budgeting procedures.

24. A fact confirmed in the 1991 *UK survey*, which reported that for 51 per cent of all respondents, overheads represented 26 per cent or more of total costs. See Davies *et al.*

25. Kaplan, 'Yesterday's Accounting', 1984, p. 96, provides another example of what, all too often, is a common situation.

26. Overhead allocation involves the allocation, apportionment or allotment of overhead costs to the appropriate cost centre or cost unit. Overhead absorption is achieved by dividing the costs involved on a suitable basis (for example, standard labour hours, direct clocked hours, direct labour costs, material costs or floor space) and then spreading them on a *pro rata* basis in line with the common factor that has been chosen.

27. The Davies *et al.*, *UK survey*, pp. 12–13, revealed that whereas 90 per cent of respondents used costs as an important factor in establishing prices, only 30 per cent 'attempted to allocate indirect/non-manufacturing costs to products on a cause and effect basis'.

28. Ibid., p. 15.

29. Simmonds, 'Strategic Management Accounting', 1988.

30. Ohmae, 'Japan: From Stereotypes to Specifics', 1982, p. 7.

# Aztec Holdings, Inc.

'Our review of actual sales during the last nine months indicates no improvement compared with our results over the past several years', concluded Roger Whinston, the general manager of Aztec Holdings.

Although we are meeting our profit objectives, we are not meeting our forecast uplift in sales and actually appear to be losing market share. To achieve sales growth in our markets, we recognize the need to achieve a major reduction in our delivery lead times. This will help differentiate our products from those of our competitors.

However, our lack of sales growth is very surprising considering the recent investments we have made to install just-in-time (JIT) manufacturing methods in the plant. It is clear that JIT has provided a major reduction in process lead times and work-in-progress inventory and that this should have helped us improve our customer service in terms of delivery speed and delivery reliability. However, we have needed to work substantial overtime hours in order to improve our delivery lead times in a period when the utilization of our factory is only running at 70–80 per cent.

## Background

Aztec Holdings manufactures industrial batteries for a wide range of applications. The company is a wholly owned subsidiary of Pittston Industries, a US-based conglomerate with diverse businesses in the health care, computer, automation and transportation industries. Both the company headquarters and the manufacturing facilities are located in Cleveland, Ohio, and serve the US, Canadian and Mexican markets.

## Marketing

'The last two decades have seen a noticeable increase in the number of applications for which motive power batteries have been used. We anticipate that the growing

This case study was written by Professors W. L. Berry (The Ohio State University) and T. J. Hill (University of Oxford). It is intended for class discussion and not as an illustration of good or bad management. © Professor W. L. Berry or AMD Publishing (UK). Enquiries in the USA to Zip Publishing, 1634 N. High Street, Columbus, Ohio 43201. Enquiries in the UK to AMD Publishing, 43 Basely Way, Longford, Coventry CV6 6QA.

concern for the environment will see this trend continue', explained Roger Whinston. 'Currently, we recognize a number of segments which reflect a wide range of applications. Our statistics indicate that the world market for industrial batteries breaks down into Europe (44 per cent), North America (32 per cent), Japan (11 per cent), and the rest (13 per cent).'

Batteries for industrial applications contain a number of cells. While the sales of industrial batteries are normally referred to in terms of batteries, manufacturing quantities are expressed in terms of cells. Industrial batteries for all applications except access platforms require about the same average number of cells per battery. Access platform applications have a larger number of cells per battery.

The North American market served by Aztec can be segmented in terms of original equipment manufacturers (OEM) and replacement sales, and by the type of battery application. Aztec sells both OE and replacement batteries in the following major areas of application: materials handling equipment, wheelchairs, industrial cleaning equipment, golf carts and access platforms. A breakdown of Aztec's sales in terms of these market segments is shown in Exhibit 1.

Aztec's sale of industrial batteries in these market segments varies substantially over the course of the year. Exhibit 2 presents monthly sales data during the past year expressed in terms of cells. It shows both the sales made directly from the plant and the sales made from the firm's field warehouses.

## Materials Handling Equipment

The sale of industrial batteries for materials handling equipment represents the largest segment for Aztec in terms of sales revenue dollars (60 per cent) and total cells (65 per cent). The split between OEM and replacement sales in terms of revenue (dollars) and cells is given in Exhibit 1.

The OEM market segment includes manufacturers of materials handling equipment. Some of these companies specialize in particular materials handling applications, such as vehicles designed for use in warehouses with narrow aisles. Other manufacturers offer materials handling equipment for vehicle applications such as in manufacturing plants, the logging industry and cargo handling. As is the case for all the market segments served by Aztec, the company offers batteries of both standard and customized design to equipment manufacturers.

As a consequence of the major inroads into the North American market made by Japanese materials handling equipment manufacturers, the battery price in the OEM market is much more sensitive than in the relevant replacement market. The order size for OEM customers is relatively large, and a failure on delivery reliability can result in a loss of business. These customers place schedules that specify, for 90 per cent of their requirements, delivery within 14 days with the remaining 10 per cent for delivery in 15 days or more.

The replacement market includes industrial and government customers who have purchased equipment and have experienced a battery failure. When a lift truck goes down the customer needs close support in order to return the vehicle to service. This

**Exhibit 1**  Sales analysis

| Market segment | Percentage total sales | Percentage sales (cells) | Percentage sales by type within segment (cells) | Percentage sales by type within segment (sales $) |
|---|---|---|---|---|
| Materials handling | 60 | 65 | | |
| OEM | | | 38 | 27 |
| Replacement | | | 62 | 73 |
| Wheelchairs | 12 | 7 | | |
| OEM | | | 71 | 70 |
| Replacement | | | 29 | 30 |
| Cleaning equipment | 9 | 5 | | |
| OEM | | | 57 | 42 |
| Replacement | | | 43 | 58 |
| Golf carts | 11 | 12 | | |
| OEM | | | 24 | 18 |
| Replacement | | | 76 | 82 |
| Access platforms | 8 | 11 | | |
| OEM | | | 26 | 22 |
| Replacement | | | 74 | 78 |
| **Total** | **100** | **100** | | |

**Exhibit 2**  Sales seasonality

| Month | Plant sales (units)[1] | Ratio to monthly sales average | Field warehouse sales (units) | Ratio to monthly sales average |
|---|---|---|---|---|
| January | 12 605 | 0.75 | 15 177 | 1.09 |
| February | 12 996 | 0.78 | 18 057 | 1.30 |
| March | 19 135 | 1.14 | 17 516 | 1.26 |
| April | 18 993 | 1.14 | 12 782 | 0.92 |
| May | 18 930 | 1.13 | 13 163 | 0.95 |
| June | 19 807 | 1.18 | 15 613 | 1.12 |
| July | 19 735 | 1.18 | 13 233 | 0.95 |
| August | 14 271 | 0.85 | 9 530 | 0.69 |
| September | 16 952 | 1.01 | 14 650 | 1.06 |
| October | 19 436 | 1.16 | 11 825 | 0.85 |
| November | 15 268 | 0.91 | 11 696 | 0.84 |
| December | 12 818 | 0.77 | 13 311 | 0.96 |
| **Monthly average** | **16 745** | | **13 879** | |

*Note*
1. Plant sales are exclusive of field warehouse sales.

requires fast delivery of the replacement battery. In fact, 60 per cent need battery replacements in seven days or less. Another 30 per cent require delivery in up to two weeks, and the remainder within 30 days.

## Wheelchairs

The sale of industrial batteries for wheelchairs is a relatively small portion of Aztec's sales in terms of sales revenue dollars (12 per cent) and total cells (7 per cent). Within this segment, OEM sales represent 70 per cent of the sales dollars and 71 per cent of the cells. Likewise, the sales of replacement units within this segment represent 30 per cent of the sales dollars and 29 per cent of the cells. The split between OEM and replacement sales in terms of revenue dollars and cells is given in Exhibit 1.

The OEM market segment includes nine US companies that manufacture wheel-chairs of standard design. Although these chairs are sold with a wide variety of customer-selected options and features, the batteries are relatively standard in design and their features vary only with the size of the wheelchair. In addition, there are numerous small companies which sell wheelchairs that are custom-built to the patient's specifications on a local basis. Recently, several Swiss and German companies have entered the North American market.

In this market segment the superior battery design gives the company an edge over its competitors, and price is not normally a major factor in winning these orders. However, delivery reliability is critical, and a failure to deliver on schedule can result in a loss of business. Seventy per cent of the orders for OEM units are placed specifying delivery within 14 days of the placement date. The remaining 30 per cent is for delivery in 15 days or more.

The customers in the replacement market segment include a wide variety of medical equipment distributors, hospitals, pharmacies and health care units that sell wheelchairs to patients. These firms provide a number of services to their customers, including both the sale and rental of wheelchairs, a medicare and insur-ance filing service, the repair and servicing of the unit and a variety of other related equipment and accessories.

Since the unit cost of a battery is significant, they are not typically stocked by replacement market customers. Therefore, it is important to provide a quick response when a battery failure occurs. Orders for replacement batteries are invari-ably required within seven days. Waiting more than seven days would not be accepted by customers who would go elsewhere.

## Industrial Cleaning Equipment

The sale of batteries for industrial cleaning equipment is also a small part of Aztec's sales in terms of sales revenue dollars (9 per cent) and total cells (5 per cent). Within this segment, OEM sales represents 42 per cent of the sales dollars and 57 per cent of the cells with the balance made up by replacement units (see Exhibit 1).

The OEM market segment includes manufacturers of industrial cleaning equipment. These companies typically manufacture units for a broad range of industrial, government and service sector applications. While their product includes a range of standard models, the customer has a wide range of optional features and accessories to select from in buying a unit for a particular application. One of these options is the engine type, which may use gasoline, LP gas or electricity as the fuel source.

As a consequence of heavy overseas competition in the North American market, price and delivery speed are major factors in the purchase of this type of equipment. Many of the industrial cleaning equipment manufacturers have been looking to their suppliers for JIT support in the manufacturing process. As a result, 70 per cent of the units are required within 7 days of the schedule placement date and the remainder within 14 days. Furthermore, a failure on delivery reliability can result in a loss of business.

The replacement market includes manufacturing companies, municipal units and private cleaning services contractors. A failure of the battery is costly to these companies because of the resulting equipment downtime and the need to maintain the cleaning schedules of their customers. Therefore, there is an overriding need for quick delivery support with seven days as the maximum delivery lead time from placement of an order.

## Golf Carts

The sale of batteries for golf carts is a relatively small portion of Aztec's sales in terms of revenue dollars (11 per cent) and total cells (12 per cent). Within this segment, OEM sales represent 18 per cent of the sales dollars and 24 per cent of the cells, with replacement units making up the balance (see Exhibit 1).

The OEM market includes several major companies that specialize in the manufacture of golf carts and a number of local companies that represent a very small share of this market. Although golf carts can be purchased with a variety of options and special features, the batteries are of a standard design with relatively few battery models. While some of the carts use a gasoline engine, about 75 per cent of the market requires an electric drive and this percentage is increasing.

The entry of overseas competition from both Asia and Eastern Europe in the golf cart market has resulted in a high level of price sensitivity for these batteries. The customer-order sizes are relatively large and are affected by the seasonal nature of this business. The golf cart manufacturers expect short delivery cycles: 70 per cent of the units are scheduled to be delivered within 14 days of the call-off date, with the remainder in up to one month.

The customers in the replacement market include distributors selling equipment for golf and other sports, golf courses and private individuals. Since these customers do not stock replacement batteries, relatively short delivery times are required, particularly in the summer. From the date of order placement, 60 per cent of the units sold require delivery within 7 days, 30 per cent are looking for up to 14 days and the remainder require delivery within one month.

## Access Platforms

The sale of batteries for access platforms accounts for 8 per cent of sales revenue dollars and 11 per cent of total cells. The OEM and replacement split is given in Exhibit 1.

The OEM market includes four major manufacturers that specialize in the design and manufacture of access platforms. Because of the governmental requirement for the certification of this product to industrial safety standards, these manufacturers tend to provide a small number of standard models, that can be fitted with a number of different optional accessories. However, a relatively large range of battery sizes and capabilities are required because of important differences in size and weight in access platform applications. Although one of the major access platform manufacturers in the world is located in Europe, overseas competition in US markets has been limited. One explanation for this has to do with the requirement for governmental certification of new products.

The sale of batteries to manufacturers of access platform equipment involves working with a customer's engineering design group as well as its purchasing department. The battery design for these units is relatively straightforward and price is often an important factor in getting the order. Because batteries for this type of equipment are very expensive, customers schedule their requirements with very short lead times. From the date of the order placement, 70 per cent of customer sales are scheduled for delivery within 7 days, and the remainder for delivery within 14 days. A failure to meet the required delivery date can result in the loss of this business.

There are a wide variety of customers in the replacement market, including companies such as commercial construction contractors, electric power companies, manufacturing plants and municipal government units. Price is not normally an important factor in the replacement market. However, because of equipment downtime caused by battery failure and the resulting problems in meeting customer schedules, the length of the delivery lead time is an important issue in this segment. Seventy per cent of customer sales are looking for delivery within 7 days, and the remainder for delivery within 14 days. Delivery on time performance against promised dates is an important but not a critical factor in this segment.

Sample customer orders that are representative of these market segments are shown in Exhibits 3 and 4. These data reflect the customer-order sizes and Aztec's delivery performance in each of the segments.

## Manufacturing

Industrial batteries are manufactured using relatively few components. A battery consists of one or more cells that are assembled into an outer container. Each cell includes a lid, a container, a number of positive and negative grid plates, a variety of electrical connectors and fittings, and fluid. The industrial battery product line at Aztec includes approximately 500 items that are mostly manufactured on a make-to-stock basis.

**Exhibit 3**    Customer-order sample

| Market segment | Customer | Product | Actual order quantity[1] | Date order placed[2] | Order reference number |
|---|---|---|---|---|---|
| Materials handling | | | | | |
| OEM | Austin | XX143 | 18 | 26/2 | 121 |
| OEM | Standard | DQ156 | 36 | 12/5 | 803 |
| OEM | Logan | CD103 | 24 | 37/4 | 568 |
| OEM | Austin | WP222 | 24 | 02/1 | 234 |
| Replacement | National | DQ102 | 12 | 13/3 | 141 |
| Replacement | Hornes | WQ431 | 50 | 21/1 | 956 |
| Replacement | Bexler | XX120 | 10 | 42/5 | 501 |
| Replacement | Scotio | WE563 | 12 | 24/2 | 172 |
| Wheelchair | | | | | |
| OEM | McKiney | QQ300 | 20 | 11/3 | 630 |
| OEM | Jones | EW345 | 5 | 24/1 | 931 |
| OEM | Wexler | WE213 | 10 | 36/2 | 719 |
| Replacement | Amer-Hos. | ER908 | 24 | 39/1 | 677 |
| Replacement | St Mary | QQ203 | 6 | 33/4 | 498 |
| Replacement | Ford | CC781 | 80 | 41/4 | 222 |
| Cleaning | | | | | |
| Replacement | Ace | AW213 | 6 | 48/4 | 403 |
| Replacement | Downtown | AW233 | 2 | 31/5 | 772 |
| Golf cart | | | | | |
| OEM | Player | WT112 | 12 | 43/2 | 861 |
| OEM | Nicholas | WW455 | 96 | 09/1 | 384 |
| Access platform | | | | | |
| OEM | Modern | TR563 | 24 | 36/4 | 555 |
| OEM | Downeys | TR234 | 45 | 05/3 | 916 |
| OEM | Speedy | RW231 | 46 | 45/1 | 119 |

*Notes*
1. These orders are prepresentative of those received by the company. The company works on a five-day-per-week basis.
2. xx/y = week number/day.

## Manufacturing Process

The battery cases, cell lids, containers, electrical hardware and fittings are purchased from suppliers. However, the positive and negative grids are manufactured by Aztec, which involves the processing of lead. The manufacturing process used consists of four main steps, as shown in Exhibit 5.

**Exhibit 4**     Customer-order delivery promise data

| Order reference number | Promised delivery date | Actual delivery date |
|---|---|---|
| 121 | 34/3 | 37/4 |
| 803 | 17/2 | 17/1 |
| 568 | 44/4 | 43/1 |
| 234 | 03/4 | 04/5 |
| 141 | 14/5 | 14/2 |
| 956 | 23/1 | 22/5 |
| 501 | 49/1 | 50/3 |
| 172 | 29/1 | 25/1 |
| 630 | 13/4 | 13/1 |
| 931 | 26/5 | 27/4 |
| 719 | 39/1 | 39/5 |
| 677 | 40/3 | 40/4 |
| 498 | 39/1 | 37/4 |
| 222 | 42/4 | 42/2 |
| 403 | 50/2 | 50/2 |
| 772 | 31/5 | 32/3 |
| 861 | 47/4 | 48/3 |
| 384 | 12/1 | 12/1 |
| 555 | 37/4 | 37/3 |
| 916 | 05/3 | 06/2 |
| 119 | 45/1 | 45/5 |

*Notes*
**1.** These orders are prepresentative of those promised by the company. The company
works on a five-day-per-week basis.
**2.** xx/y = week number/day.

The first step involves grid manufacturing. The negative and positive grids are produced to stock using grid casting machines located in separate manufacturing departments. Next, a coating is pasted on the surface of the grids in different manufacturing departments for the positive and negative grids and they are stocked in finished form. Subsequently, pickling and humid-setting operations are performed on the grids. They are then dried in a baking operation and placed into inventory.

The second and third steps in the manufacturing process are plate processing and cell assembly. These are organized into high- and low-volume production units. The high-volume units produce approximately 100 cell types, and the low-volume units manufacture about 400 different cells. Plate processing involves the production of a subassembly of positive and negative grids to meet the specifications for a particular battery cell. After plate processing, both the completed plates and a wide variety of purchased parts are stocked prior to the cell assembly operation.

**Exhibit 5**   Battery manufacturing process

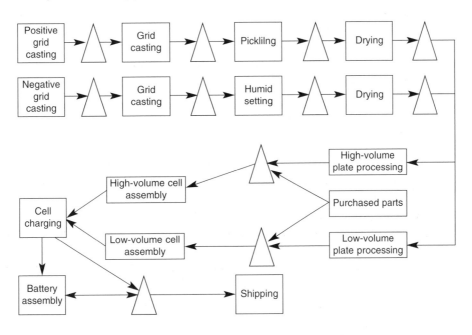

In cell assembly, the plate subassemblies, electrical connectors and fittings are assembled, placed in a plastic container and the lid is sealed. Afterwards, the cells are charged and transferred to either finished-goods inventory or the battery assembly operation.

The final step in the manufacturing process is battery assembly. Only 25 per cent of Aztec's sales require this step. Normally, the cells are shipped to the firm's field warehouses or to customer locations where they are assembled into a battery case.

## Just-in-time Manufacturing

During the past two years, Aztec has made a major investment in introducing JIT methods into the manufacturing process. Investment in new equipment and a new process layout has enabled major improvements in processing methods to be made, including substantial reductions in change-over times, and important reductions in work-in-progress inventory and process lead times.

Three parts of the process are now operated on a JIT basis: grid manufacturing, high-volume plate processing and high-volume cell assembly. As a result, the high-volume cell assembly unit is able to produce cells in small lots, and components such as plates and grids are produced as required using Kanban methods. Furthermore, the vendors for high-volume connectors and fittings, containers and lids supply Aztec on a JIT basis with daily deliveries.

Due to the wide range of products and components required, the low-volume products are still produced on a make-to-order basis. This means that production is scheduled on a batch basis in the low-volume cell assembly unit and the low-volume plate assembly unit. Since there is a relatively small range of positive and negative grids in grid casting, both the low-volume and high-volume grids are manufactured on a just-in-time basis.

## Manufacturing Lead Times

The production lead time for both the high- and low-volume cell assembly units is one day for cell assembly and 3–4 days for cell charging. However, one week is normally allowed in scheduling each of these operations. Also, one week is normally allowed for plate processing and one week for the combined operations of grid casting, pasting, pickling/humid setting, and drying. Those orders involving the assembly of cells into a battery case require a further manufacturing lead time of three days.

All purchased parts, except the plastic cell containers, are stocked by Aztec. Because of the cost and variety of height dimensions of containers, bulk orders for these items are placed on suppliers with high-volume containers supplied on a JIT basis by the suppliers. This means that daily deliveries are made by suppliers against a schedule delivery issued one week in advance.

Low-volume containers are scheduled on a make-to-order basis and require between three and eight weeks of material (purchasing) lead time. Since the containers involve relatively few width and depth (base) dimensions and material specifications, a standard-sized container is, on occasions, cut to the required height by Aztec at an extra cost in order to fill a low-volume order requiring immediate shipment.

Tight control is maintained over the inventory of the lead used by Aztec in the manufacture of grids and plates. Since lead represents 45 per cent of the manufacturing cost of a battery, both the supplier delivery times and the inventory of lead is carefully monitored by the company.

## Manufacturing Planning and Control

Aztec's manufacturing planning and control system can be characterized by the inputs and outputs shown in Exhibit 6. Sales orders are received both at the field warehouses and at the company headquarters in Cleveland. The sales administration staff enter the sales orders, indicating the required customer delivery date, using the satellite terminals of the computer-based sales order processing system. If inventory is available, sales administration allocate product to the sales order and goods are picked, dispatched and invoiced to the customer. If inventory is not available, the following guidelines are observed in making customer delivery promises:

**Exhibit 6**    Aztec's manufacturing planning and control system

| Inputs | Planning system | Outputs |
|--------|-----------------|---------|

Inputs

Sales history/forecasts $\longrightarrow$

Sales orders $\longrightarrow$

Stock replenishment orders $\longrightarrow$

Customer required dates $\longrightarrow$

Stock balance information $\longrightarrow$

Existing production orders $\longrightarrow$

Existing production plans $\longrightarrow$

Outputs

$\longrightarrow$ Production orders

$\longrightarrow$ Purchase orders

$\longrightarrow$ Production plans: assembly

$\longrightarrow$ Production plans: components

$\longrightarrow$ Management information

1. ex-stock deliveries can be quoted for 3–5 days delivery, depending mainly on the transport lead time;
2. products that are currently in the charging area can be quoted for a 10-day delivery, depending on their status in charging;
3. products for which components are available can be quoted for delivery in approximately two weeks;
4. products that require the ordering of components would require two weeks plus the material (purchasing) lead time involved.

Each warehouse carries an agreed level of finished-goods inventory, that reflects the local sales history patterns and trends. The field warehouse stock is replenished from the central warehouse at the Cleveland plant, which holds inventory in accordance with the company's overall sales history patterns. Daily computer reports advise the head office sales administration when the field warehouse stocks require replenishment and they issue stock replenishment orders to transfer inventory from Cleveland.

Each week sales administration review the past four months' sales history and the average monthly sales for the last 12 months in order to facilitate material procurement. These data are shown in Exhibit 7 for a number of representative products. Computer-generated reports indicating outstanding sales and stock replenishment orders (Exhibit 8), stock balances (Exhibit 7) and production orders for end products (their master production schedule is shown in Exhibit 9) are used in this procedure.

On a weekly basis, sales administration meet with the assembly manager and the production planning and control manager to finalize the master production schedule for the week after next. The portion of the master production schedule (MPS) covering the next six weeks for the representative products is shown in Exhibit 9. Minor revisions to next week's MPS are also made, taking into account any new and urgent sales orders. To accommodate these short-notice changes, component stocks include a 'buffer stock' level.

**Exhibit 7**  Sales history data

| Product reference number | Previous four months' sales | | | | Average monthly sales for last 12 months | Current finished-goods inventory[1] |
|---|---|---|---|---|---|---|
| | November | December | January | February | | |
| MTW55 | 198 | 0 | 29 | 2 | 230 | 71 |
| MTS24 | 362 | 304 | 382 | 552 | 625 | 49 |
| MTQ50 | 1290 | 1222 | 1561 | 1733 | 1235 | 5 |
| MTQ14 | 219 | 185 | 241 | 631 | 303 | 11 |
| MTX21 | 139 | 356 | 239 | 438 | 317 | 32 |
| MTV10 | 36 | 372 | 50 | 90 | 184 | 24 |
| MTV42 | 76 | 0 | 24 | 26 | 22 | 0 |

*Note*

1. The current finished-goods inventory is that which is on hand at the beginning of the first shift on Monday morning of week 26 after production and shipments in week 25 have been accounted for: see Exhibits 8 and 9.

**Exhibit 8**  Customer-order backlog

| Product reference number | Known delivery requirements | | | | | |
|---|---|---|---|---|---|---|
| | Week 26 | Week 27 | Week 28 | Week 29 | Week 30 | Week 31 |
| MTW55 | | | | | | |
| MTS24 | 509 | | | | | |
| MTQ50 | 742 | 250 | 482 | | | |
| MTQ14 | 192 | | | | | |
| MTX21 | | | | | | 1728 |
| MTV10 | | 50 | | 108 | | |
| MTV42 | | | | | | |

**Exhibit 9**  Master production schedule: cell assembly

| Product reference number | Master production schedule for | | | | | |
|---|---|---|---|---|---|---|
| | Week 26 | Week 27 | Week 28 | Week 29 | Week 30 | Week 31 |
| MTW55 | 50 | 50 | 100 | | 100 | 100 |
| MTS24 | | 150 | 300 | 300 | 300 | 300 |
| MTQ50 | | 900 | | 900 | | 900 |
| MTQ14 | 800 | | 500 | | 600 | |
| MTX21 | 84 | 42 | 84 | 84 | 84 | 84 |
| MTV10 | 56 | 56 | 56 | 56 | 56 | 56 |
| MTV42 | | | 36 | 72 | | 72 |

A computer-based MRP system is used to support manufacturing planning and control. The production planning and control department issues production orders for end products (their MPS) in line with the forecast supplied by sales administration. The MRP system is then run against these production orders, taking into account existing inventory and purchase-order information for low-volume components.

Manufactured components are planned and controlled in different ways, depending on their set-up and lead times. Items with short set-up and lead times (such as tubular positive plates and small parts) are controlled using a Kanban-style pull system driven by assembly usage. Items with relatively long set-up and lead times are controlled by the production planning department. In this case, weekly schedules are issued to each manufacturing department, which take into account future assembly plans and existing inventory balances.

Two types of capacity planning reports are prepared by the production planning and control manager. One, on a quarterly basis, indicates the estimated production rate (that is, the number of cells per week) for the six different production groups of tubular, flat plate, rail, BX, DX and RX. The second report is issued weekly and indicates the percentage of plant and manpower utilized during the previous week.

**Exhibit 10**  Production performance against master production schedule

| Product reference number | Week 25, MPS | Week 25, Actual |
|---|---|---|
| MTW55 | | |
| MTS24 | 350 | 314 |
| MTT42 | 150 | 137 |
| MTQ16 | 200 | 201 |
| MTC41 | | 87 |
| MTW36 | 100 | 104 |
| MTQ50 | 900 | 897 |
| MTQ14 | | 602 |
| MTX30 | 42 | |
| MTX21 | 42 | 42 |
| MTV61 | 310 | 213 |
| MTT28 | 210 | 204 |
| MTQ47 | 105 | 315 |
| MTW16 | 112 | 172 |
| MTV10 | | 56 |
| MTV42 | | |
| MTV81 | 28 | |
| Total | 2549 | 3344 |
| Percentage actual to MPS: 131% | | |

*Note:*
1. This data is a representative sample of the plant results for week 25.

**Exhibit 11**    Container stock cycle count results

| Type/part number | Description | On-hand computer | Inventory actual | Balance difference | Percentage difference |
|---|---|---|---|---|---|
| High-volume | | | | | |
| 667 | Container | 326 | 306 | −20 | −6 |
| 128 | Container | 436 | 492 | 56 | 13 |
| 424 | Container | 332 | 320 | −12 | −4 |
| 832 | Container | 1426 | 1374 | −52 | −4 |
| 527 | Container | 716 | 668 | −48 | −7 |
| Total | | 3236 | 3160 | −76 | −2 |
| Low-volume | | | | | |
| 221 | Container | 128 | 159 | 31 | 24 |
| 382 | Container | 12 | 0 | −12 | −100 |
| 112 | Container | 156 | 154 | −2 | −1 |
| 968 | Container | 84 | 84 | 0 | 0 |
| 421 | Container | 251 | 235 | −16 | −6 |
| Total | | 631 | 632 | 1 | 0 |
| **Grand total** | | **3867** | **3792** | **−75** | **−2** |

Neither of these reports translates the MPS (the number of units of each cell product item to be produced in each week over the coming six weeks) into capacity requirements for the individual manufacturing processes.

The actual assembly and component production is reviewed daily to check progress against the schedule. The overall assembly performance is reviewed weekly at a sales/production meeting held each Monday when 'panics' are identified and order priorities are established. An example of manufacturing performance against the production plan for a sample of representative products is shown in Exhibit 10. Because of the critical role played by on-hand inventory balances in Aztec's MRP system, Exhibit 11 shows the results of a recent cycle count for several representative cell container items. Although not shown, similar results should be expected for the cell finished-goods inventory.

# 2    Franklin, Singleton and Cotton

'Now that we have had the opportunity to gain sufficient understanding of this new part of our business, it is opportune to address the several areas of potential improvements we have already identified', remarked Dave Cullis, managing director of the Franklin, Singleton and Cotton (FSC) plant. He was referring to the fact that FSC had only recently been taken over by the Brannan Group and that he had assumed overall executive responsibility for this plant as well as his other executive commitments elsewhere in the group. He continued by identifying one of these opportunities as being:

> the solvent-free lamination process and the potential market opportunities that exist. As the only solvent-free process we have in Europe then we anticipate that we should now be able to compete in those segments of our overall market that require solvent-free adhesion by building on our existing business and seeking further opportunities that this alternative technology offers. Early next month we will meet to review these particular issues. This will give us a chance to consider the analysis work completed so far and to identify, and ideally provide, any other information that will help us in deciding what best to do with the additional capacity we have in this part of our business.

David Cullis was addressing the board of directors at FSC about six months after the takeover.

## Background

FSC is now a wholly owned subsidiary of the Brannan Group, an Irish-based conglomerate comprising textiles and paper as well as packaging. Located on the outskirts of Leeds in the north of England, FSC supplies a range of UK companies, with growing export sales to most EU countries.

This case study was written by Terry Hill (University of Oxford). It is intended for class discussion and not as an example of good or bad management. © AMD Publishing.

# Marketing

FSC supplies flexible packaging to a range of customers whose own end products include snacks, beverages, confectionery, food (including frozen foods, meat, poultry and dairy products) and a range of non-food products (see Exhibit 1). The packaging specification reflects the needs of each customer and can be any combination of printed or unprinted and laminated or unlaminated. (Laminated film is where two or more films are put together before or after printing. The purpose of laminates is to improve certain properties in the packaging – for example as an air/moisture barrier to improve the shelf life of a product – and thereby enhance these in terms of its end use or to protect the print or gloss levels of the base film.)

When taking over FSC, the Brannan Group not only wished to increase its market share in related segments but also recognized the opportunity of supplying new

**Exhibit 1**    Representative sample of laminated orders in the first 13 weeks of the current year

| Job number | Sector | Technical requirements | | | Sales value (£) |
| --- | --- | --- | --- | --- | --- |
| | | Flexographic | Gravure | Lamination | |
| G937 | Food | | | ✔ | 6 110 |
| G982 | Confectionery | | ✔ | ✔ | 13 612 |
| G991 | Food | | | ✔ | 14 142 |
| H022 | Confectionery | | ✔ | ✔ | 18 281 |
| H098 | Confectionery | ✔ | | ✔ | 5 128 |
| H110 | Snacks | ✔ | | ✔ | 10 410 |
| H114 | Food | ✔ | | ✔ | 16 865 |
| H120 | Food | ✔ | | ✔ | 6 451 |
| H155 | Confectionery | ✔ | | ✔ | 3 916 |
| H157 | Food | ✔ | | ✔ | 7 241 |
| H222 | Snacks | | ✔ | ✔ | 7 162 |
| H253 | Non-food | ✔ | | ✔ | 6 924 |
| H261 | Food | | | ✔ | 8 816 |
| H334 | Food | ✔ | | ✔ | 4 612 |
| H340 | Food | | | ✔ | 10 339 |
| H357 | Beverage | ✔ | | ✔ | 15 718 |
| H364 | Confectionery | | ✔ | ✔ | 6 408 |
| H389 | Non-food | ✔ | | ✔ | 4 413 |
| H402 | Beverage | | ✔ | ✔ | 17 916 |
| H424 | Food | ✔ | | ✔ | 9 778 |
| H450 | Confectionery | | | ✔ | 2 794 |
| H486 | Food | ✔ | | ✔ | 4 693 |
| H522 | Beverage | | ✔ | ✔ | 26 710 |
| H553 | Snacks | ✔ | | ✔ | 23 862 |
| H554 | Food | ✔ | | ✔ | 18 222 |
| H618 | Snacks | | ✔ | ✔ | 5 974 |

customers. In addition, the process configuration within the FSC plant matched the mix within the group as a whole, thus giving more flexibility in terms of meeting the needs of all its customers.

# Manufacturing

When the design art work has been agreed with a customer (and in many instances, the order will be for a repeat design), then either cylinders or plates will be prepared (see Exhibit 2). The orders are then scheduled into manufacturing in line with agreed specifications and delivery dates.

As shown in Exhibit 3, orders can go through a number of routes depending on which printing process is required and whether or not the product is to be laminated. Lamination can be either on the printed or unprinted side of the film. Whereas the former would have to be completed after printing (the route shown in Exhibit 3), the latter would usually be laminated first and then printed afterwards in order to minimize potential losses in the process. In addition, some products do not require printing but do require lamination.

**Exhibit 2**    An overview of the manufacturing process

All orders require a technical specification to be agreed in terms of the materials to be used and the printing required.

- *Film specification* – this concerns details of the materials to be used to form the packaging itself.

- *Artwork* – where printing is required, the designs, narrative and colours will need to be agreed by the customer. Negatives are produced from the artwork and these form the basis for making cylinders or plates.

- *Gravure process* – using copper-coated cylinders onto which designs are etched, gravure is more suited to products that would not undergo design changes and hence would attract large, cumulative volumes over many orders and often long time periods. Gravure cylinders are expensive to produce compared with flexographic plates and hence lend themselves to more stable designs.

- *Flexographic processes* – using plates as the format for transferring designs, flexographic (often called flexo) processes are best suited to shorter runs and products where packaging design changes are more frequently required.

- *Lamination* – the packaging for certain products is enhanced by putting together two or more films or substrates, which enhances the packaging by improving given characteristicts to increase shelf life. Lamination can be completed before or after printing and is also provided on unprinted film using adhesives, the basis of which can be solvents, aqueous (comprising a much reduced level of solvents) or solvent-free.

- *Finishing* – these processes slit 'parent' or 'mill' rolls into individual coils ready for loading onto customers' packaging lines.

**Exhibit 3**      Manufacturing processes: typical product flow

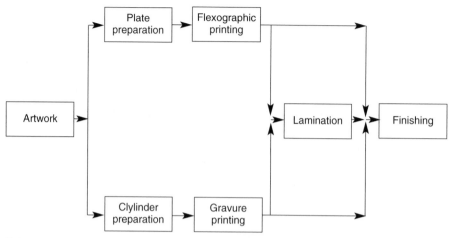

*Note*
In addition to the product flow above, products may be:
    Laminated first and then printed
    Laminated and not printed
In both instances, the product would go through the appropriate process sequence.


# Lamination

The laminator at FSC uses solvent-free adhesion and, as shown in Exhibit 3, is a separate process from that of printing. The alternative (and most frequent arrangement in the Brannan Group) is known as in-line lamination, where a product is printed and laminated as part of a sequential set of processes.

Both the printing and laminating processes are reel-to-reel formats in that the film is fed into the machine in reel form and then rereeled at the other end of the machine after being printed or laminated. Exhibit 4 gives details of a representative range of orders that were processed through the laminator in the first three months of the current year.

'Currently, the demand for products to be laminated only requires a single shift to be worked, with overtime as necessary. A working week comprises 37.5 hours with overtime working when required either to finish a job or meet a delivery date', explained Brian Sutcliffe, the manufacturing director.

The takeover by the Brannan Group has given us a real opportunity to increase our sales of packaging where solvent-free lamination is a requirement of the customer. In addition, there is also the possibility of transferring work within the group in order to make best sense of the increased capability.

The volumes processed through the lamination machine vary from one week to the next [see Exhibit 1], which reflects the number of jobs (there were 65 jobs completed in the first three months of this year) and the complexity of the lamination.

**Exhibit 4**     Representative sample of orders for laminated
products in the first 13 weeks of the current year

| Job number | Direct costs (£)[1] | Lamination machine hours |
|---|---|---|
| G937 | 4 753 | 5.0 |
| G982 | 8 379 | 18.4 |
| G991 | 2 895 | 23.0 |
| H022 | 13 825 | 24.6 |
| H098 | 4 475 | 4.8 |
| H110 | 9 333 | 3.0 |
| H114 | 11 882 | 15.3 |
| H120 | 4 773 | 4.0 |
| H155 | 3 452 | 9.5 |
| H157 | 6 298 | 4.0 |
| H222 | 7 101 | 3.1 |
| H253 | 6 281 | 6.3 |
| H261 | 6 396 | 4.8 |
| H334 | 4 648 | 3.1 |
| H340 | 7 510 | 12.3 |
| H357 | 11 797 | 10.2 |
| H364 | 6 197 | 3.3 |
| H389 | 4 622 | 3.8 |
| H402 | 12 583 | 13.4 |
| H424 | 8 302 | 4.4 |
| H450 | 1 860 | 3.3 |
| H486 | 3 295 | 3.9 |
| H522 | 20 782 | 13.0 |
| H553 | 20 077 | 14.5 |
| H554 | 14 020 | 10.5 |
| H618 | 2 402 | 3.1 |

*Note*
1. Direct costs included the direct labour and direct materials cost for
   both printing (where applicable) and laminating.

Some details of the lamination department are given in Exhibits 5 and 6.

# Future Opportunities

'The solvent-free capability of FSC's laminator appears to provide a significant opportunity to grow sales in this segment, especially given the spare capacity available', reflected Dave Cullis.

As the rest of the plant already works on a 24-hour basis over five days, then additional overhead costs will be relatively small and the infrastructure is in place. Certainly one of

**Exhibit 5**     Output (metres) in the first 13 weeks of the
                  current year

| Week | Output (metres) | Actual set-up time (hours) |
|------|-----------------|----------------------------|
| 1  | 44 700  | 2.3  |
| 2  | 179 440 | 10.1 |
| 3  | 227 550 | 6.4  |
| 4  | 224 650 | 5.9  |
| 5  | 149 150 | 11.2 |
| 6  | 120 650 | 10.8 |
| 7  | 244 300 | 4.7  |
| 8  | 179 120 | 10.3 |
| 9  | 195 610 | 14.6 |
| 10 | 145 900 | 9.5  |
| 11 | 163 050 | 11.2 |
| 12 | 240 050 | 5.4  |
| 13 | 50 500  | 10.6 |

*Note*
1. Weekly output depends, in part, on the length of the working
   week, which will be affected by national holiday closures. These
   occurred in weeks 1 and 13. Printers are highly-skilled workers
   whose pay reflect a high level of skill and effectiveness of working.

**Exhibit 6**     Some data on the lamination department in the first 13
                  weeks of the current year

| | |
|---|---|
| Total hours worked in the period | 528 |
| Normal hours per week | 37.5 |
| Overtime hours in the period | 63 |
| Number of jobs completed | 65 |
| Standard set-up time (minutes/job) | 55 |
| Standard throughput speed (metres/hours) | 9000 |

*Note*
1. There were three national holidays in the period, and these days are
   not included in this total.

our main initiatives now is to review the current orders within FSC to identify those on which we can build while looking at the larger customer base within the Brannan Group to identify opportunities for future growth.

The initial analysis of laminated orders completed at FSC shows that all of them could be completed at one or more of the other UK plants. A similar review is now being completed of the orders completed at the other plants, and then we need to get down to identify orders that could be sensibly switched and other segments or opportunities with this wider customer base. A technical review [Exhibit 7] is the step towards this – the order analysis is on the way and should be available soon.

**Exhibit 7**    Technical review of alternative laminating processes

1. Currently, there are three alternative processes by which film can be laminated:

   (a) solvent-free: as the name suggests, this is free of solvents

   (b) aqueous: low solvent base

   (c) solvent-based: high solvent base.

2. Although the adhesive material costs are similar for each process, (b) and (c) both require drying facilities with attendent energy costs.

3. Running speeds vary, depending on the process and the particular item of plant. Within the Brannan Group, the relevant running speeds are:

   (a) solvent-free: 100–200 metres/minute

   (b) aqueous: 50–100 metres/minute

   (c) solvent- based: 50–120 metres/minute.

   For (b) and (c), drying restricts relevant throughput speeds.

As with most manufacturing processes, the length of the production run also has a direct bearing on the throughput speeds achieved.

# 3

# Hoffmann Tobacco

Curt Muller sat back. He had just finished analysing last month's performance summary for the two manufacturing units, a review that confirmed the significant disparity between their results. After discussions, initiatives and promises, the Norwich plant's performance was still well short of target. In addition, this was in marked contrast to the Edinburgh plant, which seemed to go from strength to strength. The reasons for this difference were not at all apparent. In fact, the similarity of investments and approaches undertaken at each site made comparisons easier to make and contrasts easier to conclude. The problem was to identify the fundamental nature of this difference, which was marked in itself and difficult to understand given the circumstances involved.

## Background

Hoffmann Tobacco is a wholly owned subsidiary of Teison Industries, Inc., a North American holding company with interests in papermaking, printing and textiles, besides the tobacco industry. With its head office based in Virginia, the Teison Group has subsidiaries throughout North America, Europe and Australasia. Hoffmann Tobacco (HT) has two manufacturing plants within the UK (besides others in continental Europe) that produce cigarettes for both domestic and overseas markets. It was recognized that while imported cigarettes would have some appeal in overseas markets, they would inevitably lose out to other brands (particularly local products) on the basis of price. In addition, a climate of reducing demand for cigarettes in the UK and other traditional markets added to the pressure for HT to offer a wider range of products and also to reduce costs wherever possible.

## Marketing

Due to the growing recognition of the harmful effects of smoking on a person's health, the level of cigarette sales in many countries had fallen appreciably. The

This case study was written by Terry Hill (University of Oxford). It is intended for class discussion and not as an example of good or bad management. © AMD Publishing.

tobacco industry, therefore, had been forced to rethink its strategy in order to adjust for the loss of sales revenue and profit that had resulted.

In addition, the move from short to king-size cigarettes, the introduction of cut-price cigarettes from R. J. Reynolds, Philip Morris, manufacturers in Germany and own-brand labels added to the pressures for additional investment to meet new brand requirements and essential reductions in cost.

HT's marketing strategy was to increase market share at home (in an attempt to maintain current sales revenue in what was recognized to be a declining market) while increasing exports abroad. The principal target areas for growth in export sales were the Middle East, Africa, Asia and the European duty-free segments.

In broad terms, HT's marketing strategy had three principal features:

1. **Product quality**: to ensure that the product was manufactured and presented at the highest level of quality, in terms of tobacco blend, the feel and look of the cigarette itself and packaging, as a way of maintaining its position.

2. **Price**: the decline in sales had resulted in surplus manufacturing capacity within the UK cigarette industry as a whole which, together with the low-priced European cigarette imports mentioned earlier, had placed significant emphasis on the need for cost reduction. In addition, export sales had similar pressures on price due to the nature of these markets and the low-priced alternatives manufactured domestically in each of the countries or regions in question.

3. **Product range**: in response to the fact that while cigarettes were bought for many reasons, one of those clearly identified was image. Although this was in part related to product quality, the need to offer a wide range of products was a most important way of increasing both HT's share of the UK market and sales in current and future export markets.

One further feature of the UK market also emphasized many of the changes taking place. The continued growth in sales to multiple retailers (such as Tesco and Sainsbury) at the expense of the small retail outlet meant an increasing squeeze on prices similar to that which these retailers had successfully applied to food and other products in the past. This factor further emphasized the need to reduce costs in order for HT to remain competitive within its markets.

# Manufacturing

One part of the total response to declining cigarette sales and increasing competition had been a productivity improvement drive in the key manufacturing areas. In this context, the company and the Tobacco Workers Union (TWU) agreed a whole series of changes that needed both worker cooperation and substantial capital investment. The aim of the programme was to help the company survive in a competitive market while maintaining real corporate earnings, especially in future years. The changes were a combination of restructuring, process investments and changes in working methods and manning levels.

# Restructuring

In the context of declining sales for cigarettes, the need to improve the links between the marketing and operations functions was well appreciated. The previous structure had formalized the separation of these two parts of the business and was recognized as an important source of liaison, communication and coordination problems.

In order to improve these important links within the business, a policy decision was taken to allocate those products to be made at each plant in such a way as to

**Exhibit 1**    Volume of production by brand type at each factory over the three-year transition period

| Factory location | Brand type | Percentage product by volume each year | | |
|---|---|---|---|---|
| | | 1 | 2 | 3[4] |
| Edinburgh | Virginia Mild | | | |
| | UK | 33 | 47 | 61 |
| | Europe duty free[1] | 10 | 21 | 32 |
| | Hoffmann Special | 20 | 14 | 7 |
| | Hoffmann Special (plain) | 25 | 15 | – |
| | Other brands[2] | 12 | 3 | – |
| | Total | 100 | 100 | 100 |
| Norwich | Virginia Mild | | | |
| | UK | 35 | 17 | 10 |
| | Europe duty free[1] | 18 | 10 | – |
| | Hoffmann Special 10s | 15 | 18 | 19 |
| | Hoffmann Special | 16 | 15 | 17 |
| | Hoffmann Special 50s | 3 | 4 | 3 |
| | Golf Tip | 6 | 10 | 14 |
| | Hoffmann Mild[3] | – | 3 | 3 |
| | Hoffmann Special (plain) | – | 9 | 16 |
| | Mild leaf | – | 3 | 4 |
| | Other brands[2] | 7 | 11 | 14 |
| | Total | 100 | 100 | 100 |

*Notes*
1. Europe duty free is packed in both 200s and 300s.
2. The 'other brands' category at Edinburgh totalled six brand types in year 1. This category at Norwich totalled 6 brand types in year 1 and 17 brand types by year 3.
3. The Hoffmann Mild brand is produced as both a plain and tipped cigarette.
4. Year 3 is the current year to which the case study relates.

achieve greater product identity within the business as a whole. This orientation also needed to reflect the capacity requirements at each plant and was undertaken over a period of three years, as shown in Exhibit 1. Completed last year, it was agreed by all the principal functions concerned to have brought a significant improvement to the working relations, particularly between the marketing and operations functions.

## Process Investment

Multifunctional task forces were established in both plants to undertake a review of the manufacturing and distribution activities. Their broad terms of reference were to recommend the best process mix, manning levels and working practices to achieve the required production levels with associated lower costs. Considerable work was undertaken to identify the technical suitability of available processes that incorporated the latest designs and controls and offered significant improvements in terms of throughput speeds.

The principal investment proposals concerned the secondary stage of the manufacturing process, that involved the making and packing of the cigarettes themselves. The primary stage was concerned with preparation and blending, which were completed prior to the secondary stages: see Exhibit 2 'An overview of the cigarette-making process'. The throughput speeds of cigarette-making and packing machines had increased considerably since the late 1960s. The new generation of Protos could now run at speeds of 8000 cigarettes per minute (cpm) compared to the current Molins makers, which worked at speeds of 5000 cpm. In addition, the Molins HLP4 and the GD packers gave corresponding uplifts in throughput speeds. Finally, the proposals also called for the introduction of a number of conveyor/ reservoir systems with elevator arrangements that were designed to link a maker and packer together. With reservoir capacity giving storage space in excess of 50,000 cigarettes, the system comprised an automatically controlled conveyor that linked the two parts of the process together (see Exhibit 2, which gives a brief description of the cigarette-making process). As cigarette makers have much higher throughput speeds than packers, then the basic concept of linking one maker to one packer can be extended by additional conveyors enabling the linking together of machines of different speeds in order to achieve desired levels of matching and the resulting improved overall use of the capital investments involved.

The process investments centred around the provision of two major savings:

- high-speed makers and packers that would reduce the number of machines required for a given production volume and hence reduce the direct operator, indirect support and overhead requirements throughout
- secondary process investments to allow further reductions in direct and indirect employees by mechanizing certain tasks and reducing the manning levels involved in taking part-finished products from one process stage to the next.

**Exhibit 2**  An overview of the cigarette-making process

### Growing the tobacco leaf

Tobacco plants are grown in five main areas of the world: Asia, North America, Europe, South America and Africa. There are three principal varieties of tobacco (Virginia, Burley and Oriental) which are harvested differently. With both Virginia and Oriental plants, the leaves are picked selectively, starting from the bottom upward. This allows each leaf to ripen fully on the plant. The Burley plant, however, is harvested as a whole so leaves higher on the plant have less ripening time than the lower leaves. Cigarette companies take a mix of different tobaccos and blend them to meet their own product specifications in line with particular market segments. HT's recipes can use over 50 different grades of leaf, from all varieties of tobacco, to formulate a single blend, and leaves from up to three different crop years will be blended to even out any variabilities in flavour.

### Primary processing

When the blender believes the tobacco samples are ready for processing, the matured crop is brought into a cigarette-making plant (such as HT's Edinburgh and Norwich plants discussed in this case study). The primary processes comprise a number of steps. The dried and compressed leaves are first conditioned (to make them pliable) by steam moisturizing, then mixed in appropriate blend proportions in a long blending bin. The blended leaves (or lamina) then go to a compressing chamber, where they are sliced into finely cut tobacco and dried once more. The tobacco leaf stem is separately processed, being blended in a similar manner to, but cut more finely than, the leaf. After drying, lamina and stem are then blended together in precise quantities. Flavouring (such as menthol) may be added at this point in the process. The cut tobacco is now ready.

### Secondary processing

The cut tobacco, paper, filters, tipping paper and packaging are all controlled by very advanced production systems. Correct amounts of tobacco blend pass into the machines through airlocks and are combined and spread onto moving belts. The tobacco is sucked into a continuous rod, meets the paper and is sealed into shape and printed with the repeated blend name in line with the desired length of the eventual cigarette. Electronic weighing heads ensure that every cigarette contains its precise weight of tobacco. The continuous length is then cut into individual lengths, two of which are then joined to a double length filter and fused together with tipping paper for a fraction of a second. Cutters then halve the filter, and pairs of cigarettes are conveyed to the end of the line, with faulty cigarettes being eliminated by automatic scanners. Here they are loaded onto trolleys for taking to the packing area (see Exhibit 3). It is this transfer to the packing units that part of the new investments at Edinburgh and Norwich are designed to overcome. With these changes, cigarettes are conveyed directly to the packing units through the reservoir arrangement described in the case study narrative. Exhibit 3 provides an outline of the process for cigarette making. The link to packing machines would be made at the end of the process shown in this outline diagram.

As some 85 per cent of all cigarettes made are filter tip, the filter-making process is an integral part of the second processing unit. The material is processed from a bulk feed to achieve specified filter consistency. The long tube of filter is then cut into rods equal to the requirement for two cigarettes in line with particular specifications. These are then transferred to the cigarette maker, as shown in Exhibit 3, and fused to the cigarettes as described earlier.

The final stage is packing, where cigarettes are automatically packed, foil-wrapped and cartoned for delivery.

**Exhibit 3**     The layout for a typical new generation cigarette maker

Exhibit 4 summarizes the present product-mix characteristics at both plants, while Exhibits 5 and 6 list the current secondary equipment in use at Edinburgh and Norwich, the advantages to be gained and the anticipated reduction in costs.

## Current position

By involving the employees and trade union representatives at an early stage and continuing this high level of involvement throughout, the necessary reorganization and manpower reductions that had ensued were completed without any signs of animosity or disagreement from those involved. The overt and genuine wish to involve those concerned in the rationale for the proposed changes was built on many years of increasing openness displayed within the company. The result was that the relatively complex sets of arrangements were duly completed on time and the expected reductions in factory-based staff (in excess of 500) were achieved.

However, although the planned labour reduction had been accomplished within the set timescales, the anticipated profit improvements had only been achieved at the Edinburgh plant. Given the similarity of investments made and the gains in

**Exhibit 4** Overview of current blends, brands, packing sizes and product codes at each factory location

HT's current range of products reflects its need to increase the number of cigarette types as part of its competitive response in both home and export markets. In the normal way, a product code is allocated wherever there is a difference in blend, brand, length of cigarette or packing specification from one requirement to another. Thus export orders often require packing and insert changes, the number of cigarettes per pack differ to facilitate the use of slot machines,[1] and different packs are used to meet the perceived needs of customers. Below is a summary of the differences currently required at each plant.

| Number of specifications used in a typical month | Edinburgh | Norwich |
| --- | --- | --- |
| Average | | |
| Blends | 3 | 12 |
| Brands | 3 | 25 |
| Product codes | 65 | 560 |
| **Number of different packings per cigarette size (in mm)[2]** | | |
| 70 | – | 4 |
| 80 | – | 2 |
| 84 | 1 | 5 |
| 95 | – | 2 |
| 100 | – | 2 |

*Notes*
1. Slot machines refer to the coin-operated dispensing machines increasingly used in clubs, restaurants, airports and other public places. Customers serve themselves through inserting the appropriate amount of cash required.
2. The different packings used included hinged lid, shell and slide, soft cup, box and drum.

labour cost reductions that accrued, it was difficult, at least from a distance, to understand the success of one application and the relative failure of the other.

Brent Murdoch (plant manager, Norwich) was currently completing an in-depth review of the reasons behind this underperformance. He explained:

Over the last three years the market has changed. Customer lead times are now much shorter, and as many of our products are now customized at least in terms of packing, then there is increased pressure on meeting agreed delivery dates. This is particularly so in export markets and the lower-volume end of our business, which we tend to support. We estimate that ideally we need between three and five weeks to meet a delivery, depending upon the degree of customization involved. As higher-volume items are normally met from finished-goods inventory, then the total lead times estimated above [the lead times of three to five weeks quoted here comprise material lead time plus

**Exhibit 5** Principal secondary equipment at the Edinburgh and Norwich plants before and after the capital investments had taken place

| Equipment category | Edinburgh | | Norwich | |
|---|---|---|---|---|
| | **Before** | **After**[3] | **Before** | **After**[3] |
| Filter rod makers[1] | 6 | 6 | 6 | 6 |
| Free-standing plain[2] | | | | |
|   Makers | 2 | – | 4 | 6 |
|   Packers | 2 | – | 4 | 6 |
| Free-standing filter | | | | |
|   Makers | 30 | 8 | 34 | 7 |
|   Packers | 40 | 10 | 42 | 8 |
| Linked makers and packers (filter) | – | 15 | – | 20 |

*Notes*
1. Filter rod makers are the machines used to make the filter tips (see Exhibit 2).
2. The equipment for making and packing plain (or non-filter tip) cigarettes that was originally sited in the Edinburgh plant was transferred to Norwich when these products were also resited.
3. The investments involved in making these changes (new equipment, reorganizations and compensation payments) totalled £40m for both plants. About 80 per cent of this was spent on new equipment and the reorganization of existing equipment (including linking the making and packing processes) both within and between the two plants.

process lead time] are for customized products, including larger-volume orders of an infrequent nature from some less-developed countries. At our last review, about 65 per cent of all orders received were for delivery in less than five weeks, while almost 35 per cent were for less than three weeks. But, this pattern is increasingly common through businesses and certainly is mirrored in our Edinburgh plant. In addition, whereas our overall sales (both in terms of revenue [£s] and number of cigarettes sold) has slightly increased, since the decision to orient different products to the two plants the order size for our products has, if anything, declined. About half the orders received are for 100 000 cigarettes or less, with over 75 per cent for up to 500 000. Although many of these are for our higher-volume products and are, therefore, cumulated within the production scheduling system, there are also those brands of cigarettes that experience a more intermittent pattern of demand as you would anticipate with lower-volume products. Certainly this mix of work embodies a wider range and spread of volumes than before and particularly compared to Edinburgh. However, overall, the planned investments are achieving the desired labour cost reductions we anticipated. It has been a long haul, but through good working relationships we have negotiated the necessary changes and implemented them in line with the plan. On the new equipment itself we have experienced some problems [see Exhibit 7], which we are in the process of investigating. Certainly, however, the new high-speed makers and packers have made a sizeable impact on our capacity needs (and subsequent manning levels), and the concept of linking makers with packers has reduced the work-in-progress inventory and associated labour support in a most dramatic fashion. All that's left is to get Norwich's performance up to plan and on a par with that being achieved in Edinburgh.

**Exhibit 6**     Rationale supporting the capital investments summarized in Exhibit 4 and the resulting reductions in labour

The rationale supporting the capital investments in both plants was principally as follows.

The linking of a maker and packer required a conveyor and reservoir facility which provided an automatic feeding system from one process to the next. Previously (and currently with free-standing equipment) indirect labour was used to transport cigarettes from the makers to the packers. This would necessitate the movement of cigarettes loaded onto trolleys often from one floor to another and usually involving lengthy distances.

In order to decouple the maker from the packer the total holding of made cigarettes in a conveyor and reservoir system was in excess of 50,000. Thus, this afforded the two processes a practical level of independence within the linked system.

The advantages offered concerned a significant reduction in indirect labour together with small (but significant in terms of actual costs) savings on direct materials, particularly tobacco and is explained in more detail below.

The principal gains which accrued from these changes were:

(a) direct labour cost reduction: the introduction of higher-speed makers and packers, together with the increased efficiency of the new equipment,[1] resulted in a reduction in direct labour requirements;

(b) direct material cost reduction: the new equipment and concept of linked processes resulted in a reduction in material loss/waste from lower levels of rejects and damaged product in the process;

(c) indirect labour reduction: the linked process concept reduced the need for indirect support in several ways, including movement of product, storage, administrative support and maintenance/technical support for the equipment.

The expected results of these improvements were a 20 per cent reduction in factory-related staff and an anticipated 1 per cent reduction in material costs. Over 90 per cent of this planned labour reduction was achieved by the introduction of linked processes in the two plants.

*Note*

1. Efficiency in this context refers to actual output achieved compared to the expressed or standard output and came from reduced downtime and the greater level of attainment of expected throughput rates.

**Exhibit 7**    Downtime analysis experienced on the linked processes at the
Norwich plant

| Reasons for stoppage | Downtime as a percentage of total observations |
|---|---|
| **Making machine**[1] | |
| Related directly to linked process | |
|    Conveyor/reservoir fault | 2.1 |
|    Reservoir full | 3.3 |
|    Need to empty reservoir on a change-over/end of a shift | 9.4 |
|    Other | 3.8 |
|    Total | 18.6 |
| Unrelated to linked process | |
|    Maker fault | 14.2 |
|    Other | 2.5 |
|    Total | 16.7 |
| *Total for the making machine* | 35.3 |
| | |
| **Packing machine**[1] | |
| Related directly to linked process | |
|    Conveyor/reservoir fault | 2.7 |
|    Reservoir empty/waiting on a change-over/start of a shift | 12.9 |
|    Other | 2.1 |
|    Total | 17.7 |
| Unrelated to linked process | |
|    Packer fault | 16.1 |
|    Other | 2.8 |
|    Total | 18.9 |
| *Total for the packing machine* | 36.6 |

Note

1. The conveyor/reservoir faults given for both the makers and packers are independent of each other, as they are related to the feed into and out of the reservoir.

'If we are to adhere to product launch schedules, we must try every mould on receipt, then bring in the mould maker to modify it as required, regardless of whether we can then go ahead and produce initial launch quantities', said George Brett, the manufacturing director. 'If we leave mould testing until we are ready for a production run there is a risk that the need for substantial mould modification will cause us to miss launch dates.'

HQ Injection Moulding had been a major components supplier to the domestic appliance industry prior to its acquisition by one of its customers. It also, at the time, had its own range of homeware products and supplied components to other industries. Some 10 years ago, the group was restructured and notice was given that the group requirements on the company would be phased out over the following two years. At that time, the parent company accounted for over 50 per cent of existing capacity (Exhibit 1 shows the make-up of machine sizes).

This was not the only problem. The company's homeware range also faced competition from small firms who were able to compete effectively in this sector of the market.

'The consumer saw our homeware products as plastic first and homeware second', said Graham Brown, the managing director. 'The traditional image of plastic as a cheap and transient material dominated, and we competed in the marketplace on price, rather than on the basis of our products. We had to rethink how we were to compete.' The company evolved a marketing strategy to design, manufacture and sell a range of high-quality products. This would enable it to compete in a different sector of the market where price was not the dominant order-winner. Over the years, the company designed several ranges of new products and the mould introductions associated with this are summarized as Exhibit 2.

## Manufacturing

A brief outline of the process is shown as Exhibit 3. Starting with raw materials, a moulded product is produced. Certain subsequent operations (such as removing the

This case was prepared by Terry Hill (University of Oxford). It is intended for class discussion and not as an illustration of good or bad management. © AMD Publishing.

**Exhibit 1**  Details of injection moulding machines

Details of the number of machines available in each machine group defined by the company.

| Machine group | Number of machines | | |
|---|---|---|---|
| | Current year minus: | | |
| | 8 | 1 | New |
| 1 | 29 | 1 | – |
| 2 | 15 | 11 | 5 |
| 3 | 5 | 8 | 6 |
| 4 | 2 | 2 | 1 |
| Total | 51 | 22 | 12 |

Details of the 'new' machines in each group.

| Machine group | Year of purchase/new machines | | | | | | | |
|---|---|---|---|---|---|---|---|---|
| | Current year minus: | | | | | | | |
| | 7 | 6 | 5 | 4 | 3 | 2 | 1 | Total |
| 2 | – | – | – | – | 3 | 2 | – | 5 |
| 3 | 2 | 1 | 1 | 1 | – | 1 | – | 6 |
| 4 | – | – | – | – | – | – | 1 | 1 |

Details of a typical machine.

| Machine group | Features of an average machine | | |
|---|---|---|---|
| | Cost (£000s)[1] | Shot weight (ozs) | Locking pressure (tonnes) |
| 1 | 116 | 10 | 200 |
| 2 | 276 | 45 | 450 |
| 3 | 333 | 60 | 600 |
| 4 | 360 | 150 | 600 |

*Note*
1. Cost includes the purchase price of the machine and installation costs at current year prices.

sprue – that is, excess plastic from the mould passageways – by hand, knife or drill, checking the quality of the moulding and first packing operations) are all completed at the machine. The products are then transported in containers to the work-in-progress stores. From there, they are withdrawn as required by the assembly department, who complete any subassembly operations (such as glueing or welding components), assemble (for example, fit lids to bases and attach labels) and finally pack into inner and outer cartons, prior to transportation to the finished-goods warehouse. With many of the products from the original product ranges the assembly and packing was completed during the moulding process, as the work content was relatively small due to the bulk style of packaging involved.

**Exhibit 2**    Summary of the moulds introduced or planned in the last seven years

| Product range[2,3] | Number of moulds[1] | | | | | | | Current year |
|---|---|---|---|---|---|---|---|---|
| | Current year minus: | | | | | | | |
| | 7 | 6 | 5 | 4 | 3 | 2 | 1 | |
| A | – | – | 1 | 5 | – | – | – | – |
| B | – | 4 | 1 | 1 | 4 | 4 | 2 | – |
| C | 19 | 8 | 10 | 8 | 3 | 1 | – | – |
| D | 4 | 20 | – | 6 | 1 | 2 | 12 | – |
| E | 4 | 19 | – | 26 | 9 | 14 | 15 | 30 |
| F | – | – | – | – | – | 2 | – | – |

*Notes*

1. The number of moulds indicates the number of different products within each range. However, in many instances, one mould will have two or more impressions on it, so that in every moulding cycle one, two or more products would be made depending on the number of impressions on that mould.
2. Product ranges A and B belong to the original (pre-change) designs, while C to F were of the revised (post-change) designs. Further details are given in Exhibit 5, under the column headed 'Product'.
3. The dimensional sizes of old and new products vary across the different product ranges but, in overall terms, tend to be similar.

**Exhibit 3**    An outline of the manufacturing and assembly process

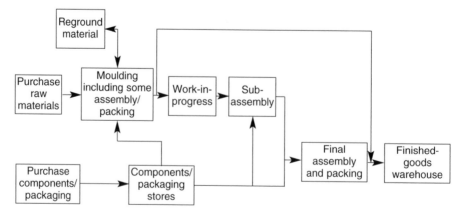

*Note*
All products do not go through each stage of the manufacturing and assembly process.

# Raw Materials

The advent of the new range of products brought with it a significant increase in raw material types and colours. In order to support the new product concept, more expensive materials were introduced and the colour range was widened. Also the old products had tended to be moulded where close colour matching was not required and material specification was less critical. Moreover, the new products were clustered around a 'matching' range of products as a strategy to enhance sales, with the purchaser who has bought one item for the home being more likely to buy another item of the set when next purchasing. This meant that it was necessary to maintain colour matches over a long period of time.

# Toolroom

Nine skilled men (including three apprentices) work days, while one skilled man provides a breakdown service for the mould shop covering the period 22.00 to 07.00 hours. About 15–20 per cent of their time is spent on new moulds and the remainder on modification and repair.

# Design

Over the years, design had expanded to become a separate function with a manager and four staff. Their job was to liaise with customers (often large department stores), agree on design detail then complete the drawings. The manager of the toolroom then undertook to make or subcontract the moulds and get them into production. The toolroom always had one draughtsperson, who dealt with mould modifications.

# Technical Services

The technical support to the mould shop is provided by John Burton, the technical manager. John has extensive knowledge of injection moulding and provides specialist help on the shopfloor. The work varies and includes:

1. Contributing to the design of a mould at the start of the mould-making process
2. Getting new moulds to a production state and establishing the settings and adjustments to be made in all future runs
3. Fine tuning a mould at the start of its production run (very important in terms of productivity)
4. Helping to determine the necessary modifications to a mould.

Before the switch in product concept, John would spend most of his day on task 3, but increasingly, due to the new product strategy, John and his staff of three technicians spend the majority of their time on the other three tasks.

Until six or seven years ago, we concentrated on thinning product wall thickness and reducing cycle times because, particularly with the long production runs associated with the old-type products, this kept the cost down. The mould was made as cheaply as possible and we used black plastic where we could so that we could use reground plastic of mixed colours. And, of course, we would use contrasting colours for lids and bases, to avoid the need to colour match.

The new products changed this. We increased wall thickness to give products greater rigidity and substance, colour match became critical, lids and bases were the same colour, quality took precedence over cycle times, packaging became far more important and quality became the order of the day. The repercussions of this on the shopfloor were considerable. A new team had to be trained and premoulding treatment of material became necessary to achieve the necessary colour and quality standards.

Many existing machines were old and often unable to meet or maintain the new product specifications. Until new machines could be justified, sanctioned and installed, many preliminary operations were necessary to overcome the inadequacies of the old machines. As an estimate, only some 25 per cent of the machines were originally up to meeting the new technical specifications required, due to wear and tear.

On the technical side, our existing fitters had to be retrained to set up moulds with complicated water circuits, heating subsystems, temperature controls and complex core-pull and ejection systems. A new class of staff, the technician, became necessary. Recruitment from outside proved fruitless, and our best setters took on this role, with the best operators replacing them as setters.

The proposed range of moulds appears bigger and more sophisticated. Overall, machine setting is now more difficult and the machine adjustment controls are inadequate for the fine level of tuning required. When several new product ranges are introduced within a short period, everyone is under pressure. The new machines due this year will have microprocessor controls with the set-up reductions it brings, justifying the 15 per cent increase in capital cost. Although we expect this margin to decrease over the next year or two, persuading top management that this additional expenditure is necessary as standard policy is a different matter. These three new machines will be groups 2, 3 and 4, with locking pressures of 450, 600 and 600 respectively.

# Maintenance

According to Phil Stokes, the maintenance manager:

many of the old machines weren't up to the quality specifications required by the change of product mix. For this reason, new machines were bought and the worst of the old machines sold. Now, besides the high-volume, low-margin products, we also make low-volume products. Our revenue and profits have both increased. For my department, this has meant fewer machines and fewer problems.

Exhibit 4 gives the financial information for the company for the last seven years.

**Exhibit 4** Some financial management information for the last seven years (year ended 31 December, all figures in £000s)

| | Current year minus: | | | | | | |
|---|---|---|---|---|---|---|---|
| | 7 | 6 | 5 | 4 | 3 | 2 | 1 |
| **Fixed assets** | | | | | | | |
| Plant | 561 | 552 | 399 | 420 | 612 | 838 | 980 |
| Moulds | 102 | 130 | 170 | 180 | 320 | 584 | 620 |
| Total | 663 | 682 | 569 | 600 | 932 | 1422 | 1600 |
| **Current assets** | | | | | | | |
| Inventory | 262 | 532 | 1029 | 1259 | 1559 | 2243 | 2567 |
| Debtors | 483 | 798 | 842 | 817 | 1321 | 963 | 1373 |
| Total | 745 | 1330 | 1871 | 2076 | 2880 | 3206 | 3940 |
| **Current liabilities** | | | | | | | |
| Creditors | 626 | 532 | 628 | 1134 | 1774 | 1744 | 1765 |
| Overdraft | 2 | 480 | 412 | 42 | 38 | 284 | 575 |
| Total | 628 | 1012 | 1040 | 1176 | 1812 | 2028 | 2340 |
| Working capital[1] | 117 | 318 | 831 | 900 | 1068 | 1178 | 1600 |
| Net assets employed[2] | 780 | 1000 | 1400 | 1500 | 2000 | 2600 | 3200 |
| **Financed by** | | | | | | | |
| Share capital | 50 | 50 | 50 | 50 | 50 | 50 | 50 |
| Retained profit[3] | 280 | 420 | 530 | 570 | 830 | 1760 | 2660 |
| Total | 330 | 470 | 580 | 620 | 880 | 1810 | 2710 |
| Group indebtedness | 450 | 530 | 820 | 880 | 1120 | 790 | 490 |
| Net capital employed | 780 | 1000 | 1400 | 1500 | 2000 | 2600 | 3200 |
| Net sales | 2552 | 2872 | 4212 | 4466 | 5810 | 5394 | 8021 |
| Net profit before tax[3] | 146 | 185 | 274 | 362 | 564 | 708 | 1050 |

*Notes*
1. Working capital = current assets − current liabilities.
2. Net assets employed = fixed assets + working capital.
3. Any difference between the net profit for any year and the increase of retained profits is due to a transfer of profit to the group.

# Mould Shop

'We are now in a totally different manufacturing situation than we were previously', was George Brett's opening comment when discussing the present situation. At the beginning of the change-over, he explained, there were several technical difficulties that had not been foreseen. These ranged from the inadequacies of many old machines to do the job, through to the moulding properties of the new materials.

He recalled how jobs had often to be allocated to a larger machine in order to achieve the required product specification (for instance, an increased locking pressure was needed to keep a mould closed during the machine cycle to avoid 'flashing'). Also, there were great difficulties experienced with colour matching, especially in the 'bright, modern' colours now being used.

> We even had to rethink our mould design, in some cases, from one that minimized the cycle time by injecting in the centre of the mould (that is, the shortest distance for the material to flow) to injecting so as to minimize the sprue mark, which lengthens the time cycle[1] and complicates the moulding process. Since then, we have overcome these initial difficulties and many more besides. But, in doing so, it has resulted in a lot of pressure, effort and cost. At times we can have seven or eight of the machines working on new products, which effectively means no production, and a complete loss of productive standard hours from some 30 per cent of our capacity. The problems of trying to complete the tasks of a development unit and a production unit under the same roof, and calling on the same capacities and skills, are enormous. The pressure of achieving deadlines, particularly when little or no slack time has been allowed in the plan (the design/customer agreement phase always absorbs whatever slack there is), requires all our attention so that normal production has to look after itself.

As shown in Exhibit 1, the available production capacity had shifted towards larger machines, sometimes in actual numbers, but markedly as a percentage of the total capacity available. To keep moulding costs down moved the argument towards multi-impression moulds, whereby every cycle produced a 'shot' with each of the impressions in the formed state (for example, two lids or two bodies, or two lids and two bodies, and so on). Of course, multi-impression moulds always become much larger and much more sophisticated. These, in turn, require larger machines and accounted, in part, for the drift away from the earlier mix of machines. In addition, mould changes and set-ups take longer and details of a representative sample of products throughout the current range is given as Exhibit 5. Besides the cost advantages inherent in multipurpose moulding, particularly with high-volume production runs, another advantage gained is that it facilitates the moulding of a product that has more than one component and where colour matching is essential.

Part of the production management's job was to consider ways of reducing costs throughout the process wherever possible. Some of these suggestions come from marketing pressure in addition to the continuous flow of ideas from manufacturing itself, with the aid of support services such as industrial engineering, toolroom and design. Exhibit 6 gives cost breakdowns for some representative products from across the current ranges.

# Assembly

The assembly department undertakes subassembly, final assembly and packing, and is located away from the mould shop in a 50,000-square-foot warehouse, which also contains work-in-progress and some of the finished-goods inventory. The work of this department has increased with the need for packing and presentation that accompanied the new products. At the other extreme, any assembly or packing of the industrial products is mainly carried out at the machine. There are, at present, some 17 assembly benches and three subassembly locations, with 27 full-time and 16 part-time packers and an indirect staff of three.

# Finished-goods Warehouse

Although the product quantities have decreased since the early 1970s, the requirement for warehousing is considerably higher. Reasons for this include:

1. subcontract industrial work for the group was moulded on a contract basis and shipped daily to the various companies
2. the traditional homewares and industrial products were (and still are) packed several together, inside a box or polyethylene bag
3. components required to assemble the new ranges of products are greater
4. the emphasis on quality means that components have to be stacked with greater care
5. the new products are packed individually in inner boxes, increasing the space requirement at the finished-goods stage.

Work-in-progress and finished-goods warehousing capacity has been increased significantly, as shown in Exhibit 7.

# Production Control

'The new range of products presents a set of production control problems, that are different from those of the old products', said Geoff Sissons, the production controller. 'The number of components and the assembly and packing requirements have increased the complexity of the process.' Exhibit 5 illustrates this.

In addition, the uncertainty inherent in the mould-testing process, the procedure for agreeing packaging and the launch dates have added factors which made planning and control far more difficult.

**Exhibit 5**  Production, sales and inventory details on several products[15]

| Product[1] | Machine group | Number of impressions[2] | Number of colours | Number of components[3] | When last moulded: Months ago | When last moulded: Colour changes | Production run (hours) Last[4] | Production run (hours) Average[5] | Production runs last 12 months | Hours to change[6] Mould | Hours to change[6] Colour | Annual sales (units) | Finished goods[7] Units | Finished goods[7] Colours | Outstanding orders Units | Outstanding orders Colours |
|---|---|---|---|---|---|---|---|---|---|---|---|---|---|---|---|---|
| *(A) General Homewares: Original Product Concept* | | | | | | | | | | | | | | | | |
| 1132 Tray | 2 | 2 | 1 | 3 | 27 | 1 | 1700 | 1700 | – | 2(½) | – | 20 686 | 67 159 | 1 | – | – |
| 2225 Bowl[8] | 2 | 1 | 8 | 2 | 1 | 3 | 192 | 248 | 6 | 2(1) | 2 | 159 120 | 33 769 | 8 | – | – |
| 1138 Bucket | 3 | 1 | 8 | 2 | 6 | 3 | 138 | 138 | 1 | 3(1½) | 2 | 13 236 | 5 829 | 5 | – | – |
| 1386 Jug | 2 | 1 | 1 | 3 | 2 | 1 | 190 | 147 | 3 | 3(1) | – | 44 237 | 34 618 | 1 | – | – |
| 1263 Tray[8] | 2 | 1 | 8 | 5 | 5 | 4 | 70 | 120 | 4 | 2½(1) | 1½ | 48 162 | 15 050 | 8 | – | – |
| 2687 Tidy | 3 | 1 | 2 | 4 | 1 | 2 | 124 | 82 | 7 | 7(3) | 2 | 50 400 | 8 280 | 2 | – | – |
| 2241 Bin | 3 | 2 | 6 | 7 | 1 | 5 | 103 | 100 | 4 | 13(5) | 2 | 47 646 | 3 642 | 5 | 195 | 1 |
| 2366 Bin | 3 | 1 | 1 | 2 | – | 1 | 156 | 120 | 6 | 7(1) | 1 | 11 779 | – | – | 288 | 1 |
| 1393 Box | 2 | 2 | 2 | 2 | 1 | 1 | 190 | 83 | 6 | 2½(1) | 1½ | 22 405 | 3 987 | 2 | – | – |
| 1267 Tub | 3 | 1 | 1 | 1 | 5 | 1 | 44 | 44 | 1 | 2½(1½) | 1½ | 13 465 | 734 | 1 | – | – |
| 8282 Bowl[9] | 3 | 4 | 6 | 3 | 2 | 6 | 220 | 250 | 2 | 10(4) | 2 | 57 840 | 480 | 6 | – | – |
| *(B) Industrial Mouldings: Original Product Concept* | | | | | | | | | | | | | | | | |
| 6900 Board | 2 | 2 | 1 | 1 | 8 | 2 | 144 | 144 | 1 | 1(–) | ½ | 6 735 | – | – | – | – |
| 6908 Basin | 4 | 2 | 1 | 2 | 2 | 1 | 62 | 62 | 1 | 22(10) | – | – | – | – | – | – |
| 6074 Lid | 2 | 1 | 1 | 2 | 3 | 1 | 45 | 45 | 1 | 3(1) | – | – | – | – | – | – |
| 6010 Tray | 4 | 2 | 1 | – | 50 | 1 | 106 | 106 | – | 3(1) | – | – | – | – | – | – |
| 6085 Knob | 1 | 5 | 1 | 1 | 16 | 2 | 125 | 125 | – | 2(½) | ½ | – | – | – | – | – |
| 6990 Frame | 3 | 1 | 1 | 4 | 2 | 1 | 163 | 163 | 1 | 24(10) | – | – | – | – | – | – |
| 6491 Cap | 1 | 6 | 1 | 1 | 6 | 1 | 110 | 511 | 6 | 2½(1) | – | 533 318 | – | – | 48 703 | 1 |
| 6209 Case | 2 | 1 | 1 | 5 | 4 | 1 | 95 | 83 | 7 | 7(3) | – | 65 159 | 1 152 | 1 | – | – |
| 8860 Tray[10] | 4 | 1 | 12 | 1 | – | 1 | 2400 | 371 | 10 | 9(3) | ½ | 159 489 | 4 804 | 6 | 19 835 | 1 |
| 8009 Case | 3 | 2 | 2 | 1 | 8 | 2 | 60 | 54 | 1 | 11(5) | ½ | 5 443 | 3 650 | 2 | – | – |
| 8010 Tray | 3 | 1 | 2 | 1 | 4 | 1 | 90 | 36 | 2 | 11(5) | ½ | 2 741 | 717 | 1 | – | – |
| *(C) General Homewares: Revised Product Concept* | | | | | | | | | | | | | | | | |
| 3910 Container | 3 | 1 | 10 | 5 | 1 | 3 | 134 | 87 | 9 | 4(2) | 3 | 35 238 | 520 | 2 | 7 917 | 3 |
| 3941 Rollholder | 2 | 1 | 3 | 8 | 10 | 3 | 55 | 55 | 1 | 13(3) | 3 | 3 312 | 610 | 2 | 432 | 1 |
| 3995 Container | 3 | 1 | 10 | 5 | 30 | 4 | 77 | 77 | – | 3½(2) | 1½ | 157 | 108 | 2 | – | – |
| 6115 No. 4 | 3 | 4 | 6 | 5 | 14 | 5 | 20 | 20 | – | 9(1) | 6 | 13 814 | 28 225 | 6 | – | – |
| 6110 No. 9 | 2 | 1 | 9 | 4 | 20 | 1 | 24 | 24 | – | 3(1) | 2 | 1 242 | 6 660 | 8 | – | – |
| 6246 No. 28 | 4 | 2 | 12 | 4 | 1 | 5 | 81 | 39 | 9 | 7(3) | 4 | 14 472 | 6 485 | 12 | 209 | 2 |
| 6151 Jug | 2 | 1 | 4 | 3 | 20 | 3 | 102 | 102 | – | 9(2) | 2 | 3 284 | 1 035 | 2 | – | – |
| 6313 Box | 1 | 1 | 4 | 6 | 30 | 1 | 24 | 24 | – | 3½(2) | 2 | 405 | 6 294 | 3 | – | 2 |
| 6332 Rack | 4 | 1 | 6 | 3 | 3 | 3 | 106 | 106 | 1 | 10(4) | 3 | 18 453 | 2 489 | 5 | – | – |
| 6846 Shelf | 4 | 2 | 2 | 9 | 4 | 2 | 42 | 92 | 2 | 8(4) | 2 | 10 598 | 2 003 | 2 | – | – |
| 6463 Clock | 3 | 1 | 4 | 10 | 14 | 3 | 78 | 78 | – | 2½(1) | 1½ | 6 393 | 1 749 | 4 | – | – |

| Product[1] | Machine group | Number of impressions[2] | Number of colours | Number of components[3] | When last moulded Months ago | When last moulded Colour changes | Production run (hours) Last[4] | Production run (hours) Average[5] | Production runs last 12 months | Hours to change[6] Mould | Hours to change[6] Colour | Annual sales (units) | Finished goods[7] Units | Finished goods[7] Colours | Outstanding orders Units | Outstanding orders Colours |
|---|---|---|---|---|---|---|---|---|---|---|---|---|---|---|---|---|
| *(D) Bathroom Ranges: Revised Product Concept* | | | | | | | | | | | | | | | | |
| 5426 Holder | 3 | 2 | 10 | 7 | – | 2 | 67 | 155 | 14 | 4(2) | 2 | 119 367 | – | – | 12 816 | 8 |
| 5229 Dish | 4 | 2 | 9 | 6 | – | 2 | 45 | 110 | 7 | 4(2) | 2 | 40 819 | 966 | 4 | 4196 | 4 |
| 5624 Holder[11] | 2 | 1 | 10 | 8 | – | 3 | 40 | 40 | 1 | 14(2) | 2 | – | 3 240 | 3 | 3 240 | 3 |
| 5315 Dish[11] | 2 | 1 | 5 | 7 | – | 3 | 20 | 20 | 1 | 14(2) | 2 | 1 080 | 1 080 | 3 | 1 050 | 3 |
| 6213 Hook | 2 | 2 | 10 | 6 | 17 | 2 | 47 | 47 | – | 4(2) | 1½ | 2 018 | 12 725 | 8 | – | – |
| 6420 Mirror | 4 | 2 | 11 | 9 | 1 | 1 | 39 | 39 | 5 | 5(2) | 1½ | 11 768 | 15 283 | 7 | – | – |
| 6428 Holder | 1 | 2 | 13 | 5 | 1 | 2 | 35 | 35 | 5 | 2½(1) | 1 | 16 913 | 21 392 | 10 | – | – |
| 6606 Beaker | 3 | 4 | 5 | 6 | 1 | 2 | 33 | 50 | 3 | 5(2) | 1½ | 24 244 | 18 785 | 4 | 3 000 | 1 |
| 6397 Caddy | 3 | 1 | 4 | 8 | 1 | 2 | 95 | 34 | 3 | 8(4) | 1½ | 10 752 | 11 167 | 4 | – | – |
| 6309 Mirror | 4 | 1 | 4 | 8 | 1 | 3 | 43 | 32 | 4 | 4(2) | 1½ | 9 720 | 3 994 | 3 | 1 500 | 1 |
| *(E) Kitchen Ranges: Revised Product Concept* | | | | | | | | | | | | | | | | |
| 4141 Bowl | 4 | 4 | 4 | 4 | 2 | 2 | 60 | 80 | 8 | 3(1) | 1½ | 58 850 | 12 280 | 4 | – | – |
| 8284 Large sieve[12] | 3 | 2 | 4 | 7 | 1 | 3 | 100 | 35 | 8 | 3(1) | 1½ | 39 638 | 96 | 1 | 8 222 | 3 |
| 4150 Small sieve[12] | 2 | 2 | 4 | 7 | 1 | 3 | 100 | 63 | 8 | | | 35 450 | 233 | 1 | 1 607 | 2 |
| 4151 Large spoon[13] | 3 | 2 | 4 | 4 | 3 | 4 | 367 | 117 | 4 | 6(3) | | 74 020 | 49 017 | 3 | – | – |
| 4156 Small spoon[13] | 3 | 2 | 4 | 4 | 3 | 4 | 367 | 140 | 4 | | 1½ | 98 828 | 4 961 | 2 | 608 | 1 |
| 4161 Scraper[13] | 4 | 4 | 4 | 4 | 3 | 4 | 367 | 144 | 4 | | | 119 765 | 26 666 | 3 | – | – |
| 4159 Jug | 2 | 4 | 4 | 4 | 3 | 3 | 143 | 72 | 7 | 9(4) | 1½ | 54 022 | 4 764 | 4 | – | – |
| 4219 Cutter[14] | 2 | 8 | 4 | 4 | 3 | 3 | 90 | 47 | 5 | 4(2) | 1½ | 162 492 | 188 261 | 4 | – | – |
| 8424 Mould[14] | 2 | 8 | 4 | 4 | 2 | 3 | 108 | 26 | 6 | 5(2) | 1½ | 122 472 | 95 994 | 4 | – | – |
| 4213 Holder | 2 | 1 | 4 | 6 | 5 | 3 | 142 | 36 | 6 | 4(1) | 1½ | 19 128 | 34 178 | 4 | – | – |
| *(F) General: Revised Product Concept* | | | | | | | | | | | | | | | | |
| 2849 Hanger | 3 | 12 | 6 | 3 | – | 5 | 183 | 50 | 9 | 11(3) | 2 | 540 615 | 58 333 | 6 | – | – |
| 6049 Bracelet | 2 | 4 | 6 | 2 | 22 | 4 | 74 | 74 | – | 2(1) | 1 | – | – | – | – | – |

*Notes*

1. In the case of several of these products there is more than one moulding involved (for example, a body and a lid); here the principal moulding (for example, the body) has been analysed as representative.
2. If a product involves only one moulding, but there are (say) two or four impressions on the relevant mould, this means that such moulds have been designed to make the product concerned in (say) multiples of two or four, each time the moulding cycle is completed (the exception to this is given in Note 11).
3. Number of components refers to the number of different components used in assembling a product. The components will usually be purchased, and typically are metal fittings and other non-plastic parts.
4. If no production runs in the last 12 months, the last order has been taken as average.
5. Average production run has been taken over the last 12 months (see above).
6. Hours to change a mould includes changing the mould, then the time taken to get the mould working to production and quality requirements, which is shown in brackets. For example, Tray 1132 2(1/2) means 2 hours to change the mould and get it working to production and quality requirements. Of this 2 hours, the adjustment process to get it working to production and quality requirements after the mould change takes 1/2 hour.
7. The colours in stock are not the same as those required for outstanding orders.
8. The colour range of these products was increased from 3 to 8 as part of extending the 'revised product concept' to products of the 'original concept'.
9. This product was in fact packed in assorted colours and held in finished stock as such.
10. The range of colours for this item was due to the fact that customers tended to prefer their own colour for reasons of brand image, recognition, and so on.
11. New product range (outstanding orders represent initial launch).
12. Both these products are on the same mould.
13. These three products are on the same mould.
14. Impressions are of different shapes: two sets of shapes × 4 impressions.
15. The products shown here are considered to be representative of both their own and the total product range.

# Exhibit 6 Cost details of representative products

## Product details | Cost details (pence per 12)[1]

| Range[2] | Item | Raw materials[3] | Labour Moulding[4] | Labour Assembly[4] | Packaging and components | Mould depreciation[5] | Overheads Moulding[6] | Overheads General[7] | Total |
|---|---|---|---|---|---|---|---|---|---|
| A | 2225 Bowl | 254 | 35 | – | 38 | 25 | 179 | 148 | 679 |
| A | 2687 Tidy | 409 | 56 | – | 78 | 40 | 303 | 242 | 1128 |
| A | 2366 Bin | 2103 | 142 | – | 272 | 160 | 787 | 957 | 4421 |
| A | 8282 Bowl | 44 | 6 | 8 | 11 | 4 | 32 | 25 | 130 |
| B | 6491 Cap | 9 | – | – | 1 | 1 | 15 | 8 | 34 |
| B | 8860 Tray | 1621 | 88 | – | 668 | 116 | 491 | 695 | 3679 |
| B | 8009 Case | 1093 | 73 | – | 515 | 83 | 406 | 496 | 2666 |
| C | 6246 No. 28 | 1799 | 110 | 103 | 435 | 280 | 609 | 839 | 4175 |
| C | 6846 Shelf | 457 | 79 | 106 | 764 | 108 | 438 | 324 | 2276 |
| D | 5426 Holder | 288 | 105 | 69 | 311 | 100 | 508 | 300 | 1681 |
| D | 5624 Holder | 163 | 92 | 88 | 272 | 77 | 440 | 232 | 1364 |
| D | 6420 Mirror | 1942 | 139 | 334 | 2469 | 317 | 773 | 951 | 6925 |
| D | 6428 Holder | 578 | 165 | 78 | 786 | 173 | 812 | 518 | 3110 |
| D | 6606 Beaker | 237 | 91 | 73 | 298 | 82 | 411 | 246 | 1438 |
| E | 8284 Large sieve | 250 | 48 | 49 | 409 | 20 | 112 | 61 | 949 |
| E | 8424 Mould | 21 | 6 | 10 | 17 | 6 | 29 | 19 | 108 |
| F | 2849 Hanger | 54 | 4 | 8 | 18 | 4 | 21 | 25 | 134 |

Notes

1. 'Pence' – one penny = one hundredth of a £.
2. The product range abbreviations A to F are detailed in Exhibit 5.
3. Raw material costs are normally adjusted twice a year.
4. Moulding and assembly labour costs are based on calculated standard times.
5. Mould depreciation is a fixed percentage of the first stage costs, which comprises raw materials, moulding overheads, mould depreciation and moulding labour.
6. Moulding overheads are based on the machine size cost below:

| Group | 1 | 2 | 3 | 4 |
|---|---|---|---|---|
| Moulding overhead allocation (£ p) | 19.48 | 22.95 | 24.60 | 24.60 |

If a product is to be moulded on a machine in Group 1, then the moulding overhead allocation will be based on £19.48, and so on. These allocations include indirect moulding labour, production staff, development, site, utilities, plant depreciation, blocks, dies and plant repairs.

7. General overheads are calculated as a fixed percentage of first stage cost.

**Exhibit 7**  Changes in components/packing, work-in-progress and finished-goods warehousing over the last seven years

| Warehousing | Current year minus: | Size (square feet) | Distance (miles) | Total (square feet) |
|---|---|---|---|---|
| Components/packing | 7 | 5 000 | – | |
| | 4 | 5 000 | – | 10 000 |
| Work-in-progress | 7 | 9 000 | – | |
| | 3 | 9 000 | – | 18 000 |
| Finished goods | 7 | 27 000 | – | |
| | 6 | 10 000 | 20 | |
| | 4 | 40 000 | 1 | |
| | 3 | (10 000) | 20 | |
| | 1 | 20 000 | 3 | 87 000 |

Then, the marketing department often requires additional colours in order to increase sales in existing markets or break into new markets [an example of such a request is shown as Exhibit 8]. These short runs and special colours often have target dates which necessitate fitting them in at all stages of the process at the expense of normal production runs. It is difficult to balance these two sets of priorities.

# Marketing

The marketing department is split into product areas and subdivided into home and export. Each subdivision has a sales manager who reports to Mark Williams, the marketing director. Mark, who has been with the company for 12 months, confirmed that the change in product direction had enabled the company to compete successfully in a new sector of the market. 'Before I joined, the company had already achieved recognition as a front runner in this section, manufacturing high-quality, well-designed products. Frankly, this was one of the reasons I took the job.'

As Mark explained, the markets for the two products the company currently manufactured and sold were very different.

Sales of the old product are normally negotiated on a large-volume contract, with call-offs to meet the agreed customer deliveries. In the new markets, retail outlets hold our ranges, but the mix of products and colours means that we often need to be able to supply orders within a few days. While this is not always possible, we have a good repu-tation from our customers for the level of support we provide. For, as they emphasize, if the exact product wanted by their customers is not available at the required time, then often the sale is lost as they spend their money on something else altogether.

Mark explained that he had continued to push this policy and had been instru-mental in bringing out several new ranges since joining the company. The latest was

**Exhibit 8**    Production details for marketing samples in new colours

| Product | Colour requests (units) | | | | | Actual time taken per product (minutes)[1] | | Allowed moulding standard time per product (minutes)[1] |
| --- | --- | --- | --- | --- | --- | --- | --- | --- |
| | Beige | Brown | Blue | Green | Total | Moulding | Colour change[2] | |
| 4012 Dish | 24 | 42 | 24 | 42 | 132 | 405 | 65 | 156 |
| 4013 Holder | 20 | 42 | 24 | 42 | 128 | 550 | 100 | 152 |
| 4014 Beaker | 24 | 42 | 24 | 42 | 132 | 480 | 60 | 111 |
| 4018 Holder | 24 | 42 | 24 | 42 | 132 | 260 | 60 | 129 |
| 4019 Holder | 24 | 42 | 24 | 42 | 132 | 670 | 110 | 132 |
| 4020 Sticks | 40 | 42 | 30 | 42 | 154 | 270 | 60 | 137 |
| 4021 Ring | 60 | 60 | 36 | 36 | 192 | 390 | 95 | 200 |
| 4023 Rack | 20 | 36 | 20 | 24 | 100 | 1140 | 220 | 175 |
| 4028 Rail | 24 | 42 | 24 | 42 | 132 | 445 | 60 | 139 |
| 4029 Frame | 24 | 42 | 26 | 42 | 134 | 530 | 120 | 137 |
| Total | 284 | 432 | 256 | 396 | 1368 | 5120 | 950 | 1468 |

*Notes*

**1**. 'Actual time taken per product' is the number of standard minutes taken to mould the quantity of the product. 'Allowed moulding time per product' is the number of standard minutes calculated to mould the quantity of the product.

**2**. Colour change time is the total time taken to change from one colour to another in this production run. It is in addition to the actual moulding time given here.

due to be launched quite soon, with another due out early this year. 'This redirection has also had a few spin-offs in the older homeware range, where we have redesigned some packaging and increased and improved the colour range.'

# Corporate Policy

'We have come a long way since those days of change', said Graham Brown, managing director.

My predecessor had the foresight to rethink corporate policy when the group restructuring created the substantial excess moulding capacity. For the past two years, I have reinforced this sound strategy. The marked increase in sales is anticipated to continue, and home and export sales support this forecast. The lower-volume products have allowed us to gradually decrease our overall moulding capacity. It is now important that we use this capacity efficiently and, in making the budgets for the coming year, we have taken account of the anticipated non-productive demands on the manufacturing facilities. But although these new product launches make large demands on the system, they are our future life blood. We must keep costs down, and so look at all areas of costs. Our decision to go towards multi-impression moulds is one way of staying competitive [see Exhibit 9]. Our recent and future product ranges reflect this perspective.

**Exhibit 9**    Technical note

### Multi-impression moulds

An important design decision to be made concerns the number of impressions to be built into a mould. A single impression would mean that with every shot only one moulding is produced. With multi-impression moulding, then two or more products (depending upon the number of impressions) are made with every shot, thus giving a significant decrease in moulding time to complete an order quantity. This could be a lid or base of the same product, two lids and two bases of the same product, two or more identical products (such as trays), or two or more products that are not identical (such as a set of spoons to be sold as a set), or two or more different products to be sold as different products in the marketplace.

- Normally the number of impressions are even-numbered to retain balance in the mould.
- The capital cost of a two-impression mould is more than twice the cost of a single-impression mould of the same item due to the increased complexity of the mould design.
- The more impressions per mould then the larger the mould size (that is, physical dimensions) and the longer it takes to set up and colour change.

### Moulding machine

With wear and tear over time, moulding machines increasingly find it more difficult to achieve the upper limits of their specification. One common problem is that when the raw material is injected into the mould under pressure, then the machine is less and less able to exert the locking pressure necessary to keep the two halves of a mould together. If it does not, then flashing will become apparent. If flashing does appear, with a low-quality item it can be trimmed off, with a high-quality item, this would normally make it a reject.

### Moulding

A mould can go onto any machine, providing that the machine is physically large enough to take the physical dimensions of the mould, has the shot weight to fill the mould and hence produce a complete moulding and has the locking pressure to keep the two halves of the mould closed during the machining cycle.

Hence the division of moulding machines into four groups reflects the fact that machines are in a range of 'sizes' (that is, physical dimensions, such as the opening to take the mould, shot weight and locking pressure). Moulds, therefore, are loaded according to the appropriate machine size. There is little opportunity to sensibly transfer one mould to another machine group.

Finally, the size of a mould is primarily a factor of the dimensional size of the product (that is, height and diameter). Similarly, the moulding cycle time (how long it takes a machine to inject material into the cavity of the mould) is a factor of product size, the wall thickness of a product and, to a much lesser extent, the condition of the machine (that is, the effects of wear and tear).

## Note

1. Cycle time is the length of time it takes for the machine to close the mould, inject the material, initial cooling, open the mould and present the moulded part for the operator to remove from the mould. In many instances, a mould is so designed as to complete this last operation on a part or wholly automatic basis.

# Jackson Precision Castings

The revised incentive scheme proposal together with the continuous improvement programmge you launched recently seem key initiatives in your efforts to continue the sales growth and improved profit performance detailed in this year's budgets. As you have explained, both initiatives will improve your internal capability to support the business's key markets. As your analysis shows, the potential sales revenue growth is there. You have highlighted the opportunity, now you need to develop the capability to exploit it.

Matt Boyd, the Group CEO of Jackson Engineering (JE), was reviewing a proposal from Jackson Precision Castings (JPC), one of the businesses which reported to him, and he looked pleased.

The remarks followed an initial decision on the proposals outlining the reasons for introducing the recent continuous improvement programme (CIP) and a revised incentive scheme proposal. The others involved were Paul Farmer (CEO of JPC), Dave Jenkins (V-P Manufacturing, JPC) and Michael Jacques, a senior partner from an international consultancy company that had been advising parts of JE over the last eighteen months. The two intitiatives which had met with such solid approval had been put forward by Paul Farmer and concerned JPC, the business for which he had responsibility. They were based on recommendations from the consultants.

'Yes', concluded Matt Boyd, 'these proposals have my full support. Let's get on with it, Paul.'

As the meeting finished and Paul, Dave and Michael made for the door, Matt called out 'And Paul, I am expecting to see the signs of an upturn in sales and profits. Soon!'

## Background

JE is a long-established, UK-based company. After growing in a haphazard fashion over many years to an annual sales revenue of some £150m, it was acquired by a US-based industrial conglomerate, AK Industrials (AKI). Over the last five to six years, AKI had been expanding its European operations particularly in the industrial sector and JE fitted well into AKI's portfolio which included automotive, precision and general engineering, injection and rubber mouldings and other general industrial companies. Matt Boyd was brought in as CEO to improve the overall profitability of the three companies within JE. One of his first actions was to decentralize the company into three autonomous businesses. There are now two larger units, each with annual sales of a little over £30m and JPC with a sales revenue of £19.8m.

The market for die castings has contracted in the UK and the rest of Europe in recent years, resulting in the closure of many small companies. Although JPC had improved its market share it still experienced reducing sales revenues over the last five years. Tight control on internal costs has kept JPC profitable, in fact above not only JE's but also AKI's corporate average. Importantly, JPC also generates a positive cash flow even though over a period of years there has been regular investment to update plant and equipment. Certainly before the change in ownership obtaining investment had not been a problem given JPC's profit and cash flow performance.

Matt Boyd's second major initiative was to ask consultants to work with each business in JE and formulate plans to improve profitability. Last year's business plan from JPC had been rejected by Matt Boyd. The reasons he gave were the company's contracting market and uncertainty about future sales revenue. The consultants were then asked to get involved in JPC with a clear instruction from Matt Boyd to start with a review of the market.

The consultants spent several months of interviewing and analysis both inside the business and talking with major customers. The market review led to a proposed strategy for growing precision casting sales.

The review was followed by an assessment of internal issues. The consultants concluded that workforce involvement had to be improved as a major factor in the overall success of the unit. They suggested the introduction of a continuous improvement programme (CIP). This was launched six weeks ago after providing relevant training for those involved. While carrying out their initial analysis the consultants examined the existing incentive scheme and concluded that it needed a major overhaul. During the period since it was introduced, the scheme had become 'loose'.[1] Paul Farmer, while agreeing with the conclusions about the current incentive scheme, felt strongly that a good, well-directed incentive scheme was an important element in achieving the projected sales and profit growth goals set within JPC's business plans.

## Market Review

The market review was organized and managed by the consultants. Michael Jacques kept an eye on the work and attended the internal meetings to discuss progress but a specialist marketing consultant, Jonathan Clarke, was brought in to work on the day-to-day analysis.

The consultants suggested visiting major customers to understand what they wanted from suppliers like JPC. The selection of customers was made by Paul Farmer to match the guidelines drawn up by the consultants. The guidelines suggested visiting enough large customers to cover over half the business's current sales revenue. Four important UK customers were selected and an export customer in France. These five companies accounted for 56 per cent of the current sales revenue. The remaining 44 per cent came from over 70 customers which were usually small companies. The chosen customers were then visited by Jim Wilson (V-P Marketing, JPC) and Jonathan Clarke.

Where possible, the team spoke with the top executives of each customer and the interviews lasted between two and four hours, depending on the availability of those involved.

The stated objectives of these visits were to:

- determine how well JPC was performing
- understand the customers' own plans for growth
- establish the basis on which customers placed their casting business, either with JPC or competitors.

Prior to the visits the consultants drew up a list of questions and this was used as a script for the interview. Exhibit 1 shows the customers, their spend on castings, the expected growth or decline in spend and the share of the current spend placed with JPC.

The main conclusions drawn from the market review were:

- as capacity for die casting had reduced throughout Europe and was now more in line with demand, the market had become less price sensitive

**Exhibit 1**     Market review – size of customer die casting spend and current JPC share

| Customer | Customer | | JPC | | |
|---|---|---|---|---|---|
| | annual die casting spend (£m) | expected growth or decline of die casting spend | current share of annual customer spend | | share of own current sales (%) |
| | | | £m | % | |
| Wilson Automotive Components | 16.6 | slow growth[1] | 3.0 | 18 | 15 |
| Gagnard Freres | 3.8 | static | 1.1 | 26 | 6 |
| Gordon Stoves | 4.2 | steady decline | 2.4 | 57 | 12 |
| Hardy-Belmont Engineering — standard / special products | 6.4 | slow decline / erratic growth | 1.4 | 22 | 7 |
| Anscombe Products | 7.4 | slow decline | 3.2 | 43 | 16 |
| Total | 38.4 | – | 11.1 | 29 | 56 |

*Note*

1. However, the potential for a rapid increase in sales is available if current decisions on Wilson Automotive Components supplying European car plants are changed.

- JPC should aim to grow share in its well-established UK market
- the European foothold should be expanded. Target customers should be identified. As a start, companies that already transacted business with other parts of JE should be on the priority list.

In fact, the French company included in the market review had been introduced through an initiative from AK1 and in 12 months had become JPC's fifth largest (£s) customer.

In addition to recommendations on the future direction of the precision castings business, the output from the review included an assessment of the factors each customer considered important when selecting suppliers for die castings (see Exhibits 2 to 6).

On the basis of the market review a new business plan was constructed. This showed that the sales growth would come from increasing share with current, major UK customers and increasing sales in Europe. The plan also proposed the introduction of continuous improvement groups and a new incentive scheme within the early part of that year. The plan had been accepted.

**Exhibit 2**     Consultant's market review report – Wilson Automotive Components

---

**Background**

Wilson Automotive Components (WAC) was a small independent manufacturing company until four years ago when it was purchased by a large automotive components group. Through the parent company's involvement it has become a supplier to two major automotive vehicle manufacturers in the UK. It supplies two main product families, each with variants, to these customers in the form of assemblies. It also supplies a variety of smaller niche manufacturers involved in both automotive and industrial applications.

In addition to original equipment sales, WAC sells spares, both components and assemblies, through its original equipment customers and independent dealers.

JPC have supplied WAC for many years.

**Location**

The WAC factory is a 45-minute drive from the JPC plant.

**Growth**

The company is shedding some of its smaller customers in order to focus on the large-volume vehicle manufacturers. Growth is based on these customers and to date has been slow, in line with a sluggish automotive market. Currently, it only supplies the UK plants of its major customers. Any move to supply other European plants would lead to large volume increases. In recent months, this is now being actively considered.

**Requirements of suppliers**

The components purchased are high-precision parts.

1. Quality conformance

'Our automotive customers are teaching us about quality' was WAC's opening comment on quality conformance. Consequently, WAC now expect its suppliers to deliver defect-free parts. No internal inspection is carried out on parts from JPC prior to use. If problems are found with parts when they are used on assembly then JPC is charged the cost of the lost assembly time, which is much higher than the cost of the part supplied.

*(continued)*

---

**Exhibit 2**     Consultant's market review report – Wilson Automotive Components (cont'd)

WAC also carries out annual, on-site audits of the quality systems of all major suppliers, including JPC.

2. Delivery reliability and delivery speed

WAC places weekly schedules on major suppliers. The schedules for the main running original equipment parts give a fixed four-week lead time. It regards delivery reliabiliy for these parts as essential.

WAC is planning to move to JIT and is already reducing inventory levels. At the moment, buffer stock is held against suppliers' failure to deliver but within 12 months this will all be removed.

For spares orders, WAC is often in competition with other suppliers who make functional replacements for WAC products. Availability usually determines who gets the order. Therefore, WAC are looking a fast response from suppliers.

3. Price

All qualified suppliers have to quote against a selection of parts on an annual basis. Competitiveness on price affects share for the following year. Spare parts are rarely sourced from a company other than an established supplier.

**Exhibit 3**     Consultant's market review report – Hardy-Belmont Engineering

**Background**

Hardy-Belmont Engineering (HBE) manufactures two types of products. Its staple product has been a range of standard motors for industrial applications. More recently it has started supplying expensive, customized motors for a variety of companies involved in large projects. Many of the projects are in the Middle East. These customers typically develop the specifications for ancillary products such as motors late in a project and being able to meet the lead times required becomes an important factor in HBE's choice of suppliers.

HBE classifies its castings as standards or specials depending on which of the two types of products they are used for.

**Location**

The company is located near Glasgow, Scotland.

**Growth**

While sales of the HBE standard range of motors has been increasing steadily throughout Europe, the demand for castings has been reducing as castings have increasingly been substituted by other technologies. The special products have led the company into a new growth area and these products will certainly use castings for at least the next five years.

**Requirements of suppliers**

HBE has always tended to source from a group of four or five castings suppliers with a strong accent on price.

For its standard parts HBE places annual, indicative orders with call-offs on fortnightly schedules to a four-week lead time. Their project work is, however, much more unpredictable and an important factor in winning this business is the ability to meet shorter delivery times than competitors. Because the castings are product specific no inventory is held while delivery promises must be met. For each project so far, HBE has asked all its regular suppliers to quote but recently it declared its intention to work with only one, or possibly two, suppliers on project work in order to cut down the time involved.

So far, JPC has supplied about 30 per cent of the parts for special projects.

**Exhibit 4**     Consultant's market review report – Anscombe Products

**Background**
Anscombe Products (AP) is a small engineering company which is part of a larger group. AP makes assemblies used in medical equipment. All the products are supplied to other parts of the group.

**Location**
AP is located about two hours' drive from the JPC plant.

**Growth**
AP is growing but the spend on castings is declining due to design changes in the end product.

**Requirements of suppliers**
Although it is a small company, AP is very efficient in its manufacturing and planning activities. It has been progressively reducing inventories and lead times over the last two to three years.

AP also has a supplier reduction programme and sets its suppliers annual targets to reduce lead times and improve delivery reliability performance. Deliveries have to be made within nominated periods on the required day.

AP is not particularly price sensitive.

**Exhibit 5**     Consultant's market review report – Gagnard Freres

**Background**
Gagnard Freres (GF) is a privately owned group. It has done business for many years with a machining company in France which is owned by AKI. The machining company was drilling and grinding castings purchased in France by GF and suggested getting quotations from JPC. This led to GF placing orders with JPC initially for one simple, high-volume part. This has now built up to three parts which make up over a quarter of GF's spend on castings. All the parts are of low complexity and involve product specifications that are not difficult to meet.

GF makes standard products for industrial applications. The demand for its products is uneven but it prefers to order from JPC in large quantities to minimise transport costs.

**Location**
GF is based in Lyon, France.

**Growth**
The market for the company's products is static.

**Requirements of suppliers**
Because the parts are so straightforward, quality conformance has not been an issue.

For GF, to source parts outside France was an important departure from its previous policy. It appears to be pleased with the results and stated that it was getting good, delivery on-time service from the UK and if this continued to be the case it would be prepared to switch more high-volume parts to JPC. However, given the variable element in its own demand, GF needs to be confident of having short response time support especially where suppliers are not close at hand.

GF seem to be happy with the prices it is paying.

**Exhibit 6**      Consultant's market review report – Gordon Stoves

---

**Background**

Gordon Stoves (GS) is one of JPC's oldest customers. It manufactures gas cookers for domestic use. Over the years it has seen its market share decline in the UK, which is its only market.

There is a lot of variety in its products and some order quantities are small.

**Location**

GS is situated approximately three hours' driving time from the JPC plant.

**Growth**

Due to a major reorganization of distribution channels, over which GS has no control, there is a lot of uncertainty about its future prospects. Over the last five years GS sales have dropped by a third.

**Requirements of suppliers**

The components purchased are a mix of simple and complex parts but with fairly straightforward tolerances. GS is very insistent that its parts must be delivered to specification and in a clean condition.

The issue of price is usually raised at an annual negotiation. Purchasing is not a strong department in GS and price pressure has never been high. Because of high product variety GS has always held large finished-goods inventory. However, financial pressures are leading GS to reduce working capital (including inventory) and it has notified major suppliers that, in future, it wants them to operate to much shorter lead times.

---

# Manufacturing

JPC makes zinc and aluminium die castings and aluminium gravity die castings. Secondary operations after casting are carried out on some parts. In addition, other parts are sent out for painting before despatch to the customer. A brief explanation of die casting is provided in Exhibit 7.

The basic layout of the factory is by groups of similar machines. The die casting equipment is generally modern reflecting the history of regular investment. Some of the machines for the secondary operations are many years old but well maintained. There is also a small toolroom that carries out basic tool maintenance. All tools are inspected after running a part and before being stored. New tools are sub-contracted using two external local suppliers who have invested heavily in modern tool-making equipment. Frequent checks are made on alternative tool markets in Europe and elsewhere in the world. To date, the local suppliers have proved very competitive on price and particularly in terms of offering short lead times.

The factory is tidy and the machines are well maintained and kept clean. Breakdowns are few and quality conformance issues with customers are infrequent. The die casting machines are normally manned for a double day shift with a much smaller night shift operating a limited number of machines. The secondary operation machines and the toolroom are manned on a single day shift basis.

The load on manufacturing fluctuates considerably. The work content of different orders varies significantly and smaller customers tend to be erratic in their require-

**Exhibit 7**    Brief explanation of die casting

Die casting is a process in which molten metal is forced by pressure into a metal mould known as a die. Because the metal solidifies under pressure, the casting conforms to the die cavity in both shape and surface finish.

The size is so accurately controlled that little or no subsequent machining is necessary. This is particularly so when zinc alloys are used. The process also eliminates such machining operations as drilling and certain types of threading.

One of the limitations of die casting is the high cost of the equipment and dies. This is not an important factor in high-volume production applications but it does limit its use in short-run jobs.

For large or complex mouldings, a single-cavity mould is used. If the quantity of castings to be produced is large and they are relatively small in size, a multiple-cavity die can then be used.

ments making forward planning difficult. Many parts can only be made to order because of the irregularity of demand. George Farmer's intention is to hold finished-goods inventory of more regular components for larger customers but to date this has happened only to a very limited extent because of problems of keeping up with overall demand. One of the next stages of the consultant's involvement is to assess inventory policy and opportunities for reducing work-in-progress. An initial analysis of customers' orders has started and a representative sample of orders for the customers interviewed in the market review is shown in Exhibits 8 and 9.

# Continuous Improvement Programme

In the early part of the continuous improvement programme (CIP), four key areas to review were agreed. These, together with other details of the activities so far, are explained in the following sections with details given in Exhibit 10.

## Manufacturing Methods Continuous Improvement Team

The objective agreed for this team was to seek opportunities for improving manufacturing methods particularly in the die casting areas. Details of the initial meetings and agreed actions are given in Exhibit 10.

## Systems Continuous Improvement Team

The objectives agreed for this team were to ensure that the company has appropriate systems in place, particularly in the areas of estimating, costing and sales documentation. Also, to evaluate the current production scheduling and control systems and to identify a future outline plan of action to implement any agreed improvements. Details of the initial meetings are given in Exhibit 10.

**Exhibit 8**     Representative sample of customer orders

| Customer | Customer order details | | | Order contribution (£s) | Date order received | | Delivery promised to customer | |
|---|---|---|---|---|---|---|---|---|
| | order number | part number | order value (£s) | | week | day | week | day |
| Gordon Stoves | 2568 | 2445A | 650 | 156 | 10 | 5 | 12 | 5 |
| | | 2445B | 750 | 195 | 10 | 5 | 19 | 3 |
| | | 7643 | 1840 | 644 | 10 | 5 | 13 | 5 |
| | | 7643C | 140 | 57 | 10 | 5 | 16 | 5 |
| | | 8904 | 800 | 224 | 10 | 5 | 20 | 5 |
| | 2889 | 2445A | 650 | 156 | 11 | 4 | 14 | 4 |
| | | 7643 | 1200 | 420 | 11 | 4 | 15 | 2 |
| | | 7643C | 90 | 37 | 11 | 4 | 17 | 4 |
| | | 9456 | 280 | 90 | 11 | 4 | 15 | 4 |
| | 4675 | 2445A | 600 | 144 | 12 | 5 | 16 | 5 |
| | | 2445B | 400 | 104 | 12 | 5 | 16 | 5 |
| | | 7643 | 880 | 308 | 12 | 5 | 16 | 2 |
| | | 7643C | 120 | 49 | 12 | 5 | 18 | 5 |
| Gagnard Freres | 1224 | 6748 | 2600 | 832 | 10 | 4 | 16 | 5 |
| | | 6749 | 2800 | 784 | 10 | 4 | 16 | 5 |
| | | 6750 | 1250 | 425 | 10 | 4 | 16 | 5 |
| | 1225 | 6748 | 2900 | 928 | 14 | 2 | 19 | 2 |
| | | 6749 | 2800 | 784 | 14 | 2 | 19 | 2 |
| | | 6750 | 1150 | 391 | 14 | 2 | 19 | 2 |
| | 1226 | 6748 | 3100 | 992 | 16 | 1 | 23 | 1 |
| | | 6749 | 2800 | 784 | 16 | 1 | 23 | 1 |
| | | 6750 | 1200 | 408 | 16 | 1 | 23 | 1 |
| | 1227 | 6748 | 3100 | 992 | 16 | 1 | 28 | 3 |
| | | 6749 | 2800 | 784 | 22 | 1 | 28 | 3 |
| | 1228 | 6748 | 2600 | 832 | 26 | 1 | 32 | 1 |
| | | 6749 | 2400 | 672 | 26 | 1 | 32 | 1 |
| | | 6750 | 1400 | 476 | 26 | 1 | 32 | 1 |
| Anscombe Products | 25013 | 12445 | 650 | 156 | 14 | 1 | 16 | 1 |
| | | 17643 | 80 | 33 | 14 | 1 | 20 | 1 |
| | | 18904 | 700 | 196 | 14 | 1 | 24 | 1 |
| | | 1945 | 360 | 115 | 14 | 1 | 17 | 1 |
| | | 1988 | 630 | 170 | 14 | 1 | 20 | 1 |
| | 25089 | 12445 | 650 | 156 | 14 | 5 | 18 | 2 |
| | | 12460 | 850 | 221 | 14 | 5 | 18 | 5 |
| | | 17645 | 1320 | 462 | 14 | 5 | 18 | 5 |
| | | 1945 | 620 | 198 | 14 | 5 | 19 | 5 |
| | | 1988 | 240 | 65 | 14 | 5 | 20 | 5 |
| | | 19885 | 150 | 54 | 14 | 5 | 20 | 5 |

**Exhibit 8**     Representative sample of customer orders (cont'd)

| Customer | Customer order details | | | Order contribution (£s) | Date order received | | Delivery promised to customer | |
|---|---|---|---|---|---|---|---|---|
| | order number | part number | order value (£s) | | week | day | week | day |
| Wilson Automotive Components | 3674 | 264405 | 6840 | 1231 | 10 | 2 | 13 | 4 |
| | | 288114 | 4860 | 778 | 10 | 2 | 13 | 4 |
| | 7610 | 11702 | 280 | 129 | 10 | 2 | 11 | 1 |
| | | 11468 | 258 | 103 | 10 | 2 | 13 | 1 |
| | | 21744 | 85 | 45 | 10 | 2 | 12 | 1 |
| | 3744 | 264405 | 6250 | 1125 | 11 | 2 | 14 | 4 |
| | | 288114 | 4380 | 701 | 11 | 2 | 14 | 4 |
| | 7643 | 11949 | 285 | 134 | 11 | 2 | 12 | 3 |
| | 3821 | 264405 | 8600 | 1548 | 12 | 2 | 15 | 4 |
| | | 288114 | 4630 | 741 | 12 | 2 | 15 | 4 |
| | 7689 | 11702 | 485 | 223 | 12 | 2 | 14 | 2 |
| | | 11468 | 35 | 14 | 12 | 2 | 13 | 1 |
| | 3927 | 264405 | 8400 | 1512 | 13 | 2 | 16 | 4 |
| | | 288114 | 4820 | 771 | 13 | 2 | 16 | 4 |
| | 7705 | 11702 | 470 | 216 | 13 | 2 | 14 | 3 |
| Hardy-Belmont Engineering | 2300 | 76609 | 800 | 120 | 10 | 1 | 14 | 1 |
| | | 76682 | 300 | 66 | 10 | 1 | 14 | 1 |
| | | 76698 | 400 | 72 | 10 | 1 | 14 | 1 |
| | | X4220 | 2500 | 750 | 10 | 1 | 13 | 4 |
| | 2400 | 76609 | 800 | 120 | 12 | 2 | 16 | 2 |
| | | 76682 | 300 | 66 | 12 | 2 | 16 | 2 |
| | | 76698 | 600 | 108 | 12 | 2 | 16 | 2 |
| | 2500 | 76609 | 800 | 120 | 14 | 1 | 18 | 1 |
| | | 76682 | 200 | 44 | 14 | 1 | 18 | 1 |
| | | 76698 | 400 | 72 | 14 | 1 | 18 | 1 |
| | 2600 | 76609 | 600 | 90 | 16 | 1 | 20 | 1 |
| | | 76682 | 600 | 132 | 16 | 1 | 20 | 1 |
| | | 76698 | 600 | 108 | 16 | 1 | 20 | 1 |
| | | X4220 | 3400 | 1088 | 16 | 1 | 19 | 1 |

*Notes*

1. The period for the sample varies by customer and not all orders for the period are shown. The orders are typical for each customer.
2. The total order value by customer will not necessarily reflect the annual split by customer or the total annual revenue.
3. For Warner Automotive Components six digit part numbers are original equipment, five digit part numbers are spares.
4. Hardy-Belmont Engineering components for special products have an X prefix on the part number.
5. The order contribution was calculated by the consultants as order value minus manufacturing cost. Manufacturing cost includes direct material, direct labour and an allocation of indirect costs such as supervision, maintenance, depreciation, rent and rates.

**Exhibit 9**    Representative sample of customer orders

| Customer | Customer order details | | Customer required delivery | | Actual delivery to customer | |
|---|---|---|---|---|---|---|
| | order number | part number | week | day | week | day |
| Gordon Stoves | 2568 | 2445A | 12 | 5 | 13 | 2 |
| | | 2445B | 14 | 5 | 19 | 5 |
| | | 7643 | 13 | 5 | 14 | 5 |
| | | 7643C | 16 | 5 | 17 | 3 |
| | | 8904 | 18 | 5 | 22 | 4 |
| | 2889 | 2445A | 14 | 4 | 14 | 4 |
| | | 7643 | 14 | 4 | 16 | 1 |
| | | 7643C | 17 | 4 | 18 | 2 |
| | | 9456 | 15 | 4 | 15 | 4 |
| | 4675 | 2445A | 15 | 3 | 17 | 2 |
| | | 2445B | 15 | 5 | 17 | 1 |
| | | 7643 | 16 | 2 | 16 | 2 |
| | | 7643C | 17 | 5 | 19 | 2 |
| Gagnard Freres | 1224 | 6748 | 16 | 5 | 16 | 5 |
| | | 6749 | 16 | 5 | 16 | 5 |
| | | 6750 | 16 | 5 | 16 | 5 |
| | 1225 | 6748 | 19 | 2 | 19 | 2 |
| | | 6749 | 19 | 2 | 19 | 2 |
| | | 6750 | 19 | 2 | 19 | 2 |
| | 1226 | 6748 | 23 | 1 | 23 | 1 |
| | | 6749 | 23 | 1 | 23 | 1 |
| | | 6750 | 23 | 1 | 23 | 1 |
| | 1227 | 6748 | 27 | 1 | 28 | 3 |
| | | 6749 | 27 | 1 | 28 | 3 |
| | 1228 | 6748 | 32 | 1 | 32 | 2 |
| | | 6749 | 32 | 1 | 32 | 2 |
| | | 6750 | 32 | 1 | 32 | 2 |
| Anscombe Products | 25013 | 12445 | 16 | 1 | 16 | 3 |
| | | 17643 | 19 | 1 | 20 | 1 |
| | | 18904 | 23 | 1 | 28 | 1 |
| | | 1945 | 16 | 1 | 16 | 4 |
| | | 1988 | 19 | 1 | 20 | 1 |
| | 25089 | 12445 | 17 | 5 | 18 | 1 |
| | | 12460 | 16 | 5 | 20 | 2 |
| | | 17645 | 18 | 5 | 19 | 2 |
| | | 1945 | 19 | 5 | 20 | 4 |
| | | 1988 | 20 | 5 | 22 | 3 |
| | | 19885 | 20 | 5 | 23 | 2 |

**Exhibit 9**  Representative sample of customer orders (cont'd)

| Customer | Customer order details | | Customer required delivery | | Actual delivery to customer | |
|---|---|---|---|---|---|---|
| | order number | part number | week | day | week | day |
| Wilson Automotive Components | 3674 | 264405 | 13 | 4 | 15 | 1 |
| | | 288114 | 13 | 4 | 14 | 5 |
| | 7610 | 11702 | 11 | 1 | 11 | 1 |
| | | 11468 | 11 | 4 | 18 | 4 |
| | | 21744 | 11 | 3 | 16 | 3 |
| | 3744 | 264405 | 14 | 4 | 15 | 5 |
| | | 288114 | 14 | 4 | 15 | 5 |
| | 7643 | 11949 | 12 | 3 | 12 | 3 |
| | 3821 | 264405 | 15 | 4 | 16 | 4 |
| | | 288114 | 15 | 4 | 16 | 5 |
| | 7689 | 11702 | 13 | 4 | 16 | 3 |
| | | 11468 | 12 | 5 | 13 | 5 |
| | 3927 | 264405 | 16 | 4 | 17 | 5 |
| | | 288114 | 16 | 4 | 17 | 4 |
| | 7705 | 11702 | 14 | 3 | 15 | 3 |
| Hardy-Belmont Engineering | 2300 | 76609 | 14 | 1 | 14 | 3 |
| | | 76682 | 14 | 1 | 14 | 3 |
| | | 76698 | 14 | 1 | 14 | 1 |
| | | X4220 | 12 | 5 | 14 | 4 |
| | 2400 | 76609 | 16 | 2 | 16 | 4 |
| | | 76682 | 16 | 2 | 16 | 1 |
| | | 76698 | 16 | 2 | 16 | 1 |
| | 2500 | 76609 | 18 | 1 | 18 | 1 |
| | | 76682 | 18 | 1 | 18 | 1 |
| | | 76698 | 18 | 1 | 19 | 2 |
| | 2600 | 76609 | 20 | 1 | 20 | 4 |
| | | 76682 | 20 | 1 | 19 | 5 |
| | | 76698 | 20 | 1 | 20 | 4 |
| | | X4220 | 19 | 1 | 19 | 5 |

*Note*
1. The orders are a representative sample of JPC's performance on delivery.

**Exhibit 10**    Details of the four teams' activities in the continuous improvement programme – initial meetings, tasks identified and actions to be taken

---

**A. Manufacturing methods continuous improvement team**

The following tasks were identified at the team's initial meetings and are numbered sequentially.

1. Introduce a rotary table for post-casting operations for high-volume jobs in order to reduce handling and associated labour costs.

2. Identify any excessive operations on existing methods in all stages of casting and secondary operations.

3. Check if untrimmed castings can go directly to the deburring and polishing area thus eliminating the cast trimming operation currently undertaken.

4. Install a drill and tap slide for high-volume work to reduce handling operations at the casting stage.

5. Establish three designated storage areas for pallets to reduce time looking for pallets by machine operators.

6. Check current cycle time on the ten highest-volume jobs loaded each week. Establish lowest times and update all records including the cost information sheets.

7. Assess reasons for casting flash. Draw up a programme of mould refurbishment to reduce post-casting operations and associated tasks.

8. Reduce energy costs in the foundry:
   - replace lids on the aluminium holding furnaces
   - pre-heat dies.

**B. Systems continuous improvement team**

1. Verify existing roles and responsibilities in the manufacturing planning and control system.

2. Review the foundry and machine shop loading system.

3. Introduce shopfloor visual loading charts for each section.

4. Review machine capabilities in the die casting areas.

5. Improve shopfloor documentation.

6. Review the current estimating system:
   - responsibilities
   - synthetic data used
   - pricing arrangements

7. Detail the current sales entry and production control procedures to reduce the steps involved and associated costs.

**C. Set-up reduction continuous improvement team**

1. Reduce set-up times on zinc and aluminium die casting machines:
   - agree priority machines and dies
   - analyse using video recordings

2. Assess availability of tools necessary for completing set-ups and consider a machine-specific tool set throughout the die casting areas.

3. Overview oil and water hose couplings as an immediate general step. Consult with coupling suppliers.

**Exhibit 10**    Details of the four teams' activities in the continuous improvement programme (cont'd)

> 4. Check lubrication arrangements for all die casting areas as a general step.
> 5. Review pre-heating arrangements on break times and times between shifts.
> 6. Review pre-heating die arrangements on change-overs.
>
> **D. Quality continuous improvement team**
> 1. Identify top five products with highest reject rates. Investigate extent and cause of rejects.
> 2. Give additional training to setters and operators on product specifications and quality conformance.
> 3. Review all rejects at the final view stage of the process. Identify cause of rejects and report back on bi-weekly basis.
> 4. Review all rejects by customers. Identify cause of rejects and report back on a bi-weekly basis.
> 5. Check each operator's ability to undertake the necessary quality conformance checks. Agree and implement a training programme to bring all operators to required levels.
> 6. Identify areas for cost-effective, corrective action to reduce rejects.

# Set-up Reduction Continuous Improvement Team

The objective of this team was to reduce the time taken to make ready and set up (change-over) the die casting machines. Details of the initial meetings are given in Exhibit 10.

# Quality Continuous Improvement Team

The objective of this team was to promote and engender a 'quality-right-first-time' culture throughout the company. Details of the initial meetings are given in Exhibit 10. Dave Jenkins (V-P Manufacturing) summed up the progress so far:

> The introduction of the continuous improvement programme has been an excellent way of formalizing employee contributions to improving key areas of the firm. Although improvement has always been a major facet of our overall activity in manufacturing, the programme has sharpened our orientation, highlighted the contributions of those involved within the organization as a whole, placed the activity within a corporate context and given a general boost to manufacturing in general and this part of our activity in particular. It's going well. The results to date have been encouraging and, as I agreed with Paul, manufacturing's role in supporting the corporate strategy of JPC has always been recognized and this continuous improvement programme will be one key element in delivering the necessary results.

# The Incentive Pay Scheme

The basis of the current incentive scheme was a measurement of standard hours produced against actual hours worked for each employee. The standard hours were based upon an agreed time for each operation completed (for example, casting) and each employee was paid an individual bonus. When the consultants examined the agreed standard times in use, they found that many had:

- not been checked for changes in work content due, for example, to alterations in methods in the last two years
- been negotiated between supervisor and the operators and the estimated times agreed had not subsequently been checked and an agreed standard time introduced.

The consultants undertook an exercise which timed a sample of jobs. This showed that many agreed times fell outside any logical pattern. It was also found that times were adjusted on occasions depending on the employee carrying out the work in order to reflect some sort of 'experience' factor and maintain pay differentials.

It was concluded that the current scheme was no longer providing a consistent incentive in terms of reflecting different levels of effort and rewarding the productivity associated with each operator's performance.

An analysis of two years' history of output was gathered by the consultants to test how the level of bonus payments varied depending on the principles of alternative schemes before a new scheme was devised. The new scheme also proposes payment based on standard hours produced compared to actual hours worked but the scheme differs from the old one in a number of important respects.

First, the scheme is a group scheme. All employees in production and associated services are paid a standard group bonus. To do this the existing scheme will have to be 'bought out'. Part of the current pay differentials between employees associated with the existing scheme are to be incorporated into their basic pay. The cost of this will be a substantial, one-off cost to the business.

Second, the standard hours achieved are calculated by a formula which allocates time based on total output. Initially the formula suggested a link with the number of components sold. However, when the formula was applied to the past two years' history of output, it was obvious that, because the parts vary in size and complexity, the number of parts produced in different periods varied substantially. This led to large fluctuations in bonus payments when the principle of number of components sold was applied to past output levels. The formula was then revised to calculate the standard hours produced on the basis of a combination of the number and weight of parts produced. The output is converted into an index figure which determines the level of bonus. The basis of the calculation is shown in Exhibit 11. To further smooth out fluctuations, the scheme would make bonus payments based on the average of the actual output achieved for the two preceding months.

The scheme is linear with a cut-off point. The bonus rises exactly in line with the increase in the index. When the bonus hits 28 per cent of basic pay, any further

**Exhibit 11**     The incentive scheme proposal

> 1. The scheme is a group incentive scheme covering all shopfloor employees. The scheme calculates a single performance figure and pays a uniform rate of bonus to each participant.
> 2. Performance is calculated for each calendar month by comparing the allowed hours for the total number and weight of castings recorded on the sales report with the total number of clocked hours for that month.
> 3. The allowed hours total is calculated by multiplying the volume figures by the standard allowed times as follows:
>    - 0.85 allowed standard minutes for each casting
>    - 4.65 allowed standard minutes for each kilogram of castings.
> 4. The performance level is the total number of allowed hours as a percentage of the total number of clocked hours. This scheme starts to pay a bonus at a performance level of 70.[2] The bonus rises linearly with increases in the index.
> 5. To smooth out large fluctuations, performance will be calculated on a two-month, rolling average basis.
> 6. The scheme will be capped when the bonus is equal to 28 per cent of average pay for the group.

increase in the index is not rewarded. Part of the agreement with employees is to review the formula every three months.

Finally, to encourage what Paul Farmer calls 'a quality mentality', the number and weight of parts returned from customers each month are deducted from the output achieved. To emphasize the importance of quality, the return figures are multiplied by a factor of two before being deducted from the 'output achieved' in the period under review.

During the development of the scheme a series of discussions with employee representatives was held. Their support was obtained to run the scheme on a trial basis for two months in parallel with the old scheme. This is planned to take place after approval of the scheme by the Group CEO.

## Notes

1. The phrase 'loose' implies that the values and measures against which performance is evaluated had not been updated as changes occurred. The result is that individual performance targets are no longer consistent with each other and that achievement and reward are no longer linked. The outcome is anomalies within the scheme and unfairness in the payments made.
2. Work ratings and performance levels are based on the 0–100 British Standard Institute (BSI) scale.

# case

# 6

# Klein Products

'Well, Alan, I think congratulations are in order', were Paul Sharman's opening comments. 'It looks as though we have a commercially viable product, now that it has come through the final phase of technical testing. The market is receptive, and two of our major customers are demanding supplies as soon as possible. The prospects look good.' Paul Sharman, managing director of Klein Products (KP), was responding to the report given by the technical director, Alan Gibson, on a plastic replacement for a major metal packaging product. 'It not only fits the relatively high technical profile of our business', he continued, 'but also presents the chance of multiplying, by a quantum leap compared to other products, the enormous commercial opportunity of exploiting technical advantage with high volumes. It comprises a large market, much greater than any of our current segments.'

## Background

KP is part of Toucon Industries, a large, diverse group of companies based in the USA, but with worldwide interests and sales in excess of $20bn. Toucon's industrial holdings include electronics, furniture, office and telecommunications equipment, food products and packaging products, in which Klein is one of several companies within the group. In addition, it has recently expanded its interests in the finance and insurance business, particularly in North America, to the extent that the non-industrials accounted for some 20 per cent of total sales revenue.

KP was purchased by Toucon Industries in the late 1980s as part of a group of companies whose principal activities were in food-related products. In group terms, KP is relatively small. However, its profit performance and ROI record in the last five years were both above the group average and the norms for the industry in which it operates. While many of its competitors are much larger, KP, with the financial backing of Toucon, is not disadvantaged in terms of investment support to help exploit viable commercial opportunities of a long- and short-term nature. Furthermore, KP's customer base has been gradually moving more and more towards large customers (with corresponding larger volumes), a fact no doubt helped by the Toucon image.

This case study was written by Terry Hill (University of Oxford) and S. H. Chambers (University of Warwick). It is intended for class discussion and not as an example of good or bad management. © AMD Publishing.

# Marketing

Currently, KP mainly sells customized packaging. In this instance, potential customers determine, often with a supplier's help, the size, shape and colour of the container they require, and the print design where applicable. With few exceptions, each product comprises a single specification in terms of the orders placed (the size, shape, colour and print are the same for each product, with only the unit quantities differing from one order to the next). To give a feel for the business, details on a representative sample of 25 products have been provided in Exhibit 1. Customers with a low annual requirement sometimes choose a standard product, which the company makes and supplies from finished-goods inventory (for example, Products 9, 18 and 25 in Exhibit 1).

Two of the distinguishing features of KP's markets are the aspects of technical competence/price and unit volume. The technical competence and price issue concerns the degree of technical competence required at the moulding and/or printing stages of production, and is explained more fully in Exhibit 2.

The company sees itself as increasingly being in the higher technical segments of its markets. However, it also recognizes that technical advantage is usually short-lived. For most products, KP can maintain a technical competence advantage for no more than two years. After this time it declines, often quite dramatically. To illustrate the relative importance of the technical competence factor, this and other relevant order-winners have been provided in Exhibit 3 for the 25 representative products referred to earlier.

'In order to help better understand our markets, we have established the order-winners for all our products, while also signalling qualifiers to which we need to pay particular attention', explained Art Hausemann, marketing director.

The sample of products in Exhibit 3 illustrates most of the issues involved. The advantage we attempt to achieve through the factor of technical competence (and correspondingly improved margin) has different levels of endurance. The typical trend is that over time, price will become an increasingly important order-winner. How quickly this transition takes place depends on several factors, including the sales volumes involved and the distinct nature of technical competence as an order-winning criterion. Where the sales volumes are large, then the stimulus for others to compete is greater, and this will, understandably, reduce the length of time we enjoy this technically-based advantage. Also, we are now entering new segments in our markets. Let me explain by using the example of Meadow Care.[1]

First, it illustrates the enormous level of success that comes from marrying technical competence and volume. This has proved difficult for us to achieve in the past, made more so by the fact that it is not possible to foresee how a segment will develop in terms of volumes, and also how long our technical competence advantage will last. With Meadow Care, the sales quantities of the medium size have grown beyond all expectations. However, our investment in the P10 printer has proved to be an important factor in our success. Although initially the customer intended to sell only the medium size, its

**Exhibit 1**  Representative sample of products listed by reducing annual sales revenue based on next year's forecast

| Reference | Product Description | Years since introduction | Annual sales quantity (000s containers) Current year minus | | | Current year | Next year's forecast | Next year's forecast Sales revenue (£000s) | Contribution as percentage of sales revenue |
|---|---|---|---|---|---|---|---|---|---|
| | | | 3 | 2 | 1 | | | | |
| 1 | Medium Meadow Care[1] | 2 | 0 | 1260 | 5630 | 11 200 | 13 460 | 555 | 68 |
| 2 | Large Antisep | 8 | 9540 | 9620 | 8460 | 7 800 | 7 320 | 390 | 34 |
| 3 | Family Disinfectant | 12 | 3300 | 3440 | 2880 | 3 010 | 3 120 | 321 | 32 |
| 4 | Giant Weedblitz | 2 | 0 | 420 | 760 | 830 | 800 | 177 | 63 |
| 5 | Small Spring Blossom | 5 | 1250 | 3300 | 6680 | 5 210 | 4 570 | 155 | 43 |
| 6 | Medium Body Care | 7 | 4200 | 4650 | 3910 | 4 240 | 3 630 | 129 | 45 |
| 7 | Small Cream Cleaner | 8 | 2190 | 2490 | 2930 | 2 800 | 2 600 | 106 | 53 |
| 8 | Family Pine Cleaner | 6 | 400 | 430 | 480 | 660 | 950 | 101 | 48 |
| 9 | Medium Standard Round | 17 | 830 | 1260 | 1410 | 1 620 | 1 690 | 95 | 72 |
| 10 | Family Harsh Cut | 2 | 0 | 710 | 1170 | 1 040 | 1 390 | 86 | 74 |
| 11 | Medium Apple Leaf | 1 | 0 | 0 | 1250 | 1 570 | 2 010 | 68 | 64 |
| 12 | Family Sterisol | 0 | 0 | 0 | 0 | 770 | 1 280 | 58 | 34 |
| 13 | Small Apple Leaf | 0 | 0 | 0 | 0 | 670 | 1 370 | 49 | 66 |
| 14 | Giant Antisep | 6 | 210 | 240 | 230 | 220 | 240 | 42 | 46 |
| 15 | Medium Siki | 7 | 800 | 1240 | 1180 | 920 | 830 | 34 | 64 |
| 16 | Medium Mouthwash Tablets | 12 | 790 | 720 | 640 | 580 | 530 | 29 | 42 |
| 17 | Large Disinfectant | 12 | 700 | 670 | 610 | 580 | 640 | 27 | 38 |
| 18 | Small Standard Tub | 17 | 950 | 920 | 790 | 830 | 800 | 23 | 83 |
| 19 | Medium Soap | 5 | 100 | 160 | 190 | 210 | 230 | 20 | 46 |
| 20 | Large Saisco | 8 | 310 | 260 | 270 | 240 | 250 | 18 | 36 |
| 21 | Large Houseplant Food | 4 | 60 | 80 | 110 | 140 | 150 | 12 | 45 |
| 22 | Medium Sabre | 0 | 0 | 0 | 0 | 180 | 170 | 10 | 35 |
| 23 | Small Antisep | 6 | 220 | 200 | 210 | 170 | 180 | 7 | 54 |
| 24 | Medium Household Wax | 1 | 0 | 0 | 50 | 40 | 40 | 3 | 70 |
| 25 | Large Standard Antiseptic | 14 | 15 | 10 | 15 | 10 | 10 | 1 | 46 |

*Note*
1. There are currently six other sizes of Meadow Care, with next year's forecast annual unit volumes ranging from 0.80 to 0.25 million units. These additional sizes were introduced this year and last year following the success of the medium size.

**Exhibit 2** A note on the corporate interpretation of the phrase *technical competence* as used in the case study

> All the products made have been reviewed by the marketing and production managers and each has been assessed for the degree of technical competence embodied in the moulding and/or printing of the product. In making this assessment, the following aspects were considered.
>
> 1. The relative level of complexity of the moulding or printing processes used. Low ratings were given to products moulded on simple, low output machinery, which could be easily adjusted and maintained to give a satisfactory quality conformance level of output. High ratings were given to processes that involved complex adjustment, precise control and considerable levels of knowledge and skill.
> 2. The degree of difficulty involved in producing the individual products. Products with complex shapes, sharp corners, very precise dimensions or difficult plastic material (in terms of moulding) increase the problems involved in achieving the required standards, and are therefore given higher technical competence ratings.
> 3. Processes developed 'in-house' for specific products. These would be given high ratings of technical competence, until the technical advantage is matched by KP's competitors.

very success stimulated the company involved to meet the demand for other sizes. However, sales of these latter products have been relatively low.

In addition, to further enhance sales of Meadow Care, the number of print types has increased as exports have been pursued. The two other suppliers of this container are both based in Continental Europe, but have neither been as fast in responding to meet the customer's needs as we have, nor in maintaining the quality levels demanded. This initiative has enabled us to increase total sales of this product. It has become clear that this type of customer-related support will increasingly become part of our overall strategy, in order to stimulate further sales volume growth.

Art Hausemann then turned the conversation towards the new product. He explained that the technical breakthrough was a 'first', and 'understandably, even a group as big as Toucon is excited'. The new product will also prove to be all new business for KP.

Currently, this market is dominated by two large companies, that together account for 70 per cent of total sales volumes. The advantage, however, of plastic over metal needs little explanation. The retailers see plastic as having so many plus points that they have shown themselves prepared to pay a price premium that is adequate to give us an acceptable return. The quantities involved are also significantly greater than anything we are in at present, with 350 million unit sales forecast for the total market this year.

Art went on to say that the feature of technical competence in the new product would be quite transient (about two years) as competitors, including those manu-

**Exhibit 3**     Weighting of order-winning and qualifying criteria for the sample products given in Exhibit 1[1]

| Product reference | Year[2] | Price[4] | Technical Competence[4] | | Delivery | | Quality conformance | Others |
|---|---|---|---|---|---|---|---|---|
| | | | Mould | Print | Speed | On time | | |
| *Market A* | | | | | | | | |
| | Current | 50 | 0 | 40 | 10 | QQ[5] | Q[5] | 0 |
| 1 | +2 | 65 | 0 | 20 | 20 | QQ | Q | 0 |
| | +4 | 60 | 0 | 10 | 30 | QQ | Q | 0 |
| | Current | 60 | 0 | 20 | 20 | QQ | Q | 0 |
| 5, 6 and | +2 | 65 | 0 | 10 | 25 | QQ | Q | 0 |
| 15 | +4 | 65 | 0 | 0 | 35 | QQ | Q | 0 |
| | Current | Q | 20 | 50 | 10 | Q | 20 | 0 |
| 11 and 13 | +2 | 20 | 20 | 40 | 10 | Q | 10 | 0 |
| | +4 | 40 | 20 | 20 | 20 | Q | 0 | 0 |
| | Current | 80 | 0 | 10 | 0 | 0 | 10 | 0 |
| 22 | +2 | 80 | 0 | 10 | 0 | 0 | 10 | 0 |
| | +4 | 80 | 0 | 10 | 0 | 0 | 10 | 0 |
| *Market B* | | | | | | | | |
| | Current | 60 | 10 | 0 | 25 | Q | QQ | 5 |
| 2, 14 and | +2 | 70 | 0 | 0 | 30 | Q | QQ | 0 |
| 23 | +4 | 70 | 0 | 0 | 30 | Q | QQ | 0 |
| | Current | 20 | 0 | 0 | 60 | 0 | 0 | 20 |
| 25 | +2 | 20 | 0 | 0 | 60 | 0 | 0 | 20 |
| | +4 | 20 | 0 | 0 | 60 | 0 | 0 | 20 |
| *Market C (unprinted)* | | | | | | | | |
| | Current | 70 | 0 | – | 30 | Q | Q | 0 |
| 3, 12 and | +2 | 70 | 0 | – | 30 | Q | Q | 0 |
| 17 | +4 | 70 | 0 | – | 30 | Q | Q | 0 |
| *Market D (unprinted)* | | | | | | | | |
| | Current | 20 | 70 | – | 0 | Q | 10 | 0 |
| 4 | +2 | 50 | 40 | – | 5 | Q | 5 | 0 |
| | +4 | 60 | 0 | – | 30 | Q | Q | 10 |
| *Market E* | | | | | | | | |
| | Current | 40 | 0 | 0 | 40 | 0 | 10 | 10 |
| 7 and 8 | +2 | 40 | 0 | 0 | 40 | 0 | 10 | 10 |
| | +4 | 40 | 0 | 0 | 40 | 0 | 10 | 10 |
| | Current | 10 | 30 | 0 | 60 | 0 | 10 | 0 |
| 24 | +2 | 30 | 10 | 0 | 60 | 0 | 10 | 0 |
| | +4 | 40 | 0 | 0 | 60 | 0 | 10 | 0 |

**Exhibit 3** Weighting of order-winning and qualifying criteria for the sample products given in Exhibit 1 (cont'd)

| Product reference | Year[2] | Price[4] | Technical Competence[4] | | Delivery | | Quality conformance | Others |
| | | | Mould | Print | Speed | On time | | |
|---|---|---|---|---|---|---|---|---|
| Market F | | | | | | | | |
| | Current | 20 | 60 | 20 | 0 | QQ | Q | 0 |
| 10 | +2 | 40 | 30 | 20 | 10 | QQ | Q | 0 |
| | +4 | 60 | 0 | 20 | 20 | QQ | Q | 0 |
| Market G (unprinted) | | | | | | | | |
| | Current | 40 | 0 | – | 40 | 0 | 0 | 20 |
| 9 and 18 | +2 | 40 | 0 | – | 40 | 0 | 0 | 20 |
| | +4 | 40 | 0 | – | 40 | 0 | 0 | 20 |
| Market H | | | | | | | | |
| | Current | 80 | 0 | 0 | 20 | 0 | 0 | 0 |
| 16 | +2 | 90 | 0 | 0 | 10 | 0 | 0 | 0 |
| | +4 | 90 | 0 | 0 | 10 | 0 | 0 | 0 |
| | Current | 60 | 0 | 0 | 40 | 0 | 0 | 0 |
| 19, 20 | +2 | 60 | 0 | 0 | 40 | 0 | 0 | 0 |
| and 21 | +4 | 60 | 0 | 0 | 40 | 0 | 0 | 0 |

*Notes*
1. Order-winner weightings. Products have been grouped together by market segment, then separated (where applicable) into subsets, with the same order-winning criteria weightings. The period chosen to reflect the life cycle of KP's products is four years.
2. +2 and +4 mean current year plus 2 years and current year plus 4 years, respectively.
3. The order-winners shown here not only highlight the importance of certain criteria for different products, but also their changing nature, particularly between the factors of technical competence and price. Where there is a gradual loss of technical competence, then the weighting given to this order-winner will reduce, while the weighting given to price will normally increase, as illustrated in the details above.
4. In assessing the factors of technical competence and price, the company considers that where the weighting points for technical competence are greater than or similar to price, then technical competence should be considered as the relevant order-winner on the technical competence/price continuum. Where the weighting for price is significantly greater than the points attributed to technical competence, then price should be considered as the relevant order-winner on this continuum.
5. Q signifies a qualifying criterion, while QQ denotes a qualifier that is order-losing sensitive.

facturing the current metal-based product, were working on a plastic replacement. 'We are aware of this', commented Art Hausemann.

Our patents will not help, as there are many alternative design approaches that could be followed by our competitors. We also anticipate that the main supplier of the existing metal products will not yield this substantial market without a fight. What we have to do is exploit our advantage over the next 24 months. In that way, it forms an ideal part of our future marketing strategy of moving from the low volume/low technical competence toward the high volume/high technical competence market segments.

# Manufacturing

The span of process within manufacturing is quite small. It comprises moulding, printing and auxiliary processes, including packing. The technical features, which manufacturing needs to provide, are in its ability to meet a product's design needs as explained in Exhibit 2.

The processes on to which products are loaded are determined at the outset, based on factors of volume and the technical demands of a product. For example, a product that requires printing comprising five colours will be routed through the five-colour printer. Exhibit 4 illustrates these differences, based on the representative products used earlier. Once the contract has been received, the company designs tooling to fit a specific process. It is, therefore, difficult subsequently to load a product on to another size of process, as the tooling is specific to the chosen process type (for example, M1). However, currently, there are several machines within each process type (for instance, in process type M3 there are 12 machines) which, to all intents and purposes, are the same in terms of loading appropriate tools (all tools designed for a process type can be loaded on to any of the machines within that type) and throughput speeds. The exception is P10, where there is only one machine. (However, within a process type, additional investment can be made to improve machine performance, on the one hand to increase throughput speed by reducing the cooling cycle or improving the take-off arrangements or, on the other hand, reducing set-up times by appropriate tooling and process modifications.)

'The provision of technical competence is not a major production problem', explains Jack Jameson, manufacturing director.

As long as the technical requirements are incorporated in the early stages in the normal way, then providing the technical edge is usually a straightforward task. We support a diverse range of products, the needs of which are provided by a number of processes. Depending on where a product is in its life cycle, then the demands of each product, in terms of what manufacturing needs to provide, can be very different, as shown in Exhibit 3. One critical part of this task is providing customer support in terms of meeting schedule changes. As the number of products grows, the need to balance production run lengths and the urgent requests from customers becomes increasingly difficult to manage. Marketing have explained that they intend to move into the higher volume segments and, if it happens, we will find that a significant help in terms of managing our processes.

At the moment, our overall sales growth has caused capacity problems on certain processes, and we are having to work weekend overtime on several moulding and printing processes. One in particular we need to look at is the five-colour printer (P10). At the moment, we are at full stretch on this one machine, and will soon be unable to meet our delivery commitments on a regular basis. The need for additional five-colour printing has been accepted: which one to purchase is the decision we need to make. Certainly, the P10 has proved to be very successful and, no doubt, was an important factor in the success of the Meadow Care business.

**Exhibit 4** The manufacturing processes and standard hours for moulding and printing the representative products[1]

| Product reference | Type of process used[2,5] | | Machine standard hours per 1000 containers | | Number of orders (current year) | Number of production runs (current year) | |
|---|---|---|---|---|---|---|---|
| | Moulding | Printing | Moulding | Printing | | Moulding | Printing |
| 1[3,4] | M2 | P10 | 1.11 | 0.23 | 12 | 3 | 3 |
| 2[3,4] | M3 | P10 | 1.21 | 0.21 | 12 | 4 | 10 |
| 3 | M3 | – | 2.45 | – | 6 | 6 | – |
| 4 | M2 | – | 3.05 | – | 4 | 4 | – |
| 5[3,4] | M2 | P9 | 1.23 | 0.25 | 12 | 3 | 10 |
| 6[3] | M2 | P9 | 0.86 | 0.25 | 12 | 1 | 12 |
| 7 | M1 | P9 | 0.86 | 0.21 | 6 | 1 | 2 |
| 8 | M3 | P9 | 2.55 | 0.21 | 2 | 2 | 2 |
| 9 | M1 | – | 2.10 | – | stock[6] | 3 | – |
| 10 | M3 | P3 | 2.88 | 0.27 | 4 | 4 | 4 |
| 11[3] | M2 | P10 | 0.85 | 0.23 | 12 | 2 | 6 |
| 12 | M3 | – | 1.75 | – | 2 | 2 | – |
| 13 | M1 | P10 | 0.68 | 0.23 | 6 | 6 | 6 |
| 14 | M3 | P9 | 4.25 | 0.20 | 2 | 2 | 2 |
| 15[3] | M2 | P10 | 1.35 | 0.23 | 12 | 4 | 8 |
| 16 | M4 | P9 | 1.44 | 0.24 | 9 | 9 | 9 |
| 17 | M3 | – | 1.30 | – | 4 | 4 | – |
| 18 | M6 | – | 0.65 | – | stock | 2 | – |
| 19 | M1 | P7 | 1.00 | 0.29 | 8 | 6 | 6 |
| 20 | M1 | P6 | 0.95 | 0.30 | 1 | 1 | 1 |
| 21 | M1 | P3 | 1.10 | 0.27 | 5 | 5 | 5 |
| 22 | M2 | P10 | 2.06 | 0.23 | 2 | 2 | 2 |
| 23 | M6 | P2 | 0.71 | 0.24 | 4 | 4 | 4 |
| 24 | M1 | P7 | 1.24 | 0.29 | 1 | 1 | 1 |
| 25 | M3 | P9 | 1.85 | 0.25 | stock | 2 | 2 |

*Notes*
1. All moulding and (some) printing processes run 24 hours a day, over five days, with weekend overtime on selected processes (for example, P10).
2. While there is some variation between the length of production runs for any given product (moulding and printing) generally these are similar, and should be considered so for purposes of analysis.
3. Products 1, 2, 5, 6, 11 and 15 are ordered on a scheduled basis, shown above as 12 orders per year.
4. Product 1 is completed on three machines, and Products 2 and 5 on two machines.
5. KP employs a range of moulding and printing processes, not all of which are shown because the sample of products has been based on representing volumes and order-winners within the business, rather than reflecting the range of processes used.
6. The word *stock* means that many orders were received for these products from many customers. The orders were supplied from finished-goods inventory, as they are not customized products.

**Exhibit 5**  Alternative mould processes and relevant investments for the new product

The following is a summary of the current position.

1. Three years of research have been conducted in optimizing the product design, selecting and testing suitable materials and in finalizing the manufacturing techniques.

2. Moulds have been purchased to fit the existing, specialized moulding process M8/1, and are undergoing extensive production trials. Early output was of a satisfactory level of quality conformance, and final trials have proved that this process is commercially viable (see the opening remarks in the case narrative).

3. The new product is not printed. Different customers will place orders for the product for a range of order quantities. They will differentiate the container by using labels at the appropriate point in their own processes. Labels are used not only to describe the contents, but also, in many instances, to further increase product differences (for example, by the use of colour).

4. Letters of intent have been received (from two of the company's main customers), giving initial requirements for a total of 3 million units in two sizes, with deliveries to commence mid-next year.

5. Mould design has been initiated for an alternative highger output process M8/2, which involves similar moulding technology.

6. Details have been obtained for processes M9/1 and M9/2. Used successfully elsewhere in the group for other high-volume products, this moulding technology is considerably more complex and has not yet been proved capable of producing the new product.

7. Estimated prices have been received for the purchase of each type of machine and associated moulds.

8. In assessing the order-winning criteria for the new product, a weighting of 70 was assigned to technical competence because of the unique combination of product design and manufacturing development associated with the product. It was recognized that the use of process M8/2 would not affect this weighting, but the use of processes M9/1 or M9/2 (which offer higher output) would further differentiate the company from competitors in terms of technical competence. These processes were assessed as having a technical competence rating of 85 for the initial period. This higher rating has been awarded to the M9/1 and M9/2 processes because it is considered that customers will perceive potential suppliers with these processes as more able to meet the higher-volume segments of these markets.

9. Comparison of processes

| Feature | Process alternatives[1] | | | |
| --- | --- | --- | --- | --- |
| | M8/1[2] | M8/2 | M9/1 | M9/2 |
| Annual output (millions of units) per machine | 1.0 | 4.0 | 10.0 | 20.0 |
| Investment per machine (£000s) | 250 | 500 | 1000 | 1500 |
| Investment per set of moulds (£000s) | 50 | 88 | 220 | 260 |
| Tool change time (hours) | 14 | 30 | 48 | 54 |
| Availability – delivery lead time for each machine (months) | – | 2 | 6 | 8 |

*Notes*
1. The new product is not printed (see 3 above).
2. The existing M8/1 process is currently used on other products, but has little, if any, available spare capacity.

10. As with any market of this size, the current metal product comprises several segments with a corresponding range of order quantities and different order-winners. Some segments involve quantities of a size similar to many of KP's present products, while others are in quantities many, many times greater.

He then went on to discuss the new product and production implications of moving into a market with different levels of volumes. 'The potential volumes are enormous', he reflected,

> and the group's imagination has been caught. The debate on where to position ourselves has been in progress now for several months, a summary of which is available [see Exhibit 5]. Given the corporate interest and accepted marketing strategy then it looks to me as though we will eventually be aiming toward the M9 machine series. The process technology will be quite something.

## Opportunities of the New Product

'The new product', explained Paul Sharman,

> symbolizes the nature of Klein's position in the market. The company has built up a substantial design and development capacity to enable it to create the technical competence advantages pursued by the company. In this way, it is able to provide the necessary product margin to support the business, while achieving acceptable levels of profit.

When summarizing the new product and the opportunities it presented for the business, Paul Sharman explained that the technical breakthrough they had achieved gave the company many advantages.

> For one, it helps create an internal image for this company within the group. We are small in group terms, but world technology firsts help build everyone's prestige. Second, it will not only help us to grow overall, but will help us to reposition ourselves within our own markets. The recent news that the new product is economically viable gives us the final piece in the jigsaw.
>
> Although it represents a quantum leap, the M9 processes must now be our next technical hurdle to overcome. For manufacturing, though, I realize that it presents a different set of problems. But that is part of the corporate game. They need to explain the options, as the investment stakes are high.

## Note

1. KP manufactures and sells plastic containers to various customers. To distinguish one product from another it uses the name of the contents to describe each container: thus, 'Meadow Care' refers to the container(s) in which this product will eventually be packed.

# Meta Products

'Our meeting with the group board was most rewarding', was Barry Levenger's opening remark to the executive team of Meta Products.

Approval was given to purchase three 500-tonne presses and one additional printer. The group board recognized the need to provide additional injection moulding and printing capacity to support the growing market in fluid containers, and proved most supportive of our corporate strategy to exploit this market opportunity. As part of their agreement, they asked for a statement of our overall strategy and what changes, if any, we are proposing to our overall approach to meeting the needs of our markets. I explained that this was now under review and timed to coincide with the introduction of these new investments in six months time. The board accepted the timing of this revision and asked to be involved in the discussion and party to its agreement. We have already recognized this as a high priority and, therefore, need to draft ideas as soon as possible.

The meeting to which Barry Levenger referred was attended by himself, as chief executive officer, and Ted Enderby, the divisional director of Meta Products, to present the application for capital investment referred to here.

## Background

Meta Products is a subsidiary of PALC Industries, a large holding company involved in a diverse range of businesses, including engineering, steel fabrication, wire-drawing, cable-making, office equipment and packaging. As part of the packaging division, Meta Products occupies two wholly owned sites in Swindon, a large and growing industrial and commercial town in southern England. Located on the main site at Bristol Road are three separate companies, two from the packaging division and one from the office equipment division. Recognizing the advantages of keeping apart businesses that are distinct, these companies (of which Meta Products is one) are organized independently of one another, while enjoying some central services (such as heating) and some functions organized on a site basis. The principal

This case was prepared by Terry Hill (University of Oxford) and S. H. Chambers (University of Warwick). It is intended for class discussion and not as an illustration of good or bad management. © AMD Publishing.

unifying factor is that all three companies are responsible to the same chief executive officer, a common feature used by the group to encourage the development of its general managers. In addition, there are the centralized functions of personnel, industrial engineering, maintenance and a toolroom. These functions occupy central office and workshop areas. Each of the three companies has its own executive team and, with the exception of the central services described earlier, is managed as an autonomous business unit, with the exception of major capital investments, which require the approval of the group board of directors. The overhead costs associated with the centralized functions described here are allocated on an agreed basis.

In addition, there is a second site close by, situated in an industrial estate adjacent to Bristol Road. This is used solely by Meta Products as a warehouse for part-finished as well as finished goods.

# Marketing

Meta Products makes a wide variety of (mainly customized) mouldings for a number of markets. Stewart Larby, the sales and marketing manager, outlined the marketing strategy. He explained that it identifies future sales growth as taking place in the food, cosmetic and fluid container markets.

'Current actual sales are up to forecast', he explained,

and the growth in fluid containers is proving to be greater than expected. This has resulted in longer lead times being currently quoted, even though we are, and have been, working weekend overtime. The additional machines will not only alleviate current capacity problems, but will give us the opportunity of developing this new market still further. Our markets can be broadly described as comprising six segments. Each of them is different, and the easiest way to explain these differences is to describe each of them in turn.

## Food Products

Food products are customized in terms of moulding and printing and are sold to large, nationally based, food processing companies. This segment comprises only a small number of customers, but involves very high annual volumes with weekly call-offs. All products (except frozen-meal packs) are printed and the variety of print designs can be as high as 20 to 25 on one item. Exhibit 1 gives details of these products, including a representative range of print varieties. Most customers, while able to give reasonably accurate weekly call-off information, tend to provide printing details only one or two days ahead of delivery requirements. As one would anticipate, all relevant aspects of quality (for example, cleanliness, product conformance and appearance) are most important. Each customer requires all suppliers to meet its own stringent quality assurance/control systems (which includes the requirement for an adequate quality control function within a supplier's manufac-

**Exhibit 1**  Details for a representative sample of food products

| Product code | | Current year | | | |
|---|---|---|---|---|---|
| | | Production runs | Colours | Print varieties | Moulded in area number |
| F098 | | 6 | 1 | – | 2 |
| F127 | | 4 | 1 | 3 | 3 |
| F186 | | 4 | 1 | 10 | 3 |
| F201 | | 5 | 1 | 10 | 3 |

| Product code | Product description | Year[1] | Relevant order-winning and qualifying criteria | | | | | | | Annual standard hours (moulding) | Print variety[5] |
|---|---|---|---|---|---|---|---|---|---|---|---|
| | | | Price | Delivery speed | Delivery reliability | Moulding quality[3] | Print quality[3] | Cleanliness | Existing supplier | | |
| F098 | Frozen-meal pack | Current | 30 | 20 | Q[2] | – | – | QQ[4] | 50 | 3220 | – |
| | | +2 | 50 | 20 | Q | – | – | QQ | 30 | 3600 | – |
| | | +4 | 60 | 30 | Q | – | – | QQ | 10 | 5000 | – |
| F127[6] | Premium butter container | Current | Q | 30 | QQ | 70 | Q | QQ | – | 5830 | 3 |
| | | +2 | 20 | 30 | QQ | 50 | Q | QQ | – | 5000 | 4 |
| | | +4 | 40 | 30 | QQ | 30 | Q | QQ | – | 2000 | 4 |
| F186 | Beverage powder container | Current | 60 | 40 | Q | – | – | Q | – | 1580 | 10 |
| | | +2 | 60 | 40 | Q | – | – | Q | – | 1200 | 10 |
| | | +4 | 60 | 40 | Q | – | – | Q | – | 800 | 10 |
| F201[6] | Luxury individual dessert | Current | Q | 50 | QQ | 50 | Q | QQ | – | 2700 | 10 |
| | | +2 | Q | 50 | QQ | 50 | Q | QQ | – | 3000 | 12 |
| | | +4 | Q | 50 | QQ | 50 | Q | QQ | – | 3500 | 12 |

*Notes*
1. +2 and +4 mean current year plus 2 years and current year plus 4 years, respectively.
2. Q denotes a qualifier.
3. Moulding quality and print quality refer to meeting the moulding and printing specifications respectively.
4. QQ denotes an order-losing sensitive qualifier.
5. Print variety refers to the number of different print designs required by customers.
6. Dimensional accuracy is a critical feature of products F127 and F201.

turing unit), while making rigorous checks on receipt of deliveries and undertaking random checks on suppliers at any time of the day, without previous notice.

## Assembled Products

Assembled products have two distinct characteristics. The first is that after moulding they all undergo one or more additional processes before completion. For example, this involves inserting one or more components into the principal moulding, joining two or more mouldings together, and/or attaching a metal fitting or applying a label, each of which requires an automatic device to complete the task. The second feature is that none of these products is printed. Within this segment there are 14 products; Exhibit 2 provides details for a representative number of these. The products are moulded on a range of machines.

## Industrial Products

Meta Products has, for many years, produced a variety of customized products for manufacturing companies. As with other market segments, the mix of products changes over time, but this type of business has remained an important part of the overall business portfolio. (Exhibit 3 provides details for a representative number of products.) Within this category, products are not printed, and moulding quality conformance concerns the absence of visual defects since the products do not demand exacting dimensional tolerances. However, this is not to imply that products are of a low design specification but more that the product specification tends not to be difficult to achieve and maintain. Given these characteristics, it is understandable that this is a price-sensitive market, as there are many small injection moulding companies able to meet the relevant customer requirements.

## Fluid Container Products

Fluid container products represent a new market segment, that has arisen as a result of the successful substitution of plastic for metal as the material to be used in making existing fluid containers. The improvements offered by plastic and, in particular, the company's mould design allowing for a single moulded unit, thus avoiding the critical problems of guaranteed sealing, has provided Meta Products with this growth opportunity. Over the last 18 months, the company has enjoyed a distinct product design advantage, which is expected to be maintained for the next two or even three years. Meta Products' design was patented two years ago but the company recognizes that other solutions are feasible. It anticipates, therefore, that competitive alternatives will be available in the next few years, which will not infringe its own patent. Most standard products are printed to customers' designs,

**Exhibit 2**  Details for a representative sample of assembled products

| Product code | | Current year | | |
|---|---|---|---|---|
| | | Production runs | Colours | Moulded in area number |
| A067 | | 4 | 2 | 4 |
| A079 | | 4 | 6 | 4 |
| A120 | | 6 | 8 | 1 |
| A125 | | 4 | 1 | 1 and 4 |
| A138 | | 6 | 1 | 4 |
| A146 | | 2 | 1 | 1 and 4 |

| Product code | Product description | Year[1] | Relevant order-winning and qualifying criteria | | | | Existing supplier | Annual standard hours (moulding) |
|---|---|---|---|---|---|---|---|---|
| | | | Price | Delivery speed | Delivery reliability | Moulding quality[4] | | |
| A067 | Labelled household item | Current | 20 | 40 | QQ[2] | 40 | – | 1250 |
| | | +2 | 30 | 40 | QQ | 30 | – | 500 |
| | | +4 | – | – | – | – | – | 0 |
| A079 | Lid assembly | Current | 100 | – | – | – | – | 645 |
| | | +2 | 100 | – | – | – | – | 400 |
| | | +4 | 100 | – | – | – | – | 400 |
| A120 | Box | Current | 20 | 50 | – | 30 | – | 460 |
| | | +2 | 30 | 50 | – | 20 | – | 500 |
| | | +4 | 40 | 50 | – | 10 | – | 600 |
| A125 | Lid assembly | Current | Q | 50 | QQ | 50 | – | 6450 |
| | | +2 | Q | 60 | QQ | 40 | – | 6500 |
| | | +4 | Q | 60 | QQ | 40 | – | 7800 |
| A138 | Hinged base | Current | 60 | – | – | Q | 40 | 920 |
| | | +2 | 60 | – | – | Q | 40 | 1000 |
| | | +4 | 60 | – | – | Q | 40 | 1200 |
| A146 | Audio insert | Current | – | 10 | Q[3] | 60 | 30 | 5200 |
| | | +2 | – | 20 | Q | 60 | 20 | 4000 |
| | | +4 | 20 | 30 | Q | 40 | 10 | 2500 |

Notes
1. +2 and +4 mean current year plus 2 years and current year plus 4 years, respectively.
2. QQ denotes an order-losing sensitive qualifier.
3. Q denotes a qualifier.
4. Moulding quality refers to meeting the moulding specification of the product.

and the print varieties are expected to increase to over 100 in the years to come (see Exhibit 4). All products undergo an assembly operation following printing to attach the appropriate handle. Current annual volumes are expected to double in the next 12 months, with similar growth levels expected in subsequent years. Customers include major chemical companies (such as Chemex) taking customized products at one end of the spectrum and small users taking standard products at the other.

## Cosmetic Products

Cosmetic products are customized in terms of moulding and printing, and sold in different volumes, depending on the level of exclusivity embodied in the final product. To ensure that the aesthetic qualities are maintained, Meta Products' customers have developed rigorous quality control procedures, which suppliers have to follow. This includes providing an independent quality control presence on a 24-hour basis and sample checks to agreed norms. Weekly schedules are provided, which are subject to changes at relatively short notice, particularly regarding printing requirements (details are provided in Exhibit 5). Current annual volumes represent a 30 per cent increase over last year. It is anticipated that volumes for the next two years will show similar levels of growth.

## Sundry Products

The final market category embraces a group of products with a wide range of applications. These include children's games, domestic applications and office sundries. Products are not printed, and details for some representative products are provided in Exhibit 6. Although this category lacks a distinct marketing orientation, it has been, and still is, an important part of Meta Products' total business. This year's sales represent a 10 per cent increase on last year.

## Manufacturing

The growth in sales, particularly with the introduction of the fluid container product range, has necessitated the purchase of additional processes and, for some products, regular overtime working. Explained Tim Wilcox, manufacturing manager:

> By and large, product types use the same moulding and, where relevant, printing processes. The exception to this is that most of the fluid container products are relatively large. Specific moulding and printing machines were, therefore, purchased to meet these size requirements and are allocated to these products on a permanent basis.
> With regard to other market categories, some products can be produced on the processes predominantly used by another category, but the need to exercise this option is

**Exhibit 3**   Details for a representative sample of industrial products

| Product code | Production runs | Current year | | Moulded in area number |
|---|---|---|---|---|
| | | Colours | | |
| I092 | 8 | 6 | | 1 |
| I104 | 3 | 1 | | 1 |
| I240 | 10 | 6 | | 2 |
| I362 | 2 | 2 | | 2 |
| I385 | 3 | 2 | | 1 |

| Product code | Product description | Year[1] | Relevant order-winning and qualifying criteria | | | | | Annual standard hours (moulding) |
|---|---|---|---|---|---|---|---|---|
| | | | Price | Delivery speed | Delivery reliability | Moulding quality[4] | Existing supplier | |
| I092 | Car trim | Current | 90 | 10 | QQ[2] | Q | – | 1720 |
| | | +2 | 80 | 20 | QQ | Q | – | 1400 |
| | | +4 | 70 | 30 | QQ | Q | – | 1000 |
| I104 | Domestic appliance clip | Current | 100 | – | QQ | – | – | 420 |
| | | +2 | 100 | – | QQ | – | – | 600 |
| | | +4 | 100 | – | QQ | – | – | 800 |
| I240 | Car component | Current | 80 | 20 | QQ | QQ | – | 2060 |
| | | +2 | 90 | 10 | QQ | Q | – | 2200 |
| | | +4 | 90 | 10 | QQ | Q | – | 2600 |
| I362 | Packaging component | Current | 90 | – | – | 10 | – | 120 |
| | | +2 | 100 | – | – | – | – | 130 |
| | | +4 | 100 | – | – | – | – | 140 |
| I385 | Industrial equipment component | Current | 100 | – | Q[3] | Q | – | 175 |
| | | +2 | 90 | – | Q | Q | 10 | 130 |
| | | +4 | 70 | – | Q | Q | 30 | 90 |

Notes
1. +2 and +4 mean current year plus 2 years and current year plus 4 years, respectively.
2. QQ denotes an order-losing sensitive qualifier.
3. Q denotes a qualifier.
4. Moulding quality refers to meeting the moulding specification of the product.

**Exhibit 4**   Details for a representative sample of fluid container products

| Product code | | Current year | | | |
| --- | --- | --- | --- | --- | --- |
| | | Production runs | Colours | Print varieties[1] | Moulded in area number |
| F2001[2] | | 4 | 1 | 6 | 3 |
| F2003[2] | | 2 | 1 | 46 | 5 |
| F2004 | | 2 | 1 | 62 | 5 |
| F2006[2] | | 4 | 1 | 30 | 4 |
| F2008[3] | | 2 | 1 | — | 5 |

| Product code | Product description | Year[4] | Relevant order-winning and qualifying criteria | | | | | | Annual standard hours (moulding) | Print variety[1] |
| --- | --- | --- | --- | --- | --- | --- | --- | --- | --- | --- |
| | | | Price | Delivery speed | Delivery reliability | Moulding quality[7] | Print quality[7] | Design | | |
| F2001[2] | 2.5-litre Vynacol | Current | Q[5] | — | Q | 30 | Q | 70 | 915 | 6 |
| | | +2 | Q | — | Q | 30 | 20 | 50 | 2 000 | 20 |
| | | +4 | 20 | — | Q | 30 | 20 | 30 | 3 000 | 25 |
| F2003[2] | 20-litre Chemex | Current | Q | — | QQ[6] | 30 | Q | 70 | 5 450 | 46 |
| | | +2 | 40 | 20 | QQ | 20 | Q | 20 | 12 000 | 75 |
| | | +4 | 60 | 40 | QQ | Q | Q | — | 15 000 | 100+ |
| F2004 | 5-litre Chemex | Current | Q | — | QQ | 30 | Q | 70 | 6 800 | 62 |
| | | +2 | 50 | — | QQ | 10 | Q | 40 | 16 000 | 100+ |
| | | +4 | 60 | 40 | QQ | Q | Q | — | 20 000 | 100+ |
| F2006[2] | 1-litre Agrite | Current | Q | — | Q | 30 | Q | 70 | 2 120 | 30 |
| | | +2 | 40 | — | Q | — | 20 | 40 | 4 000 | 60 |
| | | +4 | 80 | — | Q | — | 20 | — | 1 000 | 100+ |
| F2008[3] | 5-litre standard | Current | 30 | 40 | Q | — | — | 30 | 4 700 | — |
| | | +2 | 60 | 40 | Q | — | — | — | 6 000 | — |
| | | +4 | 60 | 40 | Q | — | — | — | 7 000 | — |

*Notes*

1. Print variety refers to the number of different print designs required by customers.
2. Products F2001, F2003 and F2006 are customized products. For example, a 5-litre Chemex comprises a standard moulding, which is then customized to Chemex's requirements at the printing stage. In addition, other changes (for example, a different coloured handle for the container) are also sometimes requested.
3. F2008 is sold as an unprinted container.
4. +2 and +4 mean current year plus 2 years and current year plus 4 year, respectively.
5. Q denotes a qualifier.
6. QQ denotes an order-losing sensitive qualifier.
7. Moulding quality and print quality refer to meeting the moulding and print specification respectively.

a decision we do not frequently need to make. However, processes have been replaced or added over the years, with the result that the moulding areas contain processes serving two or more market categories [see Exhibits 1 to 6]. We have already looked at the possibility of allocating certain moulding machines to each product type and have found this to be feasible, should we consider this to be a sensible move to take. If this course of action was followed, it would still necessitate working the same level of overtime as we currently do in order to meet the different levels of demand for the products in each market category. Following this decision, therefore, would not result in any major process difficulties or disadvantages, except that we may have to purchase the occasional moulding machine somewhat earlier than would have been the case under the present moulding arrangements.

On the issue of printing capacity, however, problems would arise if we were to attempt to allocate capacity to meet the specific needs of the food, fluid container and cosmetic market categories. Such a decision would require the purchase of additional printing capacity to cover the needs of the food and cosmetic groups, as currently they share the same printing processes – the separate requirements of fluid containers have already been recognized and separate printing process capacity has been justified and allocated to these products.

However, one issue raised at the recent capital investment application meeting with the group concerned increasing the utilization level of our current moulding capacity. Barry Levenger and Ted Enderby have commissioned me to report on this matter. Members of the group board had put forward the view that if we introduced continental shift work patterns, then we could increase our capacity from five days, plus current average overtime working, to seven days.[1] Barry and Ted confirmed that this approach had been used elsewhere in the group and had highlighted the increases in capacity that had resulted, giving details of labour costs incurred, compared to those for working a five-day week with extensive overtime. Given the large investments involved and the anticipated sales growth in the future, then it seems to make sense. Recruiting additional people should not be a problem, and we are well able to give appropriate training where necessary. A further comment they also made was that the current shift patterns lack uniformity. It's true, we do employ people using a number of different shift systems, some of which have developed over the years, but some do reflect our needs. But I take the point that to the outsider it looks somewhat ill-planned.

He then continued to outline the present organization arrangements within the manufacturing function, which have been provided as Exhibits 7 and 8. 'In order to provide the appropriate level of effort and attention to the fluid container initiative, we made special organizational arrangements', explained Tim Wilcox. 'Therefore, I will first describe the manufacturing structure for all the other products, and finish by briefly outlining the current position on fluid containers.' Tim then outlined the manufacturing scenario as follows:

Moulding is currently located in five separate areas. Part of this separation of facilities makes sense, while the remainder has been forced upon us over the years, due to the

**Exhibit 5**   Details for a representative sample of cosmetic products

| Product code | Current year | | | |
|---|---|---|---|---|
| | Production runs | Colours | Print varieties[1] | Moulded in area number |
| C068 | 4 | 1 | 3 | 1 |
| C116 | 2 | 4 | 12 | 3 |
| C210 | 6 | 1 | 6 | 3 |

| Product code | Product description[2] | Year[3] | Relevant order-winning and qualifying criteria | | | | | | | Annual standard hours (moulding) | Print variety[1] |
|---|---|---|---|---|---|---|---|---|---|---|---|
| | | | Price | Delivery speed | Delivery reliability | Moulding quality[4] | Print quality[4] | Cleanliness | Existing supplier | | |
| C068 | Facial cream tub | Current | 20 | – | – | 80 | – | Q[5] | – | 780 | 3 |
| | | +2 | 10 | – | – | 80 | 10 | Q | – | 700 | 5 |
| | | +4 | Q | – | – | 80 | 20 | Q | – | 700 | 8 |
| C116 | Supermarket moisturizer | Current | Q | 30 | Q | 30 | 40 | QQ[6] | – | 4730 | 12 |
| | | +2 | 10 | 30 | Q | 30 | 30 | QQ | – | 5000 | 15 |
| | | +4 | 20 | 20 | Q | 30 | 30 | QQ | – | 5500 | 15 |
| C210 | Skin care container | Current | Q | 40 | Q | 30 | 30 | Q | – | 1200 | 6 |
| | | +2 | 10 | 30 | Q | 30 | 30 | Q | – | 1600 | 10 |
| | | +4 | 30 | 10 | Q | 30 | 30 | Q | – | 1900 | 10 |

*Notes*
1. Print variety refers to the number of different print designs required by customers.
2. Dimensional accuracy is a critical feature of these products, particularly C068.
3. +2 and +4 mean current year plus 2 years and current year plus 4 year, respectively.
4. Moulding quality and print quality refer to meeting the moulding and print specification respectively.
5. Q denotes a qualifier.
6. QQ denotes an order-losing sensitive qualifier.

**Exhibit 6**  Details for a representative sample of sundry products

| Product code | Current year | | |
| --- | --- | --- | --- |
| | Production runs | Colours | Moulded in area number |
| S025 | 5 | 10 | 2 |
| S080 | 4 | 6 | 2 |
| S193 | 3 | 3 | 2 |
| S272 | 2 | 2 | 1 |

| Product code | Product description | Year[1] | Relevant order-winning and qualifying criteria | | | | | Annual standard hours (moulding) |
| --- | --- | --- | --- | --- | --- | --- | --- | --- |
| | | | Price | Delivery speed | Delivery reliability | Moulding quality[3] | Existing supplier | |
| S025 | Game model | Current | 50 | – | – | – | 50 | 900 |
| | | +2 | 75 | – | – | – | 25 | 1000 |
| | | +4 | 100 | – | – | – | – | 1100 |
| S080 | Office equipment item | Current | 50 | | Q[2] | 50 | – | 210 |
| | | +2 | 80 | – | Q | 20 | – | 300 |
| | | +4 | 100 | – | Q | – | – | 350 |
| S193 | Household product | Current | 100 | – | – | Q | – | 155 |
| | | +2 | 100 | – | – | Q | – | 150 |
| | | +4 | 100 | – | – | Q | – | 100 |
| S272 | Office equipment item | Current | 80 | 20 | – | – | – | 105 |
| | | +2 | 100 | – | – | – | – | 125 |
| | | +4 | 100 | – | – | – | – | 130 |

*Notes*

1. +2 and +4 mean current year plus 2 years and current year plus 4 years, respectively.
2. Q denotes a qualifier.
3. Moulding quality refers to meeting the moulding specification.

**Exhibit 7** Meta Products current organization chart

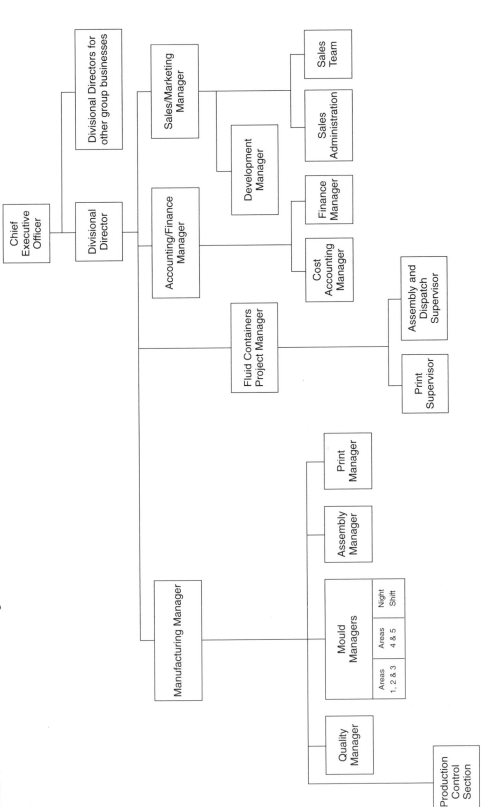

*Notes*

1. The centralized site functions report directly to the chief executive officer through their functional managers, but report for specific tasks into Meta Products as follows:

   a. personnel to the finance manager;

   b. industrial engineering and maintenance to the manufacturing manager;

   c. toolroom to the development manager;

2. Other relevant aspects of the organization are given in the case study narrative.

piecemeal purchase and sale of equipment. In order to control this, it has been necessary to provide two moulding managers, each looking after different areas [see Exhibit 7]. Furthermore, as moulding takes place on a 24-hour basis, we need to provide for a moulding manager to cover the night shift. Although the moulding managers officially work from 08.00 to 17.00 hours, working a three-shift system means that problems and decisions do not stop at the end of their working day. Consequently, these moulding managers cover most of the 24 hours and have established a sound communication system between them, which includes telephone conversations, revisits, starting early, or staying late, where required. Recently, we have been working much weekend overtime on several moulding processes, and this is covered by a combination of managers and supervisors, all of whom would be paid for their attendance.

Where products need to be assembled, these tasks are completed in a separate area, with an assembly manager responsible for all aspects of this work. We also have an evening shift from 18.00 to 22.00 hours, which has its own supervisory structure [see Exhibit 8].

On the printing side, we have a mix of arrangements to meet the demands of this part of the process. Exhibit 8 shows the relevant staffing levels, which includes printer-setters on the day shift and each of the three shifts. Their role is to set up all machines, as required, to run some of these, and to monitor the other machines (run by printers) through each shift in order to maintain quality requirements and maximize throughput levels.

With regard to quality, we employ a quality manager, whose specific role is to determine sampling and other quality procedures for in-coming materials (including packing and bought-out items), moulding, printing, assembly and packing. In addition, the job involves customer liaison on quality matters, testing current materials, assessing alternative materials and controlling the provision of necessary inspection for all hours worked. Inspectors working a three-shift pattern report on general matters to the relevant production supervisors, when the quality manager and supervisor are not on site. However, the company clearly separates the responsibility of the assurance and control of quality from that of manufacturing. In Bill Heathcote we are fortunate to have a person who is quality-oriented, appropriately qualified in terms of the materials we use (he is a chemist by training), and is well regarded by all our customers, as well as within the plant itself.

The aspect of production planning and control is organized as follows. The aspect of medium- and long-term planning falls within my own jurisdiction. The purchase of additional or replacement processes and other aspects, such as changes to shift arrangements, I retain as part of my direct responsibilities. The short-term production control activities, such as scheduling, are handled by the production control section (comprising three staff, one of whom is the section leader) who report directly to me. Their role is to schedule moulding and printing processes in line with customer requirements and agreed delivery dates and to ensure that all items necessary to run a product are available when needed. This entails coordinating materials, packaging, bought-out items, mould tool availability (for example, the toolroom checks over each mould tool before the next time it is used), and any other  items necessary to complete the work. Also, this section liaises with sales administration to discuss requests by customers to alter schedules, change priorities, or to meet changes in delivery quantities.

In addition, there are several general functions [see Exhibit 8], that link into the organization in the following way. The raw materials handler, who works on days, reports to the moulding manager for areas 1, 2 and 3. The warehouse supervisor reports to the assembly manager, the forklift drivers and cleaners are allocated to the two moulding area groupings, while all personnel within these general functions, working on nights, report to the moulding manager (night shift).

Finally, the central services of maintenance and toolroom report on an on-call basis. Unfortunately, although this does not work well, there seems little alternative. My moulding and printing managers report that the urgency and necessary orientation of these staff does not match the needs of manufacturing. The managers comment that it seems almost as though manufacturing is an inconvenience. For instance, priorities in the toolroom seem directed towards making new tools and not to refurbishing and other immediate manufacturing needs. Still, the trade-off is that we do keep associated overhead costs to a minimum – it would cost far more for each business to have its own self-contained facility. Maintenance would be less of an allocation problem, but this would need to be looked into in some depth.

Now, let us turn to the fluid container arrangements. Recognizing the importance of these products in terms of future company growth, and the levels of process investment involved, we approached this initiative in a different way to the one we use for the other parts of our business. The initial step was to appoint Keith Burns to be responsible for the project, and at a level higher, in organizational terms, than our current managers [see Exhibit 7]. In addition, we placed the responsibility for printing, assembly and dispatch under his jurisdiction. At the time, we recognized the logic of also placing moulding within a similar reporting format but, as the moulding machines were in different areas, this was not as easy. Instead, we have given him responsibility for making the scheduling and manning decisions of the appropriate plant, which he exercises by cooperating with the relevant managers and production control. One further decision, which just evolved, was to encourage direct communication with each customer. In the early days, this shortcut the current administrative procedures, thus allowing decisions to be made in discussion with our customers, and in a way best for the business as a whole. The fact that most of the companies involved also bought other products never seemed to be a problem. As the business grew, we made no attempt to change this working relationship, and not only do we think it a satisfactory arrangement, but our customers have also found it to be a sensible and practical way of meeting their day-to-day and short-term needs.

Tim Wilcox then discussed the new moulding and printing equipment, which had been sanctioned by the group. He explained that the company had recognized that the pressure on current moulding space would necessitate a review of manufacturing layouts to include the industrial estate buildings adjacent to Bristol Road.

One important reason for holding on to the industrial estate facilities was to provide the opportunity to meet our anticipated future growth. The best time to do this is before the new processes are installed, so that we can use the opportunity of additional capacity

**Exhibit 8** Current shift patterns and manning levels for manufacturing and related functions

| Location or function | Job title | Shift pattern (number per shift)[1] | | | | | |
| --- | --- | --- | --- | --- | --- | --- | --- |
| | | Days 08.00–16.00 | Three shifts[2] | Evenings 18.00–22.00 | Nights 22.00–06.00 | 12-hour shifts[3] | Total personnel |
| Areas 1, 2 and 3 (14 moulding machines) | Moulding manager[4] | 1 | | | | | 1 |
| | Supervisors | | 1 | | | | 3 |
| | Moulders | | 7 | | | | 21 |
| | Setters | 2 | 1 | | | | 5 |
| Areas 4 and 5 (12 moulding machines) | Moulding manager | 1 | | | | | 1 |
| | Supervisors | | | | | | 0 |
| | Moulders | | 8 | | | | 24 |
| | Setters | 1 | 1 | | | | 4 |
| Printing (conventional products) | Printing managers | 1 | | | | | 1 |
| | Supervisors | 1 | | | | | 1 |
| | Print-setters | 1 | 2 | | | | 7 |
| | Printers | 2 | | | 2 | | 4 |
| | Packers | 9 | | 6 | 4 | | 19 |
| Assembly | Assembly manager | 1 | | | | | 1 |
| | Supervisors | | | 1 | | | 1 |
| | Operators | 12 | | 6 | 6 | | 24 |
| | Setters | 2 | | | | | 2 |
| General functions | Night managers | | | | 1 | | 1 |
| | Raw material handlers | 1 | | | 1 | | 2 |
| | Warehouse | | | | | | |
| | Supervisors | 1 | | | | | 1 |
| | Staff | 1 | | | 1 | | 2 |
| | Forklift drivers | 2 | 2 | | | | 8 |
| | Cleaners | 2 | | | | | 2 |

## Shift pattern (number per shift)[1]

| Location or function | Job title | Days 08.00–16.00 | Three shifts[2] | Evenings 18.00–22.00 | Nights 22.00–06.00 | 12-hour shifts[3] | Total personnel |
|---|---|---|---|---|---|---|---|
| Fluid containers | Project managers | 1 | | | | | 1 |
| | Moulders | | 2 | | | | 6 |
| | Setters | 1 | | | | | 1 |
| | Assemblers | | 3 | | | | 9 |
| | Packers | | 2 | | | | 6 |
| | Assembly and dispatch supervisors | 1 | | | | | 1 |
| | Chargehands | | 1 | | | | 3 |
| | Printing manager | 1 | | | | | 1 |
| | Printers | | | | | 2 | 4 |
| Quality assurance and inspection | Quality managers | 1 | | | | | 1 |
| | Supervisors | 1 | | | | | 1 |
| | Laboratory technicians | 3 | | | | | 3 |
| | Inspectors | 2 | 2 | | | | 8 |
| Production control | Supervisors | 1 | | | | | 1 |
| | Staff | 2 | | | | | 2 |
| Maintenance and toolroom[5] | Mechanics | 6 | | | | | 6 |
| | Electricians | 6 | | | | | 6 |
| | Toolmakers | 7 | | | | | 7 |

*Notes*

1. The numbers under each category are per shift. Hence in areas 1, 2 and 3 there is a supervisor on each of the three shifts, making a total of three in the far right-hand column.
2. The 'three-shifts' pattern is organized on a rotating basis, and comprises 06.00–14.00, 14.00–22.00, 22.00–06.00 hours, with a paid-for overlap, as with all interconnecting shift arrangements.
3. The '12-hour' shifts run from 06.00 to 18.00 and 18.00 to 06.00 hours with a paid-for overlap. This arrangement is of a temporary nature, but has been formalized to ensure that the printing capacity to support fluid container products is made available at all times. When additional capacity has been provided, it is intended to change this pattern of working and this is understood by all concerned.
4. Moulding managers work from 08.00 to 17.00.
5. Although maintenance and toolroom staff are centrally based, the numbers above are permanent allocations to Meta Products. However, temporary movement takes place between Meta Products and the other companies as required.

provision to consider allocating processes to different parts of the business, as well as helping to alleviate the loss of production that will occur during plant relocation. Certainly, the space we have at both sites is sufficient to meet our immediate needs, while still offering the opportunity to accommodate further growth in the future. Our earlier foresight is now yielding important benefits.

The key issues we must address, therefore, do not concern the actual layout itself. There is sufficient space, when taking the two sites together, to meet our needs. The question concerns the rationale on which to base these decisions. We know it will incur costs, and these have been agreed in principle. A large capital investment allocation has already been agreed, with the full knowledge and support of the group.

# Development

The development manager is responsible for the development of the company's own products and also (which is by far the biggest part of his task) agreeing on the needs of customized products. For any product, this involves all aspects of moulding, printing, assembly and packaging, as required, and embraces materials, tools and machines.

# Sales Administration

Sales administration (comprising three staff, including secretarial support) reports to the sales/marketing director and is responsible for processing customer enquiries, orders and changes. To do this, it seeks information from related functions (such as production control and the relevant mould and print managers) and communicates it back to the customer. 'Processing customer order details and clarifying the requirements of our customers is one of our prime tasks', explained Pat Dodds, who was in charge of this function.

It is necessary then to seek a commitment from the relevant production managers, while liaising with production control on the other general (but essential) details. Once we have this agreement, then we go back to the customer and confirm details to all concerned. Customer schedule changes often cause the most difficulty, and in most instances this requires several telephone calls to the customer seeking additional details, which the moulding, printing and/or production control function need in order to arrive at a decision. This, as you can image, can prove very time-consuming, but it is necessary in order to ensure that our promises can be met. Being delivery-reliable is an essential element in our business.

# Future Arrangements

Barry Levenger's concluding remarks were as follows:

Securing the group's approval to purchase the additional moulding and printing processes, and the recognition of the need to consider the possibility of major structural changes involving manufacturing and other parts of the business (should they prove sensible), was the first step. What we now have to do is address the next issue, which is what makes for a sensible future arrangement. One thing is for sure, it will be costly, and will set the structure used by this business for years to come. We are committed to getting it right, and now have the opportunity to do just that. There are several options open to us. What I must ensure is that the path we follow is best for the business overall and recognizes the different needs of our customers and the demands placed upon our business.

# Note

1. Continental shifts refer to a pattern of working involving four shift teams, only three of which are involved at any one time. This provides for 24-hour coverage over seven days without involving overtime working. The description 'continental' comes from the fact that this shift pattern was first introduced by countries in Continental Europe.

# case
# 8
# Millstone Packaging

'The competitive nature of our markets is demanding on several dimensions', explained Steve Bishop, chief executive officer of Millstone Packaging.

> Our response had, therefore, been on many fronts, and much of our sustained performance is a direct result of these actions. One aspect that is a key criterion in most of our markets is that of delivery – both speed (relating to lead times) and reliability (relating to its on-time nature). In fact, our current target on delivery reliability is 98.5 per cent on all job orders.
>
> To help achieve greater control over and also reduce lead times within our total process, we have systematically invested in several areas of our pre-press (that is, pre-printing) operations. This has brought improvements in many areas including quality conformance and costs. A review of relevant aspects of our pre-press activities is underway, and early insights and analyses are now available. Our task is to continue improving in this and the other aspects of our total process in order to keep ahead and maintain our good performance and sound growth record of the past few years.

Steve Bishop was commenting on the rationale and importance for completing the analysis within the pre-press (that is, pre-printing) areas so that the necessary discussion and subsequent decisions could proceed.

## Background

Millstone Packaging is a subsidiary of Kingsbury Holdings Inc., a US conglomerate based in New Jersey with interests in food, tobacco, toiletries and domestic products. Millstone was one of eight packaging companies Kingsbury recently purchased, as part of a much larger deal, from a European-based multinational. Three of the companies (including Millstone Packaging) were based in the UK. Of the other five, one was located in France and two each in Italy and Germany. Recognizing the synergy between packaging and its other subsidiaries, Kingsbury saw this move as part of its consolidation strategy within Europe.

This case study was written by Terry Hill (University of Oxford). It is intended for class discussion and not as an illustration of good or bad management. © AMD Publishing.

# Marketing

'As with most companies', explained Marco Angeli, vice-president marketing of Millstone, 'we are continuously reviewing our markets in order to track developments and reposition ourselves to maximize opportunities for profitable sales growth'. Marco continued:

Many of these initiatives are market segment and/or customer-oriented in that we identify specific developments or opportunities and plan accordingly. Less often we make decisions concerning much broader issues. One example of the latter was identified almost two years ago and concerned reducing our dependence on line flexographic [used for designs that only comprise solid colours and text, whereas process flexographic is used where the designs include photographic or illustrated elements] work. Developments have now enabled process flexographic processes to meet the higher demands of designs that until then could only be achieved using gravure processes.[1] During the last two years, we have achieved a threefold increase in sales of process flexographic work so that it now accounts for over 20 per cent of total sales revenue. Process flexographic work has brought more sophisticated designs within the budget of more customers for lower-priced products, and there is no doubt that this trend will continue both in these and other similar products.

Today, meeting the design specification in process flexographic work is the key order-winner. In the future, as more companies will be able to meet these design specifications, this will decline in importance as it currently has for line flexographic work [see Exhibit 1]. However, this will not happen for a few years, and our increasing ability to meet the design specification for process flexographic work will continue to be the most important factor in these markets.

Delivery performance is also an increasingly important criterion in our markets. The need to respond quickly to reducing customer lead times is already important and is generally becoming more so, while failure to deliver on time will lose business quickly. Our customers use fast-throughput, high-speed processes, and if we don't get the packaging there on time then feathers fly. Similarly, an enforced change in our customers' schedules for one of a number of reasons will trigger off the need for a relatively fast response on our part.

Marco continued to describe the nature of the company's markets. While most (72 per cent) of the orders were for repeat items (that is, designs for which the artwork and flexographic plates were already available), the remainder were for amendments to existing (10 per cent) or new designs (18 per cent) (see Exhibit 2, Note 2).

Some amended and new designs can take many months to progress. The decision to introduce such a change is typically signalled some months ahead of time. A launch date will be agreed at this time and then a series of discussions will take place, centred on a customer's decision process to agree the final design. Very often the final outcome is

**Exhibit 1** Order-winners and qualifiers: current weightings and trends

| Criteria | Flexographic | |
| --- | --- | --- |
| | Line | Process |
| Quality conformance | 20↓ | 60↓ |
| Delivery reliability | QQ[1] | QQ |
| Delivery speed | 30↓ | 30↑ |
| Price | 20↓ | Q[1] |
| Sales/technical support | 30 | 10 |

*Note*
1. Q denotes a qualifying criterion; QQ, an order-losing sensitive qualifier.

rushed, so by the time we get customer clearance, the expected delivery date gives manufacturing little leeway. Our investment in origination over the last two years is aimed at gaining more control over the total process as well as the lead times in the operations process itself. Support for customers in this aspect of their requirements is most important in itself as well as for repeat orders.

# Manufacturing

Printing is relatively simple in operations terms, as the number of manufacturing processes through which a job passes is at most two or three. Although typically using high-volume batch processes, the nature of printing work demands highly skilled staff. One outcome of this is that the responsibility for all aspects of quality conformance, work scheduling and set-ups has always been part of an operator's job.

Jim Moeller, vice-president operations, explained that the company had systematically invested in machines, in part to do with supporting sales growth and also to keep abreast of process technology developments, that included customer demands for an increased number of colours within packing designs. 'In operations there is pressure on a number of dimensions. Cost reduction and quality conformance have been with us for many years', explained Jim.

Customers upgrading their own processes in order to increase throughput speeds has resulted in the need for tighter packaging specifications. This has put even more pressure on quality conformance as well as contributing to the growing importance of on-time delivery. The advent of developments in process flexographics has also allowed customers to increase the features of their packaging design, a factor that has always been an important part of a customer's own product offering. Furthermore, the company has systematically invested in pre-press activities such as origination and platemaking in order to increase its overall control and reduction of lead times and to strengthen ties with customers, a move that makes a lot of sense. In addition, we have achieved the substantial cost savings in all the pre-press areas that the investment proposals identified.

**Exhibit 2**   Sample of completed customer orders for all design types

| Customer | Design type[1,2] | Quantity (000s) | Customer placement | Delivery Agreed | Delivery Actual |
|---|---|---|---|---|---|
| Browns | R | 500 | 14 Oct | 10 Jan | 10 Jan |
| Aztec | R | 1000 | 11 Nov | 18 Jan | 18 Jan |
| Cottons | N | 200 | 15 Jan | 6 Apr | 16 Apr |
| Solent Bar | A | 400 | 7 Oct | 23 Mar | 25 Mar |
| Hartstone | A | 700 | 6 Jan | 18 Mar | 18 Mar |
| A. J. Foods | R | 5000 | 2 Dec | 17 Feb | 17 Feb |
| Browns | N | 4660 | 2 Dec | 18 Mar | 18 Mar |
| Mirror Foods | R | 850 | 17 Jan | 30 Mar | 29 Mar |
| Homewood | A | 700 | 3 Feb | 27 Mar | 29 Mar |
| Abbey | R | 450 | 3 Feb | 13 Mar | 12 Mar |
| F-lite | A | 500 | 10 Jan | 20 Mar | 28 Mar |
| Cottons | N | 750 | 8 Dec | 10 Mar | 18 Mar |
| Cottons | R | 3500 | 30 Oct | 20 Jan | 20 Jan |
| Hartstone | A | 1800 | 8 Jan | 16 Mar | 24 Mar |
| Browns | N | 250 | 10 Dec | 8 Mar | 8 Mar |
| Abbey | R | 3000 | 21 Nov | 10 Jan | 8 Jan |
| Hartstone | N | 500 | 17 Dec | 21 Mar | 30 Mar |
| A. J. Foods | A | 1500 | 4 Jan | 8 Feb | 8 Feb |
| A. J. Foods | N | 600 | 29 Nov | 7 Feb | 7 Feb |
| Farnells | R | 800 | 10 Nov | 8 Jan | 8 Jan |
| Alexon | A | 850 | 14 Dec | 10 Feb | 11 Mar |
| A. J. Foods | N | 1200 | 4 Jan | 28 Mar | 28 Mar |
| Homewood | R | 400 | 6 Jan | 25 Mar | 25 Mar |
| Cowies | N | 300 | 14 Feb | 28 Mar | 30 Mar |
| Browns | A | 900 | 10 Nov | 12 Jan | 19 Jan |
| J. B. Foods | R | 1200 | 30 Oct | 7 Jan | 7 Jan |
| Alexon | N | 650 | 11 Nov | 1 Feb | 22 Feb |
| F-lite | A | 750 | 17 Dec | 18 Jan | 16 Feb |
| A. J. Foods | N | 450 | 6 Feb | 10 Mar | 22 Mar |
| Shelleys | R | 800 | 10 Nov | 10 Feb | 10 Feb |
| Lakewood | A | 300 | 18 Oct | 7 Jan | 16 Jan |
| F-lite | N | 1500 | 25 Nov | 1 Mar | 14 Mar |
| Farnells | A | 600 | 7 Jan | 16 Feb | 16 Feb |
| Marcos | R | 200 | 1 Dec | 19 Mar | 19 Mar |
| Richards | A | 1000 | 10 Oct | 12 Jan | 21 Jan |
| JBK | A | 900 | 17 Dec | 21 Jan | 21 Jan |
| F-lite | R | 1200 | 12 Jan | 30 Mar | 30 Mar |
| A. J. Foods | N | 850 | 4 Dec | 21 Feb | 1 Mar |
| Hartstone | N | 600 | 8 Nov | 30 Mar | 18 Apr |
| Abbey | R | 1000 | 28 Oct | 18 Dec | 18 Dec |
| Shelleys | A | 900 | 14 Dec | 29 Jan | 29 Jan |
| Alexon | N | 400 | 16 Nov | 8 Feb | 16 Feb |

*Notes*

1. R = repeat design; A = amended design; N = new design.
2. The above sample gives 14 orders for each design type. However, of the orders processed in the first three months of the year, the actual breakdown between design types was: repeat, 72 per cent; amended, 10 per cent, and new, 18 per cent. In all other ways, however, the sample given is representative.

He went on to explain that the company had also moved from rubber mats to polymer plates as the medium for print transfer. Although the actual plate costs for polymer are twice that of rubber due to material costs, the former are reusable up to five or six times, whereas rubber mats could only be used once, which suited the changing mixture of the company's business to smaller, repeat orders. 'Our markets are also increasingly characterized by shorter lead times', explained Jim.

Our scheduling rules call for lead times to be in the order of 10 days to allow for all manufacturing needs to be met. Given the importance of delivery reliability, breaking into schedules may put some orders at risk in terms of delivery and will undoubtedly increase costs and invariably lead to losses in machine capacity. In fact, machines are sometimes held waiting for a job to be ready to run.

# Origination

'Three years ago', explained Tom Herbert, 'the company decided to invest in an origination capability'.

The reasons were several. The improvements in process flexographics enabled customers to undertake pack designs that previously, because they could only be completed by gravure, could not have been justified on cost grounds. We recognized that we needed to be in at the start of these developments and build on our technical capability and the strong technical image we enjoyed in the marketplace. At that time our mix of orders for line and process work was 93 and 7 per cent, respectively. Today it is 78 and 22 per cent, respectively.

Similarly, three years ago we bought in all our origination work. The artwork and customer liaison was, at that time, managed within the company, but the actual artwork and negative preparation was subcontracted. From the negatives, we make plates to go on to the machines and we have, for many years, completed this in-house. The real change has been in the preparation of artwork and the production of negatives. To be at the forefront of these changes and to offer a more complete service to our customers, we decided to undertake these tasks and have moved from a position three years ago where we bought all these services from outside to today where 82 per cent of all our needs are provided in-house.

He went on to explain that the trend in work mix towards process flexographics would continue as customers sought to improve their packaging designs as a way of enhancing sales of their own products. The rationale for investing in origination was that it offered increased control over the new design procedures, better response times, a more integrated liaison with customers and reduction of origination costs. The aim by next year was to complete almost all jobs in-house. A short synopsis of origination procedures is provided in Exhibit 3 and information relating to the department is given in Exhibit 4.

**Exhibit 3**      Origination department procedures

---

When an order is received that requires either a new design or an amendment to an existing design, it goes to a planner within the origination department. The planner then allocates it to a buyer, taking into account existing workloads and also customer knowledge where this has relevance to the smooth running of a job. A buyer then prepares the customer brief and passes it to the studio for the artwork to be completed. Currently, there are five staff members[1] working in the studio and they select the priority for completing jobs in line with customer delivery requirements. Including customer liaison, there are nine steps in the procedure before the negatives are sent to manufacturing, which then makes the plates and prints the job.

The length of time it takes to approve initial designs or subsequent changes varies with each customer. For planning purposes, the total lead times allowed were 21 days for an amended design and 22 and 25 days for a new design (for line and process, respectively). Many of these steps were, in fact, allocated one day in terms of overall planning, yet took only a few hours to complete. Also, 10 days were allocated to the artwork task in the studio even though the average time was only four hours. The 10 days were allocated in order that a realistic allowance would be made to include the backlog position in this part of the procedure.

The most difficult dimension in planning origination schedules was caused by customer delays in approving artwork and subsequent modifications. Customer placement dates recognized the lengthy lead times in this stage of the total procedure (see Exhibit 2). However, very often customer approvals were delayed until the point that delivery dates of the printed packaging were put at risk. Then all efforts had to be made to ensure that the agreed deliveries were met, which often was linked to a customer's own product launch date.

Currently, the marketing/sales team is responsible for customer liaison. The customers discuss orders of all types with the relevant sales personnel, who are the prime contacts throughout all stages of the job. The exception is distribution, as direct discussion/confirmation of delivery details are made with the customer by the distribution function.

---

*Note*
1. Of the five staff members in the studio, one is a trainee. The company has found that studio staff of the necessary experience and capability are hard to come by and can command high salaries. For these reasons it decided to train its own staff within this area.

# The Future

Steve Bishop concluded:

> Our decision to move into origination has given us much of what we hoped. It gets us closer to our customers and means that we can respond more quickly to changes in their needs. The investments involved were not large, but the cost advantages we have secured have yielded a good return. Overall our business is growing and this has been one contribution to our improved position. Certainly we feel we have the potential to gain more control over more of the process and at least afford ourselves the opportunity of reviewing lead times with the intention of reducing them and thereby supporting the key delivery-related criteria, which are a growing part of our markets.

**Exhibit 4**    Representative sample of the 491 jobs in progress in the origination department on 31 March

| Customer | Line/process[1] | Agreed delivery date | Design type[2] |
|----------|-----------------|----------------------|----------------|
| Abbey | L | 30 Jun | N |
| Browns | L | 15 Jul | A |
| Shelleys | P | 27 May | N |
| Hartstone | L | 4 Apr | A |
| Aztec | P | 11 Jun | A |
| Oaks | P | 27 Mar | A |
| A. J. Foods | L | 3 Jul | N |
| Aztec | L | 18 Apr | A |
| F-lite | L | 20 Mar | N |
| Texet | L | 2 Aug | A |
| Radcliffes | P | 4 Jun | N |
| Coles | P | 10 Mar | N |
| Texet | L | 10 Jul | A |
| Hartstone | L | 31 Mar | A |
| A. J. Foods | P | 13 Apr | A |
| J. B. Foods | L | 18 Jun | N |
| Abbey | L | 21 Jun | N |
| Cowies | L | 21 Mar | A |
| JBK | P | 20 May | A |
| Browns | L | 6 Sep | N |
| Alexon | P | 16 Mar | N |
| Crystal | L | 21 Aug | N |
| Oaks | P | 16 Apr | A |
| Marcos | L | 29 Mar | N |
| Solent | L | 18 Jun | A |
| Hartstone | P | 2 Apr | N |
| Crystal | L | 8 May | A |
| Shelleys | L | 10 Apr | N |
| Abbey | L | 2 Apr | A |
| F-lite | L | 4 Apr | N |
| Radcliffes | P | 1 May | A |
| Marcos | L | 16 Sep | N |
| Shelleys | L | 30 Aug | N |

*Notes*
**1**. L = line; P = process.
**2**. A = amendment; N = new.

# Note

1. Lower-priced consumer products, such as potato chips or potato crisps, could not justify designs that could only previously be met using gravure processes. The lower costs of flexographic processes now enabled more sophisticated designs to be used on those types of product.

# Nolan and Warner plc

In conclusion, it seems agreed that we should go ahead and quote for the two new items in the VR100 product range, one of high and one of low volume demand. I support this decision, for it is essential that we increase our sales revenue to a level where the potential for making an adequate return becomes available. Our current organizational structure, the strengths that come from our position in the market, the inherent design, manufacturing capability, available plant, and process capacity provide us with the wherewithal to take on these two new items with relatively little outlay. The products are compatible with our existing range and should present few manufacturing problems.

These were John Dyson's concluding comments at the June board meeting.

## Background

Noland and Warner plc[1] (N&W) is a wholly owned subsidiary of a UK-based automotive component supplier. As with all subsidiaries in the ATMO Group, N&W is responsible for all facets of the business, except the centralized capital funding arrangements, which operate within the group. Consequently, John Dyson, the managing director, through the group executive board, is responsible for setting N&W's corporate objectives in line with certain group-based performance criteria (for example, ROI). The meeting described in the opening paragraph is an N&W board meeting. It is at such meetings that local company decisions are made within a set of annual corporate forecasts and activities, which have to be agreed with the ATMO Group board at the start of each year.

Although N&W's markets are in the automotive component industry, the remainder of the ATMO Group is involved in other product areas, which are based on engineering, electronics, chemicals and construction.

This case was prepared by Terry Hill (University of Oxford). It is intended for class discussion and not as an illustrtion of good or bad management. © AMD Publishing.

# Marketing

Increasing competition and excess capacity has put much pressure on to N&W's markets and sales. Exhibit 1 shows the main product ranges of its business and also the unit sales during the last six years.

Rob James, the marketing director, considers the principal marketing task in this way:

> Our main aim has been, and still is, to minimize the reduction in sales revenue in real terms, and then build on the European and US demand improvements as the world economy picks up. Following the sales revenue (£s) drop five years ago, we have just about kept actual sales (£s) steady since that time. As a consequence, we have been able to minimize the revenue fall in real sales.
>
> Although the RU400 range sales have not been what the forecasts had us believe, this year (together with the known orders and forecasts for next year) shows a marked improvement over the last two years. Similarly, the VR150 and AC250 ranges are both up on the last two years' sales and the AC200 has sold more this year than ever before. In addition, the spares market is more than holding its own, as one would expect. It has been tough going over this time, and price competition has been very severe. Throughout, however, we have carefully pursued a policy of staying with all aspects of the business by attempting to meet all the demands of our customers where possible.
>
> The two products currently being discussed represent our strategy in the past and in the foreseeable future. We have to be prepared to chase the business, especially where

**Exhibit 1**  Annual unit sales by product range in the last six years

| Product range[2,3] | Unit sales for year ended 31 December[1] | | | | | |
|---|---|---|---|---|---|---|
| | Current year minus | | | | | Current year[4] |
| | 5 | 4 | 3 | 2 | 1 | |
| VR100 | 105 650 | 74 500 | 72 880 | 58 400 | 51 790 | 45 600 |
| VR150 | 74 600 | 44 850 | 45 950 | 31 250 | 30 880 | 36 040 |
| AC200 | 3 110 | 3 290 | 3 120 | 3 270 | 2 650 | 4 160 |
| AC250 | 52 620 | 34 560 | 42 360 | 28 350 | 28 520 | 37 100 |
| NT300 | 25 750 | 23 170 | 22 200 | 16 630 | 15 440 | 12 610 |
| RU400 | – | – | – | 170 | 110 | 250 |
| Total | 261 730 | 180 370 | 186 510 | 138 070 | 129 390 | 135 760 |

*Notes*

1. These are in terms of units sold and all figures have been rounded. As the unit price varies and has changed over time, it is not appropriate to relate these unit volumes to the sales revenue (£s) levels given in Exhibit 2.
2. Each product range (VR, AC, NT and RU) comprises a number of general products, each at a different stage in its own life cycle.
3. There are four main product ranges (VR, AC, NT and RU) within which there are subranges (for example, VR100 and VR150) with individual products within each of these.
4. Figures for the first eight months only of the current year are available; these have been increased on a *pro rata* basis.

we think our competitors may not be willing to go. Although this takes us into some smaller-volume products, it represents good revenue and sound business. To be able to minimize the fall in real sales (£s) has meant that we have had to increase the number of product ranges with the advent of the RU400 range two years ago and also extend the number of individual products within each range during these years. This has resulted in the need for increased efforts throughout the company, from design, product engineering, to marketing and manufacturing.

**Exhibit 2**    Balance sheet (all figures in £000s; year ended 31 December)

| | Current year minus: | | | | |
|---|---|---|---|---|---|
| | 5 | 4 | 3 | 2 | 1 |
| Total fixed assets[1] | 6 963 | 7 751 | 12 860 | 12 589 | 11 727 |
| Current assets | | | | | |
| Inventory[2] | 7 219 | 8 378 | 9 407 | 9 817 | 10 206 |
| Debtors and pre-payments | 2 893 | 2 970 | 3 010 | 2 930 | 3 209 |
| Cash | 7 | 7 | 8 | 17 | 11 |
| Total | 10 119 | 11 355 | 12 425 | 12 764 | 13 426 |
| Less current liabilities | | | | | |
| Creditors and accruals | 4 004 | 4 816 | 3 186 | 3 174 | 2 904 |
| Bank overdraft | 2 667 | 5 837 | 5 762 | 8 593 | 8 458 |
| Total | 6 671 | 10 653 | 8 948 | 11 767 | 11 362 |
| Working capital | 3 448 | 702 | 3 477 | 997 | 2 064 |
| Net assets employed | 10 411 | 8 453 | 16 337 | 13 586 | 13 791 |
| Financed by | | | | | |
| Intergroup capital account | 7 453 | 7 892 | 12 575 | 10 714 | 13 308 |
| Profit (loss) for the year | 2 958 | 561 | 1 062 | 172 | 483 |
| Intergroup loan | – | – | 2 700 | 2 700 | – |
| Total | 10 411 | 8 453 | 16 337 | 13 586 | 13 791 |

*Notes*
1. About 75 per cent of the plant investment three years ago was to provide the manufacturing process capability that the company did not have at the time to enable it to make new products. The other quarter was to help improve the process on a critical component. In turn, this improvement led to reduced manufacturing costs and a subsequent release of capacity in the related parts of the process.
2. Sales and inventory breakdown for each of the last five years are below:

| Current year minus: | Sales (£m) | Inventory (£000s) | | | |
|---|---|---|---|---|---|
| | | Raw materials | Work in progress | Finished goods | Total |
| 5 | 31.7 | 310 | 4184 | 2725 | 7 219 |
| 4 | 23.4 | 488 | 4956 | 2934 | 8 378 |
| 3 | 27.0 | 624 | 6579 | 2204 | 9 407 |
| 2 | 26.1 | 606 | 6960 | 2251 | 9 817 |
| 1 | 26.9 | 637 | 7494 | 2075 | 10 206 |

Exhibit 2 reviews the balance sheets for the period and also provides the sales information referred to by Rob James as Note 2.

# Manufacturing

The manufacturing processes are in three distinct production units. The first two units involve machining and other processes primarily laid out on a process or functional basis. In addition to the traditional areas, such as grinding and turning, there are also departments with processes to provide all or most of the operations necessary to manufacture similar components for the complete range of products. On the non-machining side, the facilities include heat treatment, degreasing and other preparatory and finishing processes. Although some of the components are bought in from outside suppliers, the policy has been, and still is, to manufacture internally wherever possible. In more recent years, the plant and process investment that has taken place has been largely to meet the requirement of new products, or for specific process improvement (for example, see Note 1, Exhibit 2). The third production unit concerns subassembly, final assembly and test. This involves subassembly and assembly processes for the higher-volume products and bench layouts to meet low-volume requirements.

Information on some representative products in each of the three production units is given in Exhibits 3 to 5. To Mike Edwards, the operations director, the manufacturing task concerned:

the introduction of new products within existing ranges and the need to reduce manufacturing costs throughout the process. Over the last year, there has also been substantial pressure to reduce inventory, in order to improve the cash-flow situation. Due to the

**Exhibit 3**    Manufacturing costs by product range

| Product range | Total manufacturing costs (per cent)[1] | | | |
|---|---|---|---|---|
| | Materials | Labour | Overhead[2] | Total |
| VR100 | 40 | 13 | 47 | 100 |
| VR150 | 39 | 13 | 48 | 100 |
| AC200 | 33 | 16 | 51 | 100 |
| AC250 | 42 | 14 | 44 | 100 |
| NT300 | 35 | 16 | 49 | 100 |
| RU400 | 43 | 15 | 42 | 100 |

*Notes*

1. The percentages given are based on three products in each range, which are currently made for original equipment (OE) sales, but reflect the spread of volumes associated with the product range reviewed. OE sales refer to orders for products, which go on to vehicles currently in production at N&W's customer's assembly plants. When vehicles are no longer being built, the orders for products revert to sales to meet the demand for spares or service only. Where a vehicle has been made for some years, then demand for products will comprise both OE and spares or service sales.
2. Overhead recovery rates are based on direct labour hours.

**Exhibit 4**   Call-offs for representative components in two of the four product ranges, with order quantity issues in the first production unit

| Product information | | | Monthly average call-offs[1] and typical order quantities[2,3] | | | |
| --- | --- | --- | --- | --- | --- | --- |
| | | | Current year minus | | | Current year |
| Range | Component | Issue details | 3 | 2 | 1 | |
| VR100 | VR108/ 1426 | Call-off | 2600 | 2520 | 1970 | 1490 |
| | | Order quantity | 4750 | 4250 | 3250 | 3500 |
| | VR111/ 3278 | Call-off | 50 | – | – | – |
| | | Order quantity | 255 | – | – | – |
| | VR115/ 1002 | Call-off | 2500 | 2500 | 2500 | 1500 |
| | | Order quantity | 2500 | 2500 | 2500 | 2500 |
| | VR116/ 2614 | Call-off | 800 | 240 | 140 | 200 |
| | | Order quantity | 800 | 800 | 440 | 400 |
| VR150 | VR151/ 1214 | Call-off | – | 400 | 1200 | 900 |
| | | Order quantity | – | 600 | 1200 | 1200 |
| | VR164/ 1019 | Call-off | 15 | 16 | 12 | – |
| | | Order quantity | 25 | 25 | 25 | – |
| | VR170/ 2630 | Call-off | – | – | 600 | 300 |
| | | Order quantity | – | – | 200 | 100 |
| | VR171/ 2710 | Call-off | – | 5 | 10 | 3 |
| | | Order quantity | – | 10 | 10 | 10 |
| AC200 | AC215/ 1186 | Call-off | 100 | 70 | 50 | 25 |
| | | Order quantity | 100 | 100 | 100 | 75 |
| AC250 | AC255/ 4914 | Call-off | 400 | 300 | 300 | 400 |
| | | Order quantity | 400 | 400 | 400 | 400 |
| | AC270/ 5300 | Call-off | 20 | 10 | 10 | 20 |
| | | Order quantity | 20 | 20 | 20 | 20 |

*Notes*

1. A call-off is the monthly delivery requirement to a customer.
2. The order quantity is the number of components issued to and processed through the first production unit (also known as batch size). These are not issued each month, but only as required.
3. Where order quantities exceed the call-off requirement, this implies that manufacturing produces, for instance, two months' sales at a time.

wider product range and the need to respond quickly to customers' changes in call-offs, this has been difficult. However, reducing inventory has to be our first priority in the future and will be an essential part of our strategic review.

In addition, the business is not making anywhere near the required return on investment. As a first step towards improving this, we have decided to close down our satellite plant at Banbury, some 30 miles away. This will mean moving the subassembly, assembly and test facilities of the short-order shop[2] at Banbury into our main site but few, if any, of the operators due to the distance involved – all components for the short-order requirements are already made on the main site.

The argument behind this move was the very necessary one to reduce costs. Spare capacity at the main factory site existed due mainly to lower unit demand and

**Exhibit 5** Summaries of typical component routings through the first production unit

| Number of machines per category[2] to complete typical components[3] | | | | Cumulative total standard time[1] | | |
|---|---|---|---|---|---|---|
| | | | | Process time per component (standard minutes) | Change-over time (standard hours)[4] | |
| A | B | C | D | | Different items | Like items |
| 6 | 5 | 4 | 5 | 126.6 | 39.0 | 27.5 |
| 3 | 7 | 2 | 2 | 29.2 | 34.5 | 18.0 |
| 6 | 4 | 3 | 4 | 55.5 | 30.0 | 11.0 |
| 7 | 5 | 3 | 3 | 47.4 | 28.0 | 10.0 |
| 6 | 4 | 2 | 3 | 64.5 | 21.5 | 14.0 |
| 2 | 2 | 3 | 2 | 120.1 | 21.0 | 15.0 |
| 6 | 4 | 3 | 1 | 162.1 | 21.5 | 12.5 |

*Notes*

1. The cumulative total standard time means that, for the first component, the total process time is 126.6 standard minutes per component, using 20 different machines from categories A to D inclusive, with a cumulative set-up time for these 20 machines of between 27.5 to 39.0 hours.
2. Machine categories are:
   A. General-purpose machines.
   B. Machines dedicated to one product range (for example, VR100).
   C. Machines dedicated to part of a product range (for example, part of VR100 range).
   D. Machines dedicated to one operation on one component by a fixture (for example, can only complete one operation on component VR108/1426).
   All machines are laid out by function or process.
3. The seven components shown are representative of the range of work involved.
4. Regarding change-over times: the 'like items' relate to a product that is similar in set-up terms to the product it is following and hence the change-over time is less than for a 'different item' that is not similar.
5. The operations do not include in-process testing.

process improvements (see Exhibit 6). It was considered that closing down the Banbury site would reduce total costs, with the manufacturing requirements being absorbed by the existing capacity on the main site.

Mike Edwards continued to explain that over the last six or seven years there has been a stringent check on process investment.

> This understandable corporate restriction has meant that, apart from the investment which has been necessary to meet new product requirements, investment has been difficult to come by. Only where significant process cost savings could be achieved has any investment been forthcoming. Consequently, we are by and large running today with the processes bought some six or more years ago.

# The Future

In addition to attempting to maintain sales revenue levels and reduce process and manufacturing costs, N&W is also seriously looking at the level of organizational

**Exhibit 6**     Process time reductions and plant utilization changes for one high-volume component on its route through the second production unit[1]

| Aspect | Current year minus | | Current year |
|---|---|---|---|
| | **5** | **2** | |
| Total standard minutes per component[2] | 8.3 | 6.3 | 4.7 |
| Plant utilization percentage | | | |
| Average | 64 | 44 | 34 |
| Low | 14 | 4 | 3 |
| High | 89 | 85 | 82 |

*Notes*

1. Although the plant utilization figures given relate to the second production unit, they are also typical of the plant utilization changes elsewhere.

2. There are fewer operations (and consequently the time taken in standard minutes is significantly shorter) through which components have to go in the second production unit compared to the first production unit.

**Exhibit 7**     Organization chart

requirements necessary to sustain the business. The present organization chart and personnel strengths are shown in Exhibit 7. The difficultly with this task is knowing where and how to make the savings.

## Notes

1. Plc means public limited company and in the USA equates to being incorporated.
2. The short-order shop handles some low-volume products and spares and is on a separate site from the main site. The three 'distinct production units' referred to earlier are all on the main site.

# Norex Printing Services

## Background

Norex Printing Services (NPS) is part of MRB Holdings, a large financial services group. NPS comprises a printing and mailing facility based in Manchester, UK. Some years ago, the board of MRB Holdings completed a strategic review that resulted in a revised mandate for NPS to operate more as an independent profit centre, seeking additional business outside the group. Until that time the major work of NPS was to provide the printing and mailing tasks for MRB's retail bank including corporate and personal bank statements and other related tasks as well as a whole range of printing and mailing work for other companies in the group.

To date NPS has achieved some notable successes in obtaining external business and this work now constitutes a substantial part of total sales revenue. It includes work for two utility companies: Telemex, a telephone company, and SEK, an electricity company. NPS is currently bidding for a major new contract with another bank, National Baking Direct, to print and mail their customer statements. The management team of NPS regard this possible contract as a further major opportunity and are confident of winning the business. As part of this growth strategy the team are preparing an investment proposal requesting the board of MRB Holdings to sanction expenditure on further printing and mailing equipment needed to provide the necessary additional capacity, and an extension to the existing buildings to accommodate some of the equipment.

## The Nature of Operations

The NPS operations are housed in one building on a large site with ample space for expansion. The two largest areas within the building are the print room and the mail room (see Exhibit 1).

Some customer contracts require both printing and mailing while others require only printing with the output despatched in bulk to the customer. Mail items and some packaged bulk output are collected at set times during the day by the Post

This case was written by Terry Hill (University of Oxford) and R. Lily. It is intended as a basis for class discussion and not as an example of good or bad management. © AMD Publishing.

**Exhibit 1**    NPS site layout

Office. There is little opportunity to changes these times as they have to fit with the times allocated by the local Post Office sorting depot in order to guarantee delivery to meet agreed schedules. Other bulk output is collected by a customer's own transport. Meeting despatch times is an essential operations task as all major contracts include a detailed despatch schedule. Because on-time delivery is such a key customer requirement, the management team of NPS is keen to ensure that the necessary print and mail capacity is available to cater for the demands of any new business. It has been assessed that the recent bid for the major contract with another bank will require additional capacity if the tender is accepted. Hence the investment proposal referred to earlier.

## The Print Room

The print room is divided into two sections – the online area, containing 15 high-speed printers, and the offline area where the output is marshalled for onward transfer. Customers' print files are delivered via high-speed data links on to the print queues on the site computer. The print operators allocate print files to individual printers, using a control console. Large applications are subdivided into several print files to enable a number of printers to work simultaneously on the same job.

The large-volume applications all use continuous stationery which is fed directly on to a printer from a large roll. Some of the smaller-volume work is fed as continuous stationery from boxes and a small amount of work uses cut sheets that are hopper fed on to a printer.

There are three types of printer in use (see Exhibit 2), reflecting the technology developments by the computer manufacturers and earlier investment decisions made by NPS. The oldest group of printers is classed as 'type 1', of which there are six. Two of the type 1 printers are dedicated to small-volume applications, requiring box-fed and cut-sheet stationery and run at 5000 feet/hour. The remaining type 1 printers are suitable for continuous stationery and run at 7000 feet/hour. The two low-volume, lower-speed machines are retained to meet long-standing jobs. For some time now new contracts have not been sought for this capacity as a matter of policy. Consequently, all capacity calculations do not include these two machines.

Type 2 printers are designated as wide printers due to the range of stationery they can accommodate. Some applications can be printed as two documents side by side, thus doubling the effective throughput of those documents. There are seven printers in this group.

The third group, type 3, comprises two fast wide printers. These are based on the most up-to-date technology and constituted a major investment. When required, these can print side by side and also have a printing speed some 50 per cent higher than the type 2 wide printers (see Exhibit 2 for details).

Three years ago, to ease the handling of printed output, a series of conveyors were installed in the print room that link the printers to the offline area. When a stack of continuous stationery output from a printer reaches a given height, it is automatically cut and the stack is pushed on to the conveyor. Four of the type 1 printers and four of the type 2 wide printers are connected to this conveyor system. However, when the newer type 3 printers were installed, the only available floor area did not have access to the conveyor system. Consequently output from these printers is accumulated in stacks at the end of the printer and periodically loaded on to trolleys by the operators and moved offline.

The site computer automatically generates an audit trail which specifies which jobs have been printed, the time taken and the print footage. An extract of this data

**Exhibit 2**    Types of printer

| Machine | | Throughput (000s feet per hour) | Manning ratio (machines per operator) |
|---|---|---|---|
| type | number | | |
| 1[1] | 4 | 7 | 2.5 |
| 2 | 7 | 7 | 2.5 |
| 3 | 2 | 10 | 2.5 |

*Note*
**1**. In addition to the four type 1 printers there are two further printers in this category. As explained in the case narrative, these are excluded from capacity calculations and so data is neither provided above nor in Exhibit 3.

is given in Exhibit 3. This is for week 14, a middle week of a month. Demand varies during a month with end-of-month weeks sometimes as much as 30–40 per cent higher than other weeks in the same period. The data is summarized by four-hour periods. The corresponding manning levels for print operators in week 14 are shown in Exhibit 4.

**Exhibit 3**   Total print footage[1] for a representative middle-of-month week (week 14) by day and four-hourly period

| Day | Machine type[2,3] | 08.00–12.00 | 12.00–16.00 | 16.00–20.00 | 20.00–24.00 | 24.00–04.00 | 04.00–08.00 |
|---|---|---|---|---|---|---|---|
| Mon | 1 | 10 224 | 9 046 | 26 450 | 92 849 | 106 022 | 66 103 |
| | 2 | 9 626 | 34 113 | 18 649 | 68 476 | 72 543 | 77 290 |
| | 3 | 0 | 0 | 8 575 | 23 841 | 62 389 | 20 370 |
| | Total | 19 850 | 43 159 | 53 674 | 185 166 | 240 954 | 163 763 |
| Tue | 1 | 11 149 | 3 784 | 24 055 | 112 219 | 108 566 | 61 270 |
| | 2 | 18 442 | 31 168 | 64 125 | 55 223 | 84 850 | 75 148 |
| | 3 | 2 453 | 0 | 7 004 | 15 793 | 60 733 | 20 936 |
| | Total | 32 044 | 34 952 | 95 184 | 183 235 | 254 149 | 157 354 |
| Wed | 1 | 3 013 | 8 637 | 47 359 | 99 376 | 108 340 | 67 597 |
| | 2 | 20 247 | 7 249 | 49 947 | 77 103 | 105 722 | 66 139 |
| | 3 | 1 091 | 655 | 10 465 | 7 165 | 66 559 | 13 467 |
| | Total | 24 351 | 16 541 | 107 771 | 183 644 | 280 621 | 147 203 |
| Thu | 1 | 44 559 | 23 550 | 31 742 | 90 621 | 100 221 | 107 405 |
| | 2 | 30 649 | 32 953 | 21 345 | 74 718 | 129 474 | 98 055 |
| | 3 | 40 220 | 13 994 | 8 685 | 18 330 | 70 443 | 23 473 |
| | Total | 115 428 | 70 497 | 61 772 | 183 669 | 300 138 | 228 933 |
| Fri | 1 | 20 699 | 33 104 | 55 144 | 108 962 | 103 971 | 9 261 |
| | 2 | 20 352 | 58 058 | 42 488 | 58 817 | 114 270 | 46 321 |
| | 3 | 28 172 | 15 935 | 21 468 | 38 585 | 66 541 | 1 739 |
| | Total | 69 223 | 107 097 | 119 100 | 206 364 | 284 782 | 57 321 |
| Sat | 1 | 11 067 | 12 581 | 573 | 1 346 | 14 640 | 950 |
| | 2 | 1 582 | 103 | 186 | 257 | 8 725 | 1 712 |
| | 3 | 849 | 0 | 0 | 0 | 0 | 0 |
| | Total | 13 498 | 12 684 | 759 | 1 603 | 23 365 | 2 662 |
| Sun | 1 | 665 | 659 | 116 | 584 | 362 | 850 |
| | 2 | 747 | 1 620 | 123 | 1 214 | 1 384 | 2 105 |
| | 3 | 0 | 0 | 0 | 0 | 0 | 0 |
| | Total | 1 412 | 2 279 | 239 | 1 798 | 1 746 | 2 955 |

*Notes*
1. Feet and footage are imperial measures. One metre is 3.3 feet.
2. The data for machine type 1 does not include the two low-volume machines referred to in the case narrative.
3. For the wide printers (types 2 and 3) one foot of output is either one foot of a single document or one foot of side-by-side documents. Thus, print footage is used as the common denominator of both demand and capacity.

**Exhibit 4**      Print operator planning levels for week 14

| Day | Four-hour period | | | | | |
|-----|-------------|-------------|-------------|-------------|-------------|-------------|
|     | 08.00–12.00 | 12.00–16.00 | 16.00–20.00 | 20.00–24.00 | 24.00–04.00 | 04.00–08.00 |
| Mon | 1 | 1 | 3 | 5 | 6 | 4 |
| Tue | 2 | 2 | 3 | 5 | 6 | 4 |
| Wed | 2 | 2 | 3 | 5 | 6 | 4 |
| Thu | 2 | 2 | 3 | 5 | 6 | 5 |
| Fri | 2 | 2 | 3 | 5 | 6 | 5 |
| Sat | 1 | 1 | 1 | 1 | 1 | 1 |
| Sun | 1 | 1 | 1 | 1 | 1 | 1 |

Some of the output needs to be separated offline and consolidated with other output for the same destination. For example, there will be a selection of different print-outs produced each night for each of the branches of the MRB bank. It is necessary to assemble a complete set for each branch. Depending on the distance of a branch from NPS's Manchester site, these sets need to be ready for collection by vans scheduled from 23.00 hours on the evening of printing through to 04.00 hours the following morning. All output to be mailed is moved by trolley down the corridor to the mail room.

## The Mail Room

A mailing machine is normally fed from a stack of continuous stationery. The machine separates each sheet and places the sheets of a statement into an envelope. In addition to the statements, up to six inserts (which normally comprise advertising material) can be added to each envelope. It is critically important that the number of envelopes produced from each stack is exactly the same as the control total printed with the stack. Much operator time is taken to ensure that the output is always reconciled with the control totals before each batch is moved away from a mailing machine. Situations where customers receive another person's statement together with their own bank statement or customers receive an empty envelope are to be avoided at all costs. Completed stacks of mailed items are then moved to the despatch area where they are collected by the Post Office.

## Customer Applications

For the main types of application with which NPS deals, the data does not become available until the end of a customer's trading day. The data is then normally processed on a customer's own computer configuration before the necessary print files are created and transmitted to the NPS site. Typically, the print files arrive mid to late evening or in the early hours of the following morning. When customers experience problems in their own internal processing, the arrival of the print files can be delayed by several hours. But even in these circumstances a customer still looks to NPS to meet the agreed despatch times from the site, if at all possible.

The print files for an application vary in volume with a recognized pattern of peak loads. For example, most personal customer bank statements are provided at the end of the month. However, even on a normal day the volumes can fluctuate substantially.

Each application has a written Service Level Agreement (SLA), which is signed by the customer and NPS. The key elements specified in the SLA are the volume of print (on key days), the time by which the customer will ensure that the files arrive on the print queue at NPS and the despatch time from the NPS site. Despatch may be specified as being more than one time, for example, 70 per cent by 24.00 hours and 100 per cent by 02.00 hours. Some examples of customer applications and the key elements of the corresponding SLA are given in Exhibit 5 with Exhibit 6 giving further details.

**Exhibit 5**     A sample of major current customer contracts

| Customer and application | | Frequency | Time on the print queue | Despatch deadlines[1] | | Print | Mail[2] |
|---|---|---|---|---|---|---|---|
| | | | | same | next | yes (✓) | |
| | | | | day | | | |
| MRB Bank | credit card statements[3] | daily | 02.00 | 12.30 16.00 | | ✓ ✓ | ✓ ✓ |
| | monthly client statements | monthly | 08.00 | 16.00 | – | ✓ | |
| | branch accounts[4] | weekly | 22.00 | 23.00 | 04.00 | ✓ | |
| | personal customer bank statements | daily | 22.00 | – | 16.00 | ✓ | ✓ |
| | special branch reports | quarterly | Friday 22.30 | Tuesday am | | ✓ | |
| Telemex | customer accounts | daily | 10.00 | within 2 days | | ✓ | ✓ |
| SEK | customer accounts[5] | daily | varied | within 24 hours | | ✓ | ✓ |

*Notes*
1. Except for MRB credit card statements, 100 per cent of all other outputs are to be despatched by the time specified. Thus the data for all MRB Bank personal customer bank statements are scheduled to arrive at 22.00 hours and all outputs need to be despatched by 16.00 hours on the day following receipt of the data.
2. Items that are mailed need to be printed to allow sufficient time for the mailing process to be completed in line with the despatch deadlines given.
3. 70 per cent of credit card statements are required by 12.30 and 100 per cent by 16.00 hours on the same day.
4. Branch accounts are despatched from 23.00 hours on one day to 04.00 hours on the next day in line with the travel time to a branch.
5. SEK cannot guarantee exact times for data delivery due to current computer capacity problems, hence the word 'varied' in the 'Time on the print queue' column.

**Exhibit 6**      Further details of the customer contract sample in Exhibit 5

> **MRB Bank credit card statements** – these record transactions up to 16.00 hours on the day before the statement is printed. In line with other credit card arrangements, customers are allocated a date in the month when the statement is closed. This date is specified by the MRB Bank in line with its own requirements.
>
> **MRB Bank monthly client statements** – these are prepared and sent to the clients' branches for personal collection. No mailing is therefore required.
>
> **MRB Bank branch accounts** – these are prepared for a branch as part of managing transactions within the branch.
>
> **MRB Bank personal customer bank statements** – these record the transactions and are mailed directly to each customer. Almost 80 per cent of customers opt to have their accounts to close in the last three days of a calendar month.
>
> **MRB Bank special branch reports** – financial reports covering the same quarter for each branch.
>
> **Telemex customer accounts** – these are quarterly telephone statements for Telemex customers. Individuals are allocated different month ends to spread the cash flow for Telemex. This means that for a customer a quarter can end at any time in a month. Furthermore, Telemex have negotiated a lower transaction cost with NPS by allowing the printing and mailing work involved to be spread over a two-day period.
>
> **SEK customer accounts** – similar to Telemex; see Note 5 on Exhibit 5.

## Management Reports

The principal reports used to control the operational performance at NPS are:

- **print output** (see Exhibit 7). This shows the total print output in feet by type of stationery. The data is given by month for the year to date with a comparison with last year also provided.

- **print productivity** (see Exhibit 8). The report covers only the roll-fed printers and records the average footage[1] produced per print operator by month.

- **mail daily report** (see Exhibit 9). The report shows the number of mailed items despatched, the level of reprints required, the number of batches not balancing with the control totals at the first check and highlights any missed deadlines.

- **mail room output** (see Exhibit 10). This lists the number of mailed items by month in the year to date.

- **missed production deadlines** (see Exhibit 11). This report shows the percentage of jobs that have missed their deadline for despatch by each month for the year to date. An additional report details all instances of missed deadlines in the current month and their causes.

**Exhibit 7**     Monthly print output report for February

| Printer type | Jan | Feb | Mar | Dec | Year to date | Previous year |
|---|---|---|---|---|---|---|
| Roll-fed laser | 15 383 | 14 143 | | | 29 526 | 163 137 |
| Box-fed laser | 525 | 494 | | | 1 019 | 17 927 |
| Cut-sheet | 520 | 694 | | | 1 214 | 6 880 |
| Total | 16 428 | 15 331 | | | 31 579 | 187 944 |
| % increase on previous month | 14.7 | −6.7 | | | | |
| % increase on previous year | 14.7 | 9.9 | | | | |

**Exhibit 8**     Monthly productivity report: roll-fed printers for February

| Month | Productivity (feet per operator) |
|---|---|
| *Target* | *880 000* |
| January | 827 090 |
| February | 834 669 |
| December | |
| Average | 830 880 |

**Exhibit 9**     Mail daily output report

| **Output despatched: 8 February** | | |
|---|---|---|
| Total number of mailed items | : | 194 666 |
| Were all items despatched to schedule? | : | Yes |
| If not, provide details | : | not applicable |
| Percentage and volume of reprints | : | 0.045%    89 |
| Percentage and volume of rejects | : | 1.011%    1972 |
| Total full batch reprints requested | : | 1 |
| Total number of batches not balancing at machine | : | 6.3% |
| Problem/duplicate batches | : | No |
| Comment | : | |
| Duplicate statements within a batch | : | No |
| Comment | : | |

**Exhibit 10** Mail room output report for February

| Printer type | Jan | Feb | Mar | Dec | Year to date | Previous year |
|---|---|---|---|---|---|---|
| Mail room staff | 36 | 36 | | | | |
| Total mailed items | 5 379 629 | 4 633 837 | | | 10 013 466 | 55 337 444 |
| % increase on previous month | 25 | −14 | | | | |
| Bank statements | 4 435 679 | 3 914 489 | | | 8 350 168 | 48 508 042 |
| % increase on previous month | 21 | −12 | | | | |
| Number of inserts | 240 000 | 225 000 | | | − | − |

**Exhibit 11** Missed production deadlines: monthly report

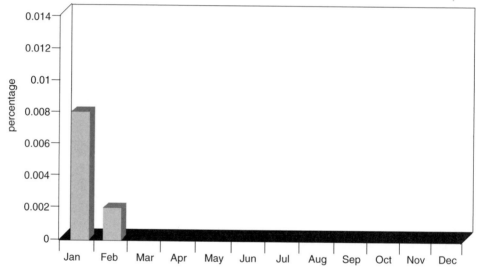

*Note*
The percentage figure is calculated by dividing missed deadlines by the number of deliveries.

## Capacity Calculations

The technical department is responsible for calculating capacity, monitoring equipment and proposing new investments. To undertake the task of calculating print capacity it uses the following guidelines:

- the two low-volume type 1 printers are not included in load or output calculations
- a manning ratio of one print operator to 2.5 print machines is assumed, so print capacity will be linked to the number of operators working at any one time

- there is only a small demand for printing on Saturday and Sunday, so all capacity and utilization analysis focuses on weekdays
- because of the specialized nature of some of the type 1 printing, a minimum average of 1.5 type 1 machines is assumed
- all capacity calculations are based on 90 per cent of the throughput speeds given in Exhibit 2
- set-ups and other tasks (such as replenishing paper and moving finished products) are completed by the operators while a machine is running. No stoppage time is, therefore, incurred.

# Contribution

As part of the initiative to develop NPS as an independent operation within MRB Holdings, a system of internal charging was introduced. Details of a representative sample of contracts are given in Exhibit 12.

# Contingency Planning

The data which NPS provide are vital for their customers' day-to-day business operation. NPS win contracts partly on the basis that they will consistently achieve the deadlines specified, even when the most extreme difficulties are encountered. Part of the operational planning for the site addresses the issue of the complete facility being unable to function, the so-called 'disaster scenario'. To cover this eventuality NPS has in place reciprocal agreements with other major print and mail facilities, including rival banking operations. The members of this consortium agree to process each other's customer data should a disaster occur.

# The Future

'The Group decision to change our mandate', explained Steve Lodge (CEO, NPS), 'has changed the way we work for the better. The contracts secured so far and the

**Exhibit 12**   Sample of runs from customer contracts

| Run number | Contract | Printer type | Price for the run (£s) | Run length (feet) | Variable cost for the run (£s) |
|---|---|---|---|---|---|
| 4628 | MRB bank statements | 2 | 620 | 17 500 | 230 |
| 5502 | SEK customer accounts | 1 | 135 | 8 400 | 100 |
| 6437 | Telemex customer accounts | 3 | 309 | 14 100 | 204 |
| 8491 | MRB branch acounts | 3 | 1 003 | 38 000 | 441 |

possible new contract to process statements for a rival bank are the type of steps we need to take in order to grow our business and meet the profit performance set by the holding company. However, more demand requires matching capacity and hence our decision to invest in additional printing and mailing capacity is appropriate. With this available we will still be able to meet the agreed contracts performance requirements.'

## Note

1. Footage relates to the imperial measure of one foot and is still used in the print and some other UK industries. As you will see, all measures of the amount of print produced are given in feet. One metre is 3.3 feet.

# case 11

# Ontario Packaging

It looks to me that we are agreed. The process investment proposals before us are sound in principle, providing we can increase throughput from present levels by some 40 per cent, as indicated in the supporting details. I know this is no easy task, but all market segments are getting more difficult, and if we are to survive and maintain current performance levels, then this type of challenge will be illustrative of many future corporate decisions. From these initial discussions it appears that the extra volume is available, even though it places a greater emphasis on price. The new process will help, in part, to reduce costs, but higher volumes are essential if we are to maintain the group's payback requirements and protect the above-average return on investment performance we have achieved in the past.

Norm Phillips, chief executive officer of Ontario Packaging, was summing up a meeting on manufacturing investment proposals, which was intended to be the initial phase of a modernization programme within the company.

## Background

Ontario Packaging is part of Texet Industries, a large group of companies with diverse interests in food, cosmetics, engineering and toys, besides a growing stake in retail holdings, and other non-manufacturing businesses. Taken over in the late 1980s, Ontario Packaging is now one of several packaging companies within the group, but the first within the province.

Having given the company time to settle down within the new corporate structure and allowing Norm Phillips to gain an understanding of the business since his transfer from within the group, some 12 months before, the executive group of Texet had recently asked the company to review its position. The review was to include an assessment of its current markets and to include any future process investment proposals it thought necessary, with an indication of why they should take place, and the anticipated impact on the business as a whole and on the various ROI measures used within the group, in particular.

This case study was written by Terry Hill (University of Oxford). It is intended for class discussion, and not as an illustration of good or bad management. © AMD Publishing.

# Manufacturing

Ontario Packaging produces a fairly wide range of cartons and other forms of packaging. Its manufacturing capability comprises various forms of printing, laminating, cutting, creasing, glueing and other auxiliary processes, together with a whole range of in-house support functions.

The investment proposals under review concern replacing current laminating equipment with an up-to-date process that would provide the same capability (see Exhibit 1). The cartons that use this process account for some 30 per cent of total production volumes (standard machine hours). At a cost of $2.5 million, the investment would give labour, material and other savings to provide a payback of 6.5 years on current volumes. However, in order to meet the Texet investment payback norm of four years it would be necessary to increase current sales revenue for these cartons by some 40 per cent. It is this higher level of volumes on which the investment proposals have been based.

Besides the basic gains accruing from increased throughput speed (a principal source of savings) and reduced material wastage, the new process would offer few additional technical advantages (set-up times were marginally faster) other than those associated with the reduced performance on existing processes resulting from wear and tear with age.

While the utilization of the current process was less than 60 per cent, the target set in the proposal for the new investment was 80–85 per cent, based on higher volumes.

# Marketing

'Ontario Packaging has, over the years, increasingly positioned itself in the higher-quality end of all its markets', explained Rod Shaw, vice-president marketing, who has been with the company for over 15 years. He added:

The cartons under review are no exception. While the technical features of the final carton are slightly less demanding than many of the rest of the product range, there is the same demand for high, reliable quality conformance. While the manufacturing process currently used is able to consistently provide the quality requirements of our products, no doubt the new process will enable us to achieve these more easily.

A recent marketing survey on the relative importance of different purchasing criteria to carton users revealed that, in the segment which the company currently serves, providing prompt quotations and samples, together with high delivery reliability and a willingness to meet schedule changes, are critical features and ones which our company has proved to be better at providing than our competitors. This represents the view our customers expressed in the survey.

While price is not an important factor in winning current orders for these products, it would increasingly be so for the new orders we would need to secure to achieve the addi-

**Exhibit 1**    Details of the investment proposal under review

As part of a strategy to upgrade its processes (as well as increase its process capability where appropriate) Ontario Packaging was proposing to invest in a state-of-the-art laminating process, which would replace the existing process capacity. Currently, some 30 per cent of the total production volumes (standard machine hours) were laminated.

The new laminator would offer significant savings in direct labour (through reduced manning), lower material costs within the laminating process and a reduced maintenance bill (although with a corresponding increase in depreciation costs).

However, in order to achieve the group payback norm of four years, the company would need to increase its sales of laminated products by about 40 per cent on current levels.

While set-up (or make-ready) times for the new process were similar to the existing equipment, throughput speeds were more than twice as fast. The order quantities currently processed averaged about 7 hours and ranged from 2 to 60 hours.

Current sales were split roughly half and half between those which were not price sensitive and those where price was an order-winning criterion at some level. However, the latter orders varied in their degree of price sensitivity: in two-thirds of this segment price was given a weighting of 20 points or less.

It was recognized that the proposed increase in sales of laminated products of about 40 per cent of current levels would be achieved in segments where price would increasingly be the important order-winner. The company, although recognizing that this would require significant sales effort, has identified the segments and customers that are available and consider the achievement of these higher volumes to be a realistic target within the required timescales.

*Notes*
1. Laminations consist of sheets of material (varying with individual specifications) that are glued together.
2. Due to space restrictions and to maintain the current, sensible flow of materials through the manufacturing process, the proposed new process will be installed where the existing equipment is positioned.
3. The current equipment comprises two machines and is run on a two-shift basis. It is also proposed to run the single replacement process on a two-shift basis.

tional volume called for by the output levels underpinning the process investment proposals being considered. However, to compensate we would be moving into higher-volume orders, which would reinforce the gains inherent in the new process in terms of the cost savings available, while obviously providing the overall volume levels associated with the whole proposal. I know we can get these additional orders, providing the price is right and we maintain all the other features of the product and necessary levels of customer service. It's a tall order, so to speak, but I know we can do it.

# 12 Peterson Carton Services

'Well, Jim', concluded Gerry Townsend, 'I do not understand why the downward trend in our financial performance is still continuing and particularly why last month does not show the improvement we expected.' Gerry Townsend, managing director of Peterson Carton Services, was discussing the management accounts for February with Jim Redman, the financial director.

With the increase in sales and manufacturing activity achieved since this time last year, the expected performance improvement has not materialized. In fact, the very opposite has happened. The financial position has now become very worrying. Well, by the end of next week we need to have prepared a summary of events and review of the actions we intend to take in order to bring about the necessary improvements. So far, the group board of directors has been patient, but at next week's meeting I am sure they will demand a clear statement of why this has happened and the steps we intend to take to turn the position around. We have to know how we are going to achieve our annual budgeted profit, having made losses in the first two months of this year amounting to £46,000 and £54,000, respectively [see Exhibit 1].

## Background

Peterson Carton Services (PCS) is situated in Lancaster, the county town of Lancashire in the north-west of England. Established in 1948, it was taken over in the late 1980s by Stebro Industries plc, a diverse group of companies involved in food processing, civil engineering, steel fabrication, general engineering, distribution, waste disposal, paper and carton making. PCS currently employs about 200 people and processes approximately 3000 tons of cardboard (referred to as *board* within the carton industry) a year, making it one of the top 30 carton manufacturers in the UK. The carton-making industry is highly fragmented, due principally to the costs of distribution, with some 250 companies serving the country. Most of these produce a wide range of general cartons for most market applications, with some

This case study was written by Terry Hill (University of Oxford) and S. H. Chambers (University of Warwick). It is intended for class discussion and not as an example of good or bad management practice. © AMD Publishing.

**Exhibit 1**  Summary of trading results and current year's budget

| Aspect | Accounting period results and current year budget | | | | | | | |
| --- | --- | --- | --- | --- | --- | --- | --- | --- |
| | Current year minus | | | Last year | | Current year | | |
| | 4 | 3 | 2 | January–June | July–December | January | February | Budget |
| Sales revenue (£000s) | 6292 | 6266 | 5505 | 3060 | 3745 | 581 | 563 | 6800 |
| Trading profit (£000s) | 283 | 135 | (151) | 79 | (321) | (46) | (54) | 236 |
| Percentage of sales margin | 4.5 | 2.2 | (2.7) | 2.5 | (8.5) | (7.9) | (9.6) | 3.5 |
| Percentage of return on investment | 2.8 | 2.5 | (4.6) | 1.4 | (12.6) | (11.8) | (14.2) | 8.0 |
| Net working capital as percentage of sales revenue | 14.1 | 14.4 | 13.2 | 14.2 | 18.1 | 18.2 | 18.1 | 10.7 |

companies also making speciality products to meet the particular needs of customers. PCS uses lithographic ('litho') printing and other traditional processes (see Exhibits 2A and B) to make its 'general' cartons (see Exhibits 3A and B) but has also developed specialized processes to make 'windowed' cartons at high speed and high quality. In addition, PCS also makes a non-carton product range of drip mats for breweries and distributors of imported wines. Also known as coasters, drip mats are sold for distribution to hotels, taverns and wine bars, where they are used to protect the surface of tables and bars. The shape and print details are customer-specified for each order.

Three years ago, the company had brought on to its main site a smaller carton business, which it had purchased some years earlier. As part of a rationalization plan, it was anticipated that this would lead to higher profits in the longer term, due to the estimated reduction in manufacturing and overhead costs resulting from this consolidation. Although cost savings did result, lower prices for existing products brought about by higher levels of competition led to a decline in profits for that year. When in the following year sales revenue also declined by 12 per cent, the company went into a loss situation (see Exhibit 1). In order to try to identify those market segments in which there was the greatest potential for sales growth, PCS completed a major market analysis, with the help of a large firm of marketing strategy consultants. This exercise reviewed the potential for sales growth in each of the main segments in which PCS operated. As a result, the consultants recommended a strategy for the company to concentrate its major sales effort in the beverages, food and 'windowed products' segments, which they identified as having the greatest potential for the rapid increase in volume necessary to sustain the required level of recovery in sales revenue and profit. The report argued that growth in these segments would be the best way to compensate for the sales revenue decline experienced in some other market segments. The reason for the sales decline in these areas was believed to be the result of intensive competition from carton companies beginning to specialize in supplying the needs of particular industries.

# Marketing

By the middle of last year, most of the consultant's recommendations had been actioned, and the increased understanding of the market was found to be useful in establishing sales revenue budgets for this year (Exhibit 4). As a direct result of the marketing thrust, sales revenue rose by 22 per cent in the second half of last year (see Exhibit 1). Details for the main segments served by PCS are given in Exhibit 4.

## Beverages

The long-established relationships with ARD Coffee and Tea Specialty Packers (two of PCS's main customers) are expected to be maintained. This is largely due to the company's reputation for high levels of product quality conformance and delivery

**Exhibit 2A**   Five-colour, offset lithographic printing machine

*Source*: Peterson Carton Services

**Exhibit 2B**   A cut and crease machine

*Source*: Peterson Carton Services

*Note*
Following printing, the printed sheets are passed through this machine, which cuts out the shape and creases the carton to enable it to be folded as required.

**Exhibit 3A**    Completed cartons waiting to be dispatched

*Note*
All cartons by their very nature are specific to a customer's needs.

*Source*: Peterson Carton Services

**Exhibit 3B**    A typical carton

*Source*: Peterson Carton Services

reliability and also because of the support given by its design function to help develop new products giving greater added value (for instance, by incorporating gold-leaf designs). All beverage cartons are printed in four or five colours and are normally delivered on completion.

The account with Maister Teas began with a small order first placed in May of last year for delivery in July. Since then, the business has grown. In fact, actual sales are substantially higher than the original forecasts given to the company. The potential for large sales with this customer is considerable for two reasons. First, its annual expenditure on cartons is significant; second, it is moving to a position of developing a long-term relationship with a smaller number of highly competent suppliers to provide all its needs. All Maister's contracts are for high-quality, five-colour products, and the company expects its suppliers to operate strict internal

**Exhibit 4**   Summary of actual sales revenue for last year and sales budgets for this year (£000s)

| Market segment | Customer | Last year's actual | Current year's forecast |
|---|---|---|---|
| Beverages | Maister Teas[1] | 335 | 610 |
| | ARD Coffees | 270 | 230 |
| | Tea Specialty Packers | 225 | 260 |
| | Others | 41 | 50 |
| | Total | 871 | 1150 |
| Industrial products | Agroparts[2] | 178 | 100 |
| | NY Equipment[2] | 174 | 50 |
| | Rotabearings | 156 | 150 |
| | F C Bruce | 104 | 90 |
| | Others | 10 | 10 |
| | Total | 622 | 400 |
| Food | Maister Cakes[3] | 256 | 475 |
| | McPhee Foods[4] | 208 | 250 |
| | Country Cuisine[4] | 20 | 60 |
| | Others | 82 | 35 |
| | Total | 566 | 820 |
| Pharmaceuticals | Pharmex | 228 | 230 |
| | AB Products | 157 | 160 |
| | HMR | 103 | 120 |
| | Others | 40 | 40 |
| | Total | 528 | 550 |
| Drip mats | Pride Ales[5] | 309 | 145 |
| | Hop Products | 128 | 95 |
| | Korolla Cola | 31 | 30 |
| | Others | 42 | 30 |
| | Total | 510 | 300 |
| Toiletries (non-luxury ranges) | Prince & Haywood | 224 | 220 |
| | SC Packers (Export) | 187 | 185 |
| | Others | 75 | 75 |
| | Total | 486 | 480 |

*(continued)*

**Exhibit 4**    Summary of actual sales revenue for last year and sales budgets for this year (£000s) (cont'd)

| Market segment | Customer | Last year's actual | Current year's forecast |
|---|---|---|---|
| Confectionery | Elizabeth Ross | 181 | 150 |
| | Others | 105 | 100 |
| | Total | 286 | 250 |
| Small electrical items[6] | GRA Electrical | 168 | 100 |
| | Domelex | 62 | 50 |
| | Others | 50 | 30 |
| | Total | 280 | 180 |
| Sundry[6] | Various general cartons | 1 025 | 870 |
| | Total | 1 025 | 870 |
| Group[7] | Various general cartons | 430 | 400 |
| | Total | 430 | 400 |
| Windowed products[8] | Various | 1 064 | 1 300 |
| | Group[7,9] | 137 | 200 |
| | Total | 1 201 | 1 500 |
| Grand total | | 6 805 | 6 900 |

*Notes*

1. The first order for Maister Teas was placed in May for delivery in July of last year.
2. The sales representative serving Agroparts and NY Equipment left PCS in September last year and joined a competitor. He is known to be arranging trial orders for these customers and is offering four-week delivery for any new orders. Given the examples in the case study narrative of what has happened in these circumstances in the past, current year budget figures reflect the position which PCS forecasts will result.
3. The first order for Maister Cakes was placed in July for delivery in October last year.
4. Both McPhee Foods and Country Cuisine are introducing just-in-time (JIT) programmes. This will require its suppliers to provide a weekly delivery of all their range of cartons. However, as part of this change to JIT, both customers are intending to reduce the number of suppliers they currently use.
5. Marketing has decided (with appropriate corporate approval) not to renew the annual contract, which is due for signature in the next two months. Contract work was not undertaken prior to last year.
6. Many of the small electrical items/sundry accounts are under severe competitive pressure from small carton manufacturers offering short lead times.
7. 'Group' refers to sales to companies within the carton division of Stebro Industries plc.
8. The major marketing initiatives commenced this January, and are now leading to improvements in sales revenues. However, reports from the field are indicating difficulties caused by PCS's current long lead times.
9. To help boost sales in this segment PCS is encouraging other companies within the Carton Division to seek suitable work, where it could provide the subcontractor windowing capacity.

quality control procedures. Orders are generally very large, but delivery is to weekly call-offs over a three-month period. In discussions on the future, Maister's buyers have stated that they wish to reduce further their own in-house carton inventory and intend to move gradually during the current year to twice-weekly deliveries on most cartons. While sales margins are low compared to general carton work, this is normal for high-volume contracts because, with considerable overcapacity existing in the carton-making industry at this time, there is strong competition for high-volume work.

# Food

Before last year, this segment was considered to comprise general carton work, with many small to medium orders being processed for a variety of customers. The marketing strategy report, however, highlighted the potential to acquire more regular, high-volume work in this segment. This was actively pursued last year, resulting in an early contract for McPhee Foods. In addition, the developing relationship with Maister Teas resulted in an introduction to Maister Cakes, another division of the same company from whom a first order was received in July of last year. The order characteristics of this work are very similar to those of Maister Teas. The only significant difference is that cartons for Maister Cakes are physically larger. As with the tea division, orders soon increased and sales levels for this account are expected to continue to grow in the current year. Last November, an order from Maister Cakes was delivered five working days late. This was due to a quality conformance problem requiring sorting to remove below-standard cartons, This late delivery brought a serious complaint from Maister Cakes and a claim for compensation to cover disruption to, and loss of output from, their own factories.

# Drip Mats

Following the marketing strategy report and corporate discussions on PCS's business as a whole, it has recently been decided to reduce the company's sales efforts in this market in order to allow the business to develop other segments deemed to be more in line with the company's needs. Keith Bowyer, sales/marketing director, explained:

> There are several factors that make this segment unattractive. Margins are generally low and the total market is declining. Although contract-type business for large, nationally based brewers (for example, Pride Ales) is ordered on an annual basis with regular call-offs, other ('promotional') orders (accounting for about 25 per cent of their business) are required relatively quickly, resulting in the need for some schedule changes to the litho print programme. These promotional drip mats are very often of a five-colour design and considerably more demanding in quality requirements. This necessitates slower running on the presses, and higher levels of rejects are typically experienced. In addition, because they form part of a one-off brand sales promotion, it is always critical that orders are delivered on time.
>
> Predominantly two- and four-colour work, drip mats are made out of thicker and lower-quality board and use the same litho printing and die-cutting/creasing (but not glueing) processes as cartons. However, the final stripping, separating and packing processes use specialized equipment dedicated to these products. This product range accounted for 7 per cent of last year's total sales revenue and current year budgets reflect the downward trend agreed for this segment in our strategy [see Exhibit 4]. The irregular nature of orders often leads to an imbalance in departmental workloads. This is particularly so in glueing, as drip mats do not require this process, whereas most other products

do. A high level of drip mat business, therefore, results in less work for some of the subsequent sections, such as glueing.

These factors have all contributed to our decision not to pursue growth in this segment and not to defend existing accounts against competitors' price reductions.

## Windowed Cartons

There is a very large number of customers for windowed cartons, each placing irregular orders, often for small quantities. Most orders are for four- or five-colour printing, generally of high-quality artwork or photographs. The function of a windowed carton is to give the eventual customer sight of the product it contains, without opening the packaging. Often quite ordinary products (such as car accessories) are packed in this way and are usually bought as gifts (for example, at Christmas).

The marketing review highlighted the considerable growth potential for this product, a fact reflected in this year's budget. It is known that very few competitors possess the necessary equipment and skills to produce high-quality windowed cartons. Of particular importance is the need for a supplier to be able to work with customers in the development of suitable designs, that would enhance their products in the desired manner. This was normally achieved by a combination of sales representatives' visits and subsequent design and prototype development by PCS's design department. Many customers use this form of packaging as a one-off marketing exercise, and hence most designs were produced once and are not subsequently reordered.

Other carton manufacturers within the Stebro Industries group do not possess windowing capacity. Therefore they will sometimes use PCS as a subcontractor to provide this service but complete all the other operations needed to make a windowed carton within their own factories. When quoting for windowing work in the group, PCS produces an estimate of the cost of this operation based on material, transport and processing costs. The latter are calculated using the normal hourly estimating rate for windowing machines. The carton division as a whole has recognized the potential for this product. Consequently, a similar sales effort in the other carton companies has been made and rapid growth is anticipated. Exhibit 5 lists a representative sample of orders for windowed cartons.

## Other Market Segments

The marketinng strategy recognized that while 'other market' business as a whole represents nearly half of PCS's sales revenue, much of this is average volume and comprises work that is of a technically undemanding nature which could be manufactured by most, if not all, carton producers. Much of this business was regular, repeat work, with only minor and infrequent design changes. Commenting on this segment, Keith Bowyer explained that it is probably retained by factors such as:

**Exhibit 5**  A representative sample of windowed cartons produced in the period July to September, last year

| Works order number | Customer | Invoiced sales (£) | Actual variable costs (£) | | | Windowing machine hours |
| | | | Material[1] | Processing | Delivery | |
|---|---|---|---|---|---|---|
| 16862 | Group[2] | 9 320 | 1 306 | 2 795 | 50 | 124.0 |
| 16893 | Panda Pottery | 12 436 | 2 140 | 1 806 | 90 | 56.5 |
| 16897 | Electronica | 17 008 | 3 670 | 2 385 | 165 | 121.5 |
| 16912 | Group | 2 451 | 625 | 541 | 25 | 24.5 |
| 16935 | Durham Foods | 8 250 | 1 710 | 902 | 60 | 26.0 |
| 16939 | Statpots | 4 241 | 787 | 447 | 25 | 19.5 |
| 16956 | Group | 6 895 | 1 651 | 1 668 | 45 | 74.0 |
| 16974 | Giftware Enterprises | 7 908 | 1 367 | 945 | 35 | 24.0 |
| 16987 | AG Camm | 4 266 | 934 | 759 | 28 | 9.5 |
| 17007 | Photo-X | 6 121 | 1 452 | 792 | 40 | 33.5 |
| 17016 | Group | 3 549 | 770 | 721 | 30 | 32.0 |
| 17089 | Ceramica | 14 733 | 2 748 | 2 368 | 210 | 51.0 |
| 17091 | Essex Confectionery | 12 236 | 2 960 | 2 129 | 185 | 46.0 |
| 17115 | Carac Gifts | 17 450 | 4 976 | 2 903 | 305 | 16.0 |
| 17144 | Group | 6 982 | 2 041 | 1 499 | 55 | 66.5 |

*Notes*
1. In the case of products processed for the group, material costs only include the windowing materials (PVC), adhesives and packaging used (for example, corrugated cardboard boxes and shrinkwrap film). Processing costs normally only relate to the windowing machine, as this process also carries out any necessary glueing.
2. The term *group* refers to another company in the carton division for which a windowing subcontract service is provided by PCS, as explained in the narrative.

- customer inertia (packaging may be low on a buyer's list of priorities)
- goodwill developed by long and successful trading relationships
- customer satisfaction with the service provided by PCS (comprising a combination of quick delivery when necessary, delivery reliability and consistent quality conformance)
- good personal relationships between PCS's sale representatives and the purchasing function of its customers
- low prices for high-volume contracts.

He continued:

> Our current marketing approach recognizes that many of our customer's orders are potentially vulnerable to competition. An example of this is illustrated by the significant amount of business we lost when a salesman (specializing in handling agreements with a number of industrial customers) left our employment and joined a competitor. Unfortunately, with his knowledge of this aspect of our business, he was able to attract many orders away from us to his new company. As we supplied nothing that could be considered unique, then he was able to take many customers with him by offering a slight improvement on one or more factors, or even just offering to guarantee the same level of overall service he, and we, had provided in the past.
>
> Our strategy is to improve our levels of service to these customers, and to defend our current business when necessary, by lowering prices. In the long term, it is intended to offset the inevitable decline in these segments by increasing sales in more profitable areas, such as windowed products – a fact that is central to the marketing review completed some 15 months ago. However, the decline in sales we experienced two years ago and the impact this had on our profit performance is a factor of which we are always mindful.

# Manufacturing

## Processes

All equipment is laid out on a functional basis. For example, there is a printing area in which all printing processes are located, a die-cutting/creasing area, containing all die-cutting and creasing processes and so on. See Exhibit 2, which shows examples of some of the plant used, and Exhibit 6, which summarizes the process capabilities and records of utilization.

In general, a machine can process any width of cardboard up to the maximum size stated (see Exhibit 6). But those responsible for planning orders aim to maximize the use of available machine widths by appropriate carton design layouts. Thus, for most products the 52-inch litho presses are capable of producing more cartons per sheet of cardboard than the 40-inch machines, resulting in lower processing costs and often less material waste per unit of output. (There is always

**Exhibit 6**  Analysis of average plant utilization

| Process | Machine manning | Basic capability | | Manned time as percentage of available time[1,2] | | | | |
|---|---|---|---|---|---|---|---|---|
| | | Maximum size | Maximum colours | Q1 | Q2 | Q3 | Q4 | Total year |
| Litho printing[3] | L1 | 40 | 2 | 97 | 77 | 73 | 61 | 77 |
| | L2 | 40 | 4 | 99 | 98 | 93 | 99 | 97 |
| | L3 | 52 | 2 | 62 | 56 | 63 | 67 | 62 |
| | L4 | 52 | 4 | 101 | 94 | 97 | 107 | 100 |
| | L5 | 52 | 5 | 78 | 93 | 113 | 127 | 103 |
| Die cutting and creasing | C1 | 40 | – | 97 | 85 | 73 | 84 | 85 |
| | C2 | 40 | – | 52 | 51 | 42 | 50 | 49 |
| | C3 | 60 | – | 89 | 81 | 78 | 99 | 87 |
| | C4 | 60 | – | 91 | 75 | 81 | 94 | 85 |
| | C5 | 60 | – | 83 | 83 | 86 | 98 | 88 |
| Glueing | G1 | – | – | 67 | 60 | 84 | 91 | 76 |
| | G2 | – | – | 69 | 58 | 77 | 81 | 71 |
| | G3 | – | – | 56 | 57 | 46 | 60 | 55 |
| | G4 | – | – | 34 | 29 | 41 | 40 | 36 |
| | G5 | – | – | 59 | 48 | 55 | 76 | 60 |
| | G6 | – | – | 56 | 52 | 40 | 45 | 48 |
| | G7 | – | – | 56 | 52 | 36 | 40 | 49 |
| Drip mat punching | D1 | – | – | 20 | 41 | 40 | 25 | 31 |
| Windowing | W1 | – | – | 64 | 52 | 120 | 70 | 77 |
| | W2 | – | – | 64 | 70 | 125 | 71 | 83 |

*Notes*

1. Manned time includes (a) all running time, including overtime, (b) all set-ups, and (c) short duration downtime (less than one hour), due to mechanical/electrical breakdowns, where it was not considered necessary to reallocate the operators involved.

2. Available time is taken as normal two-shift working (weekdays) and excludes shutdowns.

3. Any press can print fewer than its maximum number of colours; for example, L5 can print five-, four-, three-, two-, or one-colour work. Conversely, a two-colour press can print four-colour work, but this would require the cartons to be passed through a second time. Neither printing fewer colours nor passing a job through the same press twice makes sound commercial sense and it is only done as a last resort.

some material waste built into sheet design, if only at the edges. This comment refers to the fact that this inherent waste would, on a 52-inch press, be spread over more carton designs than for a 40-inch press printing the same design.) The cost of tooling (litho plates and die-cutting dies) increases approximately in proportion to the area covered, but this is usually more than compensated for by the lower processing costs inherent in a wider press. Any litho press can print fewer colours than its capability (for example, a five-colour litho printer can print four or fewer colours: see Exhibit 7, which gives a representative sample of orders completed on the five-colour printer).

All the machines, except L5 and the windowing processes, are over 10 years old and fully depreciated. More modern equipment would offer faster running speeds, marginally quicker set-ups and improved consistency of quality. However, the

**Exhibit 7**    A representative sample of work printed on L5 during last year

| Completion date (printing) | Works order number | Customer | Total machine time set-up and running (hours) | Number of colours |
|---|---|---|---|---|
| January | 16261 | ARD Coffees | 46 | 5 |
| January | 16301 | Pride Ales | 27 | 5 |
| February | 16326 | Prince & Haywood | 17 | 5 |
| February | 16349 | Tea Specialty Packers | 29 | 5 |
| March | 16407 | Agroparts | 41 | 4 |
| March | 16514 | McPhee Foods | 63 | 5 |
| April | 16527 | GRA Electrical | 21 | 5 |
| April | 16602 | S C Packers (export) | 36 | 4 |
| May | 16640 | Barking & Hollis | 32 | 5 |
| May | 16695 | Pride Ales | 11 | 3 |
| May | 16715 | S C Packers (export) | 24 | 4 |
| June | 16756 | Country Cuisine | 17 | 5 |
| June | 16809 | Hop Products | 22 | 5 |
| July | 16846 | Prince & Haywood | 55 | 5 |
| July | 16903 | Wigan Breweries | 22 | 4 |
| August | 16954 | McPhee Foods | 63 | 5 |
| August | 17001 | Group | 52 | 5 |
| September | 17063 | Maister Cakes | 10 | 5 |
| September | 17127 | Tea Specialty Packers | 62 | 5 |
| October | 17189 | Korolla Cola | 28 | 5 |
| October | 17231 | Tea Specialty Packers | 83 | 5 |
| November | 17277 | Maister Tea | 35 | 5 |
| November | 17336 | Maister Cakes | 41 | 5 |
| December | 17390 | Elizabeth Ross | 32 | 5 |
| December | 17426 | Domelex | 12 | 5 |

capital investment involved is very high. Because of the financial record of the company and current low market prices, replacement equipment has been difficult for PCS to justify in the last few years.

## Personnel

The plant is operated on two shifts of 7.5 hours per shift for five days a week, with varying levels of overtime throughout the year (see Exhibit 8). Manning levels for all the main processes are agreed nationally between the relevant trade unions and employers' federations. Thus there is an agreed manning level on a four-colour printing press and another on a five-colour printing press. Where an order specifies five colours, then it is more cost effective to print it on a five-colour press than to have to process it twice through a three- or four-colour press. PCS, as with most other businesses, conforms to these agreements, leaving only service areas (such as packing, materials handling, warehouse and quality control) where manning levels are determined by agreement between local management and the relevant trade union representatives. It is in these areas that reduction in labour could be achieved more easily by investment in equipment.

**Exhibit 8**    Overtime premium costs for January to December, last year[1]

| Month | Total overtime premium paid (£)[2] |
|---|---|
| January | 5 460 |
| February | 2 100 |
| March | 3 246 |
| April | 3 672 |
| May | 6 256 |
| June | 4 107 |
| July | 5 363 |
| August | 11 718 |
| September | 19 869 |
| October | 26 207 |
| November | 32 111 |
| December | 17 006 |

Notes
1. Overtime premium is the supplement paid to employees for working overtime and ranges from one-third of their hourly rate for short periods of weekday overtime to 100 per cent of hourly rate for Saturday afternoons and Sundays.
2. These figures do not include extra salaried costs (mainly supervisors).

## Production and Materials Control

On receipt of a customer order, the sales administration department raises a works order, which is passed to the production control department. (A works order is an internal document giving details of a customer order and providing the manufacturing function with the authorization to print a particular product in line with the volumes required. It would normally be accompanied by details of the design and the relevant litho printing plates.) At this stage, materials are ordered (board, any special inks and printing plates), and the order is scheduled using a bar chart for each machine. This procedure also shows the loading for each process.

Some excess board is always purchased to allow for both the tolerances (usually ± 10 per cent) of the manufacturer's actual supply of material and for the uncertain material yield from the processes. Customer orders are accepted on the basis of the carton industry's 'standard conditions of sale', that allow a tolerance on the quantity of cartons delivered (usually ± 10 per cent). Generally, orders are planned to produce around 10 per cent more cartons than the quantity ordered. All good cartons produced can then be delivered and invoiced at the full price. All materials are usually received within three weeks of order but this lead time can be reduced if a supplier is notified that the particular item is urgent. In addition, most specifications of board can be obtained from stockists within 24 hours but such deliveries cost about 40 per cent more than supplies direct from the manufacturers.

The prinicipal objective of the production control function is to ensure that the capacity of all processes is allocated effectively and supplies are obtained at the agreed level of quality and delivered on time to ensure that customers' orders are produced by the contracted date. However many changes in these schedules have to be catered for and are caused by factors such as:

- special customer orders are required to be produced in less than the normal lead time
- customer schedule changes to quantity and/or delivery dates
- cancelled orders
- machine breakdowns or manning problems
- quality control issues (such as faulty printing plates, inks and board), resulting in jobs being stopped and/or taken off the process until the problem can be resolved
- late deliveries from suppliers.

Furthermore, the production control function is responsible for ensuring the most efficient utilization of the processes, by sequencing jobs in such a way as to minimize set-up times and levels of work-in-progress inventory. In addition, processes with a high level of utilization must be planned to keep levels of overtime within acceptable limits, while ensuring that order backlogs do not get too long, which would result in a potential loss of orders. (Order backlogs – also known as *forward load* – refer to the number of orders that, at any one time, are waiting to go into the manufacturing system. Promised delivery dates to customers, therefore, have to take

**Exhibit 9**  Order backlog for the principal manufacturing processes (in weeks)[1,2]

| Process | Machine | Last year | | | | | | | | | | | | Current year | |
| | | Q1 | | | Q2 | | | Q3 | | | Q4 | | | Q1 | |
| | | Jan | Feb | Mar | Apr | May | June | July | Aug | Sep | Oct | Nov | Dec | Jan | Feb |
| Litho printing | L1 | 4 | 5 | 2 | 2 | 2 | 3 | 4 | 2 | 2 | 1 | 1 | 1 | 2 | 2 |
| | L3 | 2 | 6 | 3 | 3 | 5 | 4 | 4 | 3 | 4 | 6 | 4 | 3 | 4 | 5 |
| | L3 | 3 | 3 | 4 | 3 | 4 | 4 | 2 | 4 | 3 | 3 | 4 | 6 | 4 | 4 |
| | L4 | 5 | 6 | 5 | 4 | 4 | 4 | 5 | 6 | 6 | 8 | 6 | 9 | 9 | 8 |
| | L5 | 2 | 3 | 5 | 4 | 4 | 4 | 6 | 7 | 8 | 9 | 9 | 10 | 9 | 8 |
| Die cutting | C1, 2 | 2 | 2 | 0 | 1 | 1 | 1 | 2 | 1 | 2 | 1 | 1 | 2 | 1 | 1 |
| and creasing | C3, 4, 5 | 3 | 2 | 1 | 1 | 0 | 1 | 1 | 1 | 2 | 3 | 3 | 3 | 2 | 2 |
| Glueing | All | 1 | 0 | 0 | 1 | 0 | 0 | 0 | 0 | 1 | 1 | 2 | 1 | 2 | 1 |
| Windowing | All | 5 | 5 | 4 | 4 | 5 | 12 | 10 | 7 | 4 | 3 | 2 | 0 | 2 | 9 |
| Drip mat punching | – | 0 | 0 | 1 | 1 | 0 | 0 | 0 | 0 | 1 | 0 | 0 | 0 | 0 | 0 |

*Notes*
1. The information relates to the principal processes and is calculated to the nearest working week.
2. Order backlog is recorded on the last day of each month.

into account not only the process lead time – the length of time a product takes to be completed – but also the number of agreed orders ahead of it in the queue of work.)

During the second half of last year, many changes in these factors were apparently brought about by the major alterations to the work mix resulting from the new strategy. Exhibit 6 summarizes changes in utilization and Exhibit 9 is a record of the order-backlog position for all main processes.

In addition, the production control department maintains records of all material issued to production and the output of 'good' cartons. As job costing is not regularly carried out by the accounting function this information is only used by the materials planner as a guide for the purchasing and issue of board. Special analyses are sometimes carried out on new contracts to ensure that the actual material usage is in line with estimates; Exhibit 10 summarizes the data for early orders from Maister Cakes. Because the relationship between the output and input of board is shown to be within only 1 per cent of the estimate, the estimating rates are considered to be satisfactory, as some improvements in material usage would normally be made as a result of producing a particular carton on a regular basis.

## Quality Control

For most customers, quality standards are established on initial production orders, usually in the presence of a customer's representative. Samples are selected that reflect the extremes of acceptable quality, and subsequent production and future repeat orders are controlled to fall within these agreed parameters. Quality is maintained by the process operatives, with random inspections by patrolling quality control staff and the final inspection of random samples undertaken by the packing section.

For Maister Teas and Maister Cakes, the procedure has to be much more rigorous. Production trials are conducted (at PCS's expense) and control samples are selected and authorized off-site by Maister's quality assurance function. Generally, the acceptable limits are very narrow (relative to other customers' orders), and Maister also lays down strict quality control procedures, that have to be followed during production and include the frequency of patrol inspections. In addition, a specified number of cartons from each pallet of finished goods must be kept aside for subsequent inspection and referenced to the relevant pallet. When these orders are being processed, the procedures described involve two quality inspectors on a full-time basis. Delivered goods are subject to further inspection by Maister personnel and deviations from quality limits may result in returns to PCS of complete carton deliveries.

**Exhibit 10** An analysis of board usage and output of cartons for all orders from Maister Cakes during last year

| Works order reference | Month completed | Quantity of cartons ordered | | Number of cartons per board (number-up)[1] | Input: number of boards issued to production[2] | | Output: number of cartons delivered | |
|---|---|---|---|---|---|---|---|---|
| | | Number (000) | Tolerance (±%) | | Estimate | Actual | Estimate[3] | Actual |
| 17063 | September | 150 | 10 | 12 | 22 000 | 20 050 | 165 000 | 188 850 |
| 17122 | | 250 | 10 | 8 | 42 950 | 40 100 | 275 000 | 280 400 |
| 17181 | October | 200 | 10 | 12 | 25 800 | 22 950 | 220 000 | 215 600 |
| 17204 | | 175 | 10 | 8 | 33 000 | 30 000 | 192 500 | 201 350 |
| 17212 | | 1 000 | 7.5 | 12 | 95 800 | 99 750 | 1 075 000 | 1 053 300 |
| 17292 | November | 250 | 10 | 12 | 30 550 | 33 900 | 275 000 | 332 200 |
| 17336 | | 1 500 | 5 | 12 | 139 000 | 142 500 | 1 575 000 | 1 550 950 |
| 17345 | | 75 | 10 | 8 | 18 090 | 17 250 | 82 500 | 108 300 |
| 17372 | | 175 | 10 | 6 | 38 500 | 38 200 | 192 500 | 190 925 |
| 17373 | | 550 | 10 | 12 | 61 000 | 58 050 | 605 000 | 608 850 |
| 17390 | December | 450 | 10 | 12 | 50 000 | 50 000 | 495 000 | 508 800 |
| 17396 | | 2 500 | 5 | 12 | 230 000 | 225 100 | 2 625 000 | 2 474 200 |
| 17411 | | 100 | 10 | 6 | 25 820 | 26 250 | 110 000 | 120 450 |
| 17412 | | 50 | 10 | 8 | 12 170 | 14 150 | 55 000 | 81 050 |
| 17440 | | 1 100 | 7.5 | 8 | 156 400 | 166 000 | 1 182 500 | 1 160 650 |
| Total | | | | | 981 080 | 984 250 | 9 125 000 | 9 075 875 |
| Variance percentage | | | | | | +0.32 | | −0.54 |

Notes

1. Boards are normally purchased from a supplier to suit the size and specification of individual works orders. Quantities received may vary by ±10 per cent from the ordered quantities. However, as with the final product, all quantities within this tolerance band would be paid for.
2. The number of boards issued is decided by the production control department and later adjusted by the materials controller. The production controller may plan quantities slightly greater than the estimate, if he is aware that Maister has low stocks and is thus critically dependent on receiving at least the ordered quantity. The materials controller may increase the input, if the quantity of board received from the suppliers exceeds the ordered quantity (see Note 1 above).
3. The estimated output for each order exceeds the ordered quantity by a tolerance. Because of the uncertainty of quantities received from the board mills, and because of variable process material yields, the standard conditions of sale which operate throughout the carton industry allow defined maximum percentages of under- and overproduction to be delivered and charged to customers.

# Finance and Accounting

The decline in performance of the company was highlighted by the summary of trading results given as Exhibit 1. It was clear that two factors had contributed to the worsening position: increasing levels of working capital and a decline in sales margin.

## Working Capital

At a management meeting in September last year, it was shown that the major item of working capital was inventory, and it was agreed that it must be reduced this year by at least 40 per cent. In order to achieve such a reduction, all categories of inventory would have to be cut on the following basis.

### Raw Materials

The buyer was instructed to adhere rigidly to the company policy of only purchasing for customers' orders. Inventory holdings of material for drip mats would be reduced and the buffer inventory of board for regular business, such as the industrial and food segments, would be eliminated.

### Work-in-progress

Increasing levels of work-in-progress were attributed to unsatisfactory planning, resulting in occurrences such as the following:

1. Interruptions to long print or die-cutting/creasing runs (for example, Maister Teas), in order to allow the production of short-run items, where there was pressure to deliver cartons soon after receipt of raw materials and in line with a customer's requirements. Output from the interrupted order would be held as work-in-progress awaiting its later completion.

2. Overloading of certain downstream processes, resulting in work-in-progress queues.

3. Failure to ensure that orders are progressed in the best sequence to minimize work-in-progress inventory.

Apart from identifying the need to improve production scheduling procedures, the finance department proposed the introduction of a computerized planning system. This would ensure that all planning decisions resulted in a forecast level of inventory being reported. In this way, the planners would not only have a means of

**Exhibit 11** Costings for representative orders: October to December, last year

| Market/customer | Works order number | Invoiced sales (£s)[2] | Estimated contribution[1] £s | Estimated contribution[1] % of order value | Actual costs (£s) Board | Actual costs (£s) Other materials | Actual costs (£s) Processing variable[3] | Actual costs (£s) Delivery | Actual costs (£s) Total |
|---|---|---|---|---|---|---|---|---|---|
| *Beverages* | | | | | | | | | |
| Maister Teas | 17120 | 14 096 | 825 | 5.9 | 11 047 | 733 | 1 676 | 436 | 13 892 |
| | 17392 | 55 512 | 9 485 | 16.3 | 43 396 | 3 002 | 9 542 | 1 980 | 57 920 |
| ARD Coffees | 17451 | 54 450 | 9 596 | 17.0 | 41 128 | 2 202 | 7 579 | 1 649 | 52 558 |
| | 17186 | 2 836 | 1 203 | 42.7 | 401 | 188 | 1 025 | 21 | 1 635 |
| | 17347 | 30 206 | 3 672 | 12.7 | 17 483 | 2 756 | 5 541 | 1 354 | 27 134 |
| Tea Specialty Packers | 17369 | 15 542 | 6 946 | 45.4 | 3 162 | 2 091 | 3 098 | 245 | 8 596 |
| | 17242 | 4 519 | 2 333 | 52.0 | 646 | 381 | 1 130 | 29 | 2 186 |
| | 17301 | 2 374 | 1 002 | 42.2 | 356 | 286 | 705 | 25 | 1 372 |
| Eastern Teas | 17405 | 9 799 | 4 889 | 50.5 | 1 496 | 1 585 | 1 808 | 121 | 5 010 |
| | 17408 | 3 973 | 2 391 | 61.1 | 945 | 174 | 403 | 60 | 1 582 |
| *Industrial products* | | | | | | | | | |
| Agroparts | 17214 | 5 996 | 3 127 | 51.9 | 1 597 | 630 | 1 151 | 177 | 3 555 |
| | 17446 | 7 671 | 2 393 | 33.2 | 3 907 | 499 | 1 288 | 448 | 6 142 |
| NY Equipment | 17284 | 5 582 | 1 828 | 40.8 | 2 358 | 440 | 864 | 158 | 3 820 |
| | 17427 | 20 404 | 8 208 | 41.8 | 9 712 | 1 204 | 2 090 | 748 | 13 754 |
| Rotabearings | 17269 | 23 712 | 10 206 | 47.2 | 8 459 | 1 730 | 4 302 | 850 | 15 341 |
| | 17391 | 14 809 | 6 026 | 45.6 | 5 478 | 1 032 | 2 400 | 556 | 9 466 |
| F C Bruce | 17279 | 7 830 | 2 309 | 31.5 | 4 110 | 499 | 1 268 | 479 | 6 356 |
| | 17431 | 10 674 | 3 775 | 39.6 | 2 217 | 3 252 | 552 | 251 | 6 272 |
| *Food* | | | | | | | | | |
| Maister Cakes | 17122 | 15 346 | 1 571 | 10.8 | 11 423 | 1 190 | 2 563 | 677 | 15 853 |
| | 17212 | 53 366 | 8 164 | 13.9 | 40 062 | 3 963 | 10 224 | 1 712 | 55 961 |
| | 17440 | 59 971 | 9 541 | 15.4 | 44 606 | 2 953 | 11 994 | 1 838 | 61 391 |
| McPhee | 17190 | 4 403 | 1 641 | 41.8 | 1 728 | 147 | 1 191 | 123 | 3 189 |
| | 17320 | 4 766 | 1 299 | 31.0 | 1 888 | 387 | 1 519 | 125 | 3 919 |
| | 17448 | 6 397 | 4 053 | 63.4 | 1 205 | 883 | 2 738 | 249 | 5 075 |
| Country Cuisine | 17298 | 7 738 | 2 009 | 29.9 | 4 252 | 629 | 1 636 | 250 | 6 767 |

*(continued)*

**Exhibit 11**  Costings for representative orders: October to December, last year (cont'd)

| Market/customer | Works order number | Invoiced sales (£s)[2] | Estimated contribution[1] | | Actual costs (£s) | | | | |
|---|---|---|---|---|---|---|---|---|---|
| | | | £s | % of order value | Board | Other materials | Processing variable[3] | Delivery | Total |
| *Pharmaceuticals* | | | | | | | | | |
| Pharmex | 17216 | 2 560 | 1 139 | 49.0 | 654 | 172 | 795 | 20 | 1 641 |
| | 17377 | 7 082 | 4 026 | 51.4 | 2 080 | 591 | 2 041 | 55 | 4 767 |
| AB Products | 17450 | 2 205 | 908 | 46.1 | 669 | 332 | 302 | 17 | 1 320 |
| | 17323 | 1 052 | 469 | 55.7 | 156 | 52 | 262 | 11 | 481 |
| HMR | 17436 | 6 016 | 2 339 | 43.1 | 1 180 | 1 379 | 666 | 78 | 3 303 |
| | 17356 | 1 728 | 880 | 58.4 | 227 | 203 | 469 | 28 | 927 |
| *Drip Mats* | | | | | | | | | |
| Pride Ales | 17243[4] | 1 950 | 164 | 10.8 | 968 | 189 | 784 | 71 | 2 012 |
| | 17311[4] | 2 025 | 259 | 16.6 | 953 | 72 | 722 | 67 | 1 814 |
| | 17400 | 1 885 | 280 | 18.5 | 838 | 145 | 397 | 71 | 1 451 |
| | 17452 | 3 415 | 590 | 22.4 | 1 368 | 249 | 354 | 59 | 2 030 |
| Hop Products | 17261 | 5 337 | 1 974 | 52.8 | 1 191 | 197 | 505 | 85 | 1 978 |
| | 17439 | 18 333 | 7 827 | 41.4 | 8 529 | 1 120 | 2 760 | 657 | 13 066 |
| Korolla Cola | 17365 | 5 511 | 1 995 | 42.7 | 2 024 | 246 | 855 | 95 | 3 220 |
| *Toiletries* | | | | | | | | | |
| Prince & Haywood | 17276 | 29 289 | 14 143 | 47.1 | 10 498 | 2 523 | 4 304 | 903 | 18 228 |
| | 17308 | 32 868 | 11 133 | 38.4 | 12 655 | 3 307 | 5 599 | 895 | 22 456 |
| | 17415 | 20 227 | 6 840 | 39.0 | 7 277 | 2 150 | 3 466 | 524 | 13 417 |
| SC Packers (exports) | 17199 | 10 521 | 5 821 | 46.2 | 3 791 | 837 | 3 394 | 359 | 8 381 |
| | 17437 | 3 861 | 1 678 | 48.1 | 1 033 | 354 | 942 | 79 | 2 408 |
| Soap Exports | 17348 | 8 436 | 4 364 | 49.9 | 2 610 | 445 | 2 656 | 70 | 5 781 |
| *Confectionery* | | | | | | | | | |
| Elizabeth Ross | 17288 | 2 783 | 1 453 | 58.5 | 370 | 225 | 449 | 34 | 1 078 |
| | 17395 | 3 222 | 1 856 | 60.4 | 456 | 445 | 664 | 34 | 1 599 |
| Prestar | 17341 | 6 540 | 4 180 | 60.2 | 1 016 | 686 | 1 370 | 75 | 3 147 |
| *Small electrical appliances* | | | | | | | | | |
| GRA Electrical | 17208 | 12 396 | 7 033 | 52.3 | 5 908 | 1 135 | 3 680 | 332 | 11 055 |
| | 17398 | 12 064 | 5 044 | 45.9 | 3 482 | 1 342 | 3 539 | 270 | 8 633 |
| Domelex | 17423 | 6 019 | 2 821 | 48.2 | 1 165 | 1 058 | 1 741 | 78 | 4 042 |
| Exit Fans | 17257 | 3 584 | 1 574 | 52.0 | 774 | 301 | 736 | 40 | 1 851 |

| Market/customer | Works order number | Invoiced sales (£s)[2] | Estimated contribution[1] £s | Estimated contribution[1] % of order value | Actual costs (£s) Board | Actual costs (£s) Other materials | Actual costs (£s) Processing variable[3] | Actual costs (£s) Delivery | Actual costs (£s) Total |
|---|---|---|---|---|---|---|---|---|---|
| *Sundry* | | | | | | | | | |
| Jones & Straw | 17193 | 2 646 | 560 | 20.7 | 1 270 | 330 | 462 | 90 | 2 152 |
| FJ Agrichem | 17278 | 5 762 | 1 656 | 30.7 | 1 639 | 749 | 1 290 | 250 | 3 928 |
| Electronica | 17370 | 1 875 | 451 | 21.5 | 996 | 207 | 325 | 30 | 1 558 |
| London Shirts | 17454 | 2 179 | 379 | 17.2 | 1 206 | 355 | 278 | 45 | 1 884 |
| *Group* | | | | | | | | | |
| Companies in the | 17209 | 3 873 | 1 523 | 48.0 | 562 | 613 | 888 | 50 | 2 113 |
| carton division | 17318 | 6 782 | 3 809 | 62.7 | 1 024 | 443 | 2 227 | 238 | 3 932 |
| | 17359 | 5 463 | 3 360 | 60.8 | 916 | 522 | 1 711 | 318 | 3 467 |
| | 17442 | 1 600 | 1 013 | 63.4 | 301 | 221 | 685 | 62 | 1 269 |
| *Windowed* | | | | | | | | | |
| Panda Pottery | 17246 | 3 672 | 1 912 | 70.7 | 394 | 741 | 574 | 18 | 1 727 |
| Stalpots | 17420 | 7 753 | 3 684 | 68.3 | 860 | 396 | 833 | 23 | 2 112 |
| Electronica | 17443 | 9 199 | 4 249 | 66.6 | 1 018 | 752 | 1 655 | 56 | 3 481 |
| *Windowed subcontract*[5] | | | | | | | | | |
| Spa Cartons | 17352 | 8 779 | 5 547 | 63.0 | – | 2 449 | 2 099 | 50 | 4 598 |
| Stebro Packaging | 17457 | 7 369 | 3 756 | 54.2 | – | 2 225 | 1 254 | 45 | 3 524 |

*Notes*

1. Estimated contribution is the difference between the order value and the estimated variable costs of materials, processing and delivery.
2. Invoiced sales is the value of all the goods as delivered, but excludes any credit notes or returned goods.
3. Processing variable costs are calculated from the machine variable (hourly) cost rates which include:
   a. direct labour with fringe benefits
   b. energy costs
   c. consumable materials
   d. adjustments for average downtime, and
   e. repairs and maintenance materials.
   Typically, direct labour with fringer benefits accounts for less than 50 per cent of total processing variable costs.
4. These two orders are of a contract nature, as explained in the narrative. The other two orders for Pride Ales are of the promotional type.
5. This category refers to orders from other companies in the carton division, requiring only the 'windowed' process to be completed.

improving their effectiveness but would also become more aware of the results of their decisions on inventory levels.

### Finished Goods

The main categories of finished-goods inventory are:

1. overproduction (that is, output in excess of the agreed upper-tolerance level) held in anticipation of further orders;
2. inventory held awaiting call-offs due to customers delaying deliveries;
3. cartons produced to meet the whole of an order, although actual call-offs were scheduled for delivery over an extended period.

At the end of last year, 75 per cent of finished-goods inventory was in the category of awaiting call-offs, where manufacturing had made the whole of an order, with specified scheduled deliveries over the following three months. From this January, planners were instructed to manufacture only for call-offs up to six weeks ahead, and this was expected to reduce finished-goods inventory by approximately 30 per cent.

## Sales Margins

Currently, there is no job costing system but complete weekly records of process utilization are maintained. In addition, regular analyses are prepared, comparing actual and standard running speeds and set-up times for each process. It is believed that this approach highlights critical variances from standards and provides an adequate basis for management control.

Job costings are sometimes calculated on a sample basis for new orders but are found to be extremely time consuming. It has been calculated that to cost up to 1000 orders each year would require additional staff and a substantial increase in overhead costs, which could not be justified at this time. On the suggestion of the group internal auditors, a one-off job costing exercise was undertaken in February, the results of which are shown in Exhibit 11.

## Estimating

Except for very regular work (contract drip mats for national brewing companies and high-volume work for Maister), an estimate is prepared for every enquiry. Two years ago, the standard estimating procedure was computerized. This has proved to be invaluable because there were nearly 6500 enquiries processed last year and the computerized procedure has reduced the clerical staff requirement from six to three people.

The computer program allows estimators to enter details of the product specification and quantities, select the process route, enter their estimate of expected material wastage and specify delivery details. Fixed estimating data (machine throughput rates, processing costs per hour, set-up times, material costs and delivery charges) are reviewed by the accounting department every six months. The estimate provided by the computer is based on standard process running and set-up times. The estimator then applies a profit margin on the basis of advice from the salesman and sales manager, while taking into account any history of prices accepted by the customer. For large enquiries and contract renewals, the management team reviews all estimates before quotations are sent to the enquirer.

# Precision Steel plc

## Introduction

Although there are a few, small aspects of the report on which we could take issue, it seems to me that Bill Carey has, by and large, reflected the marketing changes we have been expressing and given some sound guidelines on where we must place our future energies. The emphasis given to increasing our share in all segments of the customized sections market and the need to continue and expand the customer-orientation strategy with Gambert Fabrique, one of our key accounts, seems to have struck a chord with us all, both in terms of past trends and our feel for these markets. What we now have is a strategic framework to give context and direction. This will help us to replace the more short-term response philosophy we have been using in our marketing decisions. Thanks, Bill, we have found your work helpful, and I am sure it will prove to be a document to which we will refer many times in the future.

Brian Finn, the chief executive of Precision Steel (PS) was addressing the board of directors, following a meeting to discuss a recent report titled 'Future Marketing Strategy Proposals', completed on behalf of the company. In addition to the board, Bill Carey (a senior executive from the strategic unit within the group central services, who had been responsible for preparing the report) had also attended the final part of this meeting in order to answer any queries not addressed earlier.

## Background

PS sells high-quality steel sections in a wide range of standard steel specifications, together with customer-specified material requirements. PS is part of Harbridge Industries, a large group of companies with a wide range of interests including shipping, civil engineering, electronics, fabrication and engineering, as well as steel processing. PS was established in 1932 to roll precision steel sections for the electric motor industry.

This case was prepared by Terry Hill (University of Oxford) and S. H. Chambers (University of Warwick). It is intended for class discussion and not as an illustration of good or bad management. © AMD Publishing.

Although many aspects of its activities have since changed, the rerolling of steel sections, using hot and cold processes, in a variety of steel specifications, and up to a maximum section height of 250 mm, still constitutes PS's principal business. Due to falling demand and subsequent plant closures, PS found itself, by the late 1970s (like many of its European counterparts) in a near-monopoly position, as it was now the only supplier based in the UK. However, similar businesses in Europe are always keen to export to the UK, particularly to high-volume (tonne) users.

# PS's Markets

PS buys steel sections from a limited number of suppliers (principally English Billets plc), then sells rerolled precision sections into three market segments with different characteristics. These are electric motors, stockist steel sections and customized sections, which are now described.

## Electric Motors

PS's traditional market was to provide steel sections for electric motors. While demand for this market has fallen in the last 15 years it still accounts for almost 50 per cent of PS's revenue (£s). Steel sections are rolled and subsequently precision machined by the customer. This accounts for some 50 000 tonnes per year, and details of current and past sales are given in Exhibit 1.

## Stockist Steel Sections

Sales in this market are for a range of standard sizes and shapes, all rolled from the one internationally specified steel, known by the company as PS 2000. Both home and overseas customers, therefore, order from a standard catalogue, with items being differentiated only by size and shape.

In order to compensate for the falling sales experienced in the electric motor market, the stockist steel sections segment has been built up over the last 15 years. The annual volumes processed this year totalled 30 000 tonnes, and details of representative orders are given in Exhibit 2. PS was supplying five major UK stockists and about 50 stockists overseas. Last year, PS received a major contract from a French company, Gambert Fabrique (GF), which yielded orders totalling 8000 tonnes in the following year. Apparently running at a substantial loss in its steel rerolling business, GF decided two years before to close its own rolling mill, and negotiated a contract for PS to supply its standard steel sections, using steel PS 2000. GF sells a wide range of products and is a large exporter of engineering supplies and metal sections (steel, brass and aluminium). It distributes these by a well-developed container service to its own depots and clients throughout the world.

**Exhibit 1**    Current and past sales (tonnes) of steel sections for the electric motor market

| | Current year minus | | | | Current year |
|---|---|---|---|---|---|
| | **10** | **6** | **2** | **1** | |
| Total sales (tonnes) | 79 600 | 65 300 | 55 500 | 52 000 | 50 400 |
| Average order quantity (tonnes) | 286 | 205 | 235 | 220 | 190 |
| Average number of sizes per order quantity | 20 | 20 | 29 | 27 | 26 |

*Notes*
1. There are now seven different specifications (that is, material properties) of steel raw materials (in a different range of sizes) required by this market. Each specification in all sizes is normally held in stock by PS. Ten years ago, there were only two specifications.
2. A typical order comprises several sizes of finished precision steel sections, but usually all of the same steel specification and finishing/heat treatment requirements. The various sizes will, however, be processed in separate hot mill programmes (see Exhibit 7). To explain, let's take an order from one customer for a total of 200 tonnes. If this order quantity comprised 20 sizes then, as far as manufacturing is concerned it would be similar to 20 different orders (that is, one order per size), as similar sizes (and not one customer order) are processed through manufacturing.
3. Typical delivery lead times are 6–8 weeks from receipt of an order.

The negotiations with GF resulted in agreed prices and terms for delivery by PS to its main distribution centre in Brest, an industrial port in northern France. Exhibits 3 and 4 give brief details of these agreements, as compared to other products in this segment. Last year PS initiated discussions on the possibility of direct supply to some of GF's depots. John Breen, marketing director, explained the reason for this:

> The GF contract is an important part of our customer portfolio. The annual volume is substantial, characterized by relatively large order quantities and stable schedules. But, the trade-off has been low prices. However, within a relatively short period of time, we saw the opportunity of supplying direct to GF's depots in one or more countries. The direct gains for Gambert were reduced distribution costs and for PS an increase in price.

**Exhibit 2**    Current and past sales of stockist steel sections

| | Current year minus | | | | Current year |
|---|---|---|---|---|---|
| | **10** | **6** | **2** | **1** | |
| Total sales (tonnes) | 15 100 | 17 700 | 19 400 | 28 900 | 29 700 |
| Average order quantity (tonnes) | 84 | 95 | 105 | 130 | 123 |
| Average number of sizes per order quantity | 17 | 20 | 24 | 25 | 23 |

*Notes*
1. The steel specification for this market is PS 2000 only.
2. There are 140 international standard sizes in the stockists' range.
3. GF (France) orders once a month an average of 670 tonnes in 34 standard sizes (minimum 10 tonnes per size) for delivery 6–8 weeks from receipt of an order.
4. GF (UK and Denmark) each order twice a month an average of 35 tonnes each in nine sizes (minimum 3 tonnes per size) for delivery 4–6 weeks from receipt of an order.
5. Current delivery lead times for UK stockists are 6–8 weeks from receipt of an order.

Our first successes early last year were the United Kingdom and Denmark, with each buying about 450 tonnes per year. Having received permission to negotiate directly with these two parts of the Gambert organization, we were able to satisfactorily agree higher prices than for similar products, due to the fact that GF passed on distribution costs to its customers (including parts of its own organization), as well as adding its own margin. We are now able, therefore, to take for ourselves some of that additional margin and still offer a favourable price for direct supply [see Exhibits 3 and 4]. Our policy is to encourage this, and the recent report on future marketing strategy highlights this development as one of the major planks on which we should build. We have now identified Brazil, Italy and Germany as the next areas, and early soundings seem to be favourable.

**Exhibit 3**    Some examples of typical invoiced rates per tonne (current prices)

| Markets | Billet size (mm) | £/tonne[1] |
|---|---|---|
| Electric motor: | 70 | 600 |
| XR7 material | 110 | 500 |
| | 120 | 465 |
| | 140 | 420 |
| | 190 | 425 |
| | 250 | 430 |
| Stockist steel: | 70 | 570 |
| UK stockists | 100 | 490 |
| | 120 | 475 |
| | 140 | 465 |
| | 170 | 470 |
| | 250 | 450 |
| Gambert Fabrique | 85 | 420 |
| (France) | 110 | 340 |
| | 130 | 320 |
| | 150 | 300 |
| | 190 | 300 |
| | 250 | 300 |
| Gambert Fabrique | 85 | 480 |
| (UK) | 110 | 390 |
| | 130 | 360 |
| | 150 | 350 |
| | 190 | 340 |
| | 250 | 330 |
| Customized | 85 | 810 |
| section: | 120 | 680 |
| MK 200 steel[2] | 190 | 610 |
| | 210 | 610 |

*Notes*
**1.** All prices are corrected to ex-works equivalents.
**2.** MK 200 is an expensive alloy steel.

**Exhibit 4**  Summary of estimated variable cost[1] per tonne (£) in various markets, for different tonnages per size, based on current costs

| Markets | Tonnage | Input steel height (mm) | | | | | |
|---|---|---|---|---|---|---|---|
| | | 70–85 | 100–110 | 120–130 | 140–150 | 170–190 | 210–250 |
| Electric motors (typical steel specification XR7) | 5 tonnes | 490 | 411 | 385 | 350 | 355 | 360 |
| | 10 tonnes | 460 | 386 | 363 | 330 | 335 | 340 |
| | 20 tonnes | 445 | 376 | 350 | 320 | 330 | 335 |
| Stockist steel (PS 2000 steel) | 5 tonnes | 410 | 336 | 314 | 290 | 295 | 300 |
| | 10 tonnes | 380 | 316 | 298 | 280 | 285 | 290 |
| | 20 tonnes | 365 | 306 | 290 | 275 | 280 | 285 |
| Customized sections | 5 tonnes | 635 | 550 | 520 | 500 | 490 | 490 |
| | 10 tonnes | 600 | 525 | 500 | 480 | 470 | 470 |
| | 20 tonnes | 580 | 510 | 485 | 460 | 455 | 455 |

Notes

1. Variable cost includes all direct labour, materials and other direct costs (for example, variable energy costs) and an allowance for size changes between items on a programme. It also allows for average yield losses for the market category.

In addition, we propose to consolidate our relationship with Gambert by setting up direct computer interface with Brest, which allows their buying office to link with our sales and production control systems. In this way we hope to lock them into a long-term dependence on PS.

# Customized Sections

The decline in overall sales had stimulated the need to increase sales in the customized sections segment of the market. Customized sections business refers to orders that cater for the specific needs of a wide range of manufacturing businesses, including automotive components (for example, struts), agricultural machinery and oil rig fabrication, as well as general engineering. The growth was based on converting customers from using non-precision, standard steel sections requiring extensive and costly machining and heat treatment, to purpose-rolled sections to meet their specifications in terms of dimensional tolerance, steel specification and heat treatment requirements. PS's sales force had, over the last few years, developed a broader technical knowledge in order to help increase the company's penetration in these markets. Orders can, however, involve both standard and special steels, but size and shape will always be specified by, and therefore special to, each customer. Many customers, however, place repeat orders for the same product, often on a call-off or schedule basis. Most requirements can be met by the hot rolling process, and a representative sample of orders is given in Exhibit 5. (Hot rolling is a less expensive process than cold rolling, therefore products are designed, where possible, to be made in a hot-rolled format.)

Current year's sales in this market segment totalled 20 000 tonnes, 85 per cent of which went to UK companies, with the remainder sent to all parts of the world. An important element of this growth came from sales to the oil industry.

**Exhibit 5**     Current and past sales of customized sections

|  | Current year minus | | | | Current year |
|---|---|---|---|---|---|
|  | 10 | 6 | 2 | 1 | |
| Total sales (tonnes) | 4200 | 9600 | 18 200 | 18 600 | 20 400 |
| Average order quantity (tonnes) | 18.3 | 16.6 | 11.2 | 11.8 | 12.2 |
| Average number of sizes per order quantity[1] | 1.1 | 1.2 | 1.2 | 1.2 | 1.3 |

*Notes*
1. Most orders are only for one size, but a few are for up to four different sizes.
2. Steel specification, finishing process and heat treatments are as specified by each customer. Some high-usage steel specifications are held in raw material stock at PS either against known call-offs or in anticipation of future orders.
3. Call-offs or scheduled requirements (that is, orders for a number of deliveries spread over several months) are treated in this analysis (and by the planning office and within manufacturing) as individual orders.

# Manufacturing

Steel sections pass through a series of processes, which are now briefly described. Orders differ and, whereas all products go through the hot rolling stage, requirements from then on vary in accordance with the specification. Individual customer orders are cumulated, wherever possible, by input height (often referred to as billet size) in order to maximize the tonnage processed through the high-volume hot mills. The task in the production planning office, therefore, is to combine quantities of the same billet size (irrespective of material type) and programme these through the hot mills in order to minimize the numbers of major and minor change-overs (explained later) in line with customer delivery requirements. Following this initial stage through which all steel is processed, customer orders are then separated and follow the individual process requirements to completion.

**Exhibit 6**   Characteristics of the hot rolling mills

---

**Mill C**

- Constructed 15 years ago.
- Maximum input section height: 250 mm.
- Maximum length of output: 5250 mm.
- Average output rate: 13.5 tonnes/gross hour.[1]
- Average size change time: 9 minutes within a programmed range.[2]

**Mill D**

- Constructed 10 years ago to provide efficient capacity for the high-volume electric motor sections market.
- Maximum input section height: 200 mm.
- Maximum length of output: 6000 mm.
- Average output rate: 20.3 tonnes/gross hour.[1]
- Average size change time: 10 minutes within a programmed range.[2]
- Estimated cost of upgrading to provide size capability of 250 mm sections: £550,000.

*Notes*
1. The average output rates refer to the tonnes of processed steel averaged per hour, including any size changes made. It is known as the output rate/gross hour.
2. Although size change times within a programmed range are short (between 8.5 and 10 minutes), change-overs between one range of sizes and another are much longer. Consequently, planning establishes a programme which enables these short changes to take place (which amount to small adjustments in the process) before requiring a major size change to be made. These latter changes also vary in duration depending, in turn, on the extent of the change-over. If the size alteration is itself sequential (that is, to the next size range, whether larger or smaller) then the time taken is about 1.75 hours for Mill C and 2.15 hours for Mill D. However, if the size range alteration is not sequential, then the change-over is increased by up to a further 1.5 times. Thus, the hot mill programmes are planned to minimize downtime wherever possible, while maintaining order quantity levels within the delivery requirements of customers.
3. Output rates are not significantly affected by section width, as this is not a constraining factor.
4. Both mills currently operate on a two-shift basis, 40 hours per shift week, 46 weeks a year.
5. Furnace shut down, light up, and preparations for rolling each weekend cost approximately £3000 per mill. Overnight idling of furnaces costs approximately £60 per hour (fuel and labour).
6. Company policy is to roll minimum tonnages of five tonnes per size, although authorized exceptions are allowed.

---

# Hot Rolling

Currently, two hot rolling mills are in use. One was installed 15 years ago and the second 5 years later to replace earlier mill capacity that had gradually been phased out. While the basic layout for hot rolling is similar, the process capabilities are different. This difference concerns the height and length of steel sections that can be processed. Exhibit 6 gives details.

# Hot Roll Finishing

All products go through the hot roll finishing section. The processes are simple and the set-up times are short. After initial cooling, the steel sections are lifted by an overhead crane into the work-in-progress warehousing area. The crane is, however, limited to a maximum of a five-tonne lift, which means that many order quantities are split at this stage. From this warehousing area, all products follow their own specified routing, according to the process requirements involved.

# Cold Rolling

About one-third of all products are cold rolled. The orders are drawn from the work-in-progress inventory after hot roll finishing. These processes enable higher levels of accuracy to be achieved, particularly where the product specification calls for thinner sections. They all require very long set-up times and involve expensive tooling. The specialized tooling has a three-month lead time from the suppliers, and therefore needs very careful planning. In addition, there is a disproportionate amount of tool wear at the start of a production run, until fine adjustments can be achieved.

# Other Auxiliary Processes

There are several additional processes involved, none of which have long set-up or process times. They include cold roll finishing, heat treatment, cutting to precise lengths and specified packing prior to despatch. Not all products go through all processes.

# Lead-time Calculations

The lead times used by sales in quotations are agreed annually by the sales and production directors, being occasionally adjusted as necessary by the production planning office, if overload situations seem to be arising. The following norms are currently used as a basis for calculating lead times on which delivery promises were then made: 10 weeks are allowed for the purchase of non-standard steel, 4 weeks for hot rolling, 1 week for standard heat treatment and finishing and 4 weeks for cold rolling. Non-standard finishing process lead times were calculated for each job on the basis of an assessment of the complexity involved and the degree of overall delivery speed required by the potential customer.

In all markets where customers require quicker deliveries than the total based on the above norms, shorter lead times for customer quotations are agreed by the manager of the production planning office. This is achieved by identifying areas of process-time reduction, based on current and future loading, experience and judgement. In all cases, delivery is quoted as 'ex-works' (the standard practice for the industry) and does not, therefore, include delivery arrangements. See Exhibits 7, 8, and 9, which give details of actual deliveries in a representative period.

Standard steels are assumed by the production planning office to be available from PS raw material stock holdings and thus no allowance is made in sales quotations involving standard steels to cover purchase lead time. (Most standard steels are kept in stock, as explained in the notes to Exhibit 10.) The inventory holding of each size and specification of standard steel is tightly controlled by the planning manager, using simple controls, based on average usage for the last three months, current stock and estimates of forward demand. Steel delivery is normally requested and acknowledged by suppliers as being 10 weeks from the order date. (See Exhibits 10 and 11 for information on the delivery performance of PS's steel suppliers.)

## Process Yields

Process yield is defined as saleable output divided by the input of raw material and expressed as a percentage. The yields achieved by each different process are closely monitored every month and are reported by market category. Losses (some of which are unpredictable) arise from oxidation (scale losses), damage in the process plant, cutting losses in the finishing section and quality rejects (dimensional, surface finish and metallurgical). All losses are closely monitored and investigated. They are accounted for in the estimation procedure when calculating material requirements and order pricing. Yields currently used in these calculations are based on information gathered over the last 12 months, and average 92 per cent for the electric motor and stockist steel sections markets and about 85 per cent for customized sections.

## Planning Procedures

Orders are received in the sales department, where they are recorded before being passed through to the production planning office. Exhibits 12 and 13 provide information on this activity. Orders are then collated by input height (that is, billet size) required and loaded on to the hot mills within a four-week programme. Thus,

**Exhibit 7** A representative sample of orders for UK electric motor and UK stockist steel markets

| Works order number | Tonnes ordered | Key dates (week numbers) | | |
| --- | --- | --- | --- | --- |
| | | Works order raised | Required and acknowledged delivery | Actual delivery |
| *Electric motor* | | | | |
| M864 | 10.0 | 5 | 12 | 11 |
| M866 | 15.0 | 5 | 15 | 15 |
| M878 | 8.0 | 5 | 12 | 12 |
| M879 | 5.0 | 5 | 16 | 17 |
| M880 | 10.0 | 5 | 12 | 9 |
| M881 | 8.0 | 5 | 12 | 12 |
| M910 | 6.5 | 6 | 13 | 16 |
| M912 | 12.0 | 6 | 13 | 13 |
| M913 | 12.0 | 6 | 13 | 13 |
| M914 | 15.0 | 6 | 16 | 14 |
| M930 | 8.0 | 7 | 13 | 14 |
| M936 | 5.0 | 7 | 13 | 13 |
| M937 | 10.00 | 7 | 13 | 15 |
| M938 | 8.0 | 7 | 16 | 16 |
| M939 | 8.0 | 7 | 14 | 13 |
| *Stockist steel* | | | | |
| S420 | 4.0 | 5 | 10 | 11 |
| S426 | 4.0 | 5 | 10 | 11 |
| S427 | 6.0 | 5 | 12 | 12 |
| S428 | 5.0 | 5 | 12 | 11 |
| S440 | 4.0 | 6 | 12 | 10 |
| S441 | 10.0 | 6 | 12 | 12 |
| S448 | 4.0 | 6 | 12 | 13 |
| S449 | 4.0 | 6 | 12 | 11 |
| S479 | 10.0 | 6 | 13 | 13 |
| S480 | 4.0 | 6 | 13 | 13 |
| S481 | 5.0 | 6 | 13 | 11 |
| S503 | 5.0 | 7 | 14 | 14 |
| S504 | 5.0 | 7 | 13 | 15 |
| S505 | 3.0 | 7 | 13 | 13 |

*Notes*
1. A separate works order is raised for each size within a customer order.
2. Works order numbers M866, M879, M914 and M939 were also cold rolled.

works orders for the same size (input height) of steel (the material specification is not normally a factor to be taken into account when compiling hot mill programmes) are grouped together to provide as large a quantity to be rolled as possible. However, as volumes decline, programmed quantities in the same period will decline, especially where the delivery-speed element of a market is becoming important. In these latter situations, the steel will, of course, have to be programmed into the hot mills to meet the customer delivery date, rather than to meet the programming rules used in the planning department. This would lead to lower production volumes and/or more frequent mill changes. Furthermore, when cumulative orders for the same steel size have been rolled, the individual orders are

**Exhibit 8**    A representative sample of current orders from Gambert Fabrique

| Delivery to/ works order number | Tonnes ordered | Key dates (week numbers) | | |
|---|---|---|---|---|
| | | Works order raised | Required and acknowledged delivery | Actual delivery |
| *France* | | | | |
| S463 | 10.0 | 6 | 13 | 12 |
| S464 | 25.0 | 6 | 13 | 13 |
| S465 | 25.0 | 6 | 13 | 10 |
| S466 | 20.0 | 6 | 13 | 13 |
| S467 | 16.0 | 6 | 13 | 9 |
| S468 | 28.0 | 6 | 13 | 12 |
| S469 | 35.0 | 6 | 13 | 13 |
| S470 | 25.0 | 6 | 11 | 10 |
| S471 | 20.0 | 6 | 11 | 12 |
| S472 | 20.0 | 6 | 11 | 11 |
| S473 | 15.0 | 6 | 11 | 13 |
| S474 | 25.0 | 6 | 11 | 10 |
| S475 | 10.0 | 6 | 11 | 11 |
| S476 | 20.0 | 6 | 11 | 13 |
| S477 | 20.0 | 6 | 11 | 11 |
| S478 | 15.0 | 6 | 11 | 14 |
| *UK* | | | | |
| S416 | 3.0 | 5 | 10 | 12 |
| S417 | 5.0 | 5 | 10 | 13 |
| S418 | 3.0 | 5 | 8 | 9 |
| S419 | 5.0 | 5 | 8 | 8 |
| S492 | 4.0 | 7 | 12 | 12 |
| S493 | 4.0 | 7 | 12 | 11 |
| S494 | 5.0 | 7 | 10 | 11 |
| *Denmark* | | | | |
| S412 | 4.0 | 5 | 9 | 13 |
| S413 | 4.5 | 5 | 9 | 12 |
| S414 | 5.0 | 5 | 9 | 9 |
| S415 | 4.0 | 5 | 9 | 10 |
| S489 | 5.0 | 7 | 10 | 10 |
| S490 | 5.0 | 7 | 10 | 9 |
| S491 | 3.0 | 7 | 10 | 11 |

*Notes*
1. A separate works order is raised for each size within a customer order.
2. Delivery promise for overseas destinations is acknowledged as the date the sections leave PS.

then separated to follow their own routing through the remaining processes in line with each product specification.

This results in steel sizes being processed once in each four-week cycle, so as to maintain agreed target levels of mill utilization. The procedure, therefore, is to sequence orders to minimize size of section changes and so reduce cumulative set-up times within a cycle. Exhibit 14 shows a typical hot mill rolling programme, while Exhibit 6 gives the key data for mills C and D regarding product range, output rates and change-over times on which these programmes will be established.

**Exhibit 9**  A representative sample of current UK orders received for customized sections (hot rolled and standard finishing)

| Works order number | Standard steel | Special steel | Ordered tonnes | Key dates (week numbers) | | | Total steel input (tonnes) | Total saleable output (tonnes) |
|---|---|---|---|---|---|---|---|---|
| | | | | Works order raised | Required and acknowledge delivery | Actual delivery | | |
| C026 | ✓ | | 46.0 | 5 | 10 | 9 | 49.9 | 45.4 |
| C052[1] | ✓ | | 7.5 | 5 | 15 | 16 | 8.0 | 7.3 |
| C053 | | ✓ | 3.0 | 5 | 19 | 22 | 5.1 | 4.6 |
| C057 | | ✓ | 6.0 | 5 | 20 | 20 | 7.9 | 6.4 |
| C061 | ✓ | | 10.0 | 5 | 12 | 10 | 11.0 | 9.6 |
| C082 | | ✓ | 8.5 | 5 | 19 | 20 | 8.7 | 6.9 |
| C092 | | ✓ | 3.0 | 5 | 18 | 26 | 7.5[2] | 2.2 |
| C094 | | ✓ | 20.5 | 5 | 20 | 19 | 23.1 | 19.0 |
| C099 | ✓ | | 52.0 | 5 | 11 | 10 | 58.0 | 53.3 |
| C121 | ✓ | | 10.0 | 6 | 10 | 12 | 11.0 | 10.1 |
| C126 | | ✓ | 10.0 | 6 | 22 | 21 | 13.0 | 11.1 |
| C128 | ✓ | | 20.0 | 6 | 9 | 10 | 22.5 | 20.9 |
| C132 | ✓ | | 75.0 | 6 | 12 | 12 | 83.5 | 77.1 |
| C136 | ✓ | | 15.0 | 6 | 8 | 9 | 15.5 | 15.0 |
| C150[1] | ✓ | | 20.0 | 7 | 18 | 20 | 22.5 | 19.4 |
| C151 | | ✓ | 3.0 | 7 | 21 | 21 | 4.0 | 3.2 |
| C152 | ✓ | | 15.0 | 7 | 12 | 11 | 17.0 | 15.3 |

*(continued)*

**Exhibit 9**   A representative sample of current UK orders received for customized sections (hot rolled and standard finishing) (cont'd)

| Works order number | Standard steel | Special steel | Ordered tonnes | Key dates (week numbers) | | | Total steel input (tonnes) | Total saleable output (tonnes) |
|---|---|---|---|---|---|---|---|---|
| | | | | Works order raised | Required and acknowledge delivery | Actual delivery | | |
| C160 | | ✓ | 3.0 | 7 | 24 | 21 | 4.9 | 4.2 |
| C167 | | ✓ | 10.0 | 7 | 26 | 29 | $22.0^2$ | 11.5 |
| C169 | | ✓ | 3.0 | 7 | 21 | 21 | 3.8 | 3.4 |
| C182 | ✓ | | 5.0 | 7 | 10 | 9 | 5.5 | 4.0 |
| C186 | ✓ | | 3.0 | 7 | 12 | 14 | 3.5 | 3.2 |
| C187 | | ✓ | 10.0 | 8 | 22 | 29 | $24.0^2$ | 12.5 |
| C192 | | ✓ | 12.5 | 8 | 25 | 23 | 14.0 | 13.4 |
| C193 | ✓ | | 3.0 | 8 | 12 | 12 | 3.5 | 2.6 |
| C194[1] | | ✓ | 3.0 | 8 | 28 | 28 | 3.7 | 3.1 |
| C204 | | ✓ | 3.0 | 8 | 26 | 32 | 4.2 | 2.5 |
| C207 | | ✓ | 16.0 | 8 | 25 | 24 | 20.3 | 17.3 |
| C222 | | ✓ | 4.0 | 8 | 20 | 22 | 4.0 | 2.6 |
| C231 | ✓ | | 10.0 | 8 | 14 | 12 | 11.0 | 8.9 |

*Notes*
1. These were also cold rolled.
2. Two separate rollings were necessary to achieve the required output (all or part of the first rolling was rejected by quality control).

**Exhibit 10**  A representative sample of deliveries from English Billets plc[1] for standard steel specification orders[2]

| Steel specification | Billet size (mm) | Tonnes ordered[3] | Week number: | | |
|---|---|---|---|---|---|
| | | | Ordered | Required | Received |
| PS 2000 | 100 | 250 | 25 | 36 | 44 |
| PS 2000 | 120 | 105 | 25 | 36 | 34 |
| PS 2000 | 130 | 85 | 25 | 36 | 38 |
| PS 2000 | 150 | 80 | 25 | 36 | 35 |
| PS 2000 | 190 | 130 | 25 | 36 | 34 |
| PS 2000 | 250 | 270 | 25 | 36 | 32 |
| XR 6 | 100 | 45 | 25 | 36 | 35 |
| XR 7 | 110 | 45 | 27 | 37 | 38 |
| XR 7 | 120 | 140 | 27 | 37 | 41 |
| XR 7 | 140 | 150 | 27 | 37 | 40 |
| XR 7 | 230 | 105 | 27 | 37 | 38 |
| SA 270 | 70 | 55 | 27 | 37 | 38 |
| SA 270 | 85 | 120 | 27 | 37 | 37 |
| SA 270 | 100 | 80 | 27 | 37 | 34 |
| SA 275x | 70 | 40 | 27 | 37 | 42 |
| SA 275x | 100 | 20 | 27 | 37 | 41 |
| SA 275x | 120 | 20 | 27 | 37 | 40 |
| PS 2000v | 230 | 30 | 27 | 37 | 43 |
| PS 2000x | 250 | 35 | 27 | 37 | 41 |
| PS 300 | 70 | 10 | 29 | 40 | 40 |
| PS 300 | 100 | 40 | 29 | 40 | 38 |
| PS 2000 | 70 | 115 | 29 | 40 | 42 |
| PS 2000 | 85 | 60 | 30 | 40 | 42 |
| PS 2000 | 170 | 40 | 30 | 40 | 43 |
| PS 2000v | 100 | 30 | 30 | 40 | 42 |
| PS 2000v | 120 | 35 | 30 | 40 | 40 |
| XR 7 | 70 | 80 | 30 | 40 | 39 |
| XR 7 | 85 | 90 | 30 | 40 | 41 |
| XR 7 | 100 | 40 | 30 | 40 | 41 |

*Notes*
1. English Billets plc is PS's principal raw material supplier.
2. A standard steel is classed as such by PS, if it has been processed previously, irrespective of the quantity used. This distinction from special steels signals the fact that manufacturing will have processing experience of the material, which will, in turn, lead to a reduction in problems and differences associated with one-off specials. Thus, actual process lead times are more in keeping with the norms used in lead-time calculations.
3. Most (especially the high-usage) standard steels are kept in stock by PS at levels which relate to annual usage. Orders on suppliers to replenish stocks are then made in the normal way based upon reorder levels.

**Exhibit 11** A representative sample of deliveries from English Billets plc[1] for special steels ordered for specific jobs

| Steel specification | Billet size (mm) | Tonnes ordered[2] | Week number: | | | Received tonnage |
|---|---|---|---|---|---|---|
| | | | Ordered | Required | Received | |
| 5Y102 | 100 | 28 | 27 | 37 | 40 | 22.2 |
| SD204 | 70 | 4 | 27 | 36 | 36 | 3.1 |
| BS840 | 200 | 32 | 29 | 35 | 40 | 30.2 |
| DX6DM | 170 | 16 | 29 | 35 | 36 | 15.8 |
| DN34B | 85 | 4 | 29 | 39 | 36 | 4.2 |
| DN36 | 140 | 32 | 29 | 35 | 39 | 31.9 |
| Spec 2a | 250 | 100 | 29 | 36 | 40 | 97.2 |
| DN8 | 70 | 8 | 29 | 39 | 40 | 8.7 |
| PS37 | 120 | 6 | 30 | 39 | 37 | 7.9 |
| 804/10 | 190 | 12 | 30 | 40 | 37 | 8.5 |
| DL10 | 190 | 32 | 30 | 40 | 40 | 34.8 |
| SA520 | 100 | 16 | 30 | 40 | 44 | 17.5 |
| DL12 | 100 | 4 | 30 | 40 | 36 | 3.5 |
| Spec 3b | 250 | 16 | 30 | 40 | 38 | 14.9 |
| DN8D | 140 | 4 | 30 | 41 | 42 | 5.1 |
| DN474 | 170 | 28 | 31 | 41 | 41 | 29.3 |
| C2138 | 190 | 24 | 31 | 41 | 37 | 23.1 |
| C2139 | 120 | 20 | 31 | 44 | 46 | 20.1 |
| MK200 | 230 | 120 | 32 | 38 | 37 | 116.4 |
| 550B20 | 120 | 12 | 32 | 44 | 45 | 11.9 |
| D142 | 210 | 4 | 32 | 42 | 40 | 3.7 |
| 820x | 85 | 90 | 32 | 42 | 45 | 105.0 |
| D1020 | 170 | 4 | 32 | 44 | 42 | 4.4 |
| D1022 | 130 | 4 | 32 | 44 | 42 | 4.6 |
| 540C10 | 70 | 8 | 32 | 44 | 42 | 7.9 |
| DN8D | 210 | 16 | 33 | 44 | 45 | 15.5 |
| DN36 | 100 | 4 | 33 | 44 | 43 | 4.4 |
| SA862 | 100 | 4 | 33 | 44 | 43 | 2.8 |
| DX6DM | 210 | 16 | 33 | 44 | 40 | 19.6 |

*Notes*
1. English Billets plc is PS's principal raw material supplier.
2. Special steels must be ordered in multiples of 4 tonnes up to 40 tonnes because of process restrictions (ingot sizes). The effective delivery tolerance on these orders is ± 1 tonne.

After the rolling stage, each order will then be routed according to the necessary finishing process operations to be completed. Jobs in excess of five tonnes will have to be split down after hot rolling, due to the crane-lifting limitations detailed

**Exhibit 12**    Customer order clerical processing procedures

- Customer orders are received by post, telephone, fax or e-mail.
- They are passed to the administrative department specializing in either electric motor, stockist, or customized sections.
- They are then technically and commercially appraised by experienced sales staff.
- Works orders and acknowledgement copies are raised.
- These are finally approved by both the estimating and metallurgy departments.
- Works orders are then passed to the production planning office, where orders for special steel are raised (if appropriate) and all works orders are collated in order to prepare mill programmes.

*Note*
An analysis of a representative sample of orders is provided as Exhibit 13.

**Exhibit 13**    An analysis of customer-order clerical processing times for a representative period

| Market | Average time elapsed (working days) | | |
|---|---|---|---|
| | 1 | 2 | 3 |
| Electric motor | 1.1 | 1.9 | n.a. |
| Stockist steel | 2.5 | 2.5 | n.a. |
| Customized special steels | 5.3 | 4.2 | 2.1 |
| Customized stock steels | 5.7 | 3.8 | n.a. |

*Notes*
1. This information is based on a large sample of orders which are considered to be representative.
2. The sales administration office is responsible for the processing and interpretation of customers' orders and the provision of checked works orders for production.
3. The first part of this procedure is completed in the sales office and involves commercial appraisal and appropriate administrative tasks. The average time to complete these tasks is shown in column 1.
4. The second part of this procedure is completed in the metallurgy and estimating departments for technical verification of a works order. The average time to complete these tasks is shown in column 2.
5. The final part of this procedure is compleed by the production planning office, where orders for special steels are raised. Column 3 shows the delay between this office receiving order details and the time when the order is placed; n.a. = not applicable.

earlier. The result is that delays occur in later production stages, when supervisors from these sections have to regroup part orders prior to processing in order to avoid additional set-ups.

# Corporate Decisions and Future Markets

Brian Finn reflected:

Looking back over the last decade clearly illustrates an overall volume decline in some markets. But we're in no worse a position than anyone else in this industry. In fact, looking

**Exhibit 14**     Rolling programme, March, current year

| Date | Billet size: input steel height (mm) | |
| | Mill C | Mill D |
|---|---|---|
| March | | |
| 1 | 250 | 70 |
| 2 | 150 | 70 |
| 3 | 150 | 70 |
| 4 | 140 | 70 |
| 8 | 140 | 70 |
| 9 | 110 | 85 |
| 10 | 110 | 85 |
| 11 | 120 | 85 |
| 14 | 130 | 100 |
| 15 | 130 | 100 |
| 16 | 130 | 100 |
| 17 | 190 | 100 |
| 18 | 140 | 100 |
| 21 | 140 | 100 |
| 22 | 150 | 70 |
| 23 | 150 | 70 |
| 24 | 170 | 70 |
| 25 | 170 | 120 |
| 28 | 250 | 120 |
| 29 | 230 | 120 |
| 30 | 210 | 85 |
| 31 | 110 | 85 |

*Note:*
Also refer to the details in Exhibit 6, which gives the
characteristics of these two mills, including product range,
throughput rates and change-over times.

outside our business reveals that we are doing quite well. Current return on net assets is 26 per cent, which is well above average for the manufacturing companies within the Harbridge group. Our problem is deciding what to do in the future to maintain the business position and profit returns we currently enjoy and have done for the last three years.

The key, we are certain, lies in getting our marketing strategy right. Bill Carey and his team's work in this matter is both opportune and supportive of our ideas. One advantage of being in a near-monopoly position is that we work closely with our customers and hence get good feedback on our performance in the light of their needs.

Overall our quality seems about right. A recent analysis showed few complaints, although we have recognized the need to improve the state of cleanliness of finished products, and capital investment has been sanctioned to install the necessary processes.

On the delivery side, we get complaints from our customers, but I'm told it's not too bad. Mike Sotheby (the director of purchasing and planning) keeps me informed of likely areas for complaint as we are very aware that this is important to future business. We regularly get reports from the UK Stockists and Electric Motor Manufacturers Association. This allows us to compare our delivery performance with that of our European competitors. We certainly perform as well as they do. Our records show that we achieve about 95 per cent of ordered tonnage[1] delivered on time or early.

In addition, there is also a delivery-speed factor creeping into some of our markets. Companies need deliveries quickly, and if we can meet their demands then we get the business. In these markets, the customer requires delivery in less than the 'standard' lead-time calculations we use. These are becoming more frequent in the customized sections market, and it is most important that we succeed in this segment, as it is an essential part of our intended expansion in this market overall.

The final issue is that of price. While some of our markets are price-sensitive (for example, much of the stockist steel sections and in particular Gambert Fabrique), many are not.[2] This is especially so in the customized sections market. Achieving these high margins, therefore, is important to us in terms of current and future performance. This is why we see areas of high-margin businesses as an important part of our portfolio. Bill Carey has put his finger on two and they will certainly be where we will start.

## Notes

1. Note that in all markets, PS contracts to supply (for each size) a customer order within plus or minus 1 tonne of the quantity required for each size. Also, steel suppliers to PS work within this convention.
2. Typical invoiced prices (ex-works) are shown in Exhibit 3, and some estimates of typical variable costs in Exhibit 4.

# Rumack Pharmaceuticals

Of increasing concern is the difficulty we are having in meeting our schedules and the growing customer order backlog which is resulting. For many months now there has been pressure to maintain schedules and we have been trying hard to overcome these problems. But, it appears as though it may be a permanent feature needing a long-term solution. The part which is difficult to reconcile, however, is that on paper we should have more than sufficient packaging capacity to meet current sales levels. And, no doubt, the rest of the board will also have difficulty in understanding this apparent discrepancy.

Pete Kovac, vice-president operations at Rumack Pharmaceuticals' plant in Bakersfield, California, was addressing the managers responsible for production, engineering and materials respectively (see Exhibit 1) at the weekly meeting to review current issues and progress on agreed developments.

## Background

Nine years ago, Rumack Pharmaceuticals, needing to increase capacity, decided to build a new plant in Bakersfield, California to make and pack Restolvic, one of its successful stomach indigestion products. Within three years of making the decision, the plant was in full production and it now manufactures a wide range of derivatives under the Restolvic brand name together with some of its Hedanol products, one of Rumack's pain-killing preparations.

## Marketing

Restolvic has proven to be one of the most successful products we have developed in the last decade. This is certainly so given the systematic way in which we have developed relevant variants in order to exploit the obvious sales potential. When the plant opened we had two identical lines for packing our solid products. At this time, we had more capacity than we needed and our task, therefore, has been to identify new oppor-

This case study was written by Terry Hill (University of Oxford) and R. Menda (University of Cape Town) as a basis for class discussion and not as an example of good or bad management. © AMD Publishing.

**Exhibit 1**    Part of the company's organization chart

tunities to increase sales and hence overall profits. Initially, we explored additional dosage forms which met the particular needs of consumers. Later recognizing the level of acceptance of Restolvic as a successful indigestion reliever for a wide cross-section of people, we decided to seek ways of capitalizing on the growing strength of its brand name. This led to adding further active ingredients in order to develop other OTC [over the counter] products and also prescription products such as Restolvic A (an anti-spasmodic preparation) and Restolvic E (an anti-emetic preparation). And the whole strategy has been highly successful.

Jon Prynn, vice-president marketing, then gave further details of the way in which the product line extensions and derivatives had been built on the Restolvic image and, in turn, had added to the whole, thus leading to specific gains of both an 'individual and synergistic' nature.

All products make very high margins. In fact, some of those which target specific markets will often attract a premium price and consequently even higher margins. All in all, we are a highly profitable business both in terms of total profit and as a per cent of sales.

# Manufacturing

Since the opening of the plant some six years ago, we now make and pack OTC varieties of Restolvic, some Hedanol products and more recently prescription derivatives such as Restolvic A and Restolvic E. The latter were relocated here two years ago when the Rumack Group reassessed its overall capacity requirements in the USA and decided to close one of its plants. The outcome was that the prescription Restolvic products were relocated and are now made and packed here.

Jim Lawson, production manager, went on to explain that the manufacture of pharmaceutical dosage forms is divided into two major groups of activities – processing and packaging.

Processing concerns the conversion of powdered ingredients into bulk tablet or liquid preparations. Equipment is dedicated to a single operation such as granulation, blending, tablet compression, coating and liquid mixing. These products are manufactured in bulk normally in quantities dictated by the capacity of the particular piece of processing equipment.

Filling bulk tablets and liquids produced in the processing phase of manufacturing takes place in packaging. Here tablets and liquids are bottled according to a range of sizes and on the relevant processes.

There are now four packaging lines at the plant with specific products allocated to each line.

> When we opened up the plant, we installed the relevant processing capability and also packing Lines 1 and 2, with Line 3 scheduled to come on stream 12 to 15 months later. From the start, Lines 1 and 2 worked well and this confirmed our decision to invest in three identical processes. Staying with tried and tested equipment is a significant plus point as well as the benefits for engineering support and maintenance.

Jim continued:

> When the other US plant was closed, we transferred the prescription product range and the existing packaging equipment from that plant to here, then modified and added to the process in order to bring it up to the same specification as the other three lines. The prescription range is only made on Line 4.

He added that when the Bakersfield plant was planned, sufficient floor space and facilities were allowed for in terms of future growth.

> The growth in demand for Restolvic has been rapid and this together with the transfer of products resulting from the plant closure has absorbed the excess floor space allowed for in the original plans.
>
> The capacity problems we are experiencing do not concern the processing stage of manufacturing. Here we have sufficient capacity. The problems are in packaging.

The discussion then turned to details on each of the packaging lines (see Exhibit 2 for an outline of the steps involved and Exhibit 3 for details of the four packaging lines).

**Exhibit 2**    Outline of the packaging process

> The four packaging lines referred to in the case narrative have been developed to include both the filling and packaging stage of the process. The principal steps completed within a packaging line are outlined below:
>
> 1. **Bottle unscrambling** – bottles from outside suppliers are delivered and fed into a large hopper which unscrambles and delivers them correctly positioned onto the line.
> 2. **Air cleaning** – each bottle is cleaned in terms of dust by a jet of air.
> 3. **Filling** – the appropriate number of tablet/caplets are then put into each bottle.
> 4. **Cotton insertion** – a small quantity of cotton wool is placed into the empty head space of each bottle to prevent the tablets/caplets from moving. The amount of cotton reflects the space at the top of the bottle. This adjustment forms part of the set-up for each stock-keeping unit (SKU).
> 5. **Capping** – a cap is positioned and located on each bottle.
> 6. **Induction sealing** – the cap liner and bottle is then sealed, in part as a tamper-evident feature.
> 7. **Labelling** – the appropriate label is put onto the bottle.
> 8. **Neck banding** – a PVC band is heat shrunk around the neck/cap as a final seal and as another tamper-evident feature.
> 9. **Cartoning** – each bottle is placed into its own individual carton.
> 10. **Packing** – individual cartons are then placed in a case pack in predetermined quantities.
>
> *Note*
> Stock-keeping unit (SKU) is the phrase for any individual product specification that requires a manufacturing change including packaging.

**Exhibit 3**    Details of the four packaging lines

> **Line 1** – This line fills and packs both Restolvic and Hedanol products. The selection of these products was made on the basis of bottle size. All products packed on this line use the same bottle. In this way, set-up or change-over times are reduced. Even so, they are still lengthy. Each product change means that the filler has to be stripped, cleaned and reassembled. Each line has a crew of seven, consisting of six operators and a mechanic. Three or four operators undertake the cleaning task which takes 3½ to 4 hours. The remainder work on carton and label changing which takes about the same time as the cleaning element of the change-over. So a typical change will take, at most, 4 hours. [Other details for this line are given in Exhibits 4, 5 and 6.]
>
> **Line 2** – This line is designed to accommodate three different bottle sizes.[1] Over the last two years engineering have redesigned the bottles so that the only dimension which changes is the height. This was selected as it is the easiest form of size adjustment to make on a change-over. Nevertheless, this increases the overall change-over to 5 hours. Without a bottle change then a product change would take between 3½ and 4 hours as with Line 1. Finally, all lines have the same crew make-up as explained for Line 1 and they all work on change-overs that do not require a bottle size change [see Exhibit 6].
>
> **Line 3** – This line was installed 12 months after the plant was opened. It handles all our liquid products for infants, children and adults. There are five bottle sizes here and each bottle size change takes some 8 hours. Engineering have this set-up reduction as a priority given the enormous benefits we have reaped from the improvements they made on Line 2 [see Exhibit 6]. Contamination factors and resulting set-up times restrict, for all practical reasons, the use of this line for packing non-liquid products. The result is that only liquid products are made on this line.
>
> *(continued)*

**Exhibit 3**  Details of the four packaging lines (cont'd)

> **Line 4** – This line handles the 12 product types within the Restolvic prescription range. At present, there are five bottle sizes involved and typical set-up times for bottle and product changes are similar to those on Line 3. There is spare capacity, but if OTC products are to be packed on this line then they must meet the more exacting standards of prescription and associated costs. Furthermore, equipment will need to be added to provide the additional packaging formats which are required by OTC products.[2]
>
> The current shift patterns allow us to run three lines for 24 hours a day throughout all seven days of the week. Priority is given, wherever possible, to Lines 1 and 2 as the products on these two lines have the highest demand and, therefore, require maximum capacity to allow us to meet current schedules. Lines 3 and 4 both have spare capacity and we can meet current demand by running these for two shifts and one shift per day respectively plus additional times when crews have completed their part of a change-over on another line but the mechanic has other work to do' [see Exhibit 7].
>
> Change-overs on Lines 3 and 4 are scheduled to be completed at times when the process is not manned.
>
> *Notes*
> 1. Bottle sizes differ, depending upon the two factors of tablet size and number of tablets involved.
> 2. Prescription products have simpler packaging specifications. For example, prescription products are bulk packed at the outer packaging stage where OTC products are individually packed. This additional equipment would require an investment of US$1.0m.

**Exhibit 4**  Annual volumes[1] for a number of representtive products packed on Lines 1, 2 and 3

| Product[2] | Current year minus | | | | | | Current year |
|---|---|---|---|---|---|---|---|
| | 6 | 5 | 4 | 3 | 2 | 1 | |
| AC Tablets (24) | 1148 | 1755 | 1906 | 2773 | 3844 | 3896 | 4597 |
| AC Tablets (100) | 631 | 907 | 1179 | 1053 | 1180 | 1304 | 1666 |
| AC Caplets (50) | 145 | 163 | 402 | 210 | 326 | 409 | 341 |
| AC Caplets (100) | 226 | 127 | 172 | 277 | 306 | 440 | 498 |
| IC Liquid (25 ml) | 187 | 187 | 249 | 312 | 489 | 429 | 490 |
| AC Liquid (75 ml) | 262 | 112 | 158 | 234 | 325 | 294 | 388 |
| CC Caplets (24) | | 232 | 674 | 977 | 1038 | 1356 | 1457 |
| AC Chewable (110) | | | 438 | 485 | 281 | 480 | 509 |
| IC Tablets (24) | | | 109 | 145 | 254 | 331 | 265 |
| CC Tablets (24) | | | | 151 | 151 | 165 | 127 |
| IC Tablets (12) | | | | 504 | 432 | 720 | 832 |
| CC Tablets (12) | | | | 138 | 311 | 248 | 204 |
| AC Tablets (50) | | | | | 208 | 256 | 243 |
| AC Caplets (60) | | | | | 96 | 240 | 262 |
| AC Caplets (24) | | | | | | 65 | 470 |
| Hedanol Tablets (24) | | | | | | 200 | 138 |
| Hedanol Tablets (50) | | | | | | 150 | 42 |
| Hedanol Caplets (24) | | | | | | 218 | 127 |
| Chewable (20) | | | | | | | 224 |
| Chewable (12) | | | | | | | 221 |
| Total SKUs added[3] | 17 | 20 | 22 | 35 | 37 | 45 | 51 |

*Notes*
1. Annual volumes are in 000 bottles
2. Other than the three Hedanol products, the remainder are Restolvic.
3. Total SKUs are the number of SKUs packed in each year given. Thus, currently the company packs 34 more products than it did 6 years ago. An SKU is the phrase used for any different packed item.

**Exhibit 5**   Number of production runs for some representative products on Line 1

| Product | Number of production runs Current year minus | | | | | Current year |
|---|---|---|---|---|---|---|
| | **5** | **4** | **3** | **2** | **1** | |
| AC Tablets (24) | 10 | 17 | 24 | 33 | 35 | 41 |
| CC Caplets (24) | 4 | 10 | 16 | 20 | 22 | 24 |
| IC Tablets (24) | | 4 | 6 | 9 | 10 | 10 |
| CC Tablets (24) | | | 7 | 6 | 7 | 7 |
| CC Tablets (12) | | | 6 | 9 | 8 | 8 |
| AC Tablets (50) | | | | 8 | 9 | 8 |
| AC Caplets (24) | | | | | 3 | 12 |
| Hedanol Tablets (50) | | | | | 6 | 2 |
| Hedanol Caplets (24) | | | | | 4 | 5 |

*Note*
As explained in the case narrative, there are no bottle size changes on Line 1. Where the same product but not the same quantity of tablets is packed, padding is used as a filler.

**Exhibit 6**   Run size and output data for a number of representative products packed on Line 1 during the last six months

| Products | Run size (bottles) | Average output (bottles/hour) |
|---|---|---|
| Chewable (24) | 23 352 | 4246 |
| Chewable (24) | 54 720 | 6080 |
| Chewable (12) | 17 016 | 4538 |
| Chewable (12) | 38 736 | 5165 |
| Chewable (24) | 44 664 | 4060 |
| Chewable (24) | 49 056 | 4021 |
| Chewable (24) | 58 872 | 5744 |
| IC Caplets (24) | 7 416 | 4944 |
| IC Caplets (24) | 81 720 | 6286 |
| IC Tablets (30) | 51 120 | 4987 |
| IC Tablets (30) | 164 160 | 6438 |
| CC Tablets (12) | 15 120 | 3360 |
| IC Tablets (24) | 5 208 | 3472 |
| IC Tablets (24) | 14 976 | 3744 |
| IC Tablets (24) | 29 830 | 5424 |
| AC Caplets (24) | 41 952 | 5594 |
| Hedanol Caplets (24) | 31 176 | 4454 |
| Hedanol Tablets (50) | 13 176 | 2510 |
| CC Caplets (24) | 27 696 | 5036 |
| CC Caplets (24) | 62 256 | 6445 |
| CC Caplets (24) | 62 688 | 4179 |
| CC Caplets (24) | 95 736 | 6838 |
| CC Caplets (24) | 121 272 | 7134 |
| CC Caplets (50) | 28 728 | 3591 |
| CC Caplets (50) | 29 832 | 4262 |
| CC Tablets (24) | 66 960 | 6533 |
| AC Tablets (24) | 119 808 | 6390 |
| AC Tablets (24) | 193 800 | 7112 |
| AC Tablets (24) | 286 584 | 7165 |
| CC Tablets (24) | 5 880 | 2940 |
| CC Tablets (24) | 19 008 | 5849 |
| AC Tablets (30) | 21 720 | 4137 |

*Note*
The above is a sample of the production order quantities packed on Line 1 in this period.

**Exhibit 7**    Set-up/change-over arrangements

The approach to completing the necessary set-ups/change-overs on the four packaging lines is explained below:

*Line 1*

As there are no bottle size changes on this line, the product changes are undertaken by the line crew and mechanic who are on the line at the time. A product change requires the filler to be stripped down, cleaned and reassembled. This takes about 3½ to 4 hours using four members of the team. The other members of the crew complete the labelling/carton changes with the mechanic providing support throughout. The whole change would take up to 4 hours.

*Lines 2, 3 and 4*

Product changes on these lines are undertaken in a way similar to that described for Line 1. However, where a bottle size change is also required then the packing crew would first complete the product change tasks, then move to another line which was ready but not being used. The mechanic would stay behind to complete the size change task. The length of time varies from line to line as shown below.

| | Set-up (hours) | | |
| Line | Product/packaging changes | Bottle size changes | Total for both bottle and product/packaging changes[1] |
| --- | --- | --- | --- |
| 1 | 4 | – | 4[2] |
| 2 | 4 | 5 | 5 |
| 3 | 4 | 8 | 8 |
| 4 | 4 | 8 | 8 |

*Notes*:
**1.** Size changes and product changes are completed concurrently.
**2.** No bottle changes take place on Line 1.

Further set-up reductions are constrained in two ways:

- The investment in a portable filling station and changes to existing lines to accommodate this arrangement total US$0.7m per station.
- These changes would also require additional floor space equal to 50 per cent of the existing floor space required for each packaging line. At this time floor space is at a premium.

# Engineering

The engineering manager, Rob Chow, explained how the priority for his support group was to accommodate the continued growth in the new product derivations.

We launch line extensions and new products on a regular basis in order to capitalize on the Restolvic image and brand name. And it continues to be a very successful strategy.

Our contribution is, therefore, to ensure that we can make those new products in line with the agreed launch dates. The trade-off is that we allocate little or no time to process improvements per se. Also of late, the need to work on rationalizing bottle sizes on Line 3 and working on set-ups in general has been put on a back burner. We are aware of the need to address these issues but, at the moment and for the foreseeable future, they will have to take a low priority.

# The Future

Peter Kovac summed up:

These are exciting times for our business. We have grown sales revenue and profits in line with, if not above, budget and the future looks equally promising. However, all this has been met only by making appropriate investments and the continued efforts of all concerned. The one issue of some concern is that of capacity in our packaging area. A new packaging line currently costs, including installation, some US$3.5m with a lead time of 12 months from the placement of the order before it is commissioned and up to speed. The rationale for such an investment and the case to support such a proposal will need to be carefully thought through and will understandably be questioned by the rest of the executive group given our existing capacity projections.

# Santal (SA)

As you are all aware, our automotive sales continue to grow and now account for almost 70 per cent of overall revenue. The growth is expected to continue, a fact boosted by the Group's declared policy to highlight this sector as one of its core activities. However, with growth has come increasing demands from our customers to improve the orientation of our company towards their needs. With this in mind, we have been reviewing our existing organizational structure, and now need to discuss and agree the detail of what we want to do.

Pierre Reinman, CEO of Santal (SA), was introducing a presentation reviewing the company's existing organizational structure within the context of its overall business requirements.

## Background

Santal (SA) is a subsidiary of the Albi Group, a French-based conglomerate with manufacturing plants throughout Europe and North America and involving the agriculture equipment, machine tool, aerospace and automotive sectors. Santal was founded in the early 1960s to meet the growing sealing requirements of other companies in the Group. With continued growth and increasing product range a new manufacturing facility was built near Limoges in the late 1970s. Now, Santal is a major manufacturer of elastometric seals and engineering components to companies in various industries throughout Europe and the rest of the world.

## Marketing

Santal supplies customers in both the automotive and aerospace sectors. Sales for the current year are running at the level of FF470m[1] and details of growth and split between the sectors are given in Exhibit 1.

---

This case study was written by Terry Hill (University of Oxford) and A. J. Hill (University of Manchester) as the basis for class discussion and not as an example of good or bad management. © AMD Publishing.

**Exhibit 1**    Sales revenues for the last five years

| Sales (FFm) | Current year minus | | | | Current year |
|---|---|---|---|---|---|
| | 4 | 3 | 2 | 1 | |
| Sales (million FFs) | | | | | |
| Automotive | 170 | 228 | 242 | 286 | 320 |
| Aerospace | 130 | 132 | 138 | 154 | 150 |
| Total | 300 | 360 | 380 | 440 | 470[1] |

*Note*
**1.** Based on the first 8 months of the current year and extended.

A recent report by Group Marketing together with Santal's own market reviews highlighted the potential growth opportunities within the automotive sector. Identifying the vehicle manufacturers that were likely to increase market share together with the suppliers of assemblies requiring seals (for example, fuel systems, climate control and braking systems) had given clear direction on areas and customers where potential future growth was highest.

Andre Lejet, marketing director, explained the difference between the two sectors:

The continued increase in sales within the automotive sector has been a feature of our overall corporate growth. We have recognized its growing importance over the last decade and this has been reflected in our sales and marketing efforts. At the same time we have continued our push in the aerospace sector not only because of its significance in terms of the overall business but also due to the higher margins associated with these orders.

As you can imagine, the two sectors are very different to each other. The principal areas of difference concern volumes, life cycles and the key factors in winning contracts. Aerospace comprises low-volume orders with long product life cycles necessitating support for decades after the original equipment (OE) phase[2] is ended. In fact, there is a legal requirement to provide spares if there are at least six aircraft flying anywhere in the world. Although aerospace customers continuously review price, the margins are generally higher than in the automotive sector. There are fewer suppliers and a marked demand for design and technical support by customers. On-time delivery is an important issue. Meeting customers' build schedules during the OE phase of an aircraft's life cycle is a prerequisite to being awarded a contract. When a product moves to the spares phase customer demands change. Delivery speed[3] is the key requirement, while price is even less sensitive than the OE phase due to the very low-volume intermittent nature of spares requirements.

The automotive sector is more price sensitive overall especially for contracts linked to high-volume car demand. However, spares demand changes the volume dimension and also introduces delivery speed as a factor with price becoming less important. As with aerospace, delivery reliability is necessary for both OE and spares contracts.

On the aspect of technology, there are less differences in terms of material specification but, by and large, the process technology demands of aerospace and automotive are quite similar. Certainly we use the same processes to make products for both sectors.

# Manufacturing

Bernard Benot, operations director, explained how the process of making seals was not in itself complex (Exhibit 2):

> The process of making seals is not complex in itself. The compounds are either purchased as in the case of injection moulding, or prepared in our calendering process in the rubber mill. The material is then allocated to an order (the same material may be used to mould several different seals) and prepared for the various processes in blank preparation. Following moulding, the products are inspected with some finishing (for example, trimming) requirements in the case of compression and injection moulding.

Bernard then went on to explain that products were allocated to the different processes depending upon volume:

> Based on anticipated volumes, we select the most appropriate process to cope with customer demand. Lower-volume products are most suited to compression while high-

**Exhibit 2**      Outline manufacturing processes

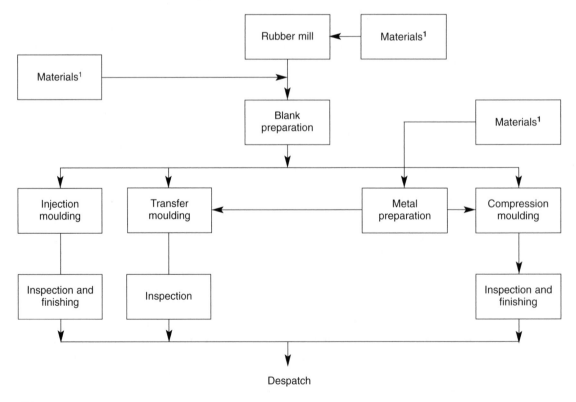

*Note*
1. Materials indicates an outside supply.

**Exhibit 3**    Manufacturing data on the representative sample of aerospace parts[1]

| Part number | Mould time per part (standard hours)[2] | Number of cavities | Press type (tonnes)[3] |
|---|---|---|---|
| 00101 | 0.0012 | 91 | 250 |
| 01422 | 0.1472 | 1 | 40 |
| 02170 | 0.0173 | 4 | 80 |
| 03742 | 0.1915 | 1 | 50 |
| 04260 | 0.0893 | 1 | 20 |
| 25252 | 0.0305 | 5 | 50 |
| 27312 | 0.0519 | 3 | 50 |
| 28280 | 0.0143 | 7 | 100 |
| 28400 | 0.0892 | 1 | 20 |
| 29112 | 0.0908 | 1 | 40 |
| 85260 | 0.0171 | 5 | 50 |
| 86052 | 0.0297 | 5 | 80 |
| 87718 | 0.0242 | 1 | 20 |
| 63162 | 0.0355 | 5 | 80 |
| 46570 | 0.0221 | 4 | 50 |
| 90034 | 0.0125 | 8 | 150 |
| 15850 | 0.0083 | 12 | 100 |
| 10260 | 0.0573 | 5 | 100 |
| 81261 | 0.0882 | 1 | 20 |
| 11340 | 0.0130 | 8 | 150 |

*Notes*:

1. All aerospace parts use compression moulding processes.
2. The mould time per part takes into account the number of cavities on a mould. Thus, for Part 00101 the moulding cycle time (that is, the length of time from the start to the finish of the moulding process) is 0.1092 standard hours. Hence, the mould time per part is

$$\frac{0.1092}{91} = 0.0012 \text{ standard hours/part}$$

3. A tonne is a metric ton.

volume products are typically allocated to injection moulding. Moulds may have a wide number of cavities [Exhibits 3 and 4]. The number of cavities is again part of the decision regarding anticipated volumes and will consequently affect the press size on to which the mould will need to be allocated. The tonnage figures [see Exhibits 3 and 4] refer to the locking pressure exerted by a press. The number of cavities on a mould (as well as the physical dimensions of the moulding) will affect the size of press necessary to meet the technical specification of the part.

He then went on to explain the shift patterns worked in the various production areas, typical set-up times by process, lead times through the different stages of manufacturing and other related data – see Exhibits 5, 6 and 7.

**Exhibit 4**      Manufacturing data on a representative sample of automotive products

| Part number | Mould time per part (standard hours) | Number of cavities | Press type[1] | Press tonnes |
|---|---|---|---|---|
| 76684 | 0.0980 | 19 | T | 500 |
| 10642 | 0.0560 | 4 | T | 45 |
| 16897 | 0.0109 | 12 | C | 50 |
| 21614 | 0.1187 | 1 | C | 30 |
| 94372 | 0.0072 | 5 | I | 135 |
| 08742 | 0.0065 | 8 | I | 135 |
| 00442 | 0.0095 | 5 | I | 135 |
| 44043 | 0.0219 | 10 | C | 100 |
| 21154 | 0.0696 | 1 | C | 40 |
| 21402 | 0.0460 | 5 | C | 50 |
| 31422 | 0.0318 | 5 | C | 40 |
| 41070 | 0.0065 | 40 | C | 100 |
| 76202 | 0.1270 | 42 | T | 100 |
| 32152 | 0.0066 | 32 | I | 190 |
| 21434 | 0.0020 | 24 | I | 135 |
| 19793 | 0.2260 | 7 | T | 50 |
| 21594 | 0.2019 | 1 | C | 100 |
| 19313 | 0.0658 | 16 | C | 50 |
| 74184 | 0.0052 | 18 | I | 135 |
| 47602 | 0.2490 | 41 | T | 50 |
| 00352 | 0.0477 | 3 | C | 50 |
| 40917 | 0.1260 | 55 | T | 100 |
| 19663 | 0.2550 | 7 | T | 45 |
| 45814 | 0.0020 | 4 | I | 250 |
| 35082 | 0.1950 | 22 | T | 100 |
| 00582 | 0.1003 | 1 | I | 250 |
| 41012 | 0.0046 | 12 | I | 135 |
| 24791 | 0.1530 | 16 | T | 50 |
| 26092 | 0.2770 | 37 | T | 100 |
| 41062 | 0.0048 | 11 | I | 135 |
| 19893 | 0.3650 | 14 | T | 50 |
| 52980 | 0.0171 | 22 | C | 100 |

*Notes*
**1.** C = compression; T = transfer; I = injection.

Notes 2 and 3 to Exhibit 3 also relate here.

**Exhibit 5**    Total quantities ordered in the last 12 months for a representative
sample of aerospace products

| Part number | Annual quantity (number of parts) | Number of production runs in the period |
|---|---|---|
| 00101 | 17357 | 11 |
| 01422 | 1638 | 7 |
| 02170 | 132 | 1 |
| 03742 | 498 | 3 |
| 04260 | 200 | 1 |
| 05252 | 4208 | 6 |
| 27312 | 276 | 2 |
| 28280 | 56 | 1 |
| 28400 | 30 | 2 |
| 29112 | 15 | 1 |
| 85260 | 155 | 2 |
| 86052 | 415 | 2 |
| 87718 | 35 | 1 |
| 63162 | 300 | 1 |
| 46570 | 122 | 2 |
| 90034 | 1376 | 1 |
| 15850 | 20 | 1 |
| 10260 | 70 | 2 |
| 81261 | 716 | 5 |
| 11340 | 118 | 4 |

# Proposed Changes

Pierre Reinmann explained the proposed changes:

> We have increasingly come to realize that we are in two distinct businesses – aerospace
> and automotive. The characteristics of both these sectors are different to one another in
> so many ways. As explained earlier, the market demands are in sharp contrast in terms of
> volumes and the way we win orders. The growth in automotive sales has brought these
> issues to the fore. It is important, therefore, to identify with the different industrial
> sectors involved.
> Understanding sector backgrounds and having knowledge of existing and future
> product programmes and key competitors are important issues and create marked differ-
> ences between aerospace and automotive. Customer contacts are also important and, in
> fact, are essential to increasing our future business in both sectors.
> To meet the growing demands of our customers and particularly to help secure the
> present growth in sales we have achieved within the automotive sector, we need to identify
> what we need to do and how best to respond to the different requirements of both sectors.

**Exhibit 6** Total quantities ordered in the last 12 months for a representative sample of automotive products

| Part number | Annual quantity (number of parts) | Number of production runs in the period |
|---|---|---|
| 76684 | 55555 | 61 |
| 10642 | 6385 | 13 |
| 16897 | 13051 | 9 |
| 21614 | 129 | 3 |
| 94372 | 64487 | 6 |
| 08742 | 27200 | 5 |
| 00442 | 8766 | 3 |
| 44043 | 27314 | 6 |
| 21154 | 298 | 3 |
| 21402 | 1250 | 6 |
| 31422 | 478 | 2 |
| 41070 | 1155767 | 90 |
| 76202 | 1784360 | 238 |
| 32152 | 193511 | 1 |
| 21434 | 126174 | 1 |
| 19793 | 2965 | 5 |
| 21594 | 50 | 2 |
| 19313 | 4000 | 6 |
| 74184 | 46879 | 3 |
| 47602 | 109365 | 22 |
| 00352 | 776 | 3 |
| 40917 | 470212 | 43 |
| 19663 | 34301 | 61 |
| 45814 | 495855 | 5 |
| 35082 | 202684 | 77 |
| 00582 | 2837 | 4 |
| 41012 | 60173 | 12 |
| 24791 | 123718 | 64 |
| 26092 | 233279 | 79 |
| 41062 | 202173 | 20 |
| 19893 | 19358 | 35 |
| 52980 | 2300 | 4 |

**Exhibit 7**  Additional manufacturing data

---

1. **Pre-moulding and post-moulding lead times**

   Typical lead times for pre- and post-moulding processes total 1 day and 3 days respectively. These can be shortened if schedules are changed and other priorities are by-passed.

2. **Shift patterns**

   - Moulding – all moulding processes work on a three-shift basis covering the 24 hours of each day.
   - Metal preparation – the shifts worked here are from 06.00–14.00 and 08.00–16.00 each day.
   - Blank preparation – this area has a double day shift system from 06.00–14.00 and 14.00–22.00.
   - Rubber mill – the shift patterns are the same as for blank preparation.

3. **Set-up times**

   Typical set-up times vary by moulding process as follows

   - Compression = 0.5 hours
   - Transfer     = 1.0 hours
   - Injection    = 4.0 hours

---

**Exhibit 8**  Overview of the proposed changes within the business

---

The proposal is to split manufacturing into two parts, one to support the aerospace and the other, the automotive business. The following provides an overview of the proposals and indicates those processes to be allocated to each business and those to be retained as a central provision.

1. **Rubber mill, blank preparation and metal preparation**

   These are to be retained as a centralized provision. Any decision to split them between the two businesses would have incurred very high additional process investments.

2. **Moulding – compression, transfer and injection**

   The report highlighted the volume differences between the aerospace and automotive sectors *per se* and the relationship between compression, transfer and injection moulding in terms of increasing volumes as explained below:

   *Aerospace* – given the low-volume nature of this sector, all the products are manufactured using compression moulding. The appropriate compression moulding processes are to be allocated to manufacture all aerospace products. This allocation will reflect the size of press and capacity requirements of this sector.

   *Automotive* – the higher-volume nature of this segment is reflected in its process allocations. The lower-volume end of this sector is served by compression moulding

   *(continued)*

**Exhibit 8**     Overview of the proposed changes within the business (cont'd)

while the higher volume is manufactured using injection moulding processes. The volume levels between these two extremes is covered by transfer moulding. As with aerospace, the appropriate compression, transfer and moulding processes are to be allocated to manufacture all automotive products. This allocation will reflect the size of press and capacity requirements of this sector.

**3. Inspection and finishing**

These activities are to be allocated to each focused unit.

**4. Despatch**

Two separate despatch areas are to be created, one to meet the needs of each business.

The proposed changes are basically to split manufacturing into two parts (see Exhibit 8). We have been discussing the form of the proposal, and consider that reflecting the market sector differences in manufacturing would best meet the needs of our current and future business.

# Notes

1. FF = French francs.
2. There are two phases in a programme – original equipment (OE) refers to the building of a new aircraft. The spares phase follows the end of the OE build. Demand for spares during the OE phase are simply added to the relevant OE schedule.
3. Delivery speed concerns meeting short customer lead times.

# Sherpin

'Growth opportunities we know to be substantial within our business overall', commented Matthew Jones, CEO of Northrop Industries. 'Given this and the profit margins we are currently able to maintain, then capitalizing on this opportunity is a corporate priority. Our concern, however, is whether manufacturing can support this future growth by meeting the needs of future customers while maintaining its support for the existing business'.

## Background

Sherpin was established ten years ago as a strategic business unit within Northrop Industries, part of the Artne Group. It has grown through an ability to provide high-quality products to industries throughout the world, and today contributes just under 10 per cent of the company's overall sales revenue (see Exhibit 1).

## Markets

Sherpin competes in four distinct markets: aerospace, automotive, industrial and motor sport. The industrial market has always been core to the overall business in that the profits generated in this market have helped the company expand into other segments. However, as these segments have grown (see Exhibit 2), it has become apparent that there are different customer demands to be met within each. As Jim Heaton (sales manager) explains:

> Our overall strategy as a business is to use our technical expertise to provide solutions to problems. Every product we make is designed specifically to meet the technical requirements of a customer. It is this capability which initially wins an order at the prototype stage, and determines the product specification which manufacturing has to meet. Once this has been achieved, there are various other demands which then have to be met as a part moves into the subsequent original equipment manufacturer (OEM) and spares

This case was prepared by Terry Hill (University of Oxford) and A. J. Hill (UMIST). It is intended for class discussion and not as an illustration of good or bad management. © AMD Publishing.

**Exhibit 1**    Actual annual sales, number of employees and gross margins for the last ten years and current year forecasts

| Year | Northrop Industries annual sales (£m) | Sherpin | | |
| --- | --- | --- | --- | --- |
| | | annual sales (£m) | number of employees | gross margin (per cent sales) |
| 1 | 65 | 1.6 | 40 | 19 |
| 2 | 70 | 2.8 | 40 | 22 |
| 3 | 76 | 4.0 | 36 | 28 |
| 4 | 85 | 5.2 | 44 | 33 |
| 5 | 94 | 6.4 | 44 | 36 |
| 6 | 105 | 7.4 | 44 | 47 |
| 7 | 118 | 8.6 | 44 | 50 |
| 8 | 130 | 11.1 | 60 | 50 |
| 9 | 140 | 14.7 | 64 | 58 |
| 10 | 162 | 17.2 | 84 | 54 |
| 11[1] | 180 | 19.7[2] | 90 | 52 |

*Notes*

**1.** Year 11 is the current year and sales figures are based upon forecasts.

**2.** Sherpin's monthly sales (£000s) for last year were:

| | | | |
| --- | --- | --- | --- |
| Jan | 1761 | Jul | 1274 |
| Feb | 1811 | Aug | 957 |
| Mar | 1710 | Sep | 1189 |
| Apr | 1564 | Oct | 1519 |
| May | 1316 | Nov | 1532 |
| Jun | 1322 | Dec | 1244 |

stages of its life cycle. These demands vary depending on the market sector within which a part competes and as explained in the next sections.

# Aerospace

The Aerospace market has historically had a traditional approach to undertaking business. This means that the relationships we initially forge and then maintain with customers are vitally important. Prototypes account for 5 per cent of total sales (£s). In this stage of a product's life cycle, new orders are won based on a combination of this relationship factor and the ability to meet the high design and quality conformance requirements within these applications. The price and delivery speed elements still play a role, but this concerns meeting norms rather than competing on price and delivery speed.[1]

However, once we move into the OEM phase the criteria change. Here price becomes more sensitive and it is necessary to be able to react quickly to a customer's short lead-time demands. In fact, at the spares stage in an aerospace product's life cycle, the requirement for fast and reliable delivery becomes vital, especially when an 'aircraft on the ground'[2] situation occurs. Due to the unpredictable nature of demand, it is often not possible to project future demand patterns in either the OEM or spares stages of a

**Exhibit 2**     Historical and projected sales by market sector

| Year | Sales by market sector (£000s) | | | |
|------|-----------|------------|------------|------------|
|      | **Aerospace** | **Automotive** | **Industrial** | **Motor Sport** |
| 1    | –    | –      | 1 605  | –      |
| 2    | 522  | –      | 2 311  | –      |
| 3    | 532  | –      | 3 469  | –      |
| 4    | 632  | –      | 4 298  | 287    |
| 5    | 702  | –      | 5 319  | 421    |
| 6    | 821  | 511    | 5 421  | 654    |
| 7    | 853  | 1 568  | 5 539  | 732    |
| 8    | 952  | 3 708  | 5 720  | 776    |
| 9    | 1564 | 4 936  | 6 844  | 1 340  |
| 10   | 1860 | 5 964  | 7 760  | 1 656  |
| 11[1,2] | 2636 | 6 808 | 8 636 | 1 616  |
| 12[2] | 3476 | 8 408 | 9 792  | 1 648  |
| 13[2] | 3276 | 11 824 | 13 624 | 1 684  |

*Notes*
**1.** Year 11 is the current year.
**2.** Sales figures for years 11, 12 and 13 are based upon forecasts.

product's life. One-off orders are, therefore, placed by customers to meet their needs in both these phases of a typical product's life cycle. We tend to find that the remaining sales (£s) for products are split evenly between these two segments.

## Automotive

Sales (£s) in this sector are split into 10 per cent prototype, 60 per cent OEM and 30 per cent spares. In the initial prototype stage of production it is our design capability which initially wins an order, although the ability, as with aerospace customers, to meet price and delivery speed requirement norms is also required. As products move into the OEM phase of their life cycle they become more price sensitive, and there is often a need to demonstrate to major customers that the Sherpin production unit has the capability and capacity to meet the required future OEM and spares volumes.

Automotive customers typically use production lines in the OEM phase of a product's life. Their aim is to cut costs by creating lean production facilities often using a just-in-time philosophy to help reduce both costs and the level of inventory holding within their process.[3] To ensure that we can support this, products are purchased from us using a contract which normally gives a view into the future of some 12 or more weeks and typically also includes a material commitment for the same period.

The spares requirement for our products is not usually handled by the same customer as OEM orders. Thus, we find that price becomes slightly less sensitive, but demand is less predictable. However, the spares companies are experienced in this market and they tend to help our production planning by using forecasting techniques to smooth their call-offs. This enables products to still be purchased using a contract with normally a 12-week commitment into the future.

## Industrial

Prototype work accounts for 10 per cent of industrial sales (£s), with the rest being divided equally between OEM and spares. Within the prototype stage of this market, orders are won primarily on our ability to react quickly to a customer enquiry. However, the proposal must also be able to meet price norms as in other markets, with design capability still an issue. Once the product moves into the next stage of its life cycle price becomes more sensitive and delivery speed less crucial. Although these demands vary depending on whether orders for products are on a contract, or one-off basis.

As with the automotive sector, some industrial customers use production lines and place purchasing contracts to help create the right environment for just-in-time manufacture in the OEM stage of a product's life. However, we find that they are not managed as effectively as in automotive, and thus there is still an element of delivery speed albeit of relatively low importance. This becomes even more apparent as a product moves into spares and wide fluctuations in demand can occur on a weekly basis. One outcome of this is that we need to be able to meet short lead times.

Unlike automotive, we find that both OEM and spares are handled by the same customer, and, due to the nature of our products, these two market segments are often supplied simultaneously. However, the spares demand is poorly managed and is merely 'front-end loaded' into the contract which gives us very little time to respond to an increase in demand. Also, because it is difficult to supply these two segments at a different price, we find that there is still a focus on price for the spares volume element of this business.

Other customers still purchase products from us using one-off orders rather than contracts in both the OEM and spares stages of their products' lives. This means that price is not as sensitive, but all other requirements remain the same. Collectively, these latter customers account for 20 per cent of total industrial sales.

## Motor Sport

The motor sport market is unique because customer requirements are the same throughout the life cycle of a product. One consequence is that price is always considered to be of very low importance. However, this is a very demanding industry and a high level of support is required within other market dimensions such as technical expertise, delivery speed, delivery reliability and quality conformance. For example, it is not unusual for us to receive a call from a customer asking for supply of a product to be used for a race in a few days' time.

In these circumstances, it is critical that we can respond to their needs, and deliver a high specification part to them on the exact date required. If there were to be any delivery reliability or quality conformance problems then we may lose the business altogether. Also, this continual focus by customers on design improvements means that modifications can occur at any stage in a product's life, and the relationship that exists between us and the customer always plays an important role in the development and maintenance of new business.

# Operations[4]

Compared with the rest of Northrop Industries, Sherpin's products require different materials and unique machining processes. Due to these factors, the decision was made to set up a facility solely dedicated to the manufacture of these parts. It comprises a number of functions including sales and marketing, commercial, design, production, purchasing and quality. Production and purchasing are now discussed in more detail.

# Production

'Presently, all products are manufactured within a small plant using a number of batch processes', explained Paul Davies. 'Components are purchased from external suppliers, and then processed in two or three days before being despatched to customers.

Operations is run on a one-shift basis and comprises goods inward, production and despatch functions. The production of a part is not complex, and normally involves two or three processes. The equipment used within these processes is inexpensive, with a new machine typically only costing between £5 000 and £10 000. The process equipment can typically be designed, manufactured and delivered in 6 to 8 weeks. However, the technical nature of these products means that the labour skill requirement is high. Thus, operators are extensively trained in the use of techniques such as statistical process control (SPC) to ensure that the quality standards are met.

The facilities are used to manufacture varying production order sizes. At one end of the scale, automotive customers tend to order weekly quantities of around 2 000 parts, which equates to somewhere between 2 and 3 days' production for one operator. Some industrial contract products are of a similar volume, but there are also one-off orders which come in sporadically and tend to comprise about 4 to 5 hours' work. Low volume parts are manufactured for aerospace and motor sport customers. Here, 2 hours' production is considered to be a large order.

# Purchasing

All products comprise a number of components which typically are purchased from several different suppliers. If any one of these components is not available, then the manufacture of a part is delayed. When suppliers fail to meet their promised delivery dates, there is often pressure to work overtime or employ temporary labour during the month end to meet sales targets and customer delivery requirements. As Bob Gilder (purchasing manager) explains:

> There is great pressure on me to ensure that Paul has all the components he requires for production. Without these our products cannot be made. In the past, the way that we achieved this was to hold buffer and safety stocks on long-running jobs where we had a good view of future demand and knew that raw materials would not become obsolete. However, in recent years one of the priorities in the Group has been to reduce inventory levels. The outcome has been continued pressure to reduce these holdings. As a result, parts are now ordered from our suppliers as and when they are required. Safety stocks have now been removed and buffer stocks reduced to a minimum.

## Order Processing

Currently, orders received into the business unit are then processed by the commercial and operations functions through a number of stages, as explained below.

# Commercial

Customer demands are received by the commercial department either as contracts,[5] or one-off[6] orders, and are immediately inputted into the computer system. Each customer has its own contact within the commercial department that processes and, when required, progresses work through operations. As Anne Ballow (commercial manager) explains:

> The idea is to create good customer relations at a personal level. By allocating a contact to each customer, we have been able to give them the service they require. This has proved a key feature for our large aerospace and motor sport accounts.

# Operations

'Once orders have been received, they are processed in the following way', explained Roy Price (SBU manager). 'Manufacturing and purchasing are run using an MRP-based computer system linked into the order processing database. This translates the customer order inputs made by the commercial department into demands for finished parts and raw materials. Orders are then raised in line with the operations standard lead times on the system.'

When the initial quotation is made at the start of a product's life preferred suppliers for the different components are selected. If the contract is secured these companies then become the sole supplier of a given component(s). Standard lead times are keyed into the computer system in line with those quoted by suppliers, and can be anything up to fifty working days (see Exhibit 3). Using these standards, products are then purchased as and when required. For example, purchasing would receive a prompt to place an order for a product usually made by Supplier D twenty working days before it is required by manufacturing. This prompt is in the form of a material requirements list printed off the computer system on a daily basis, showing which products need to be ordered that day. Lead times are reviewed regularly to ensure that they reflect the delivery agreements we have with our suppliers.

Once components have been delivered, they are held in raw material stores before being issued to production. Even though products can be manufactured in three days or less, a standard two week production lead time has been set up for all parts. The reason for this is that historically suppliers have not been reliable, and so we have put in a buffer lead time to ensure that all of the relevant components are available when required for production. However, even with this buffer, we are still sometimes unable to produce a part due to component shortages.

**Exhibit 3**     Typical operations lead-time of key suppliers

| Supplier reference[1] | Number of component types[2] | Lead time (number of working days)[3] |
|---|---|---|
| A | 2 | 45 |
| B | 233 | 10 |
| C | 21 | 7 |
| D | 35 | 20 |
| E | 24 | 37 |
| F | 11 | 17 |
| G | 77 | 17 |
| H | 28 | 18 |
| I | 64 | 27 |
| J | 13 | 45 |
| K | 25 | 10 |
| L | 103 | 27 |

*Notes*
**1.** In total there are 20 suppliers.
**2.** Each component type reflects a different stock-keeping unit.
**3.** Suppliers quote the same lead time for each component they manufacture.

**Exhibit 4**    Sales, production, despatch and labour hours data for a typical month

| Week | Sales orders received | Production | Despatches | Labour hours worked[1] |
|------|------------------------|------------|------------|------------------------|
|      | £000s | £000s | £000s | |
| 1 | 370 | 222 | 209 | 1254 |
| 2 | 350 | 347 | 180 | 1272 |
| 3 | 355 | 383 | 229 | 1308 |
| 4 | 365 | 567 | 831 | 1758 |

*Note*

**1.** The basic labour hours worked averaged 1218 per week in this typical month.

A recent analysis of the business revealed that, on average, 40 per cent of all products are delayed going into manufacturing due to a lack of materials and components. One outcome is that when the outstanding components are finally received, we find ourselves working a high level of overtime to satisfy customers' delivery requirements and month end targets. As both of these requirements are key tasks for manufacturing then it sometimes means that we make products that are due for delivery in the next period in order to meet both these targets'.

Exhibit 4 shows a typical month's production, Exhibit 5 presents delivery performance data and Exhibit 6 inventory holdings during last year.

## The Future

'Although the Sherpin business unit is only 10 per cent of our sales, it has a key role in our overall profitability. With current margin levels and future market potential (see Exhibit 7), Sherpin plays and will play a key role in our overall strategy', explained Matthew Jones.

The main opportunity for growth is in the automotive market. However, the price sensitivity of this sector means that we will be increasing sales within relatively low margin markets. Thus we must make sure that manufacturing can support this growth in terms of having sufficient capacity, and being able to support the relevant market needs, particularly re cost and delivery reliability.

In the other sectors, the growth potential is not as large, but there is scope particularly in some segments and markets. In addition, markets such as motor sport give excellent profit and keep our designers at the forefront of engineering and material technology. The requirements of markets differ markedly from one another and we need to recognize this in our developments. The challenge that faces us is how to expand successfully automotive sales, while continuing to support existing customers in other market segments.

**Exhibit 5**  Requested, promised and actual delivery date for a representative sample of customer orders within a typical month

| Order number | Market sector[1] | Delivery date | | | | | |
| --- | --- | --- | --- | --- | --- | --- | --- |
| | | requested | | promised | | actual | |
| | | day | week[2] | day | week[2] | day | week[2] |
| 72614 | Ae | 4 | 13 | 5 | 13 | 2 | 14 |
| 85221 | Au | 3 | 14 | 3 | 14 | 3 | 14 |
| 64498 | I | 2 | 12 | 2 | 12 | 3 | 14 |
| 32987 | MS | 3 | 14 | 4 | 14 | 4 | 14 |
| 21589 | I | 5 | 15 | 5 | 15 | 5 | 14 |
| 55123 | Ae | 5 | 12 | 2 | 13 | 1 | 15 |
| 19985 | Ae | 2 | 14 | 1 | 15 | 1 | 15 |
| 18754 | Au | 4 | 14 | 4 | 14 | 2 | 15 |
| 54462 | I | 2 | 12 | 2 | 12 | 2 | 15 |
| 08956 | I | 3 | 15 | 3 | 15 | 4 | 15 |
| 12587 | I | 5 | 15 | 5 | 15 | 5 | 15 |
| 56147 | Au | 5 | 15 | 5 | 15 | 5 | 15 |
| 22932 | Au | 2 | 16 | 2 | 16 | 2 | 16 |
| 46511 | I | 2 | 16 | 2 | 16 | 2 | 16 |
| 55233 | Au | 5 | 15 | 5 | 15 | 4 | 16 |
| 67859 | Ae | 5 | 14 | 5 | 15 | 4 | 16 |
| 52315 | MS | 1 | 16 | 4 | 16 | 5 | 16 |
| 59521 | Au | 1 | 16 | 1 | 17 | 1 | 17 |
| 26691 | Ae | 2 | 17 | 2 | 17 | 1 | 17 |
| 11635 | Au | 2 | 17 | 2 | 17 | 2 | 17 |
| 11279 | I | 5 | 16 | 5 | 16 | 2 | 17 |
| 41246 | Au | 5 | 16 | 5 | 16 | 2 | 17 |
| 92137 | Au | 2 | 17 | 2 | 17 | 3 | 17 |
| 27561 | MS | 1 | 17 | 3 | 17 | 3 | 17 |
| 37249 | I | 3 | 17 | 3 | 17 | 3 | 17 |
| 21234 | I | 5 | 16 | 5 | 16 | 4 | 17 |
| 57943 | MS | 2 | 17 | 3 | 17 | 4 | 17 |
| 87613 | Ae | 5 | 15 | 5 | 16 | 5 | 17 |
| 81267 | Ae | 5 | 19 | 5 | 19 | 5 | 17 |
| 11237 | Au | 3 | 19 | 3 | 19 | 5 | 17 |

*Note*
**1.** Ae = aerospace; I = industrial; Au = automotive; MS = motor sport
**2.** March is weeks 10 to 13, April is weeks 14 to 18 and May is weeks 19 to 23.

**Exhibit 6**   Value of month end inventory holding for the last year

| Month | Inventory (£000s) | | |
|---|---|---|---|
| | raw materials | work-in-progress | finished goods |
| Jan | 473 | 53 | 101 |
| Feb | 412 | 58 | 103 |
| Mar | 388 | 24 | 102 |
| Apr | 361 | 30 | 75 |
| May | 336 | 29 | 87 |
| Jun | 347 | 14 | 73 |
| Jul | 354 | 9 | 133 |
| Aug | 378 | 4 | 93 |
| Sep | 367 | 10 | 79 |
| Oct | 355 | 45 | 58 |
| Nov | 372 | 25 | 77 |
| Dec | 414 | 81 | 78 |

**Exhibit 7**   Market share by sector

| Sector | Market share (as a per cent total potential)[1] | | |
|---|---|---|---|
| | UK | Other European | US |
| Aerospace | 55 | 25 | – |
| Automotive | 10 | 7 | 2 |
| Industrial | 60 | 20 | – |
| Motor sport | 90 | 80 | 70 |

*Note*
**1.** Market share is based on last year's sales, and is estimated.

# Notes

1. Delivery speed refers to the dimension of short lead times.
2. An 'aircraft on the ground' is the term used to denote a situation where an aircraft is awaiting a spare part and, as a result, is unable to fly.
3. Within all markets, delivery reliability and quality conformance are expected by customers. However, if they are not supported for those using a just-in-time philosophy, production lines could be stopped and there is a potential to lose the business altogether.
4. The operations function comprises purchasing, production and despatch.
5. A contract is an order placed with a view into the future of normally 12 or more weeks. It typically includes a material commitment for the same period.
6. A one-off order is placed without a view to the future and is typically for an order quantity to be delivered on a specific date.

# case

# 17

# Shire Products

Over the last eight years we have recognized the need to link the marketing and manufacturing functions as an important factor in improving our competitive performance. Certainly, the level of coordination between these major parts of the business has been substantial in itself and very rewarding in terms of our overall corporate results. We have consistently been in the top three performers in the group and last year saw us at number one for the first time. Part of this has been secured by our developments in manufacturing. We have become attentive to the needs of our different markets and this has formed an important part of our total corporate support for customers. We are now reviewing some of the key elements of infrastructure to check how well we are achieving business fit in all that we do. The details before us are yet another part of this review procedure.

Jim Meadows, managing director of Shire Products, was addressing a board of directors' meeting to discuss some of the performance measures and other reviews currently used in the business.

## Background

Shire Products is a wholly owned subsidiary of Belcordia, a French conglomerate comprising engineering, electronics, textiles, building materials and packaging. Based in Toronto, Canada, Shire Products supplies a range of Canadian and US-based companies.

## Marketing

The company sells plastic bottles and containers to a range of companies in a variety of industries such as food, toiletries, chemicals, agriculture and household products. In most instances the products are customized: that is, a bottle, normally in terms of specification and print, is made only for the one customer. Some products are standard in that customers purchase a given bottle size and then either have it specifically printed or attach a label to it during their own filling and packing

This case study was written by Terry Hill (University of Oxford) and S. H. Chambers (University of Warwick). It is intended for class discussion and not as an example of good or bad management. © AMD Publishing.

operations. In all instances, however, the products are relatively high volume and orders are received over a long period of time.

'Some time ago', explained Rob Castle, 'we undertook an in-depth review of our markets and have, on a regular basis, reviewed them ever since. The latest update [given in Exhibit 1] shows the characteristics of our overall business based on a representative sample of products. With current sales revenue forecasts at $55m, we are continuing to show sustainable growth at required levels of profit.' He then continued to explain that each different market the company serves has its own order-winners and qualifiers. A brief summary of the meaning of each is given in Exhibit 2.

Rob continued:

we anticipate that the volumes of most products we are currently selling will tend to increase in years to come [see Exhibit 1]. In reality, some of these products will be superseded by new product designs, and as often is the case, we anticipate that we will continue to provide each follow-on design. Also, we do realize that we will lose some of our existing business as we know some is under a lot of competitive pressure. The figures [in Exhibit 1] provide a realistic overview of the future, even though the mix will certainly change and not all anticipated increases will line up with our forecasts.

## Manufacturing

As explained earlier, most products made by Shire Products are customized. A small quantity, both in number and revenue, are standard products sold to more than one customer. The principal manufacturing process for all products is blow moulding (see Exhibit 3). Many are then printed, with the remainder being sold as plain bottles/containers that would be labelled in the customers' own manufacturing process at the point of filling. The final step is packing, which may be of a loose nature (referred to as *jumble packed*, in that a given number of bottles/containers are loosely packed in a large container) or upright packed, which requires the containers to be stacked in a given pattern and upright.

Over the last few years, we have forged important links with the rest of the business. This has enabled the company to debate and agree the characteristics of our different markets and then to determine the response that manufacturing, as well as other functions, needs to take to best support the business. Two years ago we decided to reflect the differences in our markets by moving to focused units based on the order-winners as perceived at the time [see Exhibit 2]. We now have four of these [Exhibit 1]. By regularly reviewing how we win orders, we can monitor changes and ensure that our manufacturing developments and investments are consistent with market requirements. For example, a recent review has highlighted the investment needed to move Product D7400 from Unit D to Unit C, and we are also monitoring Products D1750 and C4505 as possible future candidates for moving to Unit B.

**Exhibit 1**   Market analysis based on representative products

| Product codes | Seasonality factor | Order-winners and qualifiers | | | | | | | | | Annual sales ($ millions) | |
|---|---|---|---|---|---|---|---|---|---|---|---|---|
| | | Price | Delivery speed | Delivery reliability | Technical competence | Quality conformance | Ramp-up capability | Product design | Product development support | Existing preferred supplier | Current year | Current year +4 |
| **Unit A** | | | | | | | | | | | | |
| A0040 | High | QQ | | QQ | | QQ | 80 | | | 20 | 6.7 | 7.7 |
| A0110 | High | QQ | | QQ | 60 | QQ | 20 | | | 20 | 5.0 | 5.6 |
| **Unit B** | | | | | | | | | | | | |
| B2011 | Zero | Q | 50 | Q | | Q | | | | 50 | 2.4 | 2.6 |
| B1046 | Medium | | 30 | QQ | | Q | 20 | 30 | | 20 | 2.8 | 3.2 |
| B3010 | Zero | | | Q | | | | 100 | | | 3.0 | 3.3 |
| B1650 | High | Q | 30 | QQ | | | 35 | 15 | | 20 | 0.9 | 1.1 |
| **Unit C** | | | | | | | | | | | | |
| C6600 | Medium | 30 | | Q | | 50 | | | | 20 | 1.1 | 1.1 |
| C4505 | Medium | | 30 | Q | | 40 | 30 | | | | 0.7 | 1.0 |
| C7100 | Zero | 100 | Q | Q | | Q | | | | | 2.4 | 2.4 |
| C1000 | Zero | 80 | QQ | Q | 20 | QQ | | | | | 0.2 | 0.3 |
| C6100 | Zero | 50 | | | 20 | | | | | 30 | 0.5 | 0.6 |
| **Unit D** | | | | | | | | | | | | |
| D1500 | Zero | Q | | QQ | Q | Q | | | 50 | | 3.7 | 4.0 |
| D1750 | Zero | Q | 25 | QQ | 50 | Q | | | 25 | | 0.4 | 0.5 |
| D4600 | Zero | Q | | QQ | 40 | | | 30 | | 30 | 0.9 | 1.2 |
| D7400 | Zero | 80 | | Q | | Q | | | | 20 | 1.2 | 1.2 |
| D8150 | Zero | Q | | Q | | Q | | | | 100 | 1.3 | 1.3 |

*Note*
Q indicates a qualifier; QQ an order-losing sensitive qualifier.

**Exhibit 2**   The order-winners and qualifiers relating to the company's markets

- *Price* – this being an order-winner means that the profit margins on the products in question are relatively low, thereby requiring cost reduction to be a priority task. Price being a qualifier signals that the company achieves relatively high profit margins and must strive to ensure that they keep price at a point where the customer considers it acceptable.
- *Delivery speed* – customer lead times are shorter than the operations lead time within the company.
- *Delivery reliability* – delivering a customer's order on the due date agreed.
- *Technical competence* – resolving the difficult technical demands of one or more aspects of a product or process when making it. This being an order-winner means that the company's ability to resolve technical problems is a factor in securing that part of a customer's business.
- *Quality conformance* – making a product to specification.
- *Ramp-up capability* – having manufacturing capability to increase the total output of a given product significantly in a short period of time (normally days). It would be linked to the seasonality factor within a market.
- *Product design* – the design perspective of the technical competence factor referred to earlier.
- *Product development support* – concerns design support for a customer both during and after product development.
- *Existing/preferred supplier* – this criterion is linked to the fact that customers often prefer not to move sourcing arrangements once the technical proving and mould/machine fit has been established. Even where tooling is wholly owned by the customer (and this is not always the case), there is a reluctance to invest the time and effort to re-establish a fresh source of supply. The exception is where the demand for products is of a high-volume nature. In these circumstances, products are often second sourced, so a customer is more willing to consider changing suppliers.

**Exhibit 3**   Outline of the manufacturing process

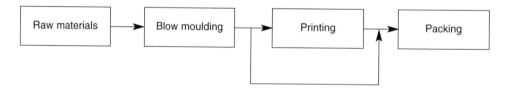

Other developments have included merging the responsibility for quality control into a machine operator's job and also moving to a four-shift continental pattern of working in Unit A to facilitate meeting the ramp-up requirements for these customers. (A four-shift continental pattern of working is an arrangement whereby four groups of operators and support staff are employed, with any three of these working at one time and the fourth resting. This arrangement allows all seven days per week over 24 hours to be covered without overtime working). The other three units work 24 hours per day over five days. In times where ramp-up is required,

**Exhibit 4**  Summary of performance reports received by the manufacturing director

| Report title | Source and frequency | Principal contents |
|---|---|---|
| Industrial engineering[1] | Industrial engineer, weekly | Output rates (bottles/hour)<br>Material as a percentage of sales value<br>Actual versus planned output percentage<br>Total output $s and bottles |
| Unit A | Unit A manager, weekly | Number of machines used<br>Effective performance percentage[2]<br>Efficiency percentage[3]<br>Rejects percentage<br>Actual versus planned unit output percentage<br>Downtime hours analysis, percentage<br>Packer effective performance<br>Overtime as a percentage of basic pay |
| Unit B | Unit B manager, weekly | As for Unit A |
| Unit C | Unit C manager, weekly | As for Unit A |
| Unit D | Unit D manager, weekly | As for Unit A |
| Distribution | Distribution manager, weekly | Number of pallets despatched<br>Pallets per warehouse man hour<br>Overtime as a percentage of basic pay |
| Toolroom | Toolroom supervisor, weekly | Overtime: actual versus planned hours<br>Downtime analysis (tool problems)<br>List of new moulds received |
| Tool development | Tooling engineer, weekly | Drawing office overtime hours<br>Machine hours used for tool development/proving<br>Hours lost due to technical problems (by unit) |

*(continued)*

**Exhibit 4**  Summary of performance reports received by the manufacturing director (cont'd)

| Report title | Source and frequency | Principal contents |
|---|---|---|
| Weekly operating statement[4] | Accounts department, weekly | Weekly output value ($s) |
| | | Raw material as a percentage of sales |
| | | Direct labour as a percentage of sales |
| | | Trading profit as a percentage of sales |
| | | Overtime cost as a percentage of sales |
| | | Variances against budgets by category |
| Unit A | Unit A manager, monthly | Effective performance percentage |
| | | Efficiency percentage |
| | | Utilization analysis (hours percentage) |
| | | Reject percentage |
| | | Scrap percentage |
| | | Output variance ($s) |
| | | Percentage returned by customer |
| | | Complaints analysis |
| | | Description of problems and plans |
| Unit B | Unit B manager, monthly | As for Unit A |
| Unit C | Unit C manager, monthly | As for Unit A |
| Unit D | Unit D manager, monthly | As for Unit A |

*Notes*

1. The industrial engineering report relates to all four units

2. Effective performance = $\dfrac{\text{standard hours produced}}{\text{actual hours worked}} \times 100$.

3. Efficiency = $\dfrac{\text{actual standard hours produced}}{\text{budgeted standard hours}} \times 100$.

4. The weekly operating statement provides the data above for each unit and as a summary.

**Exhibit 5**   Typical details/minutes for the unit managers' daily and weekly production meetings

**Unit managers' daily meetings**

No formal minutes are recorded for these meetings. Below is a summary of the format typically followed by all unit managers.

*Shift performances.* The performance of each shift is provided on the following aspects. This is given as a separate sheet for each day, which is then summarized as an average for each unit's weekly report (see Exhibit 4).

- Number of machines used
- Effective performance percentage (for blow moulding, printing and packing where relevant)
- Efficiency percentage (for blow moulding, printing and packing where relevant)
- Rejects percentage
- Actual versus planned output percentage
- Downtime hours analysis percentage.

*Tasks and problems.* A review of the tasks and problems that were addressed the previous day and a discussion and listing of the tasks and problems to be completed that day and in the near future. The latter would entail relevant details of the task or problem, identifying materials and staff requirements.

*General issues.* Basically a mechanism for general communication, particularly regarding interfunctional developments.

**Weekly production meetings**

The minutes of a particular weekly production meeting follow.

*Minutes of Weekly Production Meeting on 8 February*

| Present: | | |
|---|---|---|
| | Ron Wilcox | Manufacturing Director |
| | Paul Smith | Engineering Manager |
| | Al Holmes | Toolroom Manager |
| | Jay West | Unit A Manager |
| | Ray Hatton | Unit B Manager |
| | Ian Watts | Unit C Manager |
| | Peter Kennings | Unit D Manager |
| | Chris Johnson | Quality Manager |
| | Jim Brody | Distribution Manager |

|  |  | Action |
|---|---|---|
| 1. *Distribution* | | |
| (a) Storage space – J. B. to investigate additional external storage to cope with anticipated temporary increase in finished goods. | | J. B. |
| 2. *Unit A* | | |
| (a) Recruitment – production performance adversely affected by shortage of electricians. R. W. to see if maintenance superisor needs help to speed up selection procedure. | | R. W. |

*(continued)*

(b) Toolroom – inadequate notice has been given for tool          A. H.
preparation. The planner to investigate establishing short-term
forecasts. R. W. to be advised of action taken.

(c) Performance – Unit A consolidated performance figures for last
week were:

- effective performance, 91%
- efficiency, 95%
- average machine utilization, 76% (budget 82%)
- unit output, 94% of planned volume
- material yield, 93% (budget 94.5%)
- overtime, 6% over budget.

The reasons for the poor performance were discussed. J. W. confirmed
that this week's figures were running better than budget, which should     J. W.
restore the overall performance for the month back to budget.

3. *Unit B*
   (a) New shampoo containers (Project Rainbow) – problems with          R. H.
   establishing surface finish standards for new colours in this range.
   R. H. to liaise with sales to solve this problem. Advise R. W. of progress.
   (b) Print loading – the potential contract for 20 million containers per year
   could put a strain on print capacity. R. H. to liaise with the planning
   manager and report on the capacity implications.
   (c) Performance – Unit B consolidated performance figures for last
   week were:

- effective performance, 98%
- effiency, 101%
- average machine utilization, 81% (budget 82.5%)
- unit output, 101% of planned volume
- material yield, 96.3% (budget 95%)
- overtime, 5% over budget.

R. W. congratulated R. H. on a generally good set of figures; however,     R. H.
overtime costs should be closely watched.

4. *Unit C* } (Details similar to those of Units A and B
5. *Unit D* } were provided but have been omitted here.)

6. *Annual staff appraisals*
These should be completed by the end of this week and given to Anne        All
(R. W.'s secretary).

7. *Resin supplies*
A report that trials would begin soon using new supplies of PET raw        All
materials, which give a substantial saving through group purchasing
arrangements: probably amounting to about 2.0% reduction in costs
of PET materials throughout the group. The different physical properties
of the material and new logistics arrangement with the suppliers will
require effort from everyone to ensure that the trials are successful.

then the machine operators from Unit A would, over the weekend period, be employed in one of the other three units undertaking work to meet relevant customer demands. 'In this way', explained Ron Wilcox,

> we are always fully manned in Unit A over seven days during the many consecutive months of high demand. Before these arrangements there were times when the machine operators would be asked to work overtime every weekend for a period of up to four to five consecutive months, and, understandably, they were not always prepared to meet our needs due to the cumulative effects of working seven days per week.

As is typical elsewhere, the manufacturing function in Shire Products records and reviews a whole range of activities on a regular and frequent basis. Detailed here are the more important ways in which this is undertaken. The aspects selected concern the reports received, the meetings held, and a sample of the annual assessments completed for all personnel on a group basis. Details are given in Exhibits 4 to 9, and a brief explanation of selected aspects is provided in the following sections.

# Reports

In order to help manage a diverse set of tasks, manufacturing collects data and compiles reports on a frequent and regular basis. A summary of the performance-related reports received by Ron Wilcox is given as Exhibit 4.

# Meetings

Once a month there is a board meeting at which the functional directors review and discuss the previous month's sales and profit results. To link in with this, functional heads also undertake regular reviews of key activities in line with particular board meeting items and requests from the managing director or other directors. The systematic review of the function's activities is an integral part of managing and controlling different facets of the business.

Manufacturing holds several ad hoc meetings and is represented in meetings held by other functions. The two main meetings, however, are the daily unit managers' meeting and the weekly production meeting. Typical minutes for both are provided in Exhibit 5.

## Unit Managers' Daily Meetings

These relatively short (about 30 minutes) daily meetings involve the relevant unit manager, production supervisors and a maintenance supervisor. No formal minutes of these meetings are kept but details of what is typically included are provided in Exhibit 5.

## Weekly Production Meetings

The weekly production meeting is called by the manufacturing director for 10.00 hours each Monday. The permanent members of this meeting are the four unit managers and those managers responsible for maintenance, distribution, production planning and control, and engineering/product development. The quality assurance and purchasing managers attend on an ad hoc basis. Lasting up to three hours, all aspects of manufacturing and other relevant issues are discussed. As the manufacturing director explained, 'It not only serves as a review of what is going on and what has been achieved, but it is an excellent vehicle for communication, improving coordination, and exchanging ideas.'

## Annual Assessments

Annual assessments are an integral part of the group's policies and are undertaken down to the level of supervisor. The period of review is over 12 months, and assessments are usually undertaken by mid-February of the following year. Selected assessments are given in Exhibits 6–9.

## Concluding Remarks

'Our performance over the last five or six years is most encouraging', reflected Jim Meadows.

Many of the important parts of our corporate strategy are in place, and the outcome has been a direct contribution to the overall and sustained improvement we have achieved. Regular reviews keep us strategically alert and other important developments are in hand. We are now also looking at refining other parts of the activities and one important aspect is contained in the analyses present here. Not only will any improvements bring benefits in their own right but will also, we have found, add substantially to the overall support for the business.

**Exhibit 6**    Annual assessment (1)

| | |
|---|---|
| *Name:*    Ron Wilcox | *Job Title:*    Manufacturing Director |
| *Job Tenure:* Five years | *Appraiser:*   Jim Meadows |
| *Date:*       January 20 | |

<table>
<tr>
<td>

*Overall performance rating*

The overall rating is an evaluation of the employee's performance in the total job throughout the review process. With this in mind, take into account:

- key performance objectives
- achievement of personal improvement objective
- any additional achievements
- factors clearly outside the employee's control affecting results for which the employee was unable to compensate.

</td>
<td>

*Tick one only*

☑ Performance excellent

☐ Successful performance

☐ Employee moving towards successful performance and is perceived as being capable of achieving successful performance within an acceptable period of time

☐ Unsuccessful performance

</td>
</tr>
</table>

*Rating comments*

Ron has done an excellent job to keep his department's costs down. Made a major contribution to profit where, despite sales being down by 10%, we achieved above budget profit.

Restructured print department with resultant savings.

High Unit A demand at a time when we did a lot of reorganization. Quality improved and we kept this major customer (25% of our total sales revenue) supplied.

*Last year's objectives and results – R. D. Wilcox*

| Objectives | Results | Achieved | | Comment |
|---|---|---|---|---|
| | | Yes | No | |
| *Cost control* Decrease direct labour cost as a percentage of value added to 18.2% | Previous year the figure was 20.2%. Current year reduced to 19.8%. Depends on prices, and for some major products the company agreed price reductions to get larger share of business | ✓ | | |
| Weight of waste material discarded to be reduced to 5.0% or less of total processed *Note:* this is dependent upon production run lengths | Previous year this was 5.5%, and we reduced to 5.2% last year. Shorter run lengths were required, plus product mix changes and no weekend running of PVC machines caused figure to be higher. Therefore, not totally under his control | ✓ | | |

*(continued)*

*Last year's objectives and results – R. D. Wilcox*

| Objectives | Results | Achieved Yes | No | Comment |
|---|---|---|---|---|
| Ensure that effective performance increased in each operating unit as follows: | Only problem was Unit B, where sales volume was well below forecasts | | ✓ | |
| Unit | Standard hours/ Actual hours worked | | | |
| A | 90% | | | |
| B | 87% | | | |
| C | 84% | | | |
| D | 90% | | | |
| Install one automatic palletizer in Unit A | Achieved on time | ✓ | | |
| Extend the use of autodeflashing equipment to other Unit D machines; two completed in August and three completed in October | Four working. Decision taken by board to delay installing the last one | ✓ | | |
| Develop machine monitoring system for Unit C, which integrates with planning system by May. Extend machine monitoring system to Unit D by third quarter and Unit A by fourth quarter | Fully achieved | ✓ | | |
| Set-up reduction. Implement quick screen change proposals across all print machines by June to reduce set-up costs by up to 50% | Implemented | ✓ | | |
| *Quality* Reduce the number of bottles held for further quality control checks to 1.7% (or less) of production | Achieved. Now at 1.5% | ✓ | | |
| Reduce customer returns to 0.8% (or less) of production | Reduced to 0.69% | ✓ | | |
| *Training and development of personnel* Recruit industrial engineer/ project engineer to assist with cost control project | Used an outside consultant. New person joined 1 November | ✓ | | |

### Last year's objectives and results – R. D. Wilcox

| Objectives | Results | Achieved Yes | Achieved No | Comment |
|---|---|---|---|---|
| *Industrial relations* Obtain trade union acceptance of planned machine operator/quality control job merge and implement new assessment scheme by May | Implemented on schedule | ✓ | | |

### Next year's objectives – R. D. Wilcox

| Key result area | Objectives | Achieved Yes | Achieved No | Comment |
|---|---|---|---|---|
| Cost control | 1. Weight of waste material generated to be less than 4.5%. 2. Reduce direct labour percentage from 19.8% to 18.5%. 3. Phased installation of three autodeflashers. All three to be running by the end of May. 4. Fixed costs to be controlled within budget. | | | |
| Customer service | 1. Improve tool change performance to meet market needs. Work with outside consultant. Recommendations to be implemented by 30 September. 2. Recommend and install two second-hand PET machines to meet increased demand. Machines to be in operation by 30 June. | | | |
| Quality | 1. Internal held work to be reduced from 1.5% to 1.3% of sales. 2. Customer returns to be reduced from 0.69% to 0.6% of sales. 3. Commence TQM introductory programme yet to be agreed. | | | |
| Industrial relations | 1. Complete pay negotiations within or better than budget. | | | |
| Training | 1. Training of personnel to successfully operate machine monitoring equipment. 2. Set unit managers clear targets and objectives and measure on a quarterly basis. | | | |

*(continued)*

*Planning for future success – R. D. Wilcox*

*Strengths*
Consider and identify significant
abilities, skills, or knowledge
evident in the employee's
performance

- Knowledge of manufacturing and all the
  implications
- Good grasp of industrial relations
- Knows the blow moulding industry
- Motivates his team and focuses them
  on key result areas

*Areas for improvement*
Define areas of performance where
the employee can be more
successful in the future

- Needs to face up to people who are not
  performing rather than defending them
- Presentation skills need improving
- Apt to make his point then switch off
  from further discussion

*Ongoing coaching/training actions*
Specifically, what coaching and training
actions are planned?

- The cost control project will give
  him refined productivity

*Achievement measure*
How will the programmes be measured?

- Report due end of June

*Responsibility*
Who, in addition to the employee, is
responsible for making it happen?

- Managing director

*Timing*
When will progress be reviewed?

- Ongoing

*Employee comments (to be completed by the employee)*

A very complimentary assessment.

Signature...... *Ron Wilcox* ........................................................

Signing acknowledges that the contents of the appraisal have been discussed with you, not necessarily
that you agree.

*Appraiser comments*

He has had a good year and done an excellent job in implementing a lot of new ideas and procedures.
He has reacted well to coping with a considerable amount of work, particularly in the industrial relations
area. Ron's contribution to our cost reduction programme is particularly valued.

Signature...... *Jim Meadows* ........................................................

*Appraiser's manager's comments*

Signature........................................................................

**Exhibit 7**    Annual assessment (2)

| | |
|---|---|
| *Name:*    Peter Kennings | *Job Title:*    Unit D Manager |
| *Job Tenure:*  Three years | *Appraiser:*   Ron Wilcox (Manufacturing Director) |
| *Date:*    4 February | |

| *Overall performance rating* | *Tick one only* |
|---|---|
| The overall rating is an evaluation of the employee's performance in the total job throughout the review process. With this in mind, take into account: | ☐ Performance excellent |
| | ☑ Successful performance |
| ■ key performance objectives | ☐ Employee moving towards successful performance and is perceived as being capable of achieving successful performance within an acceptable period of time |
| ■ achievement of personal improvement objective | |
| ■ any additional achievements | |
| ■ factors clearly outside the employee's control affecting results for which the employee was unable to compensate. | ☐ Unsuccessful performance |

*Rating comments*

Peter has worked hard at the areas for improvement highlighted in his current assessment – well done.

*Contributions outside key results*

Machine performances have been improved and this is reflected in the level of utilization, which was increased from 51.8% to 62.6% (2nd half of current year = 67.7%).

Successfully completed a quality audit programme and now conducts quality audits on a regular basis.

The grinding bay and print department were restructured during the year reducing manning and improving productivity.

*Last year's objectives and results – P. Kennings*

| | | Achieved | | |
|---|---|---|---|---|
| **Objectives** | **Results** | **Yes** | **No** | **Comment** |
| Average effective performance to exceed 90% | Actual average in the period 88% | | ✓ | |

*(continued)*

*Last year's objectives and results – P. Kennings*

| Objectives | Results | Achieved | | Comment |
|---|---|---|---|---|
| | | Yes | No | |
| Material rejects to be reduced to less than 2% of the total processed | Actual was 4.4%. Represented a 0.7% reduction from previous period – Peter explained that machine wear on several key machines had contributed to this higher than targeted figure. Also, average production run lengths were lower thus increasing material wastage on change-overs | | ✓ | |
| Labour efficiency to exceed budget | Achieved. The installation of three collating tables helped to boost actual labour performance | ✓ | | |
| Tool change-overs – 80% to be completed during an eight-hour shift | Tool change leadership changed during the year under review. Monthly meetings improved level of coordination. However, 80% target not achieved. Target considered unrealistic given the increasing number of tool changes | | ✓ | |
| Meet following budgeted quality performances: | | | | |
| Customer returns <0.5% of sales | Actual returns of 0.97%, down from previous year's performance of 1.8% | | ✓ | |
| Production held <1.5% of total | Actual production held of 3.02% | | ✓ | |
| Install modification to all six 6148 machines by April of current year | Completed by end February. Showed improved actual performance of 0.07% after installation | ✓ | | |
| Resite packing conveyor by June of current year | Packing conveyor resited on time | ✓ | | |
| Complete job merge between operators and quality inspectors with necessary training | All completed to schedule | ✓ | | |
| Introduce new quality control procedures by September of current year | New procedures introduced to schedule | ✓ | | |

| | | Achieved | | |
|---|---|---|---|---|
| **Key result area** | **Objectives** | **Yes** | **No** | **Comment** |

*Next year's objectives – P. Kennings*

| Key result area | Objectives |
|---|---|
| Cost control | 1. Material rejects to be reduced to less than 2.5% of total processed. |
| | 2. Direct labour cost as a percentage of added value to average less than 21.47% blow moulding, 52.7% print. |
| | 3. Fixed costs to be controlled within budget. |
| | 4. Deflash equipment to be fitted and operational on machine 168 by end of March this year. |
| | 5. Machine monitoring system to be utilized by supervisor and machine operators to control quantity and quality of production. Machine personnel to receive feedback on the performance of their own machines. |
| | 6. Install productivity measures by June. Report to be issued by 30 June, stating targets to be achieved by end of year. |
| Quality | 1. Internal held work to be reduced from 3.02% to 2.5%. |
| | 2. Customer returns to be reduced from 0.97% to 0.75%. |
| Training | 1. Production supervisors and machine operators to be trained in the operation of new machine monitoring system. Peter is to ensure that we achieve maximum productivity increases using this new technology. |
| | 2. Assessment scheme to be used to highlight operator training requirements. Peter to ensure that adequate training is given to improve factory performance. |

*(continued)*

*Planning for future success – P. Kennings*

**Strengths**
Consider and identify significant abilities, skills, or knowledge evident in the employee's performance

- Peter is very good at analysing a situation and can be relied upon to present a considered view for immediate implementation

**Areas for improvement**
Define areas of performance where the employee can be more successful in the future

- Peter should concentrate on achieving his next year's objectives. He has the right personal qualities to be successful in these aims

**Ongoing coaching/training actions**
Specifically, what coaching and training actions are planned?

- Last year Peter completed a diploma programme in management studies and this, together with the short courses arranged, is considered sufficient at present

**Achievement measure**
How will the programmes be measured?

**Responsibility**
Who, in addition to the employee, is responsible for making it happen?

**Timing**
When will progress be reviewed?

- Production performance to be measured monthly and reviewed quarterly

**Employee comments** (to be completed by the employee)
In general I agree with the comments in this appraisal. I am keen to achieve next year's objectives and recognize the need for further training and development, both for myself and my staff.

Signature ..... *Peter Kennings* .....................................

Signing acknowledges that the contents of the appraisal have been discussed with you, not necessarily that you agree.

**Appraiser comments**
Peter works hard and should do well. He must, however, prioritize his work to ensure that his unit gives good service and helps us to achieve our demanding profit targets.

Signature ..... *Ron Wilcox* .....................................

**Appraiser's manager's comments**
A good year. Well done!

Signature ..... *Jim Meadows* .....................................

**Exhibit 8**    Annual assessment (3)

---

*Name:*    Joe Watts                    *Job Title:*    Maintenance Supervisor (all units)
*Job Tenure:* 2.5 years

---

A.  *Indicate any major achievements during the period*                    *Comments*

1.  During the period under review, with reduced labour level due to increased labour turnover, Joe has coped extremely well.

2.  Has exercised a tight control on his department's overtime costs.

3.  Holds regular meetings with department chargehands thereby improving communications. In addition, holds a monthly briefing meeting with his departmental personnel.

4.  Joe spent a considerable amount of his own time preparing and teaching a practical training programme.

5.  Joe has played a major part in installing machine monitoring throughout all units. He has also been involved in installing the planned maintenance system.

B.  *Any comments on last year's performance and on the person being assessed*

While all major objectives have been achieved, it is the opinion of the unit managers that more direct contact on the factory floor would be of considerable benefit. It would also expose Joe to problems that often require hands-on experience.

Joe has once again shown enthusiasm for the many projects carried out throughout last year in all units. The installation of a workshop computer has enabled the department to be more involved, thereby helping improve overall efficiency.

There is also some evidence that scheduled maintenance is reducing purchasing costs of spare parts.

C.  *Next year's objectives*

1.  Complete a machine overhaul on one M20 machine, with the minimum of disruption to production requirements.

2.  Complete overhaul of machines 616 and 804 as per the last overhaul of machine 680.

3.  Ensure maintenance department's involvement in Unit A's expansion of four machines to ensure minimum installation time. Essential support for key customers.

4.  Continue to use new planned maintenance system to highlight problem areas and indicate accurate individual machine costs.

5.  Seek to improve methods to reduce downtime costs by investigating problem areas and implementing solutions.

*(continued)*

D. *Overall performance rating*                                 *Comments*

(In assessing rating, achievements during the year, personal characteristics, leadership qualities and administrative ability should be taken into consideration.)

|  |  |  |  |
|---|---|---|---|
|  | Unsatisfactory performance | F | ........................ |
| 80–87% | New man gaining experience or less than adequate performance | E | ........................ |
| 88–95% | Adequate but less than fully acceptable | D | ..........✓.............. |
| 96–104% | Fully acceptable | C | ........................ |
| 105–112% | Superior sustained performance or recognition of experience | B | ........................ |
| 113–120% | Exceptionally high performance | A | ........................ |

Estimated speed through normal range: 5–7 years (when applicable).

E. *Potential*

(If and when recommended for promotion, limitations, personal qualifications, and so on)

Stay in present position

F. *Personal development*

(To include short- and long-term training.)

Signed ........C. Smith............ Appointment ................................................ Date ........Feb 9..........

Jobholder's signature ....J. Watts.................................................... Date ......Feb 9..........

**Exhibit 9**     Annual assessment (4)

---

*Name:*     David Burton                              *Job Title:*     Shift Supervisor, Unit C

*Job Tenure:* Six years

---

A.   *Indicate any major achievements during the period*                    *Comments*

   1. Frequently proposes new production methods to reduce costs,
      and if these are within his scope, he will implement them.

   2. Holds regular training sessions with shift personnel (for example,
      SPC and machine monitoring).

   3. Has become very competent in controlling all machine groups.

   4. Has made good progress in reducing cost of scrap on his shift.

   5. Achieved best productivity level of the three shifts in Unit C.

B.   *Any comments on last year's performance to also include
     the person being assessed*

   1. Last year's training in industrial engineering is now helping David
      to identify further areas for automation and cost reduction.

   2. David is keen to learn and motivated to apply his knowledge
      in the development of the unit.

C.   *Next year's objectives*

   1. Implement machine monitoring, ensuring that good production is
      recorded at two-hourly intervals, checking that reject levels are
      below set targets and corrective action is taken and recorded as
      and when needed.

   2. Factory efficiency to exceed 90%.

   3. Material wastage (purging/sweepings) to be less than 2%
      (last year = 4.1%).

   4. Quality control standards to be raised and customer
      returns/complaints to be reduced.

   5. At regular intervals (weekly), audit quality process sheets and
      check that all completed pallets that leave the shop floor have
      operators' identification number.

   6. Labour productivity to be within stated standards.

D.   *Overall performance rating*
     (In assessing rating, achievements during the year, personal characteristics,
     leadership qualities and administrative ability should be taken into consideration.)

*(continued)*

*Comments*

| | Unsatisfactory performance | F | ...................... |
|---|---|---|---|
| 80–87% | New man gaining experience or less than adequate performance | E | ...................... |
| 88–95% | Adequate but less than fully acceptable | D | ...................... |
| 96–104% | Fully acceptable | C | .........✓......... |
| 105–112% | Superior sustained performance or recognition of experience | B | ...................... |
| 113–120% | Exceptionally high performance | A | ...................... |

Estimated speed through normal range: 10 years (when applicable).

E.  *Potential*

(If and when recommended for promotion, limitations, personal qualifications, and so on)

Stay in present position

F.  *Personal development*

(To include short- and long-term training.)

Further Statistical Process Control training

---

Signed ...*J. Watts*................. Appointment ................................................. Date ............................

Jobholder's signature ............*D. Burton*..................................................... Date ............................

# Tama Electronics, Inc.

Our decision to rearrange manufacturing in line with the strategic review completed four years ago has been a major factor in the improved performance of our business. Before this change the facilities had been organized using functional/process layout principles. Even at the level of output we were recording at that time, this approach had created a high level of complexity in terms of the problems of control, high inventory, and business orientation. If we had continued to use this manufacturing approach the level of complexity that would have been created by now (particularly following our significant growth in sales) would have been difficult to imagine. One advantage we have gained at a level far above that we anticipated is the high degree of involvement demonstrated by all our employees. In fact, they have developed a proactive attitude to bringing about improvements, as illustrated by the recent proposal put forward by the manufacturing units. They have suggested that they should present their views on the type of payment system that would best suit their individual units. However, although I have no wish to dampen the enthusiasm underpinning these initiatives (and there is some logic in rewarding each unit in line with its own efforts), I feel it opportune to review the existing focus decisions to ensure that they are consistent with the current needs of the business. When this is complete, I will then feel that we will be more able to address the payment system review initiative mentioned earlier.

Gary Wilson, vice-president, manufacturing, of Tama Electronics, was summarizing an agenda item of an executive meeting entitled 'Manufacturing Strategy Developments'.

## Background

Tama Electronics (TE) is part of Colbeck Industries, Inc., a large conglomerate involving a wide range of manufacturing and service businesses. Established eight years ago, TE is a purpose-built factory, which forms part of the group's response to the expanding field of electronics. As with all parts of Colbeck Industries, TE is run as an autonomous company. As such, it presents strategic reviews for group

This case study was written by Terry Hill (University of Oxford) and S. H. Chambers (University of Warwick). It is intended for class discussion and not as an example of good or bad management. © AMD Publishing.

endorsement and is required to seek corporate approval for proposals involving major capital expenditure.

TE supplies fully assembled printed circuit boards (see Exhibit 1) and, over the years, has gained a reputation for high-quality performance and an excellent record of delivery reliability. The company only supplies to US-based companies involved in a range of industries, including televisions, domestic appliances and vending machines.

Stimulated by the corporate culture within the group, TE was very aware of the need to develop marketing and manufacturing strategies that were consistent with its business needs. As part of this, a major review of manufacturing was undertaken four years ago, which led to a reorganization of manufacturing into different units, as referred to earlier.

## Corporate Overview

Paul Hart (president of Tama Electronics) explained:

> One important corporate objective is to maintain the present level of RONA,[1] which is well above the average for this manufacturing sector. We do not wish to diversify nor to supply other market segments. Other parts of the group are serving these segments and, while not wanting to create additional competition, we also intend to stay where we are well known, our reputation is established, and where our skills and know-how lie. To enable us to continue to grow, the group has agreed on the necessary levels of capital expenditure, in terms of floor space and equipment. With regard to the latter, we have given particular emphasis to computerized test equipment, as this is where the bias of capital expenditure lies. This is not only to provide adequate capacity, but also to provide essential reports on test failures as a necessary feedback to design, manufacturing and component sourcing.

Paul then continued to explain that the working capital to sales percentage would gradually be improved as the levels of component and work-in-progress inventory are reduced.

'Future plans', he remarked, 'look for a 10 per cent actual growth over the next three years, which will need to come from an increase in market share. Our markets vary, however, and we need to provide relevant support if we are to succeed. For example, some require a high level of design and technical support and we have developed the necessary capability in computer-aided design.' He concluded that throughout the organization, the need to link markets to manufacturing, design and other capabilities is well recognized as a critical feature of strategic developments.

## Marketing

'TE sells to three distinct markets', was Steve Maskovic's (vice-president, marketing) opening comment (see Exhibit 2). 'Over the years we have been

**Exhibit 1**    Basic manufacturing stages of a typical product

Manufacturing Stage                           Diagram or Description

1. Printed circuit board (pcb)
   preparation and initial manual
   assembly of mechanical
   components.

2. Sequencing and auto-insertion
   of axial electronic components.

3. Manual assembly of remaining
   electronic components onto
   pcb.

4. Flow solder                             pcb passed over a wave of solder in
                                           specialized equipment, giving
                                           mechanical and electrical connection
5. Intermediate test                       of components to the board.

6. Manual rectification                    Computerized testing of components'
                                           properties and correct location.

7. Final assembly (manual)
   (a) Insert additional                   Resoldering or replacement of 'faulty'
       mechanical components               components.
       (for example, brackets
       and heat sinks)
   (b) Identification
   (c) Overlacquer (to prevent
       corrosion)
   (d) Encasement, if required
       (see across)

8. Final test – computerized to
   check functionality and ability
   to withstand enviromental
   conditions when in day-to-day
   use.

9. Packing

10. Warehousing and despatch

*Note:*
The product illustrated here has been considerably simplified to show the principal manufacturing stages.
Typical products would incorporate between 100 and 300 components, of which the majority would be
auto-inserted.

increasing our sales revenue in all markets through a combination of replacement and additional applications. The easiest way to explain these differences is to provide a short overview of each one in turn.' The sections that follow summarize Steve's explanation of the different markets.

## Television, Radio and Video Products

This market is characterized by high-volume products, where customers use several suppliers engendering high levels of competition. One common development with this market is the movement towards JIT supply agreements. (This refers to the requirement by customers that suppliers deliver regularly – sometimes daily or even twice daily – in line with a given schedule in order to reduce inventory levels and associated production and inventory control costs.) As a consequence, delivery reliability is becoming even more important and an essential characteristic of supplier performance. It is recognized that one way to increase market share is to continue to achieve total delivery reliability where competitors' performance on this dimension becomes suspect.

## Domestic Appliance Products

Compared to the previous market, this market segment has a wider range of volumes and product types. The result is that for some high-volume products the level of price competition is very high, whereas with others it is less so. One characteristic of this market is that some customers are seeking a high level of design change and the relevant technical support from suppliers to achieve this. In addition, and somewhat related to the characteristics of design change, there is a higher level of schedule change also required for certain products. The future in this segment is seen to be one of moderate growth but, as at present, when product designs have been agreed, then typically the characteristic of this market is for high-volume demand.

## Vending Machine Products

Volume in this market has shown the highest level of growth in recent years, which, in part, is a result of the increased range of applications. Most products are dual sourced, but TE's ability to give design support often results in the company becoming the main supplier. Maintaining this position over time is a result of providing a high level of quality conformance and achieving reliable deliveries.

In order to assess our markets, we have provided the order-winners relating to a number of products that represent these different segments [see Exhibit 2]. As one would expect, products are at various stages in their own life cycles [see Exhibit 3], and the difference between an original equipment (OE) and spares product[2] has been reflected in this

**Exhibit 2** An assessment of the order-winning criteria for the three markets using a number of representative products

| Market | Product reference[1] | Current year | | | | In two years' time | | | |
|---|---|---|---|---|---|---|---|---|---|
| | | Price | Delivery speed | Quality[2] | Other[3] | Price | Delivery speed | Quality[2] | Other[3] |
| Television, radio and videos products | AT 79 | | 25 | | 75 | | | | 100 |
| | 130 | | 25 | | 75 | | | | 100 |
| | 131 | 100 | | | | | 25 | | 75 |
| | 157 | 100 | | | | 100 | | | |
| | 161 | 30 | 50 | | 20 | | | | 100 |
| | 261 | 50 | 50 | | | 80 | 20 | | |
| Domestic appliance products | T 04 | | | | 100 | | | | 100 |
| | 14 | 100 | | | | | 20 | | 80 |
| | 15 | | | | 100 | | | | 100 |
| | 24 | 60 | | 40 | | 80 | | 20 | |
| | SS 63 | | | | 100 | | | | 100 |
| | 101 | 100 | | | | 100 | | | |
| | 127 | | 40 | 40 | 20 | 100 | | | |
| | MC 07 | 40 | 60 | | | 50 | 50 | | |
| | 21 | 40 | 60 | | | 50 | 50 | | |
| Vending machine products | CAC 21 | 60 | | 40 | | 60 | | 40 | |
| | 43 | 60 | | 40 | | 60 | | 40 | |
| | 52 | 20 | | 70 | 10 | 30 | | 60 | 10 |
| | SS 46 | | | | 100 | | | | 100 |
| | 126 | | 40 | 40 | 20 | 50 | 25 | 25 | |
| | VLC 8 | 40 | 20 | | 40 | 40 | | 20 | 40 |
| | 11 | 80 | 20 | | | 80 | 20 | | |
| | 16 | 20 | | | 80 | 50 | | | 50 |
| | 17 | | | | 100 | 20 | | | 80 |
| | DC 39 | 20 | | 20 | 60 | 30 | | 30 | 40 |
| | 52 | 30 | | 20 | 50 | 40 | | 30 | 30 |
| | 79 | 10 | 60 | | 30 | 30 | 50 | | 20 |
| | T 32 | 40 | 60 | | | 60 | 40 | | |

*Notes*
1. Product references: AT = Amplifier/tuner; T = Timer; SS = Switching system; MC = Motor control; CAC = Coin acceptance circuit; VLC = Vending logic circuit; DC = Display control.
2. Quality refers to quality conformance.
3. 'Other' refers to non-manufacturing criteria; for example, design, technical support and being an existing supplier.
4. Delivery reliability is an order-losing sensitive qualifier for all OEM items.

analysis, a fact also shown in the order-winners for both types of products. One factor we also must bear in mind is that our delivery performance in supplying orders for spares has an impact upon future orders for OE products. Unfortunately, in recent months we have tended to deliver spares orders late on several occasions.

# Manufacturing

'Before we reviewed our approach to manufacturing', explained Gary Wilson, 'we arranged facilities on the basis of process layout, a classic approach in batch manufacturing'. As explained earlier, however, this led to a relatively high level of complexity in terms of the requirements for operations control, capacity planning, inventory control and other aspects of operations. In addition, TE had problems with employee motivation, especially regarding their lack of identification with the business and plans for growth. As a result of the strategy review, TE changed its approach to one based upon smaller manufacturing units, each focused to different aspects of our business. These units were each provided with their own relevant support functions and, as a result, had responsibility for many aspects of the total production task, including day-to-day scheduling, change-overs, maintenance and quality control. The operatives were given a broader set of responsibilities, and TE

**Exhibit 3**　　Actual and forecast sales for a number of representative products

| Product reference | Annual sales (units) | | | |
|---|---|---|---|---|
| | Current year minus | | Current year | Current year +2 |
| | 4 | 2 | | |
| AT 261 | 0 | 0 | 34 500 | 120 000 |
| CAC52 | 0 | 0 | 1 150 | 10 000 |
| DC 79 | 0 | 0 | 2 530 | 5 500 |
| SS 126 | 0 | 0 | 9 200 | 32 000 |
| SS 127 | 0 | 0 | 13 800 | 40 000 |
| T32 | 0 | 0 | 35 880 | 75 000 |
| VLC 17 | 0 | 0 | 920 | 12 000 |
| AT131 | 46 500 | 86 100 | 167 900 | 2 500 |
| AT157 | 6 450 | 76 230 | 81 420 | 90 000 |
| MC07 | 0 | 16 780 | 23 460 | 25 000 |
| MC21 | 0 | 0 | 35 650 | 48 000 |
| SS 101 | 0 | 72 150 | 80 500 | 95 000 |
| T14 | 35 620 | 260 570 | 255 300 | 3 000 |
| T24 | 0 | 0 | 56 580 | 180 000 |
| CAC21 | 7 380 | 8 100 | 8 050 | 8 000 |
| CAC43 | 2 730 | 15 710 | 16 560 | 17 000 |
| DC39 | 0 | 5 215 | 8 280 | 8 000 |
| DC52 | 0 | 0 | 13 110 | 15 000 |
| VLC8 | 915 | 1 840 | 1 840 | 2 000 |
| VLC 11 | 0 | 1 060 | 18 860 | 20 000 |
| VLC16 | 0 | 0 | 1 610 | 5 000 |
| AT79 | 1 040 | 880 | 690 | 500 |
| AT130 | 16 730 | 18 070 | 2 760 | 2 000 |
| AT161 | 26 200 | 30 900 | 4 830 | 3 000 |
| SS46 | 15 550 | 13 760 | 1 150 | 1 000 |
| SS63 | 12 600 | 36 400 | 3 590 | 3 500 |
| T04 | 136 490 | 1 090 | 460 | 400 |
| T15 | 45 250 | 45 900 | 2 990 | 3 500 |

successfully introduced statistical process control to great effect. (Statistical process control involves the use of control charts – normally completed by an operator – to monitor the process and initiate corrective action as the need arises. Thus it focuses directly on the process and tunes it as required.)

The different units have identified heavily with the aspect of the business for which they were made responsible. A healthy competition has evolved, with each unit apparently wishing to outperform the others. In addition, these units identify strongly with the initial products allocated to them, and see them as 'their products'. Certainly, when suggestions have been made to reallocate products, strong resistance has developed, such that it has been more sensible not to jeopardize the significant gains that have resulted from employee involvement. Similarly, when new products have been allocated following the initial production phase, one argument always taken into account is to try to balance demand across the units to minimize the transfer of people from one unit to another. As Gary Wilson explained, 'People management is undoubtedly a critical factor in the achievements we have made so far, and we have no wish to slow down the momentum.'

The units established four years before principally concern the assembly, test and packing of pcbs. Each unit shares the more expensive processes (such as flow solder, component sequencing, auto-insertion and any expensive testing equipment, which is centrally grouped on a process basis), but otherwise are fully equipped. Also each unit had its own managerial and supervisory structure, which includes production and industrial engineering, maintenance and production scheduling personnel, together with the responsibility for quality conformance, job training and even involvement in recruitment.

Of the four units, one is termed the 'pilot line' and is responsible for the development and introduction of products. A second was set up to handle low-volume spares requirements, while a third was made responsible for all vending machine products. A fourth unit handles the rest (see Exhibit 4).

'Because of the types of tasks involved, the "pilot line" unit was given the most skilled operators, due to the development nature of the task, which often involves using product drawings and discussing specification changes', continued Gary Wilson.

The spares unit also needs a high level of skilled labour, but often we find difficulty in resourcing both these units. Certainly, in the last year, we have experienced some capacity difficulties in the spares unit, which has affected our record of delivery reliability. The other two units require less skilled labour. Their job concerns assembling a range of quantities for different products. To do this, we installed mixed mode lines, that allow the assembly of several products [see Exhibit 4].

On the issue of payment system development, it is necessary to appreciate the background events. To facilitate the original changes in working practices, part of the agreement necessary to gain employee support was to provide a guaranteed bonus payment at the average level recorded at that time. The employees' wish to review the current method of remuneration is a desire for the payment system to reflect the changes in structure and

**Exhibit 4**  Details relating to representative products and manufacturing units

| Manufacturing unit | Product reference[1] | Market reference[2] | Labour standard (minutes/pcb) | Average weekly output (pcbs)[3] | Average number of direct operatives in unit | Total number of different products made in unit |
|---|---|---|---|---|---|---|
| 1. Pilot line | AT261 | A | 21.0 | 750 | | |
| | CAC52 | C | 15.4 | 25 | | |
| | DC79 | C | 3.9 | 55 | | |
| | SS126 | C | 10.6 | 200 | 32 | 22 |
| | SS127 | B | 12.3 | 300 | | |
| | T32 | C | 7.2 | 780 | | |
| | VLC17 | C | 46.1 | 20 | | |
| 2. Others | AT131 | A | 16.4 | 3650 | | |
| | AT157 | A | 17.9 | 1770 | | |
| | MC07 | B | 3.7 | 510 | | |
| | MC21 | B | 3.2 | 775 | 116 | 14 |
| | SS101 | B | 8.1 | 1750 | | |
| | T14 | B | 5.9 | 5550 | | |
| | T24 | B | 8.0 | 1230 | | |
| 3. Vending machines | CAC21 | C | 26.6 | 175 | | |
| | CAC43 | C | 21.7 | 360 | | |
| | DC39 | C | 4.6 | 180 | | |
| | DC52 | C | 6.1 | 285 | 60 | 20 |
| | VLC8 | C | 39.8 | 40 | | |
| | VLC11 | C | 62.0 | 410 | | |
| | VLC16 | C | 51.8 | 35 | | |
| 4. Spares[4] | AT79 | A | 14.3 | | | |
| | AT130 | A | 22.1 | | | |
| | AT161 | A | 46.2 | | | |
| | SS46 | C | 9.9 | | 24 | 46 |
| | SS63 | B | 13.6 | | | |
| | T04 | B | 4.0 | | | |
| | T15 | B | 6.7 | | | |

*Notes*
**1.** AT = Amplifier/tuner; CAC = Coin acceptance circuit; DC = Display control; SS = Switching system; T = Timer; VLC = Vending logic circuit; MC = Motor control.
**2.** A = Television, video, radio; B = Domestic appliances; C = Vending machines.
**3.** The factory is operated 46 weeks per year.
**4.** Spares demand is so variable that averages are not meaningful and are not included.

responsibility, that have taken place. We accept that this is a legitimate request and agree, in principle, the need to consider more suitable alternatives. To be frank, we must be ready to respond to the employees' initiative, as considerable interest has been generated and expectations have been raised.

## Current Performance and Future Needs

'Although we have made considerable improvements in the past few years', explained Paul Hart,

Future business is going to be even more difficult to acquire. Relevant order-winners are under even more pressure. We need to reduce costs in the high-volume segments, give technical support where necessary and provide delivery speed for other products. Furthermore, customer complaints about unreliable delivery of spares and some other products have increased in the last six to nine months. This, without a doubt, will harm future business unless we bring about the necessary improvements. One underlying factor in all this is our manufacturing strategy and we must ensure that this is kept finely tuned in line with the different market requirements. Certainly it has been important in our past success and will continue to be a major factor in the future.

## Notes

1. RONA is the acronym for return on net assets, which comprises net profit as a percentage of net assets (total assets less current liabilities).
2. OE refers to pcb supplies to customers who are currently making original equipment (such as new television sets or vending machines) as opposed to orders constituting a supply of spares.

# The Great Nuclear Fizzle at Old B & W

Everything went wrong when the venerable boilermakers turned to building pressure vessels for atomic reactors. The whole electric power industry felt the consequences.

The long-awaited transition for the US electric power industry into the nuclear age has been slowed by a number of factors, including technological difficulties and public resistance. But a specific and unexpected cause for delay has been one company's crucial failure to deliver a single vital component of nuclear power plants. The failure, basically, was a management failure, and on a scale that would be cause for concern even to a fly-by-night newcomer to the nuclear industry. The company, however, was no newcomer. It was proud old Babcock & Wilcox Co. (B & W), a pioneer of the steam generating business, whose boilers were used in one of the first central power plants ever built (in Philadelphia, in 1881). B & W had an impressive $648m in sales last year, making it 157th on *Fortune*'s list of 500 largest industrials, and it has been engaged in nuclear work in a major way for 15 years, producing, among other things, atomic power systems for Navy submarines.

Moreover, the corporation is one of only five that are engaged in building nuclear power plants in the USA. With consumption of electricity growing by nearly 10 per cent a year, the utilities are counting heavily on the new nuclear stations to avoid brownouts and power failures in the years ahead. Poor performance at B & W is thus one of those problems that could send ripples through the whole economy.

All of B & W's troubles involve a single product: nuclear pressure vessels. These are the huge steel pots – some are more than 70 feet long and weigh more than 700 tons – that contain atomic reactions. They must meet rigid specifications set by the Atomic Energy Commission (AEC), and B & W built a $25m plant at Mount Vernon, Indiana, just to fabricate them. Cockily sure that the Mount Vernon plant would operate as planned, B & W sold its entire projected output of pressure vessels for years ahead. But nothing seemed to go right at Mount Vernon. Plagued by labour shortages and malfunctioning machines, the plant produced just three pressure vessels in its first three years of operation. Late 1968, after the production snarl reached horrendous proportions, a vice-president responsible for the Mount Vernon operation committed suicide in a bizarre fashion.

Last May, B & W was forced to make a humiliating disclosure. Every one of the 28 nuclear pressure vessels then in the Mount Vernon Works was behind schedule, by as much as 17 months. For the utility industry, the news from B & W meant intolerable delays in bringing 28 badly needed nuclear plants into service, with all the added expense and problems that would be entailed. Philadelphia Electric Co. estimated that it would have to spend an extra $50 000 a day just to provide from other sources, such as high-cost gas turbines, the power that it had counted on getting from its delayed nuclear units.

## Creating its Own Competition

With so much at stake, B & W's customers could not well afford to be patient. Twenty-one of the pressure vessels tied up in Mount Vernon Works were there on subcontracts from the two giants of the nuclear industry, General Electric (GE) and Westinghouse Electric. Both companies swiftly took the almost unprecedented step of forcing B & W to turn most of their partially completed vessels over to other manufacturers. When B & W, in an ill-conceived gambit, tried to hang on to two of the transferred vessels, Westinghouse took the case to court and won. In all, 14 GE and Westinghouse vessels – perhaps $40m worth – were taken out of B & W's shops. Some of the firms that got the business had never made a pressure vessel before for use in a US reactor; B & W had managed to create hungry new competitors in its own line of work. Only four GE and three Westinghouse vessels remain at Mount Vernon.

The company itself has barely begun to pay the high price of failure. Its earnings last year were still a robust $2.04 a share. In the first six months of this year, losses associated with nuclear work pushed earnings down to 22 cents a share (not even enough to cover the 34-cent quarterly dividend). From a 1969 high of 40.5 last January, B & W stock has sagged into the low 20s. At that price, the stock is hovering around book value.

The man in the middle of all these troubles is President George Zipf (pronounced Ziff), 49, a low-key executive who started with B & W in 1942 as a metallurgical engineer. But the man who bears the main onus of responsibility is Zipf's predecessor, Chairman Morris Neilson, 65, who chose Zipf for his present job a year ago, and handed him his present problems.

## In Trouble Down by the Ohio

'All areas of the company were profitable in 1968 with the exception of automatic energy', President George Zipf told B & W stockholders, after taking over as chief executive officer from Chairman Morris Neilson in September 1968. Up to then, losses on nuclear work had never seemed particularly troublesome. They were regarded simply as the price of B & W's ticket into the automatic age; and B & W had been getting into, and prospering in, new technologies for a hundred years.

However, one segment of its nuclear venture has driven B & W into deep trouble. The plant that it built along the Ohio River at Mount Vernon, Indiana, to produce huge steel pressure vessels for atomic reactors, failed to function as expected, with all kinds of dire results. One especially unhappy result was that B & W had to give up some partially completed pressure vessels to competitors.

# Bad Boy from Blair, Nebraska

Neilson is a flamboyant leader, a big bluff man with bright blue eyes and a full head of grey-blonde hair, who has a gift for salty language. More than one secretary quit 'Doc' Neilson's employ because of his profanity, and more than one executive suffered a colourful tongue-lashing in the chairman's office.

Neilson got his nickname by virtue of being a doctor's son in Blair, Nebraska, where he was known as 'Young Doc'. That was as close to earning an academic degree as Neilson came. As a boy, he himself has said, he was 'incorrigible' and was kicked out of school 'for being a bad influence on the rest of the students'. He then enrolled in a Lincoln, Nebraska, high school and worked part-time as an embalmer. 'I got into trouble in Lincoln, too', Neilson told an interviewer a few years ago.

> One night, I came home with my nose over and under my eye. I'd been in a fight and got hit with a pair of pliers. I woke up my old man and he looked at my nose, and said, 'You're going to look like a goddamn syphilitic the rest of your life.' My old man used to tell me that there were two steps ahead of me – first reform school and then the pen.

Instead, Young Doc became a steeplejack and ironworker and in 1924 joined the corporation he was later to head. 'I came to B & W by accident', Neilson has recalled.

> I was working at American Bridge as an ironmonger on a job in Chicago, and another fellow and I got drunk. We got on the train and got off at Des Moines. We were walking past this construction job, and a fellow slid down a column and said, 'You looking for work?' We figured we were.

It was a B & W job, erecting boilers for central station power plants, and from the start Doc Neilson felt at home in the two-fisted company. 'Those construction workers were goddamn rough people. They were hard drinkers, fighters, and lived by their wits.'

By the time the Second World War came along, Neilson was superintendent of marine erection. He supervised the installation of B & W boilers in 4100 Navy and merchant-marine ships during the war. Later he headed the entire boiler division, including manufacturing, and in 1957 became president and chief executive officer.

When Neilson took charge of B & W the company was already deeply involved in nuclear work. Neilson's predecessor, Alfred Iddles, had recognized early that B & W would have to prepare for the day when the atom would challenge fossil fuels as a source of energy for central generating plants. Under Iddles, B & W attracted an outstanding stable of nuclear scientists and engineers and, in 1956, set up an extensive research facility at Lynchburg, Virginia. One of B & W's first important nuclear jobs was to build Consolidated Edison's Indian Point Plant. Another project was the reactor for the nuclear ship Savannah. B & W lost money on these jobs, but it gained the experience needed to secure a corporate toehold in the nuclear era.

Nuclear losses continued under Neilson, but he improved B & W's overall profitability dramatically. Iddles had run the company as a loose-knit grouping of semi-autonomous subsidiaries. Neilson centralized and systematized management. Every executive's areas of responsibility and authority were carefully spelled out in manuals that defined company policies and aims in all sectors of the business. Although sales stayed near or below the 1958 figure of $366m until 1963 – this was a low period in the utility buying cycle – earnings climbed year by year. Profits went from $13m in 1958 to $22m in 1963. At that point, sales also began to go up, rising by 71 per cent in the next five years. Profits peaked in 1967 at $33m, at $2.69 a share (compared to $1.05 a share in Neilson's first full year).

In view of his critics, who have lately become numerous, the seeds of B & W's present problems were planted in the years of Neilson's rich harvests. It can be seen, in retrospect, that he may have been too successful in keeping B & W lean. His determination to keep down the fat sometimes 'had the effect of cutting into good red meat', says a former B & W executive. Experienced managers found themselves stretched too thin to cover all their areas of responsibility. Worse, they did not always feel that their authority matched their responsibility (that is, men in the field were held responsible for results they did not have the power to bring about).

The most biting criticism of Neilson's regime comes from men charged with nuclear assignments. In their eyes, Neilson's lack of formal education proved a serious handicap. Explains one former B & W executive: 'Neilson created an atmosphere in which engineers and technical people just didn't feel at home. Their ideas were not treated with respect. They felt that top management didn't understand technical problems, and didn't trust those who could understand them.'

## A Touch of Corporate Arrogance

From the start, B & W had foreseen a long wait before its nuclear work became profitable. Developing the necessary skills and technologies to compete in the nuclear industry has proved to be a slow and expensive process for every company that has tried it, including GE and Westinghouse. But what B & W had not expected was to lose money on its Mount Vernon Works. When the plant was planned in the early 1960s, Neilson appeared to believe that he had found a niche in the nuclear industry that offered a quick return. A nuclear pressure vessel, though huge and manufactured to demanding technical standards, is essentially just the kind of heavy steel unit that B & W was accustomed to fabricating with ease.

While the Mount Vernon plant was under construction, US utilities went on a nuclear-plant buying spree, starting in 1965. At the time, the surge in orders seemed like a lucky break for B & W. The Mount Vernon plant was designed to produce one completed pressure vessel a month, once it was in full operation, and there had been considerable doubt during the planning stages 'if we'd ever get enough work to fill the place', a former B & W executive recalls. Orders for pressure vessels poured in, faster than anyone had predicted, and the Mount Vernon plant soon got loaded up with work. It is now clear that management made too little provision for the time it would take to get the new plant operating at full capacity. Says one B & W customer: 'I think you have to say that corporate arrogance was involved.'

The first delays at Mount Vernon were caused by suppliers falling far behind schedule in providing vital equipment. A linear accelerator, used to detect welding flaws, was not delivered until August 1966, 11 months late. Even worse, a highly automated, tape-controlled machine centre – the heart of the plant as originally conceived – arrived a full year behind schedule, in September 1967.

## The Lure of Unspoiled Labour

By then, the plant had been operating on a makeshift basis for almost two years. And it had already become apparent that B & W's century of demonstrated competence in the fabrication of heavy steel products had not protected the company from grievous error. A principal one was the site itself, a cornfield near the little farm town of Mount Vernon (population: 6200) in south-western Indiana. The location had been chosen mainly because of its position on the Ohio River, safely above any known flood level, and yet reliably accessible for deep-water barges. This was an important advantage because nuclear pressure vessels are so immense that they can best be transported by water. B & W had owned the land for a number of years, and had set up a small plant there for making boiler parts.

What Mount Vernon did not have was a pool of skilled labour. This was a serious drawback because the AEC, for safety reasons, sets rigid standards for machine work and welding on nuclear projects. Late last year, a company memorandum reviewing the Mount Vernon fiasco observed: "Production workers required a new level of knowledge, intelligence, and judgement to operate the machinery, perform operations, and maintain the very high quality standards.' At the outset, however, B & W took an optimistic view of its prospects and chose, according to that 1968 memorandum, to regard Mount Vernon as 'an unspoiled labour market'. Presumably, the company expected to find a more tractable group of workers there than it had at Barberton, Ohio, where B & W's power generator division had had its headquarters and principal manufacturing facilities for many years.

The company planned to overcome the obvious shortcomings of Mount Vernon's labour pool in two ways: first, through automation – using that sophisticated machining centre – and second, through a massive training programme that would entice farmers away from their cornfields and quickly turn them into skilled welders and machinists. In one year, B & W spent $1m just to train welders. But almost as fast as men reached the levels of skill required, they left B & W for jobs elsewhere. On 30 September 1968, only 514 of the 1060 hourly employees hired in the preceding three years were still working for B & W; in other words, the company had hired three men for each one it retained. 'Turnover of the Mount Vernon workforce has been a particularly frustrating problem, and a major reason B & W has been unable to bring its full manufacturing capabilities to bear on the situation', the 1968 memorandum concluded. Some potential workers proved to be untrainable, others had a 'general negative attitude' towards heavy industry, and 'some were not able to adjust, and therefore returned to their farms'.

## 'It Drove Us Out Of Our Minds'

Workers who remained with B & W did not prove to be as unspoiled as the company had hoped. Even before the pressure vessel plant opened, it was organized by the Boilermakers Union (which also represents B & W workers at Barberton) amid charges of unfair labour practices against the management. The plant was closed by labour disputes on several occasions. The most serious occurred when the three-year contract expired in 1967, while equipment was still being installed. The Boilermakers went on strike over wages and work rules, and the plant was down for 40 days; unnecessarily long, in the view of President Thomas Ayers of Chicago's Commonwealth Edison, who had pressure vessels tied up at Mount Vernon.

From the standpoint of production, Neilson won a victory that amounted to overkill. Under the new contract, wages remained too low to stem the flow of workers away from B & W or to attract qualified workers from other areas. The B & W memo cites the 'noncompetitiveness of our wage scale' as a reason for the high turnover rate in the Mount Vernon workforce. Even for experienced workers, welding two pieces of eight-inch steel together is a demanding task, particularly in nuclear work, in which each weld is examined by X-ray. When an imperfection is found, the weld must be 'mined out' and done over again. In most plants, less than 10 per cent of the welds must be reworked, and a rework level of less than 1 per cent is sometimes achieved. But at Mount Vernon 70 per cent or more of the welds were rejected on being inspected. 'It drove us out of our damned minds', recalls Ayers, 'So costly! So time-consuming!' Ayers and other B & W customers say that they urged the company to increase the supervisory force – which regularly worked one-and-a-half to two shifts daily – so that a closer watch could be kept on the welds as they were built up.

In addition to its problems, B & W ran into unexpected trouble with equipment. The linear accelerator for X-raying welds was installed in mid-1966 but did not go into full operation until a year later. The tape-controlled machining centre was even more of a headache, and began functioning as planned only a few months ago. In this centre, huge vessel segments are positioned on optically aligned ways, and then moved a distance of 250 feet, while a series of precise machining operations are performed simultaneously, controlled by computer-prepared tape. The concept was a good one, since nuclear pressure vessels are custom jobs, each tailored to a customer's specifications. But 'debugging' of the machinery proved unexpectedly difficult. One problem was that the plant was not air-conditioned, and temperature changes threw off the many delicate adjustments that had to be made. In addition, an earthquake – fairly rare in Indiana – shook up the plant last year and it took nearly a week to reset the machine tools. Other start-up difficulties were simply incomprehensible. For example, a vital boring mill was put out of operation for several weeks when a tool broke. There was no spare on hand.

# Death in a Dry Bathtub

The man directly responsible for the Mount Vernon plant was John Paul Craven, Vice-President in charge of the power generation division at Barberton. As head of B & W's largest division, Craven was number three man in the company, and was paid $87 000 a year. At one time, there was speculation in the company that Craven might someday become president. A gentle, upright bachelor of 60, Craven was tall and distinguished looking. An engineer by training, he had been with B & W all his working life, and he had no interests outside his job. For a while, Craven had raised roses as a hobby, but after he was made Vice-President he gave up roses in order to devote himself more fully to B & W. 'His work was his whole life', says an old friend.

As the bottleneck at Mount Vernon grew worse, Craven came to feel that neither his customers nor corporate headquarters in New York fully appreciated the difficulties of Mount Vernon's advanced machine tools. He did not believe that he was given the authority, the budget or the personnel that he needed to fulfil the plant's commitments. Says another of Craven's old friends: 'Paul couldn't bear to sit in Barberton and have all the shots called from New York – and then be expected to take responsibility for not producing.'

In September 1968, before the seriousness of the pressure-vessel crisis at Mount Vernon became generally known, Neilson stepped aside as chief executive in favour of George Zipf. For a man destined for the top at B & W, Zipf had an unusual background. All of his predecessors had been identified with boilers, but Zipf came from B & W's tubular-products division at Beaver Falls, Pennsylvania, near Pittsburgh. This division, whose work is more akin to steel manufacturing than boilermaking, produces tubing for B & W's own use and for sale to other industrial customers; it accounts for roughly 30 per cent of B & W's total sales, and more than half its profits. When he transferred to New York as executive vice-president in 1966, Zipf had been at Beaver Falls for 20 years, ever since graduating from Lehigh University. He was a stranger to the problems of the power generation division, and to that division's big corporate customers.

Less than a month after taking over as chief executive from Neilson, Zipf scheduled a meeting at the Mount Vernon plant with Craven and Austin Fragomen, Vice-

President for manufacturing. The meeting was set for a Monday morning. During the preceding weekend Craven told friends that for the first time in his life he thought his job was getting beyond him. Sometime on the Sunday afternoon or evening before his scheduled meeting with Zipf, Craven took off his clothes and climbed into a dry bathtub in his $250-a-month apartment at Akron's luxurious Carlton House. Then he slashed his ankles, cut his throat and stabbed himself in the heart with the serrated eight-inch blade of a butcher's knife.

After Craven's death, George Zipf took personal charge of the power generation division, and of the Mount Vernon works in particular. Before long, both Austin Fragomen and the Mount Vernon plant manager, Norman Wagner, resigned. That left Zipf free to put a whole new team to work on the company's pressure-vessel debacle.

## The Chairman Sells Some Stock

Beginning in 1967, both GE and Westinghouse, along with many of the utilities that were the ultimate customers for B & W pressure vessels, repeatedly expressed worry over the Mount Vernon plant's faltering operations. In the fall of 1968, B & W pacified GE to some extent by setting up a temporary welding shop on barges anchored at Madison, Indiana, where expert welders from the Louisville, Kentucky, labour pool could be obtained. But for the most part, B & W brushed aside its customers' worries with assurances that things at Mount Vernon were not really as bad as they seemed. Even after Craven's death, the B & W management continued to maintain that its optimistic scheduling, with some minor changes, would prove to be realistic.

Some utility executives who met with Zipf to express their concern left with the conviction that he did not appreciate just how serious the pressure-vessel delays had become. On some occasions, he seemed to regard his callers as bothersome intruders. 'He just sat there like a damned Budha [sic]', reported one customer after such a meeting.

Faced with such frustrations, GE and Westinghouse began to consider the drastic step of pulling some of their delayed pressure vessels out of the overloaded Mount Vernon shops. Both companies assigned teams to scout for other manufacturers that might be able to take over B & W vessels and complete them. There were not many potential candidates. Up to then, B & W and Combustion Engineering, Inc., had pretty much divided the US pressure-vessel business between them. Combustion Engineering had managed to keep close to schedule on its deliveries, and had been expanding its Chattanooga machine shops. It had unused capacity. In addition, Chicago Bridge & Iron Co., which had previously done only on-site fabrication, was setting up a pressure-vessel plant in Memphis. (On-site fabrication is a more expensive method of constructing pressure vessels, used only when it is extremely difficult to transport the massive units to a site intact.) The GE and

Westinghouse teams also looked abroad for companies that might be able to take over some of the work.

In April, while B & W's biggest customers were searching for other suppliers, Doc Neilson – who was retiring on 1 May as an officer of the company, but keeping the title of chairman – quietly sold 15 000 of his 20 000 shares of B & W stock. The price at the time was about $33 a share. A couple of weeks later B & W stockholders got their first official hint of serious trouble ahead. George Zipf revealed at the annual meeting that he expected earnings to drop by 20 to 30 per cent in 1969 because of the company's losses on nuclear business. (The actual decline, of course, has since proved to be much greater than Zipf predicted.) Before long, the price of B & W's stock sank into the 20s.

## Quick Trip to Court

On 14 May, less than a month after the annual meeting, B & W sent out telegrams brusquely letting customers know that the situation at Mount Vernon was even worse than they had suspected. Zipf and his new team had completed a gloomy re-evaluation of the plant's capabilities, and B & W was adding 2 to 12 months to earlier delivery schedules, some of which had already been stretched past the dates called for in B & W's original contracts.

On receiving this news, both GE and Westinghouse sought B & W's cooperation in transferring vessels to the other shops that they had scouted out. B & W agreed to subcontract some of its work to these plants. But an unexpected difficulty soon arose. Westinghouse had determined that Rotterdam Dockyard Co., a major shipbuilding and steel fabricating firm in the Netherlands, could take two vessels and improve on the B & W schedule, provided that the vessels were transferred promptly. Westinghouse located space on a ship that would be calling at New Orleans on the desired date and, by paying a premium, was able to arrange for the ship to cancel calls at other ports and proceed directly to the Netherlands. B & W agreed to put the two pressure vessels on barges and start them on their way to New Orleans, while it negotiated a subcontract with Rotterdam Dockyard. But negotiations broke down when B & W and Rotterdam could not come to terms. To the horror of Westinghouse officials, B & W ordered the barges back to Mount Vernon.

Westinghouse then decided to pay B & W for the work it had already done, and take over the vessels itself. But speed was required. If the barges did not continue down the river while these new arrangements were made they would miss the ship to Rotterdam. Now Westinghouse found itself at a strange impasse: it could not reach anyone at B & W who would rescind the order for the barges to return to Mount Vernon. Neilson was 'not available', and Zipf was 'out of the country'. Frustrated in its efforts to reach top management and work out an amicable settlement, Westinghouse reluctantly went into the US district court in Pittsburgh, and won a temporary restraining order to prevent B & W from taking the vessels back to Mount Vernon.

During the hearing, Federal Judge Wallace S. Gourley had a revealing exchange with John T. Black, B & W's manager for commercial nuclear components.

*Judge Gourley*: On this contract for $2 542 000, what would you say that you expect to make on this?'

*Black*: This specific contract?

*Judge Gourley*: Yes.

*Black*: I don't expect to make a profit.

*Judge Gourley*: You don't expect to make a profit?

*Black*: No, sir.

*Judge Gourley*: I don't know why you would want the material to work on. You are not in business to lose money for your stockholders.

*Black*: We do not expect to make it.

*Judge Gourley*: In other words, on this contract [for] $2 542 000, you don't expect to make a penny profit for your corporation, if you went ahead and finished it?

*Black*: No, sir.

*Judge Gourley*: How much on this other one [for] $2 304 789. What profit could you be reasonably expected to make on this contact, if you finished it?

*Black*: I would think that one probably [is] in the same condition.

*Judge Gourley*: If you went ahead and finished this, you wouldn't make a cent?

*Black*: I think on direct cost, we would cover our direct cost to labour and shop expenses.

*Judge Gourley*: I meant after everything, would you or would you not make any money on this?

*Black*: No.

*Judge Gourley*: I wouldn't think your stockholders would want you to finish. I certainly wouldn't.

## Back on the Track

After Westinghouse won possession of the two pressure vessels and sent them off to Rotterdam, B & W raised no further objections to transferring work out of its shop. Indeed, it actively cooperated with its customers to get the job done. Westinghouse sent five vessels to Combustion Engineering's Chattanooga shops and two to a French firm, Société des Forges et Ateliers du Creusot. GE turned three vessels over to Chicago Bridge & Iron and had B & W send two others to Japan's Ishikawajima-Harima Heavy Industries. In every case, these firms are expected to equal or better the delivery dates set in May by B & W.

With the load at Mount Vernon lightened, prospects look better for the 14 pressure vessels that remain there, including seven for nuclear plants that B & W itself is building. For example, the Sacramento Municipal Utility District has been notified that the vessel for its Rancho Seco nuclear plant, a B & W project, will be only a couple of months late, instead of the year that seemed likely in May. That means that the vessel for Sacramento is essentially on schedule again, since the delays now expected are no more than could be accounted for by the labour disputes and earthquake that Mount Vernon suffered.

To his utility customers, George Zipf remains very much a man on trial. But now that their pressure vessels are moving along again, some utility executives are convinced that he has quietly managed to put B & W back on the track. One move that has met their approval was the appointment in September of an experienced Westinghouse man as vice-president in charge of the power generation division (John Paul Craven's old job). Bringing in an outsider at such a level is something new for B & W, and one B & W customer believes that he knows what it means: 'I think George Zipf is really in command now.' If this is so, he will have a lot to do to restore the honoured old name of Babcock & Wilcox to its former lustre.

---

### Technical note

Nuclear equipment, as stated earlier, is manufactured in a job-shop environment, while most of the fossil equipment is manufactured in a flow-shop environment. In fossil manufacturing operations, the work stations are usually arranged in proper sequence to allow materials to enter one end of the shop, and flow sequentially to completion. The normal work mix means that some work be performed at each work station, but seldom requires the product to pass over any of the work stations more than once. All jobs follow, essentially, the same path from one work station to another. Consequentially, it is relatively easy to 'line-up' or 'load' each shop with a high degree of certainty as to work content, schedule requirements and completion capabilities. Over the years, certain rules of thumb were developed, which allowed relatively accurate manufacturing planning decisions to be made for fossil manufacturing operations.

A shipping unit for a large fossil-fired boiler, such as used in power plants, differs greatly from a shipping unit for a nuclear plant. Fossil boilers are shipped as a large number of parts, which are assembled or erected at the job site. Nuclear equipment is mostly shop assembled, whereby a small number of large, assembled components are shipped to the site for installation. Complex planning is, therefore, required for the nuclear shop operations, which produce all detail parts fabricated into various levels of subassembled, and finally into large components.

*Source*: E. D. Thomas and D. P. Covelski, 'Planning Nuclear Equipment Manufacturing', *Interfaces*, 1975, **9**(3): 18–29.

# Tyndall Furniture Company (A)

Greg Procter, vice-president of marketing for the Tyndall Furniture Company, knew that the single most important marketing decision a company made was the selection of products and markets to serve. He was acutely aware of the need to focus his firm's resources because sales growth in the most recent period had slowed significantly. Profits were also below the industry average. Further complicating the task he faced were the dramatic changes going on in the industry. He was most concerned about the increasing competition at the retail level. A major problem was the recent popularity of galleries in the retail store. He had to decide just where he would marshall his energies, both on products and on markets.

## Company Background

Established in 1898 by Henry H. Tyndall, the company remained a family-owned business until 1963 when it was bought out by Berkron Industries Inc., a large conglomerate with interests in textiles, chemicals, food, clothing, retailing and, more recently, financial services. Although predominantly based in North America, Berkron also has interests in Australasia and Europe.

Although the company had in the past been an above-average profit earner within the furniture industry as a whole, in recent years its performance had declined (Exhibit 1), a fact that led to the appointment of Matt Culley as chief executive officer two years before. As with most markets, the furniture industry was becoming increasingly more competitive and witnessing significant changes in both products and market outlets (Exhibit 2).

Sales of the company had shown significant growth in recent years but slowed dramatically in the most recently completed year (Exhibit 2). Productivity increases and judicious cost cutting, combined with some advantageous product mix changes, kept net profits growing. Unfortunately, profitability as measured by net profit percentage and return on total assets was still below the industry average. It was felt

---

This case was prepared by Professors W. L. Berry (Ohio State University), T. J. Hill (University of Oxford), J. E. Klompmaker (University of North Carolina) and W. G. Morrissey (North Carolina State University) as a basis for class discussion rather than to illustrate either effective of ineffective handling of an administrative situation. © Professor W. L. Berry, Professor J. E. Klompmaker, Professor W. G. Morrissey or AMD Publishing (UK). Enquiries in the USA to Zip Publishing, 1634 N. High Street, Columbus, Ohio 43201.

that the increasingly competitive nature of the industry was largely responsible for this below-average performance.

**Exhibit 1**    Furniture industry comparisons (per cent)

| Companies | Current year minus | | | | Current year |
|---|---|---|---|---|---|
| | 4 | 3 | 2 | 1 | |
| **Tyndall** | | | | | |
| Sales | 100.0 | 100.0 | 100.0 | 100.0 | 100.0 |
| Cost of goods sold | 79.1 | 78.3 | 78.3 | 79.2 | 78.1 |
| Net profit before tax | 4.8 | 3.7 | 4.4 | 3.5 | 4.2 |
| Return on total assets | 5.4 | 5.1 | 6.5 | 6.0 | 7.1 |
| Return on investment | – | 8.6 | 9.0 | 9.4 | 10.5 |
| Sales growth | – | 10.1 | 13.7 | 13.3 | 4.1 |
| **Average all case goods companies** | | | | | |
| Sales | 100.0% | 100.0% | 100.0% | – | – |
| Cost of goods sold | 75.9 | 75.2 | 76.7 | n.a. | n.a. |
| Net profit before tax | 7.7 | 7.4 | 7.3 | n.a. | n.a. |
| Return on total assets | n.a. | n.a. | 7.0 | n.a. | n.a. |
| **Average all furniture companies** | | | | | |
| Sales | 100.0% | 100.0% | 100.0% | – | – |
| Cost of goods sold | 75.6 | 74.6 | 75.1 | n.a. | n.a. |
| Net profit before tax | 7.6 | 8.3 | 8.4 | n.a. | n.a. |
| Return on total assets | 8.2 | 8.7 | 8.9 | n.a. | n.a. |

*Note*
n.a. signifies that the particular industry information is not available.

**Exhibit 2**    Tyndall sales analysis

| Market types | Current year minus | | Current year |
|---|---|---|---|
| | 2 | 1 | |
| **Small chains** | | | |
| Sales ($) | 1 188 189 | 1 468 848 | 1 389 077 |
| Number of outlets | 14 | 14 | 14 |
| **Small independents** | | | |
| Sales ($) | 19 417 109 | 20 005 636 | 18 162 589 |
| Number of outlets | 577 | 594 | 601 |
| **Large independents** | | | |
| Sales ($) | 1 504 000 | 1 841 000 | 1 742 000 |
| Number of outlets | 5 | 5 | 5 |
| **Galleries** | | | |
| Sales ($) | 7 655 279 | 8 534 630 | 10 307 532 |
| Number of outlets | 48 | 50 | 50 |
| **Mom and pop stores** | | | |
| Sales ($) | 6 813 000 | 4 288 000 | 4 921 200 |
| Number of outlets | 1 365 | 1 126 | 883 |
| **Mass merchandiser** | | | |
| Sales ($) | 5 576 000 | 5 285 000 | 6 242 400 |
| Number of outlets | 1 | 1 | 1 |
| Total sales ($) | 42 153 577 | 41 423 114 | 42 764 798 |
| Total outlets | 2 010 | 1 790 | 1 554 |

The company made traditional furniture for the kitchen, dining room and bedroom (referred to as case goods in the industry) in three plants, all located in the Grand Rapids, Michigan, area. Much of the furniture was made from solid wood and was designed for long wear and usefulness.

# Industry Trends

The furniture industry was undergoing significant change. Most notably, a rash of acquisitions had resulted in a dramatic increase in concentration. In fact, the top 10 producers in the industry were growing at three times that of the industry. These were all firms that were staying very focused in their acquisition activities, unlike Berkron, which was a classic conglomerate with a diverse set of holdings. These large competitors were becoming increasingly difficult to deal with at the retail

**Exhibit 3**     Furniture gallery survey

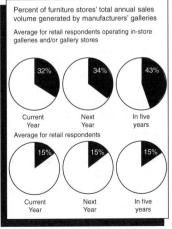

level. They were able to command large amounts of floor space in the retail sales environment, thus leaving little for the smaller producers to fight over.

Added to the problem of industry consolidation was the trend towards galleries in the retail stores (Exhibit 3). Galleries are areas in retail stores devoted entirely to the product offering of a single manufacturer. Areas can be as small as 1000 or as large as 10 000 square feet. Typically, the furniture is displayed in a setting similar to that found in a home with a room full of furniture, accessories, pictures and so on. This is in marked contrast to the traditional practice of displaying chairs in one area, couches in another, tables in another and so forth. Retailers welcome the opportunity to turn over merchandising to the manufacturer and appreciate the greater floor appeal created by the more professional display. On the other hand, they give up control of a significant amount of selling space. It also limits the number of manufacturers with which they can do business.

# Furniture Buyers

Furniture is most often viewed as a discretionary purchase, thus it is one of the first items in a family's budget that gets cut as the economy worsens. It is also still viewed primarily as a female-dominated decision even in the less traditional, more modern households. Although the industry often worries over the small portion of the typical household's budget devoted to furniture purchases, three out of five

**Exhibit 4**      Market analysis

- Fifty-five dealers operate galleries; 20 new galleries per year is the planned growth.
- The price/quality relationship is very important in Tyndall's markets. Tyndall currently enjoys a dominance in price and quality relative to its competitors.
- Tyndall's sales are to 1800 active dealer accounts with 400 key accounts.
- Sales to dealer inventories represent 95 per cent of dollar sales and 80 per cent of unit sales.
- The distribution of dollar sales by customer type is:

    small independents, 42 per cent
    galleries, 24 per cent
    mass merchandiser, 15 per cent
    mom and pop stores, 12 per cent
    large independents, 4 per cent
    small chains, 3 per cent.

- Consumers of Tyndall's furniture include: (a) an increasing population of people in the 35–55 age range who have increasing discretionary income; (b) 75 per cent of Tyndall's customers are blue-collar workers, who are hard working and want high-quality, long-lasting and traditional furniture.
- The 'ideal' customer lead time is four weeks from the receipt of the customer's order on the most popular items.

respondents to a survey by *Better Homes and Gardens* said they planned to buy some home furnishings in the next two years. Upholstery was mentioned by 59 per cent and case goods by 41 per cent. Traditional styles were favoured by 34 per cent of the respondents, with country favoured by 31 per cent.

Consumers said they visited 2.3 types of outlets before buying, with general furniture stores the most popular (62 per cent). Department stores were visited by 31 per cent and stores with brand-name furniture by 31 per cent. Brand-name furniture galleries were mentioned by 24 per cent. A store's reputation and service were the most frequently mentioned reasons for shopping at a particular store (cited by 68 per cent). Price was a reason for 63 per cent of the respondents.

Comfort (79 per cent), construction (74 per cent), durability (61 per cent) and styling/design (56 per cent) played the biggest role in the consumer's decision to buy a particular piece of furniture. Price was mentioned by 54 per cent.

Tyndall's customer profile matched much of that of the industry as a whole, but it also varied in some significant respects. Tyndall's customer could be typified as blue-collar, in the 35–55 age range, with an increasing level of discretionary income (Exhibit 4). As with other furniture manufacturers, the key decision maker is female. Tyndall's customers also tended to buy furniture in sets or collections rather than individual pieces from different lines.

# Competition

Tyndall faced a variety of manufacturers, particularly in the kitchen and dining room furniture markets. These competitors included:

- S. Bent
- Dinaire
- Virginia House
- Tell City
- Universal
- Kinkaid
- Cochran
- Temple Stuart

The firms' market share of 0.7 per cent has not suffered in competing with other large manufacturers. In this market, the price/value relationship is extremely important (Exhibit 4). Because the customer is looking for durability and wear with a style that will not go out of date, the initial purchase price is offset against the product's ability to provide years of service. Tyndall enjoys a dominance in this price and quality relationship relative to its major competitors. Through improvements in its manufacturing, the company is working on creating a technological and quality advantage. For example, the company is reducing its raw lumber costs by investing in an automated rough mill, and improving the furniture's surface finish by investing in the latest sanding technology.

**Exhibit 5**    Product line and design summary

> 1. Tyndall is building an image as a full-service manufacturer of furniture.
> 2. Tyndall focuses on solid-wood kitchen furniture in the upper portion of the medium-price range.
> 3. Tyndall manufactures five major collections of furniture:
>    (a) Lexington II: kitchen, dining room, and bedroom furniture in oak;
>    (b) Monroe: kitchen, dining room, and bedroom furniture in oak;
>    (c) Philadelphia: bedroom furniture in oak;
>    (d) Maddison: dining room and bedroom furniture in cherry;
>    (e) Scandinavian: line in oak.
> 4. Bedroom is a new high-growth area for the firm.
> 5. Dining-room furniture is a non-growth area because of the lack of capacity for chairs.
> 6. The Tyndall look is a 'safe' design that has been successful in the industry.
> 7. Six furniture groupings have been introduced by the firm in the last 11 years:
>    (a) Lexington dining room and kitchen group (eleven years ago);
>    (b) Monroe dining room and kitchen group (eight years ago)
>    (c) Philadelphia bedroom group (four years ago);
>    (d) Maddison dining room and bedroom group (three years ago);
>    (e) Lexington bedroom group (one year ago);
>    (f) Scandinavian group (last year).
> 8. The typical product life cycle for Tyndall's products is about 12 years.
> 9. Growth will come from product diversification.
> 10. Must avoid saturating a particular line.

# Marketing Strategy

## Products

Tyndall produced five major collections of furniture in oak and cherry wood
(Exhibit 5). Bedroom furniture was seen as a major growth area, while dining-room
furniture's growth was restricted by capacity constraints on chair construction.
While the typical style lasted for a 12-year period, sales over the period varied with
time. The first three to five years of a product's life saw dramatic growth. This was
followed by seven to nine years of modest growth. However, once decline set in, the
drop-off in sales was sharp. This made product design and new product introductions critical. Over the last 11 years, Tyndall had introduced six completely new
furniture groupings.

## Target Markets

Galleries were becoming an increasingly important fact of life (Exhibit 6), for a
number of reasons. Small dealers were disappearing due to consolidation in the
industry and the increasing price of entry. Also, manufacturers were finding it

**Exhibit 6**    Market trends

- A rapidly increasing number of furniture gallery outlets.
- The total number of dealers in the customer base is decreasing.
- Small dealers are concerned about manufacturers limiting their distribution of furniture.
- A reduction in the number of dealers sold to in the gallery communities.
- The furniture market includes an increasing number of 35–55 year olds who have increasing discretionary income, but the percentage of consumer discretionary income actually spent on furniture is decreasing.
- The investment barrier for becoming a dealer is increasing.
- Manufacturers have less tolerance for small customers.
- Small dealers cannot get some furniture lines.
- The big dealers are getting larger.
- The big chains are implementing acquisition programmes.
- Increasingly, the big dealers are coming to Tyndall's markets.
- The successful dealers tend to dominate their sales territories, and they tend to be 'determined' marketers with large advertising budgets.

increasingly difficult to serve a large number of small dealers. The retail market was also becoming more competitive due to the smaller portion of the typical consumer's budget being used to buy furniture.

For now, galleries, mass merchandisers and large independents seemed to offer the best growth opportunities, along with product diversification.

Geographically, Tyndall showed particular strength in the Mid-west and the North-east. Minnesota and North and South Dakota were particularly good markets for Tyndall's traditionally styled furniture. The South-west, Far West, North-west and Rocky Mountain states were not particularly strong markets.

# Pricing

Pricing of furniture varied across customers. For example, sales discounts on furniture sold by Tyndall varied from 9 per cent on products sold to mom and pop

**Exhibit 7**    Customer order data

| Customer type | Average sales discount (%) | Estimated average customer lead time (days) | Average number of end-product items shipped | Average dollars sales per year per customer ($) |
|---|---|---|---|---|
| Galleries | 21 | 35 | 52 | 206 151 |
| Mom and pop stores | 9 | 110 | 29 | 5 573 |
| Small independents | 17 | 35 | 41 | 30 221 |
| Large independents | 26 | 52 | 39 | 348 400 |
| Small chains | 22 | 44 | 43 | 99 220 |
| Mass merchandiser | 28 | 30 | 8 | 6 242 400 |

**Exhibit 8**     Average contribution to fixed costs and profit

| | Contribution per unit ($) |
|---|---|
| Product type | |
| Chairs | 24.11 |
| Tables | 125.42 |
| Case goods | 98.17 |
| Customer type | |
| Galleries | 39.77 |
| Mom and pop stores | 70.80 |
| Small independents | 52.79 |
| Large independents | 32.31 |
| Small chains | 31.09 |
| Mass merchandiser | 35.47 |

retailers to 28 per cent on products sold to the one mass merchandiser Tyndall served (Exhibit 7). Fortunately, discounters did not play much of a role in Tyndall's market or these discounts could have been even larger.

## Profitability

Because prices varied and because the product mix purchased differed from one customer type to another, average contributions also varied (Exhibit 8). Mom and pop stores yielded an average contribution per unit of $70.80, while small chains yielded only $31.09 per unit. There also was considerable variation in profitability across product types. Chairs contributed $24.11 per unit on average, while tables contributed $125.42.

## Sales Force

Tyndall did no exporting and little, if any, contract sales (to contractors, hotels, restaurants and so on). Thirty manufacturers' representatives handled the sales of Tyndall's products to its dealers, and most handled Tyndall's lines exclusively. Greg Procter was responsible for their activities and performance. He also was charged with the oversight of the production of sales literature, furniture industry journal advertising and furniture market participation.

Procter felt that a Tyndall dealer ought to have a strong financial position, be able to display the full line, be willing to place a minimum order of $3000 and do a minimum of $3000 per year of business with Tyndall. Otherwise, Procter felt that the effort to serve and maintain a relationship with a dealer could not be justified.

# Tyndall Furniture Company (B)

Don Rutkowski (vice-president, manufacturing) was just finishing his presentation of a proposal to invest in a new rough mill at the company's component plant in Grand Rapids, Michigan (see Exhibit 1). He concluded:

> It is most important that we come to a decision in the near future. As the issues involved have been discussed for some time now, the proposed investment is not something that's new to us all. However, in order to capitalize on the advantages that having a modernized rough mill will provide, an important consideration is to phase its introduction in line with marketing's plans for a new product range linked to the High Point Furniture Fair this time next year. Getting the timing right is often, as we all known, as important as the investment itself.

## Company Background

Established in 1898 by Henry H. Tyndall, the company remained a family-owned business until 1963, when it was bought out by Berkron Industries Inc., a large conglomerate with interests in textiles, chemicals, food, clothing, retailing and, more recently, financial services. Although predominantly based in North America, Berkron also has interests in Australasia and Europe.

Although in the past the company had been an above-average profit earner within the furniture industry as a whole, in recent years its performance had declined (see Exhibit 2), a fact that led to the appointment of Matt Culley as chief executive officer two years before. As with most markets, the furniture industry was both becoming increasingly more competitive and witnessing significant changes in both products and market outlets (see Exhibit 3).

This case was prepared by Professors W. L. Berry (Ohio State University), T. J. Hill (University of Oxford), J. E. Klompmaker (University of North Carolina) and W. G. Morrissey (North Carolina State University) as a basis for class discussion rather than to illustrate either effective or ineffective handling of a business situation. © Professor W. L. Berry, Professor J. E. Klompmaker, Professor W. G. Morrissey or AMD Publishing (UK). Inquiries in the USA to Zip Publishing, 1634 N. High Street, Columbus, Ohio 43201.

**Exhibit 1**    Tyndall Furniture Company (B)

---

TO: Tyndall Furniture Company Board of Directors
FROM: Don Rutkowski, Vice President of Manufacturing
SUBJECT: Proposed Rough Mill for the Tyndall Components Plant

We propose to purchase an Oliver rough mill to replace the current manual cross-cutting operation at the components plant. This mill would convert kiln-dried raw lumber into semi-finished dimension stock[1] for further processing in the fine mill, utilizing advanced computer-controlled machining and material handling systems. The new equipment would also include a Taylor edge-gluing system to increase the output of laminated dimension stock components for the chair, table and miscellaneous case goods assembly plants.

The overall impact of this proposal would be to increase the rough mill capacity to 230 per cent of the current capacity in terms of net board feet per day. All of this capacity increase will be used to decrease our dependence on outside suppliers for edge-glued dimension stock components. The purchase of edge-glued dimension stock components will decrease from the current level of 85 per cent to 15 per cent of the total requirements for these items. The overall production output of the other components produced by the components plant will not be significantly affected by this proposal.

The new equipment will increase the capacity of the rough mill and provide important cost savings in direct labour and material to enhance our competitive position in price-sensitive markets. Specific benefits include:

- Annual direct labour and dimension stock material savings of $1 million.
- Material cost savings by purchasing lower-grade raw lumber.
- Direct labour savings due to improved productivity (obtained by a 130 per cent increase in output with only a 10 per cent increase in direct labour) and reduced set-up time because families of parts can now be run on the moulding and tenoner machines.
- Reduced manufacturing lead times from four months to six weeks due to manufacturing instead of purchasing long lead-time dimension stock components.
- Improved product quality in chair-seat glued joints and other panel stock.
- Reduced work-in-progress inventory, finished component inventory, and component part shortages because of a more even flow of dimension stock material through the components plant. (Vendors currently tend to deliver material in large batches, which produces an undesirable mix of products that does not fit well with the manufacturing schedule, creating unnecessary levels of inventory.)

The investment cost of the new production process is $4.2 million. This includes the cost of extending the components plant building, the rough mill and edge-glueing equipment, the additional dry kiln capacity required, and the installation and training costs. If approved at the board of directors meeting at the end of this week, this equipment could be installed and in operation within a six-month period.

*Note*
**1**. Dimension stock is wood components ready for fine mill operations.

---

# Product Strategy

'Part of our decline', explained Greg Procter,

has been the failure in the past to offer an adequate product range. Understandably, our customers have been demanding a fuller product line as a key feature in boosting overall sales. Our principal furniture designs are Colonial and Early American, and within these 'looks' we use primarily oak and cherry woods.

**Exhibit 2**     Furniture industry comparisons (per cent)

| | Current year minus | | | | Current year |
|---|---|---|---|---|---|
| | **4** | **3** | **2** | **1** | |
| Tyndall | | | | | |
| Sales | 100.0 | 100.0 | 100.0 | 100.0 | 100.0 |
| Cost of goods sold | 79.1 | 78.3 | 78.3 | 79.2 | 78.1 |
| Net profit before tax | 4.8 | 3.7 | 4.4 | 3.5 | 4.2 |
| Return of total assets | 5.4 | 5.1 | 6.5 | 6.0 | 7.1 |
| Average all case goods companies | | | | | |
| Sales | 100.0 | 100.0 | 100.0 | – | – |
| Cost of goods sold | 75.9 | 75.2 | 76.7 | n.a. | n.a. |
| Net profit before tax | 7.7 | 7.4 | 7.3 | n.a. | n.a. |
| Return on total assets | n.a. | n.a. | 7.0 | n.a. | n.a. |
| Average all furniture companies | | | | | |
| Sales | 100.0 | 100.0 | 100.0 | – | – |
| Cost of goods sold | 75.6 | 74.6 | 75.1 | n.a. | n.a. |
| Net profit before tax | 7.6 | 8.3 | 8.4 | n.a. | n.a. |
| Return on total assets | 8.2 | 8.7 | 8.9 | n.a. | n.a. |

*Note*
n.a. signifies that the particular industry information is not available.

**Exhibit 3**     Tyndall sales analysis

| Market types | Current year minus | | Current year |
|---|---|---|---|
| | **2** | **1** | |
| Small chains | | | |
| Sales ($) | 1 188 189 | 1 468 848 | 1 389 077 |
| Number of outlets | 14 | 14 | 14 |
| Small independents | | | |
| Sales ($) | 19 417 109 | 20 005 636 | 18 162 589 |
| Number of outlets | 577 | 594 | 601 |
| Large independents | | | |
| Sales ($) | 1 504 000 | 1 841 000 | 1 742 000 |
| Number of outlets | 5 | 5 | 5 |
| Galleries | | | |
| Sales ($) | 7 655 279 | 8 534 630 | 10 307 532 |
| Number of outlets | 48 | 50 | 50 |
| Mom and pop stores | | | |
| Sales ($) | 6 813 000 | 4 288 000 | 4 921 200 |
| Number of outlets | 1 365 | 1 126 | 883 |
| Mass merchandiser | | | |
| Sales ($) | 5 576 000 | 5 285 000 | 6 242 400 |
| Number of outlets | 1 | 1 | 1 |
| Total sales ($) | 42 153 577 | 41 423 114 | 42 764 798 |
| Total outlets | 2 010 | 1 790 | 1 554 |

In order to enhance the styles they sell, many of the items are made of solid wood and, even where they use laminates, the products all look good and solid. One advantage of this has been that Tyndall enjoys relatively stable designs. In fact, their designs typically sell for 10 to 12 and even 15 years. This compares to the furniture industry as a whole, where designs sell over a much shorter product life cycle. Within these two sectors Tyndall's primary market focus is on kitchen and dining-room furniture in the upper portion of the medium-price range. In order to avoid saturating a particular line, they have in recent years been increasing efforts in the bedroom and upholstered product segments, recognizing that growth will also come from product diversification. In the last five years, they have introduced the equivalent of a new group of products each year, three of which were bedroom lines. (A group refers to a collection of products that go into one room in a home.)

Keeping marketing initiatives in line with manufacturing capabilities and capacity has been, however, an important and necessary consideration. 'It is', explained Greg, 'essential for the overall success of the business to take into account the available spare capacity within the different parts of manufacturing as one factor in new product range decisions'. While they could easily sell more kitchen furniture than they currently make, they have a problem in chair capacity that restricts overall sales. This factor has also made dining-room furniture a non-growth area. On the other hand, Tyndall now sees bedroom furniture as the new high-growth area for the firm, as they have more than adequate capacity in existing case good facilities to meet a significant increase in sales of these products. In that way, the company will best be able to improve overall company performance by increasing the utilization of existing investments in process capacity.

## Marketing Strategy

Greg went on to explain that the retail outlets for furniture sales had undergone changes in recent years (see Exhibit 4) and that recognizing these was important if the company wished to maintain its market share, let alone grow. He then continued to outline the marketing strategy being developed as having the following important features.

First, the company needs to continually review its product range. We must build on the good-quality image developed over the years by continuing to push hard in those segments in which our products already have a good position and in which we currently do well. In addition, we have recognized the need to consider other products that will help us develop new markets, both as a way to grow overall sales and to meet our customers' expectations with regard to our image as a full-service manufacturer.[1]

The second major feature is then to remain alert to the changes taking place in each of our segments. With regard to this last point, the large dealers are getting larger due to their successful acquisition programmes. In addition, we also recognize the increasing use of furniture galleries as an important means of getting our furniture in front of the

**Exhibit 4**    Furniture gallery survey

### F/T Survey: Manufacturers' Galleries at Retail

Furniture stores' average sales per sq. ft. for manufacturers' galleries

In-store $132    Free-standing $179

Percent of retail respondents operating manufacturers' galleries

In-store 47%

Free-standing 11%

**F**urniture/Today's third retail survey of manufacturers' gallery programmes outlines the current commitment furniture stores are making to gallery programmes.

The survey focuses on furniture stores only and two types of manufacturers' galleries: in-store galleries and free-standing gallery stores.

In-store galleries are those operated within a store and devoted completely to the lines of a single manufacturer. Excluded from the survey are galleries devoted to a single product, such as desks or upholstery, unless the merchandise happens to come from a single source.

Free-standing gallery stores are complete stores devoted to the lines of a single manufacturer. Examples include La-Z-Boy Showcase Shoppes and Ethan Allan stores.

Seventy-nine furniture retailers participated in F/T's survey. Twenty-one of these rank among F/T's Top 100 furniture retailers. Forty operate in-store galleries and/or gallery stores. Thirty-nine respondents operate neither.

Survey figures are based on varying numbers of respondents. Not all questions were relevant to all respondents' operations, and respondents did not answer every question. Thus the charts presented on these pages are often based on a sample of fewer than 79 retailers.

Survey information is based on the respondents experience during the past 12-month period.

Two charts on this page show the average sales per square foot manufacturers' galleries generate for furniture stores and the percentage of stores responding to the survey that operate galleries.

Other charts identify the amount of floor space devoted to and sales generated by manufacturers' galleries.

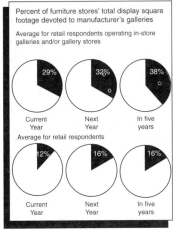

Percent of furniture stores' total display square footage devoted to manufacturer's galleries

Average for retail respondents operating in-store galleries and/or gallery stores

Current Year 29%    Next Year 32%    In five years 38%

Average for retail respondents

Current Year 12%    Next Year 16%    In five years 16%

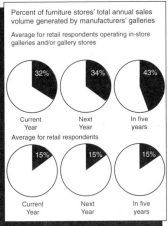

Percent of furniture stores' total annual sales volume generated by manufacturers' galleries

Average for retail respondents operating in-store galleries and/or gallery stores

Current Year 32%    Next Year 34%    In five years 43%

Average for retail respondents

Current Year 15%    Next Year 15%    In five years 15%

general public. It has been necessary, therefore, to ensure that we have an adequate presence in this segment as the total number of galleries eventually available will be limited. Fortunately, we saw this ahead of time and were early into the development. We intend to continue this initiative. Currently, we support 50 furniture galleries, and we intend to double that number in the next three years. In some ways, galleries provide two sets of advantages – on the one hand, the total segment sales are large, giving to us a homogeneous marketing thrust; while on the other, as each individual outlet is small, we do not experience the same level of customer pressure as we do with other large outlets. For this reason, we are giving considerable support to this segment, a fact that certainly is encouraging us to expand our product range, thus maximizing the level of product exposure to the public. Add the galleries initiative to our small independent market segment, and the combined sales represents two-thirds of our total sales.

We sell another 15 per cent through a mass merchandiser, which takes the overall to 81 per cent of total sales. Our policy, therefore, has been to try to keep a balance. Certainly we have deliberately limited sales to the mass merchandiser outlet as a policy of not putting too many eggs in this one basket. In addition, we are also pushing sales with small chains and large independents in order to create a more balanced portfolio within our segments. We know that mom and pops are declining and see little prospect in this segment for the future. These perspectives need to be reflected in the amount of effort and resource we are putting behind each segment. Keeping a watch on the various segments will give us the necessary balance we require while ensuring the necessary sales growth we need.

Our strategy has been aimed at contributing to the need to reverse the company's profit decline over recent years. By securing our future market outlets and expanding the product range offerings, we feel that this will not only safeguard the future but also make best use of manufacturing's capabilities and capacity in the short term.

## Manufacturing

The company has a number of plants in the Grand Rapids area. The component plant includes drying kilns, that take 'green' lumber and dry it before processing. The wood first goes through the rough mill and then the fine mill, and these components are then sent to the chair and case plants against agreed schedules. In addition, both the chair and case plants at Grand Rapids make some of the components they need while others are purchased from outside. The next stages are subassembly and assembly before a final product is finished and packed. Exhibits 5A and 5B give details of the various stages in manufacturing.

**Exhibit 5A**   Process flow chart

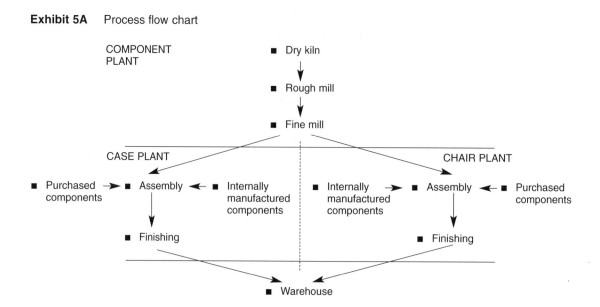

**Exhibit 5B**   Manufacturing process description

### Dry kiln

Green lumber must be dried to 6–8 per cent for use in furniture. This is accomplished through a combination of air drying and drying at elevated temperatures with forced air circulation in a dry kiln. The kiln-drying process can take from one to eight weeks, depending on such factors as species, thickness and initial moisture content. To cope with the mix required, a number of kilns are typically installed.

### Rough mill

The function of the rough mill is to convert rough lumber into blank parts that are free of defects and ready for detail machining. The defects are removed in the rough mill in the process of cutting up the boards. Depending on the parts specifications, the defect-free boards are then either edge-glued into wide panels or machined in the moulder into appropriate shapes. The processing of the lumber is performed on equipment that is normally connected by conveyors so that there is a continuous flow of the work in process. The rough mill process generates about 40 per cent waste based on the board feet of lumber brought in, and so it is an important cost-control centre in the whole manufacturing process.

### Fine mill

Parts are processed into final shapes and dimensions in the fine mill using a wide variety of machine types. The operations performed include turning, shaping, routing, sawing, bending, boring and a variety of sanding steps, with some of these operations being performed in combination on special equipment. The company has been quite creative in linking various machines together with special conveyors so that parts such as chair turnings, bent chair-back bows, chair seats, and drawer sides and backs can be economically processed in large production runs. The trade-off in these process developments has been long set-up times for low processing times and decreased work in progress. This type of equipment has been utilized most extensively in the chair plant. The machinery in the case plant is arranged so that tables, panels and solid-wood rails follow their own flow paths. This provides for easier control of the flow of these parts from operation to operation. Materials handling is by skids that are moved by 'jack boys' using hydraulic lift jacks.

### Assembly

Parts are accumulated until all of the necessary parts to complete an item are on hand. The final assembly is carried out in a variety of hand and mechanical operations that are grouped for tables, cases and chairs in separate sections of the plant. Wherever possible, these operations have been arranged on conveyors so the flow is easily controlled and paced. Various fitting and hand-sanding operations are performed along these conveyors so that when the assembled items reach the finishing room they are ready for the finishing process.

### Finishing

Tables and cases are finished on a palletized conveyor with the pallets driven through the finishing steps in a continuous flow. Chairs are placed on an overhead conveyor. The various spray booths and ovens are sized for the speed at which the conveyor is designed to operate so that there is time to perform the various spraying operations and dry the different finish coats.

'Most of our products go through the main production lines', explained Don Rutkowski,

> although some are handled (in part) in an off-line mode because of the low volumes involved. Over the years we have continuously improvised and improved our processes in order to reduce process times. This has enabled us not only to reduce direct labour costs but also to increase effective capacity. Whenever possible, we have attempted to increase throughput while ensuring that quality levels have been maintained.

The various types of product that comprise a furniture group within one of the furniture styles are made in Tyndall's own production plant. As implied by its name, the chair plant makes all the chair designs called for in any of the numerous groups within each furniture style. Currently, this totals over 60 chair types. All the other items that go into a furniture group are made in the case plant (see Exhibit 5A). Although, as explained earlier, some component parts are brought in from outside, there are very few instances when an actual furniture product is purchased complete. 'It is imperative that we retain control over our quality', explained Don, 'a factor that underlines the proposal to invest in the new rough mill facility' (see Exhibit 1). Finished items are then collated to meet outstanding customers' orders or otherwise go into inventory to support future sales.

The three plants (component, chair and case) primarily work on a single, eight-hour shift, with overtime as required. At certain times in the year the different plants do work a second shift. However, within the furniture industry there is a strong and well-established argument against double-shift working, especially with regard to maintaining high quality levels. 'In order to meet demand, it is imperative that we keep the processes well scheduled to avoid delays elsewhere', explained Don. 'The only capacity problems we have concern the chair plant, particularly in the seating and finishing processes.' He continued by explaining that overtime is worked at most times of the year, which helps keep good schedules and reduce waiting time in the plant.

'The relatively long life cycle for our typical products and the stability of our product designs generate greater total volumes over the life of a product and underpin our process improvement strategy. We are making an increasingly wide range of products', he commented, 'and the range of shopfloor order quantities varies significantly. However, we feel we are up to the task in all aspects of the job.' He then highlighted the good product designs that the company had consistently provided and the excellent image it currently enjoyed in the marketplace in terms of the quality of its products. 'Some species of wood', commented Don, 'are more difficult to process than others (for example, cherry is more demanding than oak), and this leads to a higher reject level in the process. However, we have a good quality control system, that helps maintain the high standards necessary in the segments in which we compete.'

Exhibits 6–9 show data on representative current products, and Exhibit 10 reports order-winning and qualifying criteria.

**Exhibit 6**    Representative current products[1]

| Item number | Description (year of introduction[2]) | ABC code[3] | Current year annual sales (units) | Production line | Production (units/eight-hour shift)[4] |
|---|---|---|---|---|---|
| B2089 | Table, Maddison cherry dining-room group (3) | B | 635 | Table | 133 |
| B2126 | Chair, Maddison cherry dining-room group (3) | B | 1 826 | Chair | 675 |
| B2241 | Chest, Maddison cherry dining-room group (3) | C | 70 | Case | 190 |
| C2313 | Dresser, Tyler cherry bedroom group (3) | B | 365 | Case | 145 |
| B2474 | Headboard, Maddison cherry dining-room group (3) | C | 183 | Case | 130 |
| A1073 | Table, Monroe oak kitchen group (8) | C | 155 | Table | 126 |
| A1085 | Table, Monroe oak kitchen group (8) | A | 543 | Table | 222 |
| A1106 | Chair, Monroe oak kitchen group (8) | AA | 10 841 | Chair | 1400 |
| A1024 | Table, Lexington oak kitchen group (11) | A | 2 156 | Table | 281 |
| A1145 | Chair, Lexington oak kitchen group (11) | B | 758 | Chair | 30 |
| A1126 | Chair, Lexington oak kitchen group (11) | AA | 33 170 | Chair | 1100 |
| C2201 | Chest, Lexington oak bedroom group (1) | A | 729 | Case | 300 |
| C1221 | Chest, Lexington oak bedroom group (1) | B | 214 | Case | 160 |
| C1424 | Headboard, Lexington oak bedroom group (1) | C | 15 | Case | 165 |
| C1544 | Footboard, Lexington oak bedroom group (1) | C | 10 | Case | 175 |
| C1457 | Headboard, Philadelphia oak bedroom group (4) | C | 3 | Case | 90 |
| C1567 | Footboard, Philadelphia oak bedroom group (4) | C | 1 | Case | 115 |

*Notes*

1. The products selected here are representative of the wide range of products in terms of ABC code, related annual units produced, production line and year of introduction.
2. The figure following description denotes the number of years since this item was introduced, so item B2089 was introduced three years ago.
3. The code letters in this column are the company's designation relating to the number of units produced each year: AA = Very high-volume items selected by management; A = remainder of items; B = chairs, 401–2000 units/year; cases, 201–1000 units/year; tables and pedestals, 201–800 units/year; C = chairs, 0–400 units/year; all others, 0–200 units/year.
4. Low-volume items are frequently made off-line with varying labour levels being allocated. This accounts for the low production rate in some instances (for example, A1145).
5. Tables are assembled and finished in the case plant.

**Exhibit 7**  Current year's data for representative current products[1]

| Item number | Wholesale list price ($) | Average selling price ($) | Unit variable cost ($) | Defects per 1000 units shipped[2] | Average inventory (units) | Average sales order backlog (units) |
|---|---|---|---|---|---|---|
| B2089 | 419 | 384 | 267 | 74 | 349 | 69 |
| B2126 | 100 | 96 | 60 | 18 | 735 | 179 |
| B2241 | 356 | 357 | 178 | 140 | 12 | 21 |
| C2313 | 494 | 485 | 378 | 11 | 20 | 53 |
| B2474 | 219 | 202 | 126 | 283 | 65 | 36 |
| A1073 | 418 | 384 | 138 | 19 | 23 | 11 |
| A1085 | 272 | 198 | 113 | 8 | 29 | 345 |
| A1106 | 66 | 51 | 23 | 0 | 73 | 1 806 |
| A1024 | 209 | 144 | 87 | 15 | 459 | 824 |
| A1145 | 119 | 102 | 69 | 0 | 30 | 114 |
| A1126 | 99 | 74 | 43 | 2 | 1 078 | 11 132 |
| C2201 | 159 | 159 | 130 | 0 | 476 | 370 |
| C1221 | 359 | 346 | 210 | 0 | 66 | 100 |
| C1424 | 279 | 239 | 135 | 0 | 29 | 1 |
| C1544 | 190 | 170 | 98 | 0 | 38 | 2 |
| C1457 | 303 | 250 | 119 | 0 | 29 | 1 |
| C1567 | 192 | 158 | 105 | 0 | 31 | 1 |

*Notes*
1. All figures have been rounded to the nearest whole number.
2. Average number of defects per 1000 units shipped to customers.

**Exhibit 8**  Customer order data

| Customer type | Average sales discount (%) | Contribution to fixed costs and profit/unit ($) | Average lead (days)[1] | Average defects/ 1000 units shipped | Average assembly line hours/ unit | Estimated no. of end-product items shipped to each customer type | Average sales $/year/ customer |
|---|---|---|---|---|---|---|---|
| Galleries | 21 | 39.77 | 35 | 11 | 0.0153 | 52 | 206 151 |
| Mom and pop stores | 9 | 70.80 | 110 | 7 | 0.0188 | 29 | 5 573 |
| Small independents | 17 | 52.79 | 35 | 11 | 0.0206 | 41 | 30 221 |
| Large independents | 26 | 32.31 | 52 | 2 | 0.0114 | 39 | 348 400 |
| Small chains | 22 | 31.09 | 44 | 10 | 0.0126 | 43 | 99 220 |
| Mass merchandisers | 28 | 35.47 | 30 | 7 | 0.0110 | 8 | 6 242 400 |

*Note*
1. All customers tend to want delivery of products as soon as possible. The lead times given in this column are the average delivery times which the company provides for all products and hence reflects company preference and customer leverage.

**Exhibit 9**    Current year's manufacturing data

| Production line | Sales discount percentage | Defects per 1000 units shipped | Lead Time (days)[1] | Contribution to fixed costs and expenses per unit ($) | Chair plant capacity utilization | | Percentage of items stocked in finished-goods inventory |
| | | | | | Percentage run time | Percentage set-up time | |
|---|---|---|---|---|---|---|---|
| Case goods | 2 | 41 | 8 | 74.51 | | | |
| Chairs | 24 | 2 | 44 | 30.53 | | | |
| Tables | 22 | 24 | 15 | 80.67 | | | |
| ABC categories[2] | | | | | | | |
| AA | 25 | 2 | 47 | 30.26 | 23 | 5 | 6 |
| A | 25 | 10 | 24 | 55.48 | 20 | 4 | 18 |
| B | 6 | 22 | 23 | 61.40 | 36 | 4 | 29 |
| C | 7 | 148 | 2 | 153.99 | 7 | 1 | 47 |
| Total | | | | | 86 | 14 | 100 |

*Notes*

1. Lead times are the average days taken to deliver items within each product type or category. They reflect the fact that some products are held in finished-goods inventory while others have order-backlog requirements.

2. AA = Very high-volume items selcted by management; A = Remainder of items; B = Chairs, 401–2000 units/year; cases, 201–1000 units/year; tables and pedestals, 201–800 units/year; C = Chairs, 0–400 units/year; all others, 0–200 units/year.

## Manufacturing Strategy

Don Rutkowski then outlined the rationale behind the principal investments and improvements that manufacturing had successfully introduced over the last few years. 'We have been trying to pursue a number of improvements within manufacturing to be better able to support our products in the marketplace', he explained.

Although there are numerous examples of small but important improvements in all the plants, we have been pursuing two principal activities whenever they made sense. One has been to automate processes, such as the table leg turning system, in order to reduce direct labour costs, increase output levels, maintain a more consistent level of quality, and enable us to gain a greater control over scheduling. The second initiative has been to link a number of processes together within a series so that a product goes through two or more operations before it comes out of the process. An example of this is our multiple-head boring machine. In addition to the gains similar to those secured by automation, these initiatives also have reduced work-in-progress inventory in the particular part of the process involved. Of course, and it almost goes without saying, we have also increased capacity by these investments, a factor high in our priorities.

**Exhibit 10**   Order-winning and qualifying criteria[1]

| | Small chain | | | Large independent | | | Small independent | | | Mass merchandiser | | | Gallery | | | Mom and pop stores | | |
|---|---|---|---|---|---|---|---|---|---|---|---|---|---|---|---|---|---|---|
| | C[2] | 2 | 5 | C | 2 | 5 | C | 2 | 5 | C | 2 | 5 | C | 2 | 5 | C | 2 | 5 |
| *Lexington/Philadelphia – Bedroom, High–Medium Volume (items C2201, C1221)* | | | | | | | | | | | | | | | | | | |
| Quality conformance | 60 | 60 | 55 | 60 | 55 | 50 | 60 | 60 | 60 | | 60 | 60 | 60 | 50 | 55 | 60 | 50 | 50 |
| Price | QQ[3] | QQ | 35 | QQ | 35 | 40 | QQ | QQ | 20 | | 30 | 30 | 20 | 30 | 35 | QQ | 10 | 10 |
| After-sales service | 10 | 10 | 10 | 10 | 10 | 10 | 10 | 10 | 20 | | 5 | 5 | 20 | 20 | 10 | | | |
| Delivery reliability | QQ | QQ | QQ | QQ | QQ | QQ | QQ | QQ | Q[3] | | 5 | 5 | QQ | QQ | QQ | | | |
| Design | 30 | 30 | Q | 30 | Q | Q | 30 | 30 | Q | | Q | Q | Q | Q | Q | | | |
| Design changes | | | | | | | | | | | | | | | | | | |
| New products | | | | | | | | | | | | | | | | | | |
| Customer relations | Q | Q | Q | Q | Q | Q | Q | Q | Q | | QQ | QQ | Q | Q | Q | 40 | 40 | 40 |
| *Lexington/Philadelphia – Bedroom, Low Volume (items C1424, C1544, C1457, C1567)* | | | | | | | | | | | | | | | | | | |
| Quality conformance | | | | | | | 40 | 40 | 40 | | | | 50 | 50 | 50 | 40 | 40 | 40 |
| Price | | | | | | | Q | Q | Q | | | | 10 | 10 | 10 | Q | Q | Q |
| After-sales service | | | | | | | Q | Q | Q | | | | 5 | 5 | 5 | Q | Q | Q |
| Delivery reliability | | | | | | | Q | Q | Q | | | | QQ | QQ | QQ | Q | Q | Q |
| Design | | | | | | | 60 | 60 | 60 | | | | 35 | 35 | 35 | 60 | 60 | 60 |
| Design changes | | | | | | | | | | | | | | | | | | |
| New products | | | | | | | | | | | | | | | | | | |
| Customer relations | | | | | | | | | | | | | | | | | | |
| *Tyler Cherry – Bedroom, High Volume (items C2313, B2474)* | | | | | | | | | | | | | | | | | | |
| Quality conformance | 40 | 40 | 40 | | | | 50 | 50 | 50 | | | | 50 | 50 | 50 | 55 | 55 | 55 |
| Price | 15 | 20 | 25 | | | | 20 | 25 | 35 | | | | 20 | 25 | 35 | Q | 10 | 15 |
| After-sales service | 10 | 10 | 10 | | | | 10 | 10 | 10 | | | | 10 | 10 | 10 | 10 | 10 | 10 |
| Delivery reliability | Q | Q | Q | | | | QQ | QQ | QQ | | | | QQ | QQ | QQ | Q | Q | Q |
| Design | 35 | 30 | 25 | | | | 20 | 15 | 5 | | | | 20 | 15 | 5 | 35 | 25 | 20 |
| Design changes | | | | | | | | | | | | | | | | | | |
| New products | | | | | | | | | | | | | | | | | | |
| Customer relations | Q | Q | Q | | | | Q | Q | Q | | | | Q | Q | Q | Q | | |

*Maddison Cherry – Dining Room, High–Medium Volume (items B2089, B2126)*

| | | | | | | | | |
|---|---|---|---|---|---|---|---|---|
| Quality conformance | 50 | 50 | 50 | 50 | 50 | 55 | 55 | 55 |
| Price | 25 | 30 | 20 | 25 | 30 | 20 | 10 | 20 |
| After-sales service | 10 | 10 | 10 | 10 | 10 | Q | 10 | 10 |
| Delivery reliability | QQ | QQ | QQ | QQ | QQ | Q | QQ | Q |
| Design | 15 | 10 | 20 | 15 | 10 | 35 | 25 | 15 |
| Design changes | | | | | | | | |
| New products | | | | | | | | |
| Customer relations | QQ | QQ | QQ | QQ | QQ | Q | QQ | QQ |

*Maddison/Tyler cherry – Bed/Dining Room, Low Volume (item B2241)*

| | | | | | | | | |
|---|---|---|---|---|---|---|---|---|
| Quality conformance | 40 | 40 | 40 | 50 | 50 | 40 | 40 | 40 |
| Price | Q | Q | Q | 10 | 10 | Q | Q | Q |
| After-sales service | Q | Q | Q | 5 | 5 | Q | Q | Q |
| Delivery reliability | Q | Q | Q | QQ | QQ | Q | Q | Q |
| Design | 60 | 60 | 60 | 35 | 35 | 60 | 60 | 60 |
| Design changes | | | | | | | | |
| New products | | | | | | | | |
| Customer relations | Q | Q | Q | Q | Q | Q | Q | Q |

*Monroe/Lexington Oak – Chairs/Case Goods/Tables, High Volume (items A1106, A1126)*

| | | | | | | | | |
|---|---|---|---|---|---|---|---|---|
| Quality conformance | 50 | 50 | 40 | 50 | 60 | 60 | 50 | 50 |
| Price | 40 | 40 | 50 | 40 | 20 | 30 | 40 | 10 |
| After-sales service | 10 | 10 | 10 | 10 | 20 | 10 | 10 | 10 |
| Delivery reliability | QQ | QQ | QQ | QQ | Q | QQ | QQ | Q |
| Design | Q | Q | Q | Q | Q | Q | Q | Q |
| Design changes | | | | | | | | |
| New products | | | | | | | | |
| Customer relations | Q | Q | Q | Q | QQ | QQ | Q | Q |

(continued)

**Exhibit 10**  Order-winning and qualifying criteria (cont'd)

| | Small chain | | | Large independent | | | Small independent | | | Mass merchandiser | | | Gallery | | | Mom and pop store | | |
|---|---|---|---|---|---|---|---|---|---|---|---|---|---|---|---|---|---|---|
| | C | 2 | 5 | C | 2 | 5 | C | 2 | 5 | C | 2 | 5 | C | 2 | 5 | C | 2 | 5 |
| *Monroe/Lexington Oak – Kitchen, Medium Volume (item A1085)* | | | | | | | | | | | | | | | | | | |
| Quality conformance | 55 | 50 | 45 | 55 | 50 | 45 | 60 | 55 | 50 | | | | 50 | 45 | 40 | 50 | 50 | 50 |
| Price | 35 | 40 | 45 | 35 | 40 | 45 | 20 | 30 | 40 | | | | 30 | 35 | 40 | 10 | 20 | 30 |
| After-sales service | 10 | 10 | 10 | 10 | 10 | 10 | 20 | 15 | 10 | | | | 20 | 20 | 20 | | Q | Q |
| Delivery reliability | QQ | QQ | QQ | QQ | QQ | QQ | Q | QQ | Q | | | | QQ | QQ | QQ | | QQ | QQ |
| Design | Q | Q | Q | Q | Q | Q | Q | QQ | QQ | | | | Q | Q | Q | | QQ | QQ |
| Design changes | | | | | | | | | | | | | | | | | | |
| New products | | | | | | | | | | | | | | | | | | |
| Customer relations | Q | QQ | QQ | Q | QQ | QQ | Q | Q | QQ | | | | Q | QQ | QQ | 40 | 30 | 20 |
| *Monroe/Lexington Oak – Kitchen/Dining Room, Low Volume (item A1073)* | | | | | | | | | | | | | | | | | | |
| Quality conformance | 60 | 60 | 60 | 60 | 60 | 60 | 60 | 60 | 60 | | | | 50 | 50 | 50 | 30 | 30 | 30 |
| Price | Q | Q | Q | Q | Q | Q | Q | Q | Q | | | | 10 | 10 | 10 | Q | Q | Q |
| After-sales service | 10 | 10 | 10 | 10 | 10 | 10 | 10 | 10 | 10 | | | | 10 | 10 | 10 | Q | Q | Q |
| Delivery reliability | Q | Q | Q | Q | Q | Q | Q | Q | Q | | | | Q | Q | Q | Q | Q | Q |
| Design | 30 | 30 | 30 | 30 | 30 | 30 | 30 | 30 | 30 | | | | 30 | 30 | 30 | 30 | 30 | 30 |
| Design changes | | | | | | | | | | | | | | | | | | |
| New products | | | | | | | | | | | | | | | | | | |
| Customer relations | Q | Q | Q | Q | Q | Q | | | | | | | Q | Q | Q | 40 | 40 | 40 |

*Notes*

1. Blanks indicate that these products are not (or will not be) sold to the particular type of customer.
2. C = current year; 2 = in two years; 5 = in five years.
3. Q denotes a qualifier. QQ denotes an order-losing sensitive qualifier.

## Corporate Overview

'As a company', reflected Matt Culley,

> we have been attempting to reverse the decline in profits experienced over the last 10 years. We recognize that the source of the problem lies both in marketing and manufacturing. What we make and where we sell it is a prerequisite for success. Couple the recent and proposed process investments and we should have the plant in better shape. Certainly we are looking to the substantial improvements provided by the proposed rough mill to lead the way to better profits.

## Note

1. A full-service manufacturer is a company that produces a wide range of furniture products including case and upholstered furniture.

# 22 Tyndall Furniture Company (C)

The proposal for the new shopfloor control system has been in your hands for a week now, and I would like to schedule a meeting to discuss it tomorrow morning at nine. We have all had high hopes that this would help us to improve delivery performance and productivity. Now is the time to review it and see if we feel this is the system for us.

Don Rutkowski was just concluding a meeting with his plant managers and key staff people. A great deal of work had gone into the preparation of this proposal and management was enthusiastic about it.

## Company Background

Established in 1898 by Henry H. Tyndall, the company remained a family-owned business until 1963, when it was bought by a large conglomerate, Berkron Industries Inc. The Tyndall Furniture Company had grown conservatively in its production of dining-room and bedroom furniture in primarily Early American designs. The company wanted to grow at a faster rate to take advantage of some market opportunities and to increase its profitability, which was trailing most of the industry. One of the expansion moves currently underway involved the acquisition of a nearby plant producing fully upholstered furniture, which is a new product category to Tyndall. Adding fully upholstered furniture to its line would open new opportunities in living-room furniture while increasing the company's appeal to dealers as a full-product-line supplier.

## Marketing and Product Strategy

'Sales in our market segments have been shifting somewhat over the past several years. We intend to double our in-store galleries while continuing our retreat from the mom and pop segment', stated Greg Procter.

This case was prepared by Professors W. L. Berry (Ohio State University), T. J. Hill (University of Oxford), J. E. Klompmaker (University of North Carolina) and W. G. Morrissey (North Carolina State University) as a basis for class discussion rather than to illustrate either effective or ineffective handling of an administrative situation. © Professor W. L. Berry, Professor J. E. Klompmaker, Professor W. G. Morrissey or AMD Publishing (UK). Inquiries in the USA to Zip Publishing, 1634 N. High Street, Columbus, Ohio 43201.

The mass merchandiser is obviously an important customer, but we do not want to become too dependent on a single customer, so we have tended to limit our sales with that customer. At the same time we need to stay sensitive to developments in our other market segments and remain flexible enough to respond to these changes while achieving a 10 per cent annual growth rate in total sales.

Our past product strategy has been part of our current problem in achieving more growth. We have been short of dining room chair capacity while having some surplus case capacity. This recently prompted us to bring out more bedroom groups, taking advantage of the available case capacity. It is nearly impossible to closely control our sales in each category, and it is apparent that at some point we will have to increase our production capacity in order to service our customers. In the meantime, we have kept our delivery commitments to key dealers by giving them first priority on available-to-ship products. [See Exhibit 10 in Case 21 for a review of the order winners in the company's different markets.]

# Manufacturing

The company has a number of plants in the Grand Rapids area. The component plant, which is some distance outside Grand Rapids, includes the dry kilns that take green lumber and dry it before processing. The rough mill removes all defects from the lumber to produce 'blanks', which then are processed into finished parts in the machining and sanding departments of the component plant. Some blanks are obtained from outside suppliers. The component plant supplies parts to the case plant. It is scheduled to start supplying parts to the case plant and to the fully upholstered plant in the near future. The chair plant machines all its own parts on separate facilities.

Don Rutkowski, in discussing the machining of fully upholstered parts, explained:

There is sufficient kiln capacity. Our equipment and people are more than adequate to machine these parts. Fully upholstered parts are made from lower-grade lumber, require less machining, and are not sanded so they will not materially add to our work load. The dowel joints used in upholstered furniture construction do not require the more complex machining of the products in our current product line. The typical upholstery plant has rather rudimentary equipment compared to the sophisticated machinery we have so we should have no trouble.

The plants primarily work on a single, eight-hour shift, with overtime as required. At certain times in the year the plants do work a second shift. However, within the furniture industry there is a reluctance to work a double shift because of quality and supervision problems, a view which has been substantiated over time.

'The relatively long life cycle for our typical products and the stability of our product designs generate greater total volumes over the life of a product and underpin our process improvement strategy. However, we are making an increasingly wide range of products', Don Rutkowski commented, 'and the range of

**Exhibit 1**   Current year's manufacturing data

| Production line | Customer lead time (days) | Production contribution ($) | Units | Current year's sales $ | Percentage of total |
|---|---|---|---|---|---|
| Chairs | 44 | 30.53 | 277 400 | 22 194 800 | 51.9 |
| Tables | 15 | 80.67 | 29 699 | 5 345 700 | 12.5 |
| Cases | 8 | 74.51 | 41 148 | 15 224 300 | 35.6 |
| Total | | | | 42 764 800 | 100.0 |

| ABC categories[1] | Customer lead time (days) | Contribution ($) | Percentage items in finished-goods inventory |
|---|---|---|---|
| AA | 47 | 30.26 | 6 |
| A | 24 | 55.48 | 18 |
| B | 23 | 61.40 | 29 |
| C | 2 | | 47 |
| | | 153.99 | 100.0 |

*Note*

1. AA = Very high-volume items selected by management; A = Remainder of items; B = Chairs, 401–2000 units/year; cases, 201–1000 units/year; tables and pedestals, 201–800 units/year; C = Chairs, 0–400 units/year; all others, 0–200 units/year.

**Exhibit 2**    Plant loading and scheduling rules

---

**Order point**

| ABC Class | Order point calculation | |
|---|---|---|
| | Chairs/cases lead time = 16 | Tables/pedestals lead time = 13 |
| AA | D × LT + BS | D × LT + BS |
| A | D (LT − 7) | D (LT − 7) |
| B | D (LT − 13) | 0 |
| C | 0 for 10 weeks | 0 for 13 weeks |

- D = forecasted weekly demand for an item; LT = lead time in weeks; and BS = buffer stock quantity.
- Order when available to sell < order point.
- Available to sell = inventory + on order − backlog.
- Reviewed quarterly.

**Order quantity**

Order quantity = 52D/number of cuttings per year, where the number of cuttings per year for AA = 8, A = 4, B = 2 and C = 1 (reviewed quarterly).

**Master production scheduling**

- AA and A items are loaded first.
- Schedules are created by loading forward to individual items' daily capacities and with an allowance for set-up time on critical operations.
- Schedules are created irregularly every one to four weeks.

---

production order quantities varies significantly. We do feel we are up to the task in all aspects of the job.' Don then highlighted the good product designs that the company had consistently provided and the excellent image it currently enjoys in the market-place in terms of the quality of its products.

'Greg Procter has expressed his concerns about maintaining reliable deliveries in the face of capacity problems.' Don was obviously concerned as he made these comments:

Currently I estimate that we are running at 100 per cent of our chair capacity while the table and case lines are at 90 and 80 per cent levels each [Exhibit 1]. We are going to have to do some careful analysis of this situation in view of some of the changes that are taking place. It takes two years to build and bring new capacity on-line.

## Manufacturing Planning and Control System

The current MPC system began with master production scheduling being done by Jack Joyner in the marketing division. Jack described his procedures thus:

**Exhibit 3** Representative item inventory status

| Item number | ABC code | Production line | Weekly demand | Inventory | | | Scheduled production | Backlog | | Available to sell |
|---|---|---|---|---|---|---|---|---|---|---|
| | | | | gross | weeks | allocated | | orders | weeks | |
| 7344 | A | Case | 17 | 264 | 15.5 | 13 | 99 | 238 | 14.0 | 112 |
| 6306 | A | Case | 24 | 32 | 1.3 | 32 | 341 | 183 | 7.6 | 158 |
| 3461 | A | Chair | 24 | 151 | 6.3 | 151 | 500 | 484 | 20.2 | 16 |
| 6212 | A | Chair | 112 | 928 | 8.3 | 284 | 3 500 | 655 | 5.8 | 3 489 |
| 1247 | A | Chair | 26 | 0 | 0.0 | 0 | 599 | 483 | 18.6 | 116 |
| 6011 | A | Table | 22 | 1 050 | 47.7 | 9 | 440 | 761 | 34.6 | 720 |
| 4151 | A | Table | 15 | 0 | 0.0 | 0 | 350 | 224 | 14.9 | 126 |
| 6036 | A | Table | 36 | 130 | 3.6 | 24 | 2 304 | 1 491 | 41.4 | 919 |
| 4264 | AA | Chair | 43 | −11 | −0.3 | 33 | 0 | 487 | 11.3 | −531 |
| 6261 | AA | Chair | 883 | 0 | 0.0 | 0 | 15 500 | 11 781 | 13.3 | 3 719 |
| 6186 | AA | Table | 19 | 15 | 0.8 | 3 | 342 | 129 | 6.8 | 225 |
| 4197 | AA | Table | 22 | 130 | 5.9 | 26 | 196 | 121 | 5.5 | 179 |
| 3306 | B | Case | 6 | 58 | 9.7 | 51 | 0 | 10 | 1.7 | −3 |
| 6313 | B | Case | 13 | 66 | 5.1 | 2 | 100 | 100 | 7.7 | 64 |
| 4337 | B | Case | 9 | 71 | 7.9 | 21 | 248 | 37 | 4.1 | 261 |
| 4310 | B | Case | 9 | 14 | 1.6 | 1 | 306 | 106 | 11.8 | 213 |
| 6324 | B | Case | 3 | 65 | 21.7 | 3 | 100 | 31 | 10.3 | 131 |
| 7355 | B | Case | 4 | 88 | 22.0 | 2 | 0 | 36 | 9.0 | 50 |
| 1310 | B | Case | 5 | 79 | 15.8 | 5 | 139 | 69 | 13.8 | 144 |

| | | | | | | | | | | |
|---|---|---|---|---|---|---|---|---|---|---|
| 1600 | B | Chair | 6 | 76 | 12.7 | 0 | 0 | 61 | 10.2 | 15 |
| 6296 | B | Chair | 12 | 64 | 5.3 | 26 | 0 | 55 | 4.6 | −17 |
| 1085 | B | Table | 2 | 131 | 65.5 | 0 | 0 | 22 | 11.0 | 109 |
| 6138 | B | Table | 2 | 23 | 11.5 | 0 | 50 | 23 | 11.5 | 50 |
| 4158 | B | Table | 10 | 0 | 0.0 | 0 | 198 | 113 | 11.3 | 85 |
| 4129 | B | Table | 3 | 22 | 7.3 | 0 | 100 | 17 | 5.7 | 105 |
| 1337 | C | Case | 1 | 76 | 76.0 | 0 | 0 | 8 | 8.0 | 68 |
| 7322 | C | Case | 3 | 81 | 27.0 | 0 | 0 | 32 | 10.7 | 49 |
| 6378 | C | Case | 1 | 0 | 0.0 | 0 | 30 | 3 | 3.0 | 27 |
| 7352 | C | Case | 2 | 0 | 0.0 | 0 | 40 | 11 | 5.5 | 29 |
| 1341 | C | Case | 2 | 5 | 2.5 | 1 | 39 | 12 | 6.0 | 31 |
| 6344 | C | Case | 2 | 123 | 61.5 | 0 | 0 | 25 | 12.5 | 98 |
| 1324 | C | Case | 1 | 31 | 31.0 | 1 | 100 | 13 | 13.0 | 117 |
| 6511 | C | Chair | 6 | 2 | 0.3 | 2 | 200 | 71 | 11.8 | 129 |
| 6256 | C | Chair | 1 | 79 | 79.0 | 0 | 399 | 34 | 34.0 | 444 |
| 6274 | C | Chair | 1 | 553 | 553.0 | 1 | 0 | 59 | 59.0 | 493 |
| 4270 | C | Chair | 4 | 133 | 33.3 | 0 | 0 | 60 | 15.0 | 73 |
| 4351 | C | Chair | 1 | 5 | 5.0 | 2 | 0 | 15 | 15.0 | −12 |
| 2191 | C | Table | 14 | 0 | 0.0 | 0 | 250 | 187 | 13.4 | 63 |
| 1097 | C | Table | 2 | 90 | 45.0 | 2 | 0 | 21 | 10.5 | 67 |
| 2136 | C | Table | 1 | 16 | 16.0 | 0 | 49 | 20 | 20.0 | 45 |
| 1185 | C | Table | 1 | 61 | 61.0 | 0 | 0 | 21 | 21.0 | 40 |
| 4133 | C | Table | 4 | 3 | 0.8 | 0 | 54 | 70 | 17.5 | −13 |

We usually schedule about twice a month. Our priority is to load AA- and A-class items into production first. These are classifications that were set up when we had a consultant design the system for us [Exhibit 2]. B- and C-class items are loaded as capacity is available. A list of the items and quantities is sent to Louise in the case plant and Donna in the chair plant. They actually schedule the date of production of these items and return the schedules to me. They request any change in order sequence or quantity they feel would benefit manufacturing efficiency.

Louise and Donna prepared the schedules based on the standard hours required of critical work centres. With the assistance of several clerks, they operated a simple manual shopfloor control system that allowed them to load and monitor critical operation performance rather closely. Donna stated:

> I often ask Jack for changes in the quantities of individual chair orders for class AA and A items so they are made in smaller runs. This allows us to schedule in the smaller B and C item orders that would otherwise never get made. Our chair production facilities are not geared for small runs but the customers cannot wait forever for these items.

Louise had somewhat more difficulty than Donna in that parts were supplied from the components plant that was not on the same site. She overcame this problem by means of a daily conference call between herself and the foremen and production control staff of the two plants. By means of this call she was able to impart any priorities and to anticipate when needed parts would be delivered. While dependent on the knowledge of the individuals involved, the system had proved to be simple and effective. Louise was more enthusiastic about the new shopfloor control system than Donna, who felt it would be hard to make it easier or more effective than the present system. Donna was determined to keep an open mind even though she had her doubts.

As finished case goods were packed they were placed into a large warehouse. Using the information on the inventory in the warehouse (Exhibit 3) and production schedules, customer orders were lined up for shipment, with first priority going to the mass merchandiser, galleries and key customers. In this manner reliable, short delivery cycles to critical customers had been maintained. It had become increasingly difficult over the past two years to keep this working well as chair capacity in particular became strained.

The proposed changes in the MPC system related to shopfloor controls. It was felt that a modern, computerized system would eliminate the manual work and provide information in a real-time mode. A consultant had been selected, and it was his proposal that Don Rutkowski had just received. An outline summary of the proposal's main points is shown in Exhibits 4A and 4B. The cost of the software and training was quoted at $300 000 and would require nine months to implement.

**Exhibit 4A**   Proposed shopfloor control activities

| Master scheduling | Case plant | Component plant |
|---|---|---|
| **Database development and maintenance** | | |
| | Complete master route sheets | Complete master route sheets |
| | Specific routings | Specific routings |
| | Standards | Standards |
| | Attrition levels | Attrition levels |
| | Common set-ups | Common set-ups |
| | Maintain overstock data | Maintain overstock data |
| Determine standard cutting rotation | Determine standard assembly line-up | |
| | Maintain data | Maintain data |
| **Master scheduling and production planning** | | |
| Receive cuttings from sales | Receive proposed daily assembly schedules | |
| Develop tentative and firm daily assembly schedules | Study line-up impact | |
| Produce cutting impact formats | Receive cutting impact formats | Receive cutting impact formats |
| | Study impact on work centres | Study impact on work centres |
| | Negotiate changes in assembly schedule | Negotiate changes in assembly schedule |
| Negotiate changes in assembly schedule | Make-or-buy decisions | Make-or-buy decisions |
| Input final schedule to computer for plant floor control and purchasing processing | | |
| **Plant floor control** | | |
| | Produce and distribute route sheets and drawings | Produce and distribute route sheets and drawings |
| | Daily work centre schedules | Daily work centre schedules |
| | Work centre impact | Lumber requirements projection |
| | Process report-back tickets | Process report-back tickets |
| | Produce and distribute update production reports | Produce and distribute update production reports |
| | Track inter-plant parts' progress | Track inter-plant parts' progress |
| | Morning meeting on status of production | Morning meeting on status of production |

*(continued)*

**Exhibit 4A**  Proposed shopfloor control activities (cont'd)

| Master scheduling | Case plant | Component plant |
|---|---|---|
| Track assembly readiness status | Track assembly readiness status | |
| Track assembled items' progress | Track assembled items' progress | |
| | Produce and distribute daily management reports | Produce and distribute daily management reports |
| **Resources management** | | |
| | Produce and study | Produce and study |
| | ■ Labour use analysis | ■ Labour use analysis |
| | ■ Equipment use analysis | ■ Equipment use analysis |
| | ■ Attrition variance report | ■ Attrition variance report |
| **Residual data utilization** | | |
| | Produce parts' cost analysis | Produce parts' cost analysis |

**Exhibit 4B**  Summary of reports: 1

**PROJECT SCOPE**

| Master scheduling | Plant floor control | Resources management | Integration |
|---|---|---|---|
| Cutting impact analysis | Priority scheduling | Labour | Inventory control |
| | Machine loading | Equipment | Purchasing |
| | | Materials | Costing/pricing |

**COMMUNICATIONS FORMATS**

**Master scheduling**

CP-1  Assembly schedule
CP-2  Cutting impact summary
CP-3  Work centre status projection
CP-4  Visanalysis – 4/6 weeks

*Plant floor control*
CP-5  Routine sheet – drawing on reverse

CP-6  Daily work centre schedule
CP-7  Lumber need forecast
CP-8  Daily work centre load status and
       forecast A–B

*Resources management*
CP-17  Labour utilization – department and
        individual
(a)  Weekly report
(b)  History – department/individual
(c)  Graph
(d)  Management summary

MF-1    Production control report-back ticket

CP-9    (Optional – computerized report-back)
CP-10  Parts progress analysis (optional)
CP-11  Report-back ticket analysis
CP-12  Daily work centre off-schedule report
CP-13  Daily assembly readiness report (by exception)
CP-14  Assembly item progress control (optional)
CP-15  Daily work centre status summary
CP-16  Daily management report (by exception)

CS-1    Individual parts status
CS-2    Parts off-schedule
CS-3    Parts status by case
CS-4    Work centre status analysis

*Production planning*
CP-1    Assembly schedule
CP-2    Cutting impact summary
CP-3    Work centre status projection and/or
CP-4    Visanalysis
CP-16  Daily management report
       Ref: CS-1   Individual parts status (on-line)
            CS-2   Parts off-schedule by case (on-line)
            CS-3   Parts status by case (on-line)
            CS-4   Work centre status analysis (on line)

CP-18  Work centre utilization/performance
       (a) Weekly report
       (b) History
       (c) Graph
       (d) Management summary

CP-19  Materials utilization
       (a) Attrition variance report
       (b) Parts attrition history
       (c) Management summary

Screens (on-line)
CP-20  Cost data – part/item build-up
       (a) Set-up: standard/actual variance
       (b) Run: standard/actual variance
       (c) Materials utilization

---

### SENIOR MANAGEMENT – EXECUTIVE

*Production scheduling manager*
CP-1    Assembly schedule
CP-16  Daily management report

*Case goods production manager*
Production planning
CP-1    Assembly schedule
CP-2    Cutting impact summary
CP-3    Work centre status projection and/or
CP-4    Visanalysis

*Production management*
CP-16  Daily management report
       Ref: CP-15  Daily work centre status summary
            CP-13  Daily assembly readiness report (by exception)
            CS-2    Parts off-schedule by case (on-line)
            CS-3    Parts status by case (on-line)
            CS-4    Work centre status analysis (on-line)

*Resources management*
CP-17  Labour utilization/performance summary
CP-18  Work centre utilization/performance summary
CP-19  Materials utilization summary (attrition variance)

*Vice-President, manufacturing*
CP-16  Daily management report
       Ref: All other communications as needed

*Note*
CP = computer printout; MF = manual form; CS = computer screen

**Exhibit 4C**     Summary of reports: 2

---

### PLANTS

*Production planning*
*Plant manager – area managers/superintendent*
CP-1    Assembly schedule
CP-3    Work centre status projection and/or
CP-4    Visanalysis

*Plant floor control*
*Worker*
CP-5    Route sheet/drawing
CP-6    Daily work centre schedule
MF-1    Production control report-back ticket
CP-12   Daily work centre off-schedule report

*Supervisor*
CP-6    Daily work centre schedule
CP-8    Daily work centre status and forecast
CP-12   Daily work centre off-schedule report
       Ref: CP-4    Visanalysis
             CP-15   Daily work centre status analysis

*Parts processing manager (superintendent/plant manager)*
CP-15   Daily work centre status summary
CP-12   Daily work centre off-schedule report
       Ref: CP-16   Daily management report
             CP-1     Assembly schedule
             CP-13   Daily assembly readiness report (by exception) and/or
             CP-10   Parts progress analysis (optional)

*Plant manager*
CP-16   Daily management report
       Ref: CP-15   Daily work centre status summary
             CP-12   Daily work centre off-schedule report
             CP-13   Daily assembly readiness report (by exception)
             CP-1     Assembly schedule

*Plants 30–15*
CP-13   Daily assembly readiness report (by exception) and/or
CP-10   Parts progress analysis (optional)
CP-12   Daily work centre off-schedule report
CP-11   Report-back ticket analysis
CP-16   Daily management report

*Plant 10*
CP-1    Assembly schedule
CP-13   Daily assembly readiness report (by exception) and/or
CP-10   Parts progress analysis
CP-12   Daily work centre off-schedule report
CP-14   Assembly item progress

*Control (optional)*
CP-11   Report-back ticket analysis
CP-16   Daily management report

*Rough mill special report, Plants 30–15*
CP-7　　Lumber need forecast (optional)

*General reference*
Plant manager
Area manager (superintendent)
Supervisor
Worker
Production control centres
　　　　CS-1　　Individual parts, status (on-line)
　　　　CS-2　　Parts off-schedule by case (on-line)
　　　　CS-3　　Parts status by case (on-line)
　　　　CS-4　　Work centre status analysis (on-line)

*Resources management*
Plant manager
Area manager
Foreman
Worker
Production control centres
　　　　CP-17　Labour utilization/performance
　　　　CP-18　Work centre utilization/performance
　　　　CP-19　Materials utilization (attrition variance)

*Costing*
CP-20　　Cost data/analysis (standard/actual variance)

*Note*
CP = computer print out; MF = manual form; CS = computer screen.

# Index